European Community Law
Volume I

The International Library of Essays in Law and Legal Theory
Series Editor: Tom D. Campbell

Schools

Natural Law, Vols I & II *John Finnis*
Justice *Thomas Morawetz*
Law and Economics, Vols I & II *Jules Coleman and Jeffrey Lange*
Critical Legal Studies *James Boyle*
Marxian Legal Theory *Csaba Varga*
Legal Reasoning, Vols I & II *Aulis Aarnio and Neil MacCormick*
Legal Positivism *Mario Jori*
American Legal Theory *Robert Summers*
Law and Language *Fred Schauer*
Sociological Theories of Law *Kahei Rokumoto*
Rights *Carlos Nino*
Law and Psychology *Martin Levine*
Feminist Legal Theory, Vols I & II *Frances Olsen*
Law and Society *Werner Krawietz*
Contemporary Criminological Theory *Francis Cullen and Velmer Burton*

Areas

Criminal Law *Thomas Morawetz*
Tort Law *Ernest Weinrib*
Contract Law, Vols I & II *Larry Alexander*
Anti-Discrimination Law *Christopher McCrudden*
Consumer Law *Iain Ramsay*
International Law *Martti Koskenniemi*
Property Law, Vols I & II *Elizabeth Mensch and Alan Freeman*
Constitutional Law *Mark Tushnet*
Procedure *Denis Galligan*
Evidence and Proof *William Twining and Alex Stein*
Company Law *Sally Wheeler*
Privacy, Vols I & II *Raymond Wacks*
Administrative Law *Denis Galligan*
Child Law *Harry Krause*
Family Law, Vols I & II *Harry Krause*
Welfare Law *Peter Robson*
Medicine and the Law *Bernard Dickens*
Commercial Law *Ross Cranston*
Environmental Law *Michael Blumm*
Conflict of Laws *Richard Fentiman*
Law and Religion *Wojciech Sadurski*
Human Rights Law *Philip Alston*
European Community Law, Vols I & II *Francis Snyder*
Tax Law, Vols I & II *Patricia White*
Media Law *Eric Barendt*

Legal Cultures

Comparative Legal Cultures *Csaba Varga*
Law and Anthropology *Peter Sack*
Hindu Law and Legal Theory *Ved Nanda*
Islamic Law and Legal Theory *Ian Edge*
Chinese Law and Legal Theory *Michael Palmer*
Socialist Law *W. Butler*
Japanese Law and Legal Theory *Koichiro Fujikura*
Law and Development *Anthony Carty*
Jewish Law and Legal Theory *Martin Golding*
Legal Education *Martin Levine*
Civil Law *Ralf Rogowski*

Future Volumes

Labour Law, African Law and Legal Theory, Postmodernism and Law, Law and History, Law and Ethics and Cumulative index.

European Community Law
Volume I

Edited by

Francis Snyder

Professor of European Community Law
European University Institute, Florence;
Professor, College of Europe, Bruges;
Honorary Visiting Professor of Law,
University College London

NEW YORK UNIVERSITY PRESS
REFERENCE COLLECTION

First published in the U.S.A. in 1993 by
NEW YORK UNIVERSITY PRESS
Washington Square
New York NY 10003

Library of Congress Cataloging-in-Publication Data
European community law / edited, Francis Snyder.
p. cm.—(International library of essays in law and legal theory. Areas : 18)
"New York University Press reference collection."
Includes bibliographical references.
ISBN 978-0-8147-7956-9
1. Law—European Economic Community countries. 2. Europe-Economic integration. I. Snyder, Francis. II. Series.
KJE958.E89 1993 93–9583
341.24'2—dc20 CIP

Contents

Acknowledgements

The editor and publishers wish to thank the following for permission to use copyright material.

The American Journal of Comparative Law for the essay: Koen Lenaerts (1990), 'Constitutionalism and the Many Faces of Federalism', *The American Journal of Comparative Law*, **38**, pp. 205–63.

Blackwell Publishers for essays: W.G.C.M. Haack (1983), 'The Selectivity of Economic Integration Theories: A Comparison of Some Traditional and Marxist Approaches', *Journal of Common Market Studies*, **21**, pp. 365–87; Fiona Hayes–Renshaw, Christian Lequesne and Pedro Mayor Lopez (1989), 'The Permanent Representations of the Member States to the European Communities', *Journal of Common Market Studies*, **28**, pp. 119–37; Karlheinz Neunreither (1972), 'Transformation of a Political Role: Reconsidering the Case of the Commission of the European Communities', *Journal of Common Market Studies*, **10**, pp. 233–48, and Fritz W. Scharpf (1988), 'The Joint–Decision Trap: Lessons from German Federalism and European Integration', *Public Administration*, **66**, pp. 239–78.

Department of Politics, University of Exeter for the essay: Stephen Wilks (1992), 'The Metamorphosis of European Competition Policy', RUSEL Working Paper No. 9, *Research Unit for the International Study of Economic Liberalisation and its Social and Political Effects, University of Exeter*, pp. 1–25.

Government and Opposition for the essay: Emile Noël (1992), 'Reflections on the Maastricht Treaty', *Government and Opposition*, **27**, pp. 148–57.

International Organisation for the essay: Lawrence Scheinman (1966), 'Some Preliminary Notes on Bureaucratic Relationships in the European Economic Community', *International Organization*, **20**, pp. 750–73.

Kluwer Academic Publishers for the essay: Deirdre Curtin (1990), 'Directives: The Effectiveness of Judicial Protection of Individual Rights', *Common Market Law Review*, **27**, pp. 709–39.

Legal Issues of European Integration for essays: Renaud Dehousse (1989), '1992 and Beyond: The Institutional Dimension of the Internal Market Programme', *Legal Issues of European Integration*, **1**, pp. 109–36, and Eric Stein (1983), 'On Divided–Power Systems: Adventures in Comparative Law', *Legal Issues of European Integration*, **1**, pp. 27–39.

Politics and Society for the essay: Wolfgang Streeck and Philippe C. Schmitter (1991), 'From National Corporatism to Transnational Pluralism: Organized Interests in the Single European Market', *Politics and Society*, **19**, pp. 133–64. Copyright © Sage Publications Inc. Reprinted by permission.

Revue d'Intégration Européenne/Journal of European Integration for the essay: Alex Easson (1989), 'Legal Approaches to European Integration: The Role of Court and Legislator in the Completion of the European Common Market', *Revue d'intégration européenne/Journal of European Integration*, **12**, pp. 101–19.

Sweet and Maxwell Limited for essays: Nicholas Emiliou (1992), 'Subsidiarity: An Effective Barrier Against "the Enterprises of Ambition"?, *European Law Review*, **43**, pp. 383–407; Laurence Gormley (1981), 'Cassis de Dijon and the Communication from the Commission', *European Law Review*, **6**, pp. 454–9; Hjalte Rasmussen (1988), 'Between Self-Restraint and Activism: A Judicial Policy for the European Court', *European Law Review*, **13**, pp. 28–38, and John A. Usher (1976), 'The Influence of National Concepts on Decisions of the European Court', *European Law Review*, **1**, pp. 359–74.

Every effort has been made to trace all the copyright holders, but if any have been inadvertently overlooked the publishers will be pleased to make the necessary arrangement at the first opportunity.

Foreword

This book on European Community Law, consisting of two volumes, owes its gestation and birth to many people and institutions. I wish to thank first the authors of the articles, and their original publishers, for permission to reprint their work here. Without them, a contextual approach to EC law, some fruits of which are represented in the book, would hardly be possible. I am also grateful to John Irwin of Dartmouth Publishing Company and to Tom Campbell, the general editor of the series. Both supported the project enthusiastically from the beginning and kindly agreed to publish the work in two volumes.

The European University Institute (EUI) in Florence, University College London and the College of Europe in Bruges have provided ideal settings in which to initiate and elaborate the study of EC law in context. Among my colleagues, I wish to say thanks in particular to Christian Joerges, Renaud Dehousse and Giandomenico Majone. Together with Eric Stein and David Currie during their stay in Florence in 1991, they have taught me a great deal about European Community law. In our jointly taught seminars at the EUI we have used many of these articles which are reprinted here. Most of the articles on EC institutions and constitutional and administrative law have also been used for several years in my course at the College of Europe in Bruges. My assistants in Bruges, first Jose Crespo Carrillo and then Athanassios Balodimos, helped me to explore, and demonstrate the interest of, a contextual approach to European Community law. I hope that my students, past, present and future, will agree with what has generally been the favourable judgment of their peers.

For research assistance throughout the work on this book, I am especially grateful to Nathalie Habbar. It is scarcely an exaggeration to say that, without her formidable research skills, knowledge of EC law, useful suggestions, and perseverance, this book would probably never have been completed; in any event it would have taken considerably longer. In bringing the project to completion, we have been helped enormously by the courtesy and efficiency of Anne-Lise Strahtmann, my secretary at the EUI, and Emir Lawless of the EUI European Documentation Centre, as well as other staff of the EUI Library. I also wish to thank the EC institutions, especially the Commission, the European Parliament and the European Court of Justice, for their invaluable contribution to the project.

For generous financial support, I am grateful to the European University Institute, particularly to its Research Council and to Emile Noël, its President. I wish also to thank Jacqueline Lastenouse of the Commission of the European Communities, who for some time and in a variety of ways has encouraged the development of this research. I would also like to record here my gratitude to the Nuffield Foundation, in particular Patricia Thomas, and to the British Academy for supporting earlier research which has contributed directly to this project.

Jasper Snyder and Siân Miles have contributed to this project in numerous ways, both large and small, and I am deeply grateful for their help.

Finally, I wish to thank my friends in Florence who, abandoning the search for the holy grail, have helped me in every way to understand the context of law and to put law in its place.

Series Preface

The International Library of Law and Legal Theory is designed to provide important research materials in an accessible form. Each volume contains essays of central theoretical importance in its subject area. The series as a whole makes available an extensive range of valuable material which will be of considerable interest to those involved in the research, teaching and study of law.

The series has been divided into three sections. The Schools section is intended to represent the main distinctive approaches and topics of special concern to groups of scholars. The Areas section takes in the main branches of law with an emphasis on essays which present analytical and theoretical insights of broad application. The section on Legal Cultures makes available the distinctive legal theories of different legal traditions and takes up topics of general comparative and developmental concern.

I have been delighted and impressed by the way in which the editors of the individual volumes have set about the difficult task of selecting, ordering and presenting essays from the immense quantity of academic legal writing published in journals throughout the world. Editors were asked to pick out those essays from law, philosophy and social science journals which they consider to be fundamental for the understanding of law, as seen from the perspective of a particular approach or sphere of legal interest. This is not an easy task and many difficult decisions have had to be made in order to ensure that a representative sample of the best journal essays available takes account of the scope of each topic or school.

I should like to express my thanks to all the volume editors for their willing participation and scholarly judgement. The interest and enthusiasm which the project has generated is well illustrated by the fact that an original projection of 12 volumes drawn up in 1989 has now become a list of some 60 volumes. I must also acknowledge the vision, persistence and constant cheerfulness of John Irwin and the marvellous work done by Mrs Margaret O'Reilly and Sonia Hubbard.

TOM D. CAMPBELL
Series Editor
The Faculty of Law
The Australian National University

Introduction

The European Community

This book concerns the law of the European Community (EC), the organization of countries in Western Europe which, on the basis of international treaties, have joined together for the purpose of economic and (perhaps) political integration. As these two volumes attest, EC law amounts virtually to a new legal system, possibly *sui generis* and certainly distinct both from public international law and from national (or municipal) legal systems. It involves a distinctive set of legal and political institutions. It also embraces an extremely wide – and increasing – range of areas of substantive law.

The EC consisted initially of six countries: France, Germany, Italy, Belgium, the Netherlands and Luxembourg. The United Kingdom, Denmark and Ireland became members in 1973. Greece joined with effect as of 1981. Spain and Portugal acceded to membership in 1986. Currently, the EC has 12 member-states. Further enlargement is likely in light of the recent agreement between the EC and the members of the European Free Trade Association (EFTA) concerning the establishment of a European Economic Space (EES), which was signed in Porto on 2 May 1992.

From the legal standpoint, the EC consists of three communities: the European Economic Community (EEC), the European Coal and Steel Community (ECSC) and the European Atomic Energy Community (EAEC or Euratom). Each is based on a separate treaty. The ECSC was created by the Treaty of Paris in 1951. The EEC and Euratom were established by separate Treaties of Rome in 1957. All were part of a series of projects after the Second World War designed to encourage cooperation among Western European countries and, more specifically, to foster economic and possibly political integration. Two other ventures, the European Defence Community and the European Political Community, both 'died' in August 1954 as a result of the refusal of the French National Assembly to ratify the proposed European Defence Community treaty.

Though legally distinct, the three Communities today share the same institutions. Paraphrasing the founding Treaties, the Commission represents the supranational element; the Council represents the member-states; the European Parliament represents the interests of the people of Europe, while the role of the European Court of Justice and the Court of First Instance – the judicial organs – is to ensure that the law is observed. The courts and parliaments (then called the Assembly) of the three Communities were merged in 1957; a common Commission and Council were established in 1965. As a result of the existence of shared institutions, it is common practice to use the expression 'European Community' or EC to refer to the three Communities together. More specifically, this expression also connotes the EEC which, in contrast to the other two Communities, was established for an indefinite period and is the broadest in scope. This practice will be followed here.

Since 1957 the founding Treaties have been supplemented and modified. Until recently the most significant modification was achieved by the Single European Act (SEA), adopted in 1986 and entering into force on 1 July 1987. It aimed, among other things, to improve the EC's decision-making procedures and to provide a renewed stimulus for attempts to create a Single European Market. It was thus linked directly to the EC Commission's 1985 White Paper on 'Completing the Internal Market'.[1]

Most recently, the Treaty on European Union, its annexes and Final Act were signed at Maastricht in the Netherlands on 7 February 1992. They were the result of negotiations undertaken in late 1990 and throughout 1991 in the Intergovernmental Conferences on Economic and Monetary Union and on Political Union. The Maastricht Treaty changes the name of the EEC officially to the EC, establishes a European Union, creates a European citizenship, and provides for an eventual economic and monetary union. It establishes a set of complex relations between the EC and member-states in the emerging European Union. As provided in Article 236 EEC [Treaty], the Maastricht Treaty and related texts will enter into effect once they have been ratified by all the EC member-states in accordance with their respective constitutional requirements. Assuming that ratification occurs, the Treaty on European Union will supplement and amend the Rome Treaty. It will replace the previous treaties as the EC's written constitution.

Aim and Scope of this Book

The European Community (EC) and its legal system, as well as the international political economy of which they form a part, are currently in the midst of profound change. As a result, the late 20th century is an especially exciting and challenging time for the study of EC law. These two volumes are intended not only to convey the excitement inherent in the subject, but also to illuminate some of the fundamental issues in EC law in a stimulating and thought-provoking way.

EC law is a relatively new field. It is perhaps not surprising, therefore, that most of the legal writing on the subject has been concerned mainly with the exposition and systematization of legal doctrine. In contrast, this two-volume set is intended to provide the foundation for a contextual approach to the study of EC law. The contributions give special emphasis to the operation of EC law in its economic, political and social contexts. They treat many of the standard topics of EC constitutional and administrative law, economic and social law, and foreign policy and international relations. But they explore these aspects of EC law from a variety of disciplines and theoretical and methodological perspectives.

The essays reprinted here were selected after a relatively comprehensive search of the literature published on EC law and related matters in numerous disciplines during the past 40 years. The intention of the editor was to choose papers of lasting value (so far as one can tell), which raise significant issues of EC law in a challenging way. Preference was given to essays which are (1) recent, with the exception of some classic articles which remain essential reading; (2) contextual, in the sense of being concerned with more than merely the exposition or analysis of legal doctrine; (3) capable of proposing hypotheses which go beyond the article itself; (4) explanatory or theoretical, rather than simply descriptive or expository; and (5) exemplary, novel or more than usually interesting for lawyers from the standpoint of research methods.

The book therefore includes contributions from numerous disciplines, including not only law but also history, political science, economics, sociology, anthropology, philosophy, administrative studies and international relations. The authors deploy a variety of research methods; these include case studies, statistical research, the comparative method, participant observation, the analysis of legal doctrine, the use of interviews, the use of general theory as well as analysis of the relation between law and policy. On occasion, the authors' views may diverge significantly with regard to the theories, politics, policies and perhaps even doctrine of EC law. Like other readers, however, they may at least find the papers in this book useful in the (perhaps unlikely) event that they are not aware of them already.[2]

The essays in this book deal with four different themes.[3] The first concerns the various relationships between institutions, rules, ideologies and processes. The second refers to state forms and legal pluralism, including relations between EC law, the law of member-states, and the laws, customs and practices of local communities. The third theme is the interconnection between law, economy and society. The fourth is the role of the EC and its law in the international political economy.[4] The first two themes are the subject of study in the first volume of this set, while the last two are dealt with in the second volume. The constitutional and administrative law and the substantive law of the EC are, however, intimately related. Consequently, the reader should bear in mind that both volumes contain essays which directly or indirectly, concern, each of these themes.

This first volume consists of four parts: perspectives on European integration; federalism and legal pluralism; institutions and ideologies; and rules and processes. The following paragraphs identify briefly some of the significant points of each chapter.

Part I Perspectives on European Integration

The reasons for the creation of the EC, its basic economic, social and political premises, its development from the 1950s to the present, and the fundamental aims of its legal system are often subject to disagreement and controversy. Even when facts are clearly established, they may be interpreted in different ways. Part I of this volume presents several perspectives on European integration, discussing numerous issues which underlie the more specifically legal essays which follow.

The EC is often compared to federal systems such as the US or Germany. In Chapter 1, Stein asks to what extent a comparison between the EC and the US is meaningful. Summarizing the results of an influential comparative research project,[5] he points to similarities and differences in the two systems. Similarities include the partial transfer of power from local to central authorities, the precedence of central law within its sphere of authority, as well as the role of supreme courts and, in general, their working methods. The chapter concludes that, because of their similarities and differences, each system has much to learn from the other.[6]

The role of organizations and societal processes in European integration are emphasized in Chapter 2 by Haack who presents a critical survey of different theories of economic integration.[7] He focuses on the types of questions which each theory neglects, as well as on those which it asks. Both customs union theory and neo-Marxist integration theory look at economic integration in a selective way. Haack argues that neither is sufficient in itself. Instead, integration theory should consider both the causes and the effects of integration. In his view, the crucial question concerns the objectives of government policy in embarking on the process of economic integration. He also identifies the importance of analysing the effects of further coordination of economic policy, a topic which is currently of great significance in the light of the Maastricht Treaty on economic and monetary union.

The Single European Act (SEA) of 1986 gave new impetus to European integration, though explanations of the genesis of the SEA have been subject to debate. For example, it has been cogently argued that the basic factors in the SEA negotiations, as formerly in the negotiations leading to the 1957 Treaty of Rome, were the convergence of national interests, the pro-European idealism of heads of government, and the decisive role of large member-states. In this view, pan-European business groups were relatively ineffective in influencing policy.[8] This argument is contested by Streeck and Schmitter in Chapter 3 in which they suggest that the renewed momentum for integration in the mid-1980s was due to an alignment between large European firms seeking to overcome competitive disadvantages *vis-à-vis* the US and Japan.[9] The chapter is mainly concerned, however, with the ways in which different interests are presently represented at the European level and are likely to be so represented in the future.[10] Its principal argument is that interest representation at the European level has always been more 'pluralist' than corporatist. It asks why a centralized pattern of interest politics has not (with some exceptions) emerged at the EC level in spite of being very common in national politics. The authors point to the absence of significant business factions with an active interest in having centralized negotiations with organized labour. They also suggest that the EC institutional structure, in which most power resides in the intergovernmental Council, has hindered the development of Euro-corporatism. This institutional structure is more consistent with the development of sub-national units, such as regions. The authors also propose the hypothesis that, depending on the area of policy, different levels of regulation may favour different social interests and groups. A pertinent example is 'mutual recognition' – the pre-emption by the EC of national regulation without the simultaneous establishment of EC-level regulation; this is considered in detail in other chapters.

The Treaty on European Union agreed in Maastricht in February 1992, assuming that it is ratified by all member-states, will be the most recent amendment to the EC constitution. It is based on negotiations and inter-governmental conferences which began in December 1990 and ended in the European Council in December 1991. Chapter 4 by Emile Noël, a 'quasi-participant', presents a unique view of the negotiations and their results. Noël was involved in the early phases of European integration and then served as Secretary-General of the EC Commission from 1958 to 1987; he represented the Commission in numerous negotiations, including those which led to the Single European Act.[11] The study emphasizes the political events, both inside and outside the EC, which shaped the Maastricht negotiations. It also stresses the influence of the structure and process of the negotiations on the results.[12] This analysis, together with the author's long practical experience within EC institutions, makes it possible to identify some of the most important political signals which are sent out by the negotiations and the text of the Treaty. The chapter concludes that a single currency and European defence represent two major steps towards a European federation.

Part II Federalism and Legal Pluralism

The EC is a divided-power system in which powers are divided or shared between the EC and its member-states. It differs, however, from well-known federal systems such as the US, Canada, Australia, Switzerland or Germany. Moreover, the possibility of substantial differentiation among the member-states themselves – a 'two-speed' Europe – has frequently been proposed. In addition, the importance of sub-national units, such as regions, has recently been recognized in the Maastricht Treaty. Consequently, the EC's legal and institutional structure is complex, involving several levels of authority and relations among them.[13] Some of these topics are explored in Part II.

Chapter 5 by Lenaerts argues that, except for a division of powers, a federal constitution and a federal judiciary as umpire, federal systems around the world are extremely diverse. He distinguishes two models of federalism: integrative and devolutionary. The former includes the EC, Switzerland and the US, while the latter includes Belgium, Canada and Spain. This theoretical, comparative analysis illuminates characteristics which the EC shares with 'mature' federal systems, its specific features and its potential for future development. For example, the EC equivalent of the German constitutional principle of 'executive federalism' is the duty of Community loyalty, as stated in Article 5 EEC.[14] In contrast to other divided-power systems, in the EC the smaller units play a double role: member-states are the most important participants in EC decision-making processes, and they also form a constitutional counterweight to the central authority as such. Nevertheless, all divided-power systems are characterized by tension between enumerated and residual powers; in the EC, as in others, the level of government which has only enumerated powers seeks constantly to increase its authority.[15]

The following chapter by Usher analyses the influence of national concepts on decisions of the European Court of Justice. It shows clearly how the European Court, making use of general provisions of the founding Treaties, has woven a complex doctrinal web consisting of strands derived from both national and Community sources. It gives particular attention to general principles in common use in EC law, of which the best known are proportionality, legitimate expectation and legal certainty. It also shows how the European Court fills gaps in the Treaties by means of a comparative study of the laws of member-states. It concludes that concepts derived from national sources play a fundamental role in decisions of the European Court and that – once adopted by the Court – these are applied as concepts of EC rather than of national law.

In Chapter 7, Weiler asks whether it still makes sense to refer to the EC as a supranational system and what we mean by this expression. He examines the tension in the EC between centrifugal and centripetal forces. The essay argues that, in order to understand the EC system, we need to draw a distinction between two facets of supranationalism. Normative supranationalism refers to relationships between EC policies and legal measures on the one hand, and policies and legal measures of member-states on the other hand. Decisional supranationalism concerns the institutional framework and processes of decision-making by which EC policies are formulated, adopted and executed. The study analyses the changing relations between these two facets of supranationalism. It concludes that the EC is characterized by a high degree of normative and a limited degree of decisional supranationalism. Indeed, the expansion of the former has been accompanied – and made possible – by the corresponding expansion of the latter. By virtue of this two-way process, for example, the supremacy of EC law has been actively elaborated by the European Court of Justice; however, member-states play an increasingly important, and controlling, role in the EC decision-making process. The framework is held together by what Weiler calls the 'all-or-nothing effect': though member-states retain the option of withdrawing from the EC, as long as they remain members they are constrained to apply EC law.[16]

In legal, administrative and political terms, the EC system thus depends for its day-to-day operations upon the national administrations of member-states. Chapter 8 by Scheinman focuses on the relationship between national administrations and the EC administration, in particular the Commission. It analyses key aspects of this relationship, such as working groups, committees and the Committee of Permanent Representatives (COREPER, the French acronym). It also evaluates this relationship in terms of two dimensions: first, the impact of bureaucratic interpenetration on the development of integration and, second, the impact of integration on the nature of bureaucratic power. Scheinman advances the hypothesis that the perception and use of bureaucratic interpenetration are influenced by three variables: (1) the specificity of the Rome Treaty concerning the relevant subject matter, (2) the psychological orientation of Community administrators, and (3) the constellation of political forces around the policy area in question. In general terms, bureaucratic interpenetration serves to obtain information and to generate administrative support for Commission proposals. At national level, however, it has tended to strengthen the role of technical ministries at the expense of general ones; at EC level, it has similarly tended to enhance the role of technocratic decision-making. Though rarely decisive in determining general policies, interpenetration remains the 'foundation stone, the *tissu cellulaire*' of the EC system.

Chapter 9 by Emiliou analyses the concept of subsidiarity.[17] Though it has long been part of the EC system in fact, the principle of subsidiarity was first recognized expressly in EC law in the Single European Act with regard to environmental policy. The Maastricht Treaty, once ratified, will transform it into a fundamental principle of EC constitutional law. Recognizing that no agreement exists on the definition of the concept, Emiliou refers to the Oxford English Dictionary: subsidiarity means that 'a central authority should have a subsidiary function, performing only those tasks which cannot be performed effectively at a more immediate or local level'. The author distinguishes two tendencies: subsidiarity from above and 'bottom-up' subsidiarity. Against this background, he examines the following: the historical roots of the concept; its theoretical foundations, both as a criterion for the division of competences between different levels of political power and as a guarantee for individual liberty; its role in German constitutional law; and its actual and potential importance as a principle of Community law. He argues that the Maastricht Treaty, though ambiguous, appears to give preference to the concept of 'subsidiarity from above'. He also suggests that subsidiarity is an essentially socio-political rather than legal or administrative principle. Consequently, he concludes that it is not easily amenable to judicial review.

It has often been argued that EC law, as it stands, permits substantial differentiation among member-states, subject to certain conditions and within a common legal framework. This possibility was recognized expressly by the Single European Act.[18] A classic paper by Ehlermann considered the question of such differentiation in detail.[19] He argued, first, that whether and to what extent differentiation is allowed are matters of interpretation; and, second, that economic and social differences may in principle justify differentiation, whereas purely political phenomena cannot. He concluded that the scope for differentiation in existing EC law is considerable. Its limits depend essentially on three factors: (1) the principle of nondiscrimination, (2) the prohibition of obstacles within the Community, and (3) the extent to which differentiation must be limited in time. Consequently, in his view the concept of a 'two-speed' Europe, or 'variable geometry', will not be the subject of formal Treaty amendment. The relevance of this study is increased (rather than diminished) by the fact that the Maastricht Treaty recently incorporated the UK's decision to opt out of the Social Charter and also permitted the possibility of similar differentiation with regard to a single currency. In the future the question of legally permissible differentiation is certain to remain on the EC agenda, if only because of the heterogeneity of current and foreseeable applicants for EC membership.

Part III Institutions and Ideologies

The EC has a complex institutional structure which has often been described as quadripartite,[20] thus differing, of necessity, from the classic division of powers described by Montesquieu in *L'Esprit des Lois* (1748). In the future the EC institutional structure is likely to become even more complex. For example, the Maastricht Treaty not only alters current relations among existing institutions, but also provides for the eventual creation of a European Central Bank as the centre-piece of a European System of Central Banks. The contributions in this Part and the next, without purporting to be comprehensive, consider some aspects of EC institutions. Part III is concerned with their organizational and ideological aspects;[21] Part IV deals with the relationship between rules and processes in the operation of EC institutions.

Most writers on EC institutions use the EC system as a whole as their unit of analysis and then proceed to ascribe certain functions within the system to each institution. In contrast, the essay by Neunreither (Chapter 10) begins by envisaging the Commission in isolation. It then elaborates two alternative models for its role: European government on the one hand, and European secretariat on the other hand. The author shows that each model can be applied fruitfully to analyse and explain the activities of the Commission at different times and in different sectors. Neunreither also assesses the impact of the 1966 Luxembourg Accords on the respective roles of the Commission and the Council. He argues that there has never been a generally accepted definition of the roles of EC institutions. From his analysis he draws two conclusions which have far-reaching implications for future studies of EC institutions. First, as lawyers and students of EC law, we need to consider the capacity of institutions to react to changes in the system as a whole. In the Europe of the future, for example, it will be essential to understand the flexibility and learning capacities of institutions. Second, in analysing (and evaluating) the role of institutions, we need to use criteria which are not derived directly from the system. Otherwise it is difficult, if not impossible, to assess the structure and function of institutions and to modify them so as to achieve standards of accountability, efficacy and democracy.

The greatest powers of the EC Commission currently lie in the field of competition policy. Few studies, however, delve beyond the analysis of legal doctrine and a description of administrative practice.[22] Chapter 11 by Wilks is an innovative study of organizational culture in the Commission's Directorate-General (DG) IV: Competition. It argues that a metamorphosis has taken place in DG IV which has influenced the organization's working ideology, the nature and scope of its policies, and its priorities in competition matters. After outlining the formal legal powers of DG IV, the essay traces its development since the late 1950s and analyses its recent transformation. The new assertiveness of DG IV and its expansion into previously unregulated sectors have highlighted the importance of the principle of sectoral specialization. Rapporteurs who specialize in specific sectors now have a policy-making function and play a quasi-judicial role. With these changes have come certain problems and dilemmas of transition: the shortage of resources; questions of discretion and accountability; difficulties in relations with national authorities; and the politicization of competition policy. The metamorphosis of DG IV staff from bureaucrats into regulators thus raises fundamental, enduring questions concerning EC law which are dealt with in other chapters in these volumes.

The EC institutional system is frequently envisaged in its quasi-federal aspect as consisting only of the EC and member-states – two levels of a divided-power system which are interrelated but fundamentally distinct. This picture of the EC is, however, overly simplistic and basically misleading. It neglects the vast 'grey zone' of institutions which cannot be classified easily as belonging solely either to the EC or to member-states. The phenomenon of bureaucratic interpenetration, involving the EC Commission and national administrations, was explored in general terms in Chapter 8 by Scheinman. It is also exemplified by the numerous committees and working parties composed of national experts and a representative of the Commission.

Perhaps the most prominent example of such a 'mixed' or interstitial institution is the Committee of Permanent Representatives (COREPER), composed of the ambassadors (and their deputies) of member-states to the EC. Chapter 12 by Hayes-Renshaw, Lequesne and Mayor Lopez discusses the history of COREPER, its internal organization and its role in the elaboration and negotiation of national positions in the Council. A comparative study, it analyses the examples of France, Ireland and Spain, three countries which differ in size, national political characteristics and length of EC membership. Each member-state has its own system of inter-ministerial coordination.[23] The paper discusses how COREPER helps to prepare the Council agenda and agrees much EC legislation. At the same time, the Permanent Representatives act variously as what the authors describe as 'a central post-box' and a 'benevolent censor' *vis-à-vis* their respective home capitals. The authors show clearly that, though consisting of national representatives, COREPER has long played an essential role in the EC legislative process. Today it is increasingly concerned with ensuring the effectiveness of EC law.

A central – and frequently controversial – part in the process of European integration has been played by the European Court of Justice. Chapter 13 by Easson considers the role of court and legislator in the completion of the European common market. Focusing first on the European Court of Justice, it shows how, beginning in the 1960s, the Court established the basic principles of EC law, including direct effect, the supremacy or primacy of EC law, pre-emption and fundamental rights. In doing so, the Court transformed the founding Treaties into the EC constitution.[24] In the 1970s it also fulfilled an important interpretative function, both establishing the 'four freedoms' (free movement of goods, persons, services and capital) and elaborating the relationship between directly effective Treaty provisions and secondary legislation. Easson argues that the activism of the Court must be evaluated in the context of the EC's institutional structure as a whole, particularly with regard to the virtual paralysis of the Council following the 1966 Luxembourg Accords.[25] He also argues that today '[t]he era of the judge as lawmaker . . . appears to be largely past' (p.316). The completion of the internal market since the Commission's 1985 White Paper has been largely, though not entirely, the work of the Commission, the Council and, to some extent, the European Parliament.

Though agreeing with Easson's presentation of the facts, Rasmussen offers a contrasting evaluation of the past and future roles of the European Court in Chapter 14.[26] First, he argues that the Court has been unnecessarily activist. Second, he suggests that the EC will continue to depend on the Court for further progress in economic (and political) integration. However, the main aim of the study is more general, arguing that it is not possible currently to formulate a normative theory of the interpretation of EC law because there is no consensus in the EC on fundamental values such as supranationalism or integration. Rasmussen examines the premises of judicial activism research, the proper role of the Treaty preamble and of judges' philosophies in judicial policy-making, as well as the advantages and disadvantages of a sociological method of measuring judicial activism. Instead of assessing judicial activism as a reponse to characteristics of other parts of the EC system, however, he proposes a different method for determining whether there has been actual, unwarranted judicial activism. This method consists of a careful, comprehensive analysis of reactions to the European Court's decisions by other, mainly national, authorities. These authorities are deemed (or assumed) to represent public opinion and values. The paper argues that such an analysis indicates that the European Court has often assumed functions which constitutionally belong to other parts of government. It suggests that if the European Court continues to pursue an activist policy, it will inevitably lose authority and legitimacy.[27]

Part IV Rules and Processes

The essays in the final Part of this volume consider the relations between rules and processes. Focusing primarily on EC institutions in action, they examine some of the ways in which these institutions use different types of rules, thus complementing the various issues raised in preceding chapters.

Chapter 15 by Gormley concerns a Commission 'communication' – a type of EC 'soft law' which in recent years has assumed increasing significance.[28] Gormley analyses the content and implications of the Commission's Communication[29] on the consequences of the European Court's judgment in the landmark case known as *Cassis de Dijon*.[30] The first of its kind, this Communication illustrates the legal nature, form and purposes of this new type of EC quasi-legal instrument. In addition, this particular Communication was of special importance since, in the *Cassis de Dijon* case, the European Court of Justice established the principle of 'mutual recognition'. This principle lies at the heart of the Commission's legal strategy for completing the Single European Market and is also the source of the broader EC policy of 'regulatory competition'.[31] Gormley traces the change in the Commission's strategy for economic and legal integration. The rigid harmonization of national laws by means of EC legislation, involving a Commission proposal and adoption by the Council by a unanimous vote under Article 100 EEC, was put aside. It was replaced by a strategy of selective litigation by the Commission against member-states under Article 169 EEC. Since the 1985 White Paper, this strategy of litigation has been supplemented by minimal harmonization; this is discussed by Dehousse in Chapter 19 in this volume and by several essays in Volume II.

Chapter 16 by Scharpf analyses the decision-making process in the Council. It addresses the paradox which many have discerned in the EC, especially before the adoption of the Single European Act, but also in many matters even today. Describing this paradox as 'frustration without disintegration and resilience without progress', Scharpf attempts to elaborate an institutional explanation for it. He begins with the observation that the EC resembles German more closely than American federalism: authority is shared between the two parts or levels of government rather than being allocated to either one or the other. The paper compares joint decision-making in German federalism and decision-making by the Council in the EC, arguing that both are characterized by the 'joint decision trap'. Member governments participate directly in central decision-making, with a *de facto* requirement for unanimous decisions.[32] These two conditions generate suboptimal policy outcomes as long as a 'bargaining' rather than a 'problem-solving' style of decision-making is maintained. In fact, the 'bargaining' style has prevailed in both the EC and Germany. For member governments, however, the current institutional arrangements are preferable to either greater centralization or disintegration. Scharpf helps to explain, for example, why the EC stagnated but did not collapse after the paralysis of decision-making as a result of the 1966 Luxembourg Accords; as already noted, this paralysis led directly to intense judicial activism by the European Court of Justice.

The principal type of EC legislation for completing the internal market is the directive, the regulation rarely being used in this context. According to Article 189 EEC, a directive establishes the result to be achieved, but leaves the choice of form and method for accomplishing that result up to member-states. It follows that member-states are legally obliged to transpose EC directives into national legislation. In numerous instances, however, they fail to do so. Rights conferred upon individuals by EC directives are therefore difficult to enforce. In order to resolve this difficulty, the European Court of Justice has recognized that, in certain conditions, a directive may have direct effect; that is, it may create rights which an individual may assert in his/her national court. However, such rights may only be asserted against the State or an organ of the State.[33]

The effectiveness of judicial protection of human rights which are conferred by EC directives is considered by Curtin in Chapter 17. She examines the ways in which the European Court has limited the discretion of national judges in interpreting national legislation. She also considers the extent to which EC constitutional law requires member-states to compensate individuals for damage suffered as a result of the State's breach of its EC obligations. Both of these questions have recently been considered by the European Court of Justice in important constitutional cases.[34] The author argues that, in addition, the EC legislator (that is, the Council) should act to harmonize national procedural law where necessary in order to ensure that rights derived from EC law can be enforced adequately by national remedies.

The European Parliament is sometimes considered to be the neglected institution in the EC system. Its powers have increased considerably since the late 1950s, however, partly as a result of inter-institutional agreements,[35] and partly as a result of judgments by the European Court of Justice.[36] For a long time its principal role in EC decision-making has concerned the determination of the budget. The European Parliament has tried to use its role as joint budgetary authority (together with the Council) as a means of expanding its power. Chapter 18 by Wallace is a case study of the conflict between the European Parliament and the Council concerning the 1986 budget. Emphasizing the importance of bargaining, it discusses the legal framework, the negotiation of the budget, and the case which was brought by the Council to contest the European Parliament's determination and approval of the budget.[37] It also explores the political implications of the Court's judgment for the budgetary process, concluding realistically that legal rules cannot settle such difficult issues; there is no substitute for political agreement. This paper, like that of Scharpf, emphasizes the interconnection of decision rules and policy outcomes. Like the other essays in this volume, it illustrates the operation of EC institutions in their economic, political and social contexts.

The respective roles of the main EC institutions in the internal market programme are analysed by Dehousse in the final chapter in this volume. Dehousse considers the new division of tasks between the EC and member-states, the effects of the Single European Act on EC institutions and some of the important institutional issues in the implementation of the internal market programme. These include the delegation of powers, the relation between efficiency and democracy, the problem of the legal basis of EC legislation and the role of member-states. The chapter concludes, first, that institutional reform can be achieved most easily when it is a logical implication of other political choices, instead of being undertaken for its own sake. Second, it shows that changes in the EC decision-making process paralleled changes in the perception of institutional issues, which were considered first as merely technical but subsequently as of major political importance. It demonstrates clearly that in the EC, the relationship between rules and processes is inextricably bound up with substantive law and policy.

Notes

1. Commission of the European Communities,'Completing the Internal Market' (White Paper from the Commission to the European Council, Milan, 28–29 June 1985), COM(85) 310 final (1985). See also Claus-Dieter Ehlermann (1987), 'The Internal Market following the Single European Act', *Common Market Law Review*, **24**, 361.
2. References to a limited number of other directly relevant articles, either contextual or doctrinal, are given in the footnotes. The literature on EC law is vast. For reasons of space, footnotes in both volumes refer only to English-language periodical articles, with the exception of a few references to articles or books published in languages other than English. References to books published in English are readily available elsewhere.
3. These themes were previously identified as the main areas of emphasis in the contextual study of EC law: see Francis Snyder (1990), *New Directions in European Community Law*, London: Weidenfeld & Nicolson, p.14.
4. Not all of these themes are given equal prominence in this book, partly because of gaps in the existing literature. It is not possible to give references here to all of the sources consulted in different phases of the preparation of these volumes. The editor would, however, welcome any comments or suggestions which might be useful in an eventual further edition.
5. See Eric Stein and Ted Sandalow (1982), *Courts and Free Markets – Perspectives from the United States and Europe*, Oxford: Clarendon Press, 2 volumes.
6. See also Eric Stein (1986), 'Uniformity and Diversity in a Divided-Power System: The United States Experience', *Washington Law Review*, **61**, 1081. On comparative law within the EC, see Chapter 7; also Thijmen Koopmans (1991), 'The Birth of European Law at the Cross-Roads of Legal Traditions', *American Journal of Comparative Law*, **39**, 493.
7. See also Gilbert Ziebura (1982–3), 'Internationalisation of Capital, International Division of Labour and the European Community', *Journal of Common Market Studies*, **21**, 127.
8. See Andrew Maravcsik (1991), 'Negotiating the Single European Act: National Interests and Conventional Statecraft in the European Community', *International Organization*, **25**, 19.
9. See also Wayne Sandholtz and John Zysman (1989), '1992: Recasting the European Bargain', *World Politics*, **42**, 95; also Chapter 19 in Volume II.
10. See also Francis Snyder (1990), *New Directions in European Community Law*, London: Weidenfeld & Nicolson, Chapter 2; Peter Busch and Donald Puchala (1976), 'Interests, Influence and Integration: Political Structure in the European Communities', *Comparative Political Studies*, **9**, 235.
11. See *Hommage à Emile Noël, Secrétaire général de la Commission européenne de 1958 à 1987*, Luxembourg: Office des publications officielles des Communautés européennes, 1988.
12. On this relationship, see also Chapters 16 and 18 in this volume and Chapter 7 in Volume II.
13. It has therefore been argued that classical legal theory does not account adequately for EC law, because the former has developed in conjunction with the State and largely ignores extra-State legal phenomena: see Joexerramon Bengoetxea (1991), 'Institutions, Legal Theory and EC Law', *Archiv für Rechts und Sozialphilosophie*, **77**, 195. See also Mark Jones (1984), 'The Legal Nature of the European Community: A Jurisprudential Analysis Using H.L.A. Hart's Model of Law and a Legal System', *Cornell International Law Journal*, **17**, 1; and Bert van Roermund (1991), 'Common Market and Legality: On a Possible Implicit Ecological Commitment of European Community Law', presented at the IVR Conference, Gottingen, 1991. Legal anthropology may eventually contribute to the study of EC law. See Peter Sack (ed.) (1992), *Law and Anthropology*, Aldershot: Dartmouth, particularly Francis Snyder, 'Anthropology, Dispute Processes and Law: A Critical Introduction'; Sally Merry, 'Legal Pluralism'; and Boaventura de Sousa Santos, 'Law: A Map of Misreading: Toward a Postmodern Conception of Law.
14. An excellent and detailed analysis of legal doctrine may be found in John Temple Lang (1990), 'Community Constitutional Law: Article 5 EEC Treaty', *Common Market Law Review*, **27**, 645.

15. See also Eckard Rehbinder and Richard Stewart (1985), 'Legal Integration in Federal Systems: European Community Environmental Law', *American Journal of Comparative Law*, **33**, 371; Auke Haagsmam (1989), 'The European Community's Environmental Policy: A Case Study in Federalism', *Fordham International Law Journal*, **12**, 311.
16. On this last point, see Joseph Weiler (1991), 'The Transformation of Europe', *Yale Law Journal*, **100**, 2403; see also Joseph Weiler (1982), 'Alternatives to Withdrawal from an International Organization: The Case of the European Economic Community', *Israel Law Review*, **20**, 282.
17. See also Michael Wilke and Helen Wallace (1990), 'Subsidiarity: Approaches to Power-Sharing in the European Community', RIIA Discussion Paper no. 27, London: Vlad Constantinesco (1991), 'La Subsidiarité comme Principe constitutionnel de l'Intégration européenne', *Aussenwirtschaft*, **46**, 439.
18. See Emile Noël (1989), 'The Single European Act', *Government and Opposition*, **24**, 3.
19. Claus-Dieter Ehlermann (1984), 'How Flexible is Community Law: An Unusual Approach to the Concept of "Two Speeds" ', *Michigan Law Review*, **82**, 1274–93.
20. See, in particular, Pierre Pescatore (1978), 'L'exécutif communautaire: justification du quadripartisme institué par les traités de Paris et de Rome', *Cahiers de Droit Européen*, 387.
21. For the meaning of 'ideology' in this context, see Chapter 4 of Volume II, pp. 83–112.
22. Among the exceptions in English are Frances Graupner (1973), 'Commission Decision-Making in Competition Questions', *Common Market Law Review*, **10**, 291, and Ivo Van Bael (1986), 'The Antitrust Settlement Practice of the European Commission', *Common Market Law Review*, **23**, 69.
23. See, for example, Christian Lesquesne (1987), 'L'adaptation des administration nationales à l'existence des Communautés européennes: Le cas des ministres francais', *Revue francaise d'Administration publique*, **42**, 275; Mario Chiti (1989–90), 'Il Coordinamento delle Politche Comunitarie e la Riforma degli Apparati di Governo', *Associazione per gli Studi e le Richerche Parliamentari*, **1**, 235.
24. For a detailed treatment, see Joseph Weiler (1991), 'The Transformation of Europe', *Yale Law Journal*, **100**, 2403; see also G. Frederico Mancini (1989), 'The Making of a Constitution for Europe', *Common Market Law Review*, **26**, 595; Joseph Weiler (1986), 'Eurocracy and Distrust: Some Questions Concerning the Role of the European Court of Justice in the Protection of Fundamental Human Rights within the Legal Order of the European Community', *Washington Law Review*, **61**, 1103; Francis G. Jacobs (1990), 'Constitutional Developments in the European Community and the Impact of the Single European Market after 1992', *Michigan Journal of International Law*, **11**, 887.
25. On the relationship between the respective roles of the Council and the Court, see especially Pierre Pescatore (1983), 'La carence du législateur et le devoir du juge' in *Rechtsvergleichung, Europarecht und Staatenintegration, Gedachtnisschrift für L.-J. Constantinesco*, Cologne, Berlin, Bonn and Munich. The process of decision-making in the Council is treated by Fritz W. Scharpf in Chapter 6 below. Compare however the theoretical approach advocated by Neunreither in Chapter 10 and the views expressed by Hjalte Rasmussen in Chapter 14.
26. See also Hjalte Rasmussen (1986), *On Law and Policy in the European Court of Justice: A Comparative Study in Judicial Policymaking*, Dordrecht: Martinus Nijhoff, and the review by Mauro Cappelletti (1987), 'Is the European Court of Justice "Running Wild"?', *European Law Review*, **12**, 3.
27. Empirical studies of the pattern of cases before the European Court of Justice are so far relatively rare. See however Christopher Harding (1992), 'Who Goes to Court in Europe? An Analysis of Litigation against the European Community', *European Law Review*, **17**, 105. A partial exception to the paucity of empirical studies of the Court is the research project on the use of Article 177 EEC which was conducted under the aegis of the European University Institute in Florence. The published findings of the project include J. Korte, A.E. Kellermann, W.M. Levelt-Overmars and F.H.M. Possen (1990), 'Primes Inter Pares: The European Court and National Courts. The Follow-Up by National Courts of Preliminary Rulings

ex Article 177 of the Treaty of Rome: A Report on the Situation in the Netherlands', EUI Working Paper LAW No. 90/6.

28. See generally K.C. Wellens and G.M. Borchardt (1989), 'Soft Law in European Community Law', *European Law Review*, **14**, 267. On Commission communications in particular, see Alphonso Mattera Ricigliano (1990), *Le marché unique européen: Ses règles, son fonctionnement*, Paris: Jupiter, 2nd edition, 42–46. For an analysis of EC soft law in the context of a broad range of legal instruments and strategies, see Francis Snyder (1993), 'The Effectiveness of European Community Law: Institutions, Processes, Tools and Techniques', *Modern Law Review*, **56**, 19.
29. OJ 1980 C256/2.
30. Case 120/78 *Rewe-Zentral AG v Bundesmonoplverwaltung für Branntwein* [1979] ECR 649.
31. See Chapter 13 in Volume II.
32. See also Chapter 5 in this volume.
33. See further Pierre Pescatore (1983), 'The Doctrine of "Direct Effect": An Infant Disease in European Community Law', *European Law Review*, **8**, 155; J.A. Winter (1972), 'Direct Applicability and Direct Effect: Two Distinct and Different Concepts in Community Law', *Common Market Law Review*, **9**, 425; Deirdre Curtin (1990), 'The Province of Government Determined: Delimiting the Direct Effect of Directives in the Common Law Context', *European Law Review*, **15**, 195.
34. See, in particular, Case C-106/89 *Marleasing SA v La Comercial Internacional de Alimentacion SA* [1992] 1 CMLR 305; and Joined Cases C-6/90 and C-9/90 *Andrea Francovich, Danila Bonifaci and Others v Italian Republic*, [1991] ECR I-5357.
35. See Jean Vergès (1981), 'De quelques méthodes de développement institutionnel des Communautés européennes' in *Mélanges offerts à Paul Reuter: Le droit international: unité et diversité*, Paris: Pedone.
36. See Kieran St. C. Bradley (1987), 'Maintaining the Balance: The Role of the Court of Justice in Defining the Institutional Position of the European Parliament', *Common Market Law Review*, **24**, 41; Kieran St. C. Bradley (1988), 'The Variable Evolution of the Standing of the European Parliament in Proceedings before the European Court of Justice', *Yearbook of European Law*, **8**, 27.
37. See Case 34/86 *Council v European Parliament* [1986] ECR 2155.

Part I
Perspectives on European Integration

[1]

Eric Stein*

ON DIVIDED-POWER SYSTEMS: ADVENTURES IN COMPARATIVE LAW

Of his many scholarly writings, Professor Schermers' multivolume 'International Organizations' is manifestly the most impressive one. It is also an exquisite example of an intelligent use of the comparative method as applied to intergovernmental international organisations, a family of divided-power systems.

I. ON COMPARABILITY

Two eminent comparatists tell us 'that comparisons can be useful only if the legal institutions under investigation are naturally and functionally comparable . . . . Comparative law is thus closely in tune with current trends in legal science when it asks what the function of legal institutions [in different systems] may be, rather than what their doctrinal structure is, and when it orders the solutions of the various systems upon a realistic basis by testing them for their responsiveness to the social needs they seek to fill.'[1]

This article essays a comparison between two radically different divided-power systems, the European Community, a *sui generis* international organisation, and the United States of America, a mature federation. The question is whether the two systems are 'naturally and functionally comparable' so as to make a comparison meaningful.

II. ON SIMILARITIES

In both the Community and the American federation power is allocated between central and local authorities, Community and Federal authorities on one hand, and the component state authorities on the other. Beyond

* Hessel E. Yntema Professor of Law, University of Michigan Law School.

1. Zweigert and Kötz, 1. *An Introduction to Comparative Law* 4, 39 (transl. by T. Weir, North-Holland Pub. Co., Amsterdam-New York-Oxford, 1977).

that, the two systems have certain fundamental common characteristics that support a comparative inquiry:

1. A quantum of power is transferred from local to central authority with a mechanism for reallocating central and local power in response to changing conditions;
2. The central authorities are in a greater or lesser degree independent of local authorities;
3. Within its sphere of competence, central law (federal and Community law) has precedence over local law and has direct impact on individual citizens;
4. There is a judicial mechanism for resolving disputes which arise concerning the allocation of power between the central and local authorities.[2]

There is also a similarity of the broad objectives of the two systems and of the means by which they have sought to achieve these objectives.[3] Both the Constitution and the EEC Treaty superimposed central institutional frameworks upon existing state structure with the objective of forming a 'more perfect union'. To be sure, the Constitution was intended to establish a nation, while the immediate purpose of the Treaty was limited to economic objectives, including a customs union and a 'common market'. But it is also true that, in the United States, a central reason for establishing the nation was to promote a 'common market'; and among the animating impulses for creating the European common market was the vision of an economic and political union as the culmination of the integration movement.

Comparative study of the two systems is also suggested by the reliance of each upon courts to advance their objectives. The Community is the only treaty-based system equipped with a court which may be approaching the role of a constitutional court in a federal system. The United States Supreme Court is, of course, the best known of such tribunals. By acquiescence of the political institutions, if not by design of the architects of the two systems, the courts in each have come to play a major role in defining the boundaries of central and local authorities. The interpretative techniques and the principles that the Supreme Court and the Court of Justice of the European Communities have developed in performing that role provide a fertile field for investigation.

2. On the role of the Court of Justice, see Stein, 'Lawyers, Judges, and the Making of a Transnational Constitution', 75 A.J.I.L. 1981, 1.

3. In this section of the article I rely heavily on Stein and Sandalow, 'On the Two Systems: An Overview' in Sandalow and Stein, 1. *Courts and Free Markets Perspectives from the United States and Europe* 3 (Clarendon Press–Oxford, 1982).

III. RISKS AND OPPORTUNITIES

However, any attempt to press American federation as a model for the Community would fly in the face of both history and present-day reality. In the nineteen eighties, surely Europe is in a situation radically different from that of the United States whether in 1787, or since. The egregious contextual and institutional differences need not be restated here.[4] We must not therefore expect to find that either system has developed 'solutions' that are readily transferable to the other. But the two systems today face a variety of common problems. This – and the similarities described earlier – suggests the possibility that, at the appropriate level of analysis, each system may draw on the other's experience. An examination of the manner in which each system has responded, and the reason that it has responded as it has may open some hitherto unseen opportunities for the other.

IV. ON CONTINENT-WIDE MARKETS: FREE MOVEMENT OF GOODS

A group of European and American judges, scholars and practitioners undertook such an examination, focusing specifically on the role of courts in the creation and maintenance of continent-wide free markets on both sides of the Atlantic.[5] It was in the area of free movement of goods within the two 'common markets' that functional comparison proved particularly compelling.

In the United States, the Commerce Clause of the Federal Constitution provides the cornerstone of federal authority.[6] The Supreme Court views the Commerce Clause not just as a source of Congressional power to regulate interstate commerce, but also as direct restraint on state power to affect such commerce. The EEC Treaty articles on free movement of goods[7] serve as a source of corresponding restraint on Member State action affecting movement of goods within the Community. There are significant similarities in the principles that the Supreme Court and the Court of Justice have developed for placing restrictions on state legislation that would impede interstate (intra-Community) movement of goods; and the methods that the two courts employ for determining the limits of state power are also quite similar.

4. *Ibid.* at 4–9.
5. See Vol. 1 and 2, *ibid.*
6. U.S. Constitution, Art. I, Sec. 8: 'The Congress shall have power ... [3] To regulate Commerce with Foreign Nations, and among the several States. ...'
7. EEC Treaty, Part II, Title I.

A. COMMON *VERSUS* LOCAL INTERESTS

Both courts demonstrated steadfast opposition to 'protectionist' policies. Legislation which in terms discriminates against goods from other states, by imposing restrictions not equally applicable to domestic goods, is invalid except in rare circumstances. The same is true of legislation which in terms attempts to restrict exports. Not surprisingly, both courts have had greater difficulty fashioning principles to deal with legislation which does not on its face reveal a protectionist aim, but has a disparate effect on domestic and foreign goods. Both have refused to adopt either of the extreme positions which might have been put forward, *i.e.* that all such legislation is either valid or invalid. In adjudicating the validity of such legislation, both courts have, rather, looked primarily to the aims of the legislation to ascertain whether it serves a protectionist policy or whether it promotes a legitimate interest of the state.

It has been suggested that the Court of Justice has adopted principles more restrictive of state power than those adopted by the Supreme Court. This suggestion rests upon an assessment of the attitudes of the two courts towards legislation which does not express a protectionist policy, but does none the less restrict the free movement of goods across state boundaries. The Court of Justice, it is argued, has held such legislation generally incompatible with the Treaty, while the Supreme Court has held that it is not proscribed by the Constitution. Support for this intriguing thesis can be found in the case law of the two courts, but it is not free of difficulty and rests upon an interpretation of the American decisions that is highly controversial.

The Court of Justice has on a number of occasions rendered opinions requiring the invalidation of legislation that could not fairly have been characterised as protectionist. Thus, the Court held that 'a national provision which requires, even purely as a formality. import or export licenses or any other similar procedure'[8] (such as an export declaration endorsed automatically by state customs authorities) was inconsistent with the Treaty. The Court has also ruled that the holder of a patent or trademark may not invoke a standard state industrial property law to prevent the importation of goods placed on the market in another Member State with the holder's consent.[9] Again, a Belgian charge on the import of diamonds was held illegal even though no diamonds are produced in that State and, hence, the charge did not serve to protect a domestic enterprise.[10] The Court held that any charges imposed on imports or exports, even *de minimis* fees designed to cover part of legitimate general administrative costs, are invalid unless shown to constitute

8. Case 68/76, *Commission* v. *France*, (1977) E.C.R. 515 at 530, citing Joint Cases 51 to 54, *International Fruit Company NV* v. *Produktschap voor Groenten en Fruit*, (1971) E.C.R. 1107.

9 See cases discussed by Schermers in: Sandalow and Stein, n. 3, *supra*, at 241 ff.

10. Joint Cases 2 and 3/69, *Sociaal Fonds voor de Diamant Arbeiders* v. *SA Brachfeld & Sons and Chougol Diamond Co.*, (1969) E.C.R. 211.

a fee for a public service performed exclusively for the benefit of the taxpayer or a part of the general internal taxation system.[11] These rulings, it is argued, rest upon the Court's view that the Treaty provisions expressing the free-movement-of-goods principle not only proscribe protectionism, but embody a policy of integration which supersedes state legislation that would hinder the establishment of a single, unified market. On this view, any legislation that would tend to fragment the Community-wide market is, if not *per se* invalid, at least subject to careful judicial scrutiny.

B. NON-DISCRIMINATION AND INTEGRATION

Some Americans argue that, in contrast with this view of the Community case law, the decisions of the Supreme Court do not similarly restrict state power, and that they may be explained by the single principle of 'anti-protectionism', the so-called 'non-discrimination' principle, without recourse to other 'federalist' values such as promoting a unified market and a more integrated economy. The Commerce Clause, it is argued, is a 'free trade charter' on an interstate level, but on an intra-state level the states are free to maintain a regulated, 'non-free' trading policy. The non-discrimination principle is a way of reconciling the two competing policies. Once the Court crosses the threshold of non-discrimination as the sole criterion of validity, it runs the risk – so goes the argument – of fastening upon the states an economic philosophy of *laissez-faire* that lacks constitutional warrant. During the first third of the current century the Court did, indeed, attempt to impose such a philosophy on both state and federal governments under now discredited doctrines of 'substantive due process'.[12] The unhappy consequences of that effort, it is suggested, are likely to keep the Court from making a similar effort under the Commerce Clause.

The accuracy of these differing characterisations of European and American case law is difficult to assess. To begin with, the relative paucity of European cases that raise the issue is itself an obstacle to determining whether, or to what extent, the Court of Justice is prepared to invalidate non-protectionist legislation that impedes the development of an integrated market. Of the cases cited in support of the claim that the Court applies an 'integration' principle, those involving import and export license cases may be explained without recourse to such a principle since there was at least a risk that the licence requirements might come to be administered in a way that would serve to protect the domestic market. The industrial property cases cannot be explained by the non-discrimination principle, but the history of the case law

11. See the cases discussed in Schermers, Stein and Sandalow, n. 3, *supra.* Ch. III, and Wägenbauer, *ibid.* Ch. V, *passim.*

12. *E.g. Lochner* v. *New York*, 198 U.S. 45 (1905); *Adkins* v. *Children's Hosp.*, 261 U.S. 525 (1923).

in that field suggests that the Court's concern in those cases may have been the distortion of competition as much as the free movement of goods. The strongest support for the claim that the Court has embraced a principle of integration comes from the Belgian diamond case and the cases invalidating minor cost-related charges on imports and exports. But though the rulings in these cases do seem to depend upon such a principle, the cases are plainly too few in number to permit a judgment about the depth of the Court's commitment to that principle and the circumstances in which it will be invoked.

In the United States, there is no paucity of cases, but equivalent difficulties are encountered in confidently describing the restrictions to which the states are subject under the Commerce Clause. In a series of cases involving transportation the Court has clearly gone beyond the non-discrimination principle, invalidating legislation that was not protectionist but that interfered with movement across state boundaries.[13] The state interests served by the invalidated legislation, the Court held, must yield to the national interest in an integrated transportation network. A similar principle has yet to be applied with respect to regulations affecting the movement of goods, but dicta in a number of the Court's opinions – including several of the most recent – indicate that the integration principle is in some measure applicable to that context.[14]

In evaluating the reluctance of the Supreme Court to invalidate non-protectionist state legislation, it is worth recalling that the Court is not the only agency of Government empowered to act. Congress may, under the Commerce Clause, limit state power to enact legislation which is thought to interfere unduly with an integrated national market. In the Community, similarly, the Council has power to restrict the authority of the Member States to enact such legislation if it can be shown that the legislation distorts the conditions of competition.[15] The Council may, moreover, be able to invoke its authority to harmonise national laws.[16]

C. METHOD AND PROCESS

Whether or not one concludes that the two courts apply substantially the same or different principles, it is clear that the methods they employ for determining the limits of state power are quite similar. In the past, the Supreme Court attempted to evolve diverse mechanical formulas for this purpose. The modern Supreme Court has rejected this approach. As recently

13. See Linde, 'Transportation and State Laws under the United States Constitution: The Evolution of a Judicial Doctrine' in 1 Sandalow and Stein, n. 3, *supra*, 139 ff.
14. See *e.g. H.P. Hood and Sons* v. *DuMond*, 336 U.S. 525 (1949); *Pike* v. *Bruce Church, Inc.*, 397 U.S. 137 (1970).
15. EEC Treaty Art. 101.
16. EEC Treaty Art. 100.

as 1983, the Supreme Court swept away the last debris of the 'supposedly precise division between "direct" and "indirect" effects on interstate commerce'[17] and now seeks, instead, to balance the legitimate interests of the states and the national interest in free trade among the states. State legislation which in terms restricts imports or exports is presumptively invalid and will be upheld only if it is supported by a compelling state interest. The few cases in which restrictions on imports have been upheld involved measures necessary to protect against virulent diseases. Restrictions on exports have been upheld only when necessary to protect the quality of exported goods. The validity of legislation not directly restricting imports or exports, but having a disparate effect upon them, is judged by determining whether it is supported by a legitimate state interest and, if so, whether the state interest could be served by means that would impose a lesser burden on interstate commerce.

In the Community, a similar balancing process is prescribed by the Treaty itself (Article 36) and it occurs in three stages. When the Court of Justice is faced with a state restriction on exports or imports, it will uphold it if it finds that it is justified on grounds of public health, security, or other important public policy considerations specified in Article 36, providing, however, that such a measure does not constitute 'arbitrary discrimination or a disguised restriction on trade' between the states. In applying this provision, the Court has established the so-called 'principle of proportionality' parallel to the American 'less restrictive alternative' principle, which it employs to determine whether the state interest, however legitimate, could be achieved by a measure less damaging to free trade than the one adopted. However, the Court does not engage in balancing when passing judgment upon the legality of state charges equivalent to customs duties or of discriminatory taxes since all such charges and taxes, with the narrow exceptions mentioned above, are held invalid. Similarly – in contrast with American practice – the Court will strike down restrictions applicable exclusively to exports, even if they are considered necessary to protect the quality of exported goods.[18]

'Of course, to say that the appropriate standard is a balancing test tells very little about the pattern of results that will be generated by applying the standard. Everything turns on what factors are placed on the scale, how they are characterised for purposes of evaluation, and how they are weighted

17. In overruling *Public Utilities Commission* v. *Attelboro Steam and Elec. Co.*, 273 U.S. 83 (1927) which was based on the 'direct' and 'indirect' distinction, the Court decided to follow 'the general trend in our modern Commerce Clause jurisprudence to look in every case to 'the nature of the state regulation involved, the objective of the state, and the effect of the regulation upon the national interest in the commerce". *Arkansas Elec. Co-op. Corp.* v. *Arkansas Public Com'n*, 103 S.Ct. 1905, U.S. (1983) at 1915, referring to *Pike* v. *Bruce Church, Inc.*, 397 U.S. 137 (1970) and other examples of the 'modern jurisprudence'.

18. Case 53/76, *Procureur de la République* v. *Bouhelier*, (1977) E.C.R. 197.

and ordered in the analysis.'[19] As might be expected, neither court recognises a state interest in protecting local buyers and sellers from competition with buyers and sellers from other states. On the contrary, the courts' belief that such an interest underlies legislation is virtually certain to lead to its invalidation. Thus, the Supreme Court recently struck down a North Carolina statute imposing labelling requirements on fruit allegedly for the purpose of consumer protection, but in reality to discourage competition from out-of-state fruit.[20] Similarly, in the *Cassis de Dijon* case, the Court of Justice did not hesitate to declare illegal, as applied to products imported from other Member States, a German law prohibiting the sale of certain types of liqueur with less than a fixed minimum alcohol content.[21] The Court concluded that the law was passed not to reduce the spread of alcoholism, as alleged by the German Government, but to exclude competing imported liqueurs.

Balancing occurs only when legislation is plausibly supported by legitimate interests. In the United States, the Court has, not surprisingly, given substantial weight to the state interest in the health and safety of its residents, to protecting plants and animals from disease, and to environmental protection. The Court has also been highly respectful of the state interest in maintaining the stability of markets, upholding state price regulation and compulsory marketing arrangements designed to promote that interest. Similar results have been reached by the Court of Justice, though the Court has held price regulations to be illegal restrictions on imports if they deprive foreign producers of a natural competitive advantage or interfere with the Community price systems. Moreover, rather than relying exclusively on Article 36 exceptions, the Court now appears to read Article 30 itself as excluding from its prohibition state legislation 'necessary in order to satisfy mandatory requirements relating to the effectiveness of fiscal supervision, the protection of public health, the fairness of commercial transactions and the defense of the consumer.'[22] Thus the Court upheld on health protection grounds the Belgian prohibition against selling strong alcoholic beverages in public places and a German law against night time bread baking in the face of the arguments that the laws have a distinctly protectionist impact, if not design.[23] It is interesting to note that, eschewing illusory precision in favour of realistic flexibility, the Court did not resort to formulas such as the 'direct' and 'indirect' impact distinction, although this was suggested by some authors.[24]

19. Blasi, 'Constitutional Limitations on the Power of States to Regulate the Movement of Goods in Interstate Commerce' in Sandalow and Stein, n. 3, *supra*, 174 at 185.

20. *Hunt* v. *Washington State Apple Advertising Comm'n*, 432 U.S. 333 (1977).

21. Case 120/78, *Rewe-Zentral AG* v. *Bundesmonopolverwaltung für Branntwein*, (1979) E.C.R. 649 at 662. See Everling, 'Zur neueren EuGH-Rechtsprechung zum Wettbewerbsrecht', 17 EuR 1982, 301.

22. *Ibid*. at 662.

23. Case 75/81, *Blesgen* v. *Belgian State*, (1982) E.C.R. 1211; Case 155/80, *Oebel*, (1981) E.C.R. 1993.

24. *E.g.* Waelbroeck, *Les réglementations nationales de prix et le droit communautaire*, p. 34 (Editions de l'Université de Bruxelles, 1975).

D. PRE-EMPTION

Still in the context of interstate commerce, the European participants in the above mentioned study became particularly intrigued by the case law on federal pre-emption that the Supreme Court has developed over the years in deciding whether Congressional legislation has the effect of precluding the states from legislating in areas that would be otherwise within their constitutional authority.[25] In fact, the Court of Justice engaged in a very similar thought process when it was asked to rule, for example, whether Member States may adopt marketing legislation in an area covered by a Community marketing regulation, when on its face the national legislation did not conflict with the Community law.[26] According to an eminent member of the Court of Justice, the European participants 'felt a delight not unlike that of Monsieur Joardain, Moliere's famous character, when he discovered that he had been speaking prose for years without being aware of it.'[27]

V. NO COMPARABILITY IN FOREIGN AFFAIRS?[28]

If the case can be made for comparability between the American experience in interstate commerce and the European internal market regime, can the same be said with regard to the foreign affairs functions in the two systems? Or are the institutional and contextual differences so striking that an attempt at a comparison would entail crossing Coleridge's line separating imagination from fancy?

In the first place, when it comes to foreign affairs, the United States in effect is – and has been since the Constitution – a unitary state with exclusive federal foreign affairs powers, a national diplomatic establishment and a national army. The component states have no international personality and they are excluded from participation in foreign affairs, although their activities and laws impinge on federal policy and activities.

In Europe, on the other hand, there is a complex division of foreign affairs powers between the Member States and the Community institutions. The Member States remain sovereign states with international personality, they retain full control of their armies, defence and diplomatic policies, but since

25. Cohen, 'Congressional Power to Define State Power to Regulate Commerce: Consent and Pre-emption' in 2 Sandalow and Stein, n. 3, *supra*, at 523 ff.
26. Waelbroeck, 'The Emergent Doctrine of Community Pre-Emption – Consent and Redelegation', *ibid.* at 548 ff.
27. Pescatore, *ibid.* Vol. 1 at IX.
28. See Stein (in cooperation with Henkin), 'Towards a European Foreign Policy? – The European Foreign Affairs System from the Perspective of the United States Constitution', to be published as a part of a project on 'Methods, Tools and Potential for European Legal Integration in the Light of American Federal Experience', sponsored by the European University Institute in Florence, Italy, under the direction of Professor Mauro Cappelletti.

1970, they have agreed to consult on a regular basis on their diplomatic ('political') foreign policies through the European Political Cooperation mechanism[29], a loose, extra-Community structure of committees, staffed exclusively by national diplomats under the Conference of Foreign Ministers.

In the foreign economic field, the Member States transferred specific powers to the Community institutions and they share authority with the Community. But even in the areas within the exclusive Community power, the Member States, unlike the American states, participate directly in the policy-making as a result of their role in the central Community organ, the Council of Ministers.

There are other significant differences between the two systems, not the least one the absence of single nationality for Community citizens. Moreover, the constitutive document of the United States federation is a constitution while in the Community it is a treaty among sovereign states. Yet the American Constitution was regarded by many as essentially an agreement – 'a compact' – among the thirteen sovereign states. The compact theory provided the underpinning for a variety of efforts to limit federal power, although it was rejected by the Supreme Court in *McCulloch* v. *Maryland*[30] and also, much later, in the *Curtiss-Wright* case[31] in the context of the affirmation of undivided national sovereignty over foreign affairs. The doctrine served, however, as an important political symbol of 'states' rights' until the Civil War. It is interesting to note that, although the Community was established by a treaty, as early as 1962 the Court of Justice refused to treat that treaty as an ordinary international agreement merely creating mutual obligations among sovereign states. The Court insisted instead on interpreting the treaty in a constitutional mode as creating 'a new legal order,' one in which Community law is directly applicable within its proper sphere[32] and paramount over national law[33], with an important impact on the foreign affairs powers of the Community.

VI. FINIS TO THE 'ENUMERATED POWERS' PRINCIPLE?

Another jurisprudential development in the Community suggests a comparison. In the United States, the Tenth Amendment to the Constitution lays down the principle 'enumerated powers', namely that powers not dele-

29. Stein, 'European Political Cooperation (EPC) as a Component of the European Foreign Affairs System', 43 *Zeitschrift für ausländisches Recht und Völkerrecht* 1983, 43.
30. 17 U.S. (4 Wheat.) 316 (1819).
31. *United States* v. *Curtiss-Wright Corp.*, 299 U.S. 304 (1936).
32. Case 26/62, *Van Gend & Loos* v. *Nederlandse administratie der belastingen*, (1963) E.C.R. 1 at 12.
33. Case 6/64, *Flaminio Costa* v. *ENEL*, (1964) E.C.R. 585.

gated to the federal Government are reserved to the states. In the foreign relations field, the Constitution confers certain specific powers on the federal authorities[34], not a general 'power to conduct foreign relations', as for instance the German *Grundgesetz* confers on the Federal institutions.[35] Yet the Supreme Court has made it clear that the Tenth Amendment limitation does not apply to the foreign affairs powers of the federal government. The courts have not hesitated to fill in the gaps and silences in the Constitution and to uphold federal powers not specifically transferred, through the traditional methods of interpretation, construction, the use of the 'necessary and proper' clause, and finally in 1936 through the radical doctrine in the already cited *Curtiss-Wright* case.[36] In that case, which – it should be noted – is at least in part based on a particular historical conception of the origin of the United States federation, the Supreme Court concluded that the federal foreign affairs powers do not depend on the Constitution (or on the Constitution alone), but are inherent in the national 'external sovereignty'. Thus, the status of the United States as a subject of international law, its 'international personality', determines not only the scope of its inherent foreign affairs powers in relation to other nations but also – and this is the curious aspect – the *internal allocation* of these powers to the federal authorities to the exclusion of the states.

The concept of 'enumerated powers' was clearly intended to apply as a general rule in the Community. The EEC Treaty confers specific foreign affairs powers on the Commission and the Council in a few provisions, primarily concerning foreign commercial policy.[37] In the view of a great majority of writers, the Community powers were to be viewed as limited to these specific power grants. Yet in the celebrated *ERTA* case[38], the Court of Justice, defying the learned opinion, reached a remarkable conclusion that would do away for all practical purposes with the 'enumerated powers' principle as applied in foreign affairs. The Court employed the teleological concept of '*effet utile*' and the interpretative criterion of 'the spirit, general scheme and wording of the Treaty' to hold that the Community foreign affairs power does not depend on the limited specific Treaty attributions but may be found in the general provisions as viewed in the overall Treaty system. Thus, the Community has the power to enter into international agreements with third countries on any subject which falls within its internal competence if the agreement is necessary for the achievement of a Community objective.

In the *ERTA* case, the Court buttressed its novel doctrine by referring to the 'international personality' of the Community which it found embodied in Article 210 of the Treaty.[39] The Court interpreted the article to mean

34. U.S. Constitution Art. II, Sec. 2, 3.; Art. I, Sec. 8. See generally: Henkin, *Foreign Affairs and the Constitution* (The Foundation Press, Mineola, N.Y. 1972).
35. Basic Law of the Federal Republic of Germany, Art. 32, also Art. 59.
36. See n. 31, *supra*.
37 EEC Arts. 111–116, 228–231, 237, 238.
38. Case 22/70, *Commission* v. *Council (ERTA)*, (1971) E.C.R. 263.
39. Art. 210: The Community shall have legal personality.

that 'in its external relations the Community enjoys the capacity to establish contractual links with third countries over the whole field of objectives defined' in the Treaty.[40] If the Court meant to say that the Community's international personality in international law determines the internal allocation of powers between its institutions and the Member States, it would have in effect embraced the Supreme Court rationale in the *Curtiss-Wright* case.[41] I doubt, however, that the Court had this interpretation in mind.[42]

It was obviously the need for the Member States to speak with a single voice in international economic relations that impelled the Court to define Community power in such broad terms. We may recall that on the other side of the Atlantic, some two centuries earlier, the same need to face the world more efficiently was a major impulse for the young American Republic to move from a Confederation to a Federation.

VII. THE REALITY OF FOREIGN AFFAIRS POWERS

I have explored elsewhere the structure and the means for foreign policy making in the two systems.[43] The size of this article does not permit restating the detailed findings here.

Clearly, one must avoid facile analogies between the roles of the principal actors in the foreign affairs area, the President of the United States acting alone or together with the Congress or Senate, and the Community Commission acting with the Council. Yet, not unlike the federal executive, the Commission maintains a sizeable foreign affairs establishment in Brussels and some 60 'delegations' and other offices abroad; one hundred and seventeen foreign missions are accredited to the Community in the Belgian capital.

Again, both systems face similar problems in the international economic arena and employ functionally similar means to accomplish their respective objectives. They use *autonomous* means (legislative and administrative acts) to enact and manipulate the uniform customs tariff and to adopt a spectrum of commercial policy measures such as customs, antidumping and anti-subsidy legislation and economic sanctions. They employ *conventional* means by negotiating treaties with third states. The Community, alone or

40. Case 22/70, n. 38, *supra*, at 274.
41. See n. 31, *supra*.
42. It is more likely that in the *ERTA* case the Court had in mind simply buttressing its broad systemic construction of the Treaty and rejecting the fanciful doctrine that only states – and no international organisations or groupings – can possess international personality, and that in particular the Community itself is nothing more than an agency, 'a common organ in the hands of States'. See Pescatore in: Timmermans and Völker (Eds.), *Division of Powers between the European Communities and their Member States in the Field of External Relations* (Kluwer, Deventer, The Netherlands, 1981), pp. 13–14.
43. See n. 28, *supra*.

along with the Member States, has negotiated a bewildering variety of commercial, 'association' and 'economic cooperation' agreements and it has established links with most global and regional organisations. For all practical purposes, the Community replaced the Member States in the General Agreement on Tariffs and Trade. In trade matters, the Commission negotiates under a closely circumscribed mandate from the Council, while the President's representative negotiates on behalf of the United States by virtue of a power delegated by the Congress under the Commerce Clause of the Constitution.

The comparison in the field of international responsibility becomes complicated by the inchoate state of integration in the Community, particularly if the question should arise in the context of a breach of a 'mixed agreement' to which the Community and the Member States are a party.

The judiciary in both systems has been called upon to interpret the meaning of international agreements and to determine their compatibility with the Constitution and the EEC Treaty respectively, as well as the impact of these instruments on individual citizens (the 'self-executing' effect). Generally, the area of treaty making, interpretation and application is particularly suitable for constructive comparison.

VIII. CONCLUDING OBSERVATIONS

Early in the life of the Community, a prominent member of its Court of Justice wrote: '[F]ederalist interpretation of the European treaties is particularly fruitful; . . . it is really in the thought, in the methods and in the historical experience of federalism that the future builders of Europe should seek their inspiration, much more than in the domain of international relations'.[44]

American practice, extending as it does over more than two centuries, may be helpful, especially because of its longer historical perspective and the amplitude of the material. American experience may indicate a line of thought or a particular technique which may be considered by the Community institutions; but it may also suggest what Europe should avoid, as for example mechanistic formulas in judicial interpretation or excesses of the separation-of-powers doctrine.

The American legal establishment may profit from the European developments. In some respects, such as the weight accorded to international agreements in its internal legal order or the facility for a judicial review of a treaty for 'constitutionality' before it is ratified, the Community law represents a clear advance over the American rule.

In any event, legal comparisons, adventurous as they may appear, provide deeper insights into the working of the two systems and thus contribute to much needed mutual understanding in the transatlantic dialogue among diplomats, practitioners and scholars.

44. Pescatore, 'Les rélations extérieures des Communautés européennes', (1961, II) R.C.A.D.I., 1 at 21 (*my translation*).

[2]

Journal of Common Market Studies
Volume XXI, No. 4 June 1983

The Selectivity of Economic Integration Theories: A Comparison of Some Traditional and Marxist Approaches

W.G.C.M. HAACK

Economics Faculty, University of Amsterdam

Introduction

International economic integration – or regional economic integration as it is sometimes called – is mainly a post- World War Two phenomenon. Together with the successive establishment of several economic groupings in the world a theory of economic integration has been developed, which has acquired an acknowledged place in most textbooks on international economics. In this context an enormous amount of theoretical, empirical and practical studies of all kinds of aspects of economic integration has appeared.

The results of integration research, however, are sometimes questioned. By this I do not only mean the "normal" questioning, which is an essential part of scientific progress, but a more fundamental questioning whether the questions posed, the methods used and the results obtained are the right or important ones. It is not relevant here whether one calls this a matter of paradigm or not, but it is clear that the question concerned is of vital importance for integration theory. Sometimes the need for a new and different approach is advocated, e.g. in a recent contribution of J. Pelkmans, who tries to apply the methods of the so-called "New Political Economy" to integration problems.[1]

This article is also devoted to these fundamental issues. It is largely based on the results obtained from a research project in which a comparison was made between "traditional" and "critical" – mainly neo-Marxist – theories of economic integration.[2] First we will try to discern the strong and the weak points of traditional or academic integration theory

[1] Pelkmans, 1980.

[2] Haack, 1981.

(part 2). After that a critical account will be given of a number of "critical" theories (part 3). In the concluding sections of both parts of the article some preliminary conclusions will be formulated. The last part (4) of the article examines the state of integration theory with the aid of these conclusions and tries to eleborate some suggestions for new research on this basis.

This article is limited to the analysis of international economic integration of so-called "mixed" or "capitalist" economies. Although interesting parallels can be drawn between the integration of mixed and of centrally planned economies, there are also important differences between the two. In accordance with prevailing literature we will therefore restrict ourselves to only one type of integration.

Traditional Integration theory

It is, of course, not my intention to present a complete survey of the present state of integration theory in this part of the article. This job has been done excellently by others, quite recently e.g. by Robson.[3] Instead I will focus on the sort of questions asked, the type of analysis used, to answer these questions and the main results obtained in this way. It will be shown that out of the many questions that could be asked, attention is mainly focussed on only some of them.

The literature on economic integration can be divided very crudely into two broad categories. The first is of a theoretical-analytical nature. For the largest part this literature is firmly rooted in the neo-classical micro-economic and Keynesian/monetarist macro-economic tradition. It mainly analyzes the consequences of a given integration-arrangement (or, less often, the specifics of such an arrangement to obtain given results, which is the other way around). Integration is generally conceived of in these studies as (i) a tariff arrangement, esp. a free trade area or a customs union, and/or (ii) the complete or partial liberation of factor movements, and/or (iii) the cooperation in the field of economic policy, ranging from loose forms of coordination to complete unification. It is clear that on the basis of the aforementioned measures an infinite variety of integration arrangements is in principle possible. In practice most studies limit themselves to one of the forms summed up in the well-known typology introduced by Balassa: free trade area, customs union, common market, economic union and complete economic integration.[4]

A second category of literature is of an historical-descriptive nature. It deals with the problems and achievements of factual integration arrangements. A central question in these studies is: how successful has the integration attempt been (successful in this context meaning in what

[3] Robson, 1980.

[4] Balassa, 1962.

measure the provisions of the integration arrangement are indeed realized). In this way integration itself is considered a primary goal of the arrangement. The effects on member economies generally receive attention in these studies too. Sometimes this is done by giving the theoretical concepts of the first-mentioned type of literature some empirical content. A great many of these studies are devoted to the European Economic Community, as one of the most remarkable integration arrangements attempted. In this article the treatment of factual problems will also be limited to the EEC.

In general it can be said that traditional integration theory is mainly concerned with the effects of economic integration. Some authors even explicitly limit the task of economic theory to this problem.[5] Then the question as to which effects integration theory should investigate arises. In general the answer to this question is: the effects on the availability and use of scarce goods. This can be done by the anlysis of changes in economic variables, like real national income, employment, income distribution, the balance of payments, etc. In a mixed economy these variables are at the same time objects of concern of government economic policy, in the sense that for these variables more or less precise targets are formulated. Using the aforementioned three types of possible integration measures and a list of generally accepted economic variables or objectives of economic policy we can construct the following crude scheme of the tasks of integration theory.

economic variables (policy targets)	"real" variables							"monetary variables				other policy objectives	
integration-measures	alloc.	ec. of scale	t.o.t.	ec. growth	inc. distr.	ec. struct	. . .	empl.	infl.	BoP	. . .	pol. integr.	. . .
1) tariff-arrangement:													
free trade area													
customs-union													
2) liberalization of factor movements:													
labour													
capital													
3) cooperation in economic policy:													
coordination													
harmonization													
unification													

[5] Robson, 1980.

To survey integration theory one can indicate the successive consequences of the three types of integration measures – the column – on the variables mentioned in the row. We will go the other way around and take the row variables as our starting-point and investigate how integration theory has dealt with them.

Real income analysis

Under this heading the results of research into the consequences of economic integration for the level of real national income – mainly determined by changes in allocation, production conditions and terms of trade – the growth of real income, the distribution within and between countries and the commodity and regional composition of output – the economic structure – are discussed.

The generally best known part of integration theory is the analysis of the allocative effects of the formation of a customs-union. This so-called customs union theory was initiated by Viner,[6] who introduced the famous concepts of trade creation and trade diversion. The first reflects the move toward internal free trade and Pareto-optimality, the second results from increased discrimination and violates the optimum conditions. Since then customs union theory – including the analysis of free trade areas or other preferential trading arrangements – has undergone several major theoretical refinements and extensions. Important developmets were the introduction of a general equilibrium framework of analysis and of other (apart from tariffs) distortions of competitive conditions like economies of scale.

On the basis of different assumptions a large variety of models has been developed with the aid of which the effects on allocation and terms of trade can be studied. The conclusions reached generally confirm the one drawn by Viner, that, depending on the circumstances, positive and negative effects on the level of real national income are possible. The total income of the customs union may increase, a decrease is however also possible. While one of the participating countries may gain, another may lose. The same is true for one, some or all of the third countries. One cannot say anything definite in general, all depends on the particular concrete circumstances. There is however a bias in the theoretical literature that at least one of the participating countries gains, the customs union as a whole gains and a third country is adversely affected.

Much less attention has been paid to the real income effects of the liberalization of the factors of production. It seems that in general positive effects are assumed. According to standard trade theory factor mobility would lead to an improved allocation. In the case of economic integration an extra complication arises: the internal degree of liberalization is likely to

[6] Viner, 1950.

diverge from the otherwise existing regulations. This may give rise to "diversion" in factor movements: movements between the partners substituting for movements from and to third countries. Apart from allocative effects this may have important distributional consequences. Research in this field is, however, scarce.

The real income effects of policy cooperation in principle come from two sources. The first stems from the decrease of international discrimination that results from policy cooperation and is completely similar to the effects of the customs union. The same effects on allocation, terms of trade and production conditions may result. This aspect is prominent in matters like tax harmonization, unification of legislation, etc. The second group of effects, which seems far more important, results from the content of policy cooperation. Theoretically speaking this is very difficult to analyze because it is virtually impossible to isolate the changes in national policy as a result of economic integration. So, what should be considered as an effect of integration? Apart from this theoretical difficulty a number of more practical problems arise. We will come back to this in the next paragraph.

Up to now we have summarized what are sometimes called the "static" or "once and for all" effects of economic integration on real national income. Much importance has however always been attached to the so-called "dynamic" effects of integration, i.e. the effects on economic growth. Theoretical analysis of these effects is in the main still of a rather simple nature. In general a couple of factors or mechanisms by which economic growth would be affected are listed. In these lists appear: permanent utilization of scale economies, increased competition ("the cold shower") and diminished uncertainty leading to faster technological progress and bigger investments, etc.

Several attempts have been made to measure the real income effects of the EEC.[7] There seems to be a *communis opinio* that the EEC has mainly led to trade creating, i.e. welfare improving, allocative effects. Trade diversion is only suspected to have taken place in the field of agriculture. Although the amount of trade created is often considered rather large (e.g. one half to one third of total internal EEC trade in manufactures) the resulting positive real income effect is rather disappointing, i.e. far less than one percentage point of GNP.

Empirical work on terms of trade effects is rather scarce. An optimistic conclusion is reached by Petith, who concludes that ". . . the terms of trade improvements were perhaps the major economic effects of European integration."[8] According to his opinion an improvement of 0.3–1% of GNP may have been the result of the formation of the EEC.

Empirical estimates of economies of scale are lacking. Balassa considers

[7] See f.i. Balassa, 1975.

[8] Petith, 1977.

them a part of the aforementioned dynamic effects, which he estimates at about 0.5% of GNP (in 1970).

Apart from the level and growth of real income the distribution within and between countries is an important variable. The internal distribution has not received much attention. Standard trade and factor mobility-theory suggests a tendency towards factor price equalization and a relative decrease of the renumeration of the scarce factor (i.e. labour?).[9] This conclusion is reached in a completely static framework and is based on rather restrictive assumptions (*inter alia* that factor rewards equal marginal productivities). If one of these conditions is not fulfilled the outcome is less sure. Distribution between participating countries has received somewhat more attention, e.g. in the already mentioned terms of trade analysis. The often strenuous negotiations between member countries on policy issues also suggests that the distribution of gains and losses is an important element of integration attempts. In his well-known survey article of 1972 Melvyn Krauss saw changes in income distribution within or between countries (and possibly political motives) even as the main forces behind economic integration. Although rigorous empirical research in this field is still lacking Waelbroeck on the other hand holds the opinion that "apart from the Common Agricultural Policy of the EEC this integration has not led to marked changes in the distribution of incomes among individuals or among countries."[10]

A last factor which can be treated under this heading could be called the "economic structure." By this we mean the regional, sectoral (and sometimes even the intra-sectoral) and commodity composition of production, trade and consumption. The allocative effects of integration result in a change in specialization and division of labour between member countries. Each country specializes according to comparative advantage. This leads to changes in economic structure, with the result that countries concentrate on certain products of sectors while others are abandoned. Initially it was sometimes feared (or hoped) that the establishment of the EEC would make whole sectors disappear in certain countries. In practice however the specialization took place largely within sectors. Trade between member countries became increasingly intra-industry trade. This result can be explained by the fact that the economic resources of the member countries are largely similar and specialization is mainly the result of economies of scale, product-differentiation and so-called firm-specific factors. This brings us to the study of the influence of economic integration on certain business sectors, groups of firms, competition, concentration and so on. This field is covered by the emerging literature on (European) industrial organization.[11] Initially integration may lead to increased competition.

[9] Balassa, 1976.

[10] Waelbroeck, 1976, p. 97.

[11] Jacquemin, 1975; Jacquemin and de Jong, 1978.

This may improve allocation and efficiency, mainly in the static sense. That this tendency was not frustrated by private restrictions was the main reason for the incorporation of the rules on competition in the Rome Treaty.

A larger market however offers opportunities for production on an increased scale, so integration can also be said to be conducive to concentration. Other more dynamic factors (technological developments, the importance of R and D, etc.) also favour size. Competition policy and the emerging industrial policy of the EC therefore seem to take a stand somewhere in between competition and concentration. Empirical research points to an increased degree of concentration on European markets.[12] The contribution of integration to this process however is not easy to isolate. The effect integration may have on economic structure is occasionally even put forward as a main motive for such integration. In the context of developing countries Cooper and Masell showed that a public preference for a certain sector, i.e. the industrial one, may be effectuated by the creation of a customs-union. True as this may be, it can never be an argument for integration on its own, because there are more efficient ways to create the same effect. The argument is valuable only in combination with other conditions.

Changing the national structures of production integration on the other hand may have regional and sectoral consequences, that are unacceptable and require policy action. The Treaty of Rome incorporates specific provisions in this field. Regional policy is still largely a matter for national governments. In the case of sectoral policy it is mainly agricultural policy (and quite recently the steel policy) that is a Community affair. In agriculture this policy has deliberate redistributional and allocative effects. But how far is this a result of integration?

Policy objectives

In the development of integration theory more and more attention is devoted to the influence of integration processes on the attainment of the macro-economic objectives of government economic policy, like price stability and external balance. These variables are of course not completely different from the ones treated previously. For real income (growth), distribution and economic structure governments also formulate more or less precise targets. The outcome however is largely the result of market forces, indirectly influenced by governments. The other objectives like internal and external equilibrium are more often considered the exclusive domain of the government, though private actions have a considerable influence in these fields also. The main difference probably lies in the fact that the variables treated above are largely "real" variables, whilst the

[12] Locksly and Ward, 1979.

ones we are now turning to are closely connected with monetary phenomena.

At first sight this does not seem to hold for employment, for the level of employment is intimately linked with the degree of productive activity. Negative effects of integration on employment however are mainly a result of the processes of re-allocation that will take place. So the main problem is that of the transfer of labour from the one to the other occupation, which may be effected after a transitional period. If an overall diminution of employment were to result, this could be taken as an indication that the country concerned has too high a price level according to international standards, which could be corrected by internal restrictions or a change of its exchange rate. In this way the employment or price level effects of integration are regarded as primarily temporary and eventually corrigible by an appropriate monetary and financial policy. The same reasoning can be applied to possible balance of payments problems.

It is a well-known fact however that national economic policies may conflict and frustrate the attainment of each other's policy objectives. This problem has given rise to a voluminous literature about the coordination of macro-economic policies in integration schemes, esp. monetary and fiscal policy.[13]

As a first approach "optimum currency area" theories may be mentioned. Several authors have tried to formulate criteria by which to decide whether countries ought to maintain fixed exchange rates amongst themselves or adopt a regime of flexible rates. The basis for these criteria was in general the existence of sufficient adjustment mechanisms to ensure the possibility of simultaneous achievement of internal and external equilibrium of the countries concerned. Among the criteria mentioned were e.g. a sufficient degree of factor mobility, the degree of openness of the economy, etc. As countries conform to these criteria in differing degrees a fixed exchange rate system will be more advantageous for some countries than for others; some may even lose. It is therefore sometimes suggested that it is better to study the possible advantages and disadvantages of monetary integration for specific countries. The main argument for monetary integration is the increase of efficiency by reducing uncertainty, thereby promoting improved allocation. This of course is wholly dependent on the efficiency of the market mechanism. Another frequently prevailing idea is that policy objectives are more easily or better attained by monetary integration. One has however to be careful in this respect. If monetary integration is defined – as is most often done – as the fixing of exchange rates and the complete liberalization of internal financial transactions, then the countries concerned give up an important instrument of economic policy. According to Tinbergen's rule the number of attainable policy goals

[13] Allen and Kenen, 1980.

will diminish as a consequence. This suggests that monetary integration leads to a weaker policy performance. This remains true even if monetary integration is extended by a common monetary policy. The seeming paradox is explained if it is realized that up to now policy performance is measured in terms of national goals. If union goals are adopted monetary integration in the broad sense, including an integrated monetary policy, would create the same situation as before, but for a bigger unit. In this case however, national governments have to give up national policy objectives and compromise with others. This loss of sovereignty may well be considered the main cost of monetary integration. This result is the consequence of the well-known "disciplinary" character of fixed exchange rates (which some consider as their main attraction). Other costs of monetary integration may be related to the balance of payments adjustments between different parts of the union. A possible aggravation of regional imbalances is sometimes mentioned in this respect.

In practice monetary integration in the EEC is of a limited character. In the EMS an attempt is made to maintain fixed exchange rates, while monetary policy rests in national hands.

The EC Commission clearly recognizes that national policy objectives have to be brought into line — "convergence" is a declared target of monetary integration[14] – but the discipline does not seem to work very well up till now. It shows that countries are very reluctant to hand over any competence in the field of economic policy making.

This is also illustrated in the case of fiscal policy. Some achievements have been made in this field, mainly the introduction of the VAT — but these are purely motivated by "technical" reasons, i.e. the elimination of distortions of competition (see the preceding section). There are no indications that the "political" elements of fiscal policy – level and structure of government income and expenditure – are soon to be integrated. In principle this would make it easier to attain Community goals of employment, price stability and so on. Until now the costs of the loss of sovereignty are however apparently considered too high, though the effectiveness of national policy is already somewhat impaired by the loss of the instrument(s) of commercial policy (and exchange rate policy). In this respect the European Community is an example of stagnating "spill-over".

As mentioned before sometimes integration itself is considered a policy objective. Where this is the case this objective may conflict with other policy goals. The losses in realization of these goals may be considered the costs of the integration achievements. Sometimes a real income loss is indeed defended in these terms. In view of the earlier remarks on the resistance of states to policy integration one may doubt however the priority of the integration objective. One gets the impression governments

[14] EC Commission, 1979.

may use it as an excuse if unpleasant measures have to be made acceptable.

On the other hand, integration is often seen in the light of other, more fundamental objectives of government policies. These are mainly related to the strengthening of the position of the integrated area in the world. Apart from economic considerations, such as bargaining power in trade or monetary matters, one may think of the political influence in international affairs, the defence of the existing social system, the maintenance of certain common ideological values and the preservation of a shared cultural identity. In the process of European economic integration these elements have undoubtedly played a role. It is difficult however to assess the practical importance of these "political" objectives in relation to the aforementioned "economic" policy goals. Where do these goals conflict or coincide? What are the national priorities? Are national priorities conflicting? How do national priorities develop in the course of time? etc. The detailed dynamic specification of the social welfare function that these questions call for, however, has until now not figured in integration theory. Apart from the general reference to "political objectives" the emphasis has been laid on the traditional "economic" goals that were discussed above.

Preliminary conclusions

In traditional integration theory the real income effects of different economic integration measures occupy a prominent place. Customs union theory especially, which focuses on the changes in allocation as a result of certain tariff arrangements, still holds a central position. With the aid of this theory, valuable insights are gained into the changes in international trade flows as a result of customs union formation and the condition for a welfare creating — i.e. real income increasing — customs union.

In structural and dynamic respects integration theory is much less developed. This is mainly due to the very restrictive assumptions that underlie neo-classical general equilibrium theory, in which tradition a great deal of the theory is still developed. An increasing amount of empirical research in this field – at least with regard to the EC – is however carried out.

Another problem to which integration theory rather surprisingly does not give much theoretical and empirical attention is the effect of integration or internal income distribution. Only the distribution of gains and losses between countries receive some amount of attention.

A rather recent development has been the increased attention paid to integration effects on goals of economic policy. Attention has been mainly directed to monetary integration and the achievement of internal and external equilibrium. Some promising results have been reached in this area. The contribution of "political" goals to the integration process is always recognized, but difficult to handle however. These goals are seldom really "integrated" in the analysis.

The (neo-)marxist approach

During the seventies integration problems received attention in neo-Marxist and other "critical" literature. This was mainly devoted to factual integration phenomena, i.e. the EEC, and hardly to the building of general integration theories. Partly on the basis of different theoretical backgrounds several schools of thought that emphasize different factors have developed. It is impossible to give a complete survey of the many contributions to the on-going debate. I will limit myself to a broad outline of the main arguments that are advanced.

The common basis of Marxist integration theories is of course the Marxian theory of social development, in which class conflict occupies a central role. Although we cannot go into the general theory of Marxism we have to signal two notions that play a fundamental role in integration-theory.

The first one is *capital*, which is defined as a social relationship characterized by exploitation of labour. Marx himself based it on the labour theory of value, for others the monopoly of private property forms a sufficient basis for exploitation. There is an antagonistic class relationship between capital and labour, which has to form the basis of all analysis of social phenomena. For the study of international economic integration this means that an anlaysis in terms of countries is incomplete and that an analysis on the basis of classes must be added.

The central purpose of capital is to earn a profit. In pursuing this the different parts of capital (firms and enterprises) are in a competitive relationship towards each other. This leads *inter alia* to the regular introduction of new production technologies. The speed of accumulation of individual capitals is not the same. The result is a process of concentration and centralization: competition leads more or less automatically to monopolistic market structures.

The search for profit by individual capitals is not limited by national frontiers. Capital "internationalizes" itself by international trade, foreign investment and the so-called internationalization of production practised by multinational companies. Economic integration is of course closely related with this internationalization of capital.

A second fundamental notion of Marxism that is extremely important in integration theory concerns the *state*. This is not the neutral, the general interest promoting institution of traditional economic theory, but the product of a social development dominated by class conflict. This determines the class character of the state, which has among its most important functions the maintenance of the existing social and economic order, i.e. private property on which exploitation is based. Originally in most Marxist writings the state was seen as completely dominated by the interests of capital. The state was just an instrument in the hands of the ruling class. More recently the state is approached more carefully. First of all the conflicts between individual capitals or groups of capital are acknowledged. There is no such thing as *the* interest of capital, there are just interests of different capitalists. The state is thus the battlefield of conflicting interests of different capitals. Secondly the fundamental class conflict between capital and labour is also operating on state level. State policies are the result of this conflict and not only determined by the interests of capital. A third factor is that state actions cannot always and immediately be traced down to economic interests. Political and ideological factors play an important and "relatively autonomous" role. It is important to note, however, that in Marxist theorizing state policies are in principle considered endogenous variables, that have to be explained in terms of the above-mentioned factors.

The foundations

Neither Marx or Engels has occupied himself extensively with the theory of international economic relations. In *Das Kapital* international trade is only occasionally mentioned. The world market was planned to receive adequate attention in a later volume that was, however, never written.

It was only in the beginning of the twentieth century that a broad discussion among Marxists concerning the international character of capitalist development took place, the so-called imperialism debate. A prominent place in this discussion was taken by Lenin, who emphasized the permanent conflicts of interests between the various groups of national capitals and the states that were connected with them. In this framework he also mentioned the possibility of the cooperation of European states. His remark that under capitalism a United States of Europe would be either reactionary or impossible is well-known.[15]

The modern discussion on European economic integration was greatly stimulated by a book published by the Belgian Marxist economist Ernest Mandel in 1968.[16] He saw the European Community as the beginning of a new system of government that was to transcend national states. This fitted the needs of European business that had grown to new dimensions, to which government had to adjust. This vision was severely criticized. In Germany several authors, e.g. Goralczyk and Busch have developed alternative approaches.[17] They mainly belong to the so-called "Berliner Schule" who try to extend Marx's value analysis to international competition. Mainly on the basis of the work of the political scientist Poulantzas a number of economic aspects of the internationalization of

[15] Lenin, 1915.

[16] Mandel, 1968.

[17] Goralczyk, 1975; Busch, 1978, Axt, 1978.

capital are studies by *inter alia* Palloix and Aglietta in France.[18] The point of departure of their studies is the circulation of capital as developed in the second volume of Marx's *Capital*. For the discussion on economic integration their research into the effects of international competition on national economic structures is especially important. In England integration theory is largely practised by authors from the Conference of Socialist Economists.[19] Important contributions are also coming from other non-Marxist but critical "leftist" authors like Stuart Holland. [20] In the Netherlands Marxist integration theory is developed mainly by some Amsterdam political scientists, like Van der Pijl and Stuurman.[21] Also some other not clearly Marxist, but critical authors have published on integration questions.[22]

This is the situation in Western Europe. In Eastern Europe there is also a keen interest in the process of capitalist integration. Authors like Maximova, Bogomolov and others[23] base themselves on the theory of state monopoly capitalism (Stamokap). According to this concept the national state is intensively connected with the national monopolies in the present phase of capitalist development. Attempts at international economic integration have to be explained by this fundamental characteristic. Eastern European writers also pay a lot of attention to economic technical factors leading to integration. This is undoubtedly because integration processes do not only take place in the capitalist world, but are also of importance between socialist countries. The latter, however, is beyond the scope of this article, outlined in the introduction.

Origins and effects

Although there are many differences between the various authors and schools of thought, they are in complete agreement on one point: the process of economic integration in Western Europe has to be explained by the development of capitalism as a whole. Economic integration is not an isolated phenomenon that can be studied apart from social development in its totality. The links of economic integration with this totality are numerous. It seems possible, however, to distinguish three main lines of reasoning that are based on this general point of departure, or rather, there are three clusters of arguments derived from the general proposition. Most authors treat all three, the importance attached to each of them differs among them. The first group could be called the internal European cluster.

[18] Poulantzas, 1974; Palloix, 1975; Aglietta, 1974; Deubner, 1979.
[19] Holloway, 1976.
[20] Holland, 1980; Seers and Vaitsos, 1980.
[21] Stuurman, 1974; Van der Pijl, 1978.
[22] Tudyka, 1975; Weeda, 1978.
[23] Maximova, 1973; Bognár, 1976; Bogomolov, 1976; Sedivec, 1979.

Here the fundamental influence of the concentration and centralization of capital in Western Europe is emphasized. After World War Two the expansion of certain firms was frustrated by the existing restrictions on international trade, payments and capital movements. These firms needed bigger markets and investment opportunities than the rather limited national territories could provide. Economic integration answered their needs. It created a protected, large free-trade area in which gradually capital movements would be liberalized also. Seen this way, economic integration is the economic policy reaction of the states to the needs of the internationalizing parts of the business community. Apart from these "economic" motives certain "political" internal European factors are often mentioned, e.g. the German wish to end international surveillance or the French desire to check German power. In accordance with the differences of opinion on state theory discussed above, several authors disagree about the importance that should be attached to these political factors. Against the opinion of Bognár that "political factors had a decisive say in the creation of the Community",[24] Stuart Holland thinks this is only superficially the case. He emphsized – in accordance with a more "classic" position – the importance of the economic factors.

A second cluster of factors is connected with the relations between the main capitalist (groups of) nations. These relations are characterized by rivalry and competition, as well as cooperation. In this relationship economic as well as political factors play a role. In the discussion of the effects of European economic integration on these relations certain authors emphasize the dominating influence of the United States behind the European integration process. Others on the other hand point out that integration was meant to strengthen the position of Western Europe *vis-a-vis* the United States. What arguments are advanced for both views? It is quite clear that the United States had a strong stimulating influence on the first steps towards integration in Western Europe. Whether the Americans moulded the integration process according to their own interests in later phases too is more problematic. The opinions of Poulantzas and other French writers are inclined to answer this question in the affirmative. Against this, others claim that integration was an important instrument of European business to fight American competition. Some authors even consider this the most important motive for the establishment of the EEC. We have already met the opinion of Mandel, for whom the EEC is the expression of the formation of "European", instead of "national" capitals that need the protection of a "European state" as a defence against the United States. Although he severely criticizes Mandel's concept of a "European" capital, Busch – and other authors from the "Berliner Schule" – also attach prime importance to the rivalry between the main capitalist

[24] Bognár, 1976, p. 246.

powers. He looks upon the EC as an instrument to strengthen competitive possibilities of (parts of) European business by liberalizing internal trade in Western Europe and at the same time maintain a certain degree of protectionism with regard to the United States.

European business not only meets foreign competition within Europe, but also outside this area. In this respect it is also said that the EEC is an attempt to strengthen the competitive position of Europe. Special attention in this framework has been paid to Europe's relations with developing countries. The successive association agreements are especially noted as examples of neo-colonial relationships, securing preferential markets, access to raw materials and political influence.[25]

From the last point it is only a small step towards a third group of factors that is seen to lie behind the European integration process. I mean those connected with world relations, in particular the East-West conflict after World War Two. For some west European authors this factor is much more important than inter-capitalist competition, especially for those who see a good deal of American influence behind European integration. East European authors also stress the importance of the conflict between capitalism and socialism for the integration process. In general it is claimed that by integration an attempt was made to strengthen the capitalist economic and social system against internal and external threats.

After the War capitalism in Europe was not only threatened from outside. Internally also influential groups were demanding fundamental changes. Integration would make it much more difficult for individual countries to accept such changes or to leave the capitalist system. At the same time the closer political ties and the increased economic strength of the capitalist countries would mean a stronger position against communism.

The effects Marxist authors expect from economic integration are closely related to the aforementioned clusters of factors.

For certain sections of business integration will bring increased opportunities for expansion and profit-earning. Other firms will be confronted with increased competition and will have to disappear. In general it is assumed that business has benefited and that total profits have increased, but not much empirical research is presented to back this proposition. As far as I know a detailed analysis of profit development of various groups of firms and an attempt to quantify the EEC effects in this is still lacking.

It is often said that the international concerns or multinational enterprises in particular have benefited from integration, because integration has been highly stimulating for international trade and capital movements in which these firms occupy dominant positions. Plausible as

[25] Galtung, 1976.

the argument may be, hard proofs based on empirical research are not (yet) available. Furthermore several writers note that not all, but particularly the American multinationals seem to have benefited from the EC arrangements, at least in the earlier days.

This last point brings us to the effects of integration on competitive conditions, especially between Europe and the United States. Most writers argue that the competitive position of European firms has been improved by integration. Busch, for example, presents mainly figures to underline this point. This position, however, is not uncontested. Poulantzas for example, thinks the Americans dominance is still in existence. Representatives of the French internationalization school provide support for this idea with the results of their research on the development of the economic structure of the main capitalist countries. They think it is possible to observe a new hierarchical structure in the international division of labour, in which the US ranks the highest by their specialization on knowledge-intensive production. Japan and Germany take secondary positions in this hierarchy, France's place is still lower.

There is no consensus about whether economic integration has strengthened the position of capitalism versus socialism. Sometimes an affirmative voice is heard. East European authors in general deny it. Most of them will agree with Maximova ". . . integration has by no means freed the economy of the countries concerned from the basic contradictions of capitalism. . . . Integration has by no means overcome such intensive defects of the capitalist system as the cyclic nature of economic development, inflation, monetary crises, etc."[26]

Much attention is also devoted to the effects of various kinds of economic policies that are applied within the EC. The main emphasis is on agricultural policy and monetary integration.

This last policy, which has recently found concrete form in the EMS is generally supposed to increase disequilibria. Busch for example, emphasizes structural differences in inflation that will lead to permanent balance of payments problems. Stuart Holland points to the danger that because of the external position some countries will be forced to apply deflationary policies. Whole countries may become problem areas in this way. Goralczyk stresses the dominance of German capital as a result of monetary integration. Altvater finally connects the EMS with the crisis in the world economy. He concludes that by the fixing of exchange rates an austerity policy that is deemed desirable by some countries to improve the international competitive position is forced upon other countries.[27]

On the basis of these conflicts most authors do not think further monetary integration in the future very probable. This is closely related to

[26] Maximova, 1973, p. 261.
[27] Altvater, 1979.

the position they allot to the national state in the integration process. Although there is some controversy on this, most authors hold the opinion that national states remain the central institutions that will not be replaced by newly created "supranational" institutions.

According to most Marxist authors the main characteristic of the effects of economic integration in Western Europe is an increase in disequilibria. Against advantages for one group there are disadvantages for another. While one region prospers, the other gets poorer.

Increased competition offers opportunities for some firms, others have to disappear. Advantages are generally reaped by the biggest firms, i.e. the multinationals. Disadvantages accrue to weaker firms, small farmers and labourers. In the words of Bogomolov "Integration through uncontrolled market forces brings about structural disproportions and even the decline of whole regions and branches of the national economy. The intensification of the concentration of capital and the growth of the power of the monopolies. . . have aggravated many contradictions within the EEC, have encroached on the interests of the working people, the consumer, and the average taxpayer, and have led to the ruination of many small and medium-sized enterprises".[28]

Because of these sharpened conflicts the difficulties in the integration process are not incidental, but have a structural character. The vague concept of "lack of political will" hides very concrete and vital conflicts of interests. Integration does not solve these conflicts, it rather sharpens them. In this sense integration is considered a progressive development in that it lays bare the fundamental contradictions in the capitalist system, which will ultimately lead to the renewal of society.

Preliminary conclusions

In Marxist integration theory the importance of economic forces, in the sense of the interests of firms striving for more profit, for (capitalist) integration is emphasized. Actions of national governments strongly reflect these forces. The influence of political objectives is somewhat unclear. Sometimes they are directly reduced to economic interests (ranging from the earlier mentioned profit-motive of individual firms to the maintenance of the capitalist economic system), sometimes they are given a rather autonomous role. Mostly they are placed somewhere in between.

A second characteristic of Marxist integration theory is that emphasis is laid on conflict. It is not capital in general that benefits from integration, but certain parts of capital. Between governments there is rivalry to influence the integration process and to get the best out of it. The effects of integration are likely to increase regional and structural imbalances. There is therefore less attention to the effects of integration upon countries, but

[28] Bogomolov, 1975, p. 87.

more to the effects upon different classes, groups, sectors etc. within countries.[29]

While there are many general descriptive works on integration in the Marxist traditions there is clearly a need for further theoretical and empirical economic research, especially in the field of the effects of integration on firms, sectors, regions, countries, policy objectives and so on. This could give the approach, which often makes a somewhat loose and impressionistic impression, more precision.

Comparison and conclusions

I think it is safe to conclude that both the traditional and the Marxist theories of economic integration agree that the establishment of the EEC is a result of a complicated set of interlocking causes – sometimes reinforcing each other, sometimes conflicting — and that it has an effect on many other phenomena.

The way in which both approaches fill in this rather general statement, are, however, different. While traditional theory points to a government that tries to raise the real income of the country concerned, hopes to be better able to reach its economic policy objectives and looks upon European integration as imbedded in its global cultural and ideological orientation, Marxian theories stress the profits of certain groups of firms, the interests of social groups and the struggle of capitalism against socialism.

The root of this difference lies in the way the capitalist or mixed economy is viewed. The traditional approach accepts or is at least neutral with regard to the existing economic order. There is according to this concept in principle no fundamental antagonistic relationship between the attainment of the general goals of society and the functioning of the market sector. For most Marxists on the other hand capitalism is an economic system based on exploitation and as such fundamentally incompatible with social justice. I will not go any further into this controversy which leads us into the problems of the theory of economic systems and the possibility of an optimal economic order. On the basis of this differing viewpoint, however, both conceptions approach the question of economic integration. The result is that both look at this phenomenon in a rather selective way, i.e. they tend to see, to emphasize and to interpret the things in accordance with their general background philosophy.

Selectivity as such is no evil, it is often unavoidable in social research. It has to be an explicit selectivity, however, for otherwise selectivity easily becomes partiality, prejudice, subjectivism. This seems not always to be recognised in both theories.

[29] Seers and Vaitsos, 1980.

In order to bring the discussion one step further and to contribute to a more balanced integration theory (i.e. one that may claim its selectivity to be based on an explicit valuation of all possibilities) it seems necessary to answer the following questions.

(a) Should integration theory limit itself to the research of the effects – as is mainly done in traditional theory – or of the causes – on which Marxist theories concentrate – of integration?

Neither limitation seems desirable for various reasons. The first one is that the distinction between causes and effects is not a very sharp one, for the causes of integration will generally be found in its effects. Furthermore, precisely because the motives of economic integration are, to a great extent, economic, economic theory can make an important contribution to the explanation of the causes of integration. But integration is a political process, it is often argued. This is certainly true, but political processes should not be left to political scientists exclusively, especially if they have an important economic component.

(b) As to the theoretical analysis of causes of economic integration, an interesting observation concerning the two approaches can be made. If economic integration in its formal sense is considered a government act or part of government policy, the vital question is why governments embark on such a process. In other words, what is the purpose or what are the objectives of government policy? As we have seen, traditional theory takes the objectives of economic policy as given. This means that in principle it abstains from saying anything on actual objectives. This does not mean, however, that the hypothetical objectives it postulates are completely arbitrarily chosen. For a long time the maximization of real national income was generally considered the main economic objective. This means that in a first-best world free trade would be the optimal policy and integration could only be explained by terms of trade benefits (the optimum tariff argument) or other motives (internal distribution, political motives and so on). In a second-best world in which market imperfections, tariffs and other government intervention (eventually subject to policy constraints) exist, even real income maximization could theoretically be the motive besides the other ones. After Robbins' famous dictum "there are no economic ends" in principle all social objectives are contained in the social welfare function. Both economic and political research – and here the New Political Economy to which Pelkmans refers may be useful – suggest a loss of these objectives. In a mixed economic system one of them is undoubtedly a healthy, i.e. reasonably profitable, market sector. Whether one considers this an end in itself or as a means to reach other objectives is unimportant here, for it is more or less by definition that in a mixed economy the prevalence of the private sector must be part of the social welfare function, where it may conflict with other government objectives.

Marxist theory, that has always considered the explanations of government goals as endogenous (it lacks the extreme fragmentation of the traditional social sciences), originally tends to reduce all these goals to the direct economic interests of parts of the private business community. More recently the principle of "relative autonomy" is generally accepted, which means that maybe there is only "ultimate determination". Although this may be a big step forward in theory, for practical purposes such a concept is not very concrete. It leaves room, however, for the introduction of objectives other than economic ones.

To illustrate the development in traditional and Marxist thinking one may formulate the following very crude versions of the older and newer welfare functions in both approaches (in which W = welfare, Y = real national income and R = rate of profit).

	traditional	Marxist
old	$W = w(Y)$	$W = w(R)$
new	$W = w(Y, \ldots R, \ldots)$	$W = w(R, \ldots Y, \ldots)$

So the question about the objectives of government and the way they are determined does not seem to present a real dividing line between the two approaches. Further research into how governments try to maximize their welfare functions by economic integration can best be carried out with the aid of a cost-benefit procedure. This approach is in use in the emerging economic theory of international organizations and has found promising application in the theory of monetary integration.[30] In this way the decision to embark on (or withdraw from) an integration project may be explained more carefully and completely than by saying that the governments macroeconomic policy goals are better attained or that it serves the interests of (parts of) the private sector or that it is the result of overall political motives.

(c) The above mentioned approach rests on detailed analysis of the effects of economic integration on all variables that are contained in the social welfare function. Most of these variables (e.g. justice, international stability) will be very difficult to quantify. But even if we limit ourselves to the aforementioned economic variables it will be clear that rather large and complicated models will have to be used. To analyze the effects on the "real variables" an elaborate international goods-market is necessary. For the "monetary effects" a macro-model including a monetary sector and trade in assets is required, and preferably all these relations must be integrated in one model. This is undoubtedly the direction in which traditional theory is moving.[31] This leaves room for a variety of rather complex models, the

[30] Fratianni, Pattison, 1982; Dosser, Gowland and Hartley, 1982.

[31] Allen and Kenen, 1981.

results of which will vary according to the assumptions on which they are founded. For didactic or demonstrative uses partial models may be preferred, e.g. the goods market without national income determination or a monetary sector. The results obtained with the aid of these partial models – which were mainly in use up till now – have their limitations, however.

To bring the models as close to reality as possible it is useful to introduce all kinds of distortions, e.g. market imperfections, policy intervention, etc. Among these distortions the existence of profits, to which the Marxian approach attaches so much importance, may be of special interest. It might be illuminating to incorporate profits in the goods market, e.g. by using a neo-Ricardian model. First of all this may have interesting results for the allocation effects of integration as suggested by work on tariff policy on the basis of this approach.[32] Secondly income distribution effects can be studied while the profit- wage relationship occupies a prominent place in these models. Further it may make it possible to study the effects of integration on different sectors of the economy thus gaining insight in the effects on economic structure. If it proves possible to incorporate accumulation and technological change in these models it may perhaps even throw some light on the theory of the so-called dynamic effects too.

The most important task of integration theory in the future will probably be the analysis of the effects of further economic policy coordination. As certain instruments of economic policy are taken out of the hands of national governments while most other instruments are still used nationally, which almost inevitably results in conflicting policies, there is a general loss of effectiveness of economic policy. So in principle there are gains of further coordination. This is especially true with regard to the attitudes towards third countries, but it is also applicable to internal policies. The main problem will be how eventual advantages are distributed over the countries concerned. In this context the use of the above mentioned "integrated" models seems indispensable. If these models correctly reflect country characteristics it is possible to gain insight into the costs and benefits of existing policies and policy proposals for individual countries. This way it might be easier to reach agreement on a balanced distribution of gains and losses over the partner countries.

With regard to the effects of integration on more fundamental issues such as the economic system and international relations intriguing questions can be posed to which clear answers are not easy to give. A major reason for this is the important role of value judgements in the issues concerned. In a world where economic and political divergences have reached extremely big and dangerous proportions, it is essential that the contribution of regional integration to these processes is carefully studied and discussed. The insights gained may ultimately lead to a better understanding and even some rapprochement of differing points of view.

[32] Steedman, 1979.

BIBLIOGRAPHY

M. Aglietta, *Les principaux traits contemporains de l'internationalisation du capital*, Paris, 1974.
P.R. Allen, P.B. Kenen, *Asset Markets, Exchange Rates, and Economic Integration*, Cambridge, 1980.
E. Altvater, "Internationalisierung der Austerity-Politik durch das Europäische Währungssystem (EWS)", *Tagebuch* 1-1-'79, p. 11–17.
H.J. Axt, *Staat, multinationale Konzerne und politische Union in Westeuropa*, Köln, 1978.
B. Balassa, *The theory of economic integration*, London, 1962.
B. Balassa (ed.), *European Economic Integration*, Amsterdam, 1975.
B. Balassa, "Types of economic integration," in F. Machlup (ed.), *Economic Integration: Worldwide, Regional, Sectoral*, London, 1976.
G. Basevi, "Comments," in F. Machlup (ed.), *Economic Integration: Worldwide, Regional, Sectoral*, London, 1976.
J. Bognár, "The Socio-Political and Institutional Aspects of Integration," in F. Machlup (ed.), *Economic Integration: Worldwide, Regional, Sectoral*, London, 1976.
O.T. Bogomolov, "Two types of international economic integration," *Problems of Economics*, 1975, p. 72–91.
O.T.Bogomolov, "Integration by Market Forces and through Planning," in F. Machlup (ed.), *Economic Integration: Worldwide, Regional, Sectoral*, London, 1976.
T. Buck, J. Harper, "Regional income inequality in the European Economic Community," *Tijdschrift voor Economie en Management*, nr. 3, 1978, p. 337–350.
K. Busch, *Die Krise der Europäischen Gemeinschaft*, Köln, 1978.
C.A. Cooper, B.F. Masell, "Towards a general theory of customs unions for developing countries," *Journal of Political Economy*, nr. 5, 1965, p. 461–476.
W.M. Corden, "Economies of scale and customs union theory," *Journal of Political Economy*, nr. 3(I), 1972, p. 465–475.
J. Dankert, W. Ersil, K.H. Werner, *Politik in Westeuropa*, Berlin, 1975.
Chr. Deubner, U. Rehfeldt, F. Schlupp, G. Ziebura (Hrsg.), *Die Internationalisierung des Kapitals*, Frankfurt, 1979.
D. Dosser, D. Gowland, K. Hartley (eds.), *The Collaboration of Nations, a study of european economic policy*, Oxford, 1982.
A.M. El-Agraa (ed.), *The economics of the European Community*, Deddington, 1980.
A.M. El-Agraa, A.J. Jones, *Theory of Customs Unions*, Deddington, 1981.
European Commission, *Europese Economie*, 1979, nr. 3.
B. Fine, L. Harris, *Rereading Capital*, London, 1979.
M. Frattianni, J. Pattison, "The economics of international organizations," in *Kyklos*, vol. 35 (1982), nr. 2, p. 244–263.
J. Galtung, "The Lomé Convention and neo-capitalism," *The African Review*, 1976, nr. 1.
J. Goldberg, "Was ist Integration?" in F. Rische (Hrsg.), *Arbeiterklasse und EWG*, Frankfurt a.M., 1974.
D. Goralczyk, *Weltmarkt, Weltwährungssystem und westeuropäische Integration*, Giessen, 1975.
P. de Grauwe, "Conditions for monetary integration." *Weltwirtschaftliches Archiv*, nr. 4, 1975, p. 634–646.
W.G.C.M. Haack, "Oorzaken en effekten van economische integratie in West-Europa," *Maandschrift Economie*, Nov. 1981, p. 421-440.
E.B. Haas, Ph.C. Schmitter, "Economics and differential patterns of political integration," in *International Political Communities*, Garden City, 1966.
S. Holland, *Uncommon Market*, London, 1980.
J. Holloway, "Some Issues raised by Marxist Analysis of Economic Integration," *CSE Bulletin*, May 1976.
A. Jacquemin, *Economie industrielle européenne*, Paris, 1975.
A.P. Jacquemin, H.W. de Jong, *European Industrial Organisation*, London, 1977.
H. Johnson, "An economic theory of protectionism, tariff bargaining and the formation of customs unions," *Journal of Political Economy*, nr. 3, 1965, p. 256–283.

P. Korteweg, "The European Monetary System – will it really bring more monetary stability to Europe?" *De Economist*, nr. 1, 1980, p. 15–50.

M.B. Krauss, "Recent developments in customs union theory: an interpretive survey," *Journal of Economic Literature*, nr. 2, 1972, p. 413–436.

W.I. Lenin, "Uber die Lösung der Vereinigten Staaten von Europa," *Sozial-Demokrat*, nr. 44, 1915.

G. Locksley, T. Ward, "Concentration in manufacturing in the EEC," *Cambridge Journal of Economics*, nr. 3, 1979, p. 91–97.

F. Machlup (ed.), *Economic Integration: Worldwide, Regional, Sectoral*, London, 1976.

F. Machlup, *A History of Thought on Economic Integration*, London, 1977.

E. Mandel, *Die EWG und die Konkurrenz Europa-Amerika*, Frankfurt a.M., 1968.

M. Maximova, *Economic Aspects of Capitalist Integration*, Moscow, 1973.

M. Maximova, "Comments," in F. Machlup (ed.), *Economic Integration: Worldwide, Regional, Sectoral*, London, 1976.

R.A. Mundell, "Tariff preferences and the terms of trade," *The Manchester School of Economic and Social Studies*, nr. 1, 1964, p. 1–13.

Chr. Palloix, *L'internationalisation du capital*, Paris, 1975.

J. Pelkmans, *The process of economic integration*, diss. Tilburg, 1975.

J. Pelkmans, "Economic Theories of Integration Revisited," *Journal of Common Market Studies*, nr. 4, 1980, p. 333–355.

H.C. Petith, "European integration and the terms of trade," *The Economic Journal*, nr. 87, 1977, p. 262–272.

N. Poulantzas, *Les classes sociales dans le capitalisme aujourd'hui*, Paris, 1974.

K. van der Pijl, *Een amerikaans plan voor europa*, Amsterdam, 1978.

R. Reizman, "A theory of customs-unions: the three country-two good case," *Weltwirtschaftliches Archiv*, nr. 4, 1979, p. 716–728.

P. Robson, *The Economics of International Integration*, London, 1980.

T. Scitovsky, *Economic Theory and Western European Integration*, London, 1958.

V. Sedivec, "Economic integration among advanced capitalist states," *Czechoslovak Economic Digest*, nr. 1, 1979, p. 60–75.

D. Seers, C. Vaitsos (eds.), *Integration and unequal development, The experience of the EEC*, London, 1980.

H. Siebels, H. Lenke, "Kapitalistische Vergesellschaftung der Landwirtschaft und "Gemeinsamer Agrarmarkt" in der EWG," in F. Deppe (Hrsg.), *Europäische Wirtschaftsgemeinschaft (EWG)*, Reinbek b.H., 1975.

M. Simai, K. Garam (eds.), *Economic integration, concepts, theories and problems*, Budapest, 1977.

A. Statz, "Zur Geschichte der Westeuropäischen Integration bis zur Gründung der EWG," in F. Deppe (Hrsg.), *Europäische Wirtschaftsgemeinschaft (EWG)*, Reinbek b.H., 1975.

I. Steedman, *Trade Amongst Growing Economies*, Cambridge, 1979.

S. Stuurman, *De theorie van de staat en het ontstaan van de EEG*, doct. scriptie FSW-A, Amsterdam, 1974.

D. Swann, *The Economics of the Common Market*, Harmondsworth (4e ed.), 1978.

E. Thorbecke (E. Pagoulatos), "The effects of European economic integration on agriculture," in B. Balassa (ed.), *European Economic Integration*, Amsterdam, 1975.

J. Tinbergen, *International Economic Integration*, Amsterdam (2e ed.), 1965.

R. Triffin (ed.), *EMS: The Emerging European Monetary System*, Brussels, 1979.

K.P. Tudyka, *Marktplatz Europa*, Köln, 1975.

J. Viner, *The Customs Union Issue*, New York, 1950.

J. Waelbroeck, "Measuring the Degree of Progress of Economic Integration," in F. Machlup (ed.), *Economic Integration: Worldwide, Regional, Sectoral*, London, 1976.

[3]

From National Corporatism to Transnational Pluralism: Organized Interests in the Single European Market

WOLFGANG STREECK and PHILIPPE C. SCHMITTER

ORGANIZED INTERESTS AND REGIONAL INTEGRATION

Whatever the differences between the various versions of the theory, or "pre-theory"[1] of European regional integration, organized interest groups were always assigned a prominent place in it. Especially in the "neofunctionalist" image of "Europe's would-be polity"[2] and of the path to that polity, supranational interest-group formation was expected to serve, in an important and indispensable sense, as a substitute for popular identification with the emerging new political community above and beyond the nation-state.[3] Most observers and in fact most participants in the integration process fully expected that the citizens of Europe would for a long time continue to adhere to traditional, national passions and identities. They knew that if the united Europe had to wait until its citizens began to feel as "Europeans"—rather than as the French, Germans, Italians, and so forth—it would not in any foreseeable future come about, and Europe as a political entity would in their lifetime never be more than a small bureaucracy in Brussels with very fragile support in national politics.

One reason why there nevertheless appeared to be hope was that things were believed to be different with the professional leaders of organized interest groups. Unlike the voters, they were seen as likely to orient themselves rationally and calculatedly to where the action was—that is, under the presumed logic of the neofunctionalist spillover process,[4] to "Brussels." Indeed in attitude and outlook, interest-group officials and European civil servants could easily appear as birds of a feather: both appointed rather than elected, both experts and technocrats, both susceptible to a cosmopolitan orientation and lifestyle, and both professionally interested in the smooth management of complex interdependencies and likely to be distinctly disinterested in the traditional rituals and symbolism of nationhood. Just as civil servants like Jean Monnet had been persuading, cajoling, and manipulating the elected politicians and the administrative machineries of national states into emergent supranationalism, so the *Geschaeftsfuehrer* of business associations and trade unions were expected to enlighten their elected leaders that their interests had migrated to a new place and that the offices and decisions of their representatives had to follow suit.

In fact, the relationship between European bureaucrats and the full-time managers of collective interests that was envisaged by integration theory was even more intimate. As has been pointed out, interest groups were believed to have a much better, sharper, more intense perception of the effects of spillover on the situs and locus of decisions than did the average voter and as a result were expected to make their appearance at the supranational level earlier than their less insightful fellow citizens. But more importantly perhaps, the move of organized interests onto the European scene was expected to be further accelerated by European bureaucrats who, in their search for a constituency, would be more than willing to promote interest organization on a scale coterminous with their supranational jurisdiction. Indeed in the perception of early integration theory, especially its neofunctionalist version, there was hardly anything in which "Brussels" could be more interested than in cultivating an environment, around the Commission in particular, of powerful interest organizations negotiating with Community officials and each other—as an *Ersatz* for the elusive pan-European citizen humming a pan-European supranational anthem when facing the Berlaymont office building.

Attracting a growing number of supranational lobbyists into the Community's decision-making process was seen as offering important payoffs especially for the Commission. Cooperation with organized interests would not only provide civil servants with an indispensable input of detailed factual information in complex decisions. It also and above all was to bring about the socialization of powerful forces in European civil society into a world view compatible with that of European bureaucrats and with the requirements of continued spillover. Having been drawn into the ambit of the Commission, a multitude of political players would learn from experience that management from the top, from the center, and from Brussels was more efficient and effective than national policymaking. When they returned to their national capitals, they—it was hoped and in fact predicted—would again become a lobby; this time not of their interest group vis-à-vis Brussels, but of Brussels vis-à-vis their national leaders, including their governments. By fostering a transnational system of organized interest representation, the Community and its Commission in particular would thus contribute to its own growth as a policy arena and executive body and lift itself out of the parochial entanglements of national politics and intergovernmental nondecision making into a safely anchored new world of supranational political management.

In many ways, the status provided for organized interests in the future European polity bore strong resemblance to a model of interest politics that some time later came to be known to students of politics as "neocorporatism." As in the latter, the integrated European polity was to be one that was primarily concerned with governing a "mixed economy" according to rules of technical and professional expertise whose prudent application was to help avoid social conflict and disruption. There also was to be a shift away from the territorial-electoral-parliamentary realm of politics, toward powerful mechanisms of functional representation of producer groups, and there was an emphasis on close linkage between state and society through privileged participation of organized interests in policy and through mutually supportive organizational arrangements between the machineries of government on the one hand and of large, centralized interest organizations on the other. Above all, there was the idea of the future European political economy being kept together by a combination of technocratic professionalism shared among all major players regardless of divergent, specific interests and a web of dense and durable, bi-, tri-, and multilateral bargaining relationships involving both public and private bodies. This bargaining system would contribute to order less through shared values and interests of the bargainers than through common strategic imperatives of self-restraint and compromise reflecting and respecting the complexity of a modern society and economy.

But while motivated speculation about the politics of a unified Europe prepared the ground for the (re)discovery of (neo)corporatism as a concept,[5] at the European level the reality of corporatism was not found. When in the early 1970s students of European integration in despair over their subject searching for new themes,[6] turned their energies to comparative politics, they recognized at the level of European nation-states something that looked conspicuously like what integration theory had long had in mind for Europe as whole. At the time, European nation-states were almost universally turning to centralized bargaining between firmly institutionalized class and sectoral interest groups. Facilitated, moderated, and supplemented by the government, this bargaining emerged as a reaction to the turmoil of 1968 and 1969 and as a recourse against the dislocations of the economic crises after 1973 and especially of the threat of inflation in societies with a strong labor movement whose governments were afraid of reneging on the postwar Keynesian welfare-state commitment to politically guaranteed full employment. In turning to "neocorporatist concertation," as it came to be called, national governments appeared to be doing precisely what integration theorists had been counseling the European Community and its

Commission. In order to integrate their political systems, they were relying more and more on deals with interest groups as distinct from electoral and parliamentary participation; they were sometimes bypassing and generally downgrading their parliaments as places of political decision making; they attempted to govern through compromises with and between organized interests; and they were generating obligations of special interests to the collective good not through legislation passed by parliamentary majority but through collective bargaining in all possible forms and manners.[7]

The Failure of Euro-Corporatism

Not that there was nothing like that at all at the European level. But compared to the paradigmatic national political systems of the time, interest representation around and within the Community was always much more "pluralist" than it was corporatist: more organizationally fragmented, less hierarchically integrated, more internally competitive, and with a lot less control vested in peak associations over its affiliates or in associations over its members. Union and business-association officials that were transferred to Brussels in the 1970s more often than not perceived this as a falling from grace at home and as a usually well-paid elimination from the excitement of domestic power games and succession struggles rather than as accession to the new center of political power. Belying the predictions of integration theory, by the mid-1970s at the latest it had become clear that the Brussels system of functional representation had failed to develop into a corporatist engine of supranationalism.

The history of organized supranational interests in Europe is short. Prior to the formation of the European Economic Community in 1958, European class, sectoral, and professional interest groups had only vague memories of collective action across national lines, and very little of it had been successful. Around the turn of the century, industry cartels among business firms, "proletarian internationalism" between trade unions, and some cooperative ventures involving professional groups emerged, but World War I seems to have put an end to most of this activity. After 1945, the insistence of the United States under the Marshall Plan that European countries act in concert on matters of postwar reconstruction laid a new foundation. But there is little evidence until the stimulus of the Treaty of Rome that national interest associations were prepared to establish permanent European-level organizations.[8]

Immediately after 1958, European peak associations began to form, especially for the representation of broadly encompassing industrial, commercial, and agricultural business interests: UNICE for industry (1958), COPA for agriculture (1958), a permanent conference for chambers of commerce (1958), UNACEE for craft industries (1958), COGECA for agricultural cooperatives (1959), BFEC for banking (1960), and GCECEE for savings banks (1963). Workers and consumers took much longer to build their peak associations: both the European Trade Union Confederation (ETUC) and BEUC were established only in 1973. SEPLIS, representing the liberal, intellectual, and social professions, was created in 1975. By then, roughly the time of the first enlargement to include Great Britain, Ireland, and Denmark, all of the major functional groups were present. Affiliated to their broadly encompassing European peak organizations were exclusively national associations most of which continued to command far greater resources than their nominally superior *Spitzenverband* and all of which reserved the right to act on their own on matters of particular importance to them. For example, demonstrating their continued autonomy, the national associations of industrialists for each member state opened their own offices in Brussels. None of the European peak associations of this first wave had individuals or firms as direct members.[9]

Meanwhile, a myriad of more specialized, sectoral associations were also being formed. Some of these did have direct membership, but then they were rarely affiliated (and never subordinated) to the European peak associations. By 1985, the number of interest associations registered in Brussels had reached 654, according to a census carried out by the Commission.[10] Associations of business interests vastly outnumbered those of labor, with 20 unions and 79 professional associations facing 332 associations from industry, 139 from commerce, 6 representing craft and artisanal interests, and 5 associations of small- and medium-sized enterprises. This mirrors a similar situation at the national level where business interests also prefer to work through a greater number and variety of specialized intermediaries than do workers.[11]

The Commission seems to have deliberately encouraged the formation of these associations[12] and very quickly established a procedure for recognizing their special European status. This implied privileged access to its deliberations[13] even if recognition was typically not limited to only one organization per category. Each of the Commission's Directorates-General soon surrounded itself with a vast number of standing, advisory, and management committees, most of which were based on functional rather than territorial principles of representation.[14] Apparently in the early stages, the Commission attempted to confine lobbying to certified European associations, but this was subsequently relaxed to permit an increasing volume of direct contacts with national interest representatives.[15]

Advisory committees and expert groups mushroomed in subsequent years. The Commission itself has never employed very many officials[16] and has depended heavily on consultation with interest representatives, national government employees, and experts for drafting its directives and monitoring compliance with them. By the time the Single European Act was signed in 1985, the number of consultative bodies had grown to about 700, and it has almost doubled since then to 1336 in 1988.[17] Interest representatives are well remunerated for attending meetings in Brussels, and indeed these payments might be interpreted as a subsidy for the development of an "appropriately structured" system of interest intermediation related and obligated to the European Community.

The corporatist capstone of the emerging system of Europe-wide functional representation might have been the Economic and Social Committee (ESC). This body was inserted in the Treaty of Rome and persists to the present day. Its 189 members (as of 1985) represent three "grand categories" of interest: employers, workers, and "others"—that is, agricultural and transportation interests, shopkeepers, artisans, consumers, environmental groups, and so forth. ESC members do not, however, represent European interest associations; rather, they are nominated as individuals by member governments and appointed by the Council of Ministers (*not* the supranational Commission) to four year terms. While the ESC likes to think of itself as the "other European Assembly"—a sort of functional shadow to the territorially based European Parliament—there is general agreement that it has, in fact, accomplished very little.[18] In particular, it was never able to serve as a privileged access point for organized interests to European-level decision making and therefore failed completely in providing focus and structure to the growing pluralist system of European interest associations. It also proved entirely unsuitable to accommodate labor's ritual demands for a "social Europe" and prevent the "common market" from remaining exactly that: a customs union committed to liberalism and free trade.[19]

For a few years after 1968, this seemed to be about to change. With the accession to power of social-democratic parties in major member countries and with national political elites still suffering from the shocks of their respective *autunni caldi*, the first Paris summit of the heads of state and government inaugurated an ambitious program to extend the domain of the European Community to a wide range of social policies. Subsequently for a short, intensive period between 1970 and roughly 1974, it seemed that labor was about to capture the same or similar substantive concessions and institutional privileges at the European level as it was picking up simultaneously in individual countries. If at all, it was then that labor leaders, in the way predicted by early integration theorists like Ernst Haas, began to take "Europe" seriously as a political arena in which to launch strategic initiatives.[20] Characteristically at that point, the ESC was set aside as too cumbersome and insufficiently *paritaire* to bear the burden of leading the Community into the era of "social partnership." Instead, the ministers of social affairs and, later, of economic and financial affairs decided to convoke a series of "Tripartite Conferences" bringing together the European peak associations and national representatives of capital and labor with officials of national governments and the Commission. These met six times until 1978—often in highly publicized settings—to discuss a wide range of macroeconomic and social policies. Their agenda paralleled that of the national concertation efforts of the same period: full employment, inflation, wage restraint, fiscal policy, worker training, and productivity measures. A standing committee on employment with tripartite representation was established, and there was even a plan for creating a set of sectoral councils wherein capital, labor, and state officials were expected to come up with proposals for governing the steel, shipbuilding, textiles, aerospace, and telecommunications industries.

All this effort came to naught in 1978 when the strongest proponent of Euro-corporatism, the ETUC, withdrew its support under complaints about lack of progress and also confronted with rising dissent within its ranks. Especially after the defeat in the councils of Europe of the draft European company statute that was to expand co-determination from Germany to companies incorporated in Community law and with the demise in the 1970s of the draft directive on consultation and information in multinational enterprises (the so-called "Vredelinck Directive"), there was not much left that would have justified the enormous effort labor had invested in the building of a corporatist "Social Dimension" for the Community. By the end of the 1970s, all that remained of Euro-corporatism was the standing committee on employment and a few specialized working groups that continued to recycle the by now tattered idea of concertation.

Why was it that a centralized pattern of interest politics did not emerge at the European level when it was so common in national polities? Rather than in neofunctionalist terms, the answer to the puzzle of the stagnant record of European interest politics has to be given in a language that recognizes the significance of conflict and power and does not submerge politics in the technicalities of managing sectoral spillovers. In particular, our argument emphasizes the importance for the growth of a centralized, publicly institutionalized interest politics of highly developed organizational and political capacities of *labor* during a polity's formative period—adding to whatever incentives *capital* may have on its own to get organized as well as contributing to the emergence of an active, interventionist, nonliberal *state* which may then in turn institutionalize labor as well as capital as principal participants in a centralized structure of political bargaining. That latter relation, we believe, is in itself crucial for the (further) growth of labor's political capacity as is the availability of partners for mutually centralizing cross-class alliances on the side of capital. In a nutshell, our point is that in uniting supranational Europe, it was not only the case that labor was, and continues to be, *underorganized* but there also was never a real possibility of a mutually organizing *interaction effect*, a *Wechselwirkung*, between labor and the two other major players in the political economy, capital, and the state.

As to labor itself, there is no doubt that as a European actor labor is afflicted by *specific disabilities* that are not usually present at the national level and that do not in the same way affect business. Business, for example, finds it easier than does labor to overcome the problems posed by different national languages (at least nine in the Europe of the Twelve). It also is much less hampered by ideological divisions between different political orientations like that most prominently on the labor side between communists and social-democrats. More importantly, however, the low organizational capacities of labor at the European Community level also reflect the wide regional disparities in Europe and the resulting divisions of interest between national labor movements.[21] The vast divergence in union concerns and strategies to which this gives rise are reflected, among other things, in the traditionally low significance for their affiliates of European sectoral and intersectoral union confederations. While for unions from advanced economies a joint European strategy is unlikely to offer improvements over what they have already gained on their own, to unions from weaker countries common demands tend to appear unrealistically ambitious and remote from their everyday practical concerns. Moreover to unions in rich countries, common labor standards, even if they are intended to do no more than set a floor, may appear to threaten their own, higher standards. Still and at the same time, they may *exceed* the marginal productivity of the workforces of less wealthy countries thereby undermining their ability to take advantage of increased capital mobility and attract foreign investment.[22] While it is *also* true that common standards may help unions in weaker economies to make more progress than they otherwise would and while they may make it easier for more affluent working classes to defend their employment against capital migration, bringing the different interests together and finding a compromise acceptable for both sides is far from simple. Indeed uniting national union movements behind European programs and policies always required great political effort and skill. Even where these were successfully applied, the joint platforms that were in the end adopted often had to be left deliberately vague and rarely were more than symbolic in character.[23]

As a consequence of fundamental national differences, European union officials always had to face tendencies among their constituents either to seek national solutions for their problems and ignore the supranational level altogether or to pursue their "European" interests through intergovernmental channels, using their access to home governments to work either through the national embassy in Brussels lobbying the Commission or, more likely, through the Council of Ministers.[24] Frequently such initiatives were coordinated with the respective national peak associations of employers, resulting in trilateral national coalitions pursuing joint objectives in competition with other countries and thereby effectively cutting out or starving off the European system of functional representation.

On the other hand, labor fragmentation had originally been a condition in many countries whose labor movements later proved able to propel themselves into a trajectory of growing unification and centralization. Indeed we believe that the specific disabilities of European labor are often overrated in comparison to two other factors *that would have frustrated progress toward comprehensive organization of labor and toward corporatist modes of interest intermediation and concertation even in the best of circumstances.*

The first of these factors is the complete absence of significant *business* factions with an active interest in centralized negotiations with labor. While European capital is strongly represented in Brussels by both lobbyists for individual firms and sectoral and subsectoral trade associations, the interests that these defend are primarily those of enterprises and industries demanding protection and/or (de)regulation of their *product markets.* Although sometimes the same channels are also used to address social policy and labor market concerns—for example, in the 1970s to defeat the European Community directives on workforce participation and consultation—this is not their principal purpose. In fact, the *producer interests* pursued by firms and trade associations in Brussels are by and large and more or less tacitly shared by their workforces, with business interests often functioning in effect as vertical associations representing important firm-specific or sectoral interests of labor as well as of capital.[25]

By comparison, the interests of firms *as employers* are typically not directed at extracting favorable policies from Community bodies. European business has from the beginning refused to contribute to a transfer of social policy matters from the national arenas to (tripartite political bargaining in) Brussels. While firms and their associations are always available to European officials for formal and informal consultations, binding decisions are opposed usually with reference to the widely different conditions in member states and the economic need for "flexibility." It is important to note in this context that getting its will and keeping supranationalism and tripartism from growing did not require major organizational efforts from business. To protect the Brussels body politic from contagion by the neocorporatist disease that befell European nation-states in the 1970s, all business had to do was refuse its European peak associations the competence to enter into binding obligations on behalf of their national constituents. A trilateral polity can exist and grow only if all three sides are sufficiently centralized to take part in it. By not delegating authority upward to the European level, employers were, and still are, able to confine institutions like the Social Dialogue to a strictly nonbinding, consultative status. The growing frustration of European unions in the late 1970s with the minuscule results of long and complicated discussions in Brussels and increasingly with the European Community as such, was in large part due to the *political strength business was able to draw from its organizational weakness.*

Nowhere else is the neofunctionalist image of interest groups centralizing their organizations and activities at European level and thereby pushing regional integration forward as far from reality as it is in the case of European business associations. The implicit assumption in much of neofunctionalist writing is that in a set of interdependent economies a centralized pursuit of group interests is always and unproblematically the superior alternative to traditional, national, or subnational strategies. The evidence shows, however, that there may indeed be policy arenas such as social policy and industrial relations where *different levels of regulation favor different social interests* and where groups that are favored by decentralized regulation or by the unfettered operation of "market forces" find it easy to *prevent centralization of regulatory capacity simply by refusing to build the organizations necessary for them to be able to make binding commitments at the central level.* The result is growing interdependence between national economies due to progressing market integration without proportionate growth of regulatory institutions—with the consequence of *integration and deregulation becoming one and the same.*

The second factor that frustrated progress is the presence inside the European Community's quasi-state, or *nonstate*, of a strong *centrifugal center*, in the form of the Council of Ministers that halted any attempt by supranational bodies, especially the Commission and the Parliament, to cultivate a strong constituency of organized interests that would in turn have enhanced the status of supranational Community institutions as an incipient sovereign government. No comparable barrier to central state formation and state growth has ever been present in a traditional nation-state. It should be noted that "intergovernmentalism," as it came to be called, had the same discouraging impact on the organization of business as it had on labor with opposite consequences for the realization of the respective interests. This is because under the unanimity principle of decision making, which is the hallmark of intergovernmentalism, a European interest group that wants to *prevent* a specific decision needs just one national government willing to veto that decision in the Council, frustrating even the most sophisticated lobbying efforts vis-à-vis the Commission. Where such a veto is not cast on ideological or interest-political grounds, a class like business, whose interest was and is essentially not in *shaping* but rather in *preventing* a centralized European social policy, could always hope to find allies in national governments concerned about their *sovereignty.* Intergovernmentalism thus made both encompassing organization and centralized negotiations with labor largely dispensable for European business whose social-policy interests, under the specific configuration of markets, national states, and supranational institutions that is the European Community tend to be realized as it were by default.

Much of the corporatist debate of the 1970s was on the question of whether a strong state is a precondition for strong associations or whether strong associations can develop without, and may even substitute for, a strong state. Based on national observations and cross-national comparison, what seemed to emerge as a tentative consensus assigned a prominent place to the indispensable contribution of public power even in cases of "societal corporatism."[26] The European Community has never been permitted to develop the organizational design capacities necessary to reshape powerful interest organizations rooted in civil society. Whatever capacity it may have in this respect is vastly inferior to that of the Community's nation-states from which it is derived in the first place. Moreover the policymaking process in the Community is too fragmented and dispersed to place a high premium on interest organizational centralization at the European level. In the history of the Community up to the present, intergovernmentalism and the veto powers of individual nations were always strong enough to preempt or modify centrally made decisions. Organized interests thus had no other choice even if they were otherwise inclined, than to maintain a strong national base and to cultivate established national channels of influence. This, as has been pointed out, holds in particular for groups and in policy arenas *where the interest is more in nondecisions than it is in decisions.* As long as the Community—that is, its nonintergovernmental institutions such as the Parliament and the Commission—cannot autonomously determine the range of policy issues that come under its jurisdiction, its ability to influence the structure of organized group interests will remain low indeed.

CORPORATISM, THE NATION-STATE, AND THE DEREGULATION OF EUROPEAN ECONOMIES

There are, however, more and equally important and vexing relationships between corporatism, nationalism, supranationalism, and the distribution of power in the political economy. The heyday of corporatism in the 1970s was a period of distinctly *national* responses to the catastrophic deinstitutionalization of the capitalist world economy that started in the late 1960s and to the domestic and international disorder that ensued. Apart from the United States where the absence of a European-style resurgence of labor militancy in 1968[27] had set the stage for a strategy of economic recovery through deunionization and deregulation, governments almost everywhere experimented with centrally negotiated "social contracts" of all sorts. These agreements served as a homemade replacement or functional equivalent for the now defunct set of international institutions that had in the past provided at least some form of stability for and among competing capitalist nations by, for example, imposing and enforcing external "balance of payments constraints" that helped national governments keep domestic "discipline." To an important degree, corporatist concertation in the 1970s must be understood as a sometimes desperate turn to domestic political and institutional resources in a search for solutions to what really were international problems—a turn that reflected the almost complete absence on the eve of the crisis, in spite of three decades of international institution building, of technically viable and politically legitimate mechanisms of international cooperation.[28]

Member states of the European Community in particular had recourse to corporatism or attempted corporatism in the early 1970s. Indeed if the Community was mentioned in Europe at all during that period, it was to point out how useless it had proven as an instrument for tasks like the restoration of a stable monetary environment, for working out a common energy policy with the United States and perhaps OPEC, or for fighting inflation and unemployment. The "dark age" of the European Community was above all a time when European national elites seemed to believe as a matter of course that the supranational European institutions they had set up in the 1950s and 1960s, embedded in a relatively stable world order, could not serve as a suitable tool for the restoration of that order and that therefore everybody had to find their own national solutions.[29]

National corporatism, we have maintained, was adopted as an alternative to an international response including a European one. At the same time, the use of domestic concertation on a large scale was bound to make international concertation even more difficult and thus contributed further to bringing the process of European integration, including the building of a European-level system of interest politics, to a halt. This was not only because emerging national corporatisms diverted the attention of policy makers and association officials away from "Brussels" and back to national capitals or because attempts at international cooperation would have added further complexity to the domestic bargaining process thus reducing the elites' degrees of freedom and making compromise more difficult. It was also, and more importantly, because different countries turned out to be differently equipped institutionally for corporatist concertation. While corporatism worked in some places, it failed dismally in others, and in yet others it worked for a while but created accumulated problems that later came home to roost. The economic performance of different capitalist economies thus became more divergent than ever in the 1970s, and as the history of European integration testifies, divergent performance is not at all conducive to countries giving up a share of their sovereignty—the weak ones being afraid of becoming subservient to the strong ones and the strong ones seeing no need to dilute, and even being afraid of diluting, their national success.

Second it almost follows from the above that the resurgence of European integration, as signified by the Single European Act and the internal market project, was more than just incidentally related to the demise of national corporatism in the early 1980s. If anything, it had been the rapid decline of their "effective sovereignties"[30] that had undermined the capacity of national states in the developed capitalist world to sustain the kind of social contracts that they had entered into in response to the crisis. The neocorporatist exercises of the 1970s had in large part been attempts to shore up the systems of economic and social policymaking that had been put in place under the postwar settlement[31] and to prolong their lives beyond that of the international environment in which they had originally been embedded. Ultimately it turned out that this was not possible. The changes in the international position of the United States that had exhausted its capacity to act as a benevolent hegemon had gradually given rise in the 1970s to a domestic move away from the New Deal compromise, to a political economy that sought competitiveness through deregulation and deunionization and abandoned the social-democratic principle that wages and social conditions were to be taken out of competition. After the final defeat of the Labor Law Reform Act in 1978, the Federal Reserve could feel free to respond to the second oil crisis with a dramatic increase in interest rates, ending inflation at the price of deindustrialization and causing a further, probably irreversible, decline in union organization. In the early 1980s, with effectively deregulated worldwide integrated capital markets, the destruction of American trade unions paid off handsomely in that it gave the United States the "flexible" markets and the "confidence" of financial investors required to underwrite an expansionist fiscal policy that has been ironically characterized as "Keynesianism in one country."

From the perspective of other capitalist countries, that term would appear to have carried a particularly ominous connotation. As the French socialist government after 1981 was soon to find out under the watchful eyes of other political elites, the dynamics of the international political economy after the second oil shock were governed by the old Roman imperial maxim, *quod licet Jovi non licet bovi*. Keynesianism had ceased to be universally available; it had become limited not just to one but to *only* one country. Being so much larger than everybody else and as a consequence so much less internationalized, having broken its unions, being still in control of the *de facto* world currency while no longer accepting the responsibilities of world banker, and for all these and other reasons being able to attract and maintain the confidence of what is euphemistically called "the financial markets" in spite of gigantic and growing deficits in its budget and foreign trade—the United States could effectively and successfully apply fiscal stimulus whereas the others could do so only at the expense of their capital running away and holders of financial assets dropping their currencies at their doorsteps.

The important point here is that some sort of effective Keynesian-expansionist capacity seems indispensable for the kind of corporatist concertation and social contract bargaining that was to stabilize non-American capitalism in the 1970s. As much as these systems may otherwise have differed, under the rules of corporatist bargaining a state that cannot with any reasonable prospect of success promise to apply its fiscal and monetary policy tools to alleviate unemployment cannot possibly hope to gain concessions from unions or to influence settlements between unions and employers by, for example, offering to improve the terms of the bargain through a corresponding economic policy.[32] To put the use of its sovereignty up for negotiation, a state needs to have sovereignty in the first place. As the effective sovereignty and subsequently the Keynesian capacity of European nation-states faded, so did corporatism and with it the social-democratic project of politically guaranteed full employment.

Of course, not all of the causes for the demise of sovereignty and, therefore, national corporatism originated in the deinstitutionalization of the international economy or in the internal politics of the United States and the deflationary bias it introduced in the world capitalist system. A more general explanation lies in the growing interpenetration of capitalist economies that has now increased the external contribution to a typical west European country's national accounts to a level where it can no longer be treated as a mere addition to a primarily domestic economy. As the French have learned and as everybody else has learned from the French, interdependence does not make it impossible to create jobs by Keynesian stimulus, but unless a country has the size, the currency, and the social system of the United States, chances are that many of those jobs will emerge outside the territory whose government has increased the national debt to create them. Given the absence of international institutions to manage such interdependence, governments in the early 1980s felt hard pressed, or saw a golden opportunity depending on their political complexion, to withdraw the political full employment promise of the postwar period and yield control over the restoration of prosperity and employment in their internationalized national economies to "the market," including a deregulated labor market thereby in effect accepting the increasingly demanding conditions placed by capital holders on industrial investment and conceding what Burnham once called "domestic sovereignty" to what is referred to in the jargon of international capitalism as "market forces."

It is true that the decay of national corporatism in the late 1970s and in the 1980s was also rooted in domestic developments like qualitative changes in social structures, in the economy, and in domestic political systems that had imperceptibly at first eaten away at corporatism's structural and perhaps cultural foundations. While this is not the place to review these trends in any detail, three of them will be briefly discussed, adding to the reasons why a restoration of neocorporatism at either national or supranational level has become unlikely now and in the future.[33]

1. *Increasing differentiation of social structures and collective interests in advanced capitalist societies.* Neocorporatism assumed an underlying social structure that could be plausibly conceived of as polarized in two large producer classes, "capital" and "labor." With hindsight, that assumption appears to have been already highly counterfactual when western European countries in the late 1960s were increasingly moving toward neocorporatist forms of governance. While the *corporatist working hypothesis of a bipolar organization of societal cleavages and identities* was never more than a *heroic simplification* of a much more complex reality, it could be kept alive with the help of the powerful institutional reinforcement that both business and labor as organized actors had received from their beleaguered governments. Underneath the organizational and institutional structures, however, social

change continued and perhaps even accelerated. In addition to strengthening the institutional position of labor movements, 1968 was also the birthdate of a new, highly educated, and politically outspoken *middle class* that increasingly found its specific concerns insufficiently represented in the post-1968, class-political institutional setup. Subsequently during the 1970s and 1980s, the substantive content of interest conflicts and the focus of policy attention shifted away from class-based lines of cleavage toward a panoply of discrete issues focusing on consumer protection, quality of life, gender, environmental, ethical, and other problems each with their respective movements. As is well known, in most countries this weakened the capacity of social-democratic parties to govern or alternatively strained the alliance between social democracy and the union movement. Neither was conducive to corporatist governance.

2. *Market instability and volatility and pressures on firms to increase the "flexibility" of their product ranges, technologies, and social organization.* New production technologies based on microelectronics and cutting across traditional job classifications and professional categories have created possibilities for flexible production in relatively small units. In one sense, these processes increased the need for active assent on the part of workers and therefore the need for employers to bargain with them over the quality as well as the quantity of their contribution. But in another sense, they are occurring in highly differentiated settings that are not easy to cover by a standard contract and difficult for intermediaries to control. Indeed both unions and employer associations are today finding themselves increasingly shut out of an expanding range of workplace-specific deliberations and bargaining between their respective local constituents.
3. *Changing roles and structures of interest associations.* In the new social and market environment, negotiations aimed at establishing standard national solutions for the regulation of the employment relationship appear of decreasing relevance and at times may even be counterproductive when what is demanded are policies tailored to improving the productivity and international competitiveness of specific sectors and individual enterprises. As a result, the role of intermediary institutions especially trade unions and employer associations changed from the point of view of members and interlocutors both of whom are searching for more differentiated mechanisms of representation. While decentralization may have taken very different courses in different countries, what it inevitably had in common was a weakening of the center, and it is there that corporatist bargains are traditionally struck.

Moreover the shift of employment from traditional manufacturing to the services and in some cases to public employment in a number of countries changed the character of unions in that unions from the public and private service sector became the largest units in national confederations. This seems to have weakened the organizational discipline that was traditionally maintained by unionized manual workers, especially from the metalworking sector.[34] These unions, whose industries were exposed to world market competition, have in the past typically been willing to observe wage restraint in exchange for political concessions. Their sectors have often been hard hit by deindustrialization, and such workers as remained after successful restructuring— if they joined unions at all—were employed in more scattered sites with much more individuated tasks. The very categories upon which macrocorporatist compromises were built have thus become disaggregated and dispersed, and as a result centralized negotiations on wages, benefits, and working conditions came under severe pressure. In some cases (for example, that of Sweden), the system only survived by shifting to a sectoral level.

Deregulation thus spread from the United States to Britain, the country with the most open capital markets, and from there to the European continent, meeting with declining resistance in changing domestic political economies. What it involved was a more or less forceful, and more or less successful, attack on the accumulated "rigidities" that more than three decades of "mixed economy" had installed. In many cases, this included the dismantling or at least the disregard of structures of collective bargaining and domestic compromise that already under the late Keynesian regime had more and more been perceived as obstructing industrial adjustment. Where dismantling got stuck, the proven inability of governments to deliver on employment, and their growing unwillingness to try, together with the insistence of unions on concessions and institutional monopolies that capital and governments felt they no longer needed to provide, created the atmosphere of "Euro-pessimism" and "Euro-malaise," not to mention "Euro-sclerosis" that was so pervasive in Europe during the first half of the 1980s. The internal market project emerged at this time and in this context.

THE RELAUNCHING OF THE EUROPEAN COMMUNITY: CUTTING THE CURRENCY OF NATIONAL POWER RESOURCES

If one wants a shorthand explanation for the renewed momentum of European integration in the mid-1980s,[35] one would probably account for it as the result of an alignment between two broad interests—that of large European firms struggling to overcome perceived competitive disadvantages in relation to Japanese and U.S. capital and that of state elites seeking to restore at least part of the political sovereignty they had gradually lost at the national level as a result of growing international interdependence. Unlike in the crisis years of the 1970s, European large firms seem to have resolved at some point in the early 1980s that the increased size of production runs and investments required for world market competitiveness made it counterproductive to use their clout in national political arenas to get protection from foreign competition through subsidies, technical standards serving as nontariff trade barriers, or privileged access to public procurement contracts. Instead of trying to benefit from the economic nationalism that made European integration grind to a halt in the 1970s, business throughout Europe seems to have become willing in the 1980s to join forces with political elites which, under the impact of their economies' poor performances and with worldwide policy coordination with the United States and Japan out of reach, found themselves under pressure to seek a *supranational pooling of eroded national sovereignties over economic policy*, to recapture collective autonomy in relation to the United States, and to begin to organize a competitive response to the Japanese challenge.

The main concession governments seem to have made in return for business giving up previous claims for national protection was that the future European political economy was to be significantly less subject to institutional regulation—*national or supranational*—than it would have been in the harmonization-minded *and* social-democratic 1970s when employers found themselves forced to struggle against a Community directive that would have made German-style co-determination obligatory for all large European firms. In the 1992 compromise, the project of European integration became finally and formally bound up with a deregulation project. While 1992 is all about sovereignty, it is about sovereignty vis-à-vis Europe's external environment, *not* its domestic economy. Indeed part and parcel of the pooling of sovereignties[36] under the Single European Act and of the political deals that made it possible is a redefinition of the relationship between the Community's "domestic" institutions and "the market" under which the latter stands to gain unprecedented freedom from intervention by the former. The mechanism to accomplish this, and a powerful reassurance for business that supranational sovereignty will indeed be used exclusively for the *external reassertion of*, as opposed to *internal intervention in*, the European economy, is "negative integration" through preemption of national regulatory regimes without a simultaneous supranational restoration of regulatory capacity. The adoption of "mutual recognition" as a novel method of defining and governing the internal market—a method that for all practical purposes amounts to a subtle form of deregulation[37]—can only be fully explained in this light.

Seen from a national perspective, 1992 amounts to a formal devaluation of vast political resources that have come to be organized in and around the nation-state. Declining effective sovereignty had long been chopping away at the value of investments in national political power that had been accumulated and cultivated for more than a century; this after all was why corporatism was eventually becoming untenable. The 1992 principle of mutual recognition may well be understood in analogy to the cut of a collapsed currency—an inevitable but nevertheless painful adjustment to reality with significant distributional side effects in that currency holders are more severely affected than are owners of real estate or productive capital. In present-day European nation-states with the successive layers of political, industrial, and social rights that have been built into them in the domestic struggles of the nineteenth and twentieth centuries, it is clearly labor that is in the former and capital that is in the latter position. *While mutual recognition and the resulting interregime competition devalue nationally institutionalized power resources, they leave property rights untouched or even increase their value*. As neocorporatism has always been conditional on a measure of political strength of organized labor, the prospects for its restoration in the post-1992 European nation-states are therefore dim.

This is not to say that everything that, in the analyses of the 1970s and 1980s, has come to be associated with corporatist modes of governance will disappear in Europe. Pragmatic sectoral partnerships between state agencies and groups of business firms, oscillating as it were between agency capture and *Selbstverwaltung*, are likely to continue to the extent that they are comfortably embedded in national policy styles and as long as they do not run afoul of European Community competition law, which well may happen. Especially if they have been labor-exclusive "private interest governments" from the beginning as we have called them elsewhere,[38] they may remain viable for some time due to the savings on transaction costs they entail and regardless of the weakening of their sponsors in national state and legal systems. Multiemployer collective bargaining arrangements between trade unions and employers associations, where they already exist, may not disappear either—at least, again, for the time being. But corporatism as a national-level accord between encompassingly organized socio-economic classes and the state by which an entire national economy is comprehensively governed would seem to be a matter of the past.

TOWARD A NEW EUROPEAN INTEREST POLITICS

The character of the emerging European polity has puzzled the literature on European integration from its beginnings. As it became clear that "regional integration" was an exclusively European phenomenon—the number of cases being no higher than one—the question became irrepressible of what the "dependent variable" was that integration theory expected to explain,[39] toward what "final state" (if at all) the integration process was moving, and what "the nature of the beast" was that students of European integration—like in the parable of the blind men and the elephant—were trying to grasp.[40]

Unlike in the early, "motivated" theorizing (until de Gaulle rehabilitated realism, both with and without a capital "R"), today hardly anybody[41] expects that the supranational European polity of the future will be a replication of the European nation-state of the past. Wherever else students of European politics may disagree, and they like to disagree a lot, as a minimum it now seems to be accepted that the political system of the post-1992 European Community will be fundamentally and by a quantum leap *more complex* than anything that has preceded it. For example, while Europe as whole will undoubtedly exist as a unified political entity of some as yet undetermined sort, the *nation-states* that now constitute the European Community will not disappear in that entity but will coexist with it.[42] Nor will Europe be simply an institutionalized system of *international or intergovernmental relations*; yet at the same time such relations will continue to play an important part in Europe alongside, and in interaction with, others.[43] And similarly Europe will have *supranational institutions* contributing to the governance of what will be a domestic western European polity, but these will have to share authority with national as well as with a dense web of international and transnational institutions which, too, will be constitutive elements of the emerging political system of western Europe.[44]

Europe's future polity, that is to say, will be composed of traditional domestic relations *within countries*, traditional international relations *between countries*, less traditional transnational relations between both individuals and organizations across national boundaries, and entirely nontraditional supranational relations *between European-level public institutions* on the one hand and, on the other, a *European civil society* consisting of domestic, international, and transnational forces and relations and including both nation-states and, in manifold national and cross-national combinations, their constituents. The possible dynamics of this unique and uniquely complex system of governance are as yet only poorly understood, and there is very little theory, if any at all, to guide such understanding. This applies not the least to the literature on *state formation* and the role of *class conflict* in it. While there always were more and other actors involved in the shaping of state structures than in the shaping of socioeconomic classes—for example, regional, ethnic, and cultural communities and interest groups—in the case of European integration classes, as well as other forces in civil society, have to compete for control over the newly emerging central level of governance with a qualitatively different set of players: a number of already existing, sovereign (or better and increasingly "semisovereign") nation-states. One reason why the latter's continued presence inside the European polity makes a difference is that the international boundaries between them constitute powerful, additional lines of cross-cutting cleavage inside classes and interest groups that stand in the way of their fast and effective politywide organization. Moreover unlike in the nineteenth century when the system of European nation-states was formed, social structures today appear too differentiated and political problems too variegated to be easily organizable along bipolar class lines—a condition that, while it is gradually yet fundamentally transforming the political make-up of established nation-states, can be expected to exert a much more powerful formative influence on the only now emerging polity of the integrated European Community.

There is, furthermore, a growing suspicion that conventional models of the growth of the *modern European welfare state* may not be applicable to the European Community. For some time to come, whatever will occupy the place of the supranational Single European State governing the Single European Market, will likely resemble a *pre-New Deal liberal state*, with, in Marshall's terms:[45]

- A high level of *civil rights* enabling citizens to engage freely in contractual relationships inside and across national borders, accompanied by well-protected *human rights* to equal treatment before the law, freedom of movement, and so forth. Here the European Court of Justice is of crucial importance and also the Council of Europe although the latter is not, of course, a European Community institution.

- A low level of *political rights*, with the European Parliament continuing to play only a minor role in the system of European institutions. This holds in spite of the fact that the Parliament's direct election and its new powers under the Single European Act have vastly improved its status over what it was in the mid-1970s.

- An even lower level of *social rights*, these being essentially limited to a set of European-wide health and safety standards. Historically intervention on health and safety matters represents the earliest stage in the history of the modern welfare state. Present efforts to attach a "Social Dimension" to the internal market by starting with a set of generally binding health and safety standards are aimed at replicating the familiar national trajectory of welfare state development. But in the face of the retarded advancement of European-level political rights, there is little reason to expect such efforts to be particularly successful, given in addition

- The almost complete absence of a European system of *industrial citizenship* that would give workers and unions rights to representation in industry as a functional domain at the European level, separate from the territorial domain of electoral politics. The closest the European Community will come to being a source of industrial citizenship—that is, to creating and safeguarding European-wide institutions of industrial relations and collective bargaining—is in providing for some form of labor participation under the European company statute. But, whatever this will in the end entail, it is likely to pale into insignificance when compared to some of the national systems of union rights that were part of the post-World War II national settlements.

The emerging shape of the European supranational nonstate—or even "post-Hobbesian" state[46]—does not bode well for a reappearance of neocorporatism above the disorganizing nation-state. We will now try to trace some of the implications of what we think we know about the future contours of the European polity for the structure and function of organized interests at the two newly emerging, additional levels of policymaking and interest articulation in Europe: the subnational, or regional, and the supranational levels. Together with the member states, regional and supranational political entities share in the diffuse and fragmented sovereignty of the Community, blending into a highly interdependent but incompletely unified, loosely coupled, and diverse institutional complex—the new type of state that is the European Community—that confronts an at least equally diverse civil society acting in what after 1992 will be an integrated market.

Interest Politics at the Subnational Level

At the core of the 1992 process is the abolition of national boundaries between the markets of the 12 member states of the European Community.[47] As a result, the 12 formerly national economies will turn into *regional subunits* of a larger economic entity—a *region* being defined as a *territorial society without sovereignty over its borders.* Also, the existing regional subunits of European nations, being no longer fenced in by common, national economic boundaries, will themselves become subunits in their own right of the larger, integrated European economy. This transformation of national into regional economies and of subnational regions into subunits of a supranational economy amounts to a *regionalization of Europe* as well as at the same time a *Europeanization of its regions.*

The potential importance of the regional level for the developing politics of Europe is underlined by the rich literature on *industrial districts.*[48] Its common theme is that of a strong, positive contribution of a dense, social-institutional infrastructure to the vitality of regional economies, like Baden-Wuerttemberg in west Germany or parts of the "Third Italy," that engage in "high valued-added," "flexibly specialized,"[49] or "diversified quality"[50] modes of production. In many of these prosperous and world market-competitive areas, interest associations and apparently often including unions seem to play an indispensable part in the negotiation of distributional compromises, the building of growth and productivity coalitions, the formation of public-private interfaces, the provision of a protective institutional exoskeleton for small, innovative firms, the generation of collective factor inputs, and the creation of institutions that allow for nonzero-sum cooperation among firms as well as between capital and labor at the workplace and beyond.

Recent developments seem to indicate that the former regional subunits of European national economies may be about to become independent actors on the European Community stage.[51] A number of European regions, most prominent among them Catalunia, Lombardia, and Baden-Wuerttemberg, have set up permanent offices in Brussels that bear conspicuous resemblance to embassies.

Moreover their heads of government have met several times to discuss strategy and form coalitions concerning their interests vis-à-vis the European Community. If this trend were to continue, regions would join nations, classes, sectors, and firms as participants in European-interest politics, adding another category of players and further complexities to a scene that is already highly complex and pluralistic.

Europeanization of regional interests, and especially interregional political competition for Community resources, is far from being universally welcomed.[52] For one thing, while it would improve the position of the Commission, it would also and ipso facto tend to weaken further what is left of sovereignty at the national level, which is why national governments have been found to resent actively the formation of direct connections between Brussels and "their" subnational territories. Also if regions are admitted to European politics, regional subunits of *federal* states, having independent powers of legislation, taxation, budgeting and so on, will likely have an advantage over regions in more centralized countries; namely, the absence from the above list of, say, the Midlands in England.

An important question with respect to the possible emergence of a regional level of European-interest politics concerns the sources and conditions of labor inclusiveness of regional regimes—especially whether regional power resources of labor can be generated *endogenously* inside the region or need to be mobilized *exogenously* using national power resources under the protection of a sovereign border. Regions, as has been pointed out, are societies that lack control over their borders. As European nation-states turn into regions of an integrated market economy, nationally legislated labor-market regimes are likely to lose much of their force, and the same holds for protective barriers against cross-border competition; this after all is what the expected deregulatory effect of 1992 is all about. The survival and growth of regional labor-inclusive institutions inside the integrated internal market and with it perhaps that of regionally based nonprice-competitive production, would then have to depend on nonnational, regionally indigenous forces or would require that functional equivalents for national-level supports be found at the supranational level to balance the decline in national political capacities that is associated with 1992.

Much of the literature on regional political economies seems to take the position that the composition and survival of their regimes is indeed, and always was, largely independent from national institutions. Typically the institutional infrastructure of economically successful European regions is described as based in *local* cultures, traditions, and politics that, by implication, would be unlikely to be destabilized by an attenuation of national sovereignty. Apart from the fact that culture and tradition may rapidly lose vitality in the modernizing, internationalizing post-1992 European economy, however, a case could be made that, certainly as far as the presence of unions and of a tripartite power balance in regional economies is concerned, this severely underestimates the role played in the past by *national* power resources,[53] like labor law creating or supporting various overt or covert mechanisms of union security or protective monetary and trade policies.

Regions, not being states, are by definition unable to insert *coercive power* in the voluntary contractual and communitarian relations between their citizens. Their social organization is that of a civil society largely undistorted, as it were, by public intervention. In particular, regions would seem to lack the capacity to provide the kind of public support that has generally been found to be required to transform unstable, voluntaristic, pluralistic unions into institutionally "mature" ones that are capable of looking in corporatist fashion beyond the individual enterprise or occupational group to the sector, the country or for that matter the region *as a whole*. Regionally based unionism in the European Community would have to do without external sources of associational monopoly, without authoritative stabilization of bargaining arenas, and without recourse to a public sphere balancing the manifold advantages employers enjoy in the marketplace. It is not easy to see how the disabling effects on union movements of the erosion of institutional supports at the national level should be counterbalanced by unions turning to the regional level where such supports have never existed.

In any case, even if it was somehow possible to create stable tripartite systems of regional governance, referring to this as "regional corporatism" may be highly misleading. Corporatism requires encompassing organizations that internalize a significant part of the externalities of a group's collective action and interests, and allow for hierarchical coordination between different levels of interest aggregation and group activity. Neither condition would be met in a Europe of regional tripartisms. If national-level corporatism has been undermined by growing international interdependence beyond the control of the parties at the bargaining table, regional arrangements are even more affected by the shrinking effective size of modern polities. The tyranny of external effects, as it has been called, may be and clearly is on the advance at the national level; but it certainly is incomparably more severe in the much smaller action space of a subnational region especially after the demise of national regulations that in the past have taken a core set of social and constitutional conditions out of interregional competition.

Moreover in moving their organizational center of gravity toward the region, as most of the industrial district literature more or less explicitly advises them to do, unions would write off any aspiration they may have had for playing a role in the political management of interregional externalities. Regionalized unions would inevitably be partners, junior or not, of regional capital trying to survive in interregional free market competition. Such unions would have to cease trying to act as agents of interregional redistribution. While the *mezzogiorno* policy of Italian unions in the 1970s, which relied on the movement's centralized, national power to demand regional development programs for the impoverished south of the country, may not have been particularly successful; a regionally decentralized union movement would have been unable to agree on any such policy in the first place. Today regionalized unionism would for the same reasons be incapable of a political, as opposed to a market-driven, response to the deep interdependence of regional economies with the larger European and global economic context—a condition that has become more profound than ever and that incidentally fundamentally distinguishes today's regional economies from those of the past.

It is conceivable that political control over economic interdependence is presently beyond recapture and that union organizational domains may for a long time or forever be bound to be significantly narrower than whatever the relevant "market" may be. But decentralization of unions and industrial relations toward regional arenas will clearly not remedy this condition, and to the extent that it ratifies the possibly inevitable fragmentation of organized interests, it actually amounts to the very opposite of corporatism. The emergence of regional arenas of interest politics seems to advance, not the organization of labor or for that matter of capital, but rather its *disorganization*. In the 1992 environment in particular, new opportunities for interest articulation at the regional level would appear to increase actors' range of *choice* between political channels widely beyond what would be compatible with the orderly world of corporatism. In addition to the enterprise, the sector, the nation, and perhaps Europe as a whole, struggling factions inside interest associations, including unions, would have yet another option for pursuing sectional interests separately and on their own in coalition with other categories of equally fragmented interests or with ambitious local governments. By undermining associational monopoly and interassociational hierarchy, the fragmentation of interests and the pluralist proliferation of political opportunities that is entailed in the "regionalization of Europe" adds to the decomposition of national-level corporatisms as well as to the obstacles to its supranational resurrection.

Interest Politics at Supranational Level

Tripartism never really worked in Brussels,[54] and where it was tried, it was always too encapsulated and marginal to come in any way close to a neocorporatist model of governance. There is no reason to believe that this will change. The negative integration mode of the 1992 process—the move away from harmonization to mutual recognition—ensures that the eroded domestic sovereignty of nation-states will only partly, if at all, be recreated at the Community level. Unlike older, more naive images of regional integration, allowance has to be made today for the possibility that national political arenas, themes, and regulatory instruments that are rendered obsolete by integration are not always and necessarily reconstructed at the level of the emerging supranational polity. Rather than being moved upward, they are as likely to dissipate in a larger, less orderly, or less mature institutional complex and may thereby more or less intentionally be turned over to, or replaced by, the voluntarism of market and civil society. Where this happens, it deprives what might aspire to become a European federal government of a range of subject matter and decisional discretion that it otherwise could use and indeed would need to build the mutual give-and-take in and between interest groups and public bodies that is the indispensable basis for stable neocorporatist exchange.

A case of limited state capacity at the European level reducing the incentives for comprehensive organization of economic interests is the absence of a *European central bank.*[55] Historically tripartite corporatist bargaining has typically involved the government's use not only of fiscal but also of monetary policy instruments. The need to be represented in bargaining over monetary policy was an important reason for socioeconomic interests, in particular for employers, to get organized. The European system of central banks, however, provided it will some day come into being, will be carefully shielded from political pressures, not least by its diffuse and decentralized internal structure. Moreover a European central bank is likely for a long time to continue to be subject to strongly institutionalized deflationary, "monetarist" preferences[56]—if only because the European Community as an imperfectly unified actor in the world economy will need time to get used to the reflationary possibilities offered by a large economy with a currency that could in principle compete for the role of world money.

Another important ingredient of 1970s-style neocorporatism—*centralized collective bargaining between capital and labor*—is entirely missing at the European level, and nothing is in sight that would indicate its impending appearance. In national industrial relations systems, centralized collective bargaining was often advanced by encompassing employers associations forcing unions to unify their policies and organizational structures.[57] No such support will be forthcoming at the European level in the foreseeable future, not least because the interregional mobility of capital will perhaps indefinitely now exceed that of labor and because centralization would deprive capital of the strategic advantages of competition-driven industrial relations at regional or enterprise level. The same applies to the other historical source of external facilitation, government intervention. Europe-wide institutions are unlikely to develop a capacity to serve as carryover mechanisms from the unionized to the nonunionized sector so as to protect employers in the former from competition by employers in the latter.

The emergence of European-level collective bargaining is further impeded by *mutual incompatibility of existing national industrial relations systems.* While in some countries collective agreements are negotiated at the *enterprise* level, in others they are concluded for all firms that belong to a specific *sector* on a given national or subnational *territory.* The latter, in addition to requiring the presence of strong employers associations and preferably state-sponsored extension mechanisms making agreements binding on nonaffiliated firms, depends crucially on the large and more prosperous firms being included in the territorially defined bargaining units; otherwise industrial unions would be deprived of the opportunity to increase their bargaining power in small firms by enlisting as their ally the willingness to settle and the ability to pay of large firms. In the absence of supranational employer associations and facilitating state intervention, however, all unions can hope to accomplish in building what the Commission has euphemistically called a "European industrial relations system"[58] are consultations and perhaps negotiations with the headquarters of large multinational firms.[59] But while this would be compatible with national industrial relations systems based on enterprise bargaining, European enterprise agreements would over time inevitably tend to exempt the national subsidiaries of the respective enterprises from the domain of sectoral-territorial bargaining. The result would be a weakening of existing national multiemployer bargaining regimes. Since sectoral-territorial bargaining is used by unions to reduce regional and interfirm wage differentials, unions would have not just organizational but also political reasons for objecting to European enterprise-level bargaining even if this is likely to be the only form of supranational collective bargaining on offer.

Also there is no reason to believe that an increase in political opportunities for labor at the European level, assuming that it will ever come to pass, will make consensus-building in European labor organizations less difficult. In fact, if outcomes matter more, interest differences assume more weight. Organizational, political, and ideological divergence may be even less crippling in this respect than would different national labor market structures, training systems, or living standards.[60] Trade unions from rich countries traditionally offer their poorer counterparts assistance in the pursuit of aggressive demands for wages, holidays, social security benefits, and so forth. But what to them may appear to be internationalist concern for their fellow-workers' rights and well being, the latter may eventually perceive as designed to protect their richer brothers and sisters from capital outflow and subsequent job loss.[61] As long as calls for Community-wide labor standards have no practical consequences, they are likely not to be opposed by unions in weaker economies. When confederal policies may have a real impact, their formulation could become more contested.[62]

European-level relations between capital and labor, instead of constituting the core of the European political economy, will for the foreseeable future remain compartmentalized in the private sphere of large multinational enterprises and will thus be essentially nonpolitical and voluntaristic in character. Where labor-capital relations enter the political arena, they will mainly take the form of a set of discrete "labor" and "social policy" issues. As such, they will lend themselves to being dealt with by bureaucrats, experts, and intergovernmental committees in the same way as are, for example, labeling rules regarding the cholesterol content of palm oil or regulations for the recycling of mineral water containers. Rather than driving the constitutional bargain underlying the political system, the traditional class issues of industrial society will have to compete on an equal plane with "postindustrial" themes like environmental protection, consumer rights, equality between men and women, and so forth—issues that by their nature defy integration into an encompassing framework of "class" politics.[63]

The evolutionary alternative to neoliberalism as a model for the European political economy is clearly not (German or Scandinavian) neocorporatism. More likely appears an American-style pattern of "disjointed pluralism" or "competitive federalism," organized over no less than three levels—regions, nation-states, and "Brussels." As in the United States and perhaps more so, this system would be characterized by a profound *absence of hierarchy and monopoly* among a *wide variety of players of different but uncertain status*. Interest associations, and quite a few of them, will certainly be among those players. But they will have to compete for attention with national states, subnational regions, large firms, and specialized lobbyists, leaving their constituents with a wide range of choices among different paths of access to the Community's political center and enabling them to use threats of exit to coerce their representatives into pluralist responsiveness. Just as fundamental constitutional questions of sovereignty and hierarchy inside the Community's quasi-state—concerning, for example, the relative status of regions, nations, and supranational bodies—will remain unsettled and uncertain, so will the hierarchical relations between firms, sectoral associations, and peak associations in its system of functional representation.

Given the constitutional bargain that underlies the relaunching of the European Community in the 1980s, no mechanism is in sight that could rationalize its political system, help crystallize its *melange* of actors and processes, and establish corporatist monopolies of representation, interassociational hierarchies or for that matter a predominant position for the Commission's bureaucracy and technocracy. Whatever turn the European Community may take after 1992, it will not reverse the tide and reorganize European capitalism in the neocorporatist cast.

NOTES

1. Ernst B. Haas, "The Study of Regional Integration: Reflections on the Joy and Anguish of Pretheorizing," in *Regional Integration: Theory and Research*, Leon N. Lindberg and Stuart Scheingold, eds. (Cambridge, Mass.: Harvard University Press, 1971), pp. 3–42.

2. Leon N. Lindberg and Stuart A. Scheingold, *Europe's Would-Be Polity: Patterns of Change in the European Community* (Englewood Cliffs, N.J.: Prentice Hall, 1970).

3. On the following, see in particular Ernst B. Haas, *The Uniting of Europe: Political, Social and Economic Forces 1950–1957* (London: Stevens and Son, 1958).

4. Which was of course the core concept of Haas' seminal, "neofunctionalist" theory of European and regional integration. Haas, *The Uniting of Europe*.

5. See especially Philippe C. Schmitter, "Still the Century of Corporatism?," in *Trends Towards Corporatist Intermediation*, Philippe C. Schmitter and Gerhard Lehmbruch, eds. (London: Sage, 1979), pp. 7–52; "Corporatism (Corporativism)," forthcoming in *The Encyclopedia of the Social Sciences*; Philippe C. Schmitter, "A Sketch of an Eventual Article on The European Community as an Extreme Example of a Newly Emergent Form of Political Domination," unpublished manuscript, 1989.

6. Ernst B. Haas, "Turbulent Fields and the Theory of Regional Integration," *International Organization* 30, no. 2 (Spring 1976): 173–212.

7. Gerhard Lehmbruch, "Liberal Corporatism and Party Government," in *Trends Towards Corporatist Intermediation*, Schmitter and Lehmbruch, eds.

8. The exceptions seem to be CIC (professional association of executive workers, founded in 1951), FIPMEC (small business associations for artisanal and craft trades, 1951), CEA (business association for the insurance industry, 1953), CIF (association for public service employees, 1955), COCCEE (trade and commerce, 1957), and EUROCOOP (association of consumer cooperatives, 1957).

9. It should be noted that many of these associations affiliated national associations from countries that are not, or were not at the time, members of the European Community. For example, UNICE had 27 affiliates in 1980 of which 14 were from (then) non-European Community countries. The ETUC has, in addition to most union confederations from the 12 member nations, representatives from all EFTA countries and from Malta, Cyprus, and Turkey. For by now more or less outdated descriptive surveys of European-level interest organizations, see Alan Butt Philip, "Pressure Groups in the European Community," *UACES Occasional Essay 2* (London: University Association for Contemporary European Studies, 1985); Economic and Social Committee of the European Communities, *European Interest Groups and Their Relations to the Economic and Social Committee* (Farnborough, Eng.: Saxon House, 1980); Emil J. Kirchner and K. Schwaiger, *The Role of Interest Groups in the European Community* (Farnborough, Eng.: Gower, 1981); J. Meynaud and D. Sidjanski, *Les groupes de pression dans la Communauté Européenne* (Brussels: Institut de Sociologie, 1971).

10. Commission of the European Communities, *Repertoire des Organisations Professionelles crées dans le cadre des Communautés Européennes* (Brussels: Edition Delta, several editions).

11. Wolfgang Streeck, "Interest Heterogeneity and Organizing Capacity: Two Class Logic of Collective Action?" in *Rational Actors in Institutional Settings*, Roland Czada and Adrienne Windhoff-Heretier, eds. (Boulder, Colo.: Westview Press, 1990).

12. For example, Sicco Mansholt seems to have played a major role in the founding of COPA (Lindberg and Scheingold, *Europe's Would-Be Polity*, p. 173). In the extreme case of EUROFER, the Community sponsored the creation of a Europe-wide cartel (Butt Philip, "Pressure Groups," p. 45).

13. Lindberg and Scheingold, *Europe's Would-Be Polity*, p. 173; Jane Sargent, "Corporatism and the European Community," in *The Political Economy of Corporatism*, Wyn Grant, ed. (London: Macmillan, 1985) pp. 229–253.

14. Not all access to these committees was, however, restricted to functional representatives. Many involve "experts," which admittedly may often be difficult to distinguish

from lobbyists. For a description of 46 of these consultative bodies, see Economic and Social Committee of the European Communities, *European Interest Groups*, pp. 23–52.

15. J.A. Caporaso, *The Structure and Function of European Integration* (Pacific Palisades, Calif.: Goodyear, 1974), pp. 23–52.

16. As of 1989, there were 3277 officials assisted by 9202 staff personnel in the employ of the Commission.

17. Jurgen Grote, "Guidance and Control in Transnational Committee Networks: The Associational Basis of Policy Cycles at the EC Level," unpublished manuscript, 1989.

18. N. Nugent, *The Government and Politics of the European Community* (Durham, N.C.: Duke University Press, 1989); J. Lodge and V. Herman, "The Economic and Social Committee in EEC Decision-Making," *International Organization* 34, no. 2 (Spring 1980): 265–284. Even the Committee's own propaganda literature admits that "it was regarded as the most unobtrusive of Community institutions" (Economic and Social Committee of the European Communities, *The Other European Assembly* [Brussels: ESC Press, Information and Publications Division, 1986], pp. 13–14).

19. Where, in addition, the principal lines of cleavage were not between capital and labor but rather between "Gaullists" and "Atlanticists" and between the proponents of supranationalism and national sovereignty. As these conflicts began to dominate and eventually block the Community's agenda in the 1960s, introducing social questions in addition was a hopeless endeavor from the outset.

20. Not that Haas would have predicted or approved the substance of those initiatives which to a large part was clearly outside the spectrum of the "pluralist industrialism" of the 1950s, and in the eyes of many observers, signaled a return to "class conflict" and "ideology." See Haas, "Turbulent Fields."

21. D.C. Campbell, "Multinational Labor Relations in the European Community," *ILR Report* 27, no. 1 (Fall 1989): 7–14; J. Alexander, "Divergent European Community Unionism: A Threat to Single Market Unification?," unpublished manuscript, 1989; Jelle Visser, "Trade Union Diversity in Western Europe: Dimensions, Origins, and Consequences," paper presented at the IRRU conference on *Industrial Relations and the European Community*, University of Warwick, Coventry, Eng., 1989).

22. Tommaso Padoa-Schioppa, "Questions About Creating a European Capital Market," in *1992: One European Market?*, R. Bieber, R. Dehousse, J. Pinder, J.H.H. Weiler, eds. (Baden-Baden, Ger.: Nomos Verlagsgesellschaft, 1988), pp. 283–292.

23. P. Cressey, "Trade Unions and the Social Dialogue," paper presented at the IRRU conference on *Industrial Relations and the European Community*, University of Warwick, Coventry, Eng., 1989. In that sense, the encompassingness of labor's organizational structure at the European level, as indicated by the low number of unions compared to business associations, is illusory. If the internal policymaking capacities of European union confederations are taken into account, the picture changes dramatically.

24. For a case study, see Paul Teague, "Trade Unions and Extra-National Industrial Policies: A Case Study of the Response of the British NUM and ISTC to Membership in the European Coal and Steel Community," *Economic and Industrial Democracy* 10, no. 2 (May 1989), 211–237.

25. On the difference between class and producer interests and its reflection in the organizational structures and strategies of business, see Streeck, "Interest Heterogeneity and Organizing Capacity."

26. Alan Cawson, ed., *Organized Interests and the State: Studies in Meso-Corporatism* (London: Sage, 1985); Wyn Grant, ed., *The Political Economy of Corporatism* (London: Macmillan, 1985).

27. See the book by Colin Crouch and Alessandro Pizzorno, eds., *The Resurgence of Class Conflict in Western Europe Since 1968*, 2 vols. (London: Macmillan, 1978).

28. Paul McCracken et al., *Towards Full Employment and Price Stability: A Report to the OECD by a Group of Independent Experts* (Paris: Organisation for Economic Co-operation and Development, 1977).

29. Of course, as has been pointed out, the period in question was also notable for attempts by unions and social-democratic governments to move the European Community to the left. With hindsight, this may be seen as another manifestation of the general confusion and indecision of the time when the left was still benefiting from the momentum of 1968 while the right was beginning to launch its counterattack with the support of, as it were, 1973. Moves toward a "social Europe" may in this situation have been an important reason for business and its political allies to hold back on European integration. Having not been able to escape national corporatism after 1968, it made little sense for them to accept supranational corporatism in addition at a time when the tide was already beginning to turn in their favor.

30. Stanley Hoffmann, "The European Community and 1992," *Foreign Affairs* no. 4 (Fall 1989).

31. Peter Gourevitch, *Politics in Hard Times* (Ithaca, N.Y.: Cornell University Press, 1986).

32. Marino Regini, "Political Bargaining in Western Europe During the Economic Crisis of the 1980s," in *Economic Crisis, Trade Unions and the State*, O. Jacobi et al., eds. (London: Croom Helm, 1986) pp. 61–76.

33. On the following, see Philippe C. Schmitter, " 'Corporatism is Dead! Long Live Corporatism!' Reflections on Andrew Shonfield's 'Modern Capitalism'," *Government and Opposition* 24, no. 1 (Winter 1989): 54–73.

34. Colin Crouch, "Trade Unions in the Exposed Sector: Their Influence on Neo-Corporatist Behavior," unpublished manuscript, 1988.

35. For more detail, see J. Sandholtz and J. Zysman, "1992: Recasting the European Bargain," *World Politics*, no. 1 (October 1989); Wolfgang Streeck, *The Social Dimension of the European Economy: A Discussion Paper Prepared for the 1989 Meeting of the Andrew Shonfield Association* (London: Andrew Shonfield Association, 1989).

36. Robert O. Keohane and Stanley Hoffmann, "European Integration and Neo-Functional Theory: Community Politics and Institutional Change," unpublished manuscript, 1989.

37. Hoffmann, "The European Community"; Streeck, "The Social Dimension of the European Economy."

38. Wolfgang Streeck and Philippe C. Schmitter, "Community, Market, State—and Associations? The Prospective Contribution of Interest Governance to Social Order," *European Sociological Review* 1, no. 2 (September 1985): 119–138.

39. Ernst B. Haas, *The Obsolescence of Regional Integration Theory* (Berkeley: Institute of International Studies, University of California–Berkeley, 1975).

40. Don Puchala, "Of Blind Men, Elephants and International Integration," *Journal of Common Market Studies*, no. 3 (March 1972): 267–284.

41. The exception being the "federalist" tradition of thinking about the European Community with its strongholds in Italy (the tradition of Spinelli) and remarkably in the United Kingdom (compare Michael Burgess, "Federalism and European Union: Past, Present and Future in the European Community," unpublished manuscript, 1989).

42. Puchala, "Of Blind Men."

43. Keohane and Hoffmann, "European Integration and Neo-Functional Theory."

44. Schmitter, "A Sketch of an Eventual Article."

45. Th. H. Marshall, *Class, Citizenship and Social Development* (Garden City, N.Y.: Doubleday, 1964).

46. Schmitter, "A Sketch of an Eventual Article."

47. R. Bieber, R. Dehousse, J. Pinder, J.H.H. Weiler, "Introduction. Back to the Future: Policy, Strategy and Tactics of the White Paper on the Creation of a Single European Market," in *1992: One European Market?*, Bieber et al., eds., pp. 13–31; Michael Calingaert, *The 1992 Challenge from Europe: Development of the European Community's Internal Market* (Washington, D.C.: National Planning Association, 1988).

48. Sebastiano Brusco, "The Emilian Model: Production Decentralization and Social Integration," *Cambridge Journal of Economics* 6, no. 2 (June 1982): 167–184; Charles F. Sabel, "Flexible Specialization and the Re-emergence of Regional Economies," in *Reversing Industrial Decline? Industrial Structure and Policy in Britain and Her Competitors*, Paul Hirst and Jonathan Zeitlin, eds. (New York: St. Martin's, 1989), pp. 17–70.

49. Michael J. Piore and Charles F. Sabel, *The Second Industrial Divide: Possibilities for Prosperity* (New York: Basic Books, 1984).

50. Arndt Sorge and Wolfgang Streeck, "Industrial Relations and Technical Change: The Case for an Extended Perspective," in *New Technology and Industrial Relations*, Richard Hyman and Wolfgang Streeck, eds. (Oxford, Eng.: Basil Blackwell, 1988).

51. For a strong statement to this effect, see G. Majone, "Preservation of Cultural Diversity in a Federal System: The Role of the Regions," unpublished manuscript, 1989.

52. The following discussion owes much to a set of unpublished papers by Gary Marks.

53. Walter Korpi, *The Working Class Under Welfare Capitalism: Work, Unions and Politics in Sweden* (London: Routledge and Kegan Paul, 1978).

54. Sargent, "Corporatism and the European Community."

55. E. Holm, "The Politics of Europe's Money," in *European Self-Assertion: A New Role for Europe in International Affairs*, B. Crawford and P. Schulze, eds. (forthcoming).

56. Committee for the Study of Economic and Monetary Union, "1989: Report on Economic and Monetary Union in the European Community."

57. Peter Swenson, *Fair Shares: Unions, Pay and Politics in Sweden and West Germany* (Ithaca, N.Y.: Cornell University Press, 1989).

58. Commission of the European Communities, *The Social Dimension of the Internal Market: Interim Report of the Intergovernmental Working Party*, Special Edition of *Social Europe (1988)*.

59. Campbell, "Multinational Labor Relations."

60. While this condition has existed for a long time, it was exacerbated in the mid-1980s by the accession to membership of three mediterranean countries: Spain, Portugal, and Greece. Today regional disparities in Europe are much wider than they are in the United States. According to *Eurostat Review 1977–1986*, hourly labor costs in Portugal for manual and nonmanual workers in 1984, expressed in ECU, amounted to 16

percent of German labor costs. The respective figure for Greece was 28 percent (UK: 63; France: 86). Later data or more exact measures are not at present available.

61. Wolfgang Streeck, "More Uncertainties: West German Unions Facing 1992," *Industrial Relations* (forthcoming, 1991).

62. We owe this point to a recent, as yet unpublished, paper by Peter Lange (1990).

63. To this extent, they would be subject to a "policy style" that is specifically "European"—that is, Community-European. In brief, the Brussels policy process seems to depend on successful decontextualization and depoliticization of the issues at stake—"pragmatically" isolating them from "ideological" meanings and as much as possible avoiding their incorporation in any coherent political symbolism. Didactically helpful for this kind of exercise is the recurrent discovery in European Community bodies that apparently identical political arrangements and outcomes can sometimes be of completely contrary significance in different national, political, and ideological environments—for example, legally based co-determination rights at the workplace in Britain and Germany. After policy "issues" have been divested of their emotional and ideological aura and fragmented and individualized, their treatment can be assigned to "experts"—specialists, that is, in comparative inventories of decontextualized and depoliticized problems, positions, and compromises and in the extraction of the smallest common denominator from such inventories.

Politics & Society 19, no. 2 (1991): 133–164.

[4]

Emile Noël

Reflections on the Maastricht Treaty

THE CONCLUSIONS REACHED AT THE MEETING OF THE European Council in Maastricht, on 9 – 10 December 1991, on economic and monetary union and also on political union, form an impressive and complex whole, in which undertakings of major importance coexist with other more timid ones. A detailed analysis would overstep the limits of an article. Moreover, there are still some problems to be cleared up before the final drafts are agreed, even if the principal political decisions have already been taken. The remarks which I would like to submit here will therefore deal more with general questions, and I will limit myself to the more significant provisions of the Maastricht agreements.

One need not be surprised by the heterogeneity of these agreements. The plan for economic and monetary union had been maturing for a long time, ever since the Single European Act came into force in July 1987. The report resulting from the work of the Delors Committee (governors of the central banks and some independent personalities who were requested by the European Council to meet in 1988-89 under the chairmanship of President Delors) had prepared the ground. Moreover, this report was the basis for the work of the Conference on monetary union, the conclusions of which reproduced some of its main elements.

It was only in April 1990 that President Mitterrand and Chancellor Kohl proposed to the other heads of government to open negotiations on political union. We were then on the eve of German unification. The Chancellor, like the French President, intended to underline Germany's commitment to Europe: German unification was to take place within a European framework and unified Germany was to devote itself to the political strengthening of the Community.

Several general themes were proposed to the European Council: a common foreign and security policy, the strengthening of the institutions, the *democratization* of the Community by increasing the role of the European Parliament. In June 1990 it was decided to call an intergovernmental conference but, during the Italian presidency (the second half of 1990) it became obvious that the disagreements went much further than the traditional British reservations. The advisability of establishing a common European security policy (even a common defence policy) while the new objectives of the Atlantic Alliance were being discussed, divided the Twelve and gave rise to reservations on the part of the United States. Germany and France, the protagonists of this initiative, did not attach the same importance to the reform of the institutions and to the increase in the powers of the European Parliament. The *conclusions* of the Presidency, at the end of the Rome meeting of the European Council, in December 1990, were cast in the form of a list of the tasks to be undertaken rather than of a genuine summary of the decisions, so numerous were the public reservations (those of Great Britain) and the less clearly expressed reluctance of others. Starting from such different bases, the two Conferences, on economic and monetary union on the one hand, and on political union on the other, were bound to adopt different methods of work. In spite of appeals for cohesion, the negotiations, which should in theory have formed a single whole, did not advance at the same pace, and there was little interaction between them. The gap between the two parts of the treaty was the direct consequence of this imbalance.

THE ECONOMIC AND MONETARY UNION

Conducted at a slow pace (negotiating meetings of the personal representatives of the ministers took place every fortnight) the discussions on economic and monetary union made steady progress by following the general scheme laid down by the Delors report. The committee of the governors of the central banks and the Monetary Committee were drawn upon to contribute (it was the governors who prepared the draft statute of the European Central Bank). A patient identification of the divergences, then a search for compromise took place over the ensuing months, so that by the last autumn there remained only a few questions needing political decisions. These political decisions were taken by the ministers of finance in several informal or official meetings before Maastricht and during Maastricht at a last meeting held alongside the European Council itself. The latter did not have to intervene directly, apart from the political pressure it brought to bear on the work of the ministers, a pressure which was of major importance in the adoption of the last compromises. This is the classic behaviour of ministers of finance, who do not like interventions from outside, be they those of their heads of state or of government.

The result is a *good* treaty in the style of the Treaty of Rome and of the Single European Act. The political negotiations before Maastricht and at Maastricht itself had both improved and strengthened it. The so-called opting out clauses, for the benefit of the United Kingdom and, to a lesser extent, of Denmark, were finally entered in two separate protocols for each of these countries, in conformity with the practice established since the first community treaties, and not in a general clause, included in the Treaty itself (as by the Dutch President initially proposed). The decision to pass on to the last stage of economic and monetary union (that of the Central European Bank and of a single currency) will be taken by qualified majority and a deadline (1 January 1999) has already been laid down for its implementation.

The strength of the Treaty of Rome, which set up the European Economic Community (as also that of the Treaty of Paris, which established the first Community, that of coal and steel) lay in the clarity of its undertakings, the precision of its timetable, the solidity of its institutions and the irreversible character of the process which had been engaged upon, which could not be blocked by a state or by a minority of states. This resulted in a dynamism of progress, which is still felt today, and in confidence on the part of economic actors, thus making a major contribution to the success of the undertaking.

These same characteristics are to be found in the Treaty of Economic and Monetary Union (I am referring to those parts of the Maastricht agreements which relate to these questions). The pledge of eleven states to proceed towards monetary union was taken unequivocally: the opportunity given to the United Kingdom to be *exempted* from progressing to the last stage in no way affects the commitment of the rest of the partners. The case of Denmark is slightly different. The Danish constitution makes it necessary to hold a referendum before Denmark can take part in the final stage of the monetary union. The result of this referendum cannot be prejudged, even though the political engagement of the government, and probably of the parliament, is total. The Danish protocol takes into account the possibility of a negative outcome of the referendum, which would lead to the granting of an exemption.

The timetable for these stages was firmly fixed as in the Treaties of Paris and Rome: 1 January 1994 for the passage to the second stage, 1 January 1997 or at the latest (as we have seen) 1 January 1999 for the passage to the final stage.

Alongside the existing institutions, the Treaty foresaw a new body, the European Central Bank, supported by the European system of central banks. The independence of the Central Bank, legally guaranteed, was strengthened by a supranational structure very much stronger than that of the existing European institutions. The board of the Central Bank has in fact only six members (for twelve states) and decisions by the Council of the European System of Central Banks are taken by majority voting, each member having only one vote. This is a great improvement on the European Commission (seventeen members, each state having to have at least one national) and on the Council of Ministers, which votes by a two-thirds majority of the weighted votes.

Lastly, the process once embarked on is irreversible. On the one hand, the key decisions on the passage to the final phase are to be taken by a qualified majority, *even when the Council sits at the level of Heads of State or of Government.* This is an interesting innovation. On the other hand, at the final date (1 January 1999) the transition to Economic and Monetary Union will take place regardless of the number of states participating (on 1 January 1997 the participation of at least seven states will be necessary).

CONTROVERSIAL QUESTIONS

What can one think however of the three questions which have proved most controversial during the negotiations: the special position of the United Kingdom, the role given to the European Parliament and the position of the European Commission?

As far as the special position of Great Britain was concerned, as I do not wish to intrude into the internal affairs of that country, I shall simply refer to a precedent which is almost forgotten today. There is in the Treaty of Rome a special protocol relating to France, which was hard-fought at the time. This would have allowed France to maintain the import duties and the subsidies on exports (that is to say the very negation of a customs union) which it was then (in 1957) applying in order to prop up its ailing currency... This protocol was *never* applied. The economic and monetary reform decided on in December 1958 (on the eve of the first measures for opening up the markets) by the government of General de Gaulle rendered it superfluous. It is not impossible to foretell that the same fate will befall the protocol regarding Great

Britain attached to the treaty of monetary union. It must be left to the British Parliament (as the protocol stipulates) to weigh up the risks and to decide with the well-known wisdom and realism of the Mother of Parliaments.

The inter-institutional conferences which bring together from time to time the ministers taking part in the intergovernmental conferences, the Commission and a delegation from the European Parliament have enabled the Parliament to put forward its demands concerning the treaty of economic and monetary union (although it was above all on the treaty on political union that the work of these conferences was concentrated). Recognizing the need to ensure the independence of the Central Bank, the Parliament insisted that it too should be completely involved in the relevant decisions of the Council, either by right of co-decision, or by that of assent. Although some of these demands met with little support in the conference, the latter did, however, ensure the Parliament's participation in the whole process, but principally in a consultative role. The Parliament thus takes part in the adoption of all the important measures, regulations or decisions (including the passage to the final stage) as well as in those determining the making of economic policy. This is a first step in a new function. As we shall see presently when we come to the Treaty of Political Union, the increase in the powers of the Parliament is proceeding gradually and the last word has not been spoken on the future powers of the Parliament when it comes to economic and monetary matters.

The discussions on the role of the Commission aroused more anxiety. Several delegations seemed to have reservations about the impartiality or the sense of responsibility of the Commission, which should undoubtedly consider this fact, especially in view of the further revision of the Treaty which is already forecast for 1996. The exclusive right of the Commission to make proposals has been called into question. Several delegations would have preferred that such a right should be shared with the member states, although this would have been a serious regression towards intergovernmentalism.

Even if the final result is satisfying from an orthodox point of view, the Commission has not secured a strengthening of its role proportionate to the new competences of the Community. Several of the Council's decisions, and indeed among the most important, will be taken on the simple *recommendation* of the Commission (and not on its proposal). This will give a greater freedom of manoeuvre to the Council (a proposal can be modified by the

Council only by a unanimous vote). Moreover, the Commission will have to share this right of recommendation with the European Central Bank, in matters falling especially within the latter's competence. To be sure, this procedure had already been used in the Treaty of Rome, but only in a few rare cases (for example, in the starting of negotiations). But now it is obviously extended.

THE POLITICAL UNION

The Treaty of Political Union, (namely that part of the Maastricht agreements which concerns political union) seems to be much less impressive than the Treaty on Monetary Union and the efforts of the Heads of State or of Government have led only to very limited improvements when compared to the *copy* of the Ministers of Foreign Affairs. A great distance separates the intentions proclaimed in the spring of 1990 by Chancellor Kohl and President Mitterrand (mentioned at the beginning of this article) and the final result. At that time the purpose was to bind Germany, on the eve of its unification, even more firmly to Europe. This has been well and truly forgotten today.

The European Parliament and the European Commission fixed their sights very high, both in the resolutions of the Parliament (adopted on the basis of reports by its Committee on International Affairs), and in the communications made by the Commission. What they aimed at was the communitarization of matters which had lain until then within the sphere of intergovernmental cooperation (foreign affairs, justice, internal problems) and they aimed also at the attribution of a wide legislative power to the Parliament. That these two objectives are well-founded is undeniable. But they were very far from what the majority of the delegations were prepared to accept. Thus the impact of the proposals on the negotiations themselves was minimal. The *inter-institutional conferences* devoted to political union have often given the impression of whistling in the dark and the parliament's threat (too often repeated) to refuse to approve the final results of the inter-governmental conferences did not have much effect.

As for the Commission, it found itself sometimes on the defensive, having to fight (and successfully) to maintain its present prerogatives, notably in matters concerning its right of initiative or of representation of the Community in negotiations, or being refused some extensions of the qualified majority vote in the Council (for instance, in matters of research and development). We have also seen the same reservations on the subject of economic and monetary union.

As for the Parliament, it is interesting to see that its more precise demands were satisfied in the last hours of the negotiations, and namely the synchronization of the Commission's mandate (both duration and terms) with the Parliamentary legislature, and recognition of the *indispensable* role of the European parties. It is probable that the Parliament could have achieved more of its aims had it adopted this tactic more systematically during the last months of the intergovernmental conference without sacrificing its principles.

This being said, the Treaty of Political Union is characterized more by the political signals it sends out than by real results; but the signals are important. They give hope for the future. They also enhance the value of the decision to call a new intergovernmental conference in 1996, even if the aims of the revision to be undertaken then, have been carefully veiled. I shall try to identify some of the signals, but they are not the only ones.

One political signal is that the European Parliament has obtained legislative power. Obviously, the procedure which organizes the *co-decision* with the Council is clumsy and complex, and anonymous, because the negotiators have hesitated to use the word *co-decision*. Nevertheless, well-handled (and the European Parliament has already proved its efficiency in the handling of the procedures of *cooperation* as instituted in the Single European Act), the new procedure should normally lead, at the end of a conciliation process, to the acceptance of the same text by the Council and the Parliament. The legislative acts thus approved will be signed by the presidents of both the Parliament and the Council.

Admittedly, in the event of failure of the conciliation procedure, a *third reading* has been provided for, during which the Council's position should prevail, unless the Parliament rejects the text adopted by the Council. The MEPs have justifiably stressed that this arrangement would be tantamount to the exertion of excessive pressure on the Parliament as it gives a negative character to its intervention (that of a rejection). It is to be hoped that the *third reading* will rather be an instrument of dissuasion which would induce the Council and the Parliament to agree during the negotiations.

The new procedure of *co-decision* will be applied in an important number of cases. The heads of government brushed aside some of the reservations expressed by the Ministers of Foreign Affairs. There will, therefore, be a significant innovation in the role of the Parliament, and the principle of the European Parliament's genuine legislative power is now established. It will be for future negotiators (in 1996, or before) to make things simple, rather than complicated, as today, in the words of President Delors.

Another political signal is the decision to synchronize the duration and the terms of the mandate of the European Commission with those of the European legislature, as already mentioned. The membership of the Commission will have to be approved by the Parliament from now on before appointments are made by the governments (the Parliament preserving at the same time its power to censure the existing Commission). This group of measures considerably increases the Parliament's ability to exercise political control over the work of the Commission: the part played by the Parliament in the appointment of the Commissioners will probably be made on the basis of a *legislative programme* which will in turn give full significance to any possible motion of censure.

These measures will lead also and perhaps especially to the accentuation of the political character of the Commission. Very soon the preliminary approval of its membership by the Parliament will be the decisive factor; the final appointment by the governments will retain only a formal character. The (malicious) reproach which is often heard that the Commission is an *appointed* body will become groundless. Moreover, in any immediate or long-term perspective one should fully recognize the consequences for the Council of the strengthening and politicization of the Parliament and the Commission, both of them truly *European* institutions.

Another political signal is the formulation of European citizenship in the Treaty, even if in modest terms. Notably the principle of the right of all European citizens to vote and to stand for election in their own place of residence is laid down, not only for the European elections (putting an end to some absurd situations) but also for local elections, which will mean significant changes in many countries. The President of the French Republic, for instance, has already announced that he will propose the necessary constitutional changes in France for the implementation of this clause in the treaty. This illustrates the importance of this measure — it encourages one to hope that the possibility of extending the rights of European citizens, specifically provided for in the Treaty, will not remain a dead letter.

Yet another political signal is the advance in social policy for eleven member states, without the United Kingdom (for the time being at least). Undoubtedly, the legal construct prepared at Maastricht is not perfect and its implementation will give a lot of trouble to the lawyers of the institutions. But its meaning is clear: the veto can no longer be used among the Twelve, even in an intergovernmental negotiation. Therefore, the veto is all the more impossible within the framework of the Council and it has become inconceivable that one country, whichever it is, could block an important step forward which the other partners were ready to take.

Already in the past, the possibility of action by eleven member states had been considered but the step was not taken and the Twelve finally came to an understanding. Today this kind of taboo is excluded. One cannot be sure that it will be to the advantage of the countries which hesitate most when the future evolution of the Community is considered.

Finally, a major signal: it is no longer *security* or *defence policy* that the Twelve are taking as their objective, but the common defence, the European defence, without affecting the Atlantic Alliance; it is the objective of the unanimous agreement of the Twelve, with the backing of the United States and of the other partners of the Alliance. None of this seemed possible even a year ago. This result has been achieved because of the clarification obtained before and after the Atlantic summit in Rome and also because of some constructive initiatives, like the common British-Italian proposal put forward on the eve of the final meetings.

Certainly, the formulation is still extraordinarily cautious. The purpose is *the eventual framing of a common defence policy, which might in time lead to a common defence*. But nevertheless, the word common defence is pronounced and it answers so much to the present needs in the new Europe of the 1990s that one can predict a rapid and vigorous growth of this frail graft inserted in the last hour in the Maastricht agreements.

The implementation of these policy directions is based on a triangular cooperation between the European Union, the Western European Union (WEU) and NATO. The annexes to the Treaty set out the terms of this cooperation. It will require a permanent effort of good will and imagination.

CONCLUSIONS

In conclusion, the Maastricht agreements have led to two major steps forward which deeply affect the future of our countries and of Europe. It is these two steps forward which, all things considered, should be the decisive argument for approving of these agreements.

First, the single currency. One remembers the long quarrels over the introduction of the word *federal* into the text of the Treaty (*a union with a federal vocation* should have been presented as the final objective). One may well regret that a vaguer and more elusive formulation was preferred to those terms which were themselves modest — but it does not really matter if the word *federal* has disappeared if the federal reality has begun to exist. For a single currency supported by the internal market is one of the foundations of a European federation. Before the end of the century we shall for the first time be facing an irreversible advance.

Secondly, the European defence. These words, which were barred from the official language since the failure of the European Defence Community, have resurfaced after almost forty years. The principle of a European defence (in the future) has been laid down within the framework of the Atlantic Alliance and without affecting or weakening that Alliance. The Atlantic summit in Rome and the European Council in Maastricht have put an end to decades of misunderstanding since France withdrew from the military organization of the Alliance.

In a changing world the Atlantic Alliance and the European Community seem to be elements of coherence and stability, points of reference and poles of attraction. Maastricht strengthened the Community, finally giving it the federal dimension through the single currency. Maastricht also established the solidarity and the complementarity between the Atlantic Alliance and the European Community (or Union). Even if more could have been done, the heads of state and of government have given in Maastricht a first answer to the challenges of the present time. This first answer will allow for other answers, even more ambitious, which will be required in order to face the upheavals and the dangers of the end of the century.

January 1992

Part II
Federalism and Legal Pluralism

[5]

KOEN LENAERTS

Constitutionalism and the Many Faces of Federalism

As a system of divided powers, federalism proceeds from the very essence of constitutionalism[1], which is limited government operating under the rule of law.[2]

This article argues, on the one hand, that it is the proper function of the federal constitution, umpired by the federal judiciary, to strike the appropriate balance of powers between the federation and its component entities[3], and on the other hand, that beyond this

---

KOEN LENAERTS Judge, Court of First Instance of the European Communities, and Professor of European Community Law, University of Leuven (Belgium). This article is the revised version of a paper delivered at the Harvard Law School colloquium on "Constitutionalism: The American Experiment in Wider Perspective", organized in observance of the bicentennial of the United States Constitution (April 6-9, 1989).

1. Constitutionalism is linked to federalism in the Tenth Amendment of the U.S. Constitution. The tenor of this Amendment is still subject to debate. Thus, in 1941, Justice Stone (later Chief Justice) wrote in an opinion of the Court: "The Amendment states but a truism that all is retained which has not been surrendered." [United States v. Darby, 312 U.S. 100, 124 (1941)]; but, in 1976, Justice Rehnquist (now the Chief Justice) states in another opinion of the Court: "While the Tenth Amendment has been characterized as a 'truism' stating merely that 'all is retained which has not been surrendered', it is not without significance. The Amendment expressly declares the constitutional policy that Congress may not exercise power in a fashion that impairs the States' integrity or their ability to function effectively in a federal system". [National League of Cities v. Usery, 426 U.S. 833, 842-843 (1976)]. Although the Supreme Court's ruling in this latter case was overturned in Garcia v. San Antonio Metropolitan Transit Authority, 469 U.S. 528 (1985), Justice's Rehnquist statement as to the significance of the Tenth Amendment remains valuable, since it really amounts to an *obiter dictum* on which the Court's ruling was not centrally based; see, in this sense, the convincing argument of Field, "Comment. 'Garcia v. San Antonio Metropolitan Transit Authority': The Demise of a Misguided Doctrine", 99 *Harv. L. Rev.* 84, 89-95 (1985).

2. See Laurence H. Tribe, *American Constitutional Law* 2 (1988); N.O. Nwabueze, *Constitutionalism in the Emergent States*, 1-21 (1977): "The Concept of Constitutionalism". Compare Thomas M. Cooley, *A Treatise on the Constitutional Limitations which Rest Upon the Legislative Power of the States of the American Union* 9-10 (1868): "The government of the United States is one of enumerated powers; the national Constitution being the instrument which specifies them, and in which authority should be found for the exercise of any power which the national government assumes to possess. In this respect it differs from the constitution of the several States, which are not grants of power to the States, but which apportion and impose restrictions upon powers which the States inherently possess"...

3. See, e.g., Ableman v. Booth, per C.J. Taney, 21 *Howard* 506, 516 (1859): "The powers of the general Government and of the State, although both exist and are exercised within the same territorial limits, are yet separate and distinct sovereignties, acting separately and independently of each other, within their respective spheres". Compare James Bryce, *The American Commonwealth*, 407-408 (1888); Andrew McLaughlin, *The Foundations of American Constitutionalism*, 145-149 (1966 ed).

common denominator federal systems around the world differ as to the content of the balance and the mechanisms provided for its judicial umpiring.[4]

In view of this double argument, it is further submitted that the many faces of federalism — seen as the many faces of federalism - related constitutionalism — can be propounded by contrasting the models of integrative and devolutionary federalism.[5] Both models present a natural tendency to reinforce their centripetal or centrifugal drive, while drawing on the same concepts of federal theory.

American constitutional history offers a conceptual reference for these two basic models of federalism, however divergent they are in their actual operation.

Integrative federalism refers to a constitutional order that strives at unity in diversity among previously independent or confederally related component entities. The goal of establishing an effective central government with direct operation on the people inside its sphere of powers is pursued under respect of the powers of the component entities, at least to the extent that the use by the latter of these powers does not revert into divisiveness. If need be, the system is fully capable of acknowledging the existence of societal pluralism from one component entity to another. The European Community and Switzerland are studied under this label with background references to the United States.

Devolutionary federalism, on the contrary, refers to a constitutional order that redistributes the powers of a previously unitary State among its component entities; these entities obtain an autonomous status within their fields of responsibility. The principal concern is to organize diversity in unity. The system will only be in balance when the shift from a single-sovereign towards a multi-sovereign structure is no longer resented as a merely centrifugal movement threatening national cohesion. Belgium, Canada[6] and Spain,

4. Compare the "concluding remarks" of Peter Hay & Ronald D. Rotunda, *The United States Federal System*, 347-359 (1982). See also Pescatore, "Foreword" in Terrance Sandalow & Eric Stein (eds.), *Courts and Free Markets* (1982): "It would rather seem that federalism is a political and legal philosophy which adapts itself to all political contexts on both the municipal and international level, wherever and whenever two basic prerequisites are fulfilled: the search for unity, combined with genuine respect for the autonomy and the legitimate interests of the participant entities".

5. This is a bipartite reformulation of Edward McWhinney's triadic scheme classifying federalism as monistic, pluralistic, or dualistic, in *Comparative Federalism*, 16-17 (1965).

6. In its present constitutional structure, Canada is regarded by Donald P. Kommers as a system of "dualistic federalism" (in the triadic scheme defined by McWhinney, supra n. 5), while in an earlier historical period Canada was clearly "monistic", see his comments in Mauro Cappelletti, Monica Seccombe & Joseph Weiler

whose component entities represent some kind of societal pluralism, are analyzed in this rubric.

The constitutional systems quoted in relation to both integrative and devolutionary federalism are five national ones (including the United States) and a supranational one (the European Community).

Belgium, Canada, Spain and Switzerland clearly meet the rule-of-law principles governing American federalism: they have a dual constitutional structure[7]; their central and component entities' governments act directly upon the people, each of them within its own sphere of powers; and the balance of powers between these governments is the core of a divided sovereignty, umpired by a central judiciary under central constitutional standards. These features guarantee the significance of these countries within the framework of the proposed analysis.

In 1990, it can safely be said that the one supranational system of federalism to be considered also conforms to these principles, even though this has not readily been apparent. Firstly, the question arose whether the European Community, whose existence rests on a "treaty"[8], could be said to have a central "consti-

(eds.) *Integration Through Law*, volume 1, book 1, 609 (1985). This development over time in the balance of powers inherent in Canadian federalism can adequately be seized under the concept of "devolutionary federalism".

7. Some reservation must, however, be made in respect of Belgium. The constitution of its component entities is part of the central constitution and special laws governing the organization of the country as such. In spite of this formal unity of the constitutional instruments applicable to the national government and the governments of the Belgian "Communities" and "Regions", the substance of the constitutional structure is dual, as each level of government is subject to the specific provisions relating to its operation and its powers. See, inter alia, Articles 59bis, 59ter and 107quater of the Belgian Constitution and the Special Law of August 8, 1980, Moniteur belge of August 15, 1980, as amended by the Special Law of August 8, 1988, Moniteur belge of August 13, 1988.

8. The European Community rests not only on the Treaties which have established the three European Communities (Treaty establishing the European Coal and Steel Community, signed in Paris on April 18, 1951; Treaty establishing the European Economic Community, signed in Rome on March 25, 1957; and Treaty establishing the European Atomic Energy Community, signed in Rome on March 25, 1957), but also on the annexes and protocoles to these Treaties (which have the same normative force as the Treaties themselves - see Articles 84 of the ECSC Treaty, 239 of the EEC Treaty and 207 of the EAEC Treaty). These Treaties have been amended on several occasions, inter alia, through the Convention on certain institutions common to the European Communities (signed in Rome on March 25, 1957), the so-called "Merger Treaty", establishing a Single Council and a Single Commission of the European Communities *Official Journal of the European Communities*, hereafter *O.J.E.C.* 1967, No. 152), the Treaty amending Certain Budgetary Provisions (*O.J.E.C.*, 1971, No. L 2), the Treaty amending Certain Financial Provisions (*O.J.E.C.* 1977, No. L 359), the Act concerning the election of the representatives of the European Parliament by direct universal suffrage (*O.J.E.C.* 1976, No. L 278), and the Single European Act (*O.J.E.C.* 1987, No. L 169). In addition, there are three Acts of Accession, adjusting the original Treaties, the Act of 1972 on the accession of Denmark, Ireland and the United Kingdom (*O.J.E.C.* 1972, No. L 73), the Act of 1979 on

tution."[9] Secondly, it was in no way obvious from the outset, how Community law could operate directly upon the people in the Member States.[10]

However, these two questions were solved in such a way that they no longer form an obstacle to the characterization of the European Community as a federal system, as will be demonstrated through some preliminary remarks.

The constitutionalization of the European Community Treaties

In its early case law, the Court of Justice of the European Communities[11] traced the two basic dimensions of European Community constitutionalism.[12]

Still during the ECSC period, it found the principle of a *horizontal* separation of powers[13] in "the balance of powers which is characteristic of the institutional structure of the Community" and described it as "a fundamental guarantee granted by the Treaty" to the subjects of law coming under the jurisdiction of the Community.[14] Over the ensuing decades, the Court of Justice repeatedly

---

the accession of Greece (*O.J.E.C.* 1979, No. L 291) and the Act of 1985 on the accession of Portugal and Spain (*O.J.E.C.* 1985, No. L 302).

9. Trevor C. Hartley observed in 1986 that "the Constitution of the Community takes the form of a series of international treaties", but considered that "there is no reason to believe that this form, in itself, disqualifies the Constitutive Treaties from being regarded as a constitution", "Federalism, Courts and Legal Systems: The Emerging Constitution of the European Community," 34 *Am. J. Comp. L.* 229, at 231 (1986), with reference to Stein, "Treaty-Based Federalism, A.D. 1979: A Gloss on Covey T. Oliver at the Hague Academy", 127 *U. Pa. L. Rev.* 897, 900-905 (1979). See also Buxbaum, "The European Community: "Federalism and Legitimacy", in *Federalism: Studies in History, Law and Policy.* Papers From the Second Berkeley Seminar on Federalism, 141ff. (1988).

10. See Monaco, "The Limits of the European Community Order", 1 *European Law Review* (hereafter *E. L. Rev.*) 169 (1976); Beutler, Bieber, Pipkorn & Streil, *Die Europäische Gemeinschaft - Rechtsordnung und Politik*, 37-69 (1987).

11. In the period 1953-1958, the Court acted as Court of Justice of the European Coal and Steel Community. Since 1958, it is a "common institution" to the ECSC, the EEC and the EAEC. Its official name became therefore "Court of Justice of the European Communities". The Court consists of thirteen judges, six advocates-general and one registrar (see Articles 165 to 168 of the EEC Treaty).

12. Hahn has described these dimensions as follows: "The term 'constitution' may not only designate the system or rules according to which a State . . . is governed and which affects the distribution as well as the exercise of sovereign power in the State. As the word stands for a general legal concept. . . it is also an appropriate name for the international act instituting an intergovernmental entity devoted to the pursuit of specific purposes, setting up its principal organs, specifying the relationship of these organs to one another, defining the position of the international organisation vis-à-vis its Member States." [in "Constitutional Limitations in the Law of the European Organisations", *Recueil des Cours de l'Académie de Droit International de La Haye* I, 195-196 (1963)].

13. See Articles 3 of the ECSC Treaty, 4 of the EEC Treaty and 3 of the EAEC Treaty.

14. Case 9/56, Meroni v. High Authority, judgment of June 13, 1958, *European Court Reports* (hereafter *E.C.R.*) 139, 152 (1958). Compare the hailing of the merits of "our system of checks and balances" in the Steel Seizure case, Youngstown Sheet

stepped in to uphold the interinstitutional balance in the Community's decision-making process.[15]

The other dimension, the *vertical* division of powers between the Community and the Member States, was equally constitutionalized when the Court had to explain in the landmark *Van Gend & Loos* ruling of 1962 that although the EEC Treaty presents itself as a compact among sovereign States, it is in reality - due to its substance - a "constitution" of a central legal order, federally related to the legal orders of the Member States.[16] In the case at hand, the Federal Republic of Germany, Belgium and the Netherlands had voiced the view that some caution was in order for the Court, when interpreting the EEC Treaty, because the latter is a treaty and consequently should be treated as such.[17] The Court did not seem to be impressed by this argument, as it adopted an attitude which reminds us of Chief Justice Marshall's pronouncement in *McCulloch v. Maryland*: "In considering this question, then, we must never forget that it is *a constitution* we are expounding".[18] Marshall used the phrase as a final stroke against the argument of the State of Maryland, which "deemed it of some importance, in the construction of the Constitution, to consider that instrument not as emanating from the

& Tube Company v. Sawyer, 343 U.S. 579, 593-594 (1952), concurring opinion per J. Frankfurter (only six years earlier).

15. For a full overview of these cases, see Koen Lenaerts, *Le juge et la constitution aux Etats-Unis d'Amérique et dans l'ordre juridique européen* (1988).

16. Case 26/62, Van Gend & Loos, judgment of February 5, 1963, *E.C.R.* 10, 12 (1963): "The objective of the EEC Treaty, which is to establish a Common Market, the functioning of which is of direct concern to interested parties in the Community, implies that this Treaty is more than an agreement which merely creates mutual obligations between the contracting States. This view is confirmed by the preamble to the Treaty which refers not only to governments but to peoples. It is also confirmed more specifically by the establishment of institutions endowed with sovereign rights, the exercise of which affects Member States and also their citizens. Furthermore, it must be noted that the nationals of the States brought together in the Community are called upon to cooperate in the functioning of this Community through the intermediary of the European Parliament and the Economic and Social Committee.

In addition, the task assigned to the Court of Justice under Article 177, the object of which is to secure uniform interpretation of the Treaty by national courts and tribunals, confirms that the States have acknowledged that Community law has an authority which can be invoked by their nationals before those courts and tribunals". See also Case 6/64, Costa v. ENEL, judgment of July 15, 1964, *E.C.R.* 585 (1964). But compare the critical remarks of Wyatt, "New legal Order, or Old?", 7 *E. L. Rev.* 147 (1982).

17. For a comment, see Hamson, "Methods of Interpretation - A Critical Assessment of the Results" in Reports of the Judicial and Academic Conference, September 27-28, 1976, Luxembourg, Office for Official Publications of the European Communities, 1976, II, and compare Pescatore, "International Law and Community Law - A Comparative Analysis", 7 *Common Market Law Review* (hereafter *C. M. L. Rev.*) 167 (1970).

18. 4 *Wheaton* 316, 407 (1819).

people, but as the act of sovereign and independent States."[19] Thus, Marshall reasoned as the Court of Justice was to do in 1962, but his task was easier, because - apart from the historical facts - the Preamble to the U.S. Constitution contains the solemn proclamation by the "People of the United States" of their intent "to form a more perfect Union" (of States)," whereas the EEC Treaty opens with the just as solemn declaration by six Heads of State that they are "Determined to lay the foundations of an ever closer union among the peoples of Europe". Moreover, the American people did "ordain and establish this Constitution for the United States of America", whereas Article 1 of the EEC Treaty comes no further than the declaration that "by this Treaty, the High Contracting Parties establish among themselves a European Economic Community".

At present, the constitutional character of the European Community Treaties stands beyond doubt.[20] In 1986, the Court of Justice even ruled that "the European Economic Community is a Community based on the rule of law, inasmuch as neither its Member States nor its institutions can avoid a review of the question whether the measures adopted by them are in conformity with the basic constitutional charter, the Treaty."[21]

The direct operation of European Community law

The direct operation of Community law can best be understood through an analysis of the "distinct and different concepts"[22] of "direct applicability" and "direct effect" of Community law. First of all, there is the concept of *direct applicability*. Whenever Community law states its direct applicability in the Member States the latter may not incorporate that law into national law. Even a literal duplication of directly applicable Community law into national law is prohibited,[23] since the direct applicability of Community law means that this law is "binding as such" inside the national legal orders and prevails over all conflicting rules of these legal orders.[24]

19. 4 *Wheaton* 316, 402 (1819). See further Frankfurter, "John Marshall and the Judicial Function", 69 *Harv. L. Rev.* 217 (1955).

20. For a more recent illustration of the attitude taken by the Court of Justice, see Case 270/80, Polydor v. Harlequin & Simons, judgment of February 9, 1982, *E.C.R.* 329 (1982). Compare Jones, "The Legal Nature of the European Community: a Jurisprudential Analysis Using H. L. A. Hart's Model of Law and a Legal System", 17 *Cornell International L. J.* 1-59 (1984).

21. Case 294/83, Parti écologiste "Les Verts" v. European Parliament, judgment of April 23, 1986, *E.C.R.* 1339, 1365, paragraph 23 (1986).

22. The expression is that of Winter, "Direct Applicability and Direct Effect: Two Distinct and Different Concepts in Community Law", 9 *C. M. L. Rev.* 425 (1972).

23. Case 34/73, Variola, judgment of October 10, 1973, *E.C.R.* 981, 990-991, paragraphs 9-11 (1973); Case 50/76, Amsterdam Bulb BV, judgment of February 2, 1977, *E.C.R.* 137, 146-147, paragraph 7 (1977).

24. See, e.g., Case 14/68, Walt Wilhelm v. Bundeskartellamt, judgment of February 13, 1969, *E.C.R.* 1 (1969); Case 106/77, Simmenthal, judgment of March 9, 1978, *E.C.R.* 629 (1978). In this connexion, countries such as the United Kingdom and Ire-

The following rules of Community law are directly applicable: all Treaty provisions, EEC/EAEC regulations,[25] ECSC general decisions[26] and, with more limited scope of application, EEC/EAEC decisions[27] and ECSC individual decisions.[28]

The case of EEC/EAEC directives and ECSC recommendations is more difficult to appreciate in this respect. Although "binding, as to the result to be achieved, upon each Member State to which it is addressed" (Articles 189, third paragraph, of the EEC Treaty and 161, third paragraph, of the EAEC Treaty), or "binding as to the aims to be pursued. . . to those to whom the recommendations are addressed" (Article 14, third paragraph, of the ECSC Treaty), the directive and ECSC recommendation do not constitute a legal rule that is "binding as such" within the internal legal order of the Member States.[29] They do indeed require a formal incorporation into the laws of the Member States.[30] Thus, the directive somehow appears as the mirror image of the regulation.[31]

---

land, with an outright dualistic tradition regarding the relationship between international and internal law, had to undertake no less than a *quadrature du cercle* in order to make accession to the European Community possible. They were to adapt their constitutional practices so as to guarantee the immediate reception of directly applicable provisions of Community law. The solution reached in Britain is contained in the "European Communities Act" of 1972, whose section 2 (1) reads as follows: "All such rights, powers, liabilities, obligations and restrictions from time to time created or arising by or under the Treaties, and all such remedies and procedures from time to time provided for by or under the Treaties, as in accordance with the Treaties are without further enactment to be given legal effect or used in the United Kingdom. . ." In addition, section 2(4) of the European Communites Act of 1972 guarantees the supremacy of Community law over national law within the British legal order, in spite of the principle of sovereignty of Parliament, under which a Parliament cannot bind its successors. To that effect, a rule of interpretation was introduced: any future statute will be interpreted so as to have it conform to Community law, unless Parliament clearly and expressly states in a future Act that it is to override Community law. See, on this point, Trevor Hartley, *The Foundations of European Community Law* 244 (1981). For an application of section 2 (1) and (4) of the European Communities Act of 1972, see the opinions of Lord Denning, M.R., delivered in the Court of Appeals case of McCarthys v. Smith, July 18, 1979, 3 *All E.R.* 325, 329 (1979) and April 17, 1981, 1 *All E.R.* 111, 120 (1981).

25. Articles 189, second paragraph, of the EEC Treaty and 161, second paragraph, of the EAEC Treaty.

26. Article 14, second paragraph, of the ECSC Treaty, read in combination with Article 33, second paragraph, of this Treaty. ECSC general decisions perform the same function as EEC/EAEC regulations.

27. Articles 189, fourth paragraph, of the EEC Treaty and 161, fourth paragraph, of the EAEC Treaty.

28. Article 14, second paragraph, of the ECSC Treaty, read in combination with Article 33, second paragraph, of this Treaty. ECSC individual decisions perform the same function as EEC/EAEC decisions.

29. Case 102/79, Commission of the E.C. v. Kingdom of Belgium, judgment of May 6, 1980, *E.C.R.* 1473 (1980).

30. Pescatore, "L'effet des directives communautaires, une tentative de démythification", *Dalloz chronique* 171 (1980); Pescatore, "The Doctrine of Direct Effect: An Infant Disease of Community Law", 8 *E. L. Rev.* 169 (1983).

31. Compare the cases quoted supra, n. 23.

Secondly, the concept of *direct effect* deserves some comments. Directly applicable Community law does not necessarily have direct effect in the Member States. Such effect will only be present, when the rule of Community law, whether a Treaty provision or a normative act adopted by the Community institutions, is sufficiently clear, precise and unconditional, so as not to leave any margin of discretion at the stage of its implementation either for the Community institutions themselves or for the Member States.[32] In other words, the rule itself states rights and duties which can be enforced by national courts.[33]

Direct operation of a rule of Community law logically requires that it be at the same time directly applicable (binding as such) *and* directly effective (having the said content). Only then will Community law operate on the people in a similar way as federal law does in the United States. If, however, one of these aspects is lacking, a further normative intervention is required for Community law to become fully operative. In the case of a directly applicable rule of Community law whose content is too vague to create rights and duties, it must first be executed.[34] The reverse case can also occur. When a rule of Community law has a content that makes it capable of having direct effect in the internal legal order of the Member States, but that rule does not claim to be directly applicable, it must first be formally incorporated into national law. This constellation applies to a whole range of EEC directives.[35] To the extent that a

32. Henry G. Schermers & Denis F. Waelbroeck, *Judicial Protection in the European Communities* 125, § 239 (4th ed. 1987): "(The) direct effect of a provision depends mainly on whether the courts, and finally the Court of Justice, feel able and sufficiently equipped to apply the provision without any further act by the authorities of the Community or of its Member States".

33. Case 12/81, Garland, judgment of February 9, 1982, *E.C.R.*, 370-371, paragraph 15 (1982). The Commission has published a list of provisions of the EEC Treaty, obviously all directly applicable, that have been recognized to be directly effective in the case law of the Court of Justice, *O.J.E.C.*, 1983, No. C 177/13-14.

34. An example is a regulation whose content is not clear. It will need further implementation before reaching its goals and thus cannot have direct effect. Such effect will only exist when the regulation creates rights and duties enforceable in law. See, e.g., Case 43/71, Politi, judgment of December 14, 1971, *E.C.R.* 1039, 1048-1049, paragraph 9 (1971); Case 93/71, Leonesio, judgment of May 17, 1972, *E.C.R.* 287, 293, 295-296, paragraphs 5 and 22 (1972).

35. Timmermans, "Directives: Their Effect within the National Legal System", 16 *C.M.L. Rev.* 533-555 (1979). Moreover, the national provisions incorporating the directive into the internal legal order must be in conformity with the directive's content; this can always be checked by the courts of the Member States at the request of an interested party. See Case 51/76, Verbond van Nederlandse Ondernemingen, judgment of February 1, 1977, *E.C.R.* 113 (1977); Case 38/77, Enka BV, judgment of November 23, 1977, *E.C.R.* 2203 (1977); 21/78, Delkvist, judgment of November 29, 1978, *E.C.R.* 2327 (1978); Case 14/83, Von Colson & Kamann, judgment of April 10, 1984, *E.C.R.* 1891 (1984); Case 79/83, Harz, judgment of April 10, 1984, *E.C.R.* 1921 (1984); Case 222/84, Johnston, judgment of May 15, 1986, *E.C.R.* 1651 (1986). For a comment on the judicial decision-making as to this conformity issue, see Curtin, "Ef-

Member State fails, in infringement of its obligations, to undertake such incorporation, the directive cannot be enforced by its courts in litigation between private parties,[36] or else at the request of a public authority against a private party.[37] The Court of Justice only accepts that in the absence of incorporation into national law of a directive whose content meets the conditions to be directly effective, a private litigant may rely on such directive against the public authorities of the Member State concerned, in order to see the rights enforced that (s)he should draw from the directive, if it had been correctly incorporated into the internal legal order of that State. The defending Member State is indeed estopped from pleading its own fault not to have incorporated the directive into national law.[38]

We can now turn to the core of the analysis, which looks at integrative and devolutionary federalism from the standpoint of the division of powers (part I) and the judicial umpiring of the constitutional balance (part II).

I. The Division of Powers Between the Central Government and the Component Entities in a Multi-Sovereign Constitutional Order

A. *Integrative Federalism*

A.1. The European Community

(a) Community power vs. Member State power - general principles

The Community has the powers which it received in the Treaties, while the Member States hold all residual powers.[39] In order to

fective Sanctions and the Equal Treatment Directive: The Van Colson and Harz Cases", 22 *C.M.L. Rev.* 505 (1985).

36. Case 152/84, Marshall, judgment of February 26, 1986, *E.C.R.* 723 (1986).

37. Joined Cases 372-374/85, Traen, judgment of May 12, 1987, *E.C.R.* 2141 (1987); Case 14/86, "Pretore" di Salo, judgment of June 11, 1987, *E.C.R.* 2545 (1987); Case 80/86, Kolpinghuis Nijmegen BV, judgment of October 8, 1987, *E.C.R.* 3969 (1987).

38. Case 148/78, Ratti, judgment of April 5, 1979, *E.C.R.* 1629 (1979); Case 102/79, Commission of the E.C. v. Kingdom of Belgium, judgment of May 6, 1980, *E.C.R.* 1473, 1487, paragraph 12 (1980), compare also Case 8/81, Becker, judgment of January 19, 1982, *E.C.R.* 53 (1982); Case 70/83, Kloppenburg, judgment of February 22, 1984, *E.C.R.* 1075 (1984).

39. This principle follows from Article 3 of the ECSC Treaty, Article 4 of the EEC Treaty and Article 3 of the EAEC Treaty. In its early case law, the Court of Justice once fell back on the principle in a rigid wording that would not be used anymore thereafter: "The Treaty rests on a derogation of sovereignty consented by the Member States to supranational jurisdiction for an object strictly determined. The legal principle at the basis of the Treaty is a principle of limited competence. The Community is a legal person of public law and to this effect it has the necessary legal capacity to exercise its functions but only those". [Joined Cases 7/56, 3-7/57, Algera v. Common Assembly, judgment of July 12, 1957, *E.C.R.* 39 (1957-58)]. For a comment, see Anna Bredimas, *Methods of Interpretation and Community Law* 109

understand the division of powers between the Community and the Member States, it seems appropriate to study first the participation of the latter in the decision-making process of the former. The less specific the powers granted to the Community are, the more intense the participation of the Member States will be with regard to the Community's exercise of these powers. Examples are the power "to issue directives for the approximation of such provisions laid down by law, regulation or administrative action in Member States as directly affect the establishment or functioning of the common market" (Article 100 of the EEC Treaty) and the power "to take the appropriate measures" in cases where "action by the Community should prove necessary to attain, in the course of the operation of the common market, one of the objectives of the Community and this Treaty has not provided the necessary powers" (Article 235 of the EEC Treaty). The substantive scope of these powers being absolutely open-ended, the Council (composed of one cabinet-level representative per Member State) must act unanimously on a proposal from the Commission (a body of independent members "chosen on the grounds of their general competence" and "appointed by common accord of the Governments of the Member States") and after consulting the European Parliament (the representation of the peoples of Europe constituted through direct elections in the Member States).[40] As can be seen, the decision lies with the Council, in which none of the Member States should voice opposition against it.[41]

With the exception of these powers, the Community holds specific powers.[42] This is important because, on the one hand, the Community may resort to a non-specific power only when a specific power is lacking as a basis for its action, and on the other, the decision-making process differs from one specific power to another.[43]

In some instances the Council decides by a simple majority of its

(1978); compare Alexander J. MacKenzie Stuart, *The European Communities and the Rule of Law* 36 (1977).

40. On the composition and mode of operation of the three political institutions of the Community, see Articles 137-144 of the EEC Treaty (on the European Parliament), Articles 145-154 of the EEC Treaty (on the Council) and Articles 155-163 of the EEC Treaty (on the Commission).

41. A unanimous vote within the Council does not require, indeed, that all members of this institution vote in favor of the act to be adopted; see Article 148(3) of the EEC Treaty: "Abstentions by members present in person or represented shall not prevent the adoption by the Council of acts which require unanimity".

42. They can be found throughout the EEC Treaty. Examples are all the matters decided by a simple or a qualified majority vote within the Council, listed infra, notes 44 and 45, by reference to the relevant Treaty articles.

43. See Case 45/86, Commission v. Council, judgment of March 26, 1987, *E.C.R.* 1493 (1987), defining the admissible scope of the Council's reliance on Article 235 of the EEC Treaty; and Case 68/86, United Kingdom v. Council, judgment of February 23, 1988, *E.C.R.* 855 (1988), relating to the reach of Article 43 of the EEC Treaty (spe-

members,[44] more often though by a qualified majority,[45] and for politically sensitive specific powers a unanimous vote is required.[46] A proposal from the Commission is almost always needed.[47] Depending on the subject matter dealt with, the European Parliament has either no role to play,[48] or it is to be consulted by the Council,[49] or else it must cooperate with the Council.[50]

More exceptionally, the Commission holds the prerogative of legislative decision.[51] Most Member States will be particularly on their guard as to the substantive scope recognized to this kind of specific powers for the Community.[52]

---

cific power in agricultural matters) in contrast to Article 100 of the EEC Treaty (non-specific power to approximate the laws of the Member States).

44. Article 148(1) of the EEC Treaty: "Save as otherwise provided in this Treaty, the Council shall act by a majority of its members". For applications of this general rule, see Articles 128, 151, 152, 153, 213 and 236 of the EEC Treaty.

45. Article 148(2) of the EEC Treaty: "Where the Council is required to act by a qualified majority, the votes of its members shall be weighted as follows: Belgium 5, Denmark 3, Germany 10, Greece 5, Spain 8, France 10, Ireland 3, Italy 10, Luxembourg 2, Netherlands 5, Portugal 5, United Kingdom 10. For their adoption, acts of the Council shall require at least: - fifty-four votes in favor where this Treaty requires them to be adopted on a proposal from the Commission, - fifty-four votes in favor, cast by at least eight members, in other cases". After the amendment of the EEC Treaty by the Single European Act, which entered into force on July 1, 1987, the cases of qualified majority voting within the Council have become very numerous (normally on a proposal from the Commission). See Articles 7, 8B, 28, 43, 49, 54, 55, 56, 57, 59, 63, 69, 70, 73, 75, 79, 84, 87, 92, 94, 98, 100A, 100B, 101, 103, 108, 112, 113, 114, 116, 118A, 126, 127, 130E, 130K, 130L, 130M, 130N, 130P, 130S, 154, 203, 204, 206, 206ter and 212 of the EEC Treaty.

46. See, e.g., Articles 51, 99, 121, 130D, 130I, 130O and 130S of the EEC Treaty.

47. Such proposal will always be needed when the Council performs, through its decision-making, a properly legislative function; the Commission has no right of proposal when the Council adopts its own rules of procedure (Article 151) or formulates a request to the Commission within the meaning of Article 152. See also Articles 153 and 154 of the EEC Treaty.

48. See, e.g., Articles 8B, 51, 113 and 128 of the EEC Treaty.

49. See, e.g., Articles 43, 54, 75, 99, 121, 126, 127, 130D, 130I, 130O, 130S and 236 of the EEC Treaty. The observance by the Council of its duty to consult the European Parliament is an essential procedural requirement, whose infringement leads to the invalidity of the act adopted, see Case 138/79, Roquette Frères SA v. Council, judgment of October 29, 1980, *E.C.R.* 3333 (1980) and Case 139/79, Maizena GmbH v. Council, judgment of October 29, 1980, *E.C.R.* 3393 (1980). For a comment, see Jacobs, "Isoglucose Resurgent: Two Powers of the European Parliament Upheld by the Court", 18 *C.M.L. Rev.* 219 (1981).

50. As to the content of the cooperation procedure, which involves in fact an increased right to dialogue for the European Parliament, both with the Commission and the Council, see Article 149(2) of the EEC Treaty. Applications are to be found mainly in Articles 7, 49, 100A, 118A, 130E, 130K, 130L, 130M, 130N and 130P of the EEC Treaty. The case law mentioned in the previous note is definitely to be transposed to the respect of the different stages of the cooperation procedure on the part of the Council.

51. See, e.g., Articles 90(3), 118 and 130H of the EEC Treaty.

52. Joined Cases 188 to 190/80, French Republic, Italian Republic and United Kingdom of Great Britain and Northern Ireland v. Commission of the E.C., judgment of July 6, 1982, *E.C.R.* 2545 (1982); Joined Cases 281/85, 283, 284 and 285/85 and 287/85, Federal Republic of Germany, French Republic, Kingdom of the Nether-

It is in relation to one of these powers that the Court of Justice seized the opportunity to stress the two-fold function of the Treaty provisions establishing a specific power in favor of the Community.[53] These provisions shape at once the division of powers between the Community and the Member States and the allocation of institutional prerogatives in the decision-making process relating to the subject matter at hand. This second aspect determines the participation of the component entities (the Member States) in the operation of the central government (the Community), acting within its sphere of powers.

When their input in the Community's decision-making process is at its lowest ebb, because the Commission has the last say on the matter, some Member States appear inclined to reduce the extent of the specific power granted to the Community by the Treaty provision in question. In case of success, this strategy forces the Commission to supplement the power base of its policy with other Treaty provisions (most often a non-specific one), which inevitably leads to a decision by the Council on a proposal from the Commission.

The Court of Justice, however, does not play this game lightly. It rather stands out as a beacon to defend the organic independence - against the Member States - of the Community's decision-making process in the areas where the Treaties provide for it. The Court is not ready to give a restrictive interpretation to a specific power of the Community, simply because the Commission, instead of the Council, takes the final decision as to its exercise.[54]

It even accepts to that effect that some implicit but necessary aspects of a specific power conferred upon the Community must be linked to the definition of this power.[55]

Thus, the Court of Justice does not pronounce on the division of powers between the Community and the Member States by way of a simple definition of the powers granted to the Community as opposed to those which remain for the Member States. Its jurispru-

---

lands, Kingdom of Denmark and United Kingdom of Great Britain and Northern Ireland v. Commission of the E.C., judgment of July 9, 1987, *E.C.R.* 3203 (1987).

53. See the judgment of July 6, 1982, quoted supra, n. 52 at 2574, paragraphs 8-10; and the judgment of July 9, 1987, also quoted supra n. 52, paragraphs 29-32.

54. Judgment of July 6, 1982, ibidem at 2573, paragraphs 5-6 (1982).

55. Judgment of July 9, 1987, quoted supra n. 52, paragraph 28. On the role of the theory of implied powers in the Community legal order, see Bredimas supra n. 39 at 117-118; and for an extensive analysis of the concept in the case law of the Court of Justice, see Lenaerts, quoted supra n. 15, at Nos. 393-405. The Court's reasoning is reminiscent of the ruling in McCulloch v. Maryland, per Marshall 4 *Wheaton* 316, 421 (1819): "Let the end be legitimate, let it be within the scope of the Constitution, and all means which are appropriate, which are plainly adapted to that end, which are not prohibited, but consistent with the letter and spirit of the Constitution, are constitutional." For a comment, see David P. Currie, *The Constitution in the Supreme Court* 160-168 (1985).

dence should rather be characterized as a *continuum* delineating the *specific powers* of the Community and possibly the *implied powers* linked to them, the *non-specific powers* of the Community and, finally, as a "leftover category", the *residual powers* of the Member States (which, in some cases, are voluntarily exercised in common by the latter meeting within the Council on an intergovernmental basis).

(b) The division of powers in practice - ERASMUS as a case study

By Decision 87/327/EEC of June 15, 1987, the Council of the European Communities adopted the European Community Action Scheme for the Mobility of University Students (ERASMUS).[56] The ERASMUS Decision tackles the quest for student mobility by its most ambitious, and thus its most difficult, side, *i.e.* the integration of a period of study of three months to one year spent at a university in another Member State into the requirements set by the student's home university, where the diploma will be earned. The universities can achieve that result only through agreements. Their respective national legislations must leave sufficient room for such agreements.

In its proposal that led to the ERASMUS Decision, the Commission indicated Article 128 of the EEC Treaty as the legal basis for the decision.[57] In its opinion on the proposal from the Commission, the European Parliament only referred to Article 128.[58] Yet, with a unanimous vote, the Council modified the legal basis proposed by the Commission and included in it Article 235 of the EEC Treaty.[59]

The Commission brought an action for annulment of the ERAS-

56. *O.J.E.C.* 1987, No. L 166/20. The Decision is a "Beschluss", i.e. a binding act, unnamed in Article 189 of the EEC Treaty, in contrast to the "Entscheidung" (see the said Article 189). However, only the substance of the act is relevant with a view of determining its true nature, cf. Case 22/70, Commission v. Council, judgment of March 31, 1971, *E.C.R.* 263, 277, paragraphs 38-42 (1971).

57. Article 128 of the EEC Treaty provides as follows: "The Council shall, acting on a proposal from the Commission and after consulting the Economic and Social Committee, lay down general principles for implementing a common vocational training policy capable of contributing to the harmonious development both of the national economies and of the common market".

58. *O.J.E.C.*, 1986, No. C 148/124.

59. The last paragraph of the preamble purports to justify this modification of the proposal of the Commission: "Whereas this action programme includes aspects relating to education which, at the present stage of development of Community law, may be regarded as falling outside the scope of the common vocational training policy as provided for in Article 128 of the Treaty; whereas these aspects of the programme can, together with the vocational training objectives to which they are closely linked, contribute to the harmonious development of economic activities throughout the Community; whereas to this extent the Treaty has not provided the necessary powers, and action for this purpose appears necessary to attain, in the course of the operation of the common market, one of the objectives of the Community", *O.J.E.C.*, 1987, No. L 166/21.

MUS Decision before the Court of Justice, preferably to the extent only that this Decision mentions as its legal basis Article 235 besides Article 128 of the EEC Treaty.[60]

The stakes were high, because the addition of Article 235 to Article 128 of the EEC Treaty as legal basis for the ERASMUS Decision had the effect of transforming a decision-making process requiring only a simple majority within the Council into one relying on a unanimous vote.[61]

The Court of Justice ruled in favor of the Council on the narrow ground that the ERASMUS Decision contained some research aspects which could not be based on Article 128 alone. It was thus legitimate for the Council to add Article 235 to the legal basis of the Decision proposed by the Commission. However, the Court rejected the arguments of the Council calling for a restrictive reading of Article 128 in relation to the educational aspects of the ERASMUS Decision. As to those aspects, the Court found for the Commission, considering that the ERASMUS student-mobility mechanism would be concerned mainly with "vocational training" as this latter concept was defined in earlier Court rulings.[62] The Advocate General had submitted to the Court an opposite view on the basis of a comparison of the wording of Article 128 with that of other provisions of the EEC Treaty, granting powers to the Community. The Court simply refused to engage in such comparative reading of the different Treaty articles in order to give weight to the more cautious character of the text of Article 128. In so doing, it was - as one author wrote - "stretching the Community competence to its utmost, contrary to expectations."[63]

In the wake of the entry into force of the Single European Act, the Commission seems very keen on defending the constitutional possibilities for majority voting within the Council. This should preserve the institutional position of the Commission to the extent that

60. Case 242/87, action brought on August 7, 1987 by the Commission of the European Communities against the Council of the European Communities, *O.J.E.C.*, 1987, No. C 242/4, decided by judgment of May 30, 1989, *E.C.R.* (1989), not yet reported.

61. Article 128 does not specify how the Council should vote, so that it is one of the rather few cases in which "the Council shall act by a majority of its members", Article 148(1) of the EEC Treaty. Most other examples relate to the institutional operation of the Council, see, e.g., Article 151(1) of the EEC Treaty (now Article 5 of the Merger Treaty) and Articles 152-153 of the EEC Treaty. For a more detailed analysis of the case, see Lenaerts, "ERASMUS : Legal Basis and Implementation", in, Bruno de Witte (ed.) *European Community Law of Education* 113ff. (1989).

62. Most notably Case 293/83, Gravier v. City of Liège, judgment of February 13, 1985, *E.C.R.* 593 (1985); and Case 24/86, Blaizot v. University of Liège, judgment of February 2, 1988, *E.C.R.* 379 (1988); see Arnull, "Of strip cartoonists, vets and gunsmiths", 13 *E. L. Rev.* 260 (1988).

63. Lonbay, "Education and Law: the Community context", 14 *E. L. Rev.* 363, at 369 (1989).

the Council can adopt a proposal from the Commission with a simple (or a qualified) majority when the applicable legal basis provides for this voting procedure. The Commission indeed participates in the decision-making process that takes place within the Council (experts' groups, COREPER, Council itself).[64] A recent amendment of the Council's Rules of Procedure even increases the role of the Commission, where Article 5(1) now reads: "The Council shall vote on the initiative of its President. The President shall, furthermore, be required to open voting proceedings on the invitation of a member of the Council or of the Commission, provided that a majority of the Council's members so decides" (amendment adopted by the Council on July 20, 1987).[65]

When a provision of the EEC Treaty, such as its Article 128, serves as legal basis, the new Article 5(1) of the Council's Rules of Procedure enables the Commission to force a vote, once a simple majority of the members of the Council (seven out of twelve) agrees on the merits of its proposal and, in addition, is ready to adopt it by making use of the said majority through a vote called pursuant to Article 5(1).

In most "legal basis" cases, the stakes are less spectacular. They involve the shift from a qualified majority needed under the provision of the EEC Treaty proposed as legal basis by the Commission, to the unanimity required in one of the provisions finally withheld by the Council (most often Article 235 of the EEC Treaty).

Since 1987, a considerable number of cases have been submitted to the Court by the Commission against the Council. The ERASMUS case was one of them.[66] In the cases involving Article 235 of the EEC Treaty, the analysis always turns on the question whether "this Treaty has not provided the necessary powers". This analysis is an "objective" one, so that it is subject to judicial review.[67]

In litigation about the legal basis of an act of the Council, the Court first determines whether the specific provisions of the Treaty can serve as a sufficient legal basis for the act. Only when this is not the case, may Article 235 come into play, "if action by the Community should prove necessary to attain, in the course of the operation of the common market, one of the objectives of the Community". This latter judgment, undertaken by the Council, acting unani-

64. See the Council's Rules of Procedure, adopted by the Council on July 24, 1979, on the basis of Article 5 of the Treaty of April 8, 1965 establishing a Single Council and a Single Commission of the European Communities, *O.J.E.C.*, 1979, No. L 268/1, Articles 3 (2) and 16 (3).

65. *O.J.E.C.*, 1987, No. L 291/27.

66. See supra n. 60.

67. Case 45/86, Commission v. Council, judgment of March 26, 1987, *E.C.R.* 1493 (1987), paragraph 11.

mously on a proposal from the Commission and after consulting the European Parliament, will not be reviewed by the Court.[68]

The different approach followed by the Court as to the two requirements stated in Article 235 of the EEC Treaty for allowing the Council to act under this provision seems fully justified. Just as the Council does not have the choice to act on an intergovernmental rather than a Community basis, because such choice would alter the constitutional division of powers between the Community and the Member States,[69] it does not have the choice between either one or another provision of the EEC Treaty as the basis of its Community action, because such a choice would alter the constitutional allocation of prerogatives among the Community institutions themselves in the decision-making process and thus affect the rights to participation in that process which the Member States indirectly hold or do not hold under the Community's constitution.[70]

Keeping the balance struck by the Founding Fathers is the watchword. But, once it is established that there is no specific legal basis in the EEC Treaty for action by the Community, it is a matter of political discretion entrusted by Article 235 to the Council, acting in accordance with the stated procedure, to decide on the necessity of such action.

(c) The absence of a constitutionally protected nucleus of sovereignty for the Member States

The residual powers of the Member States have no reserved status. The Community may indeed exercise its specific, implied or non-specific powers in the fullest way possible, without running into any inherent limitation set to these powers as a result of the sovereignty which the Member States retain as subjects of international law. There simply is no nucleus of sovereignty that the Member States can invoke, as such, against the Community.[71]

68. Cf. Case 22/70, Commission v. Council, judgment of March 31, 1971, *E.C.R.* 263, 283, paragraphs 93-95, (1971), Case 8/73, Hauptzollamt Bremerhaven v. Massey-Ferguson, judgment of July 12, 1973, *E.C.R.* 897, 907-908, paragraphs 2-6 (1973).

69. Opinion 1/78, October 4, 1979, *E.C.R.* 2871, 2907-2908, paragraph 31 (1979).

70. Cf. Case 45/86, supra n. 67, paragraph 12; Joined Cases 281/85, 283, 284 and 285/85 and 287/85, Federal Republic of Germany, French Republic, Kingdom of the Netherlands, Kingdom of Denmark, United Kingdom of Great Britain and Northern Ireland v. Commission, judgment of July 9, 1987, *E.C.R.* 3203 (1987), paragraph 31: "Consequently, since Article 118 provides a specific basis for the Commission's decision there is no need to consider whether the outcome sought by the decision in question might have been achieved through other general provisions of the Treaty or other procedures necessitating action on the part of other institutions".

71. Joined Cases 6 and 11/69, Commission of the E.C. v. French Republic, judgment of December 10, 1969, *E.C.R.* 523 (1969). France had maintained and even increased temporarily - over the objections of the Commission stated in an EEC Decision - the advantage granted to French exporters by the preferential rediscount rate applied by the Banque de France for short and long-term credits given for ex-

This is equally the case when the Treaty expressly acknowledges the existence of residual powers for the Member States. For instance, under Article 36 of the EEC Treaty, barriers to interstate trade, which are in principle prohibited by Articles 30 to 34 of the EEC Treaty, may be justified on grounds of public morality, public policy or public security, the protection of health and life of humans, animals or plants, the protection of national treasures of artistic, historic or archeological value, or the protection of industrial and commercial property. The final sentence of Article 36 adds that the national measures cannot "constitute a means of arbitrary discrimination or a disguised restriction on trade between Member States". Some Member States claimed that insofar as they remained short of violating this latter prohibition, Article 36 of the EEC Treaty offered constitutional protection to a list of reserved powers of the Member States, which they continued to enjoy as sovereign nations.[72]

The Court of Justice cut short this line of reasoning with some straightforward sentences pronounced in judgments during the late 1970's.[73] In the view of the Court, "the purpose of Article 36 of the Treaty is not to reserve certain matters to the exclusive jurisdiction of the Member States; it merely allows national legislation to derogate from the principle of the free movement of goods to the extent to which this is and remains justified in order to achieve the objectives set out in the article."[74]

This is no longer the case, according to the Court, "when, pursu-

---

ports to countries of the Community. It claimed to exercise reserved powers as the measures were part of the national monetary policy which falls outside the scope of the EEC Treaty. The Commission, on the contrary, relied on its authorization power stated in Article 108(3) of the EEC Treaty, to attach restrictive conditions to the freedom to act which it would be ready to leave to France. The Court ruled as follows, in paragraphs 15 to 17 of its judgment, ibidem at 539-540: "Articles 108(3) and 109(3) confer powers of authorization or intervention on the Community institutions which would be otiose if the Member States were free, on the pretext that their action related only to monetary policy, unilaterally to derogate from their obligations under the provisions of the Treaty and without being subject to control by the institutions. The solidarity which is at the basis of these obligations as of the whole of the Community system in accordance with the undertaking provided for in Article 5 of the Treaty, is continued for the benefit of the States in the procedure for mutual assistance provided for in Article 108 where a Member State is seriously threatened with difficulties as regards its balance of payments.

The exercise of reserved powers cannot therefore permit the unilateral adoption of measures prohibited by the Treaty."

As to the significance of this case, see A. Toth, "Legal Protection of Individuals in the European Communities" (I. The Individual and Community Law) 4 (1978).

72. See Barents, "New Developments in Measures Having Equivalent Effect", 16 *C.M.L. Rev.*, 271, 283-295 (1981).

73. Case 120/78, Rewe-Zentral AG v. Bundesmonopolverwaltung für Branntwein (Cassis de Dijon), judgment of February 20, 1979, *E.C.R.* 649 (1979); Case 148/78, Ratti, judgment of April 5, 1979, *E.C.R.* 1629 (1979); Case 153/78, Commission of the E.C. v. Federal Republic of Germany, judgment of July 12, 1979, *E.C.R.* 2555 (1979).

74. Case 153/78, quoted supra n. 73 at 2564, paragraph 5.

ant to Article 100 of the Treaty, Community directives provide for the harmonization of measures necessary to ensure the protection of the health of humans and animals and establish Community procedures to supervise compliance therewith."[75]

Since the purpose of Article 100 of the EEC Treaty, stating a non-specific power in favor of the Community, is to strike down, step by step, the national barriers to interstate trade, the Member States cannot continue to resort to the escape clause of Article 36 in order to keep in force measures that run afoul of EEC legislation adopted in accordance with the procedure of decision-making provided for in Article 100, *i.e.* on the basis of a unanimous vote within the Council.

Thus, the European Community undoubtedly satisfies the statement made by Justice Blackmun for the majority of the Supreme Court in *Garcia v. San Antonio Metropolitan Transit Authority*: "In short, the Framers chose to rely on a federal system in which special restraints on federal power over the States inhered principally in the workings of the National Government itself, rather than in discrete limitations on the objects of federal authority. State sovereign interests, then, are more properly protected by procedural safeguards inherent in the structure of the federal system than by judicially created limitations on federal power."[76] Although suiting the constellation of the European Community, this statement appears to be problematic in American constitutional law.[77]

The opinion of Justice Blackmun continues to hold true for the

75. Case 148/78, quoted supra n. 73, at 1644, paragraph 36. The Court continued, ibidem, that in this case, "recourse to Article 36 ceases to be justified and the appropriate controls must henceforth be carried out and the protective measures taken in accordance with the scheme laid down by the harmonizing directive." If a legislative act, based on Article 100 of the EEC Treaty, can undo the constitutional protection which the Member States apparently enjoy under Article 36, it must mean that this protection is not absolute but conditional, just as Member States enjoy, in most fields, a concurrent power as long as the Community has not itself acted. See, in this respect, infra, I, A.1, (d).

76. See supra n. 1. The Court thus adhered to the doctrinal thesis presented by Wechsler, "The Political Safeguards of Federalism: The Role of the States in the Composition and Selection of the National Government", 54 *Col. L. Rev.* 543 (1954). At the same time, however, the Court made clear that it was aware of the limits of the argument: "We realize that changes in the structure of the Federal Government have taken place since 1789, not the least of which has been the substitution of popular election of Senators by the adoption of the Seventeenth Amendment in 1913, and that these changes may work to alter the influence of the States in the federal political process". Nonetheless, for the majority of the Court, there was no "sacred province of State autonomy", id. at 554.

77. Compare Howard, "Garcia and the Values of Federalism: On the Need for Recurrence to Fundamental Principles", 19 *Georgia L. Rev.* 789 (1985); and Casper, "Federalism and the United States Constitution", in Koen Lenaerts (ed.) *Two Hundred Years of U.S. Constitution and Thirty Years of EEC Treaty. Outlook for a Comparison* 43 (1988).

European Community after the introduction in 1987, by the Single European Act, of Article 100A in the EEC Treaty.

By way of derogation from Article 100 of the EEC Treaty, Article 100A empowers the Council, acting by a qualified majority,[78] to adopt the measures needed for the approximation of national laws in view of the establishment and functioning of the internal market. Even though Article 100A contains a "specific" Community power because its scope is limited to the concept of the internal market,[79] the substance of this power remains rather open-ended, so that the Member States should normally have protected their interests through the process value of unanimous voting within the Council. Yet they gave it up, which made up the essence of the constitutional reform of 1987, but by way of compensation secured a process value of another kind, as a means of protecting their most basic interests. Community legislation adopted under Article 100A will not be water tight in all circumstances against the continuing operation of national measures based on Article 36, as EEC directives issued pursuant to Article 100 always are.[80]

A dissenting Member State cannot block a qualified majority of Member States ready to have the Council decide in a given way, but it will keep the right, stated in Article 100A(4), to further "apply national provisions on grounds of major needs referred to in Article 36, or relating to protection of the environment or the working environment", even if these provisions are in contradiction with the Community law adopted on the basis of Article 100A. The Commission must consent to such national provisions. In case of a persistent disagreement between the Commission (or another Member State) and the dissenting Member State the Court of Justice decides whether the defending Member State is justified to rely on Article 100A(4).

To sum up, Community power under Article 100A can be exercised through a qualified majority vote within the Council up to the outer limit of this power. There is no inherent limitation set to this power due to the fact that the decision does not rest on a unanimous vote. But a different process value serves to uphold the residual powers of a dissenting Member State, if - in objective terms - need be. This dispassionate judgment must in last analysis be made by the Court of Justice.[81]

---

78. See supra n. 45.

79. As to the definition of this concept in Article 100A, reference is made to Article 8A of the EEC Treaty, whose second paragraph provides as follows: "The internal market shall comprise an area without internal frontiers in which the free movement of goods, persons, services and capital is ensured in accordance with the provisions of this Treaty".

80. See supra n. 75. Compare Morse, "Harmonisation of Laws. Direct Effect of Harmonizing Directives: Relationship with Art.36", 5 *E.L. Rev.* 142-145 (1980).

81. See Forwood & Clough, "The Single European Act and Free Movement", 10

(d) The relationship between Community and Member State powers

The Member States ordinarily keep a concurrent power over the subject matter entrusted to the Community to the extent that the latter has not acted upon them.

As a rule, the powers granted to the Community contain only a potential for it to exercise them; in the absence of such exercise, the Member States remain competent to act, albeit they may not, in doing so, hurt in any way the Community's interests.[82]

The present state of Community constitutional law relating to this matter can best be summarized in the words used by Chief Justice Taney in his concurrence in the License Cases: "The mere grant of power to the general government cannot upon any just principles of construction be construed to be an absolute prohibition to the exercise of any power over the same subject by the States. . . The State may. . . make regulations. . ., and such regulations are valid unless they come in conflict with a law of Congress."[83]

The question then is whether the regulations of a Member State come in conflict with a law adopted by the Community. The criterion developed by the U.S. Supreme Court in its *Hines v. Davidowitz* ruling, that the State regulation may not constitute any obstacle "to the accomplishment and execution of the full purposes and objectives of Congress",[84] also those which are merely implicit in Congress' legislation,[85] can readily be transposed to the case law

E.L. Rev. 383, 397-408 (1985); Flynn, "How will Article 100A(4) work? A Comparison with Article 93", 24 *C.M.L. Rev.* 689 (1987); but compare Pescatore, "Some Critical Remarks on the 'Single European Act' ", 24 *C.M.L. Rev.* 9-18 (1987). This author expresses the fear that the common market might be weakened if the Court is not severe enough vis-à-vis dissenting Member States, in its judgments made under Article 100A(4) of the EEC Treaty. Such severity seems, however, likely, since it would correspond to the Court's previous posture when it interpreted Articles 30 and 36 of the EEC Treaty in order to allow national courts to verify the compatibility of Member State law with the free movement of goods throughout the Community. See supra, note 73; to the cases quoted there, the "German beer" case may be added, in which a long-standing German law prescribing the purity of all beer commercialised in Germany, was held to be contrary to Article 30 of the EEC Treaty, without being justified by Article 36, because it excluded in effect the importation of beer manufactured in other Member States, see Case 178/84, Commission of the E.C. v. Federal Republic of Germany, judgment of March 12, 1987, *E.C.R.* 1227 (1987); there was a parallel Case 176/84, Commission of the E.C. v. Greece, judgment of March 12,1987, *E.C.R.* 1193 (1987).

82. Article 5, second paragraph, of the EEC Treaty reads: "They (the Member States) shall abstain from any measure which could jeopardize the attainment of the objectives of this Treaty".

83. 5 *Howard* 504, 579 (1847).

84. 312 U.S. 52, 67 (1941).

85. See Rice v. Santa Fe Elevator Corporation, 331 U.S. 218 (1947) - out of the preparatory works of the federal legislation at issue, Justice Douglas concluded that Congress' intent was to provide for a uniform and comprehensive regulation, so that the States were not allowed to do better by adding requirements; but in Zook v. Cali-

of the Court of Justice.[86]

The preemption by Community legislation of the concurrent power of the Member States over the same subject matter presents particular difficulties, when in the absence of an actual conflict between the texts of national and Community law, the argument is made - mostly by the Commission representing the Community's interests - that the silence of the Community legislator on a specific aspect of an otherwise regulated matter, reflects the intention that this aspect remain free from any regulation and, therefore, Member State power over it is preempted, just as it is in relation to those aspects which have been regulated by the Community.

The issue is well known in American constitutional law, where the Court of Justice might even find some encouragement as to the delicate lines to be drawn. It was indeed Thomas Reed Powell who, in 1937, declared with regard to the then peaking concept of the "silence of Congress,"[87] used both to curtail State power and to make that curtailment reversible by Congress: "Now Congress has a won-

---

fornia, 336 U.S. 725 (1949), the concrete terms of a similar analysis led to the opposite outcome.

86. Compare Berardis, "The Common Organization of Agricultural Markets and National Price Regulations", 17 *C.M.L. Rev.* 539-540 (1980): "Community power in agricultural matters is. . .in the spirit of the Treaty, even after the end of the transitional period, not exclusive. Community powers and those of Member States in agricultural matters are 'concurrent' therefore in the sense that where Community law takes precedence the powers of Member States diminish as Community power increases. Action by a Member State is unlawful if it is incompatible with action taken by the Community". See also Usher, "The Effects of Common Organizations and Policies on the Powers of a Member State", 2 *E.L. Rev.* 428, 430-436 (1977); Waelbroeck, "The Emergent Doctrine of Community Pre-Emption - Consent and Redelegation", in, Terrance Sandalow & Eric Stein (eds.) *Courts and Free Markets* 548 (1982); Lenaerts, "Les répercussions des compétences de la Communauté européenne sur les compétences externes des Etats membres et la question de 'preemption' ", in Paul Demaret (ed.) *Relations extérieures de la Communauté européenne et marché intérieur: aspects juridiques et fonctionnels* 37 (1988).

87. Bowman v. Chicago and Northwestern Railway Company, 125 U.S. 465 (1888); Leisy v. Hardin, 135 U.S. 100 (1890). Both cases involved Iowa statutes, the first putting a constraint on the transportation of liquor, the second on the sale of it. The statutes were invalidated. In the first case, it was said that the regulation constituted "an unauthorized breach and interruption of that liberty of trade which Congress ordains as the national policy, by willing that it shall be free from restrictive regulations." In the second case, the Court held as follows: "Hence, inasmuch as interstate commerce is national in its character, and must be governed by a uniform system, so long as Congress does not pass any law to regulate it, or allowing the States so to do, it thereby indicates its will that such commerce shall be free and untrammeled". Congress "overrruled" both decisions in the Wilson and Webb Kenyon Acts. For the Court, it was rather easy to uphold the laws, since the Bowmann and Leisy rulings were based on the implicit will of Congress to leave the matter free. If afterwards it appeared that the Court erred in searching for Congress' intent as expressed through its silence or if Congress changed its mind, the Court had to follow the move based on the same logic. See In Re Rahrer, 140 U.S. 545 (1891); Clark Distilling Company v. Western Maryland Railroad Company, 242 U.S. 311 (1917).

derful power to keep silent, Congress can regulate interstate commerce just by not doing anything about it. Of course, when Congress keeps silent, it takes an expert to know what it means. But the judges are experts. They say that Congress by keeping silent sometimes means that it is keeping silent and sometimes means that it is speaking."[88]

This is precisely what the Court of Justice will say, if need be, in relation to the Community legislator's silence. In its Amsterdam Bulb judgment of 1977, the Court in effect decided that, by keeping silent, the Community legislator meant that it was keeping silent, so that the power of the Netherlands to fill the normative gap left by the Community had not been preempted.[89] The Court considered that the silence of the Community legislator had no meaning in terms of policy, but simply resulted from the fact that the matter at hand had not been dealt with at the level of the Community.[90]

The opposite conclusion was reached in the Van den Hazel judgment, some three months later,[91] when the Court stated in respect of Council Regulation No. 123/67 on the common organization of the markets in poultry,[92] "that the absence of measures concerning the withdrawal, where necessary, of products from the market does not stem from an omission or from an intention to leave measures of

88. Powell, "The Still Small Voice of the Commerce Clause", in Proceedings of the National Tax Association, Washington, D.C., 1937; compare the analysis of the doctrine by Biklé, "The Silence of Congress", 41 *Harv.L. Rev.* 200 (1927).

89. Case 50/76, Amsterdam Bulb BV v. Produktschap voor siergewassen, judgment of February 2, 1977, *E.C.R.* 137 (1977).

90. There is a similarity between the attitude of the Court of Justice in this case and the position defended, in 1942, by Chief Justice Stone in his dissent in Cloverleaf Butter Company v. Patterson, 315 U.S. 148, 176-177 (1942): "It is one thing for courts in interpreting an Act of Congress regulating matters beyond State control to construe its language with a view to carrying into effect a general though unexpressed congressional purpose. It is quite another to infer a purpose, which Congress has not expressed, to deprive the States of authority which otherwise constitutionally belongs to them, over a subject which Congress has not undertaken to control. Due regard for the maintenance of our dual system of government demands that the courts do not diminish State power by extravagant inferences regarding what Congress might have intended if it had considered the matter, or by reference to their own conceptions of a policy which Congress has not expressed and is not plainly to be inferred from the legislation which it has enacted". With this rather straightforward criticism of the majority opinion drafted by Justice Reed, the Chief Justice discredited in fact the old line of cases in which a large federal preemption had been upheld under the label of the "occupation of the field" by Congress beyond the actual legislation relating to such field. See, as an illustration, the opinion of the Court by Justice Lamar in the case of Southern Railway Company v. Railroad Commission of Indiana, 236 U.S. 439 (1915). The Cloverleaf dissent contributed to laying the ground-work for the later Supreme Court decisions on preemption, such as those quoted supra n. 85.

91. Case 111/76, Officier van Justitie v. Van den Hazel, judgment of May 18, 1977, *E.C.R.* 901 (1977).

92. Council of the European Economic Community, June 13, 1967. For the content of the Regulation, see ibidem, at 908, paragraphs 6-8 (1977).

this nature to the appraisal of the Member States but is rather the consequence of a considered choice of economic policy of relying essentially on market forces to attain the desired balance."[93] This judicial assessment of the tenor of the legislator's silence rested to a large extent on an analysis of the deliberations that had led to the legislation in question.[94]

In more exceptional cases, the mere grant of power to the Community entails a total loss of power for the Member States.[95] Such Community power is said to be constitutionally exclusive, because Member States are excluded from its concurrent exercise irrespective of any action or inaction on the part of the Community.

The exclusive character of a particular power of the Community is generally not stated in the Treaties,[96] it rather flows from a judicial appraisal of the intrinsic content of the power under consideration. In this connexion, the line of reasoning pursued by Justice Johnson in his concurring opinion in *Gibbons v. Ogden*, advocating the exclusive character of the power over interstate commerce held by Congress under Article I, Section 8, of the U.S. Constitution, ech-

93. Id. at 910, paragraph 16 (1977).

94. Id. at 909-910, paragraphs 14-15 (1977). Compare, in this respect, the political process values that appear to be important to the outcome of preemption cases in the United States. See the opinion of the Court per J. Brennan, in the case of Florida Lime and Avocado Growers, Inc. v. Paul, 373 U.S. 132, 143, 150-151 (1963). See also Tribe, "California Declines the Nuclear Gamble: Is such a State Choice Preempted?", 7 *Ecology L.Q.* 679, 690 (1979): "By refusing to construe ambiguous legislation expansively, the Court can act to prevent Congress from avoiding hard questions of federal-State relations and thus can increase the likelihood that Congress will give full attention to the interests of the States and of those groups whose interests parallel the States' ".

95. Thus, the Community holds exclusive powers with regard to the regime of supply of fissile materials (chapter VI of the EAEC Treaty), see Case 7/71, Commission of the E.C. v. French Republic, judgment of December 14, 1971, *E.C.R.* 1003, 1018-1019, paragraphs 18-26 (1971). Likewise, the Community powers derived from Article 113 of the EEC Treaty (common commercial policy towards third States) are normally exclusive, see Case 41/76, Donckerwolcke v. Procureur de la République, judgment of December 15, 1976, *E.C.R.* 1921 (1976); Opinion 1/75 of November 11, 1975, *E.C.R.* 1355 (1975); Opinion 1/78 of October 4, 1979, *E.C.R.* 2871 (1979). Finally, the Community's power to take conservation measures in order to prevent the depletion of fish stocks, is exclusive under Article 102 of the Act of Accession of 1972, see Case 804/79, Commission of the E.C. v. United Kingdom, judgment of May 5, 1981. *E.C.R.* 1045 (1981).

96. In the "Draft Treaty for a European Union" adopted by the European Parliament on February 14, 1984, the powers listed in favor of the Union were explicitly characterized as "exclusive" or "concurrent". The present Treaties lack, however, this kind of clarity. Bieber considers "that the Community has exclusive powers if it can clearly be deduced from the wording of the Treaties that such powers have been conferred upon it or if a provision cannot be properly applied if this were not the case (e.g. the setting-up of the Common Customs Tariff in accordance with Article 21(2) EEC, provisions concerning the institutional system)". ["On the Mutual Completion of Overlapping Legal Systems: The Case of the European Communities and the National Legal Orders", 13 *E.L. Rev.* 147, 150 (1988)].

oes through in the relevant case law of the Court of Justice.[97]

The judicial protection of the exclusive powers of the Community is not, however, a straightforward undertaking. A great deal of imagination is often needed for the Court of Justice to reconcile the conflicting interests of the Community in protecting the constitutionally exclusive reach of its power, and of a Member State acting in the name of an overriding policy concern that, in its view, cannot await the coming into force of Community legislation (which will occur only when the complex legislative process taking place within the Community has come to an end). The Court developed mainly two mechanisms to relieve the tensions inherent in any such conflict.

Firstly, legislation enacted by the Community pursuant to one of its exclusive powers may contain a "specific authorization by the Community" in favor of the Member States.[98] This is a remarkable ruling, because it allows that legislation, when it is specific to that effect, cuts through the exclusive character of the Community's power derived from the constitution. In adopting it, the Court of Justice fell however in line with the U.S. Supreme Court opinions in *Cooley v. The Board of Wardens of the Port of Philadelphia*[99] and *Prudential Insurance Company v. Benjamin*:[100] the States may not, in principle, interfere with national matters relating to interstate commerce because of the constitutionally exclusive reach of Congress' power as to these matters; but one of the ways for Congress to "regulate" them is to abide by the several States' proposals and to let them carry these out.

The Court of Justice went even further in its Bulk Oil judgment of February 18, 1986,[101] when it considered that the mere fact for the Community not to have regulated a particular aspect of the common commercial policy toward third States (in this case, the export of crude oil) constituted a "specific authorization by the Community" in favor of the Member States to act upon the matter. Thus, the United Kingdom was empowered to limit its crude oil exports to Israel. The Court's reasoning rested in fact on the existence of concurrent powers for the Member States, since the absence of a Community regime of export measures applicable to crude oil, be it in relation to Israel or any other country, was in itself considered sufficient to accept that the Member States still adopt the measures

97. 9 *Wheaton* 1, 227 (1824).

98. Case 41/76, Donckerwolcke v. Procureur de la République, judgment of December 15, 1976, quoted supra n. 95 at 1937, paragraph 32.

99. 12 *Howard* 299 (1851).

100. 328 U.S. 408 (1946).

101. Case 174/84, *E.C.R.* 559 (1986).

which they deem to be appropriate as to this matter.[102] National legislation would only be preempted, when the Community was to act upon the matter.

The conclusion must be that the Court effectively applies a scheme of "selective exclusiveness" to the different subject matters that are part of the common commercial policy toward third States (Article 113 of the EEC Treaty). For some of these subject matters, such as quantitative restrictions to exports, the Court reasons on the basis of the "concurrent powers" doctrine (this is the core of the Bulk Oil ruling), whereas for other subject matters, such as customs regulations,[103] the "exclusive powers" doctrine is enforced in so absolute a way as not even to leave the possibility for the Community legislator to expressly delegate powers back to the Member States.[104] By striking this balance, the Court of Justice discovered, one hundred and thirty five years after the U.S. Supreme Court, the wisdom inherent in the words of Justice Curtis with regard to the Commerce Clause power of Congress: "Either absolutely to affirm, or deny, that the nature of this power requires exclusive legislation by Congress, is to lose sight of the nature of the subjects of this power, and to assert concerning all of them, what is really applicable but to a part."[105]

Secondly, the Court of Justice had to be rather imaginative in the case of the exclusive power of the Community to take conservation measures in the matter of sea fisheries.[106] The Council was unable to conclude its deliberations on the legislative proposals submitted by the Commission. Measures were, however, urgently needed in order to avoid the depletion over a short time of the Com-

102. Id. at 586-587, paragraphs 32-33 (1986). Compare Dominick, "EEC-Israel Agreement and the Common Commercial Policy", 11 *E.L. Rev.* 466, 470 (1986): "Better, perhaps, that the Court. . .had acknowledged in more straightforward fashion the emergence of a more flexible pre-emption doctrine". See also the annotation of the Bulk Oil judgment by E. Völker in 24 *C.M.L. Rev.* 105-109 (1987).

103. Joined Cases 37-38/73, Indiamex, judgment of December 13, 1973, *E.C.R.* 1609 (1973).

104. In this sense the Court of Justice is more severe than the Supreme Court as to the scope of the exclusivity of the central powers, see the U.S. case law quoted supra n. 100, and compare the cases in which the Council was criticized by the Court for having broken the exclusive effect of a Treaty provision, Case 59/75, Pubblico Ministero v. Manghera, judgment of February 3, 1976, *E.C.R.* 91 (1976), Joined Cases 80 and 81/77, Société Les Commissaires Réunis v. Receveur des Douanes; Sàrl Les Fils de Henri Ramel v. Receveur des Douanes, judgment of April 20, 1978, *E.C.R.* 927 (1978); Case 37/83, Rewe, judgment of February 29, 1984, *E.C.R.* 1229, 1248-1249, paragraph 18 (obiter dictum) (1984); and Case 41/84, Pietro Pinna v. Caisse d'allocations familiales de la Savoie, judgment of January 15, 1986, *E.C.R.* 1 (1986).

105. Cooley v. The Board of Wardens of the Port of Philadelphia, 12 *Howard* 299, 319 (1851).

106. As to the principle of the exclusive power of the Community relating to this matter, derived from Article 102 of the Act of Accession of 1972, see Case 804/79, Commission of the E.C. v. United Kingdom, quoted supra n. 114.

munity's fish resources, to which the fishermen of the Member States have an equal right of access. The Court chose to protect simultaneously the constitutionally exclusive reach of the Community's power and the integrity of the fish stocks, by admitting that Member States act "as trustees of the common interest" with the approval of the Commission.[107] In other words, until the Community itself would act, the Member States were authorized to adopt national measures, not as a free exercise of concurrent powers, but as caretakers for the Community and hence bound by the Community's interests protected through the Commission's supervision.

This ruling about an exclusive power of the Community contains one of the better strategic strokes made by the Court, in order to enhance the prospects for a successful operation of the Community's legislative process. It did indeed appear much easier for the Member States to agree among themselves — within the Council — with a view to adopting Community conservation measures, than to get national conservation measures approved by the Commission.[108] Thus, within two years after the Court's ruling, the Council enacted the necessary Community legislation.[109]

(e) Executive federalism within the European Community

The last issue to be considered with regard to the division of powers between the Community and the Member States, relates to the principle of "executive federalism" that found its way from German constitutional law into the Community legal order.[110] In the

107. Id. at 1075-1076, paragraphs 30-32 (1981).

108. It was indeed pointed out to the Court (by the Commission) that the Council would have been in a position to adopt the conservation measures proposed by the Commission on the basis of Article 102 of the Act of Accession of 1972, if the United Kingdom had not itself blocked the decision-making process in the Council, see ibidem, at 1070, paragraph 9 (1981).

109. See the Council's fisheries regulations of January 25, 1983, *O.J.E.C.*, 1983, Nos. L 24 and L 25. The Commission had pressured the Member States by its declaration that in approving national conservation measures, as required by the Court's judgment of May 5, 1981, it would henceforth simply base its appreciation of such measures on the proposals which it had submitted to the Council, see *O.J.E.C.*, 1982, No. C 343.

110. Compare Frowein, "Integration and the Federal Experience in Germany and Switzerland", in, Mauro Cappelletti, Monica Seccombe & Joseph Weiler (eds.) *Integration Through Law* 586-587 (1986): "The practice of shared responsibility - where federal legislation leaves room for State laws to fill in certain gaps - is also typical of the German federal system. This practice is even more important when federal legislation must be executed by Land administrative authorities. If one takes into account the important decisions which need to be taken at the level of execution, it becomes clear that this competence of the Länder is far from negligible. The notion of "Vollzugsföderalismus" (federalism in the execution of laws, etc.) describes this important phenomenon". The European Community equivalent finds its constitutional basis in Article 5 of the EEC Treaty. For a case study on this provision see

United States, it remains a touchy question whether the legislative or executive branches of the federal government may enlist the help of the political process of the States in order to have it carry out some basic choices of federal policy.[111] Admittedly, there appears to be no problem for Congress to require a State to administer and enforce a federal regulatory scheme that is clearly identifiable as such,[112] but doubts arise when Congress legislates in general terms only requiring the States to enact all further measures needed to reach a given policy outcome.[113] The main reason for these doubts is that both the federal and the State governments should bear themselves the entire responsibility for their acts, when facing the electorate; it would therefore be unacceptable to oblige the States to pass legislation which they did not freely decide upon, but for which the voters may hold their elected officials politically accountable.

Such doubts, on the contrary, are absent in the Community legal order, not in the least because the Community legislator does not receive any direct electoral mandate. The Council and, to a still lesser extent, the Commission are only indirectly legitimized through the elections that take place in the Member States.[114]

In this context, the exercise of Community powers somehow appears as another mode for the Member States to assume their own sovereignty, not any longer through autonomous, but through common decision-making. It is consistent with such scheme that the Member States transfer a number of powers to the Community so as to have it set the general rules and objectives to be observed, while they will then have the obligation to further legislate, each one of them for its territory, to satisfy at a practical level, these general

---

Lenaerts, "The Application of Community Law in Belgium", 23 *C.M.L. Rev.* 253-286 (1986).

111. See Stewart, "Pyramids of Sacrifice? Problems of Federalism in Mandating State Implementation of National Environmental Policy", 86 *Yale L.J.* 1196 (1977).

112. See the majority opinion by Justice Cardozo in Steward Machine Company v. Davis, 301 U.S. 548 (1937), sustaining the unemployment compensation provisions of the Social Security Act of 1935, and in the companion case, Helvering v. Davis, 301 U.S. 619 (1937), upholding the old age benefits provisions of the same Act.

113. See the opinion of Circuit Judge MacKinnon in the case of District of Columbia v. Train, 521 F. 2d 971 (D.C. Cir. 1975). Compare Fry v. United States, 421 U.S. 542, 547, note 7 (1975): "The (Tenth) Amendment expressly declares the constitutional policy that Congress may not exercise power in a fashion that impairs the States' integrity, or their ability to function effectively in a federal system".

114. In addition, the Commission is supervised by the European Parliament which may vote a motion of censure on the activities of the Commission, obliging the members of the latter to resign as a body, see Article 144 of the EEC Treaty. So far, it has never happened. In a judgment of September 27, 1988, the Court of Justice mentioned, however, this possibility of political control to be taken up by the European Parliament in order to defend its institutional prerogatives against the Commission and, through the Commission, against the Council, see Case 302/87, European Parliament v. Council, *E.C.R.* (1988) not yet reported.

rules and objectives.[115] Both aspects of the decision-making process rely on a single democratic legitimacy, which is the direct election of the representative bodies of government in the Member States. Thus, in the legal order of the Community, the component entities act to the greater extent as the executive branch of the central government.[116]

The lack of a full-fledged executive branch of the Community government, that is independent from the Member States, has deflected the system of horizontal separation of powers, as upheld by the U.S. Supreme Court in the Steel Seizure case,[117] into one which has become inextricably intertwined with the vertical division of powers inherent in the federal relationship between the central government and the component entities of the multi-sovereign constitutional structure of the European Community.

Finally, it should be added that apart from the obligation for the Member States to execute the laws of the Community, the latter has also the power - as the federal government in the U.S.[118] - to use its spending power in such a way as to have Member States "freely" enact the legislation necessary to qualify for the grant of Community subsidies.[119]

---

115. Compare Cappelletti, Seccombe & Weiller, supra n. 6 at 29-35.

116. Compare Case 294/83, Parti écologiste "Les Verts" v. European Parliament, judgment of April 23, 1986, quoted supra n. 21, at paragraph 23. Direct administration of Community law by an institution of the Community is, quantitatively speaking, the exception. The best known examples of it relate to antitrust and international trade law (see Articles 85 to 94 of the EEC Treaty and the antidumping and antisubsidy legislation adopted under Article 113 of the EEC Treaty).

117. Youngstown Sheet & Tube Company v. Sawyer, 343 U.S. 579 (1952); Freund, "The Supreme Court, 1951 Term-Foreword: The Year of the Steel Case", 66 *Harv. L. Rev.* 89 (1952).

118. See the quotation by Richard Stewart & James E. Krier, *Environmental Law and Policy* 468 (1978, second edition), especially note 49, of the opinion of Circuit Judge MacKinnon in the case of District of Columbia v. Train, 521 F. 2d 971 (D.C. Cir. 1975), and their comments upon it, ibidem, p.474, No.6.

119. An example is provided by the ERASMUS Decision of the Council of June 15, 1987, quoted supra n. 56. The Community will fund programs for the exchange of university students among the institutions of higher education of the Member States, provided that the latter adapt their legislation - to the extent that such adaptation is needed - with a view of allowing the students to integrate periods of study accomplished abroad into the requirements set by the law of their home country towards the obtention of the national diploma. The Community anticipates that the financial incentive given to universities and students will pressure the Member States to voluntarily accept a pattern of greater uniformity in the basic university programs. This in turn should enhance the feasibility of "a general system for the recognition of higher education diplomas awarded on completion of vocational courses of at least three years' duration", which at present awaits the Council's final approval, see the Proposal from the Commission for a Council Directive, *O.J.E.C.* 1985, No. C 217/3 and *O.J.E.C.* 1986, No. C 143/7, quoted in the preamble of the ERASMUS Decision, *O.J.E.C.* 1987, No. L 166/21.

Compare also the background document stating the Commission's policy in the field: Supplement 8/85, Bulletin of the European Communities.

This incentive mechanism cannot be seen as a threat to the autonomy of the Member States in areas not entrusted to the Community's power. The reason for this is twofold. Firstly, the Community has no general spending power similar to that held by Congress under Article I, section 8, of the U.S. Constitution. The Community must base its decisions containing a conditional grant of subsidies to the Member States on one of its specific, implied or non-specific powers; accordingly, a tailor-made legislative process will in each case ensure that Member States have serious possibilities of participation in the decision-making.[120] Secondly, the conditions set for a grant of Community subsidies must necessarily be related to the subject matter over which the spending power is being exercised; if conditions of another kind were to be imposed, the Community would simply transgress the boundaries set to its powers in the constitutional provision on the basis of which the funds are spent (this is again a consequence of the fact that the Community's spending power is not a general one).

A.2. Switzerland

In spite of its ethnical, religious and linguistic cleavages, Switzerland's national cohesion has never been at risk.[121]

This reality reflects the balance struck by Swiss federalism between unity and diversity. Societal pluralism coexists with a drive for common decision-making in economic and military affairs.

Economic and military integration stands as the countervailing force to the pre-existing cantonal diversity. The value of unity has not defied a reasonable degree of continuing cantonal diversity.[122]

Swiss federalism, therefore, is integrative, even though its main effect - if not its main purpose - is to acknowledge the existence of societal pluralism as being consistent with a constitutionally defined political unity.

The Swiss Cantons lived for over five centuries in a confederation, before concluding, in 1815, a new federal compact.[123] This compact in fact re-instituted a confederation in order to end the disruption caused to Switzerland by the French Revolution. The loosely knit confederation did not receive any significant legislative or taxing power. It served in essence only to assure the common defense. From their side, the Cantons continued to erect customs and other barriers to intercantonal and foreign commerce.

120. See supra n. 44 to 50.

121. Compare the appraisal of Frowein, supra n. 110 at 593.

122. See, generally, Hangartner, "Die Erfüllung der Staatsaufgaben durch Bund und Kantone", NF93 *Zeitschrift für Schweizerisches Recht I*, 379 (1974).

123. Fritz Fleiner & Zaccaria Giacometti, *Schweizerisches Bundesstaatsrecht* 6 (1949).

Dissatisfaction with the absence of an integrated Swiss market became widespread throughout the Cantons.[124] As to the vesting of federal power over intercantonal commerce, the Swiss constitutional history can more readily be seen as a prefiguration of the process of economic integration that presently takes place within the European Community, than as a duplication of early American developments. Successive amendments to the Swiss Constitution have first liberalized trade and industry throughout the Confederation by guaranteeing the basic right to commercial freedom upon which the people were to rely before the courts against the Cantons,[125] and only thereafter conferred regulatory powers to the Confederation over matters of national economic interest.[126] In some instances, a residual power for the Cantons is mentioned in the Constitution, either as a police power or as a power of social protection of certain groups of people.[127] The exercise of this residual power may lead to a strictly proportional limitation being placed upon the right to commercial freedom,[128] but in no case will such exercise of cantonal power be resistent against the operation of a legislative act of the

124. The constitutional situation of Switzerland at the time can be described in the terms used by Justice Joseph Story, in 1833, when he wrote about the downfall of the American Confederation, then some fifty years earlier: "(The) want of any power in Congress to regulate foreign or domestic commerce was deemed a leading defect in the Confederation. This evil was felt in a comparatively slight degree during the war. But when the return to peace restored the country to its ordinary commercial relations, the want of some uniform system to regulate them was early perceived", in Commentaries on the Constitution of the United States; with a preliminary review of the constitutional history of the colonies and States before the adoption of the Constitution, Boston, Hilliard, Gray; Cambridge, Brown, Shattuck, 1833, § 259-260. Compare also the letter written on April 10, 1787 by the French Chargé d'Affaires, Comte de Montmorin, to his Foreign Minister, in which he reports on the fundamental weaknesses of the American Confederation, reproduced in Max Farrand, *Records of the Federal Convention of 1787* 15 (1911).

125. Article 31 of the Swiss Constitution (1874). For a comment, see Y. Hangartner, *Grundzüge des schweizerischen Staatsrechts* 130-132 (1980).

126. Jean F. Aubert, *Traité de droit constitutionnel suisse* 53ff. (1967).

127. See, e.g., Article 31ter(1) (as to legislation to make the running of establishments serving food or drink depend on professional and personal qualifications and also to subordinate the number of establishments to the existence of a need whenever the very existence of this trade is threatened by excessive competition); Article 32quater(1) to (4) (as to cantonal legislation on innkeeping and non-distilled spirits); and Article 33(1) (the Cantons may require proofs of capacity from persons who intend to exercise a liberal profession). See also Hangartner, supra n. 125 at 142-146.

128. See Bundesgericht/Tribunal fédéral, judgment of March 11, 1983, Manpower S.A. v. Grand Conseil du Canton de Genève, Bundesgericht Entscheidungen (hereafter BGE) 109, IA/IB, 61 (1983) - the Geneva law on temporary placement offices was upheld as a valid exercise of the cantonal police powers although it limited to some extent the right to commercial freedom guaranteed in Article 31 of the Constitution. See especially at 70-71, No.3, a) and b), with further reference to BGE 106, Ia, 269, No.1 and the case law quoted there. Compare Bundesgericht/Tribunal fédéral, Case Griessen v. Conseil d'Etat du canton de Genève, judgment of March 3, 1971, BGE 103, Ia, 499 (1971); see further Peter Saladin, *Grundrechte im Wandel* 236ff. (1970).

Confederation.[129]

The supremacy of a federal legislative act over inconsistent cantonal law will even be upheld, when the Federal Assembly (the national legislature) has violated the constitutional limits set to its powers,[130] while the Canton in question justifies its law by reference to a residual power expressly recognized in the Constitution.[131] There could hardly be more concluding evidence of the fact that although, under Article 3 of the Constitution, "the Cantons are sovereign insofar as their sovereignty is not limited by the federal Constitution and, as such, exercise all rights which are not entrusted to the federal power,"[132] their residual powers have no reserved status. The result is that national legislative powers in Switzerland never suffer any inherent limitation due to the existence of the Cantons.[133] Only the exercise of executive powers by the central government will be subject to judicial review, so that in this context the Cantons see the reach of their residual powers safeguarded by the judiciary if need be.[134]

But each federal system has a constitutional equilibrium of its own. In Switzerland, the lack of judicial review of national legislation and the ensuing threat to the integrity of the powers of the Cantons are compensated by the prominent presence of the Cantons inside the political decision-making of the Confederation. Thus, besides a Conseil national consisting of 200 representatives of the Swiss people,[135] there is a Conseil des Etats in which the 23 Cantons delegate each two representatives.[136] A legislative act of the Confederation requires the approval of the absolute majority of the representatives taking part in the vote within the two Conseils (while these can only vote when the absolute majority of the total number

---

129. For a clear application, see Bundesgericht/Tribunal fédéral, judgment of September 22, 1971, Gemeinde Flims v. Schweiz. Eidgenossenschaft (PTT Betriebe), BGE 97, I, 524 (1971). See also M. Imboden, "Die staatsrechtliche Bedeutung des Grundsatzes 'Bundesrecht bricht kantonales Recht' ", NF 61 *Zeitschrift für Schweizerisches Recht* 203 (1942).

130. This principle follows from the explicit rejection of judicial review of federal legislation in Article 113(3) of the Swiss Constitution. For an application, see Bundesgericht/Tribunal fédéral, judgment of January 20, 1965, Fondation Nordmann v. Conseil d'Etat du Canton de Genève, BGE 95, I, 17, 19-20, No.2 (1965).

131. Compare Fleiner & Giacometti supra n. 123 at 92-103.

132. See Huber, "Gedanken über die Ausscheidung der Zuständigkeiten zwischen Bund und Kantonen", NF87 *Zeitschrift für Schweizerisches Recht I*, 481 (1968).

133. See further Fleiner & Giacometti, supra n. 123 at 931-932, 935 ff.

134. See, e.g., Bundesgericht/Tribunal fédéral, judgment of March 23, 1977, Conseil d'Etat du canton de Genève v. Confédération suisse, BGE 103, Ia, 329 (1977), in which it was decided that a decision taken by the federal executive (the "Département fédéral des transports et communications et de l'énergie") had encroached upon the cantonal powers of Geneva and therefore had to be disregarded.

135. See Article 72 of the Swiss Constitution.

136. See Article 80 of the Swiss Constitution.

of their members is present).[137] This means in practice that a majority of the Cantons must at all times be in favor of any proposed national legislation. The political oversight of the Cantons makes up for a vacuum in their judicial protection against an excessive use by the federal legislature of its enumerated powers. In addition, this oversight mechanism is strengthened by the possibility for 50,000 citizens or eight Cantons to submit the proposed national legislation to a popular vote by referendum.[138] A qualified minority of Cantons then may try to use this vote in order to defend the reach of the cantonal powers as they see it, against the majority of Cantons that went along with the Conseil national to have the Confederation legislate on the subject matter at hand.

The Cantons possess in principle a concurrent power over all matters belonging to the sphere of powers of the Confederation to the extent that the latter has not exercised its powers.[139] This is only different when the Constitution expressly states that a power of the Confederation is exclusive[140] or when this conclusion should be inferred from the nature of the power granted to the Confederation.[141]

In the normal case of concurrent powers for the Confederation and the Cantons, the supremacy of federal over cantonal law leads the Bundesgericht/Tribunal fédéral to decide whether an exercise of power by the Confederation was exhaustive or not, so as to have

137. See Articles 87, 88 and 89(1) of the Swiss Constitution. In this respect, Swiss federalism sticks to the tradition of "federal bicameralism", as described by Herrero de Miñon, "The Passing of Bicameralism", 23 *Am. J. Comp. L.* 236, 237 ff. (1975).

138. See Article 89bis(2) of the Swiss Constitution.

139. See for a particularly straightforward formulation of this principle supra n. 128 at 68-69, No.2, b), and judgment of October 28, 1982, Schweizerische Eidgenossenschaft v. Kanton Basel-Stadt, BGE 108, I, 392, 397, No.2, b): "Die Gesetzgebungskompetenzen des Bundes lassen im allgemeinen die kantonale Zuständigkeit zur Legiferierung auf den entsprechenden Gebieten solange unberührt, bis der Bund von seiner Kompetenz Gebrauch macht und eine Ausführungsgesetzgebung erlässt".

140. See Article 38 (the power to coin money), 39 (the power to issue bank-notes and other types of paper money) and 41 (the power to decide on the manufacture and sale of gunpowder) of the Swiss Constitution.

141. See, e.g., Article 24quinquies of the Swiss Constitution, which states as follows: "(1) Legislation on atomic energy is a federal concern. (2) The Confederation shall enact regulations on protection against the danger resulting from ionising rays". This provision was interpreted as laying the basis for the existence of an exclusive power in favor of the national government in the field of atomic energy, see supra n. 134 at 336, No.3, b) (1977) - the court derived the exclusive character of the federal power from "the text and the genesis" of Article 24quinquies, as well as from the obvious need for uniformity in the regulation, or absence thereof, throughout the country as a whole, in matters relating to atomic energy (see also ibidem, at 340, No.5, b)). Thus, the Canton of Geneva could not oppose the construction or operation of a nuclear power plant on its territory, as decided by the federal authorities. It was, however, empowered to set its own conditions to the siting of such power plant, because this power was not connected to Article 24quinquies of the Swiss Constitution, but to the cantonal police powers (housing and urban planning).

possibly preempted all cantonal power in respect thereof. The preemption case law of the Bundesgericht/Tribunal fédéral is entirely reminiscent of the American judicial pronouncements on the issue in that not only the text of the national legislation is analyzed,[142] but also its implications,[143] in order to assess the scope of any remainder of cantonal power that should still exist.

Finally, Switzerland displays a good deal of "executive federalism". The Constitution regularly provides for basic legislation being enacted by the Confederation, while the Cantons have the obligation to further put into effect this legislation on their territory. The political process of the Cantons is thus enlisted to implement a national scheme of legislation, but - as is the case for the Member States in the European Community - the Cantons play a predominant role in the national political process itself, so that their executive legislation must in fact be viewed as the prolongation of what they decided to do in common at the level of the Confederation. The organic link between the Confederation and the Cantons in fact paves the way towards a smooth cooperation, often on an ad hoc basis in particular fields.[144]

B. *Devolutionary Federalism*

In countries where a unitary constitutional structure prevailed before the adventure of a federal system, the division of powers between the central government and the component entities is characterized by centrifugal tendencies that a self-protecting center intends to counter as effectively as possible. Examples are Belgium and Spain.

Canada should also be considered in this category, because its Constitution of 1867 contained a number of unitary features which were only gradually overcome by constitutional practice.[145] Thus, the power for the central government to disallow or reserve provin-

142. See Bundesgericht/Tribunal fédéral, judgment of May 8, 1963, Chambre vaudoise immobilière et consorts v. Grand Conseil du canton de Vaud, BGE 89, I, 178 (1963); judgment of November 5, 1975, Schneemobil-Club der Schweiz v. Vaud, Grand Conseil, BGE 101, Ia, 565 (1975).

143. See Bundesgericht/Tribunal fédéral, judgment of January 20, 1965, Fondation Nordmann v. Conseil d'Etat du canton de Genève, quoted supra, note 130, at 23, No.5 (in fine) (1965).

144. Thus, Article 32(2) of the Swiss Constitution declares with regard to the national economic powers: "The Cantons shall be consulted prior to the enactment of executory legislation. As a rule, the execution of the federal regulations shall be entrusted to them". Compare Häfelin, "Der kooperative Föderalismus in der Schweiz", NF 88 *Zeitschrift für Schweizerisches Recht II*, 549 (1969).

145. For an overview of these features, see Soberman, "The Canadian Federal Experience - Selected Issues", in Mauro Cappelletti, Monica Seccombe & Joseph Weiler (eds.) *Integration Through Law* 515 (1986).

cial legislation was no longer used after 1942.[146] The ensuing absence of political control by the central government over the Provinces has made that the latter did not become mere decentralized administrations of the central government. Customary constitutional law now guarantees the devolutionary dimension of Canadian federalism; it recognizes the Provinces as autonomous political powers, acting besides - and not under - the central government.[147]

The balance of powers inherent in devolutionary federalism aims at reconciling societal pluralism with a decent level of national cohesion. The component entities reflect the linguistic, religious, cultural, ethnic or simply regional differences existing within the country. Sometimes, these differences coincide with economic and social cleavages among the component entities. The central government stands for solidarity among the component entities and represents the nation as a whole.[148]

The picture that surfaces is one in which the central government devolves some of its powers to the component entities by express grant, possibly widened by the recognition of the necessary implications of such grant (i.e. the implied powers) in favor of the component entities. The residuary power rests with the central government, since it is still perceived as the ordinary bearer of sovereignty.[149]

However, given the basic distrust between the central government and the component entities - a constitutional undertone which contrasts sharply with the model of integrative federalism[150] - the relationship between the powers' spheres tends to be mutually exclusive. Devolutionary federalism therefore comes close to the concept of dual federalism, which seems discredited in American constitutional law.[151]

146. Id. at 516 and n. 15. However, still in 1938, the Supreme Court of Canada held that the power of disallowance and reservation of provincial legislation, as provided in section 90 of the Constitution Act of 1867, subsisted, (1938) S.C.R. 71. Between 1867 and 1942, especially in the first part of this period, the power was often used by the national government, see John D. Whyte & William R. Lederman, *Canadian Constitutional Law* 2-12, (1977).

147. The last codification of this development came with the Meech Lake Constitutional Accord (1987), see Peter W. Hogg, *Meech Lake Constitutional Accord Annotated* 55-85 (1988).

148. See Kenneth C. Wheare, *Federal Government* 112 (1963 fourth edition).

149. Compare Chester J. Anneau, *States' Rights under Federal Constitutions* 2-4 (1984) (giving an overview of federal societies with the residuum of power in the federation).

150. The Bundestreue is also at the heart of German federalism (another application of integrative federalism), see Schnapp, "Art.20 (Bundesstaatliche Verfassung; Widerstandsrecht)", in Ingo von Munch (ed.) *Grundgesetzkommentar* 724 (1976). The same principle is underlying Article 5 of the EEC Treaty.

151. See Corwin, "The Passing of Dual Federalism", 36 *Va.L.Rev.* 1 (1950); com-

The component entities defend the full size of the powers conferred upon them, whether or not they have exercised these powers. In their view, any further interference by the central government with the exercise of the powers granted to the component entities, must be rejected on the ground that the grant of powers is exclusive. The opposition of the component entities against a concurrent power for the central government over matters belonging to their sphere of responsibility mostly stems from the fear that the central government could be dominated by a competing component entity.[152] Only a sealing-off of the sphere of powers of the component entities as opposed to that of the central government seems appropriate to achieve the independence to which each component entity aspires in order to meet the needs flowing from its own identity within the broader national context.[153]

In addition, the central government's power being residuary, an inherent limitation of this power must be observed any time that its exercise would be likely to impinge upon the integrity of the powers granted exclusively to the component entities in the constitution.[154] This will only be different to the extent that some aspects of the central government's residuary power are constitutionally reserved to it, which normally occurs by singling out a number of "exclusive" powers within the general residuary power of the central government.[155]

---

pare Beer, "Federalism, Nationalism and Democracy in America", 72 *The American Political Science Review* 9 (1978).

152. See, e.g. section 92 of the Canadian Constitution Act of 1867, stating expressly the exclusive character of the powers granted to the Provinces. In Belgium, the Constitution is less explicit in this respect, but it flows from its context that the component entities enjoy, in principle, exclusive powers as to the matters entrusted to them, see Van Bol, "Les matières communautaires et régionales", 96 *Journal des Tribunaux* 633 (1981).

153. For an excellent account of this process as it took place in Belgium, see Covell, "Possibly Necessary but not Necessarily Possible: Revision of the Constitution in Belgium", in, Richard Simeon & Keith G. Banting, *Redesigning the State* 71 ff. (1985).

154. Thus, devolutionary federalism meets, albeit through a radically different mechanism of allocation of powers between the central government and the component entities, the concern stated by Charles Black in relation to U.S. federalism, *Perspectives in Constitutional Law* 25 (1970): "Here is one of the most important questions conceivable, with respect to the legal basis of federalism. Is there an implied limitation on the federal powers, to the effect that they shall not be used to deal with some matters under State authority. The prevalent modern answer is negative. But the grave corollary is that federalism has no basis in firm constitutional law. The federal powers. . . can be used to coerce any result, however 'local' unless such an implied limitation exists, and the concept of a legally defined federalism, judicially umpired, has then no substance."

155. See, e.g., section 91 of the Canadian Constitution Act of 1867, listing twenty-nine subjects of national power in addition to the general residuary power of the central government. Likewise, the Belgian Special Law of August 8, 1988 on institutional reforms specifies a number of powers, which are reserved to the central government (responsible for the general residuary power), Moniteur belge of August 13,

In case of a concrete conflict between normative acts based on two such exclusive powers, the central government will still not automatically get the law on its side. The outcome of the conflict must depend on the characterization of the normative acts involved under the respective powers being asserted. The more conclusive characterization prevails, while the other is held to be insufficient. Consequently, the normative act resting on the latter characterization will be discarded for transgression of power.[156]

It goes without saying that such rigid division of the powers of the central government and the component entities is hardly workable in practice. There are indeed instances in which two governments enact legislation plainly within their mutually exclusive powers and yet a normative conflict erupts. The solution then must proceed from concertation and cooperation between governments.[157] In addition, cooperation may also be needed in the relations of the component entities inter se. All these factors contribute to making devolutionary federalism rather different from one country to another.

B.1. Belgium

In its present constitutional structure, Belgium consists of three

1988, see Article 4, § 8 of the Law, replacing Article 6, § 1, VI in the Special Law of August 8, 1980, Moniteur belge of August 15, 1980. It are especially the economic powers of national importance that have been so reserved to the exclusive power of the central government.

156. Compare Lejeune, "Sur les méthodes d'interprétation des règles répartitrices de compétence", 106 *Journal des Tribunaux* 267 (1987); for an example in the Belgian case law, see Cour d'arbitrage, judgment of June 26, 1986, Moniteur belge, July 15, 1986.

157. Thus, in Belgium, the Special Law of August 8, 1988, quoted supra, note 155, provides for such concertation and cooperation in a number of policy areas involving at the same time regional and transregional interests, see Article 4, §§ 15-16, inserted as § 3bis and § 4 into Article 6 of the Special Law of August 8, 1980. Likewise, in Canada, the Meech Lake Constitutional Accord has formalized the concertation to be held between the national and the provincial governments, see the Constitution Amendment 1987, inserting section 148 into the Constitution Act of 1982: "A conference composed of the Prime Minister of Canada and the first ministers of the provinces shall be convened by the Prime Minister of Canada at least once each year to discuss the state of the Canadian economy and such other matters as may be appropriate". Besides, section 50, inserted also by the Constitution Amendment 1987, provides that "(1) A constitutional conference composed of the Prime Minister of Canada and the first ministers of the provinces shall be convened by the Prime Minister of Canada at least once each year, commencing in 1988. (2) The conferences convened under subsection (1) shall have included on their agenda the following matters: (a) Senate reform, including the role and functions of the Senate, its powers, the method of selecting Senators and representation in the Senate; (b) roles and responsibilities in relation to fisheries; and (c) such other matters as are agreed upon". In other words, in Canada, intergovernmental conferences should be held yearly, not only in order to guarantee a decent functioning of the federal system as to the ordinary exercise of public authority, but also as a means of continuous development of that system itself.

Regions (the Flemish Region, the Walloon Region and the Brussels-Capital Region) and three "Communities" (the Flemish Community, the French Community and the German-speaking Community).[158] The Regions and the Communities do not coincide as to the territory over which they exercise their powers, nor as to the content of the latter. The Regions deal mainly with the local economy, employment, the environment, the policies of housing and urban planning and major aspects of highways, ports, airports and other transportation infrastructure.[159] The Communities, on the contrary, are entities empowered to legislate on matters related to the personality of their inhabitants, such as language, culture, social life and, since a constiutional reform of 1988, education.[160]

The first move towards devolutionary federalism was made by the creation in 1970 of the Communities; the second step came in 1980 with the organization of the Regions; finally, the third stage (1988) inaugurates a dramatic increase in the powers and financial means devolved by the central State on both the Communities and the Regions.

The Flemish Region is the Dutch-speaking northern part of Belgium; the Flemish Community spreads its power over the same area but includes, in addition, the Dutch-speaking socio-cultural institutions established in the Brussels-Capital Region.[161] The Walloon Region is composed of the French-speaking southern part of Belgium, augmented by the south-eastern area that is German-speaking (the "Ostkantone"). When it comes to the division of this Region into "Communities", there is on the one hand the French Community, competent for the French-speaking territory of the Walloon Region and the French-speaking socio-cultural institutions established in the Brussels-Capital Region, and on the other, the German-speaking Community with territorial competence for the "Ostkantone."[162]

As far as institutions are concerned, the Flemish Region and the Flemish Community share the same legislature (the "Flemish Council") and the same executive (the "Flemish Executive"). Besides, there is the "Walloon Regional Council" (legislature of the Walloon Region) and the "Walloon Regional Executive", the "French Com-

158. See Articles 107quater and 3ter of the Belgian Constitution.

159. See Article 6 of the Special Law of August 8, 1980, Moniteur belge of August 15, 1980, as amended by the Special Law of August 8, 1988, Moniteur belge of August 13, 1988.

160. See Article 59bis of the Belgian Constitution, as amended on July 15, 1988, Moniteur belge of July 19, 1988, and Articles 4 and 5 of the Special Law of August 8, 1980, Moniteur belge of August 15, 1980, as amended by the Special Law of August 8, 1988, Moniteur belge of August 13, 1988.

161. See Article 59bis, §§ 4 and 4bis of the Belgian Constitution.

162. See id., and Article 59ter of the Belgian Constitution.

munity Council" (legislature of the French Community) and the "French Community Executive", and the "German-speaking Community Council" (legislature of the German-speaking Community) and the "German-speaking Community Executive". It should be noted that all these legislatures are deemed to stand at the same normative level as the national Parliament for those matters belonging to their sphere of competence.[163] Thus e.g., the Flemish Council may repeal - for its territory - a national law and replace it by a regional law, if the matter dealt with falls within the constitutional definition of the regional legislative powers. There is no form of political supervision by the central State over the exercise of powers by the Regions or the "Communities".

The legislative and executive organs of the Brussels-Capital Region have been set up in 1989.[164] The legislative acts of this Region have a somewhat lesser normative status than the corresponding acts of the Flemish and Walloon Region.[165]In political terms, it is important to stress that for the time being the members of the Flemish and French/Walloon Community and regional legislatures are respectively the Dutch-speaking and the French-speaking members of the Chamber of Representatives and the directly elected segment of the Senate.[166] The same persons thus have a "double mandate": one to sit as national legislator and one to sit as Community/regional legislator. Furthermore, each legislature elects or gives its confidence to a government resting on a parliamentary majority.[167] Problems inevitably arise when the same majority cannot be found in all four legislatures (national, Flemish, French Community and Walloon Region), so that members act as part of the parliamentary majority in one legislature, yet oppose each other in the other legislature.

A further step must therefore be taken to end the "double mandate" and give the Community/regional legislatures an autonomous

163. See Article 19, § 2 of the Special Law of August 8, 1980, Moniteur belge of August 15, 1980.

164. Special Law of January 12, 1989, Moniteur belge of January 14, 1989.

165. On the basis of Article 107 of the Belgian Constitution, all courts and tribunals will have the right to rule themselves on the compatibility of the Brussels regional laws with the Constitution and the Special Law of January 12, 1989 that organizes the Brussels-Capital Region, whereas in relation to the Flemish and Walloon regional laws, they must refer the issue to the constitutional court, the Cour d'arbitrage. In addition, in some cases, the national government could intervene in regional matters so as to safeguard the position of Brussels as the country's capital and as the seat of the European Community and of some international organizations (e.g. NATO).

166. See Articles 25 and 29 of the Special Law of August 8, 1980, Moniteur belge of August 15, 1980.

167. See Article 59 ff. of the Special Law of August 8, 1980, Moniteur belge of August 15, 1980.

status through separate elections.[168] Any joint loyalty to the Nation and the Community/Region that might still exist in the minds of the members of the Chamber of Representatives and the directly elected Senators, will then disappear. When different officials represent the - often conflicting - loyalties to the Nation and the Community/Region, Belgium is to resemble Canada on the point that the central government and the component entity governments have a distinct electoral legitimacy and operate in full independence of each other.

What remains, however, for Belgium, is the protection in the Constitution of the two linguistic communities in the operation of the central government. Although 60% of the country are Dutch-speakers and 40% French-speakers, the cabinet-level ministers are equally divided among the two communities, with the possible exception of the Prime Minister.[169] Recent practice has been that he is a bilingual Flemish politician - in the jargon of Belgian politics, "un assexué linguistique" - and further that when he should be French-speaking, he must also be bilingual and will be counted on the French-speaking contingent in the cabinet. This is the political interpretation of the 60%/40% linguistic split, while it sticks to the constitutionally mandated parity among cabinet-level ministers. Moreover, the parity rule does not apply to the junior ministers (Secrétaires d'Etat, Staatssecretarissen), who are divided more or less 60%/40% among the two communities.[170]

In the national Parliament, on the contrary, both chambers are based on a proportional representation of the Belgian population as a whole.[171] As a consequence there is a considerable Flemish majority in each chamber.[172] But special constitutional rules exist in order to protect each community against the invasion of its interests by the other in the national Parliament. For some sensitive laws, a separate majority counting must take place within each linguistic group of both chambers,[173] and for all other laws, a linguistic group

168. This step implies a reform of the Senate (revision of Articles 53 and 54 of the Belgian Constitution) and is already formally announced since 1980, in the provisions of the Special Law of August 8, 1980, quoted supra n. 156.

169. See Article 86bis of the Belgian Constitution.

170. See Article 91bis of the Belgian Constitution, that explicitly excludes the operation of Article 86bis with regard to the Secrétaires d'Etat/Staatssecretarissen.

171. See Articles 32, 49 (Chamber of Representatives) and 53-54 (Senate) of the Belgian Constitution.

172. See Article 32bis of the Belgian Constitution, and the Law of July 3, 1971, Moniteur belge of July 6, 1971, under which all members of the Chamber of Representatives and the Senate belong either to the Flemish or the French-speaking group of their chamber. The division of the members of the national Parliament elected on December 13, 1987, over the two linguistic groups is as follows: out of 212 members of the Chamber of Representatives 124 are Flemish and 88 are French-speaking; out of 183 members of the Senate 105 are Flemish and 78 are French-speaking.

173. See Article 1, last paragraph, of the Belgian Constitution.

can resort to the "sonette d'alarme", a mechanism allowing it to block the ordinary legislative process and have its concerns specially considered.[174]

Devolutionary federalism in Belgium is not only a system of mutually exclusive powers between the central government and the Community/regional governments, but also a constitutional mingling of the communities within the operation of the central government (the latter sometimes looks more like a national platform for concertation among the linguistic communities than a separate authority coexisting with the Communities/Regions). In addition, at present, there remains the organic grip of the central government on the Community/regional governments, in that members of the national legislature man the Community/regional legislatures. It is odd to see a dual federalism (as to the division of powers) borne by one organic structure whose several components are intertwined in so many reciprocal and complex ways.

No wonder that practical politics often require a more straightforward dealing with the issues of the time. To that end, a concertation committee was instituted.[175] It assembles on a regular basis the representatives of the national cabinet and the Community/regional executives to discuss all matters of common interest. In a number of cases, the committee must be consulted before legislation is passed.[176] The committee also hears complaints when a Community/regional executive or the national cabinet feels that its interests are threatened by another entity's action.[177] Political issues of some importance can only be solved in Belgium, when a compromise is backed by the concertation committee.

Lastly, it should be mentioned that Belgian devolutionary federalism has had to make a deliberate effort during the last two decades to save the existence of an economic and monetary union and a common market for goods, workers, services and capital in the country as a whole.[178]

Economic competition between the Regions once led to a Walloon law imposing an "export duty" on the deliveries of water to the

174. See Article 38bis of the Belgian Constitution.

175. See Article 31 of the Law of August 9, 1980, Moniteur belge of August 15, 1980.

176. See supra n. 157.

177. For the procedure, see Articles 32 and 33 of the Law of August 9, 1980, Moniteur belge of August 15, 1980. It should be stressed that the concertation committee deals only with conflicts of interests, not with conflicts of powers. The latter are to be judged by the constitutional court, the Cour d'arbitrage, see Article 107ter of the Belgian Constitution, implemented through the Law of June 28, 1983, Moniteur belge of July 8, 1983.

178. See generally in this respect, Jean-M. Van Bol, *Politique économique et pouvoir régional* (1982); C. Vanderveeren, P. Van Rompuy, D. Heremans & E. Heylen, *De economische en monetaire unie in de Belgische Staatshervorming* (1987).

Flemish and the Brussels-Capital Region (i.e. a payment unrelated to the actual production cost of the water). Wallonia relied both on its taxing power and on its power to regulate the environment and the water industry. The national government came up against the tax, arguing that it was contrary to the concept of a Belgian common market inherent in the federal system. The Cour d'arbitrage, Belgium's constitutional court composed equally of Dutch-speakers and French-speakers, adhered to this argument. It struck down the Walloon tax on the ground that Belgium remained - even though implicitly - an economic and monetary union and a common market.[179] In 1988, the principle was written into the constitutional texts so as to increase legal certainty in this matter of primary importance for the survival of the Nation.[180]

The Walloon water tax incident deserves more than just passing attention. It demonstrates that societal pluralism coinciding with the split between the component entities of a devolutionary federal system can exacerbate centrifugal tendencies to such extent as to imperil the basics of federalism, prevailing in countries where this constitutional model is used to integrate what was previously independent rather than to disintegrate (even though formally in a limited way only) what was previously unitary.[181]

B.2. Canada

Societal pluralism in Canada is different from that existing in Belgium. Whereas Belgium is a country with two unilingual component entities and a bilingual capital and central administration, Canada in its entirety is characterized by linguistic duality coupled with the status of Quebec as a "distinct society."[182] The new section 2 of

179. Judgment of February 25, 1988, Moniteur belge of March 17, 1988. For another ruling of the Cour d'arbitrage on the existence of a Belgian economic and monetary union, albeit in a much more limited setting, see the judgment of February 25, 1986, Moniteur belge of March 19, 1986.

180. See the new version of Article 6, 1, VI, of the Special Law of August 8, 1980, adopted on August 8, 1988, Moniteur belge of August 13, 1988, providing, inter alia, as follows: "En matière économique, les Régions exercent leurs compétences dans le respect des principes de la libre circulation des personnes, biens, services et capitaux et de la liberté de commerce et d'industrie, ainsi que dans le respect du cadre normatif général de l'union économique et de l'unité monétaire, tel qu'il est établi par ou en vertu de la loi, et par ou en vertu des traités internationaux".

181. Compare the focus of Swiss federalism, achieving first the national common market as a basis for further integration, respectful of sociocultural, religious and linguistic diversity - Article 31 of the Swiss Constitution (1874).

182. See Hogg, supra n. 147 at 11-16; compare Woehrling, "La modification constitutionnelle de 1987, la reconnaissance du Québec comme société distincte et la dualité linguistique du Canada", 29 *Cahiers de Droit* 3, 11 (1988), making reference to a warning pronounced on May 27, 1987, by former Prime Minister P.E. Trudeau against a constitutional reform that would split Canada into two unilingual parts. The Meech Lake Constitutional Accord of June 3, 1987 dropped the terms "French-speaking Canada" and "English-speaking Canada", that were used in the "Meech

the Constitution Act, introduced in the wake of the Meech Lake Constitutional Accord of 1987 confirms these principles in its first paragraph: "The Constitution of Canada shall be interpreted in a manner consistent with (a) the recognition that the existence of French-speaking Canadians, centred in Quebec but also present elsewhere in Canada, and English-speaking Canadians, concentrated outside Quebec but also present in Quebec, constitutes a fundamental characteristic of Canada; and (b) the recognition that Quebec constitutes within Canada a distinct society". The division of powers between the central government and the Provinces does not depend on the operation of these principles. It flows from the constitutional text existing since 1867 and the case law of the courts as well as political practice.[183]

Federalism in Canada is somehow crossed by an effort on the part of the central government to enlist the support of the Provinces in carrying into execution national political choices. Two principal mechanisms are being used to that effect.

Firstly, there is the use of the federal spending power through grants to the Provinces conditioned on the enactment of appropriate legislation. Thus, the central government can assure that uniform standards of services to all Canadians be observed throughout the country.[184] However, the ensuing redistribution of wealth on a national scale has caused some anger with the richer Provinces, feeling that they contribute more to the central treasury than their return from it would justify.[185] In addition, the Provinces generally argue that a system of conditional grants upsets the order of their own political priorities. In Quebec, the resentment against such system was especially great, because it appeared as a threat to this Province's francophone identity making it a "distinct society" within Canada. Hence, Quebec refused to participate in some nationwide social programs based on conditional grants by the central government. It ran instead its own programs and managed to obtain - as a "distinct society" - an unconditional grant of funds by the central government.[186]

Lake Communiqué" (a kind of draft accord) of April 30, 1987, and chose instead for the wording that became the "Constitution Amendment 1987", inserted as section 2 into the Constitution Act of 1867.

183. See Soberman, supra n. 145 at 513-516.

184. Compare section 36(2) of the Constitution Act of 1982: "Parliament and the government of Canada are committed to the principle of making equalization payments to ensure that provincial governments have sufficient revenues to provide reasonably comparable levels of taxation".

185. See Judith B. Maxwell & Caroline Pestieau, *Economic Realities of Contemporary Confederation* 59-76 (1980).

186. See Richard Simeon, *Federal-Provincial Diplomacy: The Making of Recent Policy in Canada* 43-87 (1972). With the Constitution Amendment 1987, a limit is set to the spending power of the national Parliament when this power is used to estab-

Secondly, concertation among the 10 provincial governments and the national government is necessary to keep the country going. It takes place within the so-called "intergovernmental committees". In case of success of the concertation, the outcome may be a delegation of central powers to the Provinces, or else an undertaking by the Provinces to enact the legislation needed to put into effect a national legislative framework.[187] Since, as opposed to the Belgian situation, all the governments involved enjoy a real organic independence and rely on their own democratic legitimacy, the concertation turns easily into an open intergovernmental negotiation characteristic of a confederal constitutional structure.[188] The need for concertation is still increased by the fact that - again as opposed to Belgium - the Provinces have no constitutionally protected representation at the level of the central government. The Senate consists of members appointed by the national government.[189] The Lower Chamber consists of 282 members elected in single-member constituencies. All Provinces are represented, more or less in accordance with their share of the national population.[190] But the simple majority of the members of the Lower Chamber holds the government-making power proper to a parliamentary system of government as well as the legislative power. No constitutional guarantees are built into the system, so that weaker Provinces can be outvoted without any possible appeal.

With regard to the national Cabinet, the aspiration of having all

lish a nationwide shared-cost program in an area of exclusive provincial jurisdiction. The newly introduced section 106A of the Constitution Act requires that any such program must include an opting-out alternative for any Province that chooses not to participate in the national program. The latter must however receive "reasonable compensation" from the government of Canada, "if the Province carries a program or initiative that is compatible with the national objectives". For more details, see Hogg supra n. 147 at 37-42.

187. For a comparison of the Canadian intergovernmental concertation with the process of decision-making within the Council of the European Communities, see Soberman, supra n. 145 at 535-538.

188. Compare Hogg, supra n. 147 at 53-54.

189. It should, however, be noted that the Constitution Amendment 1987 introduced a new section 25 into the Constitution Act of 1867, requiring that appointments to the Senate be made from names submitted by the government of the Province to which the vacancy relates, provided that the persons whose names have been submitted are acceptable to the national government. See also section 24 of the Constitution Act of 1867, and sections 21 and 22 of this Act as to the distribution of senators among the several Provinces. The drafters of the Constitution Amendment 1987 saw the new section 25 as a transitional measure, until a more thorough reform of the Senate could be achieved on the basis of a unanimous agreement among the Provinces, see the wording of section 25(2) and section 50(2)(a) - as to this latter provision, see supra, note 157. Even in the absence of such intended reform, section 25 may contribute to a transformation of the Canadian Senate into an upper chamber in which the component entities of the federation are represented as such, albeit on an unequal basis.

190. See section 37 of the Constitution Act of 1867.

the Provinces represented is a most real one in the selection process of the ministers, but it remains a political aspiration, without any basis in the Constitution itself. Moreover, when the majority party does not count members in the Lower Chamber from a particular Province, it will be materially impossible to have a Cabinet member from that Province, as all Cabinet members are to be chosen among parliamentarians.[191]These factors make the need for intergovernmental concertation all the more pressing. At the same time, they explain why several impasses of Canadian federalism have still been aggravated by the absence of an adequately structured machinery for intergovernmental concertation as it exists in the European Community and Belgium.[192]

In Canada, linguistic and regional differences among the Provinces have also stimulated economic particularism and continue to threaten the common market. According to one commentator, the Canadian market is in several respects less integrated than the European Community market.[193]

B.3. Spain

A third country to have resorted to devolutionary federalism, in order to counter the tensions placed upon its cohesion as a consequence of societal pluralism, is Spain. The Constitution of 1978 states in its preamble that it aims at protecting all the Spanish and the peoples of Spain in the exercise of their fundamental rights, the pursuit of their cultures and traditions, their languages and institutions. Pursuant to Article 2, the Constitution is based on the undissolvable unity of the Spanish Nation, the common and indivisible fatherland of all the Spanish, and recognizes and guarantees the right to autonomy of the nationalities and regions composing it, as well as the solidarity among the latter. Furthermore, Article 3 confirms that "castillano" is the official Spanish language of the State; all Spanish have a duty to know it and a right to use it; the other Spanish languages are also official in the respective Comunidades Autónomas as provided for in their basic statutes. Linguistic diversity is even being praised in Article 3 (3) as a richness and a cultural heritage of the country as a whole, which are to be given special protection and respect.

The Spanish variant of devolutionary federalism is unique, as the Constitution sets up a permissive framework within which the component entities can be constituted, in essence on the initiative of

191. For examples, see Soberman, supra n. 145 at 533-535.
192. Id. at 532.
193. Id. at 548-552, especially No.3 at 552. But see section 121 of the Constitution Act of 1867.

the provinces concerned. Each Comunidad Autónoma elaborates its own basic statute, containing the name of the Comunidad (it must correspond to its historical identity), the delimitation of its territory, the organization of its institutions, and finally the powers taken up by the Comunidad out of a list of possible powers stated in Article 148 (1) of the Constitution.[194]

The idea is that each of the component entities determines itself the pace of its process towards regional autonomy. For some regions, autonomy comes at last as an answer to longstanding aspirations, given their linguistic or cultural identity. Examples are the País Vasco, Cataluña and Galicia, the three Comunidades Autónomas that were formed first.[195] In other regions, economic aspirations that matured over time prevailed. This was the case for the fourth Comunidad, Andalucia.[196]At present, seventeen Comunidades Autónomas are in operation, some of which represent a rather new regional identity.[197]

The precise content of the powers of each Comunidad Autónoma is not only different because another choice was made in the seventeen basic statutes as to the twenty-two possible powers listed in Article 148(1), but also because the first four Comunidades Autónomas used the possibility which was offered to them, albeit under a somewhat more demanding procedure leading to their constitution,[198] to include into their basic statutes some additional powers not listed in Article 148(1), but not granted to the exclusive competence of the Spanish State either.[199] The other thirteen

---

194. See Articles 143 and 147 of the Spanish Constitution. Compare Franck Moderne & Pierre Bon, *Les autonomies régionales dans la Constitution espagnole* 85 ff. (1981).

195. The first two received their autonomy by basic statute of December 18, 1979, the third by basic statute of April 6, 1981.

196. Basic statute of December 30, 1981.

197. In addition to the four Comunidades Autónomas that were just mentioned, they are the Principado de Asturias (basic statute of December 30, 1981), the Comunidad Autónoma de Cantabria (basic statute of December 30, 1981), the Comunidad Autónoma de La Rioja (basic state of June 9, 1982), the Región de Murcia (basic statute of June 9, 1982), the Comunidad Valenciana (basic statute of July 1, 1982), the Comunidad Autónoma dc Aragón (basic statute of August 10, 1982), the Comunidad Autónoma de Castilla - La Mancha (basic statute of August 10, 1982), the Comunidad Autónoma de Canarias (basic statute of August 10, 1982), the Comunidad Foral de Navarra (basic statute of August 10, 1982), the Comunidad Autonoma de Estremadura (basic statute of February 25, 1983), the Comunidad Autónoma de las Islas Baleares (basic statute of February 25, 1983), the Comunidad de Madrid (basic statute of February 25, 1983), and the Comunidad de Castilla y Léon (basic statute of February 25, 1983).

198. See Article 151 of the Spanish Constitution and the comments on this procedure by Moderne & Bon, supra n. 194 at 55 ff.

199. See the list of exclusive powers of the Spanish State in Article 149(1) of the Constitution, naming thirty-two subject matters. The constitutional basis for the powers claimed by the País Vasco, Cataluña, Galicia and Andalucía, in addition to those mentioned in Article 148(1) of the Spanish Constitution, is provided by Article

Comunidades will receive this possibility, five years after their initial constitution, and this through a formal amendment of their basic statute.[200] The residuary power lies with the central government. Thirty-two aspects of it are reserved in Article 149(1) as "exclusive powers" of the Spanish State. All other aspects are subject to a possible transfer to the Comunidades Autónomas or to some of them, when they make a request to that effect and the Spanish Parliament approves it.[201] These principles imply that the residuary power of the central government is not exactly the same vis-à-vis all seventeen Comunidades Autónomas. Its extent will vary according to the choices made as to the component entity's powers in the basic statute of the latter. This is how devolutionary federalism becomes flexible enough to be tuned to different degrees of maturity reached in the drive for autonomy from one region of the country to another.[202]

The substance of the twenty-two possible powers listed in favor of the Comunidades Autónomas is very similar to the powers conferred by Belgian constitutional law to the Communities and Regions, e.g. the local economy, social policy, infrastructure, environmental protection, energy policy, cultural affairs, education, etc.[203] Likewise, most of the powers explicitly reserved to the Spanish State - within the broader scope of its general residuary power - enjoy the same status in Belgium, e.g. international relations, defense, general economic cohesion within the country, and the legislation on the recognition by the State of academic degrees.[204]

The Comunidades Autónomas have a directly elected legislature, an executive relying on a majority within the legislature, and a president chosen among the members of the legislature and thereafter appointed by the King of Spain.[205] These institutions enjoy com-

148(2) which refers to Article 149 (see especially the first and third paragraphs of this Article) and must further be combined with Article 151.

200. See Article 148(2) of the Spanish Constitution, applying to all Comunidades Autónomas created under the ordinary procedure laid down in Articles 143-147; contrast Articles 151-152 as to the first four Comunidades Autónomas that already enjoy a higher status of autonomy.

201. Compare Garcia de Enterria, "La significación de las competencias exclusivas del Estado en el sistema autonómico", *Revista española de derecho constitucional* No.5, 63 (1982).

202. See Santiago Muñoz Machado, *El derecho publico de la Comunidades Autónomas* 153 ff. (1983).

203. See the list of subject matters contained in Article 148(1) of the Spanish Constitution.

204. See the list of subject matters contained in Article 149(1) of the Spanish Constitution.

205. See Article 152 of the Spanish Constitution, applicable to those Comunidades Autónomas, constituted under the procedure laid down in Article 151, and compare Article 147, which leaves more freedom with regard to the institutional framework of the Comunidades Autónomas, constituted in accordance with Articles 143-146.

plete independence from the organs of the central government.

The organic representation of the Comunidades Autónomas at the level of the central government is rather weak. It exists only in the Senate, where 46 Senators appointed by the legislatures of the Comunidades Autónomas hold a seat along with the 208 Senators who are directly elected within the provinces. Each Comunidad Autónoma has at least one Senator, increased with one per million of inhabitants.[206] Moreover, members of the legislature of a Comunidad Autónoma cannot at the same time be a member of the Lower Chamber of the Spanish Parliament.[207] This again underscores the separate institutional set-up of the several governments. But the legislature of a Comunidad Autónoma may take the initiative of national legislation and have three of its members defend a draft bill before the Lower Chamber of the Spanish Parliament.[208] In Belgium, a similar practice could in fact be followed as a result of the "double mandate" of the parliamentarians.

On the whole, the Spanish constitutional order is not described as properly federal in doctrinal writings of the last decade. One author speaks about "autonomías integradas."[209] The expression of "Estado de las Autonomías" is also used.[210] The term federalism apparently is avoided because it is somewhat hastily associated with a strictly devolutionary process while the Constitution aims in fact at the integration of the country under respect of the diversity which characterizes it. This leaves traces of a unitary posture that could threaten the power status of the Comunidades Autónomas.

Thus, Article 150(3) of the Constitution allows the central government to harmonize, in the country's general interest, the several legislative measures of the Comunidades Autónomas even in matters which belong to their sphere of powers.[211] Such national power is unthinkable in Belgian or Canadian federalism, but it could exist in the European Community (Article 100 of the EEC Treaty) or in

---

206. See Article 69(5) of the Spanish Constitution.

207. See Article 67(1) of the Spanish Constitution.

208. See Article 87(2) of the Spanish Constitution.

209. Perez Moreno, "El concepto de 'Autonomías integradas': una clave interpretación de la Constitución española", in *Comunidades Autónomas* 11-44 (1980).

210. Peces-Barba, *La constitución española de 1978*, p.172 ff. (1981). Compare the term "Estado autonómico" preferred by Luis Sanchez Agesta, *El sistema político de la Constitución española* 343 ff. (1981), and Enrique Alvarez Conde, *El régimen político español* 57 ff. (1983).

211. Compare Garcia Lopez, "El marco del Estado autonómico y la naturaleza, significado y efectos de los preceptos contenidos en el articulo 150 de la constitución", *Revista de derecho político* No.17, 85 (1983). The Tribunal constitucional made it clear, however, that Article 150(3) may not be used to encroach unnecessarily upon the powers of the Comunidades Autónomas, see Decision No.78/1983 of August 5, 1983, Boletin Official del Estado of August 18, 1983, Supplement to No.197, p.29.

the United States when properly connected to the regulation of interstate commerce.

Furthermore, Article 155 of the Constitution provides for a political supervision over the Comunidades Autónomas by the central government. When a Comunidad Autónoma does not properly implement national law[212] or acts in a way which is inconsistent with the general interest of the country, the central government may take the appropriate measures (even though in the latter case the Comunidad Autónoma acted within the formal reach of its own powers). Here again, such mechanism cannot be imagined in Belgium nor in Canada after the falling into disuse of the central government's power to disallow or reserve otherwise valid provincial legislation on political grounds. In the European Community, on the contrary, Article 5 of the EEC Treaty imposes on the Member States a general obligation of "Gemeinschaftstreue", that is a duty to observe the Community's interest even when they deal with matters that fall within their sphere of residual powers. A violation of this obligation is not to be redressed in a political way, but it may lead to an action brought before the Court of Justice by the Commission under Article 169 of the EEC Treaty.

The conclusion therefore must be that Spain follows its own path towards devolutionary federalism. The Constitution of 1978 contains all elements as to the division of powers between the central government and the component entities to consider such federalism present in its essence. Differing with the Belgian and Canadian advocates of this type of federalism, however, the Spanish constitutional draftsmen have put a more efficient integrative brake on the centrifugal forces put into motion by the natural diversity existing in the country for centuries. Still, as the State structure immediately preceding the Constitution of 1978 was a unitary one, the main tenor of the new system of divided powers is devolutionary, even if counterbalanced by integrative mechanisms which appear to be absent in other systems of devolutionary federalism such as Belgium and Canada.

The general conclusion to the first comparative theme dealt with so far, must be that the tension between enumerated powers and residual powers is common to both integrative and devolutionary systems of federalism, whatever the precise terms of it are in each system considered by itself. In addition, the government hold-

212. The Spanish Constitution does not elaborate in any coherent and express way a system of "executive federalism", but it proceeds manifestly from such system in all of its structural features; see Tribunal constitucional, Decision No.35/1982 of June 14, 1982, Boletin Official del Estado of June 28, 1982, Supplement to No. 153, p.18. Compare Eduardo Garcia de Enterria & Tomas R. Fernandez, *Curso de derecho administrativo* 309 ff. (1983 fourth edition).

ing the enumerated powers has a natural tendency to increase its authority, whether it is the central government (integrative federalism) or the component entity's government (devolutionary federalism). The means used to that end are an extensive interpretation of the expressly listed powers and, at times, an acceptance of implied powers, "necessary and proper" to carry into execution the express powers.[213] The government retaining the residuary power is more likely to be threatened. It therefore tries to "reserve" (make "exclusive" in its favor) the most sensitive - or possibly all - aspects of this power. This effort led to the dual sovereignty thesis developed as to the powers of the American States or the Member States in the European Community, but it largely failed. A similar effort was made - this time with greater success - by the central government holding the residuary power in the systems of devolutionary federalism that have been analyzed. It even seemed the only way to save a vital degree of national cohesion in these systems. The Belgian, Canadian and Spanish Constitutions all lend support to this thesis.

II. THE JUDICIAL UMPIRING OF INTEGRATIVE AND DEVOLUTIONARY FEDERALISM

The second major aspect of comparative federalism concerns the "umpiring" of the relationship between the central government and the component entities within the common constitutional order.[214]

This expression applies to the role played by the supreme judicial body in integrative as well as in devolutionary federal systems. As a unique balance of power between the central government and the component entities structures every exercise of public authority in both varieties of federalism, it follows that they share the same need for a final umpire whose judgment may be requested by any

213. Thus, the Belgian Communities/Regions may claim the implied powers which appear to be "indispensable" to the exercise of their enumerated powers, Article 10 of the Special Law of August 8, 1980, Moniteur belge of August 15, 1980. The term "indispensable" was to guarantee that the use of implied powers be kept at a minimum, somewhat in the line of the anti-federalist interpretation of the Necessary and Proper Clause during the early decades of the American Union, see John A. Garraty, *A Short History of the American Nation* 88 (1974). In Belgium, however, the pressure on the concept of implied powers has been in the direction of a more flexible reasonableness standard. In order to express that development, the Special Law of August 8, 1988, replaced the word "indispensable" by the less rigid "necessary" (Article 8), Moniteur belge of August 13, 1988. The main difference with the United States as to the relaxation of the boundaries of the constitutionally recognized implied powers is that in American constitutional law it works in favor of the Union, bearer of the enumerated powers (centripetal movement), whereas in the Belgian context it strengthens the devolution of powers to the country's component entities (centrifugal movement). Or in other words, the technique is similar, but its effects are divergent in the two types of federalism.

214. See Freund, "Umpiring the Federal System", 54 *Col.L. Rev.* 561 (1954).

government which feels threatened in its powers, whether it be the central government or the government of a component entity.

The mechanisms of judicial umpiring, however, differ from one federal system to another. Equally different are the basic features of each common constitutional order that determine the significance of the pronouncements made by the central judiciary as umpire of the federal system and the latitude that legislatures still enjoy towards these pronouncements. These considerations will now be dealt with in consecutive order.

(a) The mechanisms of the judicial umpiring of the federal system

It would seem appropriate to take as a starting point the view held by Supreme Court Justice Oliver Wendell Holmes with regard to U.S. federalism: "I do not think the United States would come to an end if we lost our power to declare an Act of Congress void. I do think the Union would be imperiled if we could not make that declaration as to the laws of the several States".[215]

This view neatly suits Swiss federalism, in which the Bundesgericht/Tribunal fédéral cannot, under Article 113(3) of the Constitution, declare an act of the national legislature void, whereas it can "make that declaration as to the laws of the several (Cantons)".[216] It goes without saying that national coherence is not "imperiled" in Switzerland as a consequence of this one-way-only characteristic of the judicial umpiring of Swiss federalism. The question, however, would rather seem to be whether the constitutional autonomy of the Cantons is not "imperiled". As already indicated, the answer must be negative, because of the presence of the Cantons within the operation of the central government and the final political oversight of the people by referendum organized at the request of a minority of eight Cantons (out of 23).[217]

In the other federal systems here under consideration, the judiciary is competent to review central legislation on its compatibility with the division of powers contained in the constitution.[218] But

215. Oliver Wendall Holmes, *Collected Legal Papers* 295-296 (1920).

216. See Hangartner, supra n. 125 at 196-198.

217. Compare Aubert, "Le referendum populaire", NF91 *Zeitschrift für Schweizerisches Recht I*, 481 (1972).

218. See, with regard to the Court of Justice of the European Communities, Articles 173, 177 and 184 of the EEC Treaty and comments by Lenaerts, supra n. 15 at chapter V. As to the operation of the Belgian Cour d'arbitrage, a special judicial body to which the enforcement of the constitutional division of powers both against the central and the component entities' legislators has been entrusted, see Jean-Paul Lagasse & Serge Moureaux, *La Cour d'arbitrage. Juridiction constitutionnelle* (1984). In Canada, an additional hurdle had to be overcome, due to the English tradition of parliamentary sovereignty, not subject to judicial review, see Lederman,

there are signs of judicial restraint when it comes to overseeing the legislature of the judge's own level of government. Considerations inherent in the principle of separation of powers then necessarily cross the enforcement of the constitutional division of powers between the central government and the component entities.[219]

The phenomenon is well known since Chief Justice Marshall recognized a wide scope to the concept of implied powers vested in Congress under the Necessary and Proper Clause.[220] It was in fact quite a strategy to make an extensive reading of this constitutional provision and yet to couch it into a posture of judicial deference towards a legislative judgment made by Congress under the Constitution.[221]

The Court of Justice took a similar attitude when it had to rule about the reach of Community powers defined in the Treaties. It showed a readiness to normally uphold the Commission's view about the content of a particular Community power, including the implicit aspects of such power, except when the Commission's "legislative" judgment appeared to be manifestly incompatible with the constitutional text.[222]

In the European Community, the procedure which allows the Court of Justice to declare central legislation void, is very straightforward, since Member States, the Council, and the Commission may initiate it without having to demonstrate any concrete interest

"Review of B.L. Strayer, Judicial Review of Legislation in Canada", 16 *McGill L. J.*, 723, 725-727 (1970-71). As to Spain, see Articles 161 to 165 of its Constitution, commented by Pierre Bon, Franck Moderne & Y. Rodriguez, *La justice constitutionnelle en Espagne* 136-141 (1984).

219. In Belgium, this concern received still another expression. Since the country traditionally lived under a regime of unreviewability of the acts of Parliament (in line with the English parliamentary system), the practical need to have a judicial umpire of the newly created federal system (1980) was only accepted to the extent that the "court" would not only consist of professional judges. The idea was that somehow the judgments to be made by such court are in greater part political, so that they should not be left entirely to non-politicians. The compromise reached is stated in Articles 21 and 22 of the Law of June 28, 1983, Moniteur belge of July 8, 1983 - the Cour d'arbitrage has 12 members, 6 Flemish and 6 French-speakers, while each linguistic group consists of 3 members with five years seniority in high judicial or university legal occupations, while the other 3 are former members of the Senate or the Chamber of Representatives with at least eight years of seniority (they may, of course, have had a legal training, but this is in no way required; presently, several members of the court never studied law).

220. 4 *Wheaton* 316, 423 (1819).

221. Compare Frankfurter "John Marshall and the Judicial Function", 69 *Harv. L. Rev.* 217 (1955); see also Tribe, supra n. 2 at 303.

222. See, e.g., Joined Cases 281, 283-285 and 287/85, Federal Republic of Germany, French republic, Kingdom of the Netherlands, Kingdom of Denmark and United Kingdom of Great Britain and Northern Ireland v. Commission of the European Communities, judgment of July 9, 1987, *E.C.R.* 3203 (1987). Compare Shapiro, "Comparative Law and Comparative Politics", 53 *S. Cal. L. Rev.* 537, 540 (1980).

at their action.[223] The European Founding Fathers, all representing their Member States, intended to assure a wide access to an objective mechanism of judicial umpiring of the supranational system of divided powers, at least as far as the delimitation of the Community's powers was concerned.[224]

They were much less concerned about the second part of Justice Holmes' statement, that the Court of Justice be able to "make that declaration as to the laws of the several (Member) States". And as it happened, the Court did not receive the power to declare the law of a Member State void.[225] So, the fear expressed by Justice Holmes, that this flaw would imperil the Union (the Community), soon erupted in the Community legal order.[226] The Court of Justice, therefore, went as far as it could to reach the same practical outcome as the one that would be obtained through a direct invalidation of Member State law.[227]

To that effect, the Court widened the scope of the preliminary rulings procedure provided for in Article 177 of the EEC Treaty, which enables it to interpret Community law at the request of national courts. The Court interprets Community law in a most concrete way, so as to make certain that possible conflicts between national law and Community law will come to the surface.[228] Then it goes on to say that, under Article 5 of the EEC Treaty, Member State courts must leave aside the application of any rule of national law that contradicts Community law.[229] The same obligation rests

223. Article 173(1) of the EEC Treaty, explicited in Case 45/86, Commission of the E.C. v. Council of the E.C., judgment of March 26, 1987, *E.C.R.* 1493 (1987), paragraph 3. For a comment, see Arnull, "Legal Principles and Practical Politics", 12 *E.L.Rev.* 448, 449 (1987).

224. See Bice, "Studying the Court of Justice: What Messages for Federal Jurisdiction?", 53 *S. Cal. L. Rev.* 527, 531 (1980): "The Community's 'federal' system allocates far less governmental power to the central government and thus allocates far more of the attributes of sovereignty to the member States than our federal system does. Hence, member States are more significant political entities in the Community than the States are in the United States. This more important status as sovereign nations may partially explain some of the differences in court practice between the European and American systems. Because they are more significant sovereigns, States of the Community can gain access to the Court of Justice, essentially by simply requesting it. Their lower courts are afforded a significant role in defining the contours of Community law and furthermore, are not subject to direct appellate review by the Court of Justice."

225. See Case 6/60, Humblet c. Belgium, judgment of December 16, 1960, *E.C.R.* 559 (1960).

226. Compare Hay, "Supremacy of Community Law in National Courts", 16 *Am. J. Comp. L.* 524 (1968).

227. For examples, see, inter alia, Case 26/62, Van Gend & Loos, judgment of February 5, 1963, *E.C.R.* 1 (1963); Case 293/83, Françoise Gravier v. City of Liège, judgment of February 13, 1985, *E.C.R.* 593 (1985).

228. For a recent application, see Case 311/85, Vereniging van Vlaamse Reisbureaus, judgment of October 1, 1987, *E.C.R.* 3801 (1987).

229. Case 106/77, Simmenthal, judgment of March 9, 1978, *E.C.R.* 629 (1978).

on the Member State courts when they are facing a rule of national law whose enactment caused the Member State concerned to infringe its Treaty obligations within the meaning of Article 169 of the EEC Treaty.[230] Once the Court of Justice has declared that such infringement took place, the Member State — and thus its judiciary — is under a Community law duty to take all necessary remedial steps.[231] For the courts, this duty at least requires not to apply any longer the rule of national law which constitutes the infringement committed by the Member State. The Court's pronouncement will also be authoritative for the judges of the other Member States.[232]

The abidance by the Court's rulings on the part of Member State judges is not, as such, enforceable before the Court of Justice at the request of interested parties.[233] They can only lodge a complaint with the Commission, if a national judge should decide not to follow a Court's ruling. It is then for the Commission to sue the Member State in question before the Court of Justice, on the grounds that it infringed its Treaty obligations within the meaning of Article 169 of the EEC Treaty, through the decision of its judge.[234] The defending government will often have no power over "its" judiciary to have it change the previous decision, due to the separation-of-powers principle governing the national constitutional order. This judicial remedy therefore tends to be ineffective from the standpoint of the interested parties. They would rather need a right of direct appeal before the Court of Justice, which so far is absent from the scene of the Community legal order.[235] At a difference with the U.S. Supreme Court, the Court of Justice has indeed no "appellate jurisdiction" over Member State courts.[236]

230. Joined Cases 314 to 316/81 and 83/82, Procureur de la République v. A. Waterkeyn and others, judgment of December 14, 1982, *E.C.R.* 4335 (1982); see the annotation by Roth in 20 *C.M. L. Rev.* 583 (1983).

231. See Banks, "National Enforcement of Community Rights - A Boost for Damocles", 21 *C.M.L. Rev.* 669 (1984).

232. Compare Case 283/81, C.I.L.F.I.T., judgment of October 6, 1982, *E.C.R.* 3430 (1982); see Lenaerts, "La modulation de l'obligation de renvoi préjudiciel", 19 *Cahiers de droit européen* 471 (1983).

233. See Bebr, "The Rambling Ghost of 'Cohn-Bendit': Acte clair and the Court of Justice", 20 *C.M.L. Rev.* 439 (1983).

234. See Nicolaysen, "Vertragsverletzung durch mitgliedstaatliche Gerichte", 20 *Europarecht* 368 (1985).

235. See supra n. 224.

236. In the United States, the appellate jurisdiction of the Supreme Court on matters of federal law assures the necessary uniformity in the interpretation and application of that law in an absolutely binding way, see Martin v. Hunter's Lessee, 1 *Wheaton* 304, 347-348 (1816), opinion of the Court per Justice Story.

(b) The relationship between the judiciary and the legislature as to the umpiring of the federal system

Another aspect of the judicial umpiring of federalism concerns the relationship between the judiciary and the political branches of the central government as to their right to make the final judgment about the constitutional division of powers.[237] The question is whether the line drawn by the judiciary can be further modulated by the legislature, or else whether that line is as absolute as the constitution itself (which means in fact the constitution as the judiciary is "expounding" it).[238] The answer depends on the role assigned to the judiciary as umpire of the federal system. It differs especially in a comparative American-European context.

In the United States, Congress has the right to consent to State legislation that the federal judiciary held to be incompatible with the "negative implications of the Commerce Clause" (e.g., because it discriminates against out-of-State business).[239] The judicial judgment based on the "negative implications" of the constitutional text is thus subordinated to a later legislative judgment based on the positive grant of power to Congress contained in this same constitutional text.[240] It follows that the pronouncements made by the judiciary on the limitations of the powers of the States flowing implicitly from the Commerce Clause have a provisional character, until Congress speaks out pursuant to the explicit power it holds under that Clause.[241]

The line drawn by the judiciary on the basis of the negative implications of the Commerce Clause is not absolute, so that State power can further be extended or reduced through legislative enact-

237. See Dowling, "Interstate Commerce and State Power", 27 *Va. l. Rev.* 1 (1940), and "Interstate Commerce and State Power - Revised Version", 47 *Col. L. Rev.* 547 (1947).

238. McCulloch v. Maryland, 4 *Wheaton* 316, 407 (1819); see the dissenting opinion per Justice Black, joined by Justices Frankfurter and Douglas, McCarroll v. Dixie Greyhound Lines, 309 U.S. 176, 183 (1940), advocating a greater role for Congress to say what is admissible for the States under the Commerce Clause of the U.S. Constitution.

239. Prudential Insurance Company v. Benjamin, 328 U.S. 408 (1946); Cohen, "Congressional Power to Validate Unconstitutional State Laws: A Forgotten Solution to an Old Enigma", 35 *Stan. L. Rev.* 387 (1983). Compare Monaghan, "Foreword: Constitutional Common Law", 89 *Harv. L. Rev.* 1, 15-17 (1975).

240. Compare Sholley, "The Negative Implications of the Commerce Clause", 3 *U. Chi. L. Rev.* 556 (1936).

241. See Cohen, "Congressional Power to define State Power to Regulate Commerce: Consent and Pre-emption", in Sandalow and Stein, supra n. 4 at 523 ff., especially at 534 and 537. But compare Richard M. Buxbaum and Klaus J. Hopt, *Legal Harmonization and the Business Enterprise, in Integration through Law* 47-48, v. 4 (1988), pointing to the rarity of such legislative override by Congress.

ments of the central government.[242]

There appears to be more controversy about the flexibility of the line drawn by the judiciary with regard to the enforcement power held by Congress under § 5 of the Fourteenth Amendment.[243] Any legislative interpretation of a substantive right protected through this Amendment, which would be more extensive than the basic content read into such right by the judiciary, indeed entails the risk that Congress, by making use of its enforcement power, intrudes more deeply into the legal order of the States than a balanced process of judicial umpiring of the federal scheme could tolerate. This was the objection made by Justice Harlan to the Supreme Court ruling that upheld Congress' power to forbid literacy tests as a condition of eligibility, under § 5 of the Fourteenth Amendment, in spite of the fact that the Court had previously decided that such tests were compatible with the said Amendment.[244] In Justice Harlan's view, the power of Congress could not be sustained, "except at the sacrifice of fundamentals in the American constitutional system - the separation between the legislative and judicial function and the boundaries between federal and State political authority".[245]

The concern of Justice Harlan relates to the integrity of the autonomous status of the States within their constitutionally recognized sphere of powers.[246] Congress could not threaten that

---

242. Compare the opinion of the Court by Justice Jackson in H.P. Hood & Sons v. Du Mond, 336 U.S. 525, 534-535 (1949), suggesting that the Court should have a more definitive say over the extent of the negative implications flowing from the Commerce Clause for the States.

243. See Cox, "Foreword: Constitutional Adjudication and the Promotion of Human Rights", 80 *Harv. L. Rev.* 91 (1966); compare Cohen, "Congressional Power to Interpret Due Process and Equal Protection", 27 *Stan. L. Rev.* 603 (1975).

244. Lassiter v. Northampton County Board of Elections, per J. Douglas, 360 U.S. 45, 51-52 (1959): "(. . .) Residence requirements, age, previous criminal record are obvious examples indicating factors which a State may take into consideration in determining the qualifications of voters. The ability to read and write likewise has some relation to standards designed to promote intelligent use of ballot. Literacy and illiteracy are neutral on race, creed, color, and sex, . . . Literacy and intelligence are obviously not synonymous. Illiterate people may be intelligent voters. Yet in our society where newspapers, periodicals, books and other printed matter canvass and debate campaign issues, a State might conclude that only those who are literate should exercise the franchise." Yet, seven years later, the Court upheld the power of Congress to make the opposite judgment under § 5 of the Fourteenth Amendment. See Katzenbach v. Morgan, per J. Brennan, 384 U.S. 641, 651 (1966): "Correctly viewed, § 5 is a positive grant of legislative power authorizing Congress to exercise its discretion in determining whether and what legislation is needed to secure the guarantees of the Fourteenth Amendment."

245. 384 U.S. 641, 659 (1966).

246. Compare Alexander Bickel, *The Supreme Court and the Idea of Progress* 48 (1978): "The Framers of the Fourteenth Amendment explicitly rejected the option of an open-ended grant of power to Congress freely to meddle with conditions within the States, so as to render them equal in accordance with Congress' own notions. Rather federal power, legislative as well as judicial, was to be limited by the terms of the Amendment."

integrity beyond the line that the judiciary has drawn, even if its purpose is the rather benign one to increase the level of protection of the people's fundamental rights.[247]

In the European Community, a similar concern prevails, albeit in the other direction. The Court of Justice pursues a constitutional model in which the legal orders of the Community and the Member States are as strictly separated as possible.[248] The judicial line drawn between these legal orders must be absolute in all respects.

The principle of separation of the legal orders of the Community and the Member States leads to a kind of "dual federalism", which - in contrast to the ordinary meaning of this concept in American constitutional law[249] - aims at protecting the sphere of powers of the Community against possible intrusions by the Member States.[250] It would indeed be inadmissible that the Member States use their right to participation in the decision-making process of the Community with a view to regaining powers which they have transferred to the latter. To allow the legislature (the Council), through its political judgment, to empower the Member States to adopt legislation otherwise prohibited by the Treaties as interpreted in the case law of the Court of Justice, would bring to an end the coherence of the Community legal order.[251] The Council must respect the integrity of the Community's powers, just as the Member States are obliged to do so.[252] If the judicial line were not to be absolute in this

247. But see Archibald Cox, *The Warren Court. Constitutional Decision as an Instrument of Reform* 68 (1977): "The lines that must be drawn lend themselves better to the arbitrariness of political adjustment than to the rationalization of a systematic body of judge-made law. Congress has far greater flexibility in framing remedies and providing for their administration, especially remedies correcting the underlying social and economic conditions." Compare the balanced conclusion to the debate, suggested by Tribe, supra n. 2 at 350, especially note 98.

248. As an illustration, see Case 159/73, Hannoversche Zucker, judgment of January 30, 1974, *E.C.R.* 121 (1974).

249. See Beer, "Federalism, Nationalism and Democracy in America", 72 *The American Political Science Review* 9 (1978): "Federalism as the mutually exclusive allocation of powers between the general and the State governments - dual federalism, it may be called - belongs to the past. Dual federalism was indeed a feature of the original design and broadly speaking, characterized our system of multilevel government until the New Deal. Federalism in this sense does not apply, and given the realities of our times, could not be made to apply to that system today". Compare Tribe, supra n. 2 at 382-383, note 18 in fine: "In the area of conflict between federal and state regulation, the Court has clearly rejected dual sovereignty: 'This is not a controversy between equals', in Sanitary District v. United States, 266 U.S. 405, 425 (1925)".

250. See, generally, Tizzano, "The Powers of the Community", in, Office for Official Publications of the European Communities, *Thirty Years of Community Law* 43 ff. (1983), especially pp.63-67.

251. See Case 59/75, Pubblico Ministero v. Manghera, judgment of February 3, 1976, *E.C.R.* 91 (1976).

252. See Joined Cases 80 and 81/77, Société Les Commissaires Réunis v. Receveur des douanes; Sàrl Les Fils de Henri Ramel v. Receveur des douanes, judgment of April 20, 1978, *E.C.R.* 927 (1978); Case 37/83, Rewe-Zentrale AG v. Direktor der

respect, the Member States acting collectively within the framework of the Council could make a legislative judgment on behalf of the Community, which would empty the substance of the European supranational powers according to the fluctuating political circumstances of the time.[253]

Thus, the attitude adopted by the Court of Justice towards the Council's legislative judgments must be the exact opposite of that adopted by the U.S. Supreme Court towards Congress' legislative judgments which run contrary to its own rulings interpreting and shaping the negative implications of the Commerce Clause.

This difference in the judicial role performed by the two Courts as umpire of their federal system is moreover reflected in the American and European Community constitutions. There is indeed no grant of power to the Community, in the EEC Treaty, equivalent to the general power conferred on the U.S. Congress by the Commerce Clause. In fact, the EEC Treaty starts the other way round: instead of a grant of power to the Community which would by the same token limit to a certain extent the power of the Member States,[254] it provides for express prohibitions for the Member States to introduce import and export duties or to set up quantitative restrictions of whatever nature with regard to trade between the Member States.[255]

The Court of Justice then finds a stronger textual basis in the Community constitution to enforce these prohibitions against the Member States and, if need be, against the Council, than the U.S. Supreme Court does in the Commerce Clause. The latter can only found the prohibitions weighing on the States through its "negative implications". The judicial pronouncements made by the Court of Justice draw directly on the constitutional text so as to justify the absolute character of the line which runs between the Community and the national legal orders. The absence of any possible cross-over by the Community legislature in favor of some or all Member States

---

Landwirtschaftskammer Rheinland, judgment of February 29, 1984, *E.C.R.* 1229 (1984); and Case 41/84, Pietro Pinna v. Caisse d'allocations familiales de la Savoie, judgment of January 15, 1986, *E.C.R.* 1 (1986).

253. Compare Waelbroeck, "The Emergent Doctrine of Community Pre-emption - Consent and Re-delegation", in Sandalow and Stein, supra n. 4 at 572-575.

254. Such negative implication attached to a grant of power to the central government has not at all times been easy to accept in the United States either, see the dissenting opinion by Chief Justice Taney in the case of Pennsylvania v. Wheeling & Belmont Bridge Company, 13 *Howard* 518, 587 (1852): "Indeed, . . . I cannot perceive how the mere grant of power to the Legislative department of the Government to regulate commerce can give to the judicial branch the power to declare what shall, and what shall not be regarded as an unlawful obstruction; how high a bridge must be above the stream, and how far a wharf may be extended into the water, when we have no regulation of Congress to guide us".

255. See Articles 9 to 17 and 30 to 36 of the EEC Treaty.

is at the heart of the European version of dual federalism.[256]

In the United States, the possibility of such legislative cross-over is precisely characteristic of the judicial umpiring of the division of powers based upon the Commerce Clause; it is this possibility which lies at the heart of cooperative federalism in the United States.[257]

A comparative analysis of the judicial umpiring of American and European federalism seems influenced in a decisive way by the political reality that decision-making within the American Union is organically independent from the States, whereas in the European Community the Member States themselves play the double role of participants in the Community decision-making and of antipodes to the legal order of the Community as such.[258]

Thus, as central decision-making becomes more federal (i.e. autonomous from the States), federalism as a whole tends to be "cooperative"; on the contrary, as central decision-making sticks to the confederal stage (i.e. basically depending on the consent of the Member States), federalism (or supranationalism) tends to be "dual", in order to prevent a silent flow-back of powers from the central level of government to the Member States through the "unanimous" decision-making by the latter.

As a general conclusion to the second comparative theme, it can be said that the judicial umpiring of the federal system is oriented towards a cooperative federalism in the United States and a dual federalism in Europe, whereas from a procedural point of view, the enforcement of these models of federalism rests on the reverse image, i.e. judicial dualism between State and federal courts in the United States and judicial cooperation between national courts and the Community Court in Europe.

The difference as to both aspects of the judicial umpiring of American and European federalism proceeds in the end from the more significant sovereignty retained by the Member States of the European Community in their relation to the latter.[259]

---

256. This finding is not enervated by the Court's ruling in Case 41/76, Donckerwolcke v. Procureur de la République, judgment of December 15, 1976, *E.C.R.* 1921, 1937 (1976), that "as full responsibility in the matter of commercial policy was transferred to the Community by means of Article 113(1) measures of commercial policy of a national character are only permissible after the end of the transitional period by virtue of specific authorization by the Community" (paragraph 32). Such authorization must indeed be specific and may not run contrary to any rule laid down in the Treaties as interpreted by the Court of Justice, see id. at 1938 (paragraphs 38-40).

257. Compare Gerald Gunther, *Constitutional Law* 327-331 (1985 eleventh edition).

258. See Kutscher, "Über den Gerichtshof der Europäischen Gemeinschaft", 16 *Europarecht* 392 (1981); Waelbroeck, "Le rôle de la Cour de justice dans la mise en oeuvre du traité CEE", 18 *Cahiers de droit européen* 347 (1982).

259. Compare, generally, Barav, "The Judicial Power of the European Economic Community", 53 *S. Cal.L. Rev.* 461 (1980).

III. General Conclusion

Federalism is present whenever a divided sovereignty is guaranteed by the national or supranational constitution and umpired by the supreme court of the common legal order. Both sovereigns enact laws with direct operation upon those to whom they are addressed. There is — in principle at least — no political oversight of one sovereign over the other. The normal enforcement mechanism of the constitutional balance is of a judicial nature and in case of conflict between validly enacted federal and component-entity laws, the former prevail over the latter.

These essential features appear to be common to both the integrative and devolutionary variant of federalism. These features do not, however, determine the true shape of a given federal system.

Such shape will rather depend upon the way in which the division of powers (enumerated as opposed to residual powers, exclusive or concurrent powers, express and implied powers, participation of the component entities in the central government, executive federalism) is understood against the historical background of the federal system in question. Federalism can express both a drive for integration and for devolution and American constitutional tradition relating to federalism is just as frequently invoked in order to promote integration (European Community or Switzerland) or devolution (Belgium, Canada, Spain). The truth of the matter obviously is that independent from its integrative or devolutionary drive, each federal system is constantly faced with the task of keeping the appropriate balance between the autonomy of the component entities, favoring the values of societal pluralism and checks and balances inherent in the principle of constitutionalism, and the effectiveness of the central government, favoring the values of national or supranational cohesion and decision-making at the level of the common legal order when this seems the better option in terms of policy.

That the balance must and can be kept through mechanisms of judicial umpiring under the rule of law which governs the common legal order — whatever be the push and pull of changing politics over decades or even centuries — is the outstanding legacy of American constitutionalism on the threshold of its third century. The European Community and many countries around the world (not just those covered by the present study) will not fail to meet the challenge.

[6]

The Influence of National Concepts on Decisions of the European Court

By John A. Usher

Legal Secretary, European Court

I. Background and development

"The Court shall ensure that in the interpretation and application of this Treaty, and of the rules laid down for the implementation thereof, the law is observed." This formula was first used in Article 31 of the ECSC Treaty, and is repeated (with the omission of the phrase "and of the rules laid down for the implementation thereof," which in itself has been of no practical significance) in Article 164 EEC and in Article 136 Euratom.

Early in the history of the Court of Justice of the Coal and Steel Community, as it then was, it was realised that Treaty provisions and the rules laid down for their implementation were not necessarily sufficiently comprehensive to resolve disputes which might arise within the context of the Community. As Advocate-General Lagrange pointed out in his Opinion in Case 8/55, *Fédération Charbonnière de Belgique* v. *High Authority*,[1] citing Article 4 of the French Civil Code,[2] the Court could not be absolved from giving judgment because of a lacuna in Community law. Even before this, it had been stated by Advocate-General Roemer in his Opinion in Case 6/54, *Netherlands* v. *High Authority*,[3] that account must be taken of the law of the different Member States in order to interpret Community law.

Indeed, in one of the leading staff cases to arise under the ECSC Treaty, the Court went so far as to mention specifically rules applicable in the law of individual Member States to the situation before it.[4] In this case, the Assembly had decided, on the eve of the adoption of the then new Staff Regulations, that the applicants were to be admitted to the benefit of the Staff Regulations and had indicated the grade they were to hold. However, a few months later, a grading structure common to all four Community institutions was agreed, and the applicants were informed of their grades under the new structure, which they refused to accept (and this eventually

---

1 Rec. 1955, pp. 199, 264.

2 "Le juge qui refusera de juger, sous prétexte du silence, de l'obscurité ou de l'insuffisance de la loi, pourra être poursuivi comme coupable de déni de justice."

3 Rec. 1954, pp. 201, 232.

4 Joined Cases 7/56 & 3-7/57, *Algera and others* v. *Assembly*, Rec. 1957, pp. 81, 114-116.

resulted in a decision effectively removing the applicants from the benefit of the Staff Regulations, which was the main point in the action). *Inter alia,* the Court had to decide whether the initial decisions as to grading could be revoked, which, as it said, was a problem of administrative law well-known in all the then Member States, but which was not provided for by the Treaty. The Court added that unless it was to be guilty of a denial of justice, the problem would have to be resolved on the basis of rules recognised by legislation, academic authorities and case-law in the Member States. The Court found that if the act in question were legal, and individual rights had been acquired under it, then it could not be revoked, because of the need to protect the expectations thus created (a concept of which more will be said). On the other hand, it was found that if the act was illegal, then all the Member States recognised that it could be revoked, with variations notably as to the time during which this could be done, and the Court made specific reference to the provisions of French, German and Italian law in this respect. In the result, although the applicants were otherwise successful, it was held that the Assembly had no power to draw up a grading structure independently, and that the initial decisions were revocable in this respect.

However, it is more common for specific provisions of national legal systems to be discussed in the Opinions of Advocates-General rather than in the Court's Judgments; so it is no surprise to discover that in Case 14/61, *Hoogovens* v. *High Authority,*[5] a comparative study of the revocability of administrative acts, this time of those declaratory of rights rather than of those creating rights, was carried out by the Advocate-General, M. Lagrange [6] but not by the Court.

One of the great innovations of the EEC Treaty is its Article 177, enabling courts in Member States to refer questions of interpretation of Community acts to the Court of Justice for a preliminary ruling. In the first reference heard under this Article, Case 13/61, *De Geus* v. *Bosch,*[7] an appeal had been lodged against the decision of the domestic court, and the question arose as to the effect of the appeal on the reference (a question, incidentally, that has had to be considered on several subsequent occasions). The point is not covered by Article 177, but rather than consider the matter in the abstract, Advocate-General Lagrange discussed the practice in those Member States whose domestic systems use a preliminary ruling procedure, notably France and Germany, and concluded that the mere lodging of an appeal did not affect the existence of the reference [8]; the Court, for its part, succinctly noted that its jurisdiction was dependent solely on the existence of a request for a preliminary ruling.[9]

For the most part the national concepts used by the Court are more general in nature—what in the original Member States is termed "unwritten law"—although in Case 108/63, *Merlini* v. *High Authority,*[10]

[5] [1962] E.C.R. 253, [1963] C.M.L.R. 73.
[6] [1962] E.C.R. at pp. 280–283.
[7] [1962] E.C.R. 45, [1962] C.M.L.R. 1.
[8] *Ibid.* at pp. 58–61.
[9] *Ibid.* at p. 50.
[10] [1965] E.C.R. 1, 10, [1965] C.M.L.R. 109.

where it was claimed that the High Authority was estopped from fixing the equalisation contributions due from the applicants on the ground that it had earlier asked for a smaller sum, the Court found it necessary to state specifically that "the fact that such a rule" (*i.e.* estoppel) "is not mentioned in written law is not sufficient proof that it does not exist."

Before listing some of the concepts derived from the laws of the Member States currently used by the Court, it is worth noting that in some of its modern judgments the Court has felt itself able at least in the matter of fundamental rights even to take account of rules derived from international law insofar as they are binding upon the Member States. In Case 4/73, *Nold* v. *Commission*,[11] where the applicant alleged the infringement of its property rights and its right to the free pursuit of business activity, the Court stated that fundamental rights form an integral part of the general principles of law of which it ensures the observance and in safeguarding which it is bound to draw inspiration from constitutional traditions common to the Member States, and added: "international treaties for the protection of human rights on which the Member States have collaborated or of which they are signatories, can supply guidelines which should be followed within the framework of Community law." More specifically, in Case 36/75, *Rutili* v. *French Minister of the Interior*,[12] a reference for a preliminary ruling made in an action brought by an Italian national against the French authorities challenging restrictions placed on his right of residence in France as a result, *inter alia*, of his participation in certain trade union activities, the Court, after referring to the restrictions imposed by Community legislation on the powers of Member States to control migrant workers, stated that:

> "these limitations . . . are a specific manifestation of the more general principle, enshrined in Articles 8, 9, 10 and 11 of the Convention for the Protection of Human Rights and Fundamental Freedoms, signed in Rome on 4th November 1950 and ratified by all the Member States, and in Article 2 of Protocol No. 4 of the same Convention."

However, although the European Court may use principles derived from the laws of the Member States to fill in the outlines laid down by Community legislation, thus creating rules applicable throughout the Community, it is not usually open to individual Member States to fill in lacunae in Community law by reference to their own national law. This is particularly so where there exists a common organisation of an agricultural market. In Case 159/73, *Hannoversche Zucker* v. *Hauptzollamt Hannover*,[13] where the question arose as to the sugar marketing year to which excess production should be allocated, in the absence of any specific provision in the relevant regulations, the Court stated that "the rules of the common organisation of the market in sugar must be regarded as forming a complete system in the sense that it does not leave the Member States the power to fill such a lacuna by resorting to their national law."

11 [1974] E.C.R. 491, 507, [1974] 2 C.M.L.R. 338.
12 [1975] E.C.R. 1219.
13 [1974] E.C.R. 121, 129.

II. General principles in common use

(i) *Identification*

Some concepts derived from national sources have now become so well established in the case-law of the Court that they have virtually become principles of Community law in their own right, although they may still be distinguished from those general principles of Community law derived from the Treaties as such, examples of the latter being: in external trade the concept of Community preference [14]; in social affairs the notion of equality of treatment of nationals of other Member States, which has been generalised from the provisions of the EEC Treaty relating to the free movement of workers [15] and the right of establishment [16]; in business law the requirement that competition should not be eliminated [17]; and, between Member States, the duty of " solidarity." [18]

One problem which is encountered in listing those principles of Community law which have been derived from national sources is that in some cases what is in effect the same principle may be known by more than one " tag."

(ii) *Proportionality*

Probably the best known of these concepts is the principle of proportionality. This first made its appearance in Community law in the judgment of the Court in Case 8/55, *Fédération Charbonnière de Belgique* v. *High Authority*.[19] In this case the applicants had argued that rather than fix Belgian coal prices by general decision, the High Authority could ensure that such prices reached the desired level by withdrawing compensation payments (intended to compensate for the high cost of coal production in Belgium) from those enterprises which did not make a sufficient reduction in price. The Court, however, rejected this proposition and stated that " in application of a generally accepted rule of law," action of the High Authority in response to a wrongful act of an enterprise must be proportionate to the gravity of that act. In the context, this might not seem to say more than the truism that the punishment must fit the crime, and indeed the principle has often been invoked in cases where the High Authority or Commission has imposed a fine.[20] However, it is in the sense defined by Advocate-General Dutheillet de Lamothe in his Opinion in Case 11/70,

[14] See Case 5/67, *Beus* v. *Hauptzollamt Munich* [1968] E.C.R. 83, 98, [1968] C.M.L.R. 131, invoking Art. 44 (2) EEC.

[15] See Case 152/73, *Sotgiu* v. *Deutsche Bundespost* [1974] E.C.R. 153, 164.

[16] See Case 2/74, *Reyners* v. *Belgium* [1974] E.C.R. 631, 651, [1974] 2 C.M.L.R. 305.

[17] Derived from Arts. 2, 3, 85 and 86 EEC: see Case 6/72, *Europemballage and Continental Can* v. *Commission* [1973] E.C.R. 215, 244, [1973] C.M.L.R. 199; Joined Cases 6 & 7/73 *Commercial Solvents* v. *Commission* [1974] E.C.R. 223, 252, [1974] 1 C.M.L.R. 309.

[18] See Case 39/72, *Commission* v. *Italy* [1973] E.C.R. 101, 116, [1973] C.M.L.R. 439.

[19] Rec. 1955, pp. 199, 304.

[20] See Case 8/56, *A.L.M.A.* v. *High Authority*, Rec. 1957, pp. 179, 192; Case 7/72, *Boehringer* v. *Commission*, Rec. 1972, pp. 1281, 1290, [1973] C.M.L.R. 864.

Internationale Handelsgesellschaft mbH v. *Einfuhr- und Vorratsstelle für Getreide und Futtermittel* that the principle has its real importance in Community law: "citizens may only have imposed on them, for the purposes of the public interest, obligations which are strictly necessary for those purposes to be attained." [21]

In this sense, it is the Germans who have a word for it, "*Verhältnismässigkeitsgrundsatz*," which has been held to be the principle underlying Articles 2 and 12 of the Basic Law, laying down certain basic freedoms and the limits within which they may be exercised, even though no specific mention is made of the principle.[22] It is interesting to read the views of M. Dutheillet de Lamothe on this matter [23]; after mentioning the existence of the rule in Germany, he stated that the legality of a Community measure can never be judged in the light of national law but that fundamental principles of national legal systems "contribute to forming that philosophical, political and legal substratum common to the Member States from which through the case-law an unwritten Community law emerges," and he concluded, referring to the earlier case-law, that the principle of "proportionality" was already guaranteed by the general principles of Community law. Recently, the principle has been used as a criterion to test Community measures designed to combat the problems arising, particularly in agricultural matters, from fluctuating exchange rates. Indeed, in one reference for a preliminary ruling, Case 5/73, *Balkan-Import-Export* v. *Hauptzollamt Berlin-Packhof*,[24] the question was specifically asked whether Council Regulation 974/71,[25] introducing the system of monetary compensatory amounts, conflicted with the principle of proportionality. The Court declared that it was not satisfied that the Council had "imposed burdens on traders which were manifestly out of proportion to the object in view,[26] but it did state that "the Institutions must ensure that the amounts which commercial operators are charged are no greater than is required to achieve the aim which the authorities are to accomplish." [27]

(iii) *Legitimate expectation*

Another concept which is at present frequently invoked before the Court and would appear to have German origins, at least in its common formulation, is the principle of the protection of legitimate expectation [28] (*protection de la confiance légitime—Vertrauensschutz*). In fact this principle has not always been clearly distinguished from the general concept

[21] Rec. 1970, pp. 1125, 1148, [1972] C.M.L.R. 255.

[22] See cases cited in Schmidt-Bleibtrau and Klein, *Kommentar zum Grundgesetz*, 3rd ed. 1975, at pp. 168 and 246.

[23] Rec. 1972, pp. 1148–1149.

[24] [1973] E.C.R. 1091.

[25] J.O. 1971 L106/1.

[26] [1973] E.C.R. 1091, 1112.

[27] *Ibid.* at pp. 1111–1112.

[28] This was originally translated into English as "protection of legitimate confidence," but it was thought that the technical meaning of "confidence" in English law made this misleading, and the term "expectation" is now thought to be more appropriate—see Opinion of Advocate-General Warner in Case 2/75, *Einfuhr- und Vorratsstelle Getreide* v. *Mackprang* [1975] E.C.R. 607, 622.

of legal certainty or from the French one of *droits acquis* or established rights, as is evidenced by the following extract from Case 1/73, *Westzucker* v. *Einfuhr- und Vorratsstelle Zucker* [29]:

> " It is asked . . . whether the regulation . . . infringes a principle of legal certainty by which the confidence of persons concerned deserves to be protected. . . . It seems difficult to consider the amendment of a provision which was capable, because of its inflexibility, of causing losses or gains for those concerned, as adversely affecting any established position which they hold."

Again, the German Court, in its order for reference, mentioned *Vertrauensschutz,* another principle held by the German courts to underly certain provisions of the Basic Law, notably Article 2,[30] but in his Opinion Advocate-General Roemer specifically mentioned the fact that similar concepts, *i.e.* the principle that there must be no infringement upon " well-established " rights, can also be found in French and Belgian case-law.[31] It was held in fact that the regulation in question [32] did not infringe any such principle, even though it affected advance fixing certificates for the export of sugar issued before it entered into force in so far as the importation had not yet taken place by providing for an optional adjustment of the export refund following alterations in the intervention price instead of the previous automatic adjustments.

However, the rule has been applied, as a general principle of Community law, in circumstances where it is difficult to say that any " established " rights were affected and where what was protected was purely and simply an " expectation." The *locus classicus* is the judgment of the Court in Case 81/72, *Commission* v. *Council.*[33] It was necessary in this case to decide whether a Decision taken by the Council on March 21, 1972, to apply for a period of three years a particular system of adjusting the salaries of Community staff had a binding effect so as to prevent the Council from validly adopting a Regulation [34] which was not in accordance with its terms. In the words of the judgment:

> " Taking account of the particular employer-staff relationship, . . . the rule of protection of the confidence that the staff could have that the authorities would respect undertakings of this nature, implies that the Decision of March 21, 1972, binds the Council in its future action.
>
> Whilst this rule is primarily applicable to individual decisions, the possibility cannot by any means be excluded that it should relate, when appropriate, to the exercise of more general powers."

It is noteworthy that the Court, in so deciding, did not follow the Opinion of Advocate-General Warner [35] citing case law in the Member States and, in particular, English and French authorities.

[29] [1973] E.C.R. 723, 729–730.
[30] Schmidt-Bleibtrau and Klein *Kommentar zum Grundgesetz* 3rd ed. 1975, pp. 164–166.
[31] [1973] E.C.R. 723, 739.
[32] Council Reg. 1048/71 of May 25, 1971, J.O. 1971 L114/10.
[33] [1973] E.C.R. 575, 584, [1973] C.M.L.R. 639.
[34] Council Reg. 2647/72, J.O. 1972, L283/1.
[35] [1973] E.C.R. 575, 592–595.

More recently, the principle has even been used as the basis for liability on the part of the Communities. As is well known, Article 215 EEC (and Article 188 Euratom) provides that in the case of non-contractual liability, the Community shall, "in accordance with the general principles common to the laws of the Member States, make good any damage caused by its institutions or by its servants in the performance of their duties." Without wishing to enter here into a detailed discussion of this provision, it is well-established that in order to recover damages for a legislative act, it is necessary to show that a "sufficiently flagrant violation of a superior rule of law for the protection of the individual has occurred."[36] There have been several attempts to establish liability on the part of Community institutions on the basis that general principles of law can constitute such superior rules, usually by alleging that the regulation or other act alleged to have caused harm was illegal as infringing such a principle: in one series of cases the principle of "equality of treatment" or "non-discrimination."[37] The principle of proportionality has also been invoked in Joined Cases 63–69/72, *Werhahn Hansamühle and others* v. *Council and Commission*,[38] where it was alleged (unsuccessfully) that a series of acts managing the market in (particularly) durum wheat during the marketing year 1971–72 infringed the principle of proportionality and caused damage to the applicants. However, it is with regard to the protection of legitimate expectation that the most significant development has occurred, because it has now been decided in the *CNTA* case that a Community institution can be liable for harm caused by an act infringing this principle (by failing to allow a transitional period before abolishing a system of compensatory amounts) even where the legality of the act itself is not in question.[39] The applicant in this case claimed that the withdrawal by Commission Regulation 189/72[40] of the compensatory amounts applicable to colza and rape seeds violated the principle of legal certainty in that it had retroactive effect and in that it ignored the legitimate expectation of persons concerned that compensatory amounts would be maintained for current transactions. The Court decided that the Regulation did not have retroactive effect in the strict sense[41] and so considered the question of legitimate expectation. It was held that although the system of compensatory amounts cannot be considered as a guarantee for traders against the risks of changes in exchange rates, their application in practice avoids the exchange risk, so that even a prudent trader might be induced to omit to cover himself against such risk.[42]

> "In these circumstances, a trader may legitimately expect that for transactions irrevocably undertaken by him because he has obtained,

[36] Originally formulated in Case 5/71, *Zuckerfabrik Schöppenstedt* v. *Council*, Rec. 1971, pp. 975, 985.

[37] Case 5/71, *supra*; Joined Cases 9 & 11/71, *Cie. d'Approvisionnement* v. *Commission*, Rec. 1972, p. 391, [1973] C.M.L.R. 529; Case 43/72, *Merkur* v. *Commission* [1973] E.C.R. 1055.

[38] [1973] E.C.R. 1229.

[39] Case 74/74, *CNTA* v. *Commission* [1975] E.C.R. 533.

[40] J.O. 1972, L24/25.

[41] [1975] E.C.R. 533, 548.

[42] [1975] E.C.R. 533, 549–550.

> subject to a deposit, export licences fixing the amount of the refund in advance, no unforeseeable alteration will occur which could have the effect of causing him inevitable loss, by re-exposing him to the exchange risk.
>
> In the absence of an overriding matter of public interest, the Commission has violated a superior rule of law, thus rendering the Community liable, by failing to include in Regulation 189/72 transitional measures for the protection of the confidence which a trader might legitimately have had in the Community rules."

A limitation was, however, imposed on the applicant's right to recover in that:

> "the protection which it may claim by reason of its legitimate expectation is merely that of not suffering loss by reason of the withdrawal of those amounts"

since the maintenance of the system was in no way guaranteed and the applicant could not legitimately expect under all circumstances to make the profits which would have accrued under the previous system.

(iv) *Legal certainty*

It will have been noticed that protection of legitimate expectation is often associated with the broader concept of legal certainty. This is a principle so general that it cannot really be ascribed to any particular national source, yet it is of considerable importance in the case law of the Court. Just two aspects of its current application can be mentioned here. First, like many of the general principles, it is now often used as a means of interpreting Community acts in such a way as to ensure their validity rather than as a criterion for determining their validity. An example appears in the two *Deuka* cases.[43] In the first of these it was asked whether Commission Regulation 849/70[44] was invalid in so far as it provided that an increased denaturing premium should be discontinued even in respect of wheat purchased by the denaturer before the Regulation came into force. Having found that a denaturing undertaking may well arrange its programme on the basis of an entire crop year, "for the sake of legal certainty, Regulation 849/70 had to be applied in such a way that there might still benefit from the previous system . . . those quantities of goods . . . purchased before the coming into force of the Regulation, provided the request (for a premium) was made to the intervention agency before the expiry of the time-limit arising from the Regulation."[45] Interpreted in this way, the Regulation was held to be valid. In the second case, similar questions arose concerning the validity of Regulations 2859/73[46] and 175/74,[47] respectively, reducing and abolishing the relevant denaturing premium, and

[43] Case 78/74, *Deuka* v. *Einfuhr- und Vorratsstelle Getreide* [1975] E.C.R. 421, [1975] 2 C.M.L.R. 28; Case 5/75, *Deuka* v. *Einfuhr- und Vorratsstelle Getreide* [1975] E.C.R. 759.

[44] May 11, 1970, J.O., 1970, L102/7.

[45] [1975] E.C.R. 421, 433.

[46] O.J. 1973 L293/31.

[47] O.J. 1974 L20/28.

a similar answer was given: the Court stated that where there has been a "commitment to denaturing" before the expiry of the periods stipulated in the Regulations, "it is right to apply, in the interests of legal certainty, for the computation of the amount of the denaturing premium, the provisions in force at the time the application was lodged, even if the technical mixing is not done until a subsequent date." [48]

The second important modern use of the principle of legal certainty has been in the field of competition, following the decisions in the second *Brasserie de Haecht* [49] case and in *B.R.T.* v. *SABAM* [50] to the effect that Articles 85 (1) and 86 EEC produce direct effects and could not therefore be modified or limited by Regulation 17 of the Council.[51] This left, *inter alia*, problems as to the extent to which national courts could apply the notion of "provisional validity" to agreements before them and as to possible conflicts of jurisdiction between national courts and the Commission. In relation to the former, the Court decided, in the *Brasserie de Haecht* case, that there was room for distinguishing agreements made before and after the implementation of Article 85 by Regulation 17, and that in the case of "old" agreements, "the general principle of contractual certainty requires, particularly when the agreement has been notified in accordance with the provisions of Regulation 17, that the court may only declare it to be automatically void after the Commission has taken a decision by virtue of that Regulation." [52] With regard to the latter, it was held in the *SABAM* case that if the Commission initiates a procedure in application of Article 3 of Regulation 17, a national court may, if it considers it necessary for reasons of legal certainty, stay the proceedings before it while awaiting the outcome of the Commission's action.[53]

(v) *Other general principles*

There are many other general principles common to the laws of the Member States (or, in some cases, to the laws of the original Six) which are applied by the Court, but within the scope of this article it is difficult to do more than note their existence. They include the concepts of good faith,[54] the right to be heard, of which more will be said in the context of the *Transocean* case,[55] and *force majeure*, the precise meaning of which, according to the Court, has to be decided by reference to the legal context in which it is intended to operate, but which is not limited to absolute impossibility [56]; indeed, in one recent case [57] the Court implied a *force*

[48] [1975] E.C.R. 759, 771.

[49] Case 48/72, *Brasserie de Haecht* v. *Wilkin-Janssen* [1973] E.C.R. 77, [1973] C.M.L.R. 287.

[50] Case 127/73, *B.R.T.* v. *SABAM* [1974] E.C.R. 51, [1974] 2 C.M.L.R. 238.

[51] J.O. 1962, 204.

[52] [1973] E.C.R. 77, 86–87.

[53] [1974] E.C.R. 51, 63.

[54] See *e.g.* Case 44/59, *Fiddelaar* v. *Commission*, Rec. 1960, pp. 1077, 1099.

[55] Case 17/74, *Transocean Marine Paint Association* v. *Commission* [1974] E.C.R. 1063, [1974] 2 C.M.L.R. 459.

[56] Case 158/73, *Kampffmeyer* v. *Einfuhr- und Vorratsstelle Getreide* [1974] E.C.R. 101, 110.

[57] Case 64/74, *Reich* v. *Hauptzollamt Landau* [1975] E.C.R. 261, 268–269, [1975] 1 C.M.L.R. 396.

majeure clause into a regulation that did not contain one, on the basis that such clauses were contained in parallel Regulations. The Court has also considered a doctrine of estoppel, sometimes under the Latin tag *non venire contra factum proprium*, though this has rarely been applied.[58] It has, however, applied a concept of unjust enrichment,[59] has given a Community definition of legitimate self-protection (the *légitime défense* of French-derived systems),[60] and has, in staff disciplinary matters, applied the rule that a person may not be punished twice for the same offence (*non bis in idem*).[61] Finally, under the ECSC Treaty, reference was made in several cases to the French concept of *égalité devant les charges publiques*,[62] but this now seems largely to be subsumed in the wider principle of equality of treatment or non-discrimination,[63] which is regarded as a general principle flowing from the Treaties.

III. The use of technical rules

As will have been evident from the earlier sections of this article, technical lacunae may occur in the framework created by the Treaties, and have to be filled by resorting to a comparative study of the laws of the Member States.

At the simplest level, comparative studies may be carried out by the Court's staff to supply background information relevant to a case before the Court, whether it be as to the availability of maintenance grants to enable children to stay at school after school-leaving age, as in Case 9/74, *Casagrande* v. *Landeshauptstadt München*,[64] or as to the position of parallel imports under the industrial property laws of the Member States, as in the *Centrafarm* cases.[65]

Technical points of substance do nonetheless arise, and recently there have been several cases where detailed aspects of *locus standi* have had to be considered. One of the more straightforward (legally speaking) of these has been the question of the rights of trade unions, or more accurately, staff associations of officials of the Communities, to appear before the Court. The Court decided in Case 175/73, *Union Syndicale* v. *Council*[66] and Case 18/74, *Syndicat Général* v. *Commission*,[67] that "under the general principles of labour law," the freedom of trade union activity recognised under the Staff Regulations means not only that officials have the right without hindrance to form associations of their own choosing,

[58] See *e.g.* Joined Cases 17 & 20/61, *Klöckner* v. *High Authority* [1962] E.C.R. 325, 342. For an application, see Case 6/72, *Europemballage* v. *Commission* [1973] E.C.R. 215, 241, [1973] C.M.L.R. 199.

[59] Case 36/72, *Meganck* v. *Commission* [1973] E.C.R. 527, 534.

[60] Case 16/61, *Modena* v. *High Authority* [1962] E.C.R. 289, 303.

[61] Joined Cases 18 & 35/65, *Gutmann* v. *Commission* [1966] E.C.R. 103, 119.

[62] See Joined Cases 14, 16, 17, 20, 24, 26 27/60 & 1/61, *Merioni* v. *High Authority*, Rec. 1961, 319, 338.

[63] See *e.g.* Case 148/73, *Louwage* v. *Commission* [1974] E.C.R. 81, 89.

[64] [1974] E.C.R. 773, [1974] 2 C.M.L.R. 423.

[65] Case 15/74, *Centrafarm* v. *Sterling Drug* [1974] E.C.R. 1147; Case 16/74, *Centrafarm* v. *Winthrop* [1974] E.C.R. 1183, [1974] 2 C.M.L.R. 480.

[66] [1974] E.C.R. 917, 925, [1975] 1 C.M.L.R. 131.

[67] [1974] E.C.R. 933, 944, [1975] 1 C.M.L.R. 144.

but also that these associations are free to do anything lawful to protect the interests of their members as employees, and the Court further stated that "the right of action is one of the means available for use by these associations."

A more complex problem arose in Case 90/74, *Deboeck* v. *Commission*,[68] a staff case heard by the First Chamber. The question here arose as to whether an applicant challenging the validity of an act of a Community institution needs to show an interest in the grounds put forward for annulment. The action was for the annulment of an internal competition for the recruitment of secretarial assistants, and one submission of the applicant was that the notice of competition had not been preceded by a notice of vacancy as required by the Staff Regulations.[69] The Court held that she had no interest to raise the point, since she was not eligible for transfer or promotion (the procedures which may precede the holding of a competition) without taking part in the competition. This followed an Opinion delivered by Advocate-General Warner[70] in which he briefly reviewed the situation in the Member States, contrasting the tradition in French law and French derived systems whereby a person having an interest in the result[71] may raise any ground for the annulment of the act in question, with the view, *inter alios*, of Lord Wilberforce in *Malloch* v. *Aberdeen Corporation*[72] that a "breach of procedure, whether called a failure of natural justice, or an essential administrative fault, cannot give [the appellant] a remedy in the courts, unless behind it there is something of substance which has been lost by the failure"; and decisions by the Danish, Dutch and German courts that a plaintiff cannot complain of irregularities which have not caused him any harm.

However, what is interesting in this matter is not so much the result of the comparative study as the fact that both Chambers of the Court had previously reached the same conclusion despite the French view having been forcefully put. This illustrates both the difficulty of being able to make a definite pronouncement as to the origin of general principles applied by the Court—the nine judges cannot really be separated from their legal heritage, even if no specific mention is made of comparative analyses—and the danger of regarding Community law as an extension of French administrative law.

The problem arose clearly in Case 37/72, *Marcato* v. *Commission*,[73] a decision of the Second Chamber. One question there raised was whether the notice of competition should have contained an age limit. Advocate-General Mayras put forward the classical French view:

> "A candidate not admitted to a competition has an incontestable interest in challenging the working of the competition from which he considers himself to have been illegally excluded. He cannot be

68 [1975] E.C.R. 1123.
69 Art. 4 (2).
70 [1975] E.C.R. at p. 1141.
71 Conseil d'Etat, January 17, 1947, *Recueil*, p. 668.
72 [1971] 1 W.L.R. at p. 1595.
73 [1973] E.C.R. 361.

> held to be precluded from pleading a point of law, whatever it may be." [74]

The Second Chamber, however, did not apply this rule, and looked instead to the interest of the applicant in having an age limit fixed:

> "The setting of an age limit could only have resulted either in eliminating the applicant himself from the competition, which would have been directly contrary to his interest, or else in eliminating other, possibly qualified, candidates, which in the circumstances cannot be recognised as a legitimate interest of his." [75]

Perhaps the most striking example is in Case 29/74, *De Dapper* v. *Parliament.*[76] There the applicant claimed the annulment of certain promotions on the grounds, *inter alia*, that the persons promoted remained in the same grade. Although the applicant was successful in the result, the First Chamber rejected this contention on the following basis:

> "Such a submission can only be relied upon by those adversely affected by the illegality, assuming that this were proved, in the present case only the officials promoted." [77]

IV. A case-study: the Transocean case [78]

A study may now be made of the techniques involved in applying national concepts in a case before the Court.

In 1967 the Commission had granted an exemption under Article 85 (3) EEC with regard to the agreement between the undertakings forming the Transocean Marine Paint Association, subject to a condition obliging the Association to keep the Commission informed, *inter alia*, of any change in the composition of its membership.[79] In December 1973 [80] this exemption was renewed subject to certain new conditions, including Article 3 (1) (*d*) which required members of the Association to inform the Commission without delay of "any links by way of common directors or managers between a member of the Association and any other company or firm in the paints sector or any financial participation by a member of the Association in such outside companies or vice versa including all changes in such links or participations already in existence."

The applicants brought an action to annul this provision of the decision, on the basis that, since it had neither been mentioned in the Commission's "Notice of Objections" nor raised at the hearing before the Commission, the Commission had infringed the rules of procedure laid down in Regulation 99/63,[81] in particular Articles 2 and 4 thereof.

---

[74] [1973] E.C.R. at p. 374.
[75] *Ibid.*, p. 368.
[76] [1975] E.C.R. 35.
[77] *Ibid.* p. 40.
[78] Case 17/74, *Transocean Marine Paint Association* v. *Commission* [1974] E.C.R. 1063, [1974] 2 C.M.L.R. 459.
[79] Decision of June 27, 1967, J.O. 1967, 163/10, [1967] C.M.L.R. D9.
[80] Decision of December 21, 1973, O.J. 1974, L19/18, [1974] C.M.L.R. D11.
[81] Commission Reg. 99/63 of July 25, 1963, J.O. 1963, 2268.

The Commission had in fact indicated that it was willing to renew the exemption for five years, subject to certain fresh conditions and obligations. One of these was that the Association should, according to the literal English translation, "notify any change in the participatory relationships of the members," which could be interpreted, amongst other things, as requiring merely that the information which had already had to be supplied under the 1967 decision be supplemented by the notification of any links which might exist between the undertakings which were members of the association.

On the question of Regulation 99/63, Advocate-General Warner suggested in his Opinion,[82] and the Court in fact decided,[83] that Articles 2 and 4 of Regulation 99/63 concern the objections which would either bring an agreement within Article 85 (1) or prevent it being granted an exemption under Article 85 (3) and do not deal with conditions which may be imposed upon a grant of an exemption.

However, the Court is not dependent solely upon the arguments which the parties choose to put before it. Its purpose is to ensure as far as possible the uniform application of Community law and to a certain degree it has its own staff which it can use to enable it to do this. There exists a "Library and Research Division," [84] the members of which when requested by members of the Court provide research notes on points of law. In this particular case, as Advocate-General Warner was of the opinion that, at any rate in English law, this would be a situation where *audi alteram partem* could be invoked, he requested a comparative study of the laws of the other Member States to see whether this was a principle generally accepted in other Member States.

It should hardly be necessary in this *Review* to cite the well-known English cases on the question,[85] although in fact the *dictum* which is perhaps most appropriate to the facts of that particular case was pronounced in an extra-judicial capacity by Lord Morris of Borth-y-Gest when he said that "if someone has a right to be heard he must be entitled to know what he needs to be heard about. He must know what is the case against him. He must know what he has to meet." [86]

Turning then to the various national legal systems, and looking first at French law, it is interesting to note that an English text book on French administrative law [87] states that the French concept, *droits de la défense*, is much wider than the English concept of *audi alteram partem*; on the other hand, a French writer, Professor Vedel,[88] is of the opinion that the rule *audi alteram partem* is much wider than the principle of *droit de la*

---

[82] [1974] E.C.R. 1063, 1087.

[83] *Ibid.* p. 1079.

[84] Of which the present writer was a member at the time.

[85] *e.g. Cooper* v. *Wandsworth Board of Works* (1863) 14 C.B. (N.S.) 180; *Ridge* v. *Baldwin* [1964] A.C. 40.

[86] *Current Legal Problems*, 1973, p. 11.

[87] Brown and Garner, *French Administrative Law* 2nd ed., p. 124–125, citing *Trompier-Gravier* (Conseil d'Etat, May 5, 1944, *Sirey* 1945, 3, 14) and *S.A. Co-opérative d'H.B.M. de Vichy-Cusset-Bellerive* (Conseil d'Etat, April 24, 1964, *Recueil*, p. 244).

[88] *Droit Administratif*, p. 281; *Cours de Droit Administratif*, p. 536.

défense in French law, largely because he is of the opinion that the doctrine of *droit de la défense* only applies where the administrative measure in question has been taken by reason of the character or personal conduct of the person concerned. However, other writers take a somewhat wider view, notably Professor Waline, in a contribution to a publication celebrating the centenary of the Luxembourg Conseil d'Etat,[89] where he deduces from the many specific statutory instances, as well as the case-law, that the principle is in the course of development.

In the case of the Federal Republic, it is interesting to note that Article 103 of the Basic Law provides only that the right to be heard applies before the ordinary civil law courts. There is no specific provision for it in administrative law. However, commentators seem to agree that the principle applies despite the absence of any legislative necessity for it. In fact one text book[90] manages to quote 14 pre-Federal Republic decisions supporting the general idea that the right to a hearing (*das rechtliche Gehör*) is an essential element of correct procedure not by virtue of principles of written law but by principles of unwritten law, *i.e.* as a general principle of law.[91] This principle has been taken up by the Federal German courts and a clear illustration is a decision of the Verwaltungsgerichtshof of Kassel in 1956[92] concerned with an administrative decision to change what might be termed a "milk-catchment area" (*Milcheinzugsgebiet*). It was stated there that even without any express provision of a statute the administration must, as a requirement of the rule of law, hear the persons affected before taking a decision imposing any burden on them.

Similar formulations can be found, for example, in the case-law of the Luxembourg Conseil d'Etat, which has held that in the case of administrative decisions which might affect proprietary interests, the administration must hear those affected, even if the actual legislation in question is silent upon the point.[93]

The same would appear to be true in Ireland,[94] Scotland[95] and Denmark.[96] As far as Belgian law is concerned, there do not appear to be any decisions directly in point though academic opinion is in favour of giving a person affected by an administrative decision the right to be heard.[97] It appears, however, that there is no general right to be heard in Dutch administrative law, and the problem is complicated by the fact that there is no general right of appeal against administrative decisions, in the absence of a special statutory provision. However, a law of June 20, 1963,

---

[89] *Livre Jubilaire*, 1957, pp. 495–506; see also his *Droit Administratif*, 9th ed., at pp. 460, 552, 586 and 606 for specific examples.

[90] Forsthoff, *Lehrbuch des Verwaltungsrechts*, 10th ed., p. 235 *et seq.*

[91] See *e.g.* Decision of administrative court of Saxony (Sächs OVG), October 24, 1908, *Jahrbuch* t. 13 p. 97.

[92] May 18, 1956, *Neue juristische Wochenschrift*, 1956, p. 1940.

[93] August 5, 1966, Aff. No. 5968, *Roth* v. *Ministres de l'Intérieur, de la Santé Publique et des Travaux Publics*—the number of Ministers involved was the result of the subject-matter of the action, a refusal of an authorisation to work a quarry so as to protect underground water supplies.

[94] Kelly, *Fundamental Rights in the Irish Law and Constitution*, pp. 313–314.

[95] *Malloch* v. *Aberdeen Corporation* [1971] 1 W.L.R. 1578.

[96] Andersen, *Dansk Forvaltningsret*, at pp. 337 and 339.

[97] See *e.g.* Dembour, *Droit Administratif*, p. 266.

provides for appeals against the administrative acts of the central government authorities.[98]

Finally, in Italy, it has been held that the right to be heard is not protected by the Constitution in administrative proceedings[99] and that there is no general principle of administrative law requiring the Administration to communicate preparatory acts to those liable to be affected to enable them to put their view.[1]

Mr Warner reviewed the position under the various national legal systems in his Opinion and concluded that the right to be heard forms part of those rights which " the law " referred to in Article 164 EEC upholds and of which accordingly it is the duty of the Court to ensure the observance.[2]

The way the Court introduced this general principle into its judgment was to state that notwithstanding the cases specifically dealt with in Articles 2 and 4 of Regulation 99/63, the Regulation is an application of " the general rule that a person whose interests are perceptibly affected by a decision taken by a public authority, must be given the opportunity to make his point of view known."[3] Under the Court's formulation it was stated that the rule requires that an undertaking be clearly informed in good time of the essence of conditions to which the Commission intends to subject an exemption and it must have the opportunity to submit its observations to the Commission. " This is especially so in the case of conditions which, as in this case, impose considerable obligations having far-reaching effects."

The Court deduced from this that breach of the rule would be regarded as a breach of an essential procedural requirement under Article 173 of the Treaty, and that this was the case with regard to Article 3 (1) (*d*) of the Decision. Since this condition was severable, it alone was annulled, and the rest of the decision was allowed to stand whilst the Commission was given the opportunity to reach a fresh decision on the point after hearing the observations or suggestions of the members of the association.[4]

V. Conclusion

It is hoped that this article will have shown the importance of concepts derived from national sources in the case-law of the European Court, subject always to the proviso that once adopted by the Court, they are applicable as principles of Community law, not as rules of national law.

From the point of view of English readers, it will be evident from the account of the *Transocean* case that English concepts are beginning to make their presence felt. However, it will also have been noticed that certain of the most important principles applied by the Court can be

[98] See Van Wijk, Netherlands Report, *8 International Congress of Comparative Law* 1970, pp. 303 *et seq.*

[99] Cons. di Stato, Sez. IV, 9 nov. 1971, n. 959, Rass. Cons. di Stato 1971, I, p. 2076.

[1] Cons. di Stato, Sez. IV, 15 mai 1970, n. 345, Rass. Cons. di Stato 1970, I, p. 828 (834).

[2] [1974] E.C.R. 1063, 1089.

[3] [1974] E.C.R. 1063, 1080.

[4] The new Decision was in fact taken on October 23, 1975, O.J. 1975 L286/24.

regarded as derived from German sources or at least as having become principles of Community law in a formulation closely resembling that current in the Federal Republic, a point which may not be totally unconnected with the fact that of the 353 cases referred to the Court by national courts up to the end of 1975, no fewer than 167 were referred by courts in the Federal Republic. In the nature of things, judges tend to regard as common principles those which they hear cited before them day-in, day-out; perhaps there is something of a moral here for English (and Scottish) courts and lawyers.

[7]

The Community System: the Dual Character of Supranationalism* †

JOSEPH WEILER‡

Does it still make sense to refer to the Community[1] as a supranational system? And, indeed, what do we mean when speaking of such a system? The term supranationalism is evocative of an earlier era of high aspirations which seems at odds with recent developments: a resurgence of overt national political resistance to the Community,[2] a less open but even more dangerous measure of non-compliance with Community obligations[3] and a continuous cycle of political crises[4] the solutions to which seem increasingly elusive. And yet, despite all this, the Community displays a surprising measure of institutional resilience, an impressive record of substantive integration and a relevance in fields initially not contemplated.[5] These apparent contradictions in the practice of the Community may find their analogue in a more abstract conceptualization of the system.

On the one hand, to speak of the Community as supranational in the literal meaning of '... over and above individual states'[6] gives too general and antiquated a notion of the system. For we know that whatever the dreams of the past, the Community's present structure and process involve 'bits and pieces of the national governments ...'[7] with a crucial say in all aspects of Community activity. But even so, in the transfer of certain

† In memory of Sir Andrew Shonfield.

‡ European University Institute, Florence. I am indebted to Professors Cappelletti, Daintith, Jacobs, Rehbinder, Soberman as well as Mr Faull and Miss Seccombe for valuable advice and encouragement. I alone am responsible for errors of fact or weaknesses of opinion.

[1] Unless otherwise indicated 'the Community' will refer to EEC, ECSC and Euratom together.

[2] E.g. the British Labour Party EEC Policy and the French Debré-Foyer Bill. See *Proposition de Loi portant rétablissement de la souveraineté de la République en matière d'énergie nucléaire*, No. 917, Assemblée Nationale, 2ème session extraordinaire de 1978–1979.

[3] We must distinguish between several types of Community law infraction by States. Most common are inadvertent 'prelitigation' legislative or administrative violations and, less common, deliberate evasions (e.g. French-Italian 1981 'wine war'). Effective judicial remedy in respect of both is usually available. 'Post-litigation' defiance may consist in dilatory compliance by the Member States (e.g. Case 7/68 *Commission* v *Italian Republic* [1968] ECR 4) or even outright defiance (e.g. Case 232/78 *Commission* v *French Republic* [1979] ECR 2729. Cf joined Cases 24/80R and 97/80R *Commission* v *French Republic* [1980] ECR 1319). National courts may evasively apply Community law (e.g. *Secretary of State for the Home Department, ex parte Santillo* [1981] 2 All ER 917) or even deliberately defy it (e.g. *Cohn-Bendit* case, Conseil d'Etat (CE) 22 December 1978, *Dalloz* (D) 1979, 155). The cases of deliberate judicial and executive defiance are of course most troublesome. See 'Editorial Comment' *CML Rev* (1980) 311.

[4] cf Everling, *JCM Stud* (1980) 217.

[5] Particularly noticeable in the field of foreign policy in relation to political cooperation.

[6] Robertson, *Recueil des Cours* (*RDC*) (1957) 105, 143.

[7] A. Shonfield, *Europe: Journey to an Unknown Destination* (Allen Lane 1972) 17.

functions to Community organs and in relation to certain constitutional hierarchies there remains a measure of 'aboveness' in the old sense. Further, like all 'federal' models,[8] the Community presents a tension between the whole and the parts, centrifugal and centripetal forces, central Community organs and Member States. In some ways the balancing of this tension in the Community system departs, perhaps even radically, from most other 'federal' models.

The primary purpose of this paper will be then to examine the evolution of these tensions with a view to identifying the ensuing balance and explaining in what sense, if at all, one may still speak of a Community 'aboveness'. The analysis will be limited to the structure and process of the Community and will not deal with its actual operation, be it successful or otherwise, in substantive fields. In addition I shall be concerned to see whether through this analysis we might not find the elements for a working hypothesis as to what are the necessary characteristics which render a system supranational. In this way I hope to give tentative answers to the questions posed at the beginning of this paper.

A. Supranationalism – an amorphous concept

1. The Definitional Problem

The need to revert to a novel term in characterizing the Community was an indication that existing terminology was felt not to give adequate expression to the new venture.[9]

In the early treatments the concept was tackled by reference to the known juridicial-political categories of public international law (which embody the formal traditional modes of international organization) and municipal law (which embody the variety of non-unitary State arrangements).

In a powerful study of synthesis, Hay[10] analyses the most important of these attempts. Few writers adopted extreme positions of total assimilation.[11] More often the analyses, using an analogical method, characterized supranationalism as *veering towards* one or other of the two known systems. Insistence on finding a unique definition could only resolve itself in characterizing the system as sui generis. But so to characterize it with no more was hardly helpful.[12] Since the new term, supranationalism, derived

[8] The term 'federal' is used in its widest sense of sharing in governance. '[T]he original use of the term deals with contractual linkages that involve power sharing – among individuals, among groups, among states. This usage is more appropriate than the definition of modern federations' D. Elazar (ed), *Self Rule/Shared Rule* (Turtledove 1979) 3.

[9] For antecedents see Keeton in G. W. Keeton and G. Schwarzenberger (eds), *English Law and the Common Market* (Stevens and Sons 1963) 1 and Smith, *Yearbook of World Affairs* (1950) 191, esp 207–212. See also H. G. Schermers, *International Institutional Law Vol 1* (Sijthoff 1972) 20.

[10] P. Hay, *Federalism and Supranational Organizations* (University of Illinois Press 1966).

[11] See e.g. C. A. Nørgaard, *The Position of the Individual in International Law* (Munksgaard 1962) (international law approach) and Kohnstamm *RDC* (1956) 1 and comments thereon in Hay, supra n 10.

[12] Cf Hay, 12 *Am J Com L* 39 (1963).

from, indeed was the explication of, the phenomenon it sought to define, a measure of circularity was inevitable. For one had to employ the distinguishing features of the Community to give meaning to the term supranationalism which in turn was the concept used to express the distinctions between the Community and other international organizations. Even if one could agree on some a priori formula for defining supranationality, say in the ability to by-pass the nation-State's formal autonomy and exclusivity in both adopting policy and legislation as well as dealing directly with the citizen,[13] one would still be left in difficulty in trying to define those elements which would render a system supranational in this sense.[14]

2. The Dynamic Nature of the Supranational System – the Community Experience as a Process

In attempting to fix these elements there is a danger of failing to give expression to the dynamic nature of the supranational system. The Community experience has not been a static one, either in its substantive activities or, more significantly for our discussion, in the internal principles of its operation, be they in the institutional framework, the location and exercise of decision-making power, or, generally, the relationships between the Community as a whole and its constitutent parts. Thus, for instance, studies which concentrated, as the primary distinguishing factor, on the ability of Community organs to take decisions immediately binding on individuals within the national legal systems[15] would, today, in the light of subsequent developments in the Community, no longer reflect the mature evolution of that factor.

3. Evaluating the Supranational Process – The Cleavage Between Political and Legal Assessment

Acceptance of the processual character of supranationalism and its subject, European integration, entails the possibility of evaluating it in the sense of establishing, with whatever measure of precision, the progress or retrogression of supranationalism and integration. It has been common to divide the process of European integration into 'phases' and 'periods' characterized by different degrees and levels of supranationalization and integration. The cleavage between the legal and political evaluation of the progress of European integration and the supranational system is most apparent by reference to contrasting assessments of different 'phases' in the process.

[13] Cf Heathcote, *JCM Stud* (1966) 140, 141.

[14] It is, of course, possible to adopt an a priori deductive definition. The most accomplished attempt is by Schermers who suggests a useful list of supranational criteria but even he is then pushed to conclude that since to be 'completely supranational, an international organization should fulfil all [these criteria] . . . no such supranational organization exists.' Schermers, supra n 9, 21.

[15] E.g. Robertson, supra n 6, 145.

The chasm appears both in the choice of phases[16] and, more strikingly, in the evaluation of progress. Thus in a useful study synthesizing three decades of political theories on European integration, the period of 1958–1969 is signalled out as a 'distinct phase'.[17] Evaluating this period the writer comments that '[t]hroughout [these] eleven years during which General de Gaulle [who was "allergic to anything supranational"] remained in power, no notable progress could be made in integration, either in the political domain, the *institutional domain*, the monetary domain or in the geographical extension of the Common Market'.[18] Yet, from the juridical point of view, as will be shown in detail below, it was precisely during this period that certain fundamental facets of the supranational system took crucial, even revolutionary, strides ahead, establishing for example the doctrines of direct effect and supremacy of Community law.[19] Political scientists[20] and lawyers[21] alike may fall into the trap. To be sure, the departure point of each discipline is different. The political theories of European integration were largely wedded to a certain notion about the outcome of the process and embodied a certain predictive element about continuous progress. In addition, political theory laid great emphasis on the social, political and economic substantive achievements and less emphasis on ways and means. The starting point was thus one of high expectation and failure to maintain the visible social/political momentum led to a measure of disillusion in the reassessment of European integration.[22]

The juridical point of departure was different. The constituent instruments of the Communities were traditional multi-partite international treaties. Although including certain novel institutional features they were, in line with precedent, expected to be interpreted in accordance with the normal canons of treaty interpretation, one of which is a presumption against loss of sovereignty by States. The process of integration which in the legal sphere was accomplished by a 'constitutionalisation' of the Treaties[23] was set against limited initial expectations. Thus among lawyers this conditioned a sense of continuous progress of integration.[24]

4. The 'Diffuse' Nature of the Supranational System

In discussing the definitional problem we noted the need to rely on a multiplicity of distinguishing attributes (hallmarks) to give meaning to the

[16] Compare E. Stein, P. Hay, M. Waelbroeck, *European Community and Institutions in Perspective* (Bobbs-Merrill 1976) 10–13. R. Pryce, *The Politics of the European Community* (Butterworths 1973) 1–27. Greilsammer, 2 *Jerusalem Journal of International Relations* 129 (1976). R. Dahrendorf, *A Third Europe*? (EUI Florence, 1979 – Third Jean Monnet Lecture).

[17] Greilsammer, supra n 16.

[18] Ibid, 141 (emphasis added).

[19] The major decision on direct effect was given on 5 February 1963; on supremacy on 15 July 1964.

[20] An extremely pessimistic assessment in the mid-sixties – with statements such as 'Supranational structures may not survive into 1966' – is that of Heathcote, *JCM Stud* (1966) 140, 170.

[21] See e.g. devastating remarks by Shapiro, 53 *Southern California L Rev* 537, 538 (1980).

[22] Cf Puchala, *JCM Stud* (1972) 267, 267 and Haas, *JCM Stud* (1967) 315, 325–331.

[23] See Stein, 75 *American Journal of International Law* (*AJIL*) 1 (1981).

[24] See e.g. P. Pescatore, *The Law of Integration* (Sijthoff 1974).

system. We also noted the evolutionary nature of supranationalism reflecting the developments in the Community. But how are these two factors to be related? The difficulty may best be illustrated by reference to the relationship between sovereignty and supranationalism.

Hay correctly suggests that [w]ith few exceptions, . . . the criteria for the loss of sovereignty coincide with those which much of the literature regards as the elements of supranationalism. Thus, the concept of a transfer of sovereignty may be the legal-analytical counterpart of the political-descriptive notion of supranationalism.'[25]

The 'independence of the organization and of its institutions from member states . . .'; the '. . . ability of an organization to bind its member states by a majority or weighted majority vote'; the '. . . direct binding effect of law emanating from the organization on natural and legal persons'; the attribution to the organization of certain powers, functions and jurisdictions which in terms of sheer quantity result in a qualitative difference from non-supranational organizations; the nature of supranational institutions (principally the Parliament and Court), are the criteria which Hay distilled from the literature as elements of a supranational system.[26] Although it is essential to comprehend supranationalism as containing a multiplicity of factors, a different danger is created: that of treating them as an *integrated complex* progressing or retrogressing as one whole. A cursory examination of the list of criteria cited above will reveal that it is quite possible that in respect of some there may have been 'a loss of sovereignty' whereas in relation to others much less or none at all.

B. Normative and decisional supranationalism

In order to overcome some of the difficulties outlined above it is submitted that a distinction should be drawn, if only for use as a tool of analysis, between two facets of supranationalism. For convenience, I shall call them normative and decisional.[27]

Normative supranationalism is concerned with the relationships and hierarchy which exist between Community policies and legal measures on the one hand and competing policies and legal measures of the Member States on the other. Decisional supranationalism relates to the institutional framework and decision-making processes by which Community policies and measures are, in the first place, initiated, debated and formulated, then promulgated and finally executed.[28] The make-up of both these terms may

[25] Hay, supra n 10, 69. [26] Ibid, 31ff.

[27] I prefer 'decisional' to 'institutional' since the former conveys the need to look at the actual processes and not merely at formal assignment of functions. A more elaborate model is Lindberg *JCM Stud* (1967) 359 and L. Lindberg and S. Scheingold, *Europe's Would-be Polity: Patterns of Change in the European Community* (Prentice Hall 1970). But the limited framework here is probably sufficient since I am not directly concerned with the development of substantive policies and their evaluation.

[28] Puchala, supra n 22, 278, illustrates the complexity of a full model as regards the substantive sectors. I have to content myself with a general Community analysis even if this involves a sacrifice of sophistication.

include factors which can be stated at a sufficient level of generalization so as to serve as criteria for evaluating the progress or retrogression of the two particular facets of supranationalism.

A high measure of normative supranationalism will denote, in general, a hierarchy in which Community measures will take effective precedence over national ones. The choice of criteria is relatively simple since we may use the traditional principles by which relationships between, on the one hand, national and/or State law and, on the other, federal, confederal and international law are expressed: the principle of self-execution (direct effect), the principle of supremacy and the principle of pre-emption. The hallmarks will be the specific manifestation of these principles in the Community.

The centrality of the Member States in the institutional set-up and the absence of an autonomous popularly elected 'Community legislature and government' were basic structural choices taken when setting up the Community. Yet the decisional process in the Treaty may be seen as an attempt to achieve a model of '*Community* decision-making' which despite these structural choices would depart as far as possible from traditional diplomacy and intergovernmentalism and would, in the literal sense, be supranational. (Or at least above the *individual* State). In the Community context a high measure of decisional supranationalism would thus be indicated in relation to decisions taken (*a*) by Community organs the composition and mode of operation of which are autonomous (*communautaire*) and not intergovernmental in the traditional sense, or (*b*) by Community organs the composition and political functions of which are intergovernmental but the process of decision-making, for example the voting procedure, is not strictly that of intergovernmental diplomacy, or (*c*) in pluri-institutional decision-making where the role of the autonomous organs may be said to be critical, and in which the execution of these measures will be (*d*) either directly by, or under the supervisory authority and responsibility of, the autonomous bodies.[29]

Although all four factors are expressed in relation to the institutions of the Community, by virtue of the composition of these institutions, they contain the involvement, both direct and indirect, of the Member States in the decision-making process.

The separate treatment of these two facets of supranationalism covers the essence, if not the detail, of both the 'juridical' approach which focuses on formal relationships, demarcation of competences and resolution of conflicts, and the more 'political' approach which is concerned with the actualities, influenced by legal and non-legal factors, of cooperation and coordination of the different elements in the association of States. Having a clearer view of developments in both spheres may be helpful in drawing composite conclusions. A final supranational factor, relating to the Community's powers, explicit and implied, falls uneasily between the two facets and will consequently be treated separately.

[29] For a more detailed breakdown see Lindberg's 'scale of decision locus', supra n 27, 356–357.

Having introduced these distinctions we may now analyse and trace the evolution of the legal-political framework of the Community and draw some conclusions as regards the meaning of a supranational system.

C. The dynamics of normative and decisional supranationalism: Diverging trends – and a resulting balance

Examination of the European Community's evolution in the last three decades reveals the apparently paradoxical emergence of two conflicting trends. One may have expected in the process of integration a parallel evolution in the transfer of power from the periphery to the centre – an increase in central normative competence accompanied by a strengthening in the 'centralized' decision-making process. In the Community, however, we can trace on the one hand a more or less continuous process of *approfondissement* of normative supranationalism whereby the relationship between the (legal) order of the Community and that of the Member States has come to resemble increasingly a fully fledged (USA type) federal system. On the other hand, and contemporaneously, we can detect a more or less continuous process of *diminution* of decisional supranationalism, stopping, in some respects, only just short of traditional intergovernmentalism. The very existence of supranationalism in both its forms itself distinguishes the Community from most other international organizations. The divergence in the evolution of the two forms may be one of the special, perhaps even unique, features of the Community as a process of integration and as a form of governance. The possible meaning to be given to these diverging Community trends will be discussed and assessed below. First, however, I will examine in greater detail the two facets of supranationalism with a view to a clearer understanding of their meaning and so as to illustrate the respective evolutionary processes.

1. Normative Supranationalism: The Process of Approfondissement

The evolution of normative supranationalism is a well-known story and a reminder of the major landmarks will be sufficient for present purposes.

(a) *Self-executing measures – the doctrine of direct effect*

The first distinguishing feature, or hallmark, of supranationalism in its early ECSC days was the power vested in the Community's main autonomous institution, the High Authority, to adopt self-executing measures which were directly binding on individuals – mainly undertakings in the coal and steel sectors.[30] Once the Treaty of Paris was ratified by the Member States this power could be executed *regardless of the monist or dualist character of the municipal legal order of the Member States.* Despite the novelty of this

[30] Art 14 and 15 of the ECSC Treaty.

feature, at least in modern times, the international law character of the Treaty of Paris remained largely unaffected, since this manifestation of self-executing rule-making power was explicitly agreed upon by the Member States which were signatories to the Treaty.

Later, however, this first characteristic of normative supranationalism was judicially developed in relation to the Treaty of Rome. In a series of landmark decisions the European Court of Justice, throughout the 1960s and 1970s, took this doctrine far further than the limited provisions in the Treaties.[31]

It held in 1963, in the first major step in the 'constitutionalisation' of the Treaty of Rome, that under certain conditions provisions of the Treaty would have direct effect in the Community bestowing enforceable rights as between individuals and the Member States.[32] Thus Member States, vis-à-vis individuals, could no longer break their international treaty obligations relying on the weakness of traditional public international law: a weakness based in part on the exclusion of the individual as a direct subject of rights and duties (and of individual standing to sue) and on the traditional tardiness of States in bringing international claims on behalf of individuals when their national interest is not involved.

Since that 1963 decision the doctrine of direct effect has been extended, deepened and become a general rule of construction applicable to much of Community law. Important steps in its evolution have been its extension to create directly enforceable Treaty rights between individuals inter se[33] and its application, step by step, even to types of Community legislation (e.g. directives) which are addressed to Member States and which on their face would not suggest the possibility of bestowing rights and duties on individuals.[34] The process of refinement continues to date.

(b) The doctrine of supremacy

During the same period the European Court evolved its second crucial doctrine, the doctrine of supremacy, which, again, encapsulates a major aspect of fully fledged federal systems. In *Costa* v *ENEL*[35] the Court established a clear hierarchy of norms. In its view, Community law within the sphere of competence of the Community, be it primary or secondary, is superior to Member State law even if the latter is subsequently enacted and of a constitutional nature. As in the case of 'direct effect' the derivation of supremacy from the Treaty depended on a 'constitutional' rather than international law interpretation.[36] The Court's reasoning that supremacy was enshrined in the Treaty was contested by the governments of Member

[31] The literature on the doctrine is immense. For lucid up-to-date statements see, e.g., D. Wyatt and A. Dashwood, *The Substantive Law of the EEC* Chap 3 (Sweet and Maxwell 1980); J. Usher, *European Community Law and National Law* (G. Allen & Unwin 1981) 17–30.

[32] Case 26/62 *Van Gend en Loos* v *Nederlandse Administraitie der Belastingen* [1963] ECR 1.

[33] See Wyatt and Dashwood, supra n 31, 29–30.

[34] Usher, supra n 31, 18, 26–30.

[35] Case 6/64 *Costa* v *ENEL* [1964] ECR 585.

[36] For the constitutional character of secondary Community law see Case 38/69 *Commission* v. *Italian Republic* [1970] ECR 56.

States in this case and others. Acceptance of this view amounts in effect to a quiet revolution in the legal orders of the Member States. For, in respect of any matter coming within the competence of the Community – not always an easy matter to determine[37] – the legal *Grundnorm* will have been effectively shifted, placing Community norms at the top of the legal pyramid.

It follows that the evolutionary nature of the doctrine of supremacy is necessarily bi-dimensional. One dimension is the elaboration of the parameters of the doctrine by the European Court. But its full reception, the second dimension, depends on its incorporation into the constitutional orders of the Member States and its affirmation by their supreme courts. It is relatively easy to trace the evolution of the Community dimension of the doctrine from *Costa* v *ENEL*, where the Court was concerned with the paradigmatic conflict between substantive national and Community law, through the ambiguous *Walt Wilhelm*[38] and *Simmenthal*.[39] In the former, the Court accepted the possible legitimacy of having national competition policy operating beside the Community policy, with each proceeding '... on the basis of the considerations peculiar to it'.[40] Thus the issue was not about the possible co-existence of conflicting substantive law. But despite the legitimacy of having a parallel national competition policy which the Court did not dispute, the principle of supremacy required that a national court in cases of national competition law must keep an open eye that its decisions, even in their procedural, civil or penal aspects, would not prejudice any concurrent Community proceedings.[41] In the *Simmenthal* case the issue was not whether supremacy should exist but which court, in the national order, should decide this. The European Court, controversially,[42] but seemingly consistently with its earlier jurisprudence,[43] insisted on the immediacy of supremacy so that even national procedural rules which did not deny the ultimate supremacy of Community law but designated internal procedures as to the court in which the review of the national legislation should take place, were prohibited. The Court was aiming at establishing supremacy not as a question of substantive conflict but as a principle which would dictate the replacement of national law.

As regards the second dimension, the evolutionary character of the process is more complicated. It should be remembered that in respect of the

[37] See text to n 59, infra.

[38] Case 14/68 *Walt Wilhelm and Others* v *Bundeskartellamt* [1969] ECR 1. This is an ambiguous case. See e.g. Korah, *EL Rev* (1981) 14, 26 and n 50.

[39] Case 106/77 *Italian Finance Administration* v *Simmenthal* [1978] ECR 629.

[40] Recital 3 of judgment.

[41] Recitals 7–9 of judgment.

[42] See Sorrentino, 'Lo Sviluppo della Forma di Governo Italiana nella Giurisprudenza della Corte in Materia Communitaria' in *Convegno sulla Corte Costituzionale e Sviluppo della Forma di Governa Italiana* (Mimeo, Univ degli Studi di Firenze, Facoltà di Giurisprudenza 1981).

[43] The Court's judgment may seem to beg the question. It prohibits interference with a '... national Court having jurisdiction to apply such law ...'. But that is the point at issue. By virtue of the decision of the Italian Constitutional Court, (Case 205/76 of 4 August 1976, 99 *Il Foro Italiano* [*Foro It*] 2299 (1976) it could be said that lower courts have no jurisdiction in this situation.

original Member States there was no specific constitutional preparation for this European Court inspired development. The process of *approfondissement* may thus be seen in the gradual acceptance of the doctrine by the 'supreme courts' of the Six. The pattern although uneven is clearly progressive. In some Member States the reception of the principle caused no major problems (Benelux),[44] in others, the Courts accepted the doctrine with reservations regarding either the procedural implications of the doctrine (Italy) or the possible incompatibility of Community law with fundamental human rights enshrined in their constitutions (Italy, Germany).[45] Now that the European Court has indicated its willingness to review Community law itself in relation to a 'higher law' of human rights based, in part, on the common constitutional traditions, these objections will have become more theoretical.[46] In others still, the judiciary split, with one branch accepting the doctrine and the other refusing it (France).[47] As regards the new Member States, especially those with a written constitution, since at the time of accession supremacy was already an established principle it could be regulated formally in the process of accession.[48] In the UK, where the theoretical possibility of a shift in the *Grundnorm* of the type discussed above is problematic, the matter is not fully resolved since no clear case involving UK legislation contradicting earlier Community law has come before the higher courts. The House of Lords has, judiciously, avoided making an abstract pronouncement on the subject and the Court of Appeal under the tutelage of Lord Denning has see-sawed, eventually settling on a halfway-house acceptance.[49]

So far we have treated the doctrine of direct effect and supremacy as distinct concepts, whereas analytically, linked by the Court's vision of the exigencies of a cohesive and integral legal order and its insistence on the principle of uniform interpretation and application of Community law, the two are tightly connected. In this sense supremacy is consequential of direct effect. Consideration of this connection will highlight another aspect of the evolutive nature of normative supranationalism. In *Van Gend en Loos* the Commission and the Advocate General although reaching different conclusions were ad idem in seeing the inevitable link between supremacy and direct effect, once the need for uniformity was established. It is submitted that the fact that the Court rejected this cue and preferred to introduce the two concepts into the Community legal order in two separate cases (even if, inevitably, using the very similar 'uniformity' argumentation) indicated a

[44] See generally, Bebr *CML Rev* (1974) 3 and R. Plender and J. Usher, *Cases and Materials of the European Communities* (Macmillan 1980) 173–220.

[45] For Italy see n 42 supra. For Germany see H. G. Schermers, *Judicial Protection in the European Communities* (Kluwer 1979) 92–97, and note in *CML Rev* (1967–68) 483.

[46] Cf now German Federal Constitutional Court decision of 25 July 1979 [1980] 2 CMLR 531.

[47] See generally Weiss, *Legal Issues of European Integration* (LIEI) (1979) 51.

[48] See e.g Temple-Lang, *CML Rev* (1972) 167; Due and Gulman, *CML Rev* (1972) 456; Evrigenis, *CML Rev* (1980) 157.

[49] The British position is succinctly stated in L. Collins, *European Community Law in the U.K.* (Butterworths 1980) 25–26.

deliberate and politically wise attempt to phase in the progressive evolution of normative supranationalism so as to ensure as far as possible a smooth reception in the national legal and political orders.

(c) *The principle of pre-emption*[50]

It is here that one finds the third hallmark of normative supranationalism. In its purest and most extreme form pre-emption means that, in relation to fields in which the Community has policy-making competence, the Member States are not only precluded from enacting legislation contradictory to Community law (by virtue of the doctrine of supremacy) but they are pre-empted from taking any action at all. Initially, before the full ripening of the doctrine, the European Court achieved this objective by forbidding the disguise of the Community nature of regulations.[51] Subsequently, the principle came into its own even though it is still in an evolutionary stage. The Court of Justice is striving to attain an equilibrium between, on the one hand, the wish to promote Community policy-making and, on the other hand, the pragmatic necessity of regulation in fields in which the Community has competence but in which, for various reasons such as problems in its decision-making processes, it has not been able to evolve comprehensive Community policies. The Court has felt that in these situations the policy lacunae should be filled by Member State action, implying a more flexible rendering of the pure pre-emption principle. In this the Court has followed most federal systems, none of which apply pure pre-emption. This shift in the Court's formulation may be illustrated by a number of decisions in the field of external economic relations. One of the questions in the *ERTA* case[52] was whether the competence to negotiate and conclude an international agreement in the transport field rested in the Community or the Member States. Since in its Transport Chapter the Treaty does not refer specifically to Community competence to engage in international agreements, it was argued that such matters were to be left within Member State powers. In a judgment, the importance of which goes beyond the specific question before us, the Court laid down an emphatic absolute principle of pre-emption:

> [E]ach time the Community, with a view to implementing a common policy envisaged by the Treaty, adopts provisions laying down common rules, whatever form these may take, the Member States no longer have the right, acting individually or even collectively, to undertake obligations with third countries which affect those rules. As and when such rules come into being, the Community alone is

[50] I am indebted to Professor M. Waelbroeck's paper in Bellagio, July 1979 entitled 'Community Preemption and Related Problems'. See also D. J. Gijlstra et al (eds), *Leading Cases and Materials on the Law of the European Communities* (Kluwer 1977) 88–95 and Louis *Revue d'Integration Européene* (1979) 355.

[51] See e.g. Case 34/73 *Variola* [1973] ECR 990; Case 39/72 *Commission v Italy* [1973] ECR 113. See also *Amministrazione delle Finanze dello Stato v Ditte Fratelli Grassi e Greco Rocco Michele* (1976] I *Giurisprudenza Costituzionale* 1292.

[52] Case 22/70 *Commission v Council* [1971] ECR 273.

in a position to assume and carry out contractual obligations towards third countries affecting the whole sphere of application of the Community legal system.[53]

In the case of *Kramer*[54] there is a certain retreat from the earlier emphatic position in *ERTA*. The Court stated that despite the fact that the Community had adopted internal measures, these '. . . limit themselves to providing the Community institutions with the power to take measures similar to those which the Member States . . . did take. . . . [T]he Community not yet having fully exercised its functions in the matter . . . the Member States had the power to assume commitments . . . and . . . the right to ensure the application of those commitments within the area of their jurisdiction.'[55] In the *International Rubber Agreement* case[56] the Court accepted concurrent jurisdiction of the Member States in a field 'occupied' by the Community '[i]f . . . the financing (of the agreement in question) is to be by the Member States'. The Court acknowledged that as '. . . no formal decision has been taken on the question [as to whether the Community or Member States should finance the agreement, and as] there is no certainty as regards the attitude of the various Member States. . . . The exclusive competence of the Community could not be envisaged in such a case'.[57] Here we find a retreat even in respect of a policy the Community exclusiveness of which was already established. In general a pragmatic approach was to replace the purist principle evoked in *ERTA*.

On its face then it would seem that in relation to the principle of pre-emption there has been a retardation rather than a deepening of the scope of the principle in the Community legal order. For, in the terminology aptly adopted by Professor Waelbroeck, there seems to have been a shift by the Court from a 'conceptualist-federalist approach' which corresponds to pre-emption in its purest and most exclusive form to a 'pragmatic approach' which leaves the Member States concurrent competence with the Community. It should first be pointed out that in its second approach the Court has displayed, characteristically, a measure of political acumen. To insist on pure pre-emption when the Community institutions are not yet ready for their task could be retrogressive for the general evolution of the Community. At the same time the Court has insisted that in certain cases the pragmatic approach is transitory in nature. With the full occupation of a field by a Community policy, national measures (even if not contradictory and thus not in violation of the supremacy principle) could become prohibited per se. In other cases concurrent jurisdiction may remain constant. The *approfondissement* of pre-emption may thereby be explained in two ways. First, by its maturing from a crude even dogmatic statement of pure

[53] Recitals 17–18 of judgment.
[54] Joined Cases 3, 4 and 6/76 *Cornelis Kramer and Others* [1976] ECR 1279.
[55] Recitals 35–39 of judgment.
[56] Opinion 1/78 [1979] ECR 2871.
[57] Recitals 57–60 of judgment.

principle to a relatively sophisticated doctrine sensitive to Community needs. Secondly, pre-emption is seen to be spreading from one substantive field of Community law to another. It now affects sectors such as fisheries, competition policy and agriculture.[58]

(*d*) *Limits to jurisdiction?*

Direct effect, supremacy and pre-emption are the core attributes not only of supranationalism, but can be found also in fully fledged federal systems. Whence then, the acknowledged paramountcy of the Member States in the Community system?

First, it should be recorded that even today the Community remains, functionally, a *multi-sectoral condominium.*[59] The Community legal order, with all its above attributes, extends only to those fields over which the Community has competence. There are many fields, some even critical such as defence, aspects of fiscal and monetary policy and education policy, to mention just a few, which remain for the time being outside the Community sphere. But this alone would not be sufficient explanation. Several developed federal systems are equally based on a doctrine of enumerated powers which[60] did not prove an obstacle to subsequent wholesale expansion. Indeed the evolution of European integration from the limited spheres of the Coal and Steel Community to an 'Economic Community' indicated a great increase in the number and breadth of these sectoral condominiums. Further, the Common Market itself has seen a continuous process of extending the limits of Community competence, often through the Community's own variant of judicially created doctrines of implied powers.[61]

Despite the existence of Article 236 of the EEC Treaty which specifies the Treaty method of constitutional amendment, indicating that theoretical limits do exist to this expansion, from the normative point of view the European Court of Justice, true to its integrationist ethos, has consistently attempted to narrow those limits, interpreting widely and creatively existing provisions so as to allow jurisdictional expansion without recourse to complicated Treaty amendment.[62] Here too the jurisprudence indicates a measure of *approfondissement.* In the early cases the language of the Court resembled that of international law tribunals using a narrow rendering of the effectiveness principle to give *textual* meaning to specific Treaty provisions.[63] By contrast in *ERTA* the Court had come to rely on a much

[58] See Gijlstra, supra n 50.

[59] Whereby, unlike the territorial condominium in which there is joint national control over territory, here there is joint control over economic and other sectors of policy.

[60] Cf Tenth Amendment to US Constitution.

[61] See e.g. Gijlstra, supra n 50, 1–9. Schwartz 27 *ICLQ* 614 (1978); Olmi, in II *Mélanges Fernand Dehousse* (F. Nathan, Ed. Labor, 1979) 279.

[62] See e.g. Case 22/70, supra n 52 (external relations-transport policy); Opinion 1/78, supra n 56 (common commercial policy); Case 91/79 *Commission* v *Italian Republic* [1980] ECR 1099 (environmental policy).

[63] See Case 8/55 *Fédération Charbonnière Belgique* v *High Authority* [1954–1956] ECR 292, 299 ff. The narrow textual approach was even more noticeable when powers were refused: see Case 20/59 *Italy* v. *High Authority* [1960] ECR 325, 336 ff.

broader effectiveness principle, using the language of a constitutional rather than an international court.[64] Likewise the Court has taken a very lenient view towards, and effectively sanctioned, the use of Article 235 of the EEC Treaty as codified 'implied powers'. The expansive approach adopted by the Court is explicable, at least partially, by the different political structure of the Community, a structure which highlights in another way the centrality and paramountcy of the Member States. For in Europe, unlike the USA, national governments are responsible, by and large, for decision-making both at the national level and at the Community level. When policies are adopted, even at the jurisdictional limits of the Treaty and beyond, the central decision-making organs of the Member States will have partaken in the process, thereby being 'politically estopped' from challenging expansion and diffusing what in other non-unitary systems has been the classical federal debate over competences.[65]

This then is another clue to Member State centrality. For the principles of normative supranationalism provide only a framework into which substantive rules and policies must be fitted. The Community system did not opt for a classical federal governmental structure characterized by a federal legislature directly elected 'by the people', and a federal executive likewise selected, both bodies separate and independent of their would-be national counterparts. Instead the Treaty provides for a system in which the Member State governments play a key role in 'filling in' the normative framework. However, the Fathers of the Treaty hoped that by creating a hybrid structure of decision-making, which would differ substantially in its operation from traditional intergovernmental organisations, the Community interest would prevail despite the prominence of the Member States. Decision-making was also to be supranational. We must turn then to examine the evolution of decisional supranationalism.

2. The Diminution of Decisional Supranationalism

Decisional supranationalism and its expression in the evolution of decision-making in the Community are, by comparison to normative supranationalism, less easy to trace and analyse. Several reasons account for this difficulty. Strangely (or, perhaps, wisely) the Treaties are rather cryptic in their institutional provisions. A literal reading of texts gives little vision as to the function of the institutions and only a formal indication as to their competences and powers. Inevitably, there is an enormous gap between these formal provisions and the *Realpolitik* manifestation of power in Community life. We noted, in discussing normative supranationalism, the pre-eminent role played by the European Court of Justice in widening and

[64] Most writers on Community affairs accept the jurisprudential evolution although they differ as to its terminological characterization. Cf R. H. Lauwaars, *Lawfulness and Legal Force of Community Decisions* (Sijthoff 1973) 94–105 with Olmi, supra n 61.

[65] The 'political estoppel' operating against governments is illustrated in Case 91/79, supra n 62, 1103 (observation of Italian Government).

deepening the scope and meaning of normative supranationalism. The judicial process is characterized by a high measure of transparency which facilitates the task of the Community observer. It was possible to identify with relative ease and precision the evolving stages of normative supranationalism. By contrast the process of political decision-making and policy formulation is much more obscure and its evolution is marked less by clear-cut landmarks (although some critical ones exist) and more by a subtle process of institutional interplay.[66] The tension between 'whole and parts' is, naturally, a constant feature of this field as well. It manifests itself here in two, sometimes converging, axes: 1) Community versus Member States; and, within the Community, 2) non-intergovernmental versus more intergovernmental institutions. It would be far too simplistic to suggest that decision-making may be explained by simple reference to these axes; the formulation of Community policies is a complicated and multi-phased process and the duality of axes manifests itself at almost each stage.[67] This will be illustrated below. At the same time, if a global view is adopted it is possible to detect a clear enough evolutionary line in decisional supranationalism, namely its decline. This decline is apparent in relation to all criteria which were used to characterise decisional supranationalism:

(i) The independence and the autonomous policy-and decision-making role of the intergovernmental institutions is declining;

(ii) the weight of non-intergovernmental institutions in pluri-institutional decision-making processes is declining;

(iii) within quasi-intergovernmental institutions there is a decline of their unique supranational features;

(iv) in the execution or detailed legislative implementation of Community policies there has been a shift to Member State domination.

To understand this decline we must first discuss briefly the political institutions themselves and then turn to the decision-making process.

The main European Community institutions are sufficiently well known and do not need detailed description here. In the first three decades of Community life, apart from the Court, the institutions which dominated the scene were, clearly, the Commission (and High Authority) and the Council of Ministers. Also clear enough is the general role assigned to both organs. The Commission and its staff, although reflecting the national composition of the Community,[68] is undoubtedly the more *communautaire* and less intergovernmental of the two. The Commissioners are required by the Treaty '[i]n the performance of [their] duties [neither to] seek nor take instructions from any Government or from any other body. . . . Each Member State undertakes to respect this principle and not to seek to

[66] See C. Sasse et al, *Decision Making in the European Communities* (Prager Publishers Inc 1977) and H. Wallace et al (eds) *Policy Making in the European Community* (John Wiley and Sons 1976).

[67] See Wallace et al, supra n 66, esp Webb, 1–31; and H. Wallace, 33–68.

[68] But note that 'the need to cater for the differing interests of the Member States and to accept national quotas, however unofficial, . . . inhibits the development of an elite corps of policy-makers. . .'. H. Wallace, supra n 66, 53.

influence the members of the Commission in the performance of their tasks.'[69]

The Commission as a body is thus notionally autonomous and specifically free to pursue the Community interest. The functions of the Commission are varied. It has the exclusive role of initiating legislation (in the formal sense); according to this scheme it is also the central administrative organ of the Community;[70] it has a potentially important 'diplomatic' role in acting as broker between the Member States; it acts as 'federal agency' in those spheres where the Community has fully fledged federal powers (e.g. competition policy); it supervises the execution of the Treaties and Community law by Member States and acts as the Treaties and Community law by Member States and acts as a 'supranational public attorney general' in cases of violation. According to early theory of the Community it was to be the technocratic 'functional' core which would engineer and precipitate the famous spillover leading the Community towards political union.

The Council of Ministers by contrast is the main formal legislator, clearly indicating the centrality of the Member States. It would be wrong, stricto sensu, to characterise the Council as an intergovernmental institution. Its rules of voting and procedure, the role of the President and the formal reliance on Commission draft legislation distinguish it from classical intergovernmental organs and characterize it as supranational as well – albeit in a limited way.[71] Also, one important feature must be emphasized if the supranational character of the Council is to be fully appreciated. It is true that the Council can refuse to enact any legislation put before it by the Commission even if the policy is clearly in the interest of the Community. In rejecting such legislation, or amending it,[72] the Council can be, and often is, motivated by interests which are contrary to the 'Community spirit'. The Member States are, however, obliged to act jointly, though not necessarily unanimously, within the framework of the Council of Ministers. This is one of the striking interactions of normative and decisional supranationalism. In any given field which is regulated by Community law and for which competence has been transferred to the Community organs, the individual Member States are precluded from taking unilateral action in implementing and/or changing the policy; they must act jointly as the Council of Ministers within the normal decision-making procedures of the Community.

Thus, in the field of agriculture the Community has evolved a common policy which determines inter alia annual price rises. The Council is free to reject any proposal from the Commission or from one of its members. Any member may veto any given proposal and thus block a decision. This is an indication of the low measure of decisional supranationalism in the Council. What is, critically, not permissible is for one Member State or more

[69] Art 10, Merger Treaty.

[70] Apart from a few fields, the actual execution of Community policies is in the hands of the Member States.

[71] See Pescatore, supra n 24, 7–10.

[72] See Art 149 of the EEC Treaty.

to 'go it alone' in the face of Council deadlock. That is the expression of the high measure of normative supranationalism. If decisions in the particular field are to be taken they must be taken by the Ministers acting qua Council. At least to that limited extent the Council of Ministers remains a supranational institution.[73] In theory, then, the tandem of Commission – charged with policy initiative, a secondary legislative function and with execution and supervision tasks – and Council – charged with policy decision-making and actual 'primary' legislation thereby representing directly the interests of the Member States – was meant to achieve the balance in the decision-making process between Community and Member States. The real story has been very different, its main theme being the ever increasing strengthening in the weight of the Council and Member States and a corresponding decline of the Commission.[74] This process has manifested itself in several ways:

(*a*) *The decline of the Commission: the signs*

In the early years of the Coal and Steel Community, the High Authority enjoyed a large measure of autonomy. Its responsibilities were fairly narrow, confined to these two sectors, and its functions resembled the current Commission functions in, say, the field of competition. Its main addressees were sectoral undertakings and the governmental departments directly concerned. This relative narrowness explains perhaps its measure of autonomy. The effect of High Authority activity on the Member States was ex hypothesi rather limited. Politically it did not emerge as a serious focal point of real power. Moreover, normative supranationalism was as yet fairly embryonic. The High Authority was king in its court.

With the conclusion of the Treaty of Rome the sphere of activities of the Communities received an enormous qualitative and quantitative boost. Despite the deliberate attempt to play down the supranational character of the Community, since 1958 Community decisions have had a much greater effect on national life: establishment of the Customs Union, the pursuit of the Communities' four 'freedoms' (free movement of goods, labour, services and capital) and the creation of Community common policies inevitably and increasingly encroached on national policies, national legislative competences and national administrative freedom. One could expect an a priori greater interest and greater involvement of the Member States in the Community process. A further problem was bound to develop – the emergence of the Community 'democracy deficit'.[75] The democracy deficit has two closely connected aspects. In the first place, given the possible and often exaggerated tensions between Community interests and national interests, there was a fear that Community programmes would be developed which did not pay due respect to national interests. The European Assembly

[73] Cf Usher, n 31 supra, 47–84.

[74] Cf S. Henig, *Power and Decision in Europe* (Europotentials Press, London 1980); Sasse, supra n 66.

[75] Term borrowed from D. Marquand, *Parliament for Europe* (Jonathan Cape 1979).

(Parliament) was denied by the Treaties any meaningful say in the evolution and supervision of policies and law. Its members were not directly elected to their posts but nominated by and from national parliaments. The Commission for its part lacked any direct popular legitimacy; and the Council of Ministers, the main legislative body, represented the executives of the Member States. It was only to be expected that uneasiness about the Community legislative process would develop. In the absence of an effective democratically legitimate *Community* check on the legislator, it was inevitable that there would be a shift to *national* scrutiny. Alas, national parliaments have created largely unimpressive mechanisms for control of Community actions.[76] Instead, a powerful Council of Ministers which was, at least in theory, answerable to national parliamentary control could be seen as some answer to this aspect of the democratic deficit.[77] This solution is largely illusory. Much of the Council work is done by the civil servant COREPER members who are no more 'legitimate' than the Commission and with the possible exception of Denmark, there is little direct control, except on major issues, on ministerial work within the Council. Indeed – and this is the other aspect of the deficit, which remains unanswered to date – the national ministers may use the legislative forum of the Council so as to pass legislation which may have been checked and even vetoed in the national parliaments. The other traditional check on the legislature was of course to be the Court of Justice. In the early 1960s, however, the Court saw as its main task the evolution and consolidation of European institutions and policies. Thus, for example, when a Community measure which allegedly violated fundamental rights enshrined in a constitution of a Member State was brought before it for judicial review, the Court adopted a narrow formalistic approach and declared in effect that the Treaties did not impose a duty to respect those rights.[78] The Court was concerned not to impede in any way the function of the Community institutions nor to threaten the primacy of Community law. Later the Court learnt that the process of integration would be enhanced rather than impeded by a bold policy of judicial review[79] but the Court's early attitude added thus to the democracy deficit.

Despite these two factors, the enormous increase in the range of Community activities and competences and the emergence of the democracy deficit – both of which would seem to suggest an inevitable increase in the importance of the Council of Ministers -- the eclipse of the Commission was

[76] See Sasse in A. Cassese (ed), *Parliamentary Control over Foreign Policy* (Sijthoff & Noordhoff 1980) 147.

[77] In fact a different type of democracy deficit has emerged whereby the executive branch of the governments of the Member States is able to pursue policies which, perhaps, would be more open to challenge if conducted 'at home'. See e.g. Rogers & Bolton, 'The True Cost of Sanctions' *New Statesman* 9 January 1981.

[78] Cf Case 1/58 *Friedrich Stork & Co v. High Authority of the European Coal and Steel Community* [1959] ECR 17.

[79] See Cappelletti, *LIEI* (1979) 1. On recent developments in human rights and the Community legal order see Drzemczewski, 30 *ICLQ* 118, 128–134 (1981).

not immediately apparent. Two interrelated factors contributed to the maintenance of Commission power. First, the proximity in time to the conclusion of the Treaty of Rome bestowed legitimacy on the activities of the EEC in its first years. The Treaty and its provisions were debated in all six national parliaments and were approved. Secondly, so long as the Community was seen to be confined to an implementation of the explicit operative parts of the Treaty, the democratic deficit did not come to the fore. Given that the Commission's main task was the execution of these explicit policies – principally the establishment of the Customs Union – it did not come into major policy conflicts with the Council. (There were in fact certain personality clashes, in themselves indications of the political self-perception of the Commissioners and their President in the early years.)[80]

The Commission was thus able to gain immense prestige by the rapid and professional manner in which it coordinated the process of implementation and by its skill in fulfilling its 'broker' role in securing the agreement of, and settling the disputes among, the governments of the Member States. Once these first tasks were substantially achieved, however, the process of erosion in the Commission's position began to become more apparent.

The signs of the Commission decline are clear enough and discussed ably elsewhere.[81] Of the more important signs one should mention the rise to eminence of the Committee of Permanent Representatives (COREPER) as a powerful intermediary between the Commission and Council and the initial exclusion and subsequent toleration of the Commission in the new policy-shaping European body – the European Council. The European Council was set up outside the Treaties and became the institutionalized forum for the meeting of Heads of State and Government. Its function was not only to shape new 'second generation' policies but also to serve as the main arena for the settlement of intergovernmental disputes regarding Community issues. The rise of COREPER meant that Commission initiatives were subject to intergovernmental influence at an extremely early stage in their formulation, thereby detracting from the Commission role as representing the *Community* vision.[82] This process of national intervention occurs not only after a Commission proposal is made and before it is submitted formally to Council. 'Legislative Committees' comprising representatives of the Member States and Commission officials already scrutinize embryonic proposals closely after their conception within the Commission services and directorates-general. A proposal might be aborted because of national disagreement even before it is put on the Commission agenda. The emergence of the European Council contributed to the detraction from the

[80] See H. Wallace, supra n 67, 53.

[81] See e.g. *Report on European Institutions presented by the Committee of Three to the European Council* (Council of the European Communities 1980) (hereinafter 'Three Wise Men Report') 49–53. Henig, supra n 74, 51–63, 105–117. See also Baldi, *Rivista di diritto Europeo* (1981) 134.

[82] Cf Three Wise Men Report 54. COREPER does of course increase the efficiency and acceptability of the legislative outcome. For a positive analysis see Noel and Etienne, *Government and Opposition* (1971) 422. But see Tizzano, 'COREPER', Appendice, *Novissimo Digesto Italiano* (UTET 1981).

Commission's role as a source of fresh Community ideas and as the broker between the Member States.[83] The Commission was hemmed in by two new bodies 'usurping' both its technical and political-diplomatic functions.

(b) *The Council of Ministers – erosion of supranational features: the signs*

The erosion of decisional supranationalism has not only been apparent in the decline of the Commission vis-à-vis the Council (in both its derivatives: European Council and Council of Ministers). Within the Council of Ministers itself there has been a decline in its supranational characteristics. We have already noted the emergence of the European Council. This, it is submitted, is an indication of the failure of the Council of Ministers' 'First Eleven' – the Foreign Ministers – to assert themselves as an institutional body capable of giving direction to the Community and solving its problems. The need to resort to old-style loosely structured summitry is a clear regression in the role of the Council of Ministers qua Community body.

The second, perhaps more important landmark in the decline of decisional supranationalism was the retreat by the Council of Ministers from majority voting – which had been designed as the clearest manifestation in the decision-making process of the precedence of the Community interest over the national interest – to consensus decision-making. This move, precipitated by France and at first grudgingly accepted by the other five in the legally dubious Accord of Luxembourg,[84] was to become, with the accession of the three new Member States, an accepted Community norm. Thus, one of the truly outstanding supranational features of the Council's procedure was reduced. Majority voting itself is not entirely exceptional in international organizations. It is the law-making power of the Council and the effect of that law on and in the national legal orders as expressed in the concept of normative supranationalism which made the prospect of majority voting so unique. The existing veto power which each Member State now holds does not necessarily paralyse the Council because, as we have seen, in areas controlled by the Community the Council *must* at the end of the day take a decision if entire policies are not to come to a halt. The power to veto does not give an individual Member State the power to impose its own desire as to the eventual outcome of the decision-making process. Rather the effect had been to force the partners into 'package-deal decision-making' with compromises being sought not only as regards each policy but among various policies. This development was no doubt instrumental in the emergence of the European Council as a forum for this

[83] Three Wise Men Report 53 and passim.

[84] See R. Ducci and B. Olivi (eds), *L'Europa Incompiuta* (Cedam 1970) 411–422. See also P. J. G. Kapteyn and P. Verloren van Themaat, *Introduction to the Law of the European Communities* (Sweet & Maxwell 1973) 143–146.

high-powered political horse-trading although, as submitted above, the Council of Foreign Ministers could have assumed this function.

The Luxembourg Accord and the power of veto have not completely destroyed Community superiority in decision-making. First, there is the simple fact that, albeit by consent of the Council, many issues, noticeably the budget, are still decided by majority voting.[85] Secondly, the veto power of the Member States in itself does not necessarily entail, as most commentators assume, the blocking of the Community supranational process. What is crucial is the legislative context in which the veto is exercised. When the Treaty provides explicitly for Council unanimity in adopting certain policies,[86] the veto power thereby entailed gives the individual Member State the ability to block directly any unacceptable measure. And to the extent that the Luxembourg Accord extends this power to measures in which the Treaty provides for majority or qualified majority voting, the same ability will naturally exist.

However, Article 149 of the EEC Treaty provides that when acting on a proposal from the Commission 'unanimity shall be required for a [Council] act constituting an amendment to that proposal'. In this case, then, the veto power available to the individual Member State gives it the power to prevent any tampering with a Commission proposal, i.e. a 'supranational veto', but not the ability to force an amendment. The only way open to a recalcitrant Member State whose proposed amendments are 'supranationally blocked' by the veto of another State insisting on the Commission's original proposal, is to veto the entire measure, which of course is a much more serious matter and demands a higher threshold of national interest. Indeed Parliament made astute use of this principle in its latest budgetary wrangle with the Council. The régime of 'deadlines' in the budgetary process which prevent indefinite delays and the ability of three Member States to block by a 'qualified veto'[87] the changes which the Council wished to introduce to the 1980 Parliamentary supplementary budget led to adoption of that budget by the President of Parliament.

The strict doctrine of separation of powers, according to which the executive is concerned solely with implementation of policies adopted elsewhere, was probably never tenable and the crucial policy-making role of executives is so apparent as to obviate the need for any analysis. The definition of the executive function in the Community system is not easy. We have already noted that one traditional function of executives in contemporary Western democracies, that of initiating and submitting policy proposals to the legislative branch – a task initially associated with the Commission – has, except in the narrow technical sense, been largely taken over by the Council of Ministers and the European Council.

[85] And see also the procedure in the agricultural management committees. See text to n 93 infra.

[86] E.g. Art 126 of the EEC Treaty.

[87] I.e., where the Treaty provides for a qualified majority in Council a small number of States can veto a decision.

Has there been a similar decline in the post-legislative phase? The issues here are complex and our conclusions must be regarded as rather tentative and speculative. In some limited fields, such as competition, the Commission acts like a federal agency with full executive powers, although even here it has to rely for enforcement measures on the national systems. In most matters, however, the practical execution of Community policies and rules, be they in the field of agriculture or the application of the Common Customs Tariff, is performed by the national administrations acting as 'agents' for the Community in such things as collecting charges, issuing clearances and dispensing grants. To the extent that the 'agency' is automatic, acting directly on Community measures and Commission instructions, this feature cannot be viewed as a weakness in the executive role of the Commission and as a sign of decline in decisional supranationalism.

However, the Communities as a political system have not escaped the world-wide trend of increased government by *administrative* legislation and action. Thus, whereas the legislature (the Council) enacts enabling measures or issues policy mandates, it is left to the 'executive' to implement the policies by secondary legislative measures and administrative acts. Just as the COREPER was introduced by the 1965 Merger Treaty as an extra tier of Member State representation, designed ostensibly to facilitate the technical preparation of Council meetings but in practice precipitating an erosion in the policy initiatory role of the Commission, it is possible to identify a similar trend in the establishment of Member State committees in relation to the executive functions of the Commission. I shall focus, by way of illustration, on two aspects of this development: first, by way of micro-analysis on the role of one committee already provided for in the Treaty of Rome, and, secondly, by way of overview on the general proliferation of committees set up by Council acts.

i. *The 'Article 113 Committee'*. Article 113 of the EEC Treaty dealing, inter alia, with conclusion of trade agreements by the Community, bestows responsibility on the Commission for *negotiating* agreements although acting on a mandate given by the Council. The Commission must consult with '. . . a special committee appointed by the Council to assist the Commission in this task . . .'. This '113 Committee' was duly set up,[88] composed of representatives of the Member States, its presidency held in rotation by the Member State holding the presidency of the Council. Its mode of operation is a useful illustration of the diminishing executive role of the Commission.[89] On the one hand a Council-Member State committee would

[88] See JO 1961 71/1273; JO 1969 L 326/39. In relation to agreements based on Art 238 of the EEC Treaty, which does not provide for a consultative committee, the Council set up a group of national observers who 'constitute . . . more than token representation, although less than active intervention'. Bot, *CML Rev* (1970) 286, 294.

[89] Among commentators there is no dispute about the decline in the Commission role although opinions differ about the appraisal of the phenomenon. Castonis, *CML Rev* (1967–8) 421; Alting von Geseau, *JCM Stud* (1967) 426; and Leopold, 26 *ICLQ* 54, esp 59–62 (1977) tend to be more critical of

be useful especially if amendments to the mandate were needed and could be provided at the locus of negotiations. The committee would also ensure that agreements negotiated would receive the ultimate assent of the Council upon which the constitutional power to conclude the agreement is bestowed. At the same time it has been pointed out that the role assigned to the Committee (and to national observers in other types of Community agreements) has meant that '. . . the Member States are able to oversee the Commission's behaviour in every negotiating session and ensure that application of the mandates to concrete issues comports with their wishes'[90] and that thus the '. . . picture of the Commission . . . is that of Community spokesman and agent or, more technically, plenipotentiary of the Council. The term "negotiate" has clearly not been interpreted [by virtue of the role assumed by the Member States and the Council] to accord the Commission an authoritative role in forming EEC negotiating policies or *directing the negotiations themselves*'.[91] To the extent that the Commission has managed to re-build its role it has not relied on a re-interpretation of the Treaty provisions but on the sheer technical expertise which it can bring to the treaty-making process. But in this sense it is no more than an equivalent to a competent national civil service.

It is perhaps worth pointing out that use of a 'democracy deficit' argument to justify these developments is hardly convincing for, except in the most formal sense, curtailment of Commission power has reduced the role of one set of (European) civil servants and elevated another (national) set. The continued reluctance of the Council to increase the role of the European Parliament in the process of treaty-making[92] testifies to the fact that national interests play a greater role than does concern for democracy.

ii. *The proliferation of committees.* With the substantive expansion of Community activities, especially in the agricultural sector, a wide-ranging network of committees has been set up, many of them to partake in the 'legislative implementation' of Community policies. Some of these are advisory committees, the consultation of which is obligatory but the opinions of which once consulted are not binding.[93] Others, the management and regulatory committees, have a more decisive role.

As regards the management committees, particularly prominent in the agricultural and fishery fields, the Commission must submit its draft measures to them. The committee may approve the measure, by a qualified majority, or fail to reach a decision (if no qualified majority is reached either

this development. Bot, supra n 88, offers a more balanced approach maintaining that the exigencies of international relations and their conduct make this development largely inevitable.

[90] Castonis, supra n 89, 435.

[91] Ibid 434 (emphasis added). But see Bot, supra n 88, 309–310. See also W. Feld, *The European Community in World Affairs* (Alfred Publishing 1976) 105.

[92] See generally Weiler in Cassese, supra n 76, 151; and J. Weiler, *The European Parliament and its Foreign Affairs Committees* (Cedam Oceana, 1982).

[93] See 'Council and Commission Committees' (EC) *Bulletin* Suppl 2/80, 18–19.

way) whereupon the Commission is free to adopt the measure which will have full legislative force. If the committee manages in fact to 'reject the measure' (qualified agreement against) the Commission may still adopt the measure but this measure will come into effect only after a certain period during which the full Council may, by qualified majority, reject it. The regulatory committees' procedure is slightly more restrictive on the Commission.[94]

It is difficult to assess this proliferation of committees in relation to the power of the Commission. Unlike, say, the Article 113 Committee, the Commission presides in all these management and regulatory committees. And since executive power is exercised here through legislative means, the involvement of the Council would seem to be natural. Pragmatically, the involvement of representatives of the Member States may also contribute to the smooth functioning of whatever policy is executed regardless of the implications for the institutional balance. Besides, in the decision-making process the qualified majority rule means that, as regards Management Committees the vetoing power of a few States may actually assist the Commission in adopting the measure. All these elements would tend to point to the conclusion that the proliferation of committees serves the ends of open and efficient government[95] and as regards formal decision-making increases the supranational element. Yet, taking a longer-term view, one cannot avoid noting that these mechanisms indicate an unwillingness of the Council and Member States to entrust the execution of policy to the Commission with, say, safeguards of reporting and information. In this sense, then, the proliferation of committees may be regarded as one element in the decline of decisional supranationalism.[96]

(c) *The reasons for decline*

The decline may be expressed as an intrusion of Member State diplomatic control at all stages of the decisional process: initiative (European Council); legislative preparation (domination by COREPER); adoption (veto power); and execution (committees). The advantages of higher acceptability of Community output and a greater confidence of governments in the decisional process must be offset against a burdening of the process and a lowering of the 'community' content of measures. What then accounts for the decline?

i. We noted the early success of the Commission in implementing the explicit policies in the Treaties. The need to evolve a 'second generation' of Community policies based on broad indications in the Treaties but not explicitly set out imposed a much more delicate and politically sensitive task on the Commission. The power of 'initiative' now called for was less formal and technical, that is it no longer called for proposals which gave legislative

[94] Ibid 22.

[95] The Court of Justice has affirmed the legality of management committees and even seemed to approve their political role. Case 25/70 *Einfuhr- und Vorratsstelle* v *Köster* [1970] ECR 1161.

[96] See e.g., Working Document 115 1968–69 (30 September 1968) of European Parliament and Resolution of 3 October 1968, OJ 1968 C 108/37.

form to explicit Treaty obligations but rather it called for wide, reflective and more 'value'-prone proposals. Whereas the first generation of policies were negative – in the sense that the Member States undertook to refrain from certain actions and the Commission was charged with implementing this negative régime – the new policies were to have a positive content on which agreement was more difficult. The ability of the Commission to propose new initiatives and get them accepted was thus considerably weakened. The importance of the Council of Ministers and European Council was strengthened. It was those bodies which could give the drive to new policies and ensure their acceptability in the national orders. To be sure, the Commission retained its position as a source of ideas and vision for developments on the Community level. The environmental policy, to give but one example, would not have emerged without an internal Commission initiative. But it was for the European Council to sanction the policy, to balance it and officially to launch it. The Commission was left somewhat in the background.

ii. The need for 'second generation' policies brought the democracy deficit to the fore. What is more, with the widening of Community activities, national parliaments felt threatened by a process which would wrest even more power from them. The Commission which had little formal democratic legitimacy became an easy target for attack.

iii. The Commission itself, although growing in experience, put on much bureaucratic fat. This expressed itself not only in its numerical staff growth but also in the evolution of traditional bureaucratic ailments which significantly reduced its internal efficiency.[97] Lack of internal (lateral) coordination, distortions in the pattern of promotion, and personal and national rivalries all contributed to an internal drop in morale and an external drop in esteem. The materially privileged position of Commission employees (alongside all other Community employees) in the current harsh climate may also have contributed to this process.

iv. The independence of the Commission and its judicial impartiality began breaking down in a bizarre dialectical process. The very importance of the Commission prompted the Member States to take not only – as was constitutionally permissible – an active interest in the appointment of the Commissioners themselves but also in the promotion of personnel within the Commission and in the allocation of portfolios among Commissioners. The Commission was thus seen to be losing its impartiality, a singular handicap considering its intended mediatory role in Council disagreements. Internally, this governmental intervention strained both the collegiate nature of the Commission and the authority of its President.

v. Finally, it may be that the process of *approfondissement* of normative supranationalism, as described above, had a negative effect on decisional supranationalism both in the Council-Commission relationship and within the Council itself. Normative supranationalism meant that the impact of

[97] Spierenburg Report (Commission of the European Communities 1979).

Community policies and law was perceived as growing not only in scope – to cover more fields – but also in depth – so as to have a more immediate and binding legal effect from which the Member States could not escape. Thus, to give one example, the politically delicate issue of supremacy was countered by an insistence of the Member States on their control of the making of this 'supreme' law and their ability to block its making. This view of the role and power of national governments was emphasized strongly by 'pro-marketeers' in the 1975 UK referendum, using it (somewhat misleadingly) as a tool against charges of the 'loss of sovereignty' which Community membership entailed. It is thus suggested that the correlation between the *approfondissement* of normative supranationalism and the diminution of decisional supranationalism is not accidental but at least partly causal. As we noted, the European Court of Justice had not excluded the sensitive field of foreign economic relations from the effects of normative supranationalism, giving one of its decisive rulings – the *ERTA* decision – on the doctrine of pre-emption in relation to the treaty-making capacity of the Community. The Council of Ministers and the Member States, for their part, have ensured that in the execution of the Community's external policy the Commission is kept – by devices such as the Article 113 Committee – on a very tight rein and that the Member States, by a legal interpretation of the limits of Community competence, are active parties in many agreements.[98]

3. The Diverging Trends – an Assessment

It is this last reason which gives the clue to one possible significance of the diverging trends. For, it is submitted, the outcome of the process represents a certain balance of action and reaction, whereby the permeation and expansion of Community influence – expansion in breadth expressed by the growing number of fields where Community impact is felt and expansion in depth as expressed by the *approfondissement* of normative supranationalism – is matched by an ever closer national control exercised in the decision-making processes. To this extent the *approfondissement* and *diminution* may be regarded as antidotes to each other producing, in a two-way process, a certain balance by a cyclical interaction of the judicial-normative process with the political-decisional one. Here then is one dimension of the Community formula for attaining an equilibrium between whole and part, centripetal and centrifugal, Community and Member States. It is an equilibrium which explains a seemingly irreconcilable equation: a large, surprisingly large, and effective measure of transnational integration coupled at the same time with the preservation of strong, unthreatened, national Member States. It is this equilibrium which may perhaps explain the overall stability of the system and its resilience to recurring crises generated within and outside. It explains how the Member States were able to 'digest' a constitutionalisation of the Treaty and a

[98] The so-called 'mixed agreement'. See Kapteyn and Verloren van Themaat, supra n 84, 351 ff.

normative evolution unprecedented in other international organizations. (We shall see below that this union of high normative and low decisional supranationalism may also give a key to reformulating the meaning of a supranational system).

Shonfield, in his seminal political analysis of the Community, noted the duality juxtaposing on the one hand '. . . the extent to which the detailed operation of the Community powers is today jealously observed and controlled by the member governments'[99] with, on the other hand, two European Court cases[100] which demonstrated the high level of what I have called normative supranationalism. He created the 'bag of sticky marbles' metaphor to express this duality and correctly sought the explanation in the substantive features which both draw and repel the members of the Community: A Community characterized on the one hand by a shared historical, political and cultural background which, since repeatedly threatened by strife and conflict in the past and finding common economic and political exigencies in the present, was and is being pushed and drawn towards integration. But also a Community which is, on the other hand, equally characterized by a rich diversity which has evolved in a history of separate tribal, religious, linguistic, economic and political development the complete integration of which is neither feasible or desirable.[101] The analysis of normative and decisional supranationalism complements the substantive explanation of the 'bag of marbles' by giving it its structural expression. But it also gives a clue to another of the paradoxes and inbuilt contradictions of the supranational system. For the diminution of the decisional facet represents the rejection of the federal option and the *approfondissement* of the normative facet its affirmation only on one, albeit important, postulate: the juxtaposition, in relation to governance structures in non-unitary systems, of this federal option as against an intergovernmental one. But if we postulate a different axis, relating to the division of competences and the content of programmes and policies in non-unitary systems, an axis on which we would juxtapose the federal option against a centralist one, we would reach opposite conclusions. The normative structure and its main author the Court speak the language of centralization. The concepts of supremacy, direct effect and pre-emption are, naturally, only meaningful in a non-unitary arrangement. They do not make sense where a single source of authority exists. But their rationale in the supranational system has been based on a unitary concept of uniformity, found, substantively, in the notion of one market and, procedurally, in Article 177 of the EEC Treaty – as well as in the constitutionalising Court decisions. By contrast, the decisional decline and the resurgence of the Member States are, ironically perhaps, an assertion, on the programmatic level, of the federal principle,

[99] Shonfield , supra n 7, 10.

[100] I believe Shonfield was alluding to Case 48/71 *Commission* v. *Italian Republic* [1972] ECR 532; Case 48/69 *Commission* v. *ICI* [1972] ECR 649.

[101] Shonfield, supra n 7, 17.

and the sentiment echoed one of diversity. The divergence of the supranational trends, mirrored in the tension between uniformity and diversity, have important implications. For the Court, as we shall see in the prospective analysis, it produces challenges for which solutions are not easily found.

As regards the Commission, one has the impression that it has not always appreciated that whereas the 'federal' principle on what we have called the normative level is rooted is uniformity, when one turns to the programmatic level this same principle calls for a careful consideration of diversity claims and that an over-centralised ethos by the Commission in its programmes (based on the notion that Community law must *always* be one and uniform) may be an additional factor in burdening the decisional process.[102] The divergence between normative and decisional supranationalism indicates that many of the tools for integration in the normative armoury of the Communities – even the more subtle tools, like the directive – are likely to remain under-employed because of decisional difficulties. In the preparation of new policies and programmes the Commission will have to shift emphasis. In present conditions it is no longer sufficient to introduce grand programmes for uniform Community policies, based on a reasoned presentation of Community needs and potentials. In relation to each policy the Commission will have to engage in a micro-analysis of the barriers to Council decision-making, which may vary from issue to issue, with a view to presenting programmes particularly sensitive to decisional obstacles as well as to normative ones. The tolerance to Member State variance, especially in positive programmes, may also be reassessed with greater circumspection being exercised in relation to proposed uniform laws.[103] This will also mean that where a uniform law *is* necessary a greater insistence could be placed on the integrity of its application. In this context the discussion of committees takes a different turn. For what could be seen as a reduction in the Commission's autonomous executive role could be usefully employed, by that very Commission, as a device to *reduce* the decisional barriers. The greater the involvement of the representatives of the Member States, the less reluctant they may be towards new Commission proposals.

The Commission can, in certain fields, radically reassess its own role. Where the decisional barriers seem insurmountable it could selectively abandon its function as initiator of policies and engage in direct voluntary contact with the Member States to assist them in developing independent policies which may however serve Community ends.

Finally, relating the two facets of supranationalism provides us with a different set of terms of reference with which to examine the jurisprudence of the Court of Justice and the type of integrationalist philosophy which, as

[102] For criticism of this ethos, explicit and implicit, see e.g. Annex 3 to Three Wise Men Report 82–83.

[103] The legislative programme is at times sensitive to this call for diversity even within 'uniform' laws. See e.g. Art 5 of Council Directive 75/129 on approximation of laws relating to collective redundancies OJ 1975 L 48/29.

we saw above, was at the basis of its judicial policy. The Court's case law and judicial policy may be subjected to four different orders of analysis.

The first, the technical-legal order, is concerned with ascertaining the precise meaning and parameters of the Court's judicial decisions. The recent *Cassis de Dijon* line of cases is still troubling interpreters grappling with a new judical policy.

The second order of analysis is concerned with evaluating, in the strict legal sense, the correctness and legitimacy of the Court's case law. The debate surrounding the notion of direct effect as applied to directives is an example of this order.

The third order of analysis is concerned with the evaluation of the Court's case law as regards its impact on European legal integration. It hardly needs repeating that without the bold steps taken by the Court, the most important of which were discussed briefly in our analysis of the evolution of normative supranationalism, the legal structure of the Community would manifest only a fraction of its present cohesion. So, unlike the second order of analysis, the terms of reference here go well beyond a strict legal evaluation of the legitimacy of the Court's judicial policy. They are widened to incorporate the impact of these decisions on the general architecture of the legal order.[104] But even here the analysis is still confined to an area which flows almost directly from the Court's jurisprudence. The evaluation, to use our terminology, remains at the level of normative supranationalism.

The fourth order of analysis then will try to widen the terms of reference even further. The questions which will be asked, and to which, at this stage of research, only extremely tentative answers may be given, concern the relationship between the Court's case law and its impact in the normative field on the one hand and the decisional facet of supranationalism on the other. This is, of course, a two-way relationship. I have already suggested that in evolving its doctrine of pre-emption the Court will have been cognizant of decisional difficulties in the Communities' policy-and rule-making structure. To insist on pure pre-emption and expect it to work necessitates efficient central organs; the absence of these in the Community gives one explanation to the pragmatic, less pure, approach adopted by the Court in this instance. It was on the basis of this analysis that I had argued that what appeared as a retrogressive judicial approach was in fact part of the *approfondissement* process. One could at this stage only speculate whether the Court would have taken a different approach as regards pre-emption had the decline in decisional supranationalism not occurred. Looking at the relationship the other way round we have already suggested the possible negative effect to which *ERTA* may have contributed. One can imagine the policy difficulties if the Court were called upon to adjudicate in the debate regarding the responsibility for the expenditure of the Com-

[104] See C. J. Mann, *The Function of Judicial Decision in European Economic Integration* (M. Nijhoff 1972); A. W. Green, *Political Integration by Jurisprudence* (Sijthoff 1969).

munity budget.[105] A 'supranational' judicial decision could still be countered by a political elimination of items of expenditure over which control would be denied to the Member States.

D. The system of compliance

There remains one crucial factor missing from the structural analysis. What are the ties that keep the framework together? By what means has it been possible to preserve the integrity of the system despite the evident decline in decisional supranationalism, the outright hostility from certain national quarters and the lack of independent federal enforcement mechanisms, the evolution of which one would normally expect to accompany the development of normative supranationalism?

1. Withdrawal or Selective Application

The natural departure point for a reply would be an examination of the possibilities of Member State withdrawal from the Community. Here again we find if not a cleavage between legal and political analysis at least a sharp difference of emphasis. Juridically, in discussing withdrawal from the Community a distinction is drawn between the European Coal and Steel Community on the one hand and the European Economic Community and Euratom on the other. As regards the former, Article 97 of the ECSC Treaty provides that 'This Treaty is concluded for a period of fifty years . . .'. As regards the latter, Articles 240 of the EEC Treaty and 208 of the Euratom Treaty provide respectively that 'This Treaty is concluded for an unlimited period.' A recent study based on general international institutional law,[106] cogently argues '. . . that no right of withdrawal can be implied in the case of treaties like ECSC . . .'. The same view is reached as regards the EEC and Euratom Treaties, namely that the aforenoted Articles '. . . exclude any implied possibility of unilateral withdrawal' since '. . . no other meaning which could be given to these provisions would not make them redundant'.[107]

This juridical argument is curtly dismissed in a political analysis of the Community system: Pryce argues that '[T]he question of unilateral withdrawal is not dealt with in any of (the Treaties) – for the good reason that none of the partners was willing to tie its own hands with regard to this matter. . . . The silence on this means quite clearly that each of the signatories maintains absolute authority to take such a decision at any point in

[105] See FIDE, *Reports of the Ninth Congress, 25–27 September 1980, Vol 3: Possible Areas of Conflict between Community Institutions in the Implementation of Community Law* 4 (FIDE and Sweet & Maxwell 1980) esp Ehlermann § 3, 3.13–3.22.

[106] Akehurst, [1979] *Current Legal Problems* 143. The leading authority on withdrawal generally is Feinberg 39 *British Yearbook of International Law* (BYIL) 189 (1963), on whom Akehurst draws.

[107] Akehurst, supra n 106, 151. See also Case 128/78 *Commission* v *UK* [1979] ECR 419, 429; and Case 7/71 *Commission* v *France* [1971] ECR 1003.

the future. The fact that the Treaty of Paris was concluded for a 50-year period and the other two for an unlimited period is irrelevant in this context.'[108]

This legally erroneous statement has a strong measure of political truth behind it. Should a Member State be determined to withdraw, lack of legal consent from its partners will not be an obstacle in its way. The general Hobbesian maxim that covenants without swords are but words is accurately reflected by Pryce in his statement that in the Community '[t]here is no army to convince a reluctant partner'.[109] The real glue that binds the Community together is the bond of common vision and common interest in pursuing what has aptly been called 'Alliance politics'.[110]

Does this mean that the discussion of withdrawal is irrelevant to an understanding of the supranational system? It is submitted that the question of unilateral withdrawal is politically futile. Unlike pre-World War II practice it is rare in the life of contemporary international organizations for States to withdraw their membership.[111] The more common pattern is one of selective non-application by States of those duties and obligations of membership which seem to conflict with national interests. Given the wide range of duties and obligations which flow from Community membership such practice, if adopted, would be lethal to the Communities. Equally common is the failure of international organizations to adopt sanctions against breach and, on those occasions when measures are adopted, to enforce them effectively. The essence of what for convenience I call the 'all-or-nothing effect' in the European Communities is that whereas Member States retain the ultimate political option of withdrawing from the Community and thereby disengaging from their obligations of membership (an option which the process of economic and political enmeshment has made increasingly difficult but not impossible) as long as they opt for membership they are largely unable to practise selective application of Community obligations. I do not of course mean that infractions have become impossible; no legal system can guarantee this. Rather the supranational system of submission attaches to international norms the habit of compliance associated with national ones and provides fairly effective remedies in cases of breach. The 'all-or-nothing effect' means above all the removal of expediency as a primary incentive for compliance with individual measures and the replacement of the virtually voluntary character of State obedience which characterizes the classical international legal order with a binding judicial process. There still remain, for reasons which will be explained below, certain lacunae in the full realization of the 'effect', but it has certainly reached a stage where it can be stated as a fundamental of the supranational system.

[108] Pryce, supra n 16, 55. [109] Ibid.

[110] A. Shonfield, *European Integration in the Second Phase: the Scope and Limitation of Alliance Politics* (The University of Essex – Noel Buxton Lecture 1974).

[111] See Finberg and Akehurst, supra n 106, and examples therein. Indeed, in the few cases cited 'withdrawal' was subsequently construed as 'inactive membership'.

We have already noted the central role of the Court of Justice in the evolution of supranationalism. But the existence of a court as part of the institutional framework of an international organization is not unique and cannot, as such, explain the 'all-or-nothing effect'. Nor can the existence of a compulsory jurisdiction per se be sufficient explanation since, as was recently exemplified,[112] submission to the compulsory jurisdiction and subsequent obedience to an award are among the obligations which in the current state of international law can often be flouted with impunity. What produces the effect is rather the entire *system* of judicial review involving both national courts and the European Court, which transnationalizes mechanisms hitherto used only in the context of municipal judicial review.[113]

2. The Functional Division of Adjudicatory Tasks and Judicial Review[114]

The Community features a double-limbed system of judicial review which operates on two levels. Two sets of legislative acts and administrative measures are subject to judicial review: (*a*) (the first limb) those of the Community legislative and administrative institutions (principally Council and Commission) which are reviewable for conformity with the provisions and principles of the Treaties and with an emerging unwritten higher law based on the constitutional traditions of all Member States as well as international treaties such as the European Convention on Human Rights;[115] and (*b*) (the second limb) acts of the Member States which are reviewable, in accordance with the principle of supremacy, for conformity with Community law itself. Needless to say, in the context of compliance of Member States with Community obligations, effective review of the latter acts is the crucial issue.[116]

Judicial review may take place at the exclusive level of the Community Court. As regards the first – less critical – limb, the organs of the Community and the Member States, as well as individuals, may, in accordance with the Treaty,[117] directly challenge Community acts and measures (as well as inaction) before the European Court. As may be expected the rules of standing for individuals are quite narrowly defined and the Court has made them narrower still by interpreting them rather strictly.[118]

[112] See *Case Concerning United States Diplomatic and Consular Staff in Tehran (United States of America* v *Iran)* 19 *International Legal Materials* 555 (1980).

[113] See Cappelletti, 23 *Rivista di diritto processuale 1 (1978)*.

[114] On the system of judicial review generally, see e.g. the erudite treatment by Schermers, supra n 45; L. Neville Brown and F. G. Jacobs, *The Court of Justice of the European Communities* (Sweet & Maxwell 1977). G. Vandersanden and A. Barav, *Contentieux Communautaire* (Bruylant 1977). A. Tizzano, *La Corte di Giustizia delle Comunità Europee* (E. Jovene, 1967). Naturally my treatment here will only sketch the bare limbs of the complex system.

[115] See Schermers, supra n 45, 31–80.

[116] Cf O. W. Holmes *Collected Legal Papers* (Peter Smith, Reprint 1952) 295–296.

[117] E.g. Art 173, 175, 184 and 215 of the EEC Treaty.

[118] Cf Stein and Vining in F. Jacobs, *European Law and the Individual* (North-Holland 1976) 113.

As regards the second, critical, limb the Commission and Member States may, in accordance with the Treaty,[119] bring an action against a Member State for failure to fulfil its obligations under the Treaty. Failure to fulfil an obligation may take the form of inaction in implementing a Community obligation or enacting a national measure contrary to Community obligations. Although, as indicated above, not unique, the very existence of a non-optional judicial forum for adjudication of these types of disputes sets the Community above most international organizations. At the same time the 'intergovernmental' character of this process and the consequent limitations on its efficacy are clear enough. Four weaknesses are particularly glaring.

In the first place, the decision of the Commission and/or Member States to bring an action against an alleged violation by another Member State will often be influenced by political considerations; the Commission, for example, might not wish to prejudice delicate negotiations with a Member State.[120] Secondly, effective supervision will depend on the ability of the Commission to monitor the implementation of Community law. Given the vast range of Community measures, this becomes an impossible task.[121] Thirdly, the type of action which is likely to be brought will relate largely to abject Member State failure to *implement* a national measure required by Community law. It will be far less suited to review of the ordinary application and enforcement by Member States of Community obligations especially as they affect individuals. That type of violation becomes normally transparent only through cases and controversies affecting individuals. Even if alleged violations were brought to the attention of the Commission, it is unrealistic to expect them to take up all but the most flagrant violations. Finally, given the intergovernmental character of this process, a Member State found to have failed to fulfil an obligation may simply disregard the judgment against it.[122]

These weaknesses are to an extent remedied by the review of both limbs at the national level, a process which is possible through the functional division of judicial tasks between the European Court of Justice and national courts and which essentially produces the 'all-or-nothing effect'. It is unnecessary to stress the fundamental importance of Article 177.[123] This multifunctional Article provides inter alia that when a question concerning either the interpretation of the Treaty or the validity and interpretation of acts of the institutions of the Community is raised before national courts, the latter may (and in the case of courts of final instance, must) refer the issue for a preliminary ruling of the European Court of Justice. Once this ruling is made it will be remitted back to the national court which will give, on the basis of the ruling, the decision in the case pending before it. The national

[119] E.g. Art 169, 170 and 93 of the EEC Treaty.

[120] See Ehlermann, *The Role of the Legal Service of the Commission of the European Communities in the Creation of Community Law* (Univ of Exeter 1981).

[121] See Commission observations in Case 144/77 *Commission v Italian Republic* [1978] ECR 1307.

[122] See n 3 supra.

[123] Jacobs, 90 *LQ Rev* 486 (1974).

courts and the European Court of Justice are thus integrated into a unitary system of judicial decision making. The two limbs of judicial review exist on this level as well. A reference to the Court on the *validity* of acts of institutions is clearly a mode for judicial review of Community acts at the instance of individuals. One will note that the question of locus standi from the point of view of the European Court does not arise. Thus it may even be possible for an individual to be denied standing in a direct challenge before the European Court but have the act reviewed if he has standing in accordance with national procedural law. The individual will be able to challenge the Community act in the national courts (Community law being, of course, part of the 'law of the land'), whereupon it will be remitted to the European Court of Justice for an interpretation on validity and returned back to the national court for pronouncement.[124] Taking judicial review of Community measures as a whole, the trend, in respect of individual challenges, is one of a restrictive attitude to actions brought directly before the European Court with a shift to national courts as the forum for adjudication, using, when necessary, the preliminary reference for an interpretation or check of validity of a Community measure.[125]

Turning to the second limb concerning the judicial review of national measures for conformity with Community law, the European Court has made astute use of that part of Article 177 which provides for references on the 'interpretation' of Community law. On its face the purpose of the procedure is to guarantee uniform interpretation of Community law in all Member States. However, often the factual situation in which Article 177 is employed is when a litigant pleads in the national court that a rule or measure of national law or an administrative practice, should not be applied as it is in conflict with Community law. On remission to the European Court it renders its interpretation of Community law within the factual context of the case before it. Theoretically, a division exists in the adjudicatory tasks of the two courts: the European Court states the law and the national court applies it to the case in hand, using of course the principle of supremacy where necessary. Thus the traditional formula of the Court is to state that:

> . . . The Court of Justice ruling under Article 177 of the EEC Treaty does not hold that a given national [law] is incompatible with Community law. . . . Within the context of the judicial cooperation established by the provision it is for the national courts, applying the fundamental rule that Community law takes precedence, to uphold the right of the subjects based, under the Treaty itself, on the direct effect of [the provisions concerned].[126]

[124] On the effect of an invalidity declaration under Art 177, see Usher, *EL Rev* (1981) 284.

[125] The substantive review grounds for legality under Art 173 of the EEC Treaty and validity under Art 177 are largely similar although certain slight differences exist. See Schermers, supra n 45, 210–211. There are of course additional procedural and temporal differences between the two remedies.

[126] Case 61/79 *Amministrazione delle Finanze dello Stato v Denkavit Italiana* [1980] ECR 1205, Recital 12 of judgment.

But as has been usefully concluded in a study on the role of the European Court in judicial review:

It is no secret, however, that in practice, when making preliminary rulings the Court has often transgressed the theoretical borderline. . . . [I]t provides the national judge with an answer in which questions of law and of fact are sufficiently interwoven as to leave the national judge with only little discretion and flexibility in making his final decision.[127]

What is important, indeed crucial, is the fact that it *is* the national court acting in tandem with the European Court which gives the formal final decision on the compatibility of the national measure with Community law. The main result of this procedure is the binding effect and enforcement value which such a decision has on a Member State, coming from its own courts, as opposed to a similar decision handed down from Luxembourg by the European Court of Justice wearing its intergovernmental hat. This then is a procedural dimension of the constitutionalisation of the Treaties since through it the rule of law (of which the habit of obedience, even of the State itself, to the rulings of courts is probably the most fundamental aspect) is incorporated into the supranational system.[128] The quest for an effective law of nations in the traditional international legal order has been characterized by the creation of a succession of international courts, tribunals, arbitration bodies and other judicial and quasi-judicial fora. With a few exceptions these bodies have all been victims of the inherent weakness of the rule of law on the international plane. International jurisprudence, with all the attention it receives from scholars, has remained on the periphery of international law and international relations. By contrast, the supranational system – in a synthesis of international law and constitutional law – puts the inherently stronger *national* system in the service of the transnational order.

The above analysis helps to express the current limitations and lacunae in the 'all-or-nothing effect'. Four main limitations might be mentioned. First, not all alleged violations by Member States of Community obligations give rise to cases involving individuals. Many obligations do not produce direct effect and rest in the province of intergovernmental relations, violation of which remains a matter for the Commission and Member States. Second, even in matters potentially involving individuals there will exist inevitable 'access-to-justice' barriers. Ignorance of the European rights, the increased cost and time which the two-tier litigation involves (the procedural price of the system of compliance) and the fragmentary and diffuse character of the rights which might entail a very low stake for any one individual (in *Costa* v *ENEL* the controversy involved a sum of approximately one pound sterling) are the more obvious barriers. Third, the use of Article 177 as a method for judicial review of Member State compliance will depend on the acceptance by national courts of the utility and/or duty to make references.

[127] Rasmussen, *EL Rev* (1980) 112, 115.

[128] Could the knowledge of certain disobedience have influenced the Court in Case 104/79 *Pasquale Foglia* v *Mariella Novello* [1980] ECR 745? Cf Tizzano, 105 *Foro It* IV, 256 (1980).

The practice in this respect although encouraging is not completely satisfactory.[129] Finally, preliminary rulings, once received by the referring court, must be followed both by the court and by the national administration. Here too the system displays certain breaches either overt as in the case of the Conseil d'État or of a more subtle kind.[130]

We may now enquire whether the same type of dialectical process tentatively suggested as regards the normative and decisional structure of the Community may also occur in the relationship between the Court and its national counterparts. An even greater measure of caution is called for in assessing this problem. To be sure, negative national judicial attitudes to Community jurisprudence are usually conditioned by a variety of internal factors which have little to do with the posture of the European Court. But, on occasion, a link between Community judicial activism and national judicial hostility cannot be excluded. It is clear that the Court in *Van Duyn* failed to convince the Conseil d'Etat in *Cohn-Bendit*; that the logic of *Rutili*, in which the Court stated the Community claim to control national concepts of public policy, was equally unimpressive to Lord Denning and his colleagues in *Santillo* and that the Italian Constitutional Court in *Comavicola* was unimpressed by the decision in *Simmenthal*. But then, it is only natural to expect a measure of national judicial resistance in the face of some of the constitutionalising decisions. If the prospect of such resistance had influenced the Court, little of the normative edifice would have been created.

I believe the greater peril lies paradoxically in judicial inactivism, in the failure to act as a federal adjudicator as regards the substantive expansion of the Community's jurisdiction. We noted above that because of the peculiar supranational features of the Community as a non-unitary system, once political consensus in Council is reached as regards jurisdictional expansion this may take place without the usual problems faced in some federal systems. For once, the unison of Member State and Community interests in the Council produces the conditions which dampen national resistance. The very sharp but largely uncontested increase in the usage of Article 235 is evidence of this development.[131] Most of the criticism has concentrated on the undemocratic nature of the decision-making involved which excludes national parliaments. To be sure this is a role which may be given to the new directly elected Parliament. The Court, which itself had developed its own expansive version of implied powers, and which adopted a very liberal attitude of tacit encouragement towards political expansion, has been criticized on the same grounds: as partaking in, or sanctioning, an undemocratic process.[132] I wish to shift the argument to another level. A consistent failure of the Court to assert itself as a programmatic federal adjudicator

[129] For a useful attempt at analyzing the different patterns of references, see Mortelmans *CML Rev* (1979) 557. See also R. Lecourt, *L'Europe des Juges* (Bruylant 1976) 273–283.

[130] See *Secretary of State for the Home Department, ex parte Santillo* [1981] 2 All ER 917.

[131] This expansion is brilliantly traced by Tizzano 21 *Rivista di Diritto Europeo* 139 (1981).

[132] See e.g. Giardina, 1 *Italian Yearbook of International Law* 99, 103 (1975).

might not only leave doubts as regards the legal and democratic legitimacy of the new Community policies as well as contributing to an abstract loss of confidence in the European Court by its national counterparts; it might affect the most hallowed normative principle – supremacy. The clearest illustration of this danger may be found in the Italian Constitutional Court decision in *Frontini*. *Frontini* is traditionally read as an affirmation of the supremacy principle subject to an explicit, if muted, human rights reservation. But the basis of acceptance of the doctrine rested on the functional division of tasks between Member State and Community: '. . . there is thus made by each of the Member States a partial transfer to the Community organs of the legislative function, on the basis of *a precise criterion of division of jurisdiction* by subject-matter indicated analytically in the second and third parts of the Treaty . . .'.[133]

This rationale is echoed in the jurisprudence and constitutional amendments of most other Member States. Should the functional division be seen to be breaking down without adequate judicial control by the European Court it is difficult to guess what shape and depth national judicial resistance might take. When the Court developed its doctrine of fundamental rights its credibility was impaired since it was clearly perceived as a response to a supremacy challenge rather than a genuine concern with human rights. A similar loss in credibility would accompany a reactive rather than active Court doctrine as regards jurisdictional limits.

One cannot turn round today and condemn the Court's activism for any negative impact this may have had on the decisional structure or judicial cooperation. Not only do the defects here have, as our analysis has shown, independent causes, but without that jurisprudence we could hardly have spoken of a *Community* as we know it today; substantive achievements would be perhaps no more than, say, those of the GATT. Hamson's critique that in *Van Gend en Loos* and its progeny the Court was severing '. . . the legal world – the world in which it operates – from the world of what we call real or actual events'[134] may be turned on its head. The Court's jurisprudence was inspired perhaps by its all too familiar knowledge of that very world in which international agreements lacking a normative framework have such limited impact. But, however great the merits of the constitutionalising decisions, it may still be useful to conclude this section with the profound historical warning so elegantly sounded by Dawson:

> Judicial agencies have a peculiar power to enlist obedience and impose control – essentially . . . because they meet a deeply felt and constant need for trustworthy neutrals. . . . But there are limits to the allegiance that judges can inspire, as the experience of France reveals. The judges of pre-Revolutionary France became partisans in political strife for a reason that seemed to them persuasive – that other

[133] [1974] 2 CMLR 372, 385 (emphasis added). The Court further mentions that the Community subject-matter must correlate to the general aims of the Treaty but this cannot be read as sanctioning wholesale expansion.

[134] Hamson, *Judicial and Academic Conference* (Court of Justice of European Communities 1976) II, 9. Contra Kutscher, ibid, I, 47.

political agencies had failed. . . . In their attempt to fill a great gap in French political institutions they brought disaster on themselves and caused a lasting impairment of their own function.[135]

E. The distinction and the union of normative and decisional supranationalism: Some theoretical reflections

By way of concluding this analysis we may return to some of the theoretical problems raised earlier as regards the definition and articulation of the supranational order. The distinction between the decisional and normative facets, combined with the all-or-nothing principle enshrined in the Community system of compliance, may be useful in shedding a different light on and perhaps even clarifying some of those theoretical problems. Five brief observations may be made in this context.

First, the distinction and the different evolutionary paths alert us to the danger of adopting monolithic explanations or characterizations of the system. Studies suggesting an evolution from, say, 'federal to confederal'[136] are correct only in an extremely narrow definition of the concepts employed; so narrow as to reduce considerably their explanatory utility of a system rich in contradictions.

Although the distinction between the two facets underlined these contradictions, it enabled us to capture and to express the inevitable processual character: the evolution of two diverging trends explicable both independently but also by their interaction with one another and their ensuing unique balance.

Secondly, the distinction between the two facets of supranationalism explains, at least partially, one of the important reasons for the cleavage between legal and political structural analysis. Lawyers have tended to focus on the normative structure whereas political scientists have typically avoided this and concentrated on the decisional framework. (Naturally, in non-structural analyses, we will have to look for similar cleavages between law and economics and political science with both).

The third theoretical consideration concerns the issue of sovereignty. The contribution of a purely structural analysis to the sovereignty debate can be but limited. The transfer of sovereignty is intricately bound to the weight and importance of the substantive areas over which jurisdiction is given, or evolves, to the components of the system.[137] And yet the distinction between the two supranational facets can articulate with greater precision the often heard political notion that participation in the system does not only mean a loss of sovereignty but also a gain in terms of the influence of one State over its partners. As we saw, it is the interaction of low decisional and high

[135] J. P. Dawson, *The Oracles of the Law* (Greenwood Press, reprinted 1978) XVI.

[136] Cf Taylor 27 *World Politics* 336 (1975).

[137] L. N. Lindberg and S. A. Scheingold (eds), *Regional Integration, Theory and Research* (Harvard U Press 1971) complement legal studies by offering means of measuring the impact, esp 45–127 and 232–264.

normative supranationalism – especially in areas of exclusive Community jurisdiction – which explains this phenomenon. One Member State, even a small one, through the power of veto (low decisional) may influence important dimensions of, say, the agricultural or fisheries policies through the inability of the other partners to adopt unilateral measures (high normative). This direct influence extends beyond that possible in the normal international context. The 1981 British veto of the Fisheries Agreement with Canada is a recent example. To be sure there would be a political price to be paid for continuous obstructionism, but the explanation of the very possibility is I think sharpened by the distinction between the two facets.

Fourthly, the distinction between the two facets proved a means by which to identify the two intersecting and often contrasting axes along which the Community is oscillating as a non-unitary system: the intergovernmental-federal axis and the centralised-federal one. The tensions which this produces in terms of the competing claims of uniformity and diversity will have their effects in years to come.

Finally, for what is perhaps the most far-reaching, and hence tentative, conclusion we must consider the *union* rather than the *distinction* between the two facets in combination with the 'all-or-nothing effect'. For in this union, with its unequal weighting, we may possibly find the underlying principles of what we mean when speaking of a supranational system. In most international organizations there is a low measure of both facets. In some international organizations we find a measure of decisional supranationalism. In the UN itself there is a surprisingly high measure manifest in, say, the voting rules of the General Assembly, the Security Council (with the known exceptions) and the various committees and affiliated organs, as well as in the independent role of the Secretary General.[138] What is crucially lacking, and this accounts for the weakness of that organization, is any real measure of normative supranationalism.[139] By contrast, any multi-partite treaty with self-executing measures among monist States will display at least a measure of this normative character but to the exclusion of the decisional facet. It is the union of the two within one framework which distinguishes structurally the supranational order from other international organizations. The different weighting and especially the low level of the decisional facet sets the system apart from non-unitary (federal) States. For in these States, the separate tiers of central and (member) State power with the independent source of popular legitimacy and functional allocation which the former enjoys, always result in a high central decisional level. Likewise if the 'all-or-nothing effect', with all its current lacunae, is a valid characterization of the system of compliance (a necessary component in any organizational analysis) then we may have found the complementary principle of the

[138] See e.g. L. Gordenker, *The UN Secretary-General and the Maintenance of Peace* (Columbia U Press 1967) and Cox 23 *Int Organ* 265 (1969), and E. B. Haas, *Beyond the Nation-State: Functionalism and International Organization* (Stanford UP 1964) 119 ff.

[139] But see Henkin, 23 *Int Organ* 656, 664 and 680 ff (1969).

supranational order. For it is clear that the 'all' mechanisms are precisely those lacking from other international organizations whereas the political option of *unilateral* pacific withdrawal expressed in the 'nothing' option, is unavailable in non-unitary States. Extrapolating from the Community experience, the union of the normative and decisional facets and all-or-nothing compliance may provide a new economical way of structurally expressing the concept of a supranational system.

[8]

Some Preliminary Notes on Bureaucratic Relationships in the European Economic Community

LAWRENCE SCHEINMAN

IN his review of the Fifth General Report on the Activity of the European Community the Rapporteur for the European Parliament critically singled out certain aspects of the Commission's style in developing Community policy: the excessive importance it seemed to place on proposing only solutions which had the strongest chance of being adopted by the Council of Ministers instead of maximizing the potentiality of its power of initiative; and, as a corollary, the disturbing tendency toward increasing infusion and influence of national administrations in the policy orientations and decisions of the European Economic Community (EEC).[1]

More recently, the French government made the following point in its ten-point aide-mémoire designed to serve as a basis for the resolution of the crisis of June 1965:

> Cooperation between the Council and the Commission constitutes the driving force of the Community. This cooperation must occur at all stages. Consequently, before finally adopting a proposal of special importance to the states, the Commission must consult the governments at the appropriate level. . . .[2]

LAWRENCE SCHEINMAN is Assistant Professor of Political Science at the University of California, Los Angeles, and presently a Research Associate of the Center for International Affairs, Harvard University.
The author would like to thank the Social Science Research Council for its generous support of this research as well as several members of its Committee on International Organization who commented on an earlier draft of this article which was delivered at a SSRC Conference at Bellagio, Italy, in July 1966. Special thanks are due to Ernst B Haas, whose suggestions contributed extensively to the discussion on the measurement of bureaucratic interpenetration, and to Jacques Houssiaux, a colleague at the Center for International Affairs. The author's debt to the many officials in the EEC and the national administrations cannot be overemphasized.

[1] *Agence Europe*, October 16, 1963.

[2] *Agence Europe*, January 18, 1966. This point, as drafted, was not acceptable to France's partners and was modified considerably in the agreement reached at Luxembourg at the end of the month. The text

Granted the ambiguity of the phrase "at an appropriate level," i.e., whether it was intended to mean the ministerial or some inferior level of administration, these two critiques imply diametrically opposed conceptions of what ought to be the nature of the relationship between the Commission of the EEC and the member states. Such relationships can take any number of forms and assert themselves at many levels—meetings between ministers and commissioners, contacts between interest groups and the various representatives of the Commission, etc. This article is concerned with one particular level of relationship—a singularly evident and important one: that which obtains between the national administrations and the bureaucracy of the EEC Commission. In a preliminary and schematic fashion I shall try to show certain aspects of this relationship and to evaluate it tentatively in terms of the impact of bureaucratic interpenetration on the development of integration and the impact of integration on the nature of bureaucratic power.[3]

For the purposes of this discussion bureaucratic interpenetration is defined in two ways. In its most simple form, bureaucratic interpenetration is the intermingling of national and international bureaucrats in various working groups and committees in the policy-making context of the EEC. The intermingling of bureaucrats per se is not peculiar to the EEC and is found in other regional international organizations such as the North Atlantic Treaty Organization (NATO) (e.g., the Committee of Economic Advisors, the Committee of Political Advisors) and the Organization for Economic Cooperation and Development (OECD) (e.g., the Economic Policy Committee, the Energy Committee). Although the tasks of these various committees do not radically differ, at least on paper, the situation in the EEC must be distinguished from that of the other organizations in terms of the nature and impact of this interpenetration of bureaucratic organizations.

The source of the difference rests principally in the organizational and environmental context in which interpenetration occurs. The members of the EEC have undertaken certain commitments and obligations which go beyond simple cooperation or agreements to agree. Furthermore, they have developed

finally accepted stresses the importance of close collaboration between the Council and the Commission and provides that,

> Before adopting a proposal of particular importance it is desirable that the Commission make the appropriate contacts with the Governments of the Member States, *through the Permanent Representatives*. This procedure, however, in no way impairs the right of initiative the Commission holds under the Treaty.

(*Agence Europe*, January 31, 1966. Emphasis supplied.) It is still unclear whether the Permanent Representatives are the sole medium or merely apprised of contacts which may occur at any of several levels.

[3] Much of what follows is based on documentary and interview research in several Community sectors—competition (cartels and ententes, state aids, harmonization of legislation), the right of establishment, transport, and certain dimensions of commercial policy (development of the list of exceptions in the Kennedy Round of General Agreement on Tariffs and Trade [GATT] negotiations, development of a common commercial policy). The national administrations referred to are the French, West German, Dutch, Italian, and Belgian, which have been studied in roughly that order of priority.

an institutional framework within which these commitments are carried out. The commitment is the development of a common market and eventual economic union, not a mere free trade area; and it is linked to a timetable and transitional period in many vital sectors. The institutional framework is the system of authoritative decision making lodged in extranational organs: the Council of Ministers and the Commission. These factors create an environment which gives added meaning and impulse to the mingling of national and international administrators.

Beyond the above definition bureaucratic interpenetration also may be considered as a conceptual tool to analyze the growth pattern of integration. If we accept Haas' definition of integration as "the process of *increasing* the interaction and the mingling [of actors] so as to obscure the boundaries between the system of international organizations and the environment provided by their nation-state members"[4] then we may find bureaucratic interpenetration useful as an indicator of system transformation. In other words, we may postulate that to the degree that the level of decision making rests on the bureaucratic plane, to that degree integration has progressed; when the normative pattern of decision making is administrative problem solving rather than classic diplomatic negotiation, we can speak in terms of systemic change and adaptation.

Thus, using the degree of bureaucratic decision making as a variable we may be able to make certain judgments about the intensity of integration. This approach assumes that, normally, high policy issues, dealt with on an internation basis, will not be left in the hands of public administrators but rather will be resolved at the level of politically responsible ministers in a more or less classic diplomatic context.[5] If issues are found to be resolved at the bureaucratic level (even granted the need of a final formal imprimatur at the level of political responsibility), then we may be able to conclude that the issues in question and the policy sector they represent have become internalized, i.e., shifted from a classic diplomatic to an integrated or Community level of resolution.

To approach bureaucratic interpenetration in this manner would require its measurement. The task of measuring interpenetration in the sense of specific case studies lies beyond the pale of this article, but it may be suggested that such an undertaking would entail the analysis of three factors. One element would be the question of the level of authority at which decisions are taken

[4] Ernst B. Haas, *Beyond the Nation-State: Functionalism and International Organization* (Stanford, Calif: Stanford University Press, 1964), p. 29.

[5] On levels of decision making and styles of negotiation see Ernst B. Haas, "International Integration: The European and the Universal Process," *International Organization*, Summer 1961 (Vol. 15, No. 3), pp. 366–392; and Ernst B. Haas and Philippe C. Schmitter, "Economics and Differential Patterns of Political Integration: Projections About Unity in Latin America," *International Organization*, Autumn 1964 (Vol. 18, No. 4), pp. 705–737.

both within the member states of the Community and within the organizational context of the Community itself. We might, therefore, categorize decisions taken in the Community structure according to whether they are taken at the level of the Council of Ministers, the Permanent Representatives, or the working groups of high-level civil servants which operate under the auspices of the Permanent Representatives.

Secondly, we might want to consider the style of dialogue in the negotiating process. Is the dialogue carried on at the level of functional specialists whose principal task is to discover the technically and economically appropriate solution, or is the dialogue one among generalists operating within the framework of political instruction? What are the sources of initiative for conflict resolution? And, are the negotiations geared toward "upgrading common interests" or toward the classic diplomatic pattern?

Thirdly, we might address ourselves to the question of the kinds of circumstances and conditions under which decision making and negotiation shift from one level of operation to another. What are the conditions for administrative as distinguished from diplomatic decision making? What types of issues are typically treated in one or the other category? To what extent has there occurred a shift of conflict resolution from one level to another, and to what can we attribute such change? This list is far from exhaustive or exclusive, but it is suggestive of one *modus operandi* for attacking the problem of bureaucratic interpenetration.[6]

I

Before turning to the subject matter itself, one caveat is in order: In the realm of interadministrative activity and its relationship to integration, generalization often may be not only inopportune but even misleading. Differentiation occurs not merely from General Directorate to General Directorate of the Commission but from service to service and even from problem to problem within a given service. Bureaucratic interpenetration is conspicuously high, for example, in the sector concerned with the right of establishment[7] where a framework program, largely the handwork of experts, slowly is being filled out by still other experts. But even in this relatively narrow sphere of activity the results of penetration have been found to vary from meeting to meeting, often depending upon who happened to be chairing a particular national delegation at a given moment. In other words, within a fairly gen-

[6] The application of such a scheme will be treated in a book now in progress, provisionally entitled *Patterns of Power: Bureaucracy and the Integrative Process*. The following discussion focuses more on the mechanistic definition of interpenetration than on the attitudinal one.

[7] Right of establishment is governed by Title III, Chapter 2, of the Treaty Establishing the European Economic Community (Treaty of Rome) and refers to the free movement of non-wage-earners between the member states. These persons are to be allowed to establish themselves for business or commercial purposes in any member country on the same conditions as nationals of the state in question.

eralized structural and institutional framework of bureaucratic relationships, the basic human factor is frequently crucial. Consequently, many of the generalizations which might be offered must be taken with extreme caution.

If it were not for the qualifying phrase "at an appropriate level" and the political context in which the French aide-mémoire noted above was submitted, France's insistence on close consultation between the Commission and the national governments would appear curiously redundant of an existing state of affairs. For it is indeed a central characteristic of the Commission style, subject to variations in distribution, frequency, and utility, that there exist a large number of expert and consultative working groups composed of national administrators sent to Brussels at the request of the Commission services.[8] There are, furthermore, many personal contacts between Commission and national administrators and between national administrators themselves which fall outside the more formal framework. What is even more paradoxical in the French aide-mémoire is that at the same time as it has called for closer liaison and consultation Paris has been chafing under the bit of "working group proliferation" and subtly is seeking to pare down these groups to manageable size.[9] This attempt to limit and control the working groups should be read not only in terms of a concern for administrative efficiency but also as a peripheral attack on the Commission's prerogatives.

A great majority of the EEC administrators are marked by the conviction of the importance, if not indeed the imperative nature, of cultivating close relations with national administrations. There is less uniformity of view on the purposes to which such relationships can be most efficaciously put and on whether they are more fruitful in the conceptualization or executory phases of policy development. There appear to be three principal variables on which the perception of the use of bureaucratic interpenetration seems to turn: the specificity of the Rome Treaty regarding the subject matter, the psychological orientation of Community *fonctionnaires,* and the constellation of political forces around the policy area in issue.

[8] There are, at present, over 260 such groups which meet periodically in Brussels. More than one-third of these groups are clustered in two Directorates-General: Internal Market and Agriculture. About 55 percent of these groups consist of governmental bureaucrats only. Of the remainder, approximately 25 percent are mixed groups of governmental and private experts. The balance (about 20 percent) consists of private experts exclusively.

[9] In the first half of 1966 the French government refused to send administrative experts to Brussels to participate in working groups on three separate occasions. Two of these refusals pertained to the social field where, France insists, the Community lacks authority to act under the Rome Treaty except in a limited number of cases. The third refusal concerned the establishment of a working group to study the harmonization of penal law for the breach of Community regulations and directives.

Under any circumstances, however, manageability would appear to be a serious problem for the national governments. It is reported that in 1964, for example, close to 1,200 meetings of expert groups took place. These groups generally consist of medium- or high-level *fonctionnaires,* the delegations from each state varying from two to six members, so that including Commission personnel the average meeting consists of some twenty to 25 persons.

II

It might at first appear that there would be a close and direct relationship between the perception of the utility and of the timing of administrative penetration and the strength of the juridical foundations upon which the Commission happens to be operating. In other words, we might expect that as the commitments undertaken by the states in the Rome Treaty became more vague the importance of bureaucratic interpenetration would become correspondingly greater. Although the general tendency is in this direction the pattern does not hold uniformly true. Variations occur all along the distribution of authority continuum. They are more noticeable at the extreme where the Commission has the most authority than at the other extreme where it has the least ability to act independently. By way of example let us look briefly at several cases in point.

The Commission is vested with considerable legal authority in the cartel and in the state aids sector. In both instances treaty provisions are self-executing and binding on the member states. In the former case the Commission service has more or less shunned or minimized bureaucratic relations, thus bringing in its wake a considerable amount of ill will.[10] In the state aids sector, on the other hand, the Commission service has assiduously sought to develop close relations with national administrations for the completion of this chapter of the Treaty of Rome. Admittedly, there are particular difficulties in the state aids sector which render it more susceptible to and reliant on national administrative action.[11] The distinctions between the operational codes of these two services, however, appear to rest less on the solidity of the juridical foundations than on the combination of personal attitudes and the conceptualization of tasks confronting the bureaucratic service in question.

Further along the Treaty power spectrum, where the position of the Commission is more tenuous, as in transport or harmonization of legislation, use of bureaucratic interpenetration in the conceptualization and proposition-building phase also has markedly differed. In the case of transport policy (or, rather, the lack thereof) the interpretation of certain Treaty articles probably would sustain the argument that unanimity will be necessary for adopting regulations on basic policy issues even as voting patterns in the Council of

[10] Bureaucratic interpenetration in the cartel sector is relatively weak both in the conceptualization and executory stages. In the latter instance there is a Consultative Committee of national administrators. This committee was established under Regulation 17 (1962) to assist the Commission in the application of cartel provisions, but the Commission has sought to minimize its role by interpreting the provisions which govern it in a very restrictive fashion. The members of the committee, on the other hand, have sought to expand its role. For a partial justification of the low level of interpenetration in this field, see below, footnote 15.

[11] Unlike the cartel sector in which information can be gleaned from investigations of cartels and from other members of the industrial community, in the state aids sector information often may be exclusively in the hands of the national administrations responsible for the management of these aids.

Ministers shift more toward majority rule. Consensus is high both in and outside of the Commission that the General Directorate of Transport did not make adequate and effective use of the national administrations in developing transport policy proposals. While it would be quite erroneous to argue that transport failures have derived solely or even principally from this fact, it does remain probable that a certain amount of progress would have been made on some issues if the Commission had used more effectively the potential of bureaucratic interpenetration.[12] Harmonization of legislation, on the other hand, another area where unanimity usually is required in the Council, represents what even may be an excess in the reverse direction—the *overestimation* of the potentiality of administrative decision making. This is one of several sectors in which working group proliferation has been most noticeable and the proliferation is in part tied to the weight attributed to bureaucratic interpenetration by the responsible Commission authorities in this area.[13]

The relative importance of the specificity of Treaty provisions to bureaucratic interpenetration becomes more clear when one considers the second variable noted above—the psychological orientation of the Community administrators responsible for the sector in question. At the risk of slight distortion it appears that many of the Community's civil servants fall into one of two camps—ideologists or pragmatists.[14] An ideological orientation may derive from either or both of two sources. Many ideologists may be militant "Europeans" whose total energies are devoted to the building of a united Europe although it must be pointed out that many a dogged "European" approaches his tasks from a highly empirical point of view. The ideological approach also may be the result of self-identification with the Treaty of Rome—in other words, an intense and personal devotion to the successful and complete fulfillment of the

[12] Article 83 of the Rome Treaty provides for a Transport Committee. This committee is composed of independent experts designated by the governments of the member states, and among these experts are high-ranking civil servants from the ministries of transport. The Commission made poor use of the potential of this committee and thus increased certain tensions which already existed between the Commission bureaucracy and the national administrations. For example, the Commission would often submit to this committee problems which presupposed a nonexistent common transport policy; but questions basic to a common policy itself were rarely discussed with this committee.

[13] There is another side to this coin: the desire of the national administrations to institutionalize working groups which have been set up to prepare proposals by turning these groups into continuing consultative or surveillance committees. While a number of such committees already exist, their proliferation is not looked upon very favorably by the Council of Ministers (and especially France) largely because of the financial costs involved and also because of a concern over the deconcentration of authority.

[14] The terms pragmatic and ideological are employed here in a methodological sense. I am not referring to the degree of commitment of Community administrators to their organization and its goals but rather to the procedural code by which they operate.

Community administrators also might be categorized according to whether they are activists who seek to integrate or nonactivist "pencil pushers" who passively fulfill their assigned tasks. Indeed, there is a problem of nonactivism in the Commission and it is due essentially to the minimal direction or instruction by the Commissioners to their administrative staffs. Lack of direction also accounts for the glaring problem of overlapping jurisdictions and competition among various Commission services. The term "legalist" could be substituted for ideologist without doing violence to the distinction in question.

Treaty. To the extent that any generalization can be formulated one can sense that the tendency toward this way of thinking is higher among those with a legal than with an economic background and higher among West German and Dutch than among French or Italian administrators. When the ideological approach is found in a sector in which the Treaty is highly specific, then specificity takes on a great importance and bureaucratic relationships may be given correspondingly less weight. The cartel sector appears to fall somewhat in this category.[15] Those who are more pragmatic in their approach, on the other hand, tend to look upon and utilize bureaucratic interpenetration equally intensely whether they are working under very specific or very vague Treaty provisions.

Finally, there is the question of the political environment of the policy sector in issue. Bureaucratic interpenetration may be responsive to this factor rather than to legal or psychological conditions. Indeed, in the last analysis, the political factor is paramount. In the field of agriculture, for example, the tendency of the Commission service was to minimize the importance of administrative penetration at the conceptual stage without, however, discounting it and to sharply upgrade the importance of this level of operation in the executory phases of policy. The most striking example of administrative interpenetration occurs in the agricultural management committees *(comités de gestion)* which also probably represent the most advanced form of technocratic decision making the Community has yet developed. As Leon Lindberg's studies on the evolution of agricultural policy in the EEC attest, the hard decisions have been the result of vigorous political bargaining which extends beyond the pale of technocratic activity.[16]

Several factors may account for the agricultural policy developments which are not easily reproduced in other policy contexts. The unusually cohesive and effective team developed under Sicco L. Mansholt's auspices, coupled with a political constellation of forces which put a major Community member, France, squarely behind the bid for a common agricultural policy as a *quid pro quo* for further development in industrial policy, and a common starting

[15] It should be pointed out that under any circumstances the development of an effective dialogue on cartel problems in the Community would have been difficult. At the time the Rome Treaty went into effect Belgium, Italy, and Luxembourg lacked legislation on restrictive practices and even today Italy and Luxembourg still have not passed the necessary legislation. The absence of a body of law on the subject meant the absence of qualified individuals capable of intensively discussing cartel issues. On the other side, the Commission had to deal with the highly organized and influential West German Bundeskartelamt which sought to impose its cartel philosophy on the entire Community. Caught in this dilemma, even more pragmatic administrators might have sought to work in relative isolation rather than run the risk of becoming the prisoner of the West German cartel office or of losing valuable time in nugatory discussion. There does exist a Conference des Ententes which serves as a meeting ground for national and Community experts, but this organ has never been turned into a consensus-building body for cartel policy.

[16] Leon N. Lindberg, *The Political Dynamics of European Economic Integration* (Stanford, Calif: Stanford University Press, 1963); and Leon N. Lindberg, "Decision Making and Integration in the European Community," *International Organization,* Winter 1965 (Vol. 19, No. 1), pp. 56–80.

point of agricultural protectionism in the six member states, all provided certain advantages unlikely to be repeated in the near future in the EEC.[17] The development of a common agricultural policy did *not* rest initially on administrative consensus, and the winning of national administrative support came not at the inception but only at a later stage in the process of policy development. We should also note that in agriculture the crucial initial decision was to construct a new system rather than to seek to coordinate or harmonize existing agricultural systems. By definition, such a decision would necessitate different tactics than would be required in a sector where the Commission chose to operate through existing systems and structures entailing less radical change.

Experience may sustain the contention that bureaucratic interpenetration was less important at the developmental stage than at the management or executory stage in the agricultural sector. This probably would not hold true, however, for many other sectors such as monetary, cyclical, or medium-term policy where minimal Treaty provisions, coupled with the problem of stimulating any great public interest, and a certain esoteric quality of the subject matter in issue proportionately increase the potentialities of administrative decision making and the importance of technical knowledge. But even in other less specialized sectors, such as transport, social, commercial, or energy policy, it does not seem likely that the Commission can avoid seeking accommodation through administrative media for in these areas the probability of marshaling a team and public opinion as was done in agriculture is fairly remote. It will unquestionably take a political decision to reap any major success in these areas, but I submit that the achievement of success will follow a different path than that used in agriculture.

III

Perhaps the basic question which first must be answered is: What is the purpose and utility of bureaucratic interpenetration? A principal purpose is to secure *information*. An essential source of bureaucratic power is expertise and a Community bureaucracy largely composed of former national civil servants is not likely to overlook this vital fact. Quite aside from the question of presenting proposals likely to win Council approval there is the matter of developing proposals which are technically and economically in accordance with the facts of economic life in the member states. Such information as will contribute to this end is most likely to come from the competent national

[17] It seems likely that progress in other fields will require a stimulus equal to that which France provided in agriculture, especially given the less "Communitarian" attitude which has been developing since France vetoed British entry into the EEC in 1963. It is open to question whether such a stimulus might not have to await the entry of new members, such as the United Kingdom, to the Community. Under conditions of extended membership, however, there arises the problem of the extent to which the Community style will remain the same.

authorities. Generally speaking, EEC *fonctionnaires* feel that more objective and complete information will come from national administrations than from the *milieux intéressés* although this latter source of information is frequently resorted to as well, either to complete Community information or to serve as a cross-check.[18]

A second equally, if not more, important factor in bureaucratic interpenetration is the generation of administrative *support* for Commission proposals. The EEC is not yet an autonomous political actor and in its present stage of development has a fairly limited clientele capable of sustaining it. The existence of a "European class" in the member states is still rudimentary and insufficient to serve alone as a social support for the Commission. Also, the EEC bureaucracy is less effectively related to national pressure groups than are the national administrations with whom national pressure groups still maintain their principal dialogue. While transnational interest groups capable of rendering effective support for Commission policies do exist, their quality of organization is uneven, their representative capacity is highly disparate, and their overall impact is still often only nominal. As a consequence, national administrations emerge as potentially the most effective source of support for Community policies and often serve as the major clientele groups of the Commission. Not infrequently, Commission members and *fonctionnaires* have remarked that "you cannot integrate against the national administrations."

There are two closely related aspects to the *support* function of national administrations—a negative and a more positive one. On the one hand, there is the expectation that the acquiescence of national administrators in "Community" solutions will minimize resistance to Commission proposals at the Council level and in the discussions of the Permanent Representatives' working groups which review Commission proposals and prepare the Council meetings. The frequently heavy reliance of ministers on their experts, the immediate access of the technician to the minister, and the highly complex nature of much of the EEC's work support this expectation. This is especially true when one considers that the expert who negotiates on behalf of his government in the context of the Permanent Representatives' working groups is quite often the same expert who participated in the Commission-presided working groups which discussed or elaborated the proposal in issue. Despite the inevitable limitations imposed on the national administrator (interadmin-

[18] There is a danger in overemphasizing information and the expert knowledge it brings in its wake. Where sensitive political and economic interests are involved, expertise alone is insufficient to carry major policy proposals. It may be argued that in overemphasizing expertise in the transport sector the Commission lost sight of certain important economic and political interests, a loss which eventually cost the Commission its leadership role.

We should also bear in mind that both national and Community administrators could use the information medium to achieve particular ends and thus distort the objective flow of information. This is, in fact, a not uncommon practice of national administrations when they first learn of Commission interest in a specific sector.

istrative competition within his own government, activity of interest groups), as a rule he carries considerable weight with his minister. To ignore the national expert until the moment he appears across a negotiating table where some of his vested interests may be at stake is to court great danger of failure unnecessarily.

On the other hand, there is the hope that the Commission-presided working group can lead to a positive consensus on the policy orientation embodied in the proposal and that the spillover effect of this consensus will either induce the national participants to lobby actively for the Commission proposals or, more subtly, to avoid suggesting other equally valid policy alternatives. Given the tendency of most civil servants to avoid running unnecessary risks and to disengage themselves from political controversy, the latter alternative appears to be the medium more frequently resorted to by the national administrators interested in supporting the Commission's proposals.

One further point should be made at this juncture. There is a certain penchant for technocratic decision making among Community administrators which is frequently given tacit support by their national counterparts, and this serves as yet another factor in bureaucratic interpenetration. National administrators who are competent in given fields of activity may, and sometimes do, find quite inviting the temptations of asserting greater authority in their national context through the medium of Community policies.[19] Commission administrators, themselves marked by what might be described as administrative imperialism and operating in the same substantive channels, nourish this temptation by joining forces with the responsible national civil servants in elaborating minutely detailed proposals. The expectation is that the economic and technical logic of the proposed solution will leave little if any room for discussion at higher policy-making levels and consequently will be given almost routine approval in the Council of Ministers.

The success of such gambits is highly erratic. Occasionally, proposals which are presented in such an unimpeachable manner are so constructed as to give complete satisfaction to all the negotiating partners and in doing so really give satisfaction to none. The real problems, rather than being tackled, simply have been pushed ahead. Furthermore, it is not uncommon for highly detailed propositions to be laced with ambiguous phrases and *malentendus* allowing open season on interpretation.[20] Finally, even where such qualifying factors

[19] The planning sector would seem to be particularly amenable to such tactics. The Community policy context gives national administrators a means of escaping the influence of their clientele groups and of reshaping and reorienting national policies.

[20] Problems of this nature tend to cluster in the harmonization field. A typical example may be found in the second *projet de directive* for the harmonization of pharmaceutical legislation where the provisions for the selection of experts to pass judgment on the marketability of pharmaceutical products was sufficiently broad to accommodate the rather liberal West German and rather restrictive French systems. The result of so broad a provision was to gain the accord of all the national delegations but at the same time to leave the considerably different national systems in very much the same state that they were before the directive was drafted. In other words, harmonization was terminological only, not substantive.

are not present, there is still the problem of threading the proposal through the difficult political maze which awaits it in the meetings of the Permanent Representatives and the Council of Ministers.

The preceding commentary has dealt only with the question of institutionalized bureaucratic relations. Interpenetration is also fostered through the myriad personal contacts between national and Community administrators and contacts between national administrators themselves. These relationships derive not only from the personal friendships which develop as a result of frequent contact in the multilateral meetings discussed above but also from the fact that many Community administrators come from national administrations either on a permanent or temporary (seconded) basis. Fairly close contact is maintained with the home bureaucracy for the most part although this is more true for nationals of some states (France, West Germany, and Italy) than for those of others (the Netherlands and Belgium).[21] Despite these many individual and bilateral contacts there is a strong conviction among both Community and national administrators that whatever benefits are to be derived from bureaucratic interpenetration are more likely to be achieved in multilateral contexts. Bilateral meetings serve to clarify certain specific problems of a given state or to allow national civil servants to discuss more frankly the reasons for objections they may have raised in the multilateral reunions. Intimate knowledge of the mechanism of a national administration may permit an international administrator, familiar with the system and in contact with its personnel, to sense the advantages and dangers of particular courses of action. But, for the purposes of building bureaucratic consensus and for maximizing the potentialities of bureaucratic interpenetration, the multilateral medium appears to be the most fruitful.[22]

In sum, there is an intensive pattern of bureaucratic relationships in the European Economic Community, developed in varying degrees and utilized with greater or lesser effectiveness by the Commission bureaucracy. These relationships are generally formalized in Commission-presided consultative and working groups in which national administrators participate with a view to

[21] One of the problems the EEC must cope with is the lack of a real administrative training ground. The College of Europe at Bruges, while a sometime source for Commission recruitment, does not fulfill this need. There is a long-standing debate on whether a fully independent career administration or a seconded (but independent) administration is best suited to the needs of the EEC, and there are compelling arguments on both sides. This subject will be treated at greater length in a forthcoming article "Bureaucratic Mobility as an Integrative Factor: The Case of the EEC."

[22] One aspect of bilateral relationships which is deserving of special note is the relationship of the Commissioners and their cabinets to the national governments. Both the Commissioners and their cabinets operate at the political level in the countries of which they are nationals (and elsewhere as well). Often, Commission *fonctionnaires* resort to the cabinets in order to seek a means to neutralize or eliminate national bureaucratic resistance. Conversely, the cabinets can and do keep an eye on what the Commission services are doing in terms of national interests. As in the case of the Commission bureaucracy, however, not all the cabinets function equally effectively or efficiently, nor are all used for the same purpose by the Commissioners in charge.

protecting vested interests but often also with a view to participating effectively in the process of economic integration. From the vantage point of the Commission the principal benefits to be derived from such relations are first, to garner information, an essential requisite of bureaucratic power, and secondly, to minimize national resistance by appealing for the support of a principal national economic power wielder in the modern welfare state—the public administrator.

IV

Granted the extensiveness of these transnational bureaucratic relationships, how do they relate to the process of integration? What sort of impact does bureaucratic interpenetration have on policy orientation in an integrating context and, conversely, what impact does this context have on the nature and extent of bureaucratic power? Part of the answer may depend on how one defines the bureaucratic universe—whether one is speaking of all public officials in national administrations exclusive of the minister himself, whether one includes the ministry of foreign affairs or only the "technical" ministries, and so on. The following discussion is focused on the technical ministries but the nontechnical administrations will be reincorporated later on.

The phenomenon of bureaucratic interpenetration has been steadily increasing since the inception of the Common Market. As more subject matter areas have come to be treated in a Community context, more administrators have been drawn into the expanding network of transnational relationships. Bureaucratic influence over the shape and direction of European integration, however, has *not* followed the same linear progression. Schematically, the impact of administrators has followed a more modest path, possibly even a degressive one over a period of time. In keeping with our earlier caveat concerning generalization, we should bear in mind that there is a considerable amount of variation. Bureaucratic influence and impact were relatively high during the euphoric first years of Community life, but they have become progressively subjected to increasing environmental restraints. These restraints derive not only from the chill political atmosphere which has enveloped the EEC ever since France vetoed the United Kingdom's application for entry in 1963 but also from the fact that as the Common Market advances toward the end of the transition period, more sensitive and difficult problems come to the fore.[23]

The true impact of bureaucratic power on integration and policy making best can be felt when national and international *fonctionnaires* reach consen-

[23] I am referring here to "external" restraints. However, we must not forget "internal" restraints which derive from the growth of the organization itself. There is a lack of cohesion within the EEC administration and a good deal of interservice rivalry. This rivalry not only impedes organizational efficiency but also reduces the ability of the Community bureaucracy to maintain autonomous leadership in policy initiation and development. The problem will be examined more fully in the article cited in footnote 21 above.

sus on the nature of the solution to be applied to a given problem. However, it is no simple task to achieve consensus among experts drawn from different environments and operating under the constraints of different economic structures. The notion of an "administrative class," cohesive, continuous, and guided by a common set of ethics and values, has often been taken to task by students of national administrative systems. The clustering together of administrative actors from several countries strains even further the probabilities of technocratically imposed solutions to Community problems. Bureaucratic relationships in the Community over the past eight years have been strikingly successful and have led to certain psychological transformations which undoubtedly have simplified management of certain administrative tasks. Overall, however, they have tended to remain fairly constant between the pole of conflict and the pole of collusion, fluctuating in one direction or the other as the interests, problems, and participants have changed. In transport, commercial policy, and certain aspects of competition policy, the tendency has been toward conflict whereas in the sectors of right of establishment and harmonization of legislation, they have been somewhat less strained. In the area of general economic policy (cyclical, monetary, and budgetary policy, for example) they have even tended toward the collusive end of the continuum. One reason for this last situation may be that the dialogue is almost entirely one of *cooperation* among economic experts: There is no immediate question of a transfer of competence, the participants tend to think in the same general analytic patterns, and the Commission has never sought to impose solutions on the member states. Under crisis conditions as occurred in 1965, however, the committees formed in this policy sector are unable to sustain themselves. This is their singular weakness.

National administrators are by nature protective and conservative and even those who are firmly committed to the principle of economic integration will vigorously defend the systems and policies for which they are responsible. Despite this natural tendency toward administrative conservatism, national administrators are often caught on the horns of a dilemma. On the one hand, they do wish to minimize their sacrifices and to maintain administrative sovereignty, to *bien garder la ficelle*. On the other hand, many national administrators have a considerable interest in "Europe" from the ideological or from the professional point of view. The EEC represents a new dimension of administrative activity, more substantive and meaningful than any other transnational economic organization such as OECD or GATT. Experience would seem to indicate that over the years the system, as a whole, has been positively affected by the general interest in expanding the dimensions of economic activity. But even as the system shifts, individual administrators tend to incline toward conservatism on individual cases. This is principally true when matters of competence and the division of authority enter the picture.

Voluntary change and breaking the cake of custom are not easily achieved and this is one reason why radical innovation, such as in the agricultural sector, requires tactical operations which go beyond the administrative level. Personal friendships, mutual understanding, appreciation for the problems another administration faces, and a more cosmopolitan way of thinking are all fringe benefits derived from frequent and close contact between national and international administrators in the multilateral working groups of the Commission. The dominant experience of the EEC, however, is that the functional requisites of a man's job invariably will dominate the positions he takes.

Finally, even if consensus is achieved, there is still the critical issue of the effect of this consensus. The answer turns primarily on the political inclination of the government as well, of course, as on the weight carried by the bureaucracy in the political system and on the interplay of such forces as interest groups. If the government line is reasonably clear and not hostile to integration, administrative impact on specific government policies and on overall government orientation will be relatively high and occasionally even definitive. If the government orientation is hostile to integration, if political consensus on progress is lacking, administrative impact will be correspondingly lower. This has become fairly clear over the past several years when one considers the changing *marge de manoeuvre* of French administrators who participate in Community activity.

There is a generally widespread belief that national administrators who come to Brussels to attend Commission-presided working groups are freewheeling, uninstructed delegates who speak officiously and in no way commit their government to any course of action. This is the sort of generalization which often leads to misunderstanding. It is true that governments are not committed, juridically at least, by what their experts say and do in Brussels in the earlier phases of policy preparation. Even at the cost of some embarrassment to the government in question, long-standing commitments by experts have been reversed. It is not true, however, that these administrators come uninstructed. The pattern varies from country to country with Italian experts tending to be the least and West German experts the most instructed, but as the Community has progressed instructions have become more elaborate and restrictive in all countries.[24] The French administrators noted above used to have considerable latitude of action and were frequently able to translate consensual agreements made in Brussels into government instructions and

[24] This is highly nuanced. French instructions, for example, might be cast in the sense of "don't go beyond this and that limit" with a margin of maneuver left within this framework. (This is much less evident since the termination of the recent crisis, however.) Italian instructions, on the other hand, often may be drafted with a view to insisting on one or several points with nothing whatever being said regarding any of the other points to be discussed. Consequently, the Italian delegate may be "free" on these other matters. In any case, the instructions which are given are occasionally challenged by the Permanent Representatives either because the instructions go too far or because they don't go far enough.

policy at later negotiating stages. Now they are closely monitored and even before the most recent Community crisis French administrators were unable and unwilling to take liberties either officially or unofficially. Unfortunately for the Commission, the same attitude and pattern have spread to the other national delegations though in a more modest and less obtrusive manner.

This tendency is not simply a reflection of the changing political climate in the EEC but is also the result of the increased stakes involved in Community decisions. More sensitive economic interests and more far-reaching commitments are now at issue. It is not just a question of reducing or eliminating a tariff or paratariff barrier, of treating the nationals of another state on the same basis as a state treats its own citizens, or of allowing free movement of labor within the Community. More and more it is a question of undertaking positive commitments that entail structural, institutional, and psychological changes of far-reaching consequence. Under these conditions governments are rapidly awakening to the increasing importance of even minor "technical" decisions which, when added up, may amount to something quite substantial. In brief, both for political and economic reasons governments have become more concerned with what technicians are saying and doing. A key manifestation of this concern is the tendency to give more and closer instructions to these administrators earlier in the game.

Within the context of the foregoing, the general pattern followed by many of the Commission's services is to try to build consensus among national experts in the Commission-presided working groups. What often is sought is agreement on a Commission-sponsored *avant-projet*. There is a wide range of difference, however, between Commission *fonctionnaires* as to how far they will go in seeking to negotiate a consensus among conflicting national views. In the cartels and ententes fields, for example, the dialogue often turns into a monologue, the Commission informing the national administrations of what next must be done. Some Community pundits have dubbed the cartel sector as *"l'Université,"* especially in view of its tendency to draw heavily on independent experts in the academic community. Significantly, this field of activity has not progressed as rapidly or as far as it might have under the "strong" Treaty provisions on competition.[25] In harmonization of legislation, on the other hand, a genuine dialogue obtains and the final project usually has the unanimous or near unanimous support of the national delegations. For example, the Commission held sixteen working group meetings over a four-year period on the problem of harmonizing procedures in public works contracting in an effort to hammer out as sound and acceptable a proposal as possible. Not until every avenue of conciliation was explored did the Commission finally "take its responsibility" and submit a proposition.[26]

[25] See, however, footnote 15 above.

[26] The public contracts case, not yet decided by the Council of Ministers, also exemplifies some of the weaknesses of relying on administrative penetration to carry policy proposals. In this case the West

It is precisely this latter kind of activity that was critized by Arved Deringer, the Parliament's Rapporteur whose comments were noted on page 750. However, where unanimity is required in the Council and where the national administrations are currently responsible for the field of activity in question, this would seem to be the pragmatic and realistic approach. Even in an area such as the right of establishment, where a qualified majority suffices to pass a directive in the Council of Ministers, a similar approach usually is used. In both instances, however, when the issue has reached a point where the national administrations were unwilling or unable to go further toward conciliation, the Commission has submitted the proposal it felt most representative of the Community interest and most likely to win ultimate approval. Where there has been conflict between what is most likely to succeed and what is in the Community interest, some Community administrators claim to have given priority to the latter but others admit to having followed the path of least resistance. This is a highly significant fact in light of the frequency with which the Commission claims to represent the "Community interest." Moreover, it calls into question the extent to which the integrative process necessarily "upgrades common interests."

Bureaucratic interpenetration is more effective at the technical than at the political level of policy making. This raises the knotty problem of what constitutes a political as distinguished from a technical issue and the line is often not easy to draw. What is technical to one country may be political to another. For the Netherlands, whether the Community oil storage policy is based on a 45- or 60-day supply is simply a technical issue whereas for Italy, an oil importer with no indigenous resources, the same question is quite political given the infrastructure and cost factors involved in oil storage. Furthermore, many technical issues become politicized as they run the course from Commission to Council. This usually occurs either because an attentive interest group perceives a threat in some provision of a proposition, or because, from a government's point of view, something which may be technically sound also may be politically unpalatable. Any issue which is institutionally oriented and which may have a bearing on institutional equilibrium is treated, of course, as political.[27] Once these limitations are realized, however, there still remains a wide range of activity open to technical domination.

National administrators, despite the earlier noted inclination toward increasing the scope of their influence, tend to be circumspect in dealing with

German administration negotiated a compromise with the Commission only to be reversed at home by pressure applied by the Länder and cities which pass most of the contracts and which felt inadequately consulted by Bonn. The Commission eventually redrafted certain provisions to accommodate Germany's federal situation. In fact, it does not appear that the Commission has come to grips either with the issue of West German or Community federalism.

[27] This does not necessarily mean that the issue is treated at the political level. See, for example, the problem of "right of information" treated below.

such political issues as intrude in the discussion. The Commission *fonctionnaires* have not always been as cautious, and in the earlier years sometimes sought to negotiate with national administrators on some political questions. This could either take the form of seeking to depoliticize the issue by couching it in technical terms—a tactic which rarely escaped the attention of the Permanent Representatives—or by inserting certain provisions which, while seemingly innocuous, might be politically loaded. In the right of establishment sector, for example, the Commission on several occasions introduced provisions calling for a "right of information" on the part of the Commission. This meant that every decree, act, or implementing device designed to carry out the directive in issue would first have to be communicated to the Commission which implicitly would have the right to recommend changes, modifications, or alternative solutions. The provisions were quashed before reaching the Council of Ministers allegedly on the ground of technical complexity but actually because the provisions smacked of institutional imperialism on the part of the Commission and posed the delicate question of Community balance of power. The tendency to negotiate political questions with the national administrations is much less evident today. The Commission has found that to do so sometimes raises unnecessary problems and that in the present political environment of the Community it has limited value. For, even if there are no objections, or even if there is acquiescence by national administrators at the preproposal stage, the latter often are unable to sustain such decisions on behalf of the Commission once the real negotiations begin in the Committee of Permanent Representatives.

V

Let us now return to the question of the impact of integration on bureaucratic power. Economic union under the Rome Treaty implies increased administrative activity in the policy-making area, for the economic realm is one in which administrations have typically made the greatest inroads in the political process. As government has expanded to meet increasing socioeconomic demands, administrative activity and influence correspondingly have increased. The merging, harmonizing, or coordinating of economic sectors would seem to entail a direct and substantial impact of administration on policy development. It is undeniable that the influence and authority of the executive branch of government in all of the member states have increased as a result of the EEC. Certain traditional restraints on ministers and administrators have been weakened in the face of new and subtle decision-making processes.[28] At the same time certain short-term and long-term *intranational* ad-

[28] I am referring principally to parliamentary controls. However, the influence of interest groups should not be underestimated.

ministrative redistributions are taking place in the executive branch. We earlier noted that bureaucratic influence does not necessarily rise in direct relation to increased bureaucratic interpenetration because of the moderating influence of environmental restraints. It is to the causal role of integration in the creation and nourishment of those restraints that I would like to devote the following comments.

The dominant battle being waged in the member states at the bureaucratic level is between the technical and nontechnical ministries for control over the management of integration. It would be too simple and misleading to say that the economic ministries are in the vanguard of integration, jousting with protectionist foreign ministries, for it is often the case that it is the latter who reach the accommodation necessary to permit integration to move forward.[29] Technicians are not, by nature, more likely to reach agreement than are diplomatic personnel, especially when decisions may involve a shift of competence or a reduction of administrative autonomy. By the same token, however, there is much truth in the contention that foreign ministries are often among the last to appreciate and accept the need for certain integrating decisions. Integration then appears to have affected national bureaucratic power in somewhat the following manner.

The ministries of economic affairs, convinced of the importance of developing rational economic growth, have placed great importance on the success of the Common Market. This is strikingly evident in the case of France where many of the ideas now couched in the Rome Treaty emanated from *hauts fonctionnaires* in the Ministry of Finance and Economic Affairs. Since foreign economic relations traditionally had been directed primarily from within the ministry of economic affairs or of finance it was assumed that what previously had been done in a bilateral context now should be continued or even expanded in a multilateral context. The ministries of foreign affairs, however, have not shared this view. Except in West Germany, where a government mandate lodged authority in the hands of the Ministry of Economic Affairs, the foreign ministries have maintained a firm hand on the integration tiller.[30] They have sought to exercise surveillance largely through the medium of the Permanent Representatives who are administratively responsible to the ministry of foreign affairs in all of the member states.

A considerable proportion of the Community work is highly technical in nature and neither the foreign ministries nor the foreign economic divisions

[29] A good example is the issue of association with third states. In the cases of Greece, Turkey, and, presently, Austria, the economic experts were much less favorable to reaching agreement than the political leaders. If purely economic criteria were used or if economic technicians dominated the negotiations there probably would not be association agreements with any of these countries.

[30] In West Germany there is a balance between the Foreign Office and the Ministry of Economic Affairs insofar as the management of Common Market affairs is concerned. Despite this formula of shared responsibility there are always issues which lead to overlapping jurisdictions and consequent tensions.

in the ministries of economics have adequate personnel to manage the mass of complex materials which daily occupy the national and Community services. The result has been the increasing importance and influence of the technical ministries and services at the expense of both the ministry of foreign affairs and the external relations divisions of the ministry of economic affairs.[31] It is probable in the long run that as the EEC develops and expands, the foreign ministries will continue to lose influence and authority, for as common policies develop they become internal policies no longer the subject of traditional diplomatic negotiators. Eventually, the technical ministries and services will become the dominant actors along with their Commission counterparts in the direction and management of major economic sectors, if not the entire economy. How extensive this will be depends on political will, economic interest, and the fulfillment of spillover potential.

This is the schematic development but in the day-to-day life of the Community matters are more nuanced and complex. At present the potential power of the technical expert has been circumscribed not only by the fact that final decisions remain in the hands of politically responsible ministers but also by the assimilation of a certain level of specialized knowledge by the generalist. Furthermore, the technical ministries have been victims of their increased importance and expanding competence in the sense that the multilateralization of problems has reduced the *exclusivity* and *autonomy* of these ministries for the present. Technical ministries now may have a broader scope of action but at the same time what previously might have been done with little or no surveillance from internal political forces is now bruited about and subjected to stronger political control. Thus, multilateralization, a key derivative of the integrative process, serves to regulate administrative power at the same time that it broadens the scope of that power.

The structural component of this surveillance and control is found at both the national and Community level. National control occurs in the coordinating mechanisms established to handle European problems in the member states. Both the mechanism and its effectiveness vary from state to state, with France having the most organized and most effective coordinating mechanism and West Germany having one of the least effective though not the least well-organized coordination committees. In France, for example, the Secrétariat Général Comité Interministériel (SGCI), consisting of a ten-man staff, centralizes the flow of all information between Brussels and Paris. The authority of this institution has been steadily increasing in response to a perceived need to exert stronger controls over French administrators who are in liaison with

[31] One manifestation is the growth of councils of "technical" ministers such as agriculture, finance, and transport. Although the recent Community crisis retarded this growth, at least for France, the general trend has been in the direction of a sectorial allocation of responsibility. What then becomes crucial is the manner in which the national governments arrive at the positions they will take in the negotiations in Brussels.

the EEC. Instructions for discussion and negotiation flow from this institution and there is a very high continuity between what a French expert says and what the French government eventually does. The reason is not, however, that the administrator is charting the course of his government. It is rather that under political mandate, the autonomy of French administrators is being closely regulated to allow maximum maneuverability to the political leadership. There is some evidence that previously, French administrators, who were generally outdistancing their government in the development of Community policies, were occasionally "negotiating" compromises with the Commission administration, a situation which helped further integration. To avoid the risks of a *copinage technocratique* and to ensure careful consideration of even minor technical issues, as well as to respond to the political factor noted above, the SGCI, often in conjunction with the Quai d'Orsay, has tightened its controls. In the West German situation, on the other hand, coordination between ministries is often lacking until the issue becomes highly political, despite the existence of a coordinating mechanism in the Ministry of Economic Affairs. A political climate favorable to integration and a deep respect for ministerial autonomy in Germany largely account for weaker coordinating controls. However, continuity between what a German administrator says and what his government ultimately does is correspondingly lower than in the case of France.[32]

Structural control at the Community level is exercised through the medium of the Committee of Permanent Representatives. The review and negotiation procedures which take place in this context serve as an effective monitor over technocratic decision making and sharply curtail the ability of the national administrator to fully commit his government. On the other hand, the Permanent Representatives often have turned out to be the Commission's best friend and to have labored hard to overcome technical resistance to politically desirable integration policies. A detailed discussion of the Permanent Representatives as an actor in administrative penetration is beyond the scope of this article, but a few comments regarding this organization are in order.

Activity in the Permanent Representatives takes place on a *horizontal* plane where Commission proposals are evaluated not only in terms of their logic but also in terms of the overall impact of the singular policy decision on the general policy framework. Technically sound proposals have been altered or even rejected at this level because of their incompatibility with greater political interests. The Commission's "prenegotiations," on the other hand, are *vertical* operations largely confined to seeking economically and technically sound solutions often quite aside from their political or social impact. It is the hori-

[32] While there may be poor interministerial coordination in Bonn this does not mean that within any one ministry things might not be run autocratically, with tight controls over the individual administrator. The problem basically is that a West German administrator may be speaking only for his ministry and not for his government.

zontal review which particularly tests the Commission's mettle, for it is here that the fine art of melding economics and politics really begins.

Secondly, although some Permanent Representative delegations are more influential than others in their home governments and some are closer to the Commission than others, all delegations try to monopolize the relationships between the Commission and their capitals. They seek to minimize direct contact between Commission administrators and national administrations and insist that any written correspondence from Brussels pass through their hands.[33] Without complete information on every dossier, of course, their ability to recommend and to negotiate would be curtailed. Correspondingly, one of the main Community tensions occurs between the Permanent Representatives and the national administrations for a dominant voice in the management of the development of integration.

Despite the constraints on administrative power and at the risk of complicating the matter even further, I think it must be stressed that at each of the levels under discussion—Commission "prenegotiation," the preparation of the national government's position, and in the final phases of negotiation in Brussels—the administrative expert is always present. His influence is *not* to be underestimated. To the extent that he operates without close instructions or coordination, or to the extent that his government has no strong interest in the question, his ability to commit his government to a particular course of action is increased. The course he chooses to follow under these conditions will have considerable impact on what his government finally does, for where an administrator has been left fairly free to act on behalf of his government the probability is strong that his advice will be accepted by his minister. There also have been many instances where the political authorities, unable or unwilling to come to grips with a problem, will remit it to the experts and solutions found at this level will be ratified eventually in the Council of Ministers.

VI

In reaching any conclusions on the relationship of administrative interpenetration to Community policy making and the process of integration, it is necessary to keep in mind the level of policy about which we are speaking. The EEC is constantly operating at several levels simultaneously—the inner core fulfillment of the customs union provisions of the Rome Treaty and the outer ring development of common policies either on the basis of independent coordinated or cooperative policies or on the basis of a single Community policy. As of this time, except for agricultural policy, the principal prog-

[33] The French delegation is the most adamant on this point but Italy and the Netherlands follow close behind. The West German delegation takes a more permissive view of the situation but at the same time insists that it be kept informed of all such correspondence and interchange.

ress of the Community has been confined almost exclusively to the inner core customs union. It is precisely in this area that firm commitments, timetables, and the definition of responsibilities have been most clearly spelled out in the Treaty and accepted from the beginning by the member states. Similarly, it is in this relatively technical area, in which the emphasis is on the elimination of barriers and obstacles, that administrative decision making is most intense and predominant and where the Commission bureaucracy most skillfully exercises its ability to transcribe political issues into technical terms in conjunction with the national administrations.

From the point of view of both levels noted above, it is clear that bureaucratic interpenetration is a singularly important factor in the integrative process. It is equally clear, however, that despite its importance, bureaucratic interpenetration is rarely *the* decisive factor in *major* policy orientation. The interpenetration of administrations as an integrative factor depends largely on the political environment. Where governments simply are prepared to abide by the rules of the game, bureaucratic interpenetration can lead and has led to increased governmental parallelism which in turn maximizes the opportunity to bring proposals to a successful conclusion. In the presence of major political support, such as France gave the Commission in the field of agricultural policy, bureaucratic interpenetration plays a more modest role (in basic policy orientation) although bureaucratic influence in operationalizing political decisions obviously is quite high.

To be successful, penetration generally must involve a *dialogue* between two different types of administration. On the one hand, there is an international administration charged with integrating functions, a process which entails the carrying on of essentially political activities. On the other hand there are national administrations responsible for the administration of existing political and economic systems. The former is concerned with system transformation; the latter is inclined toward system maintenance. As a result of this difference the international bureaucracy often seeks to break out of the operational frame of reference while the national administrations seek to stay within that frame of reference.[34] The Commission cannot afford to discount this psychological factor any more than it can afford to discount national political and social factors in the shaping of Community policy proposals. Where the Commission has failed to take these factors into account, it has also invariably failed to make substantial progress.

When responsible and fairly autonomous administrators come together in a policy-making context, the extremes of collusion, which could lead toward technocratic dominance, or collision, which could lead to the neutralization

[34] We must stress once again that the rule does not hold uniformly true. The Commission is not always the leader: National administrations sometimes seek to use the EEC as a means to achieve internal change, to gain greater influence over the external environment, or to assert greater authority in the national context.

of bureaucratic power, have rarely, if ever, been found. Collusion is much more probable in the managerial or executory stage, as in the case of the *comités de gestion,* than in the policy formulation stage. There also have been occasional incidents of unremitting hostility toward change. In these cases hostilities often have been eliminated by the intercession of individual Commissioners or their cabinets at the political level of the national capital in question. Principally, however, national administrations have responded by seeking an accommodation which minimizes sacrifice, change, or loss of autonomy. The EEC experience largely has been one of preparedness of national administrations to accept technical and economic readjustment.

In sum, bureaucratic interpenetration is alone insufficient to bring major policies to bear, but without it progress becomes difficult if not sometimes impossible. The major decisions which have been taken thus far in the EEC have been reached at the political level. This is as true for acceleration and for the recent developments in the field of transport policy as it is for agriculture. Bureaucratic interpenetration, however, remains the foundation stone, the *tissu cellulaire* of the system.

[9]

Subsidiarity: An Effective Barrier Against "the Enterprises of Ambition"?

NICHOLAS EMILIOU
*Lecturer in European Law, University of Southampton**

Subsidiarity has been formally recognised as a constitutional principle of Community law by the Maastricht Agreements. It expresses both a fear and a hope: a fear that the Community will arrogate excessive competence; and a hope that subsidiarity will operate as a safeguard against a unilateral expansion of supranational powers.

Right from the start certain things become obvious: first, that there is a general confusion and disagreement as to the meaning of this concept, and secondly, that subsidiarity is by no means a novel concept. Any discussion of subsidiarity has to consider the nexus of economic, political, philosophical, social and constitutional factors of European integration.

Multi-layered political systems based on subsidiarity have been developed into successful political, social and economic models. Subsidiarity fosters social, cultural, economic and political diversity. It should not be forgotten that the strength of the Community lies in diversity.

Introduction

The principle of subsidiarity has been enshrined in the European Community legal order by Articles A(2) and B of the Treaty on European Union and Article 3(b)(2) EEC which were introduced as a result of the Maastricht Agreements of December 1991. This concept has become " . . . shorthand for a cluster of issues about the sharing of powers between different levels of government in Western Europe."[1]

Nevertheless, when it comes to the definition of subsidiarity different people mean different things depending on their viewpoint. Thus the important factor about subsidiarity is the manner in which it is defined. On this there is a general agreement that there is no agreement on the definition of this concept. A narrow approach to the content of the principle of subsidiarity may result in a very limited scope of examination. Some legal aspects which, in the opinion of others, come under the heading of subsidiarity could be neglected or even discarded. Thus the definition of subsidiarity adopted for the purposes of this paper is quite broad; essentially referring to the principle according to which "a central authority should have a subsidiary func-

* The author is grateful for the assistance in preparation of this paper from Ms. Catherine Barnard, Dr. Nicholas Green and Professor Francis Snyder, none of whom is responsible for its deficiences.

[1] M. Wilke and M. Wallace, *Subsidiarity: Approaches to Power-Sharing in the European Community*. RIIA Discussion Papers No. 27. (1990) London.

tion, performing only those tasks which cannot be performed effectively at a more immediate or local level."[2]

Two terms are commonly used to denote different tendencies: "subsidiarity from above" and "bottom up" subsidiarity. The former term involves a definition of subsidiarity which benefits central institutions. This definition of subsidiarity embodies the idea that in a particular field the power enjoyed by central institutions is limited to those areas where intervention or measures from the centre seem necessary to achieve a given goal. On the other hand the "bottom-up" approach to subsidiarity assumes that central authorities are subsidiary or auxiliary to the lower levels of power. In this sense only when action and/or measures from the lowest possible level of government are not adequate to achieve a given goal then the higher level of authority should intervene (or come to the rescue!).

Subsidiarity favours the diffusion of power among a number of substantially self-sustaining centres. This diffusion of power is known as non-centralisation. Non-centralisation is quite different from de-centralisation, which is the conditional diffusion of specific powers by a central government to local governments subject to recall. It is also more than devolution—the unilateral grant of powers to subnational units by a central government, not normally rescindable. Non-centralisation is a way of ensuring in practice that the authority to participate in exercising political power cannot be taken away from the general or the state governments without common consent.

Historical context

The most visible source of subsidiarity lies in the canon law of the Catholic Church. Pope Pius XI incorporated subsidiarity expressly in the Roman Catholic social philosophy in his Encyclical Letter, *Quadragesimo Anno* (1931).[3] The Pope, concerned with the social disorder at the time, tried to prescribe some fundamental principles for the reconstruction of the social order. In his opinion the State had assumed a large number of responsibilities and duties and had been overwhelmed by them. Responsibilities were being moved from small groups to large groups. In the Papal view:

> " . . . just as it is wrong to withdraw from the individual and commit to a group what private enterprise and industry can accomplish, so too it is an injustice, a grave evil and a disturbance of the right order, for a larger and a higher association to arrogate to itself functions which can be performed efficiently by smaller and lower societies. This is a fundamental principle of social philosophy, unshaken and unchangeable. Of its very

[2] Oxford English Dictionary. This is the definition adopted by the House of Lords Select Committee on the European Communities. *Report on Economic and Monetary Union and Political Union*. Session 1989–90 27th Report. (1990) London, HMSO, p. 14.

[3] Pope Pius XI, *Quadragesimo Anno* (London, Catholic Truth Society, 1936), p. 31 para. 79.

nature the true aim of all social activity should be to help members of the social body, but never to destroy or absorb them."

Subsidiarity has been repeatedly brought into the scene by Pope Pius XI successors. The Papal Encyclical *Pacem in Terris* (1963) stressed the role of subsidiarity as a general principle of social organisation: "The relations between the public authorities and the citizen, the family and intermediary bodies must be governed and brought into balance by the principle of subsidiarity." The role of subsidiarity in Roman Catholic social philosophy is not to be overlooked. These ideas have had, in continental Europe, a considerable influence on theories concerning the relation between the State and society and on political action based on that thinking. Subsidiarity, as a principle of social organisation, played its part in laying the basis for the effort to create " . . . a corporate structure of the State on the continent in the years before and even immediately after the Second World War."[4]

Theoretical foundations

In the years after the Second World War there was shift, especially in the Federal Republic of Germany,[5] from a socio-philosophical to a legal concept of subsidiarity. Thus the original relationship between the individual, the group and society has been extended to embrace political institutions and authorities. In the latter sense, subsidiarity establishes a presumption in favour of the lower authorities and jurisdictions. That is, certain areas of decision-making will not be subject to interference from the central authorities.[6] Thus the centre should exercise only those powers which cannot be discharged by the smaller political units. The reverse of course can be true. That is, the central authority, pointing to the autonomy of the lower level, may transfer some of their responsibilities to the latter.

One of the aspects of the Rule of Law in a democratic State is the separation and division of powers both on the vertical and horizontal axis. The idea behind this is that fragmentation of power will best protect liberty. As a result, executive, legislative and judicial functions, both at national and supranational level, are attached to different organ-groups. It is the functional and institutional interdependence of these organ-groups rather than their independence that prevents any of them from achieving dominance over the others.

Federalism[7] adds an extra safety valve to the system of checks and

[4] Kapteyn. (1990) *Community law and the Principle of Subsidiarity*. Speech delivered at the Centre for European Law, Kings College London, November 2, 1990. Unpublished.

[5] See generally in H. Stadler, *Subsidiaritatsprinzip und Foderalismus*. (1951) Freiburg.

[6] See Gretschmann in his paper for the Delors Colloquium 1991, EIPA, Maastricht on *The Subsidiarity Principle: Who Is to Do What in an Integrated Europe?* in Proceedings of the J. Delors Colloquium 1991. *Subsidiarity: The Challenge of Change*. Maastricht, pp. 48–49.

[7] For the purposes of this paper "federalism" is taken to mean a mode of political organisation that unites separate states or other polities within an overarching political system in such a way as to allow each to maintain its own fundamental political integrity. Federal systems do this

balances, which shields against abuse of power, protects the freedom of the individual and safeguards justice.[8] Power, attributed to the state by the people, is exercised under separate headings on a horizontal axis—legislative, executive and judicial arms of the state authority—and divided on a vertical axis—local government, state and central government.[9] Separation of powers and the federal state division are closely linked; in the context of competing powers and levels of authority individual rights are best protected. Federalism fosters the model of subsidiarity: that is, as many tasks as possible should be administered by small groups before making the next level responsible for them. In practical terms this implies that local government should precede state administration, which, in turn, should precede federal government.

Thus subsidiarity can only be fully understood and defined within the context of federalism.[10] Federalism is the most important element of the vertical division of powers.[11] Decentralisation and devolution as expressed by the principle of subsidiarity are the main constitutional reasons for fostering activities and responsibilities at the federal level. Since all these sources

---

by requiring that basic policies be made and implemented through negotiation in some form, so that all the members can share in making and executing decisions. See Britannica (Micropaedia) Vol. 4, p. 712. Lenaerts draws a distinction between *integrative federalism and devolutionary federalism*. Whereas the former "refers to a constitutional order that strives at unity in diversity among previously independent or confederally related component entities," the latter "refers to a constitutional order that redistributes the powers of previously unitary State among its component entities." See K. Lenaerts, Constitutionalism and the Many Faces of Federalism. (1990) 38 A.J.C.L. 205, 206. It could be argued that the European Community is moving towards the model of integrative federalism.

[8] According to Lenaerts, *ibid.*, at p. 205: "As a system of divided powers, federalism proceeds from the very essence of constitutionalism, which is limited government operating under the rule of law."

[9] F. Jerusalem, *Die Staatsidee des Foderalismus.* (1949) Tubingen, p. 12. The term horizontal separation of powers simply means that every organ-group is bound to remain within its powers as prescribed by the constitution. On the other hand, vertical separation of powers denotes division of the tasks assigned by the constitution to organ-groups exercising different level of authority; that is the division of powers between federal and state organs.

[10] On the very day (June 18, 1991) on which the Luxembourg Presidency issued its draft Treaty on the European Union, the United States Secretary of State James Baker said: "The architects of a United Europe have adopted the principle of 'subsidiarity,' something like America's 'federalism'—that is, the devolution of responsibility to the lowest level of government capable of performing it effectively." See Belmont European Policy Centre. *From Luxembourg to Maastricht: 100 Critical Days for Europe* (1991) Brussels, p. 50. According to the Prime Minister of Luxembourg Jacques Santer there are obvious and close links between subsidiarity and federalism:

> "Federalism can be seen as a pyramid and a pyramid will only be sound if its base is broad, *i.e.* if the bodies at the base are left to do everything they can do. From this point of view, the higher bodies only intervene if the lower bodies withdraw. The bodies closest to the base are inevitably also the ones closest to man. They should therefore not be deprived of their competences as long as they carry out their tasks properly. A federal or near federal system will only function satisfactorily and with respect for man, if it distributes the executive, administrative and legislative competences according to the abovementioned scheme."

See Santer, *supra*, n. 6, at p. 20.

[11] K. Loewenstein. *Political Power and the Governmental Process.* (1957) Chicago, at p. 295 *et seq.*

of power are in accordance with the basic principles of the federal constitution,[12] they strengthen its vitality. Thus issues of federalism, subsidiarity and separation of powers are inextricably interwined. The federal judicial power constitutes an aspect of the separation of powers as well as federalism; the distribution of legislative and executive responsibilities to the federation and the component States is a federal issue as well as part of the horizontal division of powers.[13]

Subsidiarity has two aspects: on the one hand, it can be used as a criterion for the division of competences between the different levels of political power; on the other hand it can help delineate the dividing line between the individual sphere and that of the State.[14]

Subsidiarity as a guarantee for individual liberty

Much of Western political thought and constitutional theory considers the distinction between the sphere of the individual and that of the State as the bedrock of the democratic system of government. The prevailing view in a democracy is that the individual is first of all a member of the community and only secondly a citizen of the state.[15] A vast variety of different groups and associations (which are the constituent parts of the "society" at large) are interposed between the individual and the state authority. This meets the vital human need to associate while, at the same time, acting as a buffer against the omnipotent state authority.

Nevertheless, as a result of the growing responsibilities of the contemporary "social state," the clear 19th century distinction between the public and private sphere has been blurred. Yet, the importance of a clear demarkation of the spheres of the individual, groups and the state as an essential prerequisite of liberty cannot be stressed enough. A near total absorption of society by the state will signal the end of liberty; weakening the state, on the other hand, will lead to a similar result because the state guarantees safety as a precondition of freedom.[16] Therefore a balance should be struck between state interest and protection of the sphere of the individual and groups formed by individual. It should always be borne in mind, however, that the state is a creation of society and the individual and voluntary associations formed by him; as a result they should not be at the mercy of the state authority.

Alexis de Tocqueville observed in 1835 that in the case America:

" . . . no other country has relied more broadly or successfully on the

[12] See Art. 28 GG and Art. IV para. 4 United States Constitution.

[13] K. Doehring, *Staatsrecht der Bundesrepublik Deutschland.* Frankfurt, pp. 107 *et seq.*; E. Stein, *Staatsrecht.* (1980) Tubingen, pp. 67 *et seq.* (1982).

[14] Delors, *supra*, n. 6, at p. 7.

[15] M. Imboden, *Politische Systeme.* (1964) Basel & Stuttgard, pp. 22 *et seq.*

[16] See E-W. Bockenforde, *Die Verfassungstheoritische Unterscheidung von Staat und Gesellschaft als Bedingung der individuellen Freiheit.* (1973) Oplanden.

'principle of association'—a principle in which political parties, professional associations, social clubs, families, labour-unions, religious organizations, and other private collectivities are thought entitled to lead their own free lives and exercises within the area of their competence and authority so effectively as to justify labelling it sovereign."[17]

According to Blackstone liberty is prior to the state and before the state.[18] Liberty is natural and therefore in defining the sphere of the individual and that of the state there should be a presumption favouring the individual. At this point subsidiarity can be helpful in the sense that in dividing responsibility between the individual, the community and the state, everything is reserved for the individual and the community, except what is granted to the state by the constitution and only in so far as the objectives of the society cannot be sufficiently achieved by individual or community action.

Subsidiarity as a principle of German constitutional law

The principle of subsidiarity[19] as discussed and introduced into German public law has been derived from the Catholic social doctrine ("*katolische Soziallehre*")[20] and was first formulated broadly by Isensee in 1968[21] who himself mentions the principle as first occurring in the goals and aims of the Paulskirchen Constitution of 1848. The principle of subsidiarity has been taken to mean that higher organisational units of government may acquire competences if and in so far as lower units cannot exercise the same powers as well or better.[22]

Subsidiarity is not expressly mentioned in the Grundgesetz (GG) but it can be traced in several articles.[23] Article 30 GG states that: "The exercise of governmental powers and the discharge of governmental functions shall be incumbent on the 'Lander,' in so far as this Basic Law does not otherwise prescribe or permit."[24] Article 72 GG is clearly a specific enunciation of the

[17] See A. Tocqueville, *Democracy in America*. 4 Vols. 1835–40.

[18] Blackstone. *Commentaries*. Book I, Chap. I.

[19] The principle of subsidiarity in German constitutional law embodies the idea that the Federal Authority should have a subsidiary function, performing only those tasks which cannot be performed effectively at a more immediate or local level. See Stadler, *supra*, n. 5, at p. 167.

[20] *Ibid.*

[21] K. Stern, *Das Staatsrecht der Bundesrepublik Deutschland*. (1984) Munchen, at Bd. IV p. 1219, names Isensee as the originator of the principle.

[22] ". . . die hoheren organisatorische Einheit nur insoweit Aufgaben an sich zieht, als die nachgeordnete Einheit sie nicht ebensogut oder besser erledigen kann"; T. Maunz and R. Zippelius, *Deutsches Staatsrecht*. (1985) Munich, p. 69.

[23] "Im Grundgesetz ist [die Subsidiaritat] nicht ausdrucklich formuliert, findet aber insbesondere in den Art. 2 I, 6, 9, 28 II, 30, 70 I, 72 II und 83 einen Ausdruck"; Maunz/Zippelius, *ibid.*

[24] The Tenth Amendment to the United States Constitution, dealing with the same issue, says: "The powers not delegated to the United States by the Constitution or prohibited by it to the States, are reserved to the States respectively, or to the people."

more general idea of subsidiarity. This provision deals with the concurrent legislative powers of the Federation and the Lander.

According to Article 72 GG:

> "I. In the field of concurrent legislative competence the Lander have the power to legislate as long and insofar as the Federation does not make use of its right to legislate.
> II. In this field the Federation will have the right to legislate to the extent that federal legal regulation is needed because:
> 1. a matter cannot be effectively regulated by the legislation of individual Lander, or
> 2. the regulation of a matter by a Land might prejudice the interest of other Lander or of the people as a whole; or
> 3. the maintenance of legal or economic uniformity or living conditions beyond the territory of any one Land, necessitates such regulation."

From the above constitutional provisions it is clear that in the first instance, all government competence is presumed to lie with the Lander,[25] so that there is a relationship of subsidiarity between Lander and the Federation.[26] The only criteria by which competence should be transferred to the federal government are whether the Bundeslander are able to handle legal competences adequately and administrative obligations effectively despite their regional limitation.[27]

The main reason for the introduction of this principle into the Grundgesetz was to limit centralisation to the absolute minimum.[28] This might be condensed into the formula "as much central government as necessary, as little central government as possible." In practice though, despite Article 30 GG, there has been a shift of powers to the Federal unit, which has turned the principle of subsidiarity almost on its head, revealing the weakness of the federal guarantee of subsidiary powers for the States.[29]

Since 1949 the tendency to strengthen federal legislative powers have led to a limitation of legislative jurisdiction of the Bundeslander.[30] Furthermore,

---

[25] See Art. 30 GG: "Ausubung der staatlichen Befugnisse und die Erfullung der staatlichen Aufgaben ist Sache der Lander, soweit dieses Grundgesetz keine andere Regelung trifft oder zulasst."

[26] "Zwischen Bund und Landern herrscht also das Verhaltnis der Subsidiaritat." S. Isensee, 225 f.

[27] "Entscheident ist alleine, ob die Lander in ihrer regionalen Begrenztheit imstande sind, eine Aufgabe sachgerecht gesetzlich zu regeln und wirksam verwaltungsmassig wahrzunehmen." See J. Isensee, *Subsidiaritatprinzip und Verfassungsrecht.* (1968) Berlin, p. 227.

[28] " . . . Leitgedanke . . . , der die Kompetenzverteilung durch den Verfassungsgeber beherrschte, dass die Zentralisierung sich auf das notwendige Mass zu beschranken habe." Isensee, *ibid.*

[29] "Die angebliche [kompetenz-] Vermutung fur die Lander kehrt sich um in eine *Vermutung zugunsten des Bundes* . . . Hier offenbart sich die Schwache der foderalistischen Vorranggarantie." Isensee, *supra*, n. 27, at p. 231.

[30] G-B. Oschatz and H. Risse, Europaische Integration und deutscher Foderalismus. In *Europa-Archiv*, (1988) vol. 43, pp. 9–16.

the transfer of powers to Community institutions took further powers from the Lander and led to what has been described as the "effect of a two-fold erosion"[31] of their powers.

Co-operative federalism and vertical separation of powers

Nevertheless the federal element in the Federal Republic is not lost. The "*Verfassungswirklichkeit*"[32] of more than four decades in Germany produced *co-operative federalism*[33] within the framework of which the Lander and the federal government share certain powers. This co-operation consists of common contracts[34] among the Lander, common agencies of the Lander, common agencies of the Lander and the federal government, and finally Lander participation in common competences at the national level.[35]

This system of government does not provide an absolute guarantee of a smooth running of the State. Rather " . . . defiance and non-compliance [of subordinate units] are characteristics of everyday relations even in a system of 'co-operative federalism.' "[36] But eventually productive confrontations are the advantage—and for this reason perhaps even the purpose—of federal systems.[37]

Both co-operative federalism and the principle of subsidiarity achieve vertical separation of powers by means of the creative force of co-ordinated initiatives working "from below" in order to accomplish common tasks.[38] German experience shows that a special relationship between the federal

[31] *Ibid.*, at p. 9

[32] Constitutional reality, often at variance to the intention and spirit of the Basic Law.

[33] The political principles that animate "co-operative federalism" emphasise the primacy of bargaining and negotiated co-ordination among several power centres; they stress the virtues of dispersed power centres as means of safeguarding individual and local liberties. On co-operative federalism see generally Maunz/Zippelius, *supra*, n. 22.

[34] The contractual sharing of public responsibilities by all state governments within the framework of the federal system appears to be a central characteristic of federalism. Sharing, in a wide sense, includes common involving in policy making, financing, and administration. Sharing may be formal or informal; in federal systems, it is usually contractual. The contract is used as a legal device to enable governments to engage in joint action while remaining independent entities. Even where there is no formal arrangement, the spirit of federalism tends to infuse a sense of contractual obligation. See Maunz/Zippelius, *supra*, n. 22, at pp. 107 *et seq.*

[35] "Diese offenbaren sich insbesondere in gemeinsamen Beschlussen der Lander, in Bund-Lander-Abkommen, in Gemeinschaftseinrichtungen von Bund und Landern, und schliesslich in der Einbeziehung von Gemeinschaftsaufgaben in das Bundesrecht." Maunz/Zippelius, *ibid.*

[36] Krislov, Ehlermann and Weiler. "The Political Organs and the Decision-Making Process in the United States and the European Community," in Cappelletti, Seccombe and Weiler (eds.). *Integration through Law. Europe and the American Federal Experience.* (1986) Berlin/NY, Vol. I, Book II, p. 93.

[37] According to Kristov/Ehlermann/Weiler, *ibid.*, p. 95 " . . . federalism, in this respect, is like marriage, which, we are told, combines the maximum of temptation with the maximum of opportunity."

[38] "Der Weg foderaler Kooperation verwirklicht das Ziel vertikaler Gewaltenteilung, nicht minder aber auch das der Subsidiaritat, durch die schopferische Kraft koordinierter Initiativen, die von unten her wirken, um eine Gemeinschaftsaufgabe zu verwirklichen." Isensee, *supra*, n. 29, at p. 235.

authority and the component units is a *sine qua* non condition for the effective implementation of federal policies.

Subsidiarity as a principle of Community law

The question of the origins of subsidiarity in Community law is subject to dispute. It is common ground, however, that subsidiarity was introduced in the debate about the future architecture of the Communities in the mid-1970s.

The McDougall Report,[39] on the role of public finance in European integration, addressed, *inter alia*, the question of which economic policy areas should be funded at Community level and the effect of Community funding on the policies that remained in the hands of national governments. The report dealt with the question of fiscal federalism "from the bottom up" and was based on the general assumption that the Community was developing beyond the pre-federal integration phase, with a federal structure as the destination of the integration process. The findings of the report were clear: "only through a comprehensive and consistent allocation of authority and initiative to appropriate levels of government would the integration process in Western Europe proceed sensibly."[40]

The report suggested for instance that social welfare services (that is, education, health, housing and social security) should remain in the province of the Member States because of their limited scope and because of the absence of significant spillover effects (that is, significant impact on cross-border policies). Macroeconomic measures, on the other hand, because of their significant cross-border impact, would require action at Community level combined with some sharing of power between the Community and the Member States in order to maximise the general welfare. The report referred to integrated economies of federal states as an example of the distribution of power between different levels in the area of public finances.

The draft European Union Treaty,[41] drawn up by the European Parliament in 1984, calling for a radical reform of the Communities, included several references to the principle of subsidiarity. The preamble to the draft Treaty makes the division of powers between the Union and the Member States subject to the principle of subsidiarity: common institutions will be entrusted " . . . only with those powers required to complete successfully the tasks they may carry out more satisfactorily than the States acting independently." Reference to subsidiarity was made, expressly or explicitly, in other provisions of the draft as well. Article 12 of the draft Treaty incorpor-

[39] Commission of the European Communities. *McDougall Report of the Study Group on the Role of Public Finance in European Integration*. (1977) OOPEC. Luxembourg. For a more detailed discussion of the report see, Wilke and Wallace, *supra*, n. 1, at pp. 23 *et seq*.

[40] Wilke and Wallace, *supra*, n. 1, at p. 23.

[41] [1984] O.J. C 77/33.

ated the principle of subsidiarity as a condition of the exercise of concurrent powers by the Union:

> "Where this Treaty confers concurrent competence on the Union, the Member States shall continue to act as long as the Union has not legislated. *The Union shall only act to carry out those tasks which may be undertaken more effectively in common than by the Member States acting separately, in particular those whose execution requires action by the Union because their dimension or effects extend beyond national frontiers.*"[42]

Following the pattern established by the German Grundgesetz,[43] Article 12 of the draft Treaty draws the distinction between exclusive and concurrent powers.[44] The notion of concurrent powers, which is familiar to German lawyers by virtue of Article 72 GG, has been widely misinterpreted in the other Member States. The most common view is that concurrent powers are those which make possible simultaneous action by the Union and the Member States. Nothing is further from the truth. As in the case of exclusive powers, concurrent powers are " . . . conferred upon the Union and upon the Union alone. The Union cannot share the exercise of such powers with the Member States."[45] The difference between exclusive and concurrent powers is the following. While the powers defined as exclusive by the constitutive Treaty can be exercised by the Union from the entry into force of the Treaty, the exercise of its concurrent powers is suspended and made subject to compliance with certain procedural and substantive conditions. Until those conditions are met, the Member States retain the right to legislate in the area concerned. This right is lost once the Union decides to exercise its legislative powers. When this decision is taken, the Union's power is of the same nature as in those cases where it has exclusive powers. This means that the Member States lose all power to act in that area unless the legislation of the Union gives them the right to enact implementation measures.

According to the scheme established under Article 12, therefore, the Union will exercise only powers attributed to it exclusively. Under Article 12(2), however, the Union will be able to take action in the field of concurrent powers provided that the criteria established by the principle of subsidiarity are observed. These criteria are:

(a) the *more effective attainment test*: "The Union shall only act to carry out those tasks which may be undertaken more effectively in common than by the Member States acting separately . . . " The question whether a task can be carried out more effectively at the level of the Union rather than at

---

[42] Author's emphasis.

[43] Arts. 71 and 72 GG. See also Commission's proposals during the preparation of the Tindemans report. EC Bulletin, Suppl. 5/75.

[44] This distinction is not novel to Community law. The Court of Justice pointed to the division of the Communities' powers into exclusive and concurrent in the field of the common commercial policy and the common fisheries policy. See, *e.g.* Opinion 1/75 [1975] E.C.R. 1355.

[45] See Capotorti, Hilf, Jacobs and Jacque. *The European Union Treaty*. (1986) Oxford. p. 77.

national level should be resolved according to objective criteria of social, economic, technical and legal character. Commentators of the draft Treaty[46] appear to have taken the view that the expression "more effectively" actually means "more satisfactorily." That phrase was intended to emphasise the fact that the question here is not one of "technocratic advantageousness" but of balancing effectiveness against other conflicting values. This balancing act is clearly a question of political judgment. Here the criterion is effectiveness, which may have a centralising effect.

(b) the *cross-boundary dimension effect*: according to which the Union shall [only] carry out the tasks which " . . . because [of] their dimension or effects extend beyond national frontiers." This test should be taken to mean that when the effects of action at the national level is clearly more advantageous for the Member States or action at the Union level is more disadvantageous for the Member States then the task in question should not be given a dimension[47] which extends beyond national frontiers. Naturally, the question whether a task has a cross-boundary dimension very much depends on what goals the Union sets for itself. Nevertheless, since the Union is assigned only those tasks whose dimension and effects extend beyond national frontiers, this criterion tends to have a decentralising effect.[48]

It could be argued that the drafters of Article 12(2) considered the cross-boundary dimension effect as a special application of the more effective attainment test.[49] The existence, however, of these two criteria side by side implies that there is a crucial political and institutional choice to be made between a federalism of a centralising nature and federalism of a decentralising nature.[50]

The Single European Act introduced the principle of subsidiarity, albeit

[46] Nickel, D. Le projet de traite instituant l' Union Europeene. (1984). C.D.E. 511 at 514.

[47] According to Constantinesco the word "dimension" in Art. 12(2) of the draft means the internal and external aspects of the task in question. See V. Constantinesco, *La distribution des pouvoirs entre la Communaute et ses Etats membres: Le equilibre mouvant de la competence legislative et le principe de subsidiarite.* (1990) Working Paper. Annual Conference of the College of Europe. Bruges.

[48] *The Principle of Subsidiarity*. EP Committee on Institutional Affairs. Rapporteur: Valery Giscard d'Estaing, (European Parliament, July 1990). DOC EN/RR/91692, p. 5.

[49] It is interesting to note that the Rapporteur of the Committee on Institutional Affairs, Mr. Valery Giscard d'Estaing, in his report of October 31, 1990, on the principle of subsidiarity refers to the more effective attainment test in conjunction with the cross boundary dimension test. Mr. Giscard d'Estaing suggested the insertion of the following provision in the Treaties:

> "The Community shall act only to fulfil the tasks transferred to it by the treaty and to achieve the objectives defined thereby. If powers have not exclusively or completely assigned to the Community, the Community shall, in carrying out its tasks, take action in so far as the achievement of these objectives requires its intervention because, by virtue of their magnitude or effects, they transcend the frontiers of the Member States or because they can be undertaken more efficiently by the Community than by the Member States acting separately."

See *The Principle of Subsidiarity*. EP Committee on Institutional Affairs. Rapporteur: Valery Giscard d'Estaing (European Parliament, October 1990). DOC EN/RR/98228.

[50] *Supra*, n. 4.

in a limited field, into the positive law of the Community. Article 130r(4) EEC provides: "The Community shall take action relating to the environment *to the extent to which the objectives referred to in paragraph 1 can be attained better at Community level than at the level of the individual Member States.*"[51]

The House of Lords dealt with Article 130r(4) EEC recently in *R.* v. *London Boroughs Transport Committee, ex p. Freight Transport Association and others.*[52] The appellant, a traffic regulatory authority acting on behalf of local authority boroughs of Greater London, imposed a night ban on lorry traffic in London in order to reduce noise and pollution. Exceptions were allowed for goods vehicles which were individually licensed for that purpose. A condition of such licence was that the vehicle should be fitted with a device to silence air brakes produced by one of three specified manufacturers. The applicants in the original action contended that this condition was unlawful because it was in breach of two Directives laying down manufacturing standards for braking devices and sound levels for exhaust systems as well as Article 30 EEC. It was argued, on the applicants' behalf, lorries which complied with the provisions of the Directives in question could not have further conditions relating to sound levels or braking systems imposed on them and that the condition did just that, and therefore the condition was unlawful as contrary to the directives and Article 30 EEC.

Lord Templeman referring to Article 130r(4) EEC said that this provision recognised that:

> " . . . London's environmental traffic problems cannot be solved, although they can be ameliorated by Council directives to control every vehicle at all times throughout the Community.
>
> The attainment of the Community object of preserving, protecting and improving the quality of the environment requires action at the level of individual member-States. A vehicle which complies with all the weight, size, sound level and other technical requirements and standards of directives issued by the Council pursuant to Article 100 and is therefore entitled to be used in every member-State throughout the Community is not thereby entitled to be driven on every road, on every day, at every hour throughout the Community. In the interests of the environment the traffic authorities of Santiago de Compostella may ban all or some Community vehicles from medieval streets. The traffic authorities of Greater London may ban all or some Community vehicles from residential streets at night."

Even though his Lordship refrained from referring to the principle of subsidiarity *expressis verbis* it is clear from the above passage that subsidiarity was the heart of his argument. It is obvious that local authorities are better

[51] Author's emphasis.
[52] [1992] 1 C.M.L.R. 5.

equipped to deal with environmental problems of urban areas including noise caused by vehicles. The Commission's Green Paper on *The Urban Environment*,[53] to which Lord Templeman referred, lends support to the above proposition. Relevant passages include the following:

> "4. *Instruments of Community Action*
> City authorities, and the national governments which provide the legislative and financial framework within which the cities operate, have the major responsibility to improve the urban environment . . .
>
> 5.2 *Urban Transport*
>
> . . . .
>
> At the Community level it is not possible to provide details of the strategy that would be appropriate for a particular city. But it is possible to identify a number of areas where progress would contribute to reducing the impact of vehicle traffic on the city . . ."

Local authorities should therefore be encouraged to protect the environment against damage in urban areas since according to the test provided for by Article 130r(4) EEC, that is, the "better attainment" test, they are better equipped to attain the objectives referred to in Article 130r(1) EEC.[54]

Article 130r(4) EEC establishes, as indicated above, the "better attainment test," that is, the Community (in the field of the environment) shall pursue only those objectives which can be better attained by the Community than Member States acting individually. According to Judge Kapteyn:

> "The better attainment test adds to the consideration of policy makers a criterion that even without this admonition they should apply: in considering how objectives may best be attained, it must be clear that action at Community level is better than at the level of the individual States. It is a test with which much is left to discretion and which is ultimately a matter of political choice."[55]

The "better attainment" test is clearly a subjective test and its inclusion in Article 130r(4) EEC constitutes an invitation to a subjective interpretation of this provision. What "can be attained better at Community level" depends on the direction which one wants to move and there is often no agreement about this. If an objective can really be attained better at Community level, why then does everyone not agree about it? The fact that there is no agreement proves that one's conception that a task can be attained better at a higher level of authority is subjective and not shared by everyone.

[53] Com. (90) 218, June 27, 1989.

[54] Art. 130r(1) EEC defines the objectives of the EC environmental policy as follows:
—to preserve, protect and improve the quality of the environment;
—to contribute towards protecting human health;
—to ensure prudent and rational utilisation of natural resources . . .

[55] *Supra*, n. 4.

396 Subsidiarity

In the Padoa-Schioppa Report of 1987,[56] dealing with the underlying issues of economic policy which arose as a result of the Iberian accession to the Communities and the project for the completion of the European internal market, subsidiarity was used as an institutional norm and a political concept. The report pointed to two guiding principles which could be used to decide whether Community intervention is necessary; that is, the cross-frontier spill-over effects and the task of dealing with unemployment. The cross-frontier spill-over effects criterion has been derived from the fundamental proposition of economics that efficiency requires that benefits should be enjoyed by those who create them while costs should be borne by those who cause them. Whenever this principle is violated, reference is made to "spill-over" effects or externalities.

An aspect of the principle of subsidiarity is that policy should be executed at the lowest possible level of government. Nevertheless, if that is not efficient and compensation mechanisms fail, then the responsibility should be transferred to the next higher level.[57] That happens when the spill-over of important cost or benefit elements to other areas leads, respectively, to over-or under-supply of public goods. As European integration advances, spill-over effects are likely to increase in importance and therefore more powers will need to be transferred to the Community level.[58]

As far as the cross-frontier spill-over effects test is concerned, the question is which level of authority is better suited to perform a particular task in an adequate manner. This test, therefore, constitutes an efficiency criterion. With respect to the priority task of dealing with unemployment, the report recognised that in the field of social policy the basic responsibility belongs to the national governments. Nevertheless, if regional unemployment is the result of common market policies, then the Community should intervene.

Further reference to subsidiarity was made in the Delors Report on Economic and Monetary Union (EMU) of 1989.[59] There subsidiarity was used as a means of balancing Community and national powers in the area of monetary and macroeconomic policy-making. According to paragraph 20 of the report:

> "The attribution of competences to the Community would have to be confined specifically to those areas in which collective decision-making was necessary. All policy functions which could be carried out at national (and regional and local) levels without adverse repercussions

---

[56] Commission of the European Communities. *Efficiency, Stability and Equity: A Strategy for the Evolution of the Economic System of the European Community (Padoa-Schioppa Report)*. (1987) Luxembourg.

[57] W. Oates, *Fiscal Federalism*. (1972). N.Y.

[58] Molle, W. *The Economics of European Integration*. (1990). Aldershot, pp. 27 *et seq.*

[59] Committee for the Study of Economic and Monetary Union. *Delors Report on the Economic and Monetary Union in the European Community*. (1989) OOPEC. Luxembourg.

on the cohesion and functioning of the economic and monetary union would remain within the competence of the member countries."

Subsidiarity is mentioned in Chapter II of the report. This concerns the final stage of economic and monetary union which implies complete freedom of movement for persons, goods, services and capital, irrevocably fixed exchange rates between national currencies and finally a single currency. Subsidiarity is referred to as "an essential element in defining the appropriate balance of power within the Community." According to Molle[60] within the framework of an economic and monetary union:

> " . . . [the Member States] tend to apply the principle of subsidiarity, that is, leaving competence as long as possible with the nation states. Transfer of competence will be agreed upon only if it can be proved to make the overall policy process more efficient."

As far as the monetary aspect[61] of EMU is concerned there is little doubt as to the application of subsidiarity. The choice made at Maastricht, to adopt a single currency by January 1, 1999, at the outside, leaves little room for manoeuvre. The adoption of a common currency implies quite a high degree of integration of macroeconomic and budgetary policies. The existence of a single monetary institution which formulates and implements a common monetary policy is the natural consequence of the adoption of a single currency. Those policies should be singularly aimed at monetary and exchange rate stability. In this area therefore the Member States are faced with a complete transfer of sovereignty to the Community.

The situation is somewhat different in the area of economic union.[62] This is a voluntary process involving sovereign states. A significant element of political acceptability is involved as far as the division of powers between the centre and the periphery is concerned. According to the Director-General of D.G. II (Economic and Financial Affairs):

> "While in monetary union there is the obligation of result, *i.e.* stability, due in particular to the independence of monetary power, and therefore also the obligation of means, the case of economic union is somewhat different. Obviously we aim at the obligation of result, *i.e.* economic convergence . . . but we leave some room to manoeuvre as regards the

[60] *Supra*, n. 58, at p. 145.

[61] Monetary union is a form of co-operation which on top of a common market (notably free movement of capital) creates either irrevocably fixed exchange rates and full convertibility of the currencies of the member states, or one common currency circulating in all member states. See Molle, *supra*, n. 58, at p. 13.

[62] Economic union implies not only a common market but a high degree of co-ordination or even unification of the most important areas of economic policy, market regulation as well as macroeconomic and monetary policies and income redistribution policies. Not only is a common trade policy pursued towards third countries, but external policies concerning production factors and economic sectors are also developed. See Molle, *supra*, n. 58, at p. 13.

choice of means which the various Member States could employ to achieve results which . . . must be opportune for the entire union."[63]

Obviously this is an area which Member States should enjoy a degree of autonomy but also where certain common rules are necessary as well. Economic union therefore constitutes an area which is subject to concurrent powers between the Community and the Member States, that is, an area bound to be governed by the principle of subsidiarity.

The preamble to the Social Charter of the European Community[64] linked the principle of subsidiarity to the social dimension of the single European market. This instrument is not legally binding. It constitutes a "political and solemn declaration" by 11 governments of Member States to the effect that the Community has a social dimension as well as an economic dimension. The Charter invites the Commission to submit, at the earliest opportunity, proposals which will turn the social rights envisaged in the Charter into binding legal rules. The preamble to the Charter states that by virtue of the principle of subsidiarity:

" . . . responsibility for the initiatives to be taken with regard to the implementation of these social rights lies with the Member States or their constituent parts or the two sides of the industry as well as, within the limits of its powers, with the European Community."

It is clear from this statement that subsidiarity in this area has only a limited scope of application. The Commission has up until now taken action in the fields of free movement of persons, protection of health and safety of workers in the workplace and labour law. There is a consensus that the first two areas require action at the Community level while the situation is less clear as far as labour law is concerned. Labour law is an area which reflects diverse national traditions and is the outcome of a process of struggle between different interest groups. The crucial element in the making of labour law is power. Another characteristic of labour law is the extent to which certain matters are governed by contractual relationships rather than legislative rules.

Subsidiarity has been a prominent principle in most national systems of labour law for quite some time. The contractual element of labour law is no more than an aspect of subsidiarity because instead of the central legislature deciding on terms and conditions of employment the matter is left to be regulated by the individual employer and employee. Thus the question in this area is not only what can be done at the national or Community level but also what can be done directly with negotiations and contractual agreements between the interested parties. Given the above it is only natural that rules

[63] See G. Ravasio, *Report of the Panel Discussion Dealing with Economic and Monetary Union*, *supra*, n. 6, at p. 85.

[64] The Community Charter of the Fundamental Rights of Workers. COM 89/658.

and practices in this area vary enormously from one Member State to another. "Subsidiarity from above," which assumes centralist tendencies, should not be allowed to undermine the progress achieved in the social field in each Member State. The Community authorities therefore have only a limited scope of intervention in this area.

The Commission has limited its proposals—some of which are fiercely opposed by a number of national governments—on matters which have a direct or indirect effect on the smooth functioning of the single European Market.[65] Subsidiarity, if interpreted properly, can help working people in the Community "... [to] shape, at different, easily comprehensible levels ... their social and political future both democratically and in solidarity with each other."[66]

After much discussion, subsidiarity was formally introduced as a general principle of Community constitutional law by Articles A(2) and B of the Treaty on European Union. Article 3b gives a definition of subsidiarity for the purposes of the European Community Treaty.

Article A paragraph 2 of the European Union Treaty provides: "This Treaty marks a new stage in the process of creating an ever closer union among the peoples of Europe, where decisions are taken as closely as possible to the citizens." This provision constitutes a clear reference to the jurisdiction of the regions within the framework of the European Union. Article B of the same Treaty provides:

> "The objectives of the Union shall be achieved as provided in this Treaty and in accordance with the conditions and the timetable set out therein while respecting the principle of subsidiarity as defined in Article 3b of the Treaty establishing the European Community."

The inclusion of the principle of subsidiarity in this provision shows that the framers of the European Union Treaty considered it to be an absolutely central concept to the construction of the Union and a guideline for future action.

According to Article 3b of the EEC Treaty:

> "The Community shall act within the limits of the powers conferred upon it by this Treaty and of the objectives assigned to it therein.
> In the areas which do not fall within its exclusive competence, the Community shall take action, in accordance with the principle of subsidiarity, only if and in so far as the objectives of the proposed action cannot

---

[65] The Commission has submitted to the Council proposals for directives on the following:
—adaptation of working time;
—information and consultation of workers employed in undertakings established in more than one Member State;
—employment relationships other than full-time and unlimited duration;
—a form of proof of an employment relationship.

[66] H. Hill, *The Social Dimension and Subsidiarity*, *supra*, n. 6, at p. 143.

be sufficiently achieved by the Member States and can therefore, by reason of the scale or effects of the proposed action, be better achieved by the Community.
Any action by the Community shall not go beyond what is necessary to achieve the objectives of this Treaty."

Article 3b(1) EEC establishes the principle that the Communities will have only the powers assigned to them exclusively or previously exercised by them. By the operation of this provision, all the powers of the Communities are derived from the Treaty, and they are assigned powers ("*competences d'attribution*") while the Member States hold all residual powers. The drafters of this provision obviously took account of the case law of the Court of Justice[67] and recognised, by virtue of the rule of effectiveness (*effet utile*), the existence of implied powers[68] vested in the Communities in order to achieve their objectives.

This provision should be read together with Article 235 EEC.[69] This provision gives the Community the power to act, in the absence of specific enabling provision, in all cases where action is required at the Community level in order to complete the Common Market. Article 235 EEC was not meant to be a means of expanding Community powers by "the back door," but rather an expression of subsidiary competences in the sense of supporting and complementary functions.[70] The express recognition of the doctrine of "implied powers" in the revised Treaty, however, has the advantage that it introduces a certain element of flexibility in the definition of the powers of the Communities thus allowing for their broad interpretation.

Article 3b(2) provides that Community action in an area of *concurrent competence* ("In the areas which do not fall within its exclusive jurisdiction, . . . ") is subject to a substantive condition, that is, observance of the principle of subsidiarity. This provision does not refer to legislation but to action by the

[67] See for example, Case 22/70 *Commission* v. *Council* (*ERTA*) [1971] E.C.R. 263. In Joined Cases 281, 283–5, 287/85 *Germany* v. *Commission* [1987] E.C.R. 3203, the Court held that whenever a provision of the EEC Treaty confers a specific task on the Commission, that provision must also be regarded as impliedly conferring on the Commission " . . . *the powers which are indispensable in order to carry out that task*."

[68] The theory of implied powers has originally been developed in the constitutional law of the United States (see *McCulloch* v. *Maryland* 17 U.S. (4 Wheat.) 316 (1819). The current formulation of this doctrine is: "The exercise by Congress of power ancillary to an enumerated source of national authority is constitutionally valid, so long as the ancillary power does not conflict with external limitations such as those of the Bill of Rights and of federalism." (See L. Tribe, *American Constitutional Law*. (1988). Mineola, NY, p. 301.) Thus the existence an expressly delegated end of power implies the existence of any power reasonably necessary to attain it.

[69] Art. 235 EEC provides:
"If action by the Community should prove necessary to attain, in the course of the operation of the common market, one of the objectives of the Community and this Treaty has not provided the necessary powers, the Council shall, acting unanimously on a proposal from the Commission and after consulting the European Parliament, take the appropriate measures."

[70] Gretschmann, *supra* n. 6, p. 54

Community which makes it possible to argue that administrative action is covered as well.

Article 3b(2) EEC makes clear that the tests to be applied are:

(a) the more effective attainment test combined with an absolute necessity test: Community institutions should take action "only if and in so far as the objectives of the proposed action cannot be *sufficiently* achieved by the Member States." The absolutely necessary test apparently lays down the requirement that the Community shall carry out new tasks only if their performance at the European level is absolutely necessary in the interest of the citizens and if their full effect can be attained only at Community level.[71] It is obvious that this test is very restrictive and if strictly applied it could seriously hamper further growth towards the ultimate goal of European integration.

(b) a combination of the better attainment and cross boundary dimension test: " . . . the objective of the proposed action . . . can therefore, by reason of the scale or effects of the proposed action, be better achieved by the Community." This test denotes a centralising conception of subsidiarity.

Given the definition adopted by the framers of Article 3(b)(2) EEC, it is clear that preference was given to the concept of "subsidiarity from above" which suggests a centralising tendency. This means that the Communities, in the field of concurrent competences, will be required to perform in so far as necessary only those tasks which can be carried out more effectively at the Community level than the national level, because of their "scale or effects" or for reasons of more effective implementation. The word "scale" could provide the Court with an extra handle should it choose to intervene in this area. The fact that the authors of Article 3(b)(2) EEC plunged into four different tests for the application of the principle can only weaken it and lead to confusion.

Since subsidiarity is applicable only in the fields where the Community does not enjoy exclusive competences, this means that the "*acquis communautaire*" will remain unaffected by the application of this principle. Theoretically, at least, Member States will retain all the powers which they are able to exercise more efficiently themselves and must transfer to the Community those powers which they are unable to use effectively. The Community should therefore intervene, in the sphere of concurrent powers, only in a subsidiary capacity and " . . . in accordance with a principle of exact appropriateness whereby each level is granted powers only because these cannot, given their nature and scope, be exercised efficiently and effectively at any other level."[72]

Article 3(b)(3) EEC does no more than restate the well established principle of proportionality in the context of institutional law. Proportionality and subsidiarity are closely related concepts but not identical. First of all subsi-

[71] See the 1987 Munich declaration of the Minister-Presidents of the German Lander.

[72] Supra n. 49.

diarity constitutes a limitation of Community powers towards Member States whilst proportionality is applicable to the relationship between the Community and its citizens. Furthermore, subsidiarity goes a step further than proportionality. Proportionality is concerned with the question whether Community action is necessary at all.[73] If Community action is unnecessary then there is a breach of the principle of proportionality. On the other hand, subsidiarity comes into place when the decision has been made that a particular measure is necessary. Subsidiarity is concerned with the question who is responsible for introducing the measure in question. Thus subsidiarity refines the principle of proportionality and takes it one step further.

Is subsidiarity justiciable? The role of the Court of Justice

Given the close affinity between proportionality, which is a judge-made principle, and subsidiarity it could be plausibly argued that subsidiarity may be justiciable. Also, the fact that subsidiarity has been written into Part I of the EEC Treaty, alongside with other basic principles to be applied in the interpretation of the Treaty such as the duty of co-operation in good faith (Article 5 EEC) and non-discrimination (Article 6 EEC),[74] is a strong indication that the drafters of the Treaty have invited the Court of Justice to adopt subsidiarity as another basic principle of judicial review.

Severe doubts have been raised, however, as to whether the Court of Justice is fitted for the task to decide whether the principle of subsidiarity has been breached in a particular case or not. The objections to the justiciability of subsidiarity can be summarised as follows:

(a) It will give power to the Court to delineate the powers of the centre and the periphery. This is a classic political decision inappropriate for a court of law.

(b) Legal certainty of Community and national legislation will be eroded since both will be open to challenges on the basis that the principle of subsidiarity has been breached. This is due to the evolutionary character of the principle. What can be lawfully decided at national level today might need to be decided at the Community level tomorrow.

(c) The Court might have to intervene in disputes of political character between Member States; and,

(d) If a strict interpretation of the concept of subsidiarity is adopted this might lead to an excessive degree of involvement by the Court in the day to day running of the Community. If, on the other hand, a more liberal approach is adopted, for instance a presumption in favour of validity of Community action, the principle will be weakened to a great extent.

---

[73] In Case 15/83 *Denkavit* [1984] E.C.R. 2171 at 2175 the Court gave the following definition to the principle of proportionality: "By virtue of the principle of proportionality, according to well established case law of the Court, measures adopted by Community institutions must not exceed what is appropriate and necessary to attain the objective pursued."

[74] The equivalent of Art. 7 EEC.

These arguments call for some further comments. Questions such as to whether Community action is more effective than is required or whether a task can better be attained at the Community rather than at the national level will inevitably allow the Court to indulge in political considerations. This might release the judges from their proper reserve in interfering with decisions on the grounds of policy, or assessment of facts or merits. This will inevitably destroy the credibility of the Court of Justice which, given its jurisprudence,[75] is arguably the Community's most effective institution.

But even if it is accepted that subsidiarity should be justiciable this does not solve the problem of political debate and negotiation. The Treaties and the powers of the Communities have to be adapted to changing political, economic and social circumstances. The history of the Communities shows that the attribution of competences and the interpretation of the Treaties has varied. The Treaties have an evolutionary character; they adapt to changing circumstances. This holds true especially in the grey areas where Community and national powers overlap. Subsidiarity may help to set the boundaries in these grey areas but will not take the political debate away from this problem. For this reason justiciability will not provide a watertight answer in those grey areas between what Brussels is entitled to do and what is the province of the national administrations.

Another problem as far as the justiciability of subsidiarity is concerned is the subjective character of the principle in question. This means that the application of subsidiarity is a policy decision which should be left to political bodies democratically answerable for their decisions. Therefore, unless subsidiarity can be formulated in an objective way judicial review will be impossible. But even in this case, judicial review should be of a limited extent and only manifest or grave disregard of the principle would nullify the challenged measures. Thus the Court will have to leave a wide margin of discretion to the decision making institutions. Such views have been adopted by the House of Lords Select Committee on the European Communities in their Report on "Economic and Monetary Union and Political Union":

> "One new role which has been proposed for the Court is that of interpreting the principle of subsidiarity. The Committee do not believe that subsidiarity can be used as a precise measure against which to judge legislation. The test of subsidiarity can never be wholly objective or consistent over time—different people regard collective action as more effective than individual action in different circumstances. Properly used, subsidiarity should determine not only whether Community legislation is necessary or appropriate at all, but also the extent to which it should regulate and harmonise national divergences, and how it should

[75] See, for example, Case 26/62 *Van Gend en Loos* [1963] E.C.R. 1 (direct effect); 6/64 *Costa* v. *ENEL* [1964] E.C.R. 565 (supremacy of Community law over national law) and more recently

be enforced. *But to leave legislation open to annulment or revision by the European Court on such subjective grounds would lead to immense confusion and uncertainty in Community law.*[76]

. . . the principle [should] be kept clearly in the minds of those who formulate Community legislation. But this should not be done so as to open the way to pointless litigation after the Council or the Commission have acted."[77]

The experience of the Bundesverfassungsgericht (BVerfGE) in reviewing the compatibility of the federal legislation with Article 72(2)GG is instructive in this respect. According to this constitutional provision, federal legislation must be necessary on three grounds, two of which are roughly equivalent to the more effective attainment test and the cross-boundary effect test, while the third is similar to the cross boundary dimension test. The BVerfGE does not deal with the question of necessity as this is considered to fall within the ambit of legislative discretion. It only examines:

(i) whether the legislature has interpreted these grounds properly;
(ii) whether it has exceeded its powers; and,
(iii) whether there had been a misuse of powers.[78]

The principle of subsidiarity as formulated in Article 3b(2) EEC concentrates on the question of distribution of powers between the Community and the Member States. Experience has, however, shown that this view is too simplistic. Subsidiarity should also determine instruments through which Community powers will be exercised. As it has been suggested:

"In essence subsidiarity is a socio-political term, not a legal or constitutional principle. As the Christian Social literature and discourse make clear, subsidiarity is not a self-standing concept, but a guideline to be applied *in combination* with other relevant principles of social action, such as stewardship or justice."[79]

If this position is to be adopted, then the proper role of subsidiarity, in the Community legal order, should be that of a guiding principle for the political institutions of the Community but not a general principle of law amenable to judicial review by the Court.

Nevertheless one could foresee situations where subsidiarity may be forced into the Court's conscience. One possible scenario is where a national authority trying to implement a Community measure is faced with a challenge by an individual before a national court on the ground that the Com-

Joined Cases C–6/90 and 9/90 *Francovich and Others* v. *Italian Republic* Judgment of November 19, 1991 (not yet reported) (state liability to individual for breach of Community law).

[76] Author's emphasis.

[77] *Supra*, n. 2 at p. 55.

[78] See Kapteyn, *supra*, n. 4, at pp. 23–24. Also Constantinesco, *supra*, n. 47, at p. 12.

[79] See Wilke and Wallace, *supra*, n. 1, at p. 4.

munity measure is in breach of the principle of subsidiarity. In this case the national court seized of the case, if it entertains any doubts as to the validity of the Community measure in question, will have no choice but to refer to the Court of Justice under Article 177(1)(b) EEC.[80] In these circumstances, of course, the Court will be under the obligation to come to grips with the question of subsidiarity.

The Court would have two alternatives to deal with such a reference. It could either simply uphold the validity of the challenged act without engaging into any evaluation, which would certainly be an unsatisfactory solution. It could also declare the reference inadmissible on the ground that it may not review the merits of the Community measure in question—and that technically in a non-contentious proceeding. Such an alternative would be excessively formalistic. Such an answer could hardly satisfy and help the national court which may be even encouraged undertake such a review itself.

A sensible course of action for the Court will be to restrict itself to a "marginal review"[81] of subsidiarity. This is the attitude which has been adopted by the Court in examining whether the Council and/or the Commission have kept within the limits of their discretion. In this case the Court examines only whether " . . . the evaluation of the competent authority contains a patent error or constitutes a misuse of powers."[82] Support for this argument may be drawn from the Court's case-law on the Community institutions' liability for damages in respect of normative acts. Here the Community will incur liability only when " . . . a sufficiently serious breach of a superior rule of law for the protection of the individual has occurred."[83]

The Court certainly may not be expected to push the extent of its judicial review, as far as subsidiarity is concerned, any further than is absolutely necessary for ensuring and respecting the Rule of Law.[84] It is idle to point out in this connection that an appropriate reasoning of a judgment supporting the Court's findings in respect of the observance of the principle of subsidiarity may be a proper guarantee for a judicial review, exercised properly and within reasonable limits.

[80] See Case 314/85 *Foto-Frost* [1987] E.C.R. 4232 where the Court said that while national courts may declare a Community act valid, they have no power to declare it invalid.

[81] Schermers uses the term "marginal review" in the cases where the Court's review is strictly confined to questions whether the administration remained within the proper bounds and did not use its authority in a manifestly incorrect manner. See H. Schermers, and D. Waelbroeck, *Judicial Protection in the European Communities*. (1992) Deventer, at paras. 313, 437, 601–603.

[82] Case 78/74 *Deuka* [1975] E.C.R. 432.

[83] This doctrine is known as the "Schoppenstedt formula"; see Case 5/71 *Zuckerfabrik Schoppenstedt* v. *Council* [1975] E.C.R. 975.

[84] In Case 294/83 *Parti Ecologiste "Les Verts"* v. *European Parliament* [1986] E.C.R. 1339, the Court emphasised that "the European Economic Community is a Community based on the rule of law, in as much as neither its Member States nor its institutions can avoid a review of the question whether the measures adopted by them are in conformity with the basic constitutional charter, the Treaty."

Conclusion

To compare the principle of subsidiarity, from the legal point of view in different legal systems presents almost insurmountable difficulties. The concept of subsidiarity is vague and heavily discussed in most European legal systems.[85] It is essentially a socio-political rather than a legal or constitutional principle. Obviously it is difficult to describe in abstract terms the precise meaning and scope of the principle in question.[86] It is a notion which partly rests on federalist divisions and powers of a kind which are reflected in the American Constitution and the German Grundgesetz. However, it is also something that comes from thinking about the relationship between the individual and the State and how to achieve a balance of responsibilities in society.[87] Here, it has been attempted to portray some general principles which form the substance of the basic idea of subsidiarity.

Comparative study shows that the concept of subsidiarity seems to be most elaborate in Germany. This can be easily explained by the fact that it was the Grundgesetz that first indirectly incorporated the principle of subsidiarity and elevated it to the status of a constitutional principle. Originally designed as a legal limit on the federal powers in the field of concurrent competences, it has given rise to the basic constitutional principle of co-operative federalism. Different rules derived from subsidiarity lead back to certain patterns of conflicts of interest between different levels of government which must be solved in the modern federal systems. This paper has shown first, that subsidiarity can only be properly understood within the framework of federalism; secondly, that it involves not only the relationship between different layers of government but also the relationship between the State, the society and the individual; thirdly, that it can be considered as a response to the historical experience that central authorities, national and supranational, function with the tendency to impair the freedom of lower levels of government; and, finally that it is not amenable to judicial review

[85] According to Gretschmann, *supra*, n. 6, at p. 49, the "many faces of subsidiarity" are "due to the complex architecture of the phenomenon subsidiarity is trying to capture." He concludes that:

> " . . . the lack of clear definition is not simply a disadvantage; on the contrary, in political terms, unspecified and even murky formulas often carry considerable political advantage. Consensus on a programme of institutional reform, painted with broad brushstrokes, can be reached more easily if the key concept is not too cutting and precise. To the extent that the concept of subsidiarity helps overcome political resistance and prejudice, due to its ambiguous nature and its open interpretability, it is a useful tool for paving the way to European integration by smoothing over and concealing political differences."

[86] According to Gretschmann, (*supra*, n. 6, p. 45):

> "By origin, and in its most abstract conception, subsidiarity is a normative recommendation, a rule for setting up institutional arrangements in such a way that decisions, affecting peoples' lives directly, should be taken as far down the chain of social organization as possible."

[87] House of Lords Select Committee on the European Communities. *Economic and Monetary Union and Political Union*. (1990). Vol. II, Evidence. London, p. 3 (*per* Dr. H. Wallace).

partly due to its evolutionary character and also because this would unduly permit the judge to intervene in policy considerations. Like all legal principles subsidiarity cannot be mechanically applied. However, its application would affirm an important principle by which all Community action should expect to be measured: that the Community should take action in a particular area only to the extent to which given objectives can be attained more effectively at the Community level than at the level of the individual Member States.

As the Communities assume new powers, democracy should be based on a clear demarcation between national and supranational powers; the acceptance of the legitimate group interests; effective legal guarantees for individuals and a system of checks and balances to control the action of the institutions. Further centralisation, by preferring a system that is supposed to produce a general will, which as a result will seek to eliminate sectional pressures and impose uniform rights and duties should be avoided. Historical experience has shown that the legacy of such centralisation is interference of the centralised institutions in almost every aspect of everyday life and the creation of new central institutions. Bureaucrats therefore multiply each with his little parcel of power. As a result the ordinary citizen becomes alienated.

Centralism is too rationalist; the idea that there is only one best possible way of solving any particular problem, and that one solution should be universally applicable results in inflexibility; ministers and departments become so rigid and isolated from each other, that the right hand does not know what the left hand is doing; that leads to a stalemate in the best of cases or to deep crises in the worst.[88] Subsidiarity may be an effective way of guarding against over-extension and overload on the Community system.[89]

[88] See the very vivid description by Zeldin of the French malaise of centralism in T. Zeldin, *The French*. (1988) London, pp. 169 *et seq*.

[89] *Supra*, n. 87.

Part III
Institutions and Ideologies

[10]

TRANSFORMATION OF A POLITICAL ROLE: RECONSIDERING THE CASE OF THE COMMISSION OF THE EUROPEAN COMMUNITIES

By Karlheinz Neunreither

I. METHODOLOGICAL DIFFICULTIES OF ROLE DEFINITION

When President Pompidou, at his press conference of January 21, 1971, outlined certain prospects for the development of the European Communities, he drew in a few sentences, from a trend that has been evident now for some years, the conclusion that was consistent with his policy. He sketched out a new role for the Council of Ministers, that of a future European government, reducing the Commission's role to that of a technical auxiliary. The rather startled reaction in the other capitals[1] suggests that in spite of all the political theories of integration, the main variables of Community development had obviously not been discussed in sufficient detail to provide at least a modicum of scientifically based background information in good time to those actively engaged in politics.

In this connection the role of the Commission of the European Communities affords an apt illustration. It can be said that political theory, almost without exception, has failed to approach the subject of the 'Commission' with impartiality; rather has it taken over, with certain modifications, the ideas as to a role originally thought out for the High Authority of the ECSC,[2] without ever critically examining in any detail the weight these early concepts could bear. Moreover, by the time it was realized that the High Authority perhaps fell far short of the role that had been assigned to it, the political theorists had long since turned their attention to the newly set up Brussels Communities.

Now praiseworthy studies such as those by Haas and Lindberg suffer from the fact that—avowedly or not—they work within a system-related concept and therefore derive their definition of the roles of indi-

[1] None of the other five Community Governments has yet (i.e. end-1971) responded officially to the French overture. In some capitals such as Bonn, the Government is quoted unofficially as believing that it would be tactically preferable to delay consideration of the French proposals until the French Government has clarified its position more fully. However, it is difficult to escape the impression that this attitude which would be perfectly credible from the tactical angle in reality conceals strategic shortcomings, if indeed a strategy exists.

[2] This applies in particular to Ernst B. Haas, *The Uniting of Europe* (London, 1958).

vidual institutions from this superordinate concept. In other words every institution must be assigned a more or less exactly defined place, as otherwise coherent assertions on the Community as a whole present the utmost difficulty. This does not, of course, rule out a dynamic conception of the role of a particular institution or other elements of the Community system, such dynamism itself, however, is again part of the development of the entire system.

To get behind the resulting difficulties, it would certainly be worth while demonstrating in a carefully thought-out monograph, that there has never been a generally accepted definition of the roles of the Community institutions, and that even at the most reliable point of departure—the relevant provisions of the Community Treaties—obscurities and possible misinterpretations creep in. To take but one example, the introductory sentence of Article 155 of the EEC Treaty, stating that the Commission is granted certain powers 'with a view to ensuring the functioning and development of the Common Market', points, under verbal exegesis and taking current legal terminology in the individual countries, to a host of possible interpretations. Since, moreover, the intentions of the parties to the Treaty are largely unknown—neither official explanatory texts nor even protocols exist—we are thrown back on the manner in which the main participants of a system interpret roles. But here we must be on our guard; clearly it appears undesirable to allow them themselves to define even rather basic elements, e.g. who belongs to the system, lest the answers would be all too divergent. This puts the researcher in the position of a *deus ex cathedra*, himself determining the parameter of his system and deciding which of the role definitions offered to him he will adopt for a particular institution and which he will discard as irrelevant.

In view of this uncertainty at the very point of departure, it seems strange that almost the entire literature on the Communities comes to somewhat apodictical assertions and neglects to develop sets of systematized variables not only for the distant future but also for each period under investigation. A scientific discussion kept 'open' to this extent would certainly have spared us a number of surprises in recent years; it would also perhaps have permitted of a broader theoretical basis for thinking on the subject.

In what follows an attempt is made to arrive, with the aid of a greatly reduced and formally modest model, at a number of critical assertions regarding the transformation of the role of the European Commission. The methodological interest of such a procedure could lie in its isolating a participant in the system and leaving to that participant the choice between a number of hypothetical basic options. For the sake of simplicity only the choice of role as between 'European government' and

'European secretariat' is dealt with. We are concerned not so much with differentiated propositions as with the verification of the working hypothesis, with the extent to which such a procedure can help in avoiding some of the difficulties of a 'closed' systematic analysis.

2. TWO HYPOTHETICAL ALTERNATIVE ROLE DEFINITIONS

The choice of two hypothetical role definitions—'European government' and 'European secretariat'—is justified because although the original constitutional mandate as laid down in the provisions of the Brussels Treaties is far from clearly defined—particularly as regards the Commission—it does permit (and this was not the case with the High Authority of the ECSC) of two different interpretations. The first is that, in contrast with the High Authority, the Commission's role should be downgraded for the following reasons:

1. The desire of the parties to the Treaty not to repeat the experiment of the Coal and Steel Community—that is, to make provision in future treaties for Member States to play a more direct part than hitherto in the decision-making process.
2. The 'outline' character of the Community inevitably bringing the Council of Ministers to the forefront as the body that decides on rule-making measures.

A second interpretation would tend to discard the original downgrading of the role of the Commission as compared with that of the High Authority as formalistic and irrelevant, and to place the political emphasis, as far as the Commission is concerned, more squarely on the concept of the development of the Treaty alluded to in Article 155 thereof. In this model a sort of overall responsibility falls on the Commission for the future development and completion of the Community; this is also echoed in unofficial formulas, such as 'guardian of the Treaty' and so on, later used by the Commission itself. Incidentally, adoption of this second interpretation by the EEC Commission inevitably did more than increase the weight it carried with the Council of Ministers; it also downgraded the functions of the other two executives—the Euratom Commission and the High Authority—because to some extent the EEC Commission also took over from them responsibilities which, though informal, are of a politically effective kind. A tendency to regard the EEC Commission as, so to speak, the forerunner of a future European government is already implicit in this interpretation.[3]

[3] To avoid possible misunderstanding it might be useful to emphasize that the denomination of the two following alternative role models should not be interpreted as a recommendation to apply the rather obsolete conception that in our political systems governmental and administrative functions could clearly be separated. The contrary is obvious. The notions of 'government' and of

A. *Hypothetical Role model: The Commission as 'European Government'*

1. The Commission must try to become as independent as it can of its main potential opponents, the Member States.
2. To this end it must become the focal point of a common centripetal grouping of forces. The remaining institutional elements of such a grouping—the European Parliament, for instance—must be brought into a dependent supporting relation to it.
3. Such a grouping must extend beyond the institutional sphere and embrace a network of European associations and parties and a European élite. For this purpose, and as a preliminary, support must also be given to close cooperation between associations, parties and trade unions as well as to European organizations, scientific congresses, fact finding missions and publications that depend on the Commission for financing.
4. The Commission must prevent Member States from forming a united front against it; it must always appear in the field of forces as the indispensable mediator between national interests.
5. The Commission and its officials must foster an *esprit de corps* based on loyalty to the Commission. Prerequisites for this are powers of internal organization and scope for recruiting staff in independence from the other participants in the system. Once a strong enough position has been built up, an attempt can be made to transfer elements of this loyalty to the national sphere, and to stir up conflicts of loyalty at least among those sections of the European élite which, like the national bureaucracies, are tied to powerful opponents.[4]
6. Building on these foundations, and by speeding up implementation of the Treaty, the Commission must keep the Council of Ministers under constant pressure and, on the basis of the 'logic of the Treaty', bring it round to taking a series of decisions previously determined by the Commission.
7. Within the limits of the powers conferred by the Treaty, proposals for weighty structural decisions must be deferred until a point of irreversibility appears to have been reached at which the danger of grave repercussions in the event of a failure to comply becomes the overriding consideration for a stubborn partner.
8. Basic political decisions lying outside the actual province of the Treaty, such as the common organization of external and defence policy or the accession of new members, should not be dealt with by the Commission—that is, brought into play politically on its own

'secretariat' as used here should therefore only be defined by the criteria given below. If one prefers, one can just call them model A and model B.

[4] See notes by David Coombes, *Politics and Bureaucracy in The European Community* (London, 1970) pp. 94 et seq.; he develops a critical analysis of the 'engrenage' concept.

initiative—until it is quite certain that in these cases too, Community bodies can force Member States into action.

B. *Hypothetical Role Model: The Commission as 'European Secretariat'*

1. The Commission recognizes the fact that the constitutional authority —the Member States—has transferred the essential powers of decision to the Council of Ministers, a body under its control, and that it itself has therefore been assigned a secondary role which appears to rule out any prospect of independence or insubordination.
2. The Commission may not therefore even attempt to become a potential focal point of a grouping either directed against or largely independent of the Member States.
3. Any attempt by the Commission to build up for itself an extra-institutional reference system of political forces would merely be a challenge to the Member States, on whose cooperation and goodwill it has to rely.
4. The Commission cannot fight against fronts formed by the Member States. All it can do, through a wise and farsighted policy, is to prevent their formation. Should this not prove possible, it would have to keep out of the firing-line of serious clashes of interests.
5. *Esprit de corps* is less important than close links with the national sphere. If necessary, the Commission's entire staff should be recruited by periodic secondment from the national authorities, so as to encourage interpenetration and avoid clashes.
6. The Commission should make use of its right of initiative only on the basis of definite obligations, in point of substance or time, imposed by the Treaty. On no account should this lead to its evolving and applying a sort of overall strategy in its relations with the Council of Ministers.
7. The Commission cannot hope, with the help of one or more Member States, to induce other partners to make serious structural concessions. At all events it cannot behave as an active driving force in such circumstances.
8. Decisions and initiatives going beyond the terms of reference laid down for the Commission in the Treaty are strictly taboo. The Commission must respect the corresponding decisions of the Council of Ministers or governments.

The two sets of criteria outlined above already contain the main elements for the construction of a rudimentary hypothetical model of behaviour. It must be repeated that they have not been derived from the concept of a system; nor are we seeking criteria for an 'ideal

Commission' as do authors like Lindberg and Scheingold.[5] Again, we are not looking for an ideal type (Max Weber) or a real type (Walter Eucken) of Commission. The sets of criteria are deliberately chosen as hypothetical points of departure with a view to arriving in the course of the investigation at a pattern of behaviour as differentiated as possible. It has already been pointed out that in the present version the schema has been greatly simplified; in a more searching investigation it would have to be applied in a far more finely classified form.[6]

3. 1958–65: A 'FEDERALIST' COMMISSION?

Any investigation of the Commission in terms of the variables of this or that possible role schema is best begun with the exercise of initiative. This sphere is the easiest to isolate and to subdivide into areas of action—a circumstance of major importance for ascertaining whether one can speak at all of a continuous role of the institution in every sphere.

The sphere of action can be broadly classified as follows:

1. Removal of internal obstacles to trade through the gradual elimination of internal customs duties and quantitative restrictions.
2. Adoption of a Common External Tariff and its defence on the appropriate international bodies.
3. Rounding off the abolition of internal customs duties by removing distortions in competition of whatever kind, harmonizing taxes and social security benefits, and ensuring freedom of movement of labour and capital.
4. Introduction of a common or coordinated economic policy including common agricultural, transport and commercial policies.
5. Enlargement of the Community through accession and associations.
6. Questions relating to a political union; continued institutional development of the Community itself.

If the initiative exercised by the Commission is judged in the light of the foregoing criteria, the following picture broadly emerges for the first eight years (1958–65), that is, for the first two phases of the transitional stage of the Common Market.[7]

[5] See Leon N. Lindberg and Stuart A. Scheingold, *Europe's Would-Be Polity* (Englewood Cliffs, 1970), pp. 93 et seq.

[6] A sophisticated classification of criteria is very difficult if we adopt—as many authors do—a value scale on the 'school mark' principle. This procedure is liable to degenerate into an obscure mixture of qualitative and quantitative methods which only simulate a scientific basis.

[7] The following is a summary of a study made by the author during the relevant period. In the abbreviated form in which it appears here it does not, of course, introduce anything new in terms of content; it is, however, justified by the conclusion it leads to, namely that it is impossible to define a unified concept as to the role of the European Commission.

1. As regards the establishment of the customs union the Commission did not wait for the expiry of the series of stages laid down in the Treaty for the elimination of internal customs duties, but as early as in February 1960 submitted a recommendation for speeding up the process. The Commission had to steer a bold course between the interests of the former high-duty countries, which at first feared these duties would be reduced too fast, and those of the former low-duty countries which were opposed to a rapid adjustment of their external tariffs to the level of the Common External Tariff. Since institutional questions too were bound up with the pace of the progressive reduction of duties, this quickened tempo resulted in a considerable strengthening of the Community bodies. The pressure on Member States to react to the Commission's proposals was intensified. The success of its first initiative encouraged the Commission in 1964 to put forward a second proposal for bringing forward the time-limit for the completion of the customs union. The Member States, however, shrank from this development and conceded to the Commission a transitional period cut by only eighteen months.
2. The Commission encountered the Common External Tariff with the Treaty; customs heads that had not been included were negotiated by the governments virtually among themselves. The main scope for political initiative was thus offered by the international negotiations on tariff questions in GATT, above all in the Dillon Round and the Kennedy Round that followed it. On the whole, the EEC Commission was unable in these negotiations to exercise anything approaching the same initiative as it had done over the internal aspect of the customs union. First, a special committee consisting of government representatives (under Article 111 of the EEC Treaty) stood in its way, and the supervisory activities of that committee soon set going a ponderous check-back mechanism which imposed a severe limitation on the Commission's scope for conducting the negotiations. The success of the two rounds of negotiations certainly enhanced the Commission's international reputation; at the same time it won greater respect from the Council of Ministers, though more as an aid in achieving the Council's aims than in its capacity of a potential opponent.
3. In the case of the internal liberalization measures that accompanied the dismantlement of tariff barriers, on the other hand, the Commission returned to a burst of activity in which it could give free play to its initiative. Fairly soon, however, it became entangled in a veritable thicket of clashing interests, for which justification was sought either on bureaucratic grounds, as in the case of frontier checks on goods, or on economic grounds, as in the case of State trading monopo-

lies and the freeing of capital movements. The Commission tried in these cases to retain a flexible approach and avoid a head-on collision with entrenched coalitions of interests in the Member States. Obviously it relied too heavily on the effect of the mounting pressure of the rapidly growing volume of trade.

4. Competition policy stands on the threshold between regulations with a purely liberalizing purpose and those of a more actively radical kind. Its more defensive aspect, namely, that concerned with restrictive trade practices, was first pushed ahead with powerful support from the Commission.[8] Its more active aspect, that concerned with facilitating mergers between undertakings, was first seen to present problems in October 1966 when it was made a political issue—with an anti-American bias—especially by the French government. The remaining areas of a common policy, with the exception of the agricultural policy, never got beyond feeble attempts at coordination during the period in question. Energy and transport policy are perfect illustrations of how the Commission's status never rose above that of a purveyor of proposals that were either rejected or not even considered. Agricultural policy, therefore, remains the outstanding exception. In this equally controversial sector one of the parties concerned, France, made the Community's survival conditional on the achievement of satisfactory results, although it was unable to put forward proposals on how things should be organized. This special situation, coupled with the fact that the department in question was headed by one of the most determined and persuasive experts of the Commission, who had already worked in the preceding years for the Europeanization of the elite both in the political sphere and in the associations, won for the Commission considerable freedom of action. On the other hand, medium-term economic policy, cyclical and commercial policy, at all events up to 1965, reflect the ever-widening gap between the Commission's constructive efforts and the reluctant attitude of the Member States.

5. Like commercial policy, accession and association are cases where the fact that general external policy covers a closely related field restricted the Commission's ability to exercise its initiative. Admittedly it did manage, by dint of repeated statements and published documents, to work out a policy line of its own in this sphere and to drive home the fact that it was, in a general way, in favour of new

[8] This of course overlooks the question of effectiveness of the policy on restrictive trade practices. The assumption is tenable that Regulation No. 17 issued by the Commission which led to a flood of restrictive trade practice notifications (about 37,000 in all) and was followed by years of indecision on the part of the Commission in reality obstructed an effective policy on restrictive trade practices. In the meantime, several group exceptions have been granted which allow them to concentrate on the hard core of distorted competition (number of cases pending on Jan. 1, 1971: 7,336).

entries and association, and in commercial policy terms, a champion of an 'outward-looking' Community. This did little, however, to influence the course of events, the less so the more the attitude of Member States was determined by strictly external policy factors. The most striking example of this was the breaking off of the first negotiations on British entry and the postponement and eventual rejection, of Israel's application for association—less spectacular, perhaps, but all the more worthy of investigation.

6. The EEC Commission's interpretation of its own role in the years 1958–65 is reflected most clearly in the structural development of the Community: the Commission as an institution believed that it had a position of primary responsibility not only in relation to the Treaty and other institutions but also to the Governments of the Member States; this responsibility was linked with the personal commitment of a majority of its members to a highly integrated Community which would eventually become a European federal State. The Commission chose primarily to back attempts to widen the area in which the Community enjoyed political freedom of action; this attitude is exemplified in its policy on the European Parliament which it hoped would be systematically upgraded and become a second part of an independent institutional tandem,[9] and also in secondary proposals such as the plan to set up a European University. This trend culminated in the Commission's proposals of March 1965 to endow the Community with its own resources which finally sparked off a serious crisis in the Community. These proposals were drawn up in such a way that the 'community' bodies, i.e. the Commission and Parliament, would have been strengthened considerably at the expense of the Council of Ministers. In submitting its proposals the Commission knew that it would incur opposition from the only Member State which was bound to reject such a change on grounds of political principle, i.e. France. Assuming that a 'point of no return' had been reached, primarily as a result of the common agricultural policy and miscalculating the freedom of action which it felt the French President still had, even though elections were in the offing, it engaged in a gambit for exceeding its role capacity. The French Government felt that the Commission had committed the sacrilege of using its right of initiative to modify the structure laid down in the Treaty. Negotiations during the subsequent crisis leading up to the famous Luxemburg agreement of January 1966, were therefore aimed more at limiting political action by the Commission than at preventing majority decisions in the Council. One might even specu-

[9] I have examined the Commission's role in relation to the European Parliament in a paper which has been published in the *Zeitschrift für Parlamentsfragen* in the autumn of 1971.

late that the limitation on majority decisions in the Council was intended simply as a safety valve to prevent France from ever being confronted again with a situation like that which arose in the spring of 1965; of course the enlargement of the areas in which majority decisions could be taken, planned for the third phase of the transitional period, would have increased the number of potential conflict situations. The decisive aspect of the Luxemburg decisions is not, however, the inclusion of this safety valve but the defeat of the Commission's limited bid to act as a European Government.

Even the briefest survey of the individual spheres in which the Commission works gives results which are so varied that it is difficult to arrive at a unified concept of the Commission's role. This is important because it departs from the conclusions reached in many publications on this subject. Though, admittedly, some authors have drawn attention to this situation it was mainly those who did not examine the community system as a whole but concerned themselves with specific aspects thereof.[10] The common method of postulating a general model for the institutions, i.e. putting forward distinct concepts as to the role of the individual institutions and then setting out supporting examples from one or two areas of activity, does not seem the most appropriate because it might easily lead to general conclusions on the Commission's behaviour from the partial areas examined in greater detail.

The difficult task of studying the Commission's individual spheres of activity in detail would therefore lead to rejection of the usual hard and fast concept of the Commission's role in favour of an extremely varied and flexible role concept. We must not, however, conclude from this that different role concepts exist side by side and that nothing more can be said. It is on the contrary important to point out that in the years 1958–65 which we have considered briefly here, the Commission's activity conformed in the main to the criteria defined initially for its 'Government' role. The principal politically relevant factor was that in some areas the Member States came to consider this partial function as the main role, i.e. in their own attitude to the Commission they tended to lend general credence to its claim to be a precursor of a European Government. This is particularly clear in instances where emotional factors come into play, e.g. in the matter of the passive right of the Commission to establish legations and the ceremonial ('red carpet') developed in this connection.[11]

[10] See David Coombes, op. cit., and Fritz Fischer, *Die institutionalisierte Vertretung der Verbände in der Europäischen Wirtschaftsgemeinshaft* (Hamburg, 1965), one of the many studies of the European Community which have been completely 'forgotten'.

[11] This problem loomed large in the government negotiations leading up to the Luxemburg decisions of January 1966. In this connection, see the decalogue originally submitted by the French delegation.

This interpretation of a partial role as the general role was particularly marked in the case of stronger opponents such as France and suggests that up to 1965 the Commission did in fact claim to be the 'policy formation centre' of the Community. The importance of this role only becomes clear when we consider the events of following years in which this claim was gradually watered down until it practically disappeared. If the Community is considered as a system of government, one important function of such a system, i.e. the preparation and implementation of policies, has not been performed since 1965 and no other institution has taken over the Commission's role in this sphere.

4. SINCE 1966 FUNCTIONAL BUREAUCRATIZATION AND BEYOND?

In analysing the role of the Commission since 1966 (the EEC Commission was replaced by the joint Commission in 1967), it is sufficient for our purposes to consider primarily those areas in which the 'Government' role was most clearly marked in previous years. Without embarking upon a detailed analysis it can be stated that performance of this role ceased to all intents and purposes after the crisis in 1965. Although it is certain that several factors played a part in this development, e.g. the partial paralysis of the Commission after its merger in 1967 because of the failure to decide on a rationalization of its administrative infrastructure, the after-effects of the shock of 1965 can still be seen as the decisive contributory factor. The Member States have learned their lesson from that year, as indeed has the Commission which, contrary to the general impression, had to bear the brunt of the attacks (see above). It is even possible to speak of a fundamental turning point in the development of the Commission; the decisions of January 1966 merely emphasized this change in direction.

The main contributory factors can be summarized as follows:

1. The Commission encountered increasing opposition to any efforts to use its right to legislate with the freedom of a European executive. The national Governments in practice claimed a right to determine the Community's progress themselves. The 'spill-over' became a carefully negotiated 'package deal'.[12]
2. The Commission ceased to make bold, comprehensive proposals and turned increasingly to studies, recommendations and above all memoranda when it wished to draw the Council's attention to a particular problem. Sometimes it only submitted proposals after

[12] The 'package deal' aims at achieving short-term equilibrium while 'spill-over' can be considered as a dynamic concept ruling out successive short-term states of equilibrium and must therefore be construed as a long-term concept, ensuring roughly equivalent benefits for all participants during the game.

Council working parties had already reached their own conclusions, e.g. in the case of the economic and monetary union. Research, energy, regional and industrial policy are further examples of a relatively informal approach by the Commission which can scarcely be said to have taken the initiative.

3. It is perhaps still more significant that the principle of unanimity in the Council, which is ultimately merely the decisional expression of negotiating positions on the lines of quasi-diplomatic standing conferences, rubbed off on the Commission. The scanty information emerging from the carefully guarded conference rooms of the Commission suggests that the wave of renationalization also affected the Commission itself. The harmful effects of this development on the Commission's claim to represent Community interests directly, especially in a confrontation with the individual interests of Member States, are evident.

In short, the Commission has abandoned its 'governing' role and tended to become little more than a high-level secretariat of the Council. This does not prevent the Commission from performing a salient function, recognized by the Member States, as a complementary body of the Council—as was recently the case with the negotiations on Britain's entry—or from blocking many initiatives originating in the Council which might lessen its independence still further.[13] On the other hand there are two factors: first the end of the Commission's claim to represent the system as a whole, i.e. the general interest, and secondly the renunciation of the associated right to take fundamental policy initiatives in major areas covered by the Treaty where there is a risk of entering into conflict with other participants in the system. In the current phase of transformation of its role, intermediate and mixed forms of Commission action prevail. It will for example be possible to argue at length which role is reflected in the Commission's proposals on industrial policy or on the reform of Euratom. Partly because of the French overture in January 1971, it seems likely that an institutional discussion will be opened which may eventually raise the veil of ambiguity which has shrouded the actual intermediate phase and lead instead to new hard and fast institutional patterns.

If we assume that up to about 1965 the Commission performed important 'governing' functions which it has since abandoned, we must then ask who will take over the role it has ceased to perform. It should be relatively safe to suppose that an economic and monetary union

[13] An interesting example of the Commission's residual capacity to block proposals is given by the attempt led by France and the Federal Republic to reduce the independence of the Commission set-up by arranging for national officials to be detached to the Commission on a rota basis. On this particular matter, the Commission has so far avoided even presenting a proposal, so that the relevant discussions in the Council are 'semi-illegal'.

within the Community and an active external commercial and development policy cannot be pursued as an accretion of individual decisions but only in the context of a genuine policy, i.e. a comprehensive and coherent concept which can be understood by the other participating parties, e.g. the parliaments, the public in the Community and non-member States. Since the European Parliament and the Economic and Social Committee as well as the European bureaucracy are clearly unable to take over this institutional role, we are bound to conclude that it is likely to be handed over to the Council of Ministers.

We can therefore assume that the French overture is not a seven day wonder but is intended as a design for a new, long-term institutional structure in the Community. Above all the Council would be empowered to draft policies which in turn would entail a considerable development of its infra-structure. The 'technical' bureaucracy of the Commission would therefore be counterbalanced by a new 'political' bureaucracy of the Council amounting in practice to a prolongation of the national bureaucratic decision-making centres. The proposed elevation of the Permanent Representatives to ministerial status is only an outward sign of this deeper transformation.

The other Community institutions, above all the Commission and European Parliament would then be forced further back from the direct centres of decision. They would have even less importance than hitherto as components of the effective Community apparatus; in the most unfavourable hypothesis they would be nothing more than a decorative appendage to which we might not even attribute Walter Bagehot's definition of a dignified part of the constitution.

The present trends and political action of at least some Member States are therefore moving towards a review of the whole institutional system, going far beyond the transformation of the Commission's role, but nevertheless following from the change in the Commission's functions in recent years. The risk for political science lies in the fact that with the inevitable time-lag in the preparation of studies, it is simply too late to design countermodels and intervene in the current discussions. Since the decision-making system of the Community cannot be considered in isolation but only in the context of national systems, it follows that the future of our national political systems is also at stake. In particular the further development of parliamentary democracy could be seriously influenced by a development along these lines.

5. LEARNING CAPACITY, INSTITUTIONAL AUTONOMY AND ROLE TRANSFORMATION

Consideration of the changing role of political institutions raises a number of difficult theoretical problems, two of which are shortly examined in our concluding remarks: the problem of the ability of the Commission to react to changes in the system and the problem of evaluating the system itself by criteria which are not derived directly from it.

With regard to the first point, some recent theories of international relations concentrate on the concept of ability to react to change as a central problem of system analysis. Too often however, study is confined to behaviouristic adaptation to an environment which cannot be influenced; the concept, therefore, becomes one-sided and is reminiscent more of the helplessness of the individual in an anonymous society of which he can no longer have any comprehensive grasp than of the active, purposeful structure of political bodies which are usually confronted by a given number of political forces whose full extent they think they can grasp and which they believe they can influence by political action. At least with a political system of the kind embodied in the European Community we are therefore faced, in the case of the individual institutions, with patterns of behaviour which—if we may venture a comparison with national economic structures—correspond to action centres in oligopolistic markets rather than in atomistic competition.[14] Passive adaptation is therefore merely one possible orientation, while the contrasting active attempt to shape the environment in a specific manner, clearly reflected for example in some of the initiatives taken by the Commission in 1958–65, points to a potential ability to insist on a particular line of action. The Commission's initiatives can be considered indicative of the active component of this ability to insist while passive, delaying components are also present. The lack of a detectable reaction to changes need not be synonymous with insufficient adaptability; it may on the contrary represent a positive act of will.

For the Commission of the European Communities, this means that the conceptual tension between learning capacity (understood as an ability to react) and the ability to insist must be considered in any attempt to define the change in its role. It would be difficult to catalogue the many different components of the Commission's activity and evaluate on the one hand the nature of its inability to react (which tends to hide behind a veil of 'political continuity') and on the other its positive ability to insist. Nevertheless, I would suggest to discuss whether it might be useful to analyse the Commission in the light of scales of activity patterns like the following:

1. Easily influenced: a change of behaviour on confrontation with an

[14] This leads on the problem (which we cannot go into here) of determining who, in a political system, defines the learning factors by whose acquisition learning performance is of course judged. It must be assumed that current studies involve some objectification which requires highly critical analysis.

actual or presumed conflicting form of behaviour (including anticipated reaction to the latter) can easily be triggered by an external stimulus.[15]

2. Adaptable: behaviour can be changed spontaneously to increase the prospect of attaining specific purposes.
3. Insufficiently adaptable: difficulties or major delays are encountered in implementing the process of adaptation although the need for it is recognized.
4. Marginal ability to insist: limited (in terms of material or time) ability to resist undesirable changes or to influence them in a particular manner.
5. Strong ability to insist: ability to oppose strong resistance to undesirable changes even on important structural matters and over a long period.
6. Absolute rigidity: inability to change an adopted attitude, generally hiding behind falsely objective arguments.

A second problem in analysing the roles of political institutions arises from the need to determine whether criteria which are not directly derived from the system should be used. Generally such criteria are not introduced and the individual parts of a system are studied primarily to determine whether they accord with the system concept, i.e. 'function' properly. Especially in studies which belong to system analysis in the narrower sense of the word there is sometimes—as mentioned earlier—not only a tendency to define roles very stringently in a manner which does not always correspond to reality, but also to elevate the system concept into an absolute value, which sometimes gives the impression that everything is good as long as it suits the system. Here again scientific theory should consider how it can make allowance for phenomena which disturb the system but are in themselves 'meaningful'. Is a properly functioning decision-making capacity in the Council of Ministers in itself so important that this capacity should not be blocked partially, e.g. to avoid unrealistically high agricultural prices?[16] The failure to consider problems such as this, which in the final analysis require reference to more comprehensive systems of other categories, can only be interpreted as a belated and scarcely recognizable offshoot of the once proud theory of the freedom from values (Wertfreiheit). It is highly

[15] On the concept of 'anticipated reaction', see in particular Carl J. Friedrich, Constitutional Government and Democracy' (Boston, 1950 rev. ed.), index.

[16] It appears that some 280 Commission proposals have not yet been dealt with by the Council of Ministers. This might be taken to indicate shortcomings in the policy output capacity of the Council. It would, however, be necessary to examine the content of each individual proposal in detail to produce scientific backing for this conclusion.

debatable whether issues such as the change in the role of the European Commission, which appear at first sight relatively clear, can be dealt with satisfactorily in scientific terms without reopening this wider discussion on which the political scientists have at present turned their backs.

[11]

The Metamorphosis of European Competition Policy

Stephen Wilks

Stephen Wilks is Professor of Politics at the University of Exeter. His research interests lie in comparative political economy and among his recent publications are *Comparative Government-Industry Relations* (Oxford, Clarenden, 1987, edited with M. Wright; and *The Promotion and Regulation of Industry in Japan* (Macmillan, 1991, edited with M. Wright).

This working paper arises from a project funded by the Economic and Social Research Council on Comparative Competition Policy. It was presented as a paper at the European Group of Public Administration Conference at Pisa, September 1992 and is reprinted in Francis Snyder (ed) *European Law in Context: A Reader*, 1992.

RUSEL Working Paper No. 9
ISBN: 1 872342 10 4

Acknowledgement

The author would like to acknowledge the generous assistance of those officials in DG IV who were kind enough to discuss at length many of the ideas explored in this chapter. Particular thanks are due to Dr. Manfred Caspari for allowing formal access to individuals and materials within DG IV and to his successor, Dr. Claus Dieter Ehlermann for generously extending that privilege. Also, to Colin Overbury and Joseph Gilchrist for their encouragement, and to Leigh Hancher and Michelle Cini for comments on an earlier draft. The support of the Economic and Social Research Council under grant R000232903 is also gratefully acknowledged.

1. Introduction

Competition policy and competition law stand in complex relationship to one another. The legal powers granted to the Commission in Articles 85-94 of the Rome Treaty have only gradually been translated into legal activism and effective jurisdiction over the past 35 years. European competition policy only came of age during the 1980s and is still in a dynamic process of mobilising latent powers. Thus the merger regulation of 1989, the actions against public undertakings under article 90, and the creation of an effective framework for controlling state aids all ensure that competition policy is continuing to generate some of the most urgent and exciting controversies in Community law.

The steady intensification and expansion of European competition law has been a political, every bit as much as it has been a legal, process. Successive Commissioners have initiated investigations, decided cases, extended powers and gone to the Court only after intense consideration of political feasibility as well as legal reasoning. There has, of course, been a powerful legal momentum. The power of precedent, the rulings of the Court, the incidence of complaints and the level of potential infractions within the Community economy have all generated their own pressure for the competition authorities to act. Thus in evaluating the nature, pace and direction of the development of competition policy, and competition law, it is necessary to evaluate the interplay of policy priorities and legal pressures. Where to begin?

The argument of this paper is that we should begin by considering the institutions through which these various pressures are mediated and evaluated. Primarily this means considering the Commission's Competition Directorate-General, DG IV, whose Commissioner from 1989-92 was Sir Leon Brittan. But the argument goes beyond the suggestion that DG IV simply registers and weighs pressures. As an organisation it has become self-confident and assertive with its own policy preferences, a distinctively free market world outlook, with distinctive competences and identifiable biases. The importance of policy choice and the exercise of administrative discretion within DG IV is at least as important as the wider political and legal considerations. Thus the modern day Kremlinologists of the legal profession study DG IV and its staff with an endearing tenacity. That is why large law firms have Brussels offices and why Management Today advises that "No significant company pursuing European alliances or ambitions, can nowadays afford not to develop this kind of (close) relationship with the European Commission" (Foster, 1990, p. 63). Yet law journals and law texts remain preoccupied with the formal law. Even Kerse's admirable procedural study barely considers the attitudes, training, competences and influences on the officials in DG IV who actually handle the cases considered (Kerse, 1988). Lawyers interested in such issues would find little help elsewhere in the academic literature. Detailed studies of the institutions, organisation and procedures of the various Directorate-Generals are very sparse indeed and there is no such study of DG IV. The following discussion proceeds some way in that very necessary direction.

Hence the second section of this chapter discusses the formal powers of the Commission in the area of competition policy. The following two sections contrast the traditional administration of those powers with a new, post 1984 exercise of self-confidence and more deliberate exploitation of latent possibilities. The fifth section then reviews some of the more significant recent policy developments and the sixth section reviews the problems and obstacles which currently confront the Directorate-General. The seventh, concluding section presents an argument that DG IV is neither strictly bureaucratic nor professional in its activities but rather that its senior officials undertake an almost ministerial role in the dual sense that their functions are quasi-judicial, and that their exercise of discretionary choice amounts to policy initiation.

2. The Powers of DG IV

The Competition Directorate-General is responsible for applying the competition provisions of the Rome Treaty, essentially articles 85 to 94. As such its major objective has always been seen to be "the furtherance of the integration of the European market" and it is the natural promoter of the internal market. If the Rome Treaty was imbued with the philosophy of the free competitive market then that philosophy has found its natural home within DG IV. Markets in modern industrialised economies are in fact highly concentrated, highly integrated and organised; furthermore, a multitude of nationalistic protective devices exist across the twelve member states. It could be anticipated that DG IV would need weapons of formidable strength to sustain competition and, indeed, it has them.

Very simply DG IV has power to prohibit cartels and restrictive practices under article 85 of the Rome Treaty and it can prohibit "abuse of dominant position" (i.e. misuse of monopoly power) under article 86. Articles 92 and 93 allow it to restrict or prohibit 'state aids' (governmental assistance and subsidy) while article 90 which allows control over nationalised undertakings. Powers have also been extended beyond the Treaty provisions as with the creation since 1990 of a new power to control large mergers throughout the Community in the form of the long awaited merger regulation. A moment's consideration of this list - cartels, agreements in restraint of trade, loans and grants by government, aid to nationalised industries, mergers - reinforces the argument that most competitive strategies of large firms, and all operations of national industrial policy, are heavily constrained by competition law.

Potentially that pressure of constraint could be translated into a power to determine corporate strategies and industrial policies. This potential for competition powers to be used to promote some form of industrial policy has been fiercely resisted by successive Commissioners and by DG IV officials. It forms a constant undercurrent of tension with other DGs, of suspicion from national governments, and is an issue that has grown in salience in the recession of the early 1990s. In earlier periods tensions were restrained by the fact that the sheer extent of potential powers was not widely appreciated outside the specialist circle of competition lawyers and, in any case, those powers were used very sparingly. The following section analyses the restrained, traditional administration of competition law but for the moment it is necessary to dwell on the procedural as well as the Treaty powers of DG IV.

First the division of labour within the Competition Directorate-General needs to be appreciated. There is a very sharp distinction between those officials responsible for operating articles 85 and 86 and the merger regulation, and those responsible for articles 92 and 93. In the former case officials deal with commercial undertakings; they are concerned with sometimes elaborate interpretation of case law; they have a regular and sometimes large case load resulting from notification and complaints, and on the whole they are qualified lawyers. In the latter case, articles 92 and 93, officials are concerned with state aid which adds an unusual and highly significant element to the orthodox 'antitrust' portfolio. Officials deal directly only with governments and government agencies, their procedures are more adversarial but, most important, assessments rest on economic analysis of industrial sectors to a greater extent than on case law and most officials here are economists. Dealing with different clients, different principles and drawing on different skills the two sides of the 'house' have relatively little routine contact. Here we will concentrate on articles 85 and 86.

In order to implement articles 85 and 86 the Commission required an accepted set of procedures. These were adopted in 1962 after 3 years work and negotiation in the form of the famous regulation 17 which is "the procedural bible" for articles 85 and 86. There is by now a formidable body of cases and interpretation attached to regulation 17 (for a flavour see Temple Lang, 1981) but essentially it provides DG IV with five sets of powers. First it allows DG IV to discover breaches through mandatory notification of new agreements by enterprises backed up with powers to require enterprises to provide necessary information and more draconian powers to carry out investigations. As Temple Lang wryly remarks,

> The most serious violations are rarely notified to the Commission since they have no chance of being approved. - There is an increasing body of evidence ... that complaints are not made about the most serious violations (Temple Lang, 1981, p.336).

Perhaps, one suspects, because smaller producers are too scared to rock the boat and will occasionally complain informally. Hence the Commission has powers to act on its own initiative and to make unannounced 'dawn raids' to seize relevant documents. Such "investigations by surprise", in search of a "smoking gun" have become more common since 1979 (see Joshua, 1987, for a review by a DG IV practitioner of the art). They have been used spectacularly in anti-cartel investigations such as the 1987 investigation of the chemical industry when Hoechst resisted official investigation physically in their offices, and legally in the German and the European courts; a resistance that was only overcome after the imposition of penalty payments and use of search warrants.

A second, interesting, power is provided by article 1 of regulation 17. It allows the Commission to "conduct a general inquiry into an economic sector" where it suspects abuse. This right has been used, as with an early investigation into the margarine industry, but is used very rarely. It is nonetheless symbolic of the Commission approach, which is to investigate cases in their economic context; and it has potential in the field of a presumptive industrial policy.

Thirdly, regulation 17 permits informal discussion and negotiation of cases allowing many to be settled by agreement, and fourthly it allows fines to punish non-cooperation and continued abuse. The fines run up to 10% of turnover and can thus be very significant. Criminal damages are excluded at European, but not at national level which in theory gives complainants an incentive to seek redress through European law in national courts.

The fifth set of powers are the most significant and deserve major emphasis. In the area of competition policy the Commission acts alone. In virtually no other area of substantive policy or administration does the Commission have such independence and freedom of manoeuvre. It does not need the approval of the Council of Ministers or the European Parliament; it has no need to use national legislation or to implement through national administrations; budgetary implications are virtually non-existent and, to complete the picture, other than the Legal Service, DG IV is relatively immune to pressure from other Directorate-Generals. Regulation 17 provides for an Advisory Committee on Restrictive Practices and Monopolies which is to be consulted on all draft decisions. The French originally wanted this to have a veto but the Germans resisted this (see Goyder, 1988, pp. 41-2) and national authorities can only advise. The outcome is nicely summarised by Jacobs who observes that to this extent "the Commission is, in effect, a federal agency, operating directly within the territory of the Member States and having exclusive competence ... in this respect competition law is unlike any other area of EEC law" (Jacobs, 1981, p. 205).

The major restraint is within the Commission itself. The Commissioner has some delegated powers to act alone, as in respect of formal requests for information, but on all major issues he has to carry a majority of his colleagues in the Commission. Other than that, the whole process of investigation and decision is subject to challenge and review by the European Court of Justice. The procedures established under regulation 17 thus give the Commission very extensive powers to police, interpret and apply articles 85 and 86. A recent authority has observed that:

> It gives to DG IV indeed powers probably greater than would be accorded to it were the Regulation now being debated ab initio, when the delegation of such de facto powers to a single DG in the Commission might be made more subject to control and intervention by Member States as well as by other institutions of the Community (Goyder, 1988, p.36).

It is perhaps a well-developed awareness of the extent of its powers that has led DG IV to be so sparing in its use of them.

3. Diffident Administration: the first twenty years of DG IV

In retrospect, and certainly by comparison with the 1980s the first twenty years of competition administration appear hesitant. There is an element of cyclical inevitability in this. New institutions take time to develop competence, self-confidence and a degree of legitimacy in the eyes of their clients. Various cycles have been at work. There has undoubtedly been a legal cycle. Until a body of case law can be built up the Commission is unsure how to define and apply articles of the Treaty and unsure whether the Court will uphold its decisions. For example, in the Quinine case, decided in 1969, the European Court confirmed that an informal "gentleman's agreement" was every bit as vulnerable to anti-cartel action as a formal, signed cartel agreement (see Swann, 1983, p. 82; Goyder, 1988, pp. 136-7). Officials now observe that European competition policy has built up in thirty years a body of jurisprudence that took three times that long to evolve in the United States but it has at times been an uncertain process.

Similarly there has been an economic cycle. The second decade of competition policy encountered a European industry in recession. State aids proliferated and became even more difficult to control. Structurally depressed industry from steel to textiles attempted collective solutions which ran counter to competitive principles and there was pressure, for instance, to approve 'crisis cartels' (which was resisted, see Swann, 1983, p. 95). The accession of the three in 1973 and pressure from governments and industry towards a more pragmatic interpretation of competition policy, to temper it, in other words, with an industrial policy, made the decade 1972-82 a difficult one for DG IV.

So also there has been a generational cycle in the personnel operating competition policy. It is a feature of much of the Commission, which is especially marked in DG IV, that there is low staff turnover. Accordingly it is possible to suggest that we have seen a first, second and third generation of staff in DG IV. The first generation joined a new, untried institution. They were the 'pioneers' of DG IV and the most senior are now retiring. They were building a new institution from scratch and were aware of the limitations of the exercise. The second generation which joined in the late sixties and the seventies could take DG IV for granted, but not its powers. They were concerned to establish procedures and to win cases in an adverse environment which made it a constant battle to expand the jurisdiction of the Directorate-General. It is no accident that DG IV in the mid-seventies was accused of bureaucratic delay and formalistic attention to detail combined with a reluctance to take on controversial new policy areas (see Groupner, 1973; Allen, 1977). A third generation joined in the eighties. Typically they regard both DG IV and its powers. They are enthusiastic, extremely competent, slightly impatient with industry and with national governments and one can detect an evangelical streak. They are concerned to employ existing powers and to expand the jurisdictional scope of the Commission. For a young lawyer the process of expanding the scope of law and making new law through new cases can be just as satisfying as breaking a cartel or protecting a consumer interest.

The nature of generational change is important because, more than most government agencies, DG IV is its staff. Here we are concerned mainly with the 200 or so 'A' grade officials. While the second generation referred to above move into the more senior and managerial posts the third generation form the more junior but immensely influential stratum of case officers. They are the 'rapporteurs' who take responsibility for individual cases, undertake economic and legal analysis, make recommendations, draft decisions and provide the momentum and the dynamism of the organisation. To understand the contrast between the hesitant seventies and the self-confident eighties it is useful to look at the organisation "from the inside out" from the point of view of the staff.

The competition authorities of the Community are entrusted with the pursuit of an ideal. That ideal is free competition. In practical terms the commitment to the perfectly competitive market is tempered by a pragmatic concern with the competitiveness of European industry, which is built into Article 85 and with social and regional considerations, built into Article 92. There is also a prime objective, in which DG IV differs from all national competition authorites, of promoting the economic integration of the Community and hence an emphasis mainly on inter-state trade. Nonetheless, there is a strong vein of free-market purism running through DG IV which provides an anchorage for many of the judgements and decisions made by officials. This is entirely to be expected, especially when one traces back the intellectual inheritance of the competition provisions. They are derived fairly directly from German competition law and Goyder (1988, p. 22) traces their antecedents to the Spaak Report and two draughtsmen, one German, one French. Behind German law lay, of course, American antitrust principles and Allen (1977, p. 93) notes the further similarity between Articles 85 and 86 and the first two articles of the Sherman Act.

This thread of American/German purism has the dangerous implication of opening up for the attention of competition authorities a huge raft of possible infractions. It provides little guidance on priorities or balances to be struck. Since all abuses of competition are sinful, and all sins are equal, all should be equally condemned. The danger of this position was illustrated graphically by the 'Christmas Message' of 1962, a notice concerning restrictions on patent licensing arrangements which resulted in the staggering total of 34,500 notifications of bilateral agreements (Goyder, 1988, pp. 45-6). It proved quite impossible to tackle this workload speedily with the staff available and the episode had two legacies. Firstly, new initiatives by the Commission challenging existing practices (such as franchising) or moving into new areas (such as insurance) are calculated partly in terms of the likely workload. Secondly, from that time onwards DG IV has been burdened by a backlog of outstanding notifications.

The case load for articles 85 and 86 comes from one of three sources, complaints, notifications and ex officio action (initiative of the Commission). The tradition has developed of treating complaints quickly and that, combined with a notification backlog, has restricted the time available for staff to take action on their own initiative. The combination of these various factors, namely lack of clear priorities; caution; and reaction to complaints and notifications, produced an administrative style in the 1970s which generated extensive criticism. The administration of competition policy was felt to be too reactive, fragmentary, without a clear sense of proportion and of priorities. There was undoubtedly truth in this perception as in the associated view that the Commission was too concerned with 'vertical agreements' - relating to control over sales and distribution; as opposed to 'horizontal agreements' between producers. But such criticisms also undervalued the dynamics of the development of jurisprudence. Without supporting case law lawyers find it difficult to predict outcomes and therefore to take initiatives and this process is by its nature incremental. Thus the 1970s saw the development of effective control over defensive cartels on the back of important cases such as the Dyestuffs case (1972) and the Quinine Cartel case (1969). As Goyder (1988, p.139) observes:

> In giving strong support to the majority of the findings of the Commission in these important cases early in the history of the Community's competition policy, the Court made an important contribution to underpinning the confidence of the Commission in preparing and bringing substantial cartel cases.

There is also, of course, the reality that the establishment of an important legal principle in an ostensibly minor case can be quickly generalised, and has a crucial 'demonstration effect'. Economic or political priorities are not necessarily a good guide to what may be legally significant.

In the very early days of DG IV its staff were seen as 'exotic technicians' applying an arcane set of legal principles to cases whose circumstances and importance were often less than clear. By the late 1970s the image had changed. The talk was of a pedantic bureaucracy. Thus Allen's assessment of the directorate-general is remarkably negative,

> the output of DG IV illustrates the growing preoccupation of the Commission with bureaucratic procedures. The tenacity with which many of those working within DG IV adhere to the exact letter of the law on relatively minor technical matters, whilst ignoring more serious infringements in politically sensitive areas, can be said to reflect either a sensible and pragmatic awareness of political realities or, perhaps more accurately, a bureaucratic desire not to rock the boat. Frequent criticism is levelled at the calibre of many of those implementing competition policy ...

His gloomy conclusion was that "if competition policy is to further develop, it is difficult to see this occurring along the lines it has followed so far" (Allen, 1977, p. 110). His criticisms drew upon an earlier and more detailed analysis of the internal decision making within DG IV undertaken by Frances Graupner (1973). She charts the complex process of consideration and examination of cases through the dossier system, derived from French administrative practice. Having prepared a recommendation for action on a particular case the rapporteur will prepare a draft which travels to at least five people within the Directorate-General, to the Commissioner's Cabinet and to the Legal Service. Since formal committee meetings are exceptional any material objection or amendment necessitates a new draft which must repeat "the snakes and ladders procedures" (Graupner, 1973, p. 299). The result is significant delay, considerable frustration and a built-in bias towards caution which can only be overcome by enthusiasm and persistence on the part of the rapporteur. In turn this enthusiasm was lacking. Michelmann's study, published in 1979, found morale in DG IV to be conspicuously low (Michelmann, 1979).

In fact both the caution and the apparently bureaucratic procedure can be defended, as discussed below. The really striking feature of this 1970s critique, however, is how inaccurate and redundant it now appears.

4. A Conspiracy of Events: Competition Policy comes of age

An attentive reader of the financial press over the last five years could hardly avoid contact with the work of DG IV. The state aids work has perhaps seen the greatest rise from obscurity. There have been dramatic cases of aid being questioned and limited, especially in relation to the motor industry and equally noteworthy cases where aid given has been ordered to be repaid. Articles 85 and 86 work has also received prominence with controversial but popular action over parallel car imports and the liberalisation of air transport, moves into financial services and insurance and the dramatic raids and huge fines associated with cartel-busting, most melodramatically in the polypropylene case. But it is the operation of the new Merger Taskforce which has generated the most spectacular coverage. When, in its fifty third case, the Task Force rejected the proposed takeover of de Havilland by Aerospatiale and Aleria it provoked a furious reaction in Paris and Rome. The story rumbled on through October 1991 to provide a nice example of the high politics of the Commission and the perennially newsworthy nature of merger policy.

This picture scarcely conforms to the picture of bureaucratic inactivity painted in the previous section, so what has changed? There have been many important and mutually reinforcing developments. Here we can examine seven. The first two are straightforward. In a metaphor beloved of the British civil service it can be said that the various institutions of the EC have begun to 'pull in the same direction' over competition policy. This applies to the European Court of Justice and to the European Parliament. It might be more accurate to say that the European Court has continued to support the Commission. Goyder (1988, p. 415) remarks that the Court would not

> annul Commission decisions on procedural grounds unless there was either a cardinal flaw in the process or a total inadequacy of economic analysis as, for example, in the Belgian Wallpapers case (1975) ... (the Commission) ... has not found itself handicapped, as have some national courts, by technical or narrow interpretations of its jurisdiction or powers.

Similarly Kerse notes that the Court has never annulled a decision on the grounds of 'abuse of power' (Kerse, 1988, pp. 279-80). DG IV is very aware of this support and is always at pains not to jeopardise it. The message of cases lost in the early eighties was that the Court would not tolerate sloppy decisions based on apparently cursory economic analysis. The Commission must do its homework. In addition, each case is carefully vetted by the Legal Service which constitutes the most effective external constraint on the activism of DG IV. The Legal Service is noted for its caution and has regarded some of the more adventurous decisions as somewhat outlandish. In this context it is interesting that a recent Director appointment in DG IV (one of only six) is of a gamekeeper turned poacher, a noted Irish specialist in competition law transferred from the legal service (John Temple Lang). The lawyers in DG IV would probably regard a secular failure to win cases in the European Court as a greater threat than either political or economic challenges.

Similar comments could be applied to the continuing support from the European Parliament. Through questions to the Competition Commissioner and through its annual resolution on the Competition Report (published in the succeeding year's Competition Report) the Parliament has constantly supported the competition priority and pressed for more forceful action even though it has made procedural criticisms.

A persistent refrain in the comments of the Parliament has been the need to progress more rapidly and decisively towards the integration of the internal market. This introduces the third reinforcing factor. To a large degree market integration has always been the prime objective of DG IV. To have it elevated to the main Commission objective is good for morale, raises the salience of competition issues and means that DG IV is taken more seriously by other Commission agencies. In fact the Internal Market White Paper says relatively little about competition policy although it affirms its importance and presses for progress in specific areas, especially financial services and the control of state aids. The Single European Act says even less. All the same, as momentum has developed the contribution of DG IV has become more apparent and its actions of more importance, both materially and symbolically. In a speech to a meeting of Commission Director-Generals in 1990 Brittan gave a forceful expression of this pre-eminence. "We are on the eve of 1992. Competition policy is now mature", he declared it "is now at the centre of politics, economics and law in the EC" (Brittan, 1990b).

As with the theory of indicative planning the 1992 vehicle is only partly a programme of administrative action, it relies also on the principle of the self-fulfilling prophecy. A fourth factor is accordingly the support given to 1992 and hence to DG IV within the Community at large. You do not have to scratch a Commission official very deeply to find scepticism about the pretensions of the Single European Market. In many respects the programme and the aspirations are quite unrealistic, as one or two studies have pointed out (see Butt Philip, 1988). 1992, as one official remarked, is "fantastic advertising" which industry takes far more seriously than many officials. It has sparked a wave of anticipatory mergers in Europe but also created a wave of enthusiasm for the concept of the internal market and its effective regulation. This helps provide the Commission with the lifeblood of any successful administrative agency, legitimacy. Opinions differ as to how far either large companies or national governments have come fully to accept (or perhaps even understand - let alone acknowledge!) the extent to which DG IV trespasses on national sovereignty. The legitimacy quotient is lower than the Commission would like but in the case of DG IV has undoubtedly been raised by the 1992 programme.

The fifth ingredient in the mixture can be found in the philosophical endorsement of the market which has been the dominant ideological feature of the 1980s. It means either that national governments are more inclined to support competition policy or, more realistically, that their opposition is more difficult for them to justify. Whether one calls it neo-liberalism or Thatcherism the move towards deregulation, privatisation and the withdrawal of the state has been of almost revolutionary proportions in the United Kingdom, it was always congenial to the Germans and has become influential in France and many of the smaller European countries. This has meant that in respect of articles 85 and 86 the Commission is now swimming with the tide and on the state aids side the environment has been transformed. National governments are now far more willing not only to concede that subsidies are heretical but also to reduce them and to accept a greater degree of Commission interventionism.

These five external factors combining to support and to raise the salience of competition policy have interacted with two internal developments: the third generation of staff and a new style of Commissioner. It is widely agreed that DG IV is becoming more popular among recruits to the Commission and is recruiting well-qualified, well-motivated staff. Such staff are distinctive in that for the most part they combine a high level of professional competence (as qualified lawyers or economists) with a commitment to the European ideal. Their work involves a high level of responsibility from the beginning and they have a very well developed sense of the sheer power at their disposal. As emphasised earlier, a rapporteur has a considerable influence in deciding (say) the acceptability of a large programme of regional aid, the conditions under which credit cards can be used across Europe, or the practical operation of patent protections which govern innovation activity within the pharmaceutical industry. Such weighty responsibility can be daunting but it can also be immensely stimulating and many officials are enthusiasts. The overall impression is of an organisation which has a strong departmental 'culture' which is, in turn, becoming more positive and self-reinforcing to produce an esprit de corps across most divisions. Hence both morale and self-confidence are at a high point. This is terribly important. If, as will be argued later, DG IV is moving from a reactive, rather negative mode of administration to one that is proactive, more managerially aware, positive and innovatory then this metamorphosis rests on staff attitudes. Staff must work confidently, be willing to be decisive and then to pursue cases with imagination and a dogged determination. In the field of science policy much has been made of the role of 'project champions' in successful processes of innovation; so DG IV relies on its officials to become 'case champions' if it is to expand its standing and jurisdiction.

Finally there is the role of the Commissioner. Legal studies of competition policy pay little attention to the Commissioner and his Cabinet but the significance of leadership from the Commissioner was established by Peter Sutherland whose success was built upon by Leon Brittan to become arguably the most forceful Commissioner in the history of DG IV and a most effective member of the 1989-92 Commission. Before Sutherland departed in 1988 the press tended, in the usual cult of the individual, to attach much of the prominence of DG IV to his personal role. That understated the importance of the six factors mentioned earlier but there is no doubt that Sutherland seized, and symbolised, the moment. He was a dynamic, charismatic character portrayed as a young (only 42 when he left office) tough Irishman who combined the legal flair of the barrister with the aggression of the rugby captain (Dawkins, 1987). But it would be wrong to regard his influence as one of direct leadership. To a surprising degree there is within the Commission a disjuncture between the Commissioner and his Cabinet on the one hand, and the Directorate-General on the other. Rather than the integration of the minister with his department so typical of Britain the European model is conducted in terms of 'us' and 'them'.

Contrary to early misgivings Sir Leon Brittan proved just as effective as Sutherland and threw himself with ill-concealed relish into his Commission responsibilities. Also relatively young (49 when entering office) Brittan was impeccably well qualified for the job. Not only was he a weighty national politician from one of the larger Member States (his immediate predecessors were from Ireland, Holland, and two from Luxembourg), he was a QC (appointed 1978), and held national office as Chief Secretary (1981-83), Home Secretary (1983-85) and Secretary of State for Trade and Industry (1985-86). Equally important, he shared the self-defined mission of DG IV, the pursuit of free competition, and was hence ideologically in tune with his officials.

Living up to the reputation he acquired at the DTI, Brittan proved to be a sophisticated operator on the Brussels scene. Although notorious for intellectual arrogance he became a decisive and determined administrator able to inspire loyalty, to impose priorities and to provide strategic leadership. More surprisingly, he and his Cabinet became adept in the vital Brussels processes of negotiation and compromise. To a greater degree than Sutherland he was willing to lobby and to cut deals, sometimes to the frustration of DG IV officials who would have preferred tougher decisions (Kellaway, 1990). Above all Brittan put an end to any sense of drift in DG IV. He had his own priorities propounded in a torrent of speeches extending well beyond the competition brief. Thus his attention focused successively on the merger regulation, finally approved in December 1989; on developing an effective state aids regime; on liberalisation of financial services; and on extending competition provisions to public enterprises.

Brittan was supported by a Cabinet widely regarded as skilled, experienced and highly effective. This has shifted the centre of gravity in DG IV somewhat away from the fonctionaires in their comfortable new offices in the Avenue de Cortenberg towards the Cabinet on the 13th Floor of the Berlaymont. This physical separation symbolises the real gulf between the Commissioner and his officials which reflects French rather than British administrative practice and tends to reinforce the formalism and legalism of the actual conduct of business. In compensation the Merger Task Force has strengthened both the number and the status of officials who are now led by a new Director General, Claus Dieter Ehlermann, appointed early in 1990. Formerly the Director-General of the Legal Service Dr. Ehlermann has been a popular appointment with a style more suited to the strategic development of policy than his more cautious predecessor, Dr. Manfred Caspari. The appointment of a German as Director General of DG IV has become almost a Commission convention and was seen as an additional reassurance to the Germans over the operation of the merger regulation. In any event, the overall combination of strong Commissioner, effective Cabinet, respected Director General and high-calibre officials makes the current DG IV a formidable organisation.

5. Manifestations of the New Assertiveness

It might be objected that the discussion so far has been abstract and speculative; what difference do these factors make in practice? We can pick up a few examples of the most important developments to illustrate the scope of the expansion of DG IV's role.

The restrictive practices/monopoly control work under articles 85 and 86 offers several significant examples involving the expansion of competition policy into previously unregulated sectors. Although the Commission had always maintained that banking and insurance were subject to articles 85 and 86 no decisions in this area were taken until 1984 (see Fourteenth Report, 1985, pp. 66-7). The Commission warned that it "intends to continue its policy of strengthening the application of the competition rules in these sectors". Here we have a massive and complex industry of great sensitivity and strong national differentiation. The fact that there have been relatively few decisions and cases reflects not inactivity but the fact that these industries are very sensitive to the regulatory environment and will adapt their procedures either before notification to the Commission or as a result of informal discussions. The move by DG IV into service industries including commodity markets and broadcasting takes it into the most quickly growing sector of the economy and a sector which in the more advanced countries, like the UK, is actually larger than manufacturing.

More recent still is the Commission's willingness to extend jurisdiction into the traditionally exempted areas of public enterprise; transport, telecommunications, energy and water. Air transport was a favoured area of activism for Peter Sutherland but Brittan has also moved forcibly into the areas of telecommunications and energy.

Progress has been rapid. In telecommunications early cases established that nationalised undertakings were 'commercial' (See the 1985 British Telecom case and Schulte-Braucks, 1986, p. 59). Subsequently DG IV decided to begin to employ the hitherto little used Article 90 to proceed against public undertakings. This allowed the Commission to adopt a Directive on competition in the market for telecommunications services in June 1990 simultaneously with the open network provision directive. These measures are seismic and very sensitive.

Telecommunications is a vital industry and its promotion, liberalisation and regulation is one of the most important items on Europe's industrial agenda. The Commission is engaging in very controversial action but is already using the same principles, and the established precedents to extend jurisdiction over energy monopolies with transport, water and possibly even defence to follow. Competition rules, it declares, will "be applied regardless of whether a company is nationalised or privatised" (Twentieth Report, 1991, p. 51).

Moves into previously unconsidered sectors of the economy is one manifestation of DG IV activism, an emphasis on certain general forms of restrictive practice is a second. In the early days of DG IV much attention was devoted to so-called 'vertical agreements' between producers, distributors and retailers. More recently emphasis has been given to 'horizontal' agreements which include cartel-type agreements between producers, joint ventures and mergers. Spectacular action involving secret investigation, raids and the imposition of very substantial fines has been taken against blatantly illegal cartels. Fines of 58 million ECU were imposed on the 15 petrochemical producers involved in the polypropylene cartel and in 1990 Solvay and ICI were fined 47 million ECU for illegal market sharing of soda ash.

The merger regulation is the most important aspect of current competition policy. It has been the subject of much discussion and comment and the adoption of the Regulation in December 1989 was seen as a great boost for DG IV and a personal triumph for Leon Brittan (for detail see Nineteenth Report, 1990, pp. 249-68; Elland, 1990). The lack of effective jurisdiction over merger activity had long been the most glaring hole in the edifice of European competition powers. The Commission put forward a draft proposal as long ago as 1973 and for eighteen years debilitating haggling had dragged on.

The merger regulation thus provides DG IV with the complete armoury of competition powers and, with the state aids competence, gives it unrivalled authority to regulate industry. Initially DG IV proceeded cautiously and pragmatically. In the first 17 months of operation, up to January 1992, the Task Force had reviewed about 80 mergers whose turnover fell above the high threshold of ECU 5 Billion. Proceedings were opened against relatively few and only the controversial decision taken in November 1991 to prohibit the de Havilland takeover had by then caused significant conflict.

While moves into new sectors and towards a more effective control of horizontal agreements represent substantive manifestations of a more active Competition Directorate-General, changes in internal organisation have also taken place. A two-stage reorganisation in 1984/85 and 1986 eliminated the old Inspection Directorate and created a new Coordination and Policy Directorate to give the organisation shown in Fig. 1. The first important change is the altered arrangements whereby rapporteurs are now responsible for collecting information through inspection. This cuts down internal paperwork and delay and it puts the specialist out in 'the field' although it is regarded as less than welcome by some rapporteurs. The second change is the restructuring of Article 85/6 into ten sectorally specialised divisions. These changes have only marginally affected state aids work.

The principle of sectoral specialisation is logical but has important implications. Background sectoral analysis, definition of the market and of competition within it is central to case work. It is the basis for legal interpretation of the "effect on competition" which is the basic evaluative principle of Article 85. Sectoral analysis is thus the basis for negative clearances, exemptions, settlements, draft decisions and eventual cases in the European Court. The intention of the reorganisation was thus to increase the level of sectoral expertise among rapporteurs and divisional heads. In practice the allocation of case work is affected also by current case load and by linguistic

Fig. 1

ORGANISATION OF DG IV

Commissioner — Sir Leon Brittan

- Cabinet (6 people) Chef. James Currie

Director-General — Claus Dieter Ehlermann

- Deputy — R. Simonnet
- Advisers and Hearings Officers

- Merger Task Force — Directeur, Colin Overbury
  - 3 operating Units
- Directorate A — Policy and Co-ordination — Directeur, Rafael Garcia-Palencia Cebrian
  - 6 Divisions
- Directorate B — Articles 85/6 I — Directeur, vacant
  - 4 Divisions
    1. Electronics and Telecoms
    2. Textiles, other manufacturing
    3. Banking, Insurance, Media
    4. Media, Consumer Electronics, Distribution
- Directorate C — Articles 85/6 II — Directeur, Gianfranco Rocca
  - 3 Divisions
    1. Metals, paper etc.
    2. Energy and base chemicals
    3. Chemical products etc.
- Directorate D — Articles 85/6 III — Directeur, John Temple Lang
  - 4 Divisions
    1. Steel and coal
    2. Transport, tourism
    3. Automobiles, transport
    4. ECSC inspection and training
- Directorate E — State Aids — Directeur, Asger Petersen
  - 6 Divisions

Note: Organisation and staff at February 1992.

competences but broadly rapporteurs are able to develop expertise within a given sector. Thus they will understand the economics and the market; be familiar with the leading firms, trade associations and research bodies; they will scrutinise the specialist press and consult informally with a whole range of experts. They will become familiar with the policy stances of governments and other commission agencies and will become known within the specialised community of legal advisers, Brussels law firms and consultancies. The implications of this are that the individuals concerned will inevitably form their own judgements and views about the sector. They will be in a position to balance legal interpretation against economic ramifications and political preferences. Contact with the officials concerned confirms that this is exactly what they do, often with a sensitive appreciation of the subtleties of given problems. In this they are not mere technicians, and they are certainly not bureaucrats in any strict usage of that term; their function is far more quasi-judicial and concerned with 'policy' for the sector concerned.

Equally important harbingers of a more comprehensive policy stance are apparent on the state aids side of the house. The control of state aids under articles 92-4 is more simple to understand but more complicated to administer than article 85-6 work. The subject matter is clear:

> The definition of state aid is a wide one including direct financial grants or loans, exemptions or deferrals of tax or duty, reduction in interest rates, the use of land or facilities at favourable rates, guarantees, reimbursement of expenses, and exemption or deferral of tax. It may even include equity investment ... It includes assistance of this kind from national, regional or local authorities or indeed from any source dispensing funds derived from the state (Goyder, 1988, p373).

Aids which distort competition are illegal but there are a series of problems with interpreting and implementing these articles. Investigations of aid is difficult. There are no equivalent powers to regulation 17 and the Commission must rely on cooperation from member states. Further, there is no power for the Commission to issue regulations. The Council may do so but in practice has not. Defining the applicability of state aid rules and the criteria and policy to be applied by the Commission thus depends on non-legally binding 'communications' and 'letters' to member states; 'frameworks' for given categories of aid which are similarly non-binding; and directives which do have the force of law but which rely on member states to enact appropriate legislation.

The state aids articles contain quite wide areas in which aids are perfectly acceptable. Interpretation can be difficult with a very modest case law and principles which have indicative rather than statutory status. Thus the Commission likes aid to be selective (preferably assisting rationalisation), transparent, finite and 'appropriate' (to its purpose). In many cases a delicate judgement is necessary. The Commission has always felt that it could not afford to apply the law too literally and to confront the member states, "the role of the Commission, therefore, had in the first place to be primarily educational rather than adversarial" (Goyder, 1988, p. 376).

A final problem lies in the sheer intransigence of some national governments. A considerable degree of ingenuity is encountered in devising new forms of aid and Commission officials can recount hair-raising stories of the lengths some national governments will go to avoid having to terminate aid. Such problems were relatively modest up to 1973 and the Commission attached a low priority to state aid, proceeding on a reactive, case-by-case basis. The following decade, up to 1983, was far more problematic as the recession and new members brought a proliferation of aid schemes. This period of trench warfare has largely come to an end with economic recovery and a more systematic and considered approach to this area has been developed.

The determination to get to grips with the state aid problem dates from the late 1970s as the Commission began to outline its approach and policy in a series of letters and communications to national governments. For example, in January 1985 the Commission issued a "Commission communication on the cumulation of aids for different purposes". This proposed that member states should notify cumulation of aids "defined as the application of more than one aid scheme to a given investment project" (Competition Rules, 1987, p. 115) and set out thresholds and definitions which should govern such notification. These various guidelines now approach a comprehensive evaluation of state aids and have been brought together in a compendium of rules which runs to 261 pages (see Competition Rules, 1987). The compendium also contains the important, broadly permissive, 1986 'Framework for State aids for Research and Development' but not the equally important 'Communication on the method for the application of Article 92(3)(a) and (c) to Regional Aid' (Official Journal, August 1988). Partly as a result of such initiatives the level of notification of aid plans rose significantly in 1987, to 326 notifications and to 429 in 1990. This, argued the Commission, is "a sign of increased acceptance of the discipline devised by the Commission" which "reflects the increased efficiency of Commission policy in controlling such aids" (Seventeenth Report, 1988, pp. 13 and 141).

There is no doubting the general consensus that a determined control of state aids is a prerequisite for realising economic gains from the completion of the internal market. In "the optic of 1992", to use the Commission's engaging phrase, state aids policy has increased salience but it is also apparent "that the Commission's knowledge of state aids has been less than complete" (Seventeenth Report, 1988, pp. 137-8). This unsurprising conclusion emerged from the work of a Task Force on State Aids set up in 1986. The Task Force provided the lead into one of the most important initiatives of the Commission in this area. It produced a report early in 1988 comprising an analysis and inventory of state aids across the Community. The exercise originated at least partly in a request from Peter Sutherland for details of the dimensions of the problem. He wanted to know the amount of aid, types, intensities, the country profile and changes over time. Officials found it impossible to give adequate answers. The Task Force drew representatives from seven Directorate Generals in addition to DG IV. It gathered information from every possible source about different forms of state aid for the period 1981-86, and proceeded to analyse it by country, instrument, industry, function, and intensity (ratio of total investment). The material has gone to form a computerised data-base which has been updated in the second survey of state aids in 1990 and can be used both for further analyses and as a method of cross-referencing with Commission approvals and decisions (see European Economy, 1991).

The Task Force White Paper won broad endorsement from national governments who agree with its findings and generally welcome the exercise. The findings revealed some startling contrasts, "the study shows that in 1986 the volume of state aids ... amounted to 93 bn ECU or 3% of GDP and represents an average of 9% of public expenditure. In the manufacturing sector state aids represent over 6% of value added and amount to 49 bn ECU in 1986. In most Member States, expenditure on aids exceeds the corporate taxes paid by companies" (Press Release, 6 June 1988). The figures provide potent ammunition and stress the profligacy of the Italians although their subsidy intensities are dwarfed by the new and exceptional need to continue state aids to East German industry. Bringing East German industry into conformity with the competition rules is proving a separate challenge in its own right.

The preparation of the White Paper proved to be something of a Pandora's Box. A full analysis of aids invited consideration of further ways in which they could and should be controlled and established a momentum.

The state aids issues were seized on by Leon Brittan as one of the first of his priority areas. He intensified control, extended coverage and embarked on the high profile confrontation with the French over repayment of aid to Renault. There are, of course, dangers in such a rapid expansion of competence into this previously passive area. The first is that such aspirations undeniably constitute a further encroachment into the economic sovereignty of member states. The ability to establish, finance, subsidise and fiscally influence industrial and commercial undertakings is one that is historically fundamental to the integrity of the modern industrialised state. National governments do not fully accept the legitimacy of Commission control in this area and are likely either to resist it or to subject it to a process of political bargaining (a possibility considered further below). The second danger is that state aids are the generic instrument par excellence of industrial policy. It has always been argued that competition policy must be understood and operated in the context of the whole range of Commission policies. The consolidation of a DG IV competence in the field of state aids raises the possibility, indeed the probability, that such competence must be operated by reference to some scheme or strategy of industrial policy. Again, this raises issues of actute ideological and practical complexity.

As if to give substance to such fears a range of Commission initiatives on state aids are indicative both of assertiveness and a more strategic orientation. The first is headline material. In a communication of November 1983 the Commission warned governments and firms that case law indicated that aid granted illegally could be required to be repaid. This policy has begun to be applied with determination and the Seventeenth Report (1988, p. 139) notes that by the end of 1987 repayments of 999 mn ECU had been ordered in 22 cases. The Belgians were the worst culprits although the forced repayments of aid by Renault and Rover attracted more attention. It is indicative of the unpopularity of this development that de facto repayment is proving very difficult to ensure. A second initiative is less spectacular but just as interesting. The Commission has put into place a framework for the notification and evaluation of state aids in the motor vehicle sector. Such frameworks have been produced before, but only for 'crisis' sectors such as steel and textiles. The Commission experienced a number of contentious recent aid cases in the motor industry and noted that the industry is second only to steel in the magnitude of aid received. Hence the objective is to consider future aid in the light of a complete sectoral picture which encompasses all aids, from all governments, to all manufacturers (excluding components). Officials from DG III might jealously consider the potential to use this sectoral evaluation as an industrial policy instrument for restructuring the industry; an argument which DG IV would earnestly resist. Further initiatives sponsored by Brittan include an extension of the aid rules to public enterprises and a systematic review of aid schemes already in operation rather than simply reacting to new notifications.

6. Problems and Dilemmas of Transition

Perhaps enough has been said above to establish the argument that DG IV is taking a range of significant initiatives. Before assessing their implications we need also to take account of a number of practical and philosophical problems which could prevent the organisation from exploiting the potential of its Treaty powers and the opportunities of a favourable decade in the Community's economic policy. We can consider four such problems, two practical, two more profound and longer-term.

Shortage of Resources. DG IV has a very considerable workload and very modest resources of staff. Officials certainly feel they are seriously under-staffed, a position encapsulated in a nice little comparison which is offered independently, on the least provocation, by most DG IV officials - namely that there are more people involved in giving state aid in Wallonia (Southern Belgium) than there are controlling state aids across the whole Community. William Dawkins heard the same story, or saw the same television programme, "It was remarkable work for a unit with a staff of 30, fewer than those assigned to administering state aid in Wallonia" (Dawkins, 1988). There is clearly an anecdotal oral tradition at work here. Dennis Swann also notes that "the EC Commission employs fewer people than Wandsworth Borough Council" (Swann, 1983, p. 196) but, whatever the most appropriate comparison it is evident that the staff of DG IV is barely sufficient. Excluding language staff the Commission currently employs around 9,700 administrative staff; of whom about 2,800 are elite 'A' grade. Of those DG IV has about 200 'A' grade officials and with a budgetary staff freeze across the Commission as a whole significant staff increases are virtually out of the question. It was hoped within the organisation that the merger regulation would break the logjam and allow greatly increased staffing levels. In fact about 40 new 'A' grade officials have been recruited to administer the regulation. This is barely adequate and will do little for the rest of the organisation. In fact it may be that talent is being drained away from other parts of the organisation into the Merger Task Force; Brittan observed that

> a Task Force has been established within DG IV and we have recruited to it some of the very best officials from within the Commission and on secondment (Brittan, 1990c).

The merger activity has undoubtedly been regarded as a glamorous and exciting posting. A chance to compensate for the serious promotion bottleneck which exists at the A.4./A.5. Principal Administrator level.

The effects are predictable. Staff must deal with the urgent rather than the important. There is less opportunity to take initiatives, to pursue ex officio cases, to undertake medium term managerial planning or longer term strategic planning. Two particular aspects of this deserve emphasis. First there is the 'notification mountain' in respect of Article 85/86 work. Ever since the mass patent notification referred to above DG IV has had to deal with a backlog of work. Recent figures show 2,734 cases pending in December 1990 of which only 375 were begun during the year. Officials are phlegmatic about the problem and point out that DG IV is no worse than most national competition authorities. Other observers have been more agitated and Goyder in particular has emphasised this problem. He concludes that:

> the chief continuing weakness of DG IV ... in the enforcement of competition policy is that its inadequate resources both in financial terms and in numbers of officials, have prevented it from ever completely digesting the overload of notified agreements.

He goes on to draw out the worrying implication of this which is that:

> This has ... led to an uncertainty about the value of notification in the case of new agreements ... and a widespread cynicism in business circles about the efficacy of the exemption process.[1]

There are some who feel that Goyder may be over-emphasising the resource question but his argument is also persuasive when he links it to procedural inadequacies. He notes an improvement in procedures and devices, such as block exemptions which greatly simplify the workload, and also notes the increased willingness to accept undertakings from companies and to close cases by 'settlement'. This introduces the second, more profound, dilemma.

Discretion and Accountability. There is no doubt that the Commission collectively has considerable discretion and independence in deciding upon competition cases. It is an old, but still relevant, critique that such discretion is to a dangerous degree arrogated to DG IV as a whole or to individual directorates, divisions, or even individual officials within it. The argument can be considered in four stages; first the critique, second the rebuttal, third the effects on the DG IV 'culture', and fourth the implications for an expansion of powers.

The main target of criticism is not so much formal decisions of the Commission. They are duly considered, published, and can be challenged in the European Court. Rather the concern is with informal discussions, the issuing of 'comfort letters' (which have no legal standing) and the closure of cases through settlement. The critique has been summarised by Van Bael who points out that over the nine years to 1984 about 96% of cases were closed through 'settlements' (the figures actually include termination and expiries). He would not be reassured to note that the rate has gone up to 97% for 1985-89. He goes on to argue that "the Commission's discretion in settling or prosecuting a case is very wide indeed". After examining a series of cases and principles he concludes that:

> the applicable rules of procedure laid down in Regulation No. 17 remain rather 'Kafkaeque' in that the Commission combines the function of prosecutor, judge and jury ... it is clear that the Commission's settlement practice, which occurs outside the due process requirements contained in Regulation No. 17, is even more in need of change. Once a proceeding is opened, the Commission should not be at liberty to set aside such minimum procedural safeguards simply by embarking on a settlement course. This creates an alternative body of secret jurisprudence ...[2]

This may seem a curiously blinkered line of criticism, especially to a British readership. In the British and in many other administrative systems ministers, and civil servants acting in their name, have very wide discretionary powers, often analysed as 'quasi-judicial' and only marginally subject to judicial review. One curious feature of DG IV is in fact the entrenched legalism which imbues every aspect of its work, it may seem perverse indeed to press for an escalation of legal process.

Nonetheless, there is an element of valid concern about the accountability of DG IV and Van Bael's comments do serve to underline the discretionary power of DG IV officials to negotiate a settlement. The rebuttal of Van Bael's basic criticism illustrates a dilemma in the administration of competition policy. On the one hand it is criticised as being too bureaucratic; on the other it is assaulted for being too cavalier. Here the criticisms relayed earlier from Graupner and Allen can be set against the criticisms from Van Bael. Why, as Graupner and Allen complain, is DG IV relatively bureaucratic in procedure, with a series of checks on dossiers internally, by the Cabinet and by the Legal Service? Well precisely to cope with the problem identified by Van Bael, that DG IV is prosecutor, judge and jury. To avoid officials misinterpreting cases, being influenced by improper considerations, or simply pursuing vendettas, dossiers are carefully evaluated, cross-checked and compared with other similar cases. The organisation needs to retain a degree of bureaucratic control, it also needs to avoid immobilisme by retaining informality and discretion. The trick is to get the balance right.

This tension between discretion and accountability has helped to produce a distinctive organisational 'culture' within DG IV. The idea of organisational culture is slippery but it is a useful shorthand to refer to the mix of attitudes, expectations and typical behaviour which constitute the norms of the organisation (see Wilks, 1986, 1990; Wilks and Wright, 1991). On the discretionary side of the balance is a pressure to settle cases both as a necessary response to the workload and due to a reluctance to engage in an adversarial process. As with a nuclear deterrent, DG IV has always felt a reluctance to use the full force of its powers. It is more realistic, and probably ultimately more successful, to persuade industry to adapt and to rely on the demonstration effect. Negative decisions are therefore to be avoided unless there is an important point of principle to be established by a leading case. But the process of securing a settlement demands informal consultation, explanation of the Commission's interpretation, a degree of reasonable compromise and advice on what would be acceptable. For the most part Commission officials are very open and accessible. They attend meetings, speak at conferences, allow themselves to be exposed to the mix of influences and pressures at large in the sector. This makes for an administrative style which gives every impression of being far more flexible, less didactic, than those of national competition authorities.

On the accountability side of the balance, however, officials must be careful to ground their expressed views in sound legal interpretation. Hence the frequent reference to articles and cases which makes such an initial impact on the visitor. There is also a limit to the openness. While officials will discuss problems with a candour that might scandalise the psychotically secretive British civil servant there is a firm threshold of specifics which remain firmly confidential. Indeed, DG IV's self-contained offices on the Avenue de Cortenberg were segregated deliberately to make possible a level of security which has been significantly strengthened as a result of the merger regulation. DG IV cannot afford too public a perception that "the importance of close contacts with DG IV officials is increasingly essential for parties involved in competition proceedings" (Belmont, 1987, p. 2) as a leading law firm remarked. Thus officials must be careful to avoid flippancy or the impression of a casual manner. They need to adopt a sober, reasoned approach which conveys authority. This is not just a facade, it is a functional necessity. To take a hypothetical example. It would be daunting for a junior official to have to telephone the chief executive of a leading British building society to tell him that his new, cherished, credit card scheme, in the view of the Commission (i.e. the judgement of the official), breached competition rules. With the added knowledge that such a judgement would be rapidly relayed through the industry creating a wide ripple effect. To be able to take such action, and to explain it, does take real authority.

This mixture of informality and authority is not easily learned, and it certainly is not taught. New officials in DG IV receive no formal training but learn the job, in the derogatory terms of the British civil service by "sitting next to Nellie". The off-the-cuff judgement is that it takes one-and-a-half to two years before the new rapporteur becomes fully effective and in that time he or she will have acquired a package of norms which constitute a set of inarticulate but quite specific procedural and judgemental standards - a 'culture'. The culture is an organisational or 'house' culture, or even perhaps an Article 85/86 culture, which is collective rather than individual. Such cultures evolve and the DG IV balance has moved from the bureaucratic towards the discretionary definition of the job.

The implications of this type of culture are wide because outsiders will find their perceptions of DG IV affected by its style as well as its formal powers. Thus, for instance, in the discussion of the new merger regulation there are (at least) two agendas at work. One is concerned with the proper scope of Community power over mergers; but another is equally concerned at how Commission officials will define and utilise those powers. The Commission in 1990 is arguably in a far better position to use the powers intelligently and judiciously than was the Commission when the original proposals were made in 1973. This must affect their acceptability.

Relations with National Authorities. As observed early in this article DG IV has used its power cautiously in the past. It has sought co-operation from national authorities who may be trade and competition authorities with Articles 85 and 86, and who will be a different group of Industry/Economics/ Treasury agencies on the state aids side. The norm has been to consult, persuade and to 'carry' national governments and ministries. This becomes more difficult as DG IV becomes more assertive and comprehensive in its administration. There is a balance to be struck between co-operation and confrontation. A little judicious confrontation is clearly helpful and begins to change the rules of the game but perpetual confrontation would be disastrous.

The specific problem here is the implementation of policy. On the one hand there is an 'implementation deficit', on the other there are moves to entrust a greater degree of implementation to national authorities. The implementation deficit can be seen especially on the state aids side. National governments are not always scrupulous in notifying aids or making them consistent with prior approvals. Similarly there appears to be a reluctance to police repayment of aid ordered by the Commission. This is perhaps comprehensible. Aid is sometimes the subject of political priorities and bargains. In some countries national politicians have a clientelistic relationship with industries or constituencies and the requirement to repay aid can cause acute political embarrassment. Nevertheless, the Commission has to make sure that its legal pronouncements are implemented.

On the other side of the coin one of the expedients favoured by the Delors Commission in order to circumvent the budget and manpower squeeze is 'subsidiarity'. This is the principle that work should be done at the lowest possible level. 'Self-policing' of competition rules is an interesting idea which would require a deliberate programme of action to implement. National officials would need to be trained, there could develop a systematic programme of exchanges and secondments between DG IV and national ministries and DG IV itself would become a policy making body analogous to a Swedish or German Federal Ministry. Although such proposals are beginning to be seriously discussed they are still speculative. They would take on a greater credibility if there existed a 'community' or 'network' of competition specialists who already shared the same concerns, attitudes and perhaps meetings. While there are indications that an embryonic community does exist on the state aids side it is surprisingly non-existent in relation to articles 85 and 86. Thus one looks in vain for a network of key officials in key ministries across Europe with a shared interest in competition issues and regular contact with one another. Here one can agree with Allen (1977, p. 109) who noted that

> integration theorists ... have looked towards the European networks of competition experts and government officials for confirmation of their theories. However ... Although the Commission's decision-making processes allow for a lot of contact among experts from member states there is little evidence of any spillover from such contact.

In this respect DG IV can appear a somewhat introverted organisation and any move towards significant decentralisation of competition administration would require fundamental changes of attitude. This does not, of course, apply to 'judicial implementation'. The Commission has always been keen to see parties bring actions under Articles 85 and 86 in the national courts. This has been very slow to develop but, for instance, in the British courts the case of Garden Cottage Foods Ltd. v. Milk Marketing Board (House of Lords, 1983) suggested not only the utility of Articles 85 and 86 to attack monopoly practices but also the possibility of significant damages.

Politics and Politicisation. The fourth problem of transition to a more activist stance is that of political opposition. When DG IV's stance was reactive and perhaps defensive it could sustain its position through professional and technical competence. But policy initiation demands a strong political presence. British civil servants like a minister who can "master his brief and fight his corner", so DG IV needs a Commissioner who can play the games of European and Commission politics. In this it has been fortunate in its Commissioners during the 1980s.

The state aids example is instructive here. Up until 1981 state aids decisions went through the Commission meetings by 'written procedure'. In other words they were written into the agenda but not specifically discussed and were passed unless objected to. The Commission has a two month time limit to examine notification and if it does not oppose them within that period they are deemed approved. The folklore of the Commission holds that in 1981 a member state managed, by a combination of delayed agendas and cancelled meetings, to prevent a decision of opposition ('contentious procedure' under Art. 93(2)) from being formally passed and hence were able to go ahead with impunity and grant aid. This apparently infuriated Roy Jenkins, then President, who instituted a new procedure whereby the Chefs du Cabinet of all the Commissioners would have state aids on a fortnightly agenda and would discuss them. They would then make recommendations for the Commission either as 'A' points (passed not discussed) or more complex cases warranting discussion. This procedure was designed to ensure first that all cases were considered, and second, that a Commission view was formed avoiding the item being 'talked out'.

This new procedure had the unfortunate side-effect of politicising state aids decisions. They are now discussed in two forums, by the Cabinets and by the Commissions. This enables national politicians, and the firms themselves, to lobby either through functional Directorate-Generals' Cabinets (e.g. DG III - Industry or DG XVI - Regional), or through the 'national' Commissioners and Cabinets. Thus the Belgians can mobilise through the Belgian Commissioner's Cabinet, regardless of his portfolio (which happens to be Transport). The big state aids cases, such as Rover and Renault, have thus become big set-piece political battles where Brittan's Cabinet has to lobby, pressure, manipulate and protest. On the whole they win their cases but the obstacles involved make for a more defensive posture and introduce presentational and populist criteria into the decision process. The Cabinet will build new angles into the case and the decision and, in a delightful verbalism, they may 'nuance' the decision. It appears that each battle is still fought from scratch. DG IV have not yet established the principle of control and won legitimacy for their opposition. One of the most notorious cases is therefore relatively recent. In 1984 the Commission opened a procedure against loans of 144 mn ECU to the French textile group Boussac. It calculated the aid element at 99 mn ECU. The recommendation from DG IV was that the aids should be declared illegal and be substantially repaid. The recommendation reportedly first went to the Commission in December 1986 and was discussed for virtually a whole day. The negative decision was not eventually approved until July 1987 after eight months politiking (Seventeenth Report, 1988, pp. 164-5).

Conclusion: From Bureaucrats to Regulators

There is a fairly well developed literature which assesses the activities of the Commission as part of the complex of European institutions and as part of a presumptive supra-national European government (see, for instance, Henig, 1983; George, 1985; Keohane and Hoffman, 1991). This paper is written at a more specific level and offers a tentative characterisation of DG IV, while accepting that a full analysis would place the organisation within the wider context of the Commission and the other European institutions.

It would seem at first sight that DG IV has gone through a series of qualitative changes in its short life. In the early days it was seen as a grouping of technical specialists but as its work and procedural arrangements expanded it came to be regarded in the mid-1970s as a rather unimaginative bureaucracy. A third broad change has taken place in the mid-1980s, or perhaps it would be more correct to say that the change is still in progress. It is tempting to describe the organisation nowadays as a body of policy-makers; certainly they adapt policy and to an extent they are policy innovators. A more specific and accurate description may be to characterise DG IV officials as 'regulators'. Here the term regulation is used in the American rather than the British sense. There is a body of analysis of contemporary American regulation which argues that regulatory bodies interpret their jurisdiction in order to secure given societal or economic goals (Hancher, 1990, Chapter 1). Regulatory changes are designed with specific policy goals in mind and are neither mechanical and defensive in nature, nor rigid and reactive in implementation (for discussion and UK comparison see Baldwin and McCrudden, 1987). American regulators are policy makers in disguise and the phenomenon reaches its apotheosis in the American Supreme Court. Contemporary analysis of the Court stresses the way in which Justices are chosen for the records and their platforms. Their analysis and findings are constructed by reference to statute and case law but are argued in terms of social, economic and political realities. At the extreme the reasoning appears inductive, reaching conclusions then presenting law and fact to justify them. In a very modest fashion the same argument could be applied to DG IV. It is a regulatory body which pursues policy change through regulative means. It is neither a technocracy nor a bureaucracy.

Of course DG IV has bureaucratic characteristics in the classic Weberian sense. It has permanent salaried officials, an elaborate hierarchy, procedures, rules and recruitment by merit. But its work is far from bureaucratic. Cases are not assessed by reference to pre-defined procedures, rules and criteria to produce a mechanical determination regardless of extraneous factors - the characteristic of bureaucracy. Neither are they assessed in terms of purely technical criteria such as the effect on competitiveness, economic prosperity, technological development or social welfare - the marks of technocracy. Rather cases are assessed in a complex amalgam which combines judicial criteria with economic analysis and political awareness; the whole overlaid with the norms of the organisation and the desired development of competition policy. Hence the work of DG IV is typified by the need to arrive at a calculated judgement and in this sense is more ministerial than administrative.

A series of influences have produced this distinctive mixture. The dominance of legal power and process has brought the professionalism of law with associated characteristics of a collegiate atmosphere arising from shared skills, and the initiative which arises from confidence in professional judgements. A European legal style has brought the clear definition and interpretation of statutory provisions which is characteristic of Roman law and avoids the abstract principles and procedural complexities of a Common Law approach. Associated with this is the willingness to use the courts which is so alien to the British administrative tradition and still, one suspects, has the ability to intimidate British officials and firms.

A French administrative style reinforces some of these legal biases. The institutions of the dossier and the rapporteur are again in sharp contrast to the committee systems typical of British central administration. It places great pressure on the individual and requires an investment of energy and enthusiasm if the natural inertia of the system is to be overcome. This can work two ways. The rapporteur may become resigned, reactive, defensive and hence ineffectual. This may have been a more widespread problem in the 1970s. Alternatively, the rapporteur may use this individual opportunity to make decisive progress. The dossier system can minimise compromise and allow the 'conviction administrator' to drive views through the system. It has been remarked that "it is difficult to block a rapporteur". He or she has the facts and presents the case. Since opposition cannot be based on a superior knowledge of the case it must usually be based on a political or policy argument which is inherently difficult to make and sustain. Hence the confident individualism of the professional can actually be reinforced by administrative process.

A third set of economic considerations are introduced by the statutory competition provisions themselves. A determination of the effect of an agreement on competition and inter-state trade requires a full analysis of the economic sector including the producer structure and the market. The necessity for this to be undertaken scrupulously and conscientiously, in both Article 85, 86 and state aids cases has consistently been underlined by European Court judgements. This approach prohibits a narrow legal interpretation and since economic principles are even vaguer than legal principles it demands an individual assessment of each case which to that extent becomes unique. There are consistencies across cases, and the ability of lawyers to think laterally and perceive them can be startling. But apart from some deliberate attempts at categorisation (as with franchising, patents or distributive agreements) the level of routine is low.

A fourth influence is that of power. As remarked earlier, DG IV has the most direct and independent power to be found within the Commission. Many cases are sizeable and important in their own right, while establishing a legal principle in a minor case may equally have wide ramifications. Officials are very aware of their power, indeed, this no doubt enhances their commitment and job satisfaction. Hence when they engage in evaluation of a case they are engaged in an individual judgement which again could be termed 'quasi-judicial'.

The intermixture of these several influences produces, it is argued, a distinctive administrative style and a distinctive organisation. There has been a metamorphosis to a 'regulatory' form of competition policy. The EC has succeeded in creating an impressive 'federal agency' whose operation provides one model for the administrative apparatus of the presumptive European federal state.

REFERENCES

Allen, D. (1977), 'Policing and Policy-Making? Competition Policy in the European Communities', in H. Wallace et al (eds.), Policy-Making in the European Communities, London, Wiley.

Baldwin, R. and McCrudden, C. (1987), Regulation and Public Law, London, Weidenfeld and Nicolson.

Belmont (1987), 'The European Community: 1986 Review and 1987 Prospects: A Competition/Anti-Trust Overview', Belmont European Community Law Office, mimeo.

Brittan, Sir Leon (1990 a)), 'New Ways for the Nineties' address to the Irish Management Institute, transcript, April.

Brittan, Sir Leon (1990 b)), Observations to the Directors General Competition Meeting, Brussels, abridged transcript, July.

Brittan, Sir Leon (1990 c)), 'The Principles and Practice of Merger Policy in the European Community', address at the Centre for European Policy Studies, Brussels, September.

Butt, Phillip A. (1988), Implementing the European Internal Market: Problems and Prospects, RIIA Discussion Paper 5, Chatham House.

Competition Law (1986), Commission of the EC, Competition Law in the EEC and in the ECSC, Compendium, Brussels.

Competition Rules (1987), Commission of the EC, Competition Rules of the EEC and the ECSC Applicable to State Aids, Compendium, Brussels.

Dawkins, William (1987), 'A Skilful run for the line' (profile of Sutherland), Financial Times, 28 September.

Dawkins, William (1988), 'Competition lawyers strike a bonanza in Brussels', Financial Times, 5 September.

Elland, W. (1990), 'The Mergers Control Regulation (EEC), No. 4064/89', EC Law Review, 3.

European Economy (1991), 'Fair Competition in the internal market: Community state aid policy', European Economy,48, Sept, pp.7-114.

Foster, G. (1990), 'Europe's Merger Maze', Management Today, July.

Fourteenth Report on Competition Policy (1985), Brussels, EC.

George, S. (1985), Politics and Policy in the European Community, Oxford, Clarendon.

Goyder, D. G. (1988), EEC Competition Law, Oxford, Clarendon.

Graupner, F. (1973), 'Commission Decision-Making in Competition Questions', Common Market Law Review, 10 (3) August, pp. 291-305.

Hancher, Leigh (1990), Regulating for Competition: Government, Law and the Pharmaceutical Industry in the UK and France, Oxford, Clarendon.

Henig, S. (1983), 'The European Community's Bicephalous Political Authority: Council of Ministers - Commissions Relations', in J. Lodge (ed.), Institutions and Policies of the European Community, London, Frances Pinter.

Jacobs, F. (1981), 'Jurisdiction and Enforcement in EEC Competition Cases', in D. Rowe, F. Jacobs and P. Jackson (eds.), Enterprise Law of the Eighties, London, ABA.

Joshua, J. M. (1987), 'Proof in Contested EEC Competition Cases: A Comparison with the Rules of Evidence in Common Law', European Law Review, 12 (5), pp. 315-53.

Kellaway, Lucy (1990), 'Tough Act of an EC Deal Maker' (profile of Brittan), Financial Times, 9 July.

Keohane, R. and Hoffman, S. (eds.) (1991), The New European Community: Decisionmaking and Institutional Change, Oxford, Westview.

Kerse, C. (1988), EEC Antitrust Procedure, London, European Law Centre, second edn.

Michelmann, H. (1979), Organisational Effectiveness in a Multinational Bureaucracy, Hants., Saxon House.

Nineteenth Report on Competition Policy (1990), Brussels, EC.

Official Journal (1988), 'Amended proposal for a Council Regulation (EEC) on the control of concentrations between undertakings', Official Journal, C130, Vol. 31, 19 May.

Schulte-Braucks, R. (1986), 'European Telecommunications Law in the Light of the British Telecom Judgement', Common Market Law Review, 23 (1) Spring, pp. 39- 59.

Seventeenth Report on Competition Policy (1988), Brussels, EC.

Swann, D. (1983), Competition and Industrial Policy in the European Community, London, Methuen.

Temple Lang, J. (1981), 'Community Antitrust Law - Compliance and Enforcement', Common Market Law Review, 18 (3) August, pp. 335-62.

Twentieth Report on Competition Policy (1991), Brussels, EC.

Van Bael, I. (1986), 'The Antitrust Settlement Practice of the European Commission', Common Market Law Review, 23, pp. 69-90.

Wilks, S. (1990), 'The Embodiment of Industrial Culture in Bureaucracy and Management' in S. Clegg and S. Redding, Capitalism in Contrasting Cultures, Berlin, de Gruyter.

Wilks, S. and Wright, M. (1991), 'The Comparative Context of Japanese Political Economy', in S. Wilks and M. Wright (eds.), The Promotion and Regulation of Industry in Japan, Basingstoke, Macmillan.

[12]

Journal of Common Market Studies
Volume XXVIII, No. 2 December 1989
0021-9886 $3.00

The Permanent Representations of the Member States to the European Communities

FIONA HAYES-RENSHAW, CHRISTIAN LEQUESNE
and PEDRO MAYOR LOPEZ*

Over fifteen years ago, the Carnegie Endowment for International Peace undertook a major research project on 'Permanent Missions Accredited to International Organisations' (Virally *et al.*, 1971–6).[1] It was perceived that, although they were an integral part of national administrations, permanent missions seemed to participate fully in the decision-making processes of international organizations. As such, they appeared to be in the privileged position of straddling the national and international bureaucracies simultaneously. The case of the European Communities (EC) was analysed by Jean Salmon in the first volume, which appeared in 1971, but no systematic work has been done specifically on this topic since then.[2]

This article aims to fill the existing lacuna of information and bring what is known about these EC bodies up to date, by looking in turn at the history of their creation, the way in which they are organized internally today, and finally the role they play in the elaboration and negotiation of the national

* Fiona Hayes-Renshaw is completing a PhD thesis on COREPER at LSE, Christian Lequesne works at the Centre d'Etudes de Relations Internationales in Paris, and Pedro Mayor-Lopez works at the Ministry of Economic Affairs in Madrid. The main body of this article was written while all three were attending the College of Europe, Bruges in 1986–7. The chief source of material for the study was a series of interviews with officials from the three permanent representations, the Commission, the General Secretariat of the Council of Ministers, and members of the national administrations in Dublin, Madrid and Paris. The authors are grateful to Dr Helen Wallace and Dr Geoffrey Edwards who have commented on earlier versions of this article.

[1]Though interesting as a first introduction to the role of the permanent representations, the data in both these studies is now somewhat out of date, albeit useful for comparative purposes. However, some of their general conclusions hold true today.

[2]Several studies have been devoted to COREPER, however. See the references at the end of this article for sources. There has been no recent study on the Council of Ministers.

position in the Council of Ministers. The aim is to document the important and complex nature of the role played by officials of national permanent representations to international organizations, the EC being a rather special case.

Since it is impossible to deal with all 12 Member State delegations in this article, three Member States — France, Ireland and Spain — which differ in a number of significant ways, have been chosen as a type of microcosm of the Community. Useful generalizations can be drawn from this study. The differences between them are largely a result of size, length of membership of the EC and national political characteristics. Although each of the delegations has the same functions to perform, and each conforms to a basically similar model, the organization, functioning and status of Member States' permanent representations will differ according to national attitudes, practices and priorities.

THE CREATION OF THE PERMANENT REPRESENTATIONS

Legal Basis and Evolution

The institution of permanent representations of the Member States is only indirectly provided for in the Community Treaties. The Treaty of Paris setting up the European Coal and Steel Community (ECSC) was silent on the subject; nonetheless,

> [f]rom the time of the first Council session in September 1952, the prevailing impression was that the Council would not be able to take decisions quickly unless they had been properly prepared. (Houben, 1964: 138)

As a result, the Special Council of Ministers decided to create a 'Co-ordination Committee' (Comité de Co-ordination — COCOR) in February 1953, under Article 10 of its provisional internal rules of procedure. This Committee, which met for the first time on 5 March 1953, had a double function: to prepare the Council's meetings and to undertake any studies commissioned by the Ministers. In order to do this, COCOR created a certain number of technical working groups, such as the committee on railways and the committee on customs problems.

The efficiency and usefulness of the Committee quickly became apparent; its work, which was of a purely preparatory nature, ensured 'more continuous and efficient ministerial action' (Delhaye, 1971: 8). However, the Committee met only about once a month, with the result that delegations were visiting, rather than permanent, and were not therefore viewed as a threat by the members of the High Authority.

Despite the generally positive experience with COCOR, analogous committees were not explicitly provided for in the 1957 Treaties, although Articles 151 EEC and 121 Euratom laid down that the internal rules of procedure of the Council '*may* provide for the creation of a committee composed of representatives of the Member States' (emphasis added).[3] The omission can be traced back to the negotiations which preceded the establishment of the two new Communities.

The question of whether the members of the EC and Euratom Councils could send representatives in their place, thereby necessitating the creation of a permanent substitute body in Brussels, first arose at the intergovernmental conference convened in 1956 to draft the treaties for the new Communities.[4] There was a general realization that the enormous amount of detailed and time-consuming work required of the Council in order to achieve the tasks set out in the Treaties would benefit greatly from advance preparation by a committee of representatives of each of the Member States.

However, there was disagreement as to whether such a body should be a committee of ministerial deputies, or a group of officials with a purely administrative preparatory function. The Ministers of Foreign Affairs finally opted for a less precise formula, which appears in both of the Rome Treaties: the creation of a 'committee of representatives of the Member States', whose tasks and competences would be decided by the Council.[5]

The members of the interim committee continued to work *de facto* under the title of 'qualified representatives' after the entry into force of the Rome Treaties. The function of 'permanent representative' was officially instituted by the Ministers of Foreign Affairs at a meeting on 6–7 January 1958, as was the Committee of Permanent Representatives, generally known by its French acronym, COREPER.[6] Each of the Member States then appointed its permanent representative to the Communities, beginning with Italy and Luxembourg in February 1958, and ending with West Germany in June of the same year. Each Ambassador was surrounded by a team of national officials and the permanent representations were formed.

[3]In fact, a committee had already been created before 1 January 1958, the date on which the Treaties of Rome officially came into force. This was known as the 'interim committee' and was created by the Ministers of Foreign Affairs at the official signature of the Treaties on 25 March 1957. Its remit was to prepare the entry into force of the Treaties and it consisted of the heads of the national delegations attending the intergovernmental conference — i.e. senior officials from each of the Member States.

[4]The decision to convene such a conference was taken by the Ministers of Foreign Affairs of the Six at the Venice conference on 28 May 1956. This decision was taken on the basis of a recommendation from an intergovernmental committee, headed by the Belgian Foreign Minister, Paul-Henri Spaak, which had in turn been created by the Foreign Ministers meeting in Messina on 1 and 2 June, 1955. The committee had been charged with studying the ways in which a new phase on the way to European integration could be set in motion.

[5]Articles 151 EEC and 121 Euratom.

[6]This Committee has so far been composed of the heads (who are of ambassadorial rank) of the permanent representations, even though this linkage was never laid down by the founding fathers.

122 THE PERMANENT REPRESENTATIONS OF THE MEMBER STATES

Formation of the French, Irish and Spanish Permanent Representations

Legally, the permanent representations are diplomatic missions created by a unilateral act of the relevant government. In fact, there is no accrediting procedure in the strict sense for permanent representations to international organizations, including the EC; Member States are free to set up such bodies if they so wish, and letters of credence are not required.

There is no explicit mention of the privileges and immunities to be accorded to permanent representations in any text of the Treaties. Yet their status needed to be decided upon at an early stage, since it would determine the seniority of the persons sent to head and staff these bodies. The Belgian government eventually decided that Article 10 of the Rome Treaty's Protocol on Privileges and Immunities[7] would apply to the permanent representations of the Member States. As a result, these bodies and their members have enjoyed the same rights as traditional embassies on Belgian territory since 1958. These provisions do not apply to the Belgian delegation.

As one of the founder members of the EC, France's permanent representation in Brussels dates back to April 1958, when the first French permanent representative to the EEC and Euratom took up office, surrounded by a team of several officials, most of whom were diplomats. It was only during the period of office of the third Permanent Representative, Jean-Marc Boegner,[8] that the French mission began to take on its present administrative structure. As he wished to

> abstract himself sufficiently from the technicality of the dossiers (which he understood very well) in order to get a clear and political overview of the situations which arose. (de l'Ecotais in Rideau *et al.*, 1975: 411)

he sought to delegate power by adding further advisers, including diplomats and officials from the technical ministries in Paris — a practice which became more widespread among all the Member States. By the time he was replaced in February 1972 — the year of the Community's first enlargement — the French permanent representation had acquired its present organization, rhythm of work and its relationship with Paris.

Ireland officially joined the European Communities on 1 January 1973, along with Denmark and the UK. However, Dublin had requested the opening of diplomatic negotiations with the Communities as far back as 1959

[7]This article became Article 11 of the Protocol on the Privileges and Immunities of the European Communities annexed to the Treaty on the Merger of the Executives of 8 April 1965.

[8]The periods of office of each of the French permanent representatives to date are as follows: Eric De Carbonnel (1958–9); Georges Gorse (1959–61); Jean-Marc Boegner (1961–62); Etienne Burin des Roziers (1972–5); Jean-Marie Soutou (1975–7); Luc de la Barre de Nanteuil (1977–82); Jacques Leprette (1982–5); Luc de la Barre de Nanteuil again (1985–6), François Scheer (1986–8) and Philippe Louet (1988 to the present).

(Coombes, 1983). A permanent mission to the Communities, attached to the Irish Embassy to Belgium and Luxembourg (which was located in Brussels), was set up to monitor and keep abreast of developments in the EC. An official request for accession was made in 1961, but it was rejected in 1963 at the same time as the British candidature. Since Dublin regarded membership of the Communities as merely a matter of time, the Irish permanent mission was detached from the embassy in 1967 and became an independent body, its main task being that of negotiating Irish accession. The three or four senior officials from the Ministries of Foreign Affairs and Agriculture were quickly joined by other colleagues from Dublin. On the eve of accession, the Irish mission consisted of about 20 officials — a number which has remained fairly static over the years.[9]

As in the Irish case, the Spanish permanent mission to the European Communities predated its membership; it existed from 1964 onwards, and became an independent body in 1970. After the establishment of the constitutional monarchy, the Suarez government made its official request for accession on 25 July 1977. The permanent mission became Madrid's main posting during the nine years of negotiation, along with a task-force set up in Madrid. It was composed mainly of diplomats, who enjoyed a considerable degree of autonomy of decision, in some senses greater than at present. The permanent representation, created by royal decree in January 1986,[10] is headed by a career diplomat.[11]

This short description of the background to and creation of the three permanent representations under analysis has provided a first indication of the perceived importance of their role. This is further reflected in the way in which each representation is organized and the functions attributed to it.

COMPOSITION AND ORGANIZATION OF THE PERMANENT REPRESENTATIONS

Although they are essentially national bodies, each of the permanent representations has the same two major functions to fulfil — representing the views of their Member State in Brussels, and keeping the capital informed about what is happening in the Community. Each is organized in a broadly similar fashion, although their numbers differ, as does the mix between diplomats and other officials (see Table 1). These divergences are the result of geographic factors on the one hand, and national priorities and characteristics on the other.

[9] The periods of office of the Irish permanent representatives to date are as follows: Sean Kennan (several months during 1973); Brendan Dillon (1973–82); Andrew O'Rourke (1982–6); John Campbell (1986 to the present).

[10] Royal Decree No. 260/1986, *Boletin Oficial des Estado*, 13.02.1986.

[11] Ambassador Carlos Westendorp y Cabeza.

Table 1
Officials in the Permanent Representations, 1988

	Total no. of officials	Diplomats no. (%)		Technicians no. (%)	
Spain	32	11	34	21	66
France	28	11	39	17	61
Ireland	24	11	46	13	54
Average of the 3		11	40	17	60
Total Community	383	156	41	227	59

The total number of personnel[12] in each of the three permanent representations under analysis varies: the Spanish mission has 103 people, the French 60 and the Irish 53. During the period of the Presidency, held by each Member State in turn for a period of six months, these figures may show a slight increase, although again differences will be a result of such factors as geography, experience and different attitudes towards the Presidency. (For more information on the Presidency, see Edwards and Wallace, 1977 and, more recently, O'Nuallain and Hoscheit, 1985.)

Spain undertook its first Presidency of the Communities in 1989 (1 January–30 June); it is therefore impracticable as yet to attempt to gauge the possible repercussions on its administrative organization as a result of this responsibility. In the case of Ireland, about six extra officials are sent to Brussels for the duration of the Irish Presidency, i.e. an increase of about 25 per cent. So far, there has been no similar provision in the French case.

The relatively small number of French officials is striking[13] and can be at least partly explained by the geographical proximity of the French and Belgian capitals; the French team in Brussels can be quickly augmented by Paris-based officials, when necessary. The Spanish representation was staffed by 48 officials in 1987 (making it second only to the 59 strong Greek mission), partly because, as a new Member State, there was a need to educate as many of their officials as possible in a relatively short time about the Community, and partly because of the distance separating Madrid from Brussels.

The number of administrative-grade officials can, in turn, be divided into diplomats and line-department officials (or technicians), the mix providing interesting insights into the perceived functions of the representations, and the interests and priorities of each of the Member States. It is interesting to

[12]Including all categories, both administrative and secretarial.

[13]The numbers are as follows for the other large Member States: West Germany — 42, Italy — 36, and the UK — 40.

note that a greater number of officials from the line departments than career diplomats is evident in each of the three cases, as well as across the Community as a whole.[14] This can no doubt be explained by the fact that highly-detailed technical Community dossiers cover an increasing range of issues and can take considerably longer than the relatively short-lived negotiations required for accession — thereby necessitating a greater complement of 'specialists' than 'generalists' on the spot to protect national interests. Given this tendency, it is significant that the post of permanent representative has continued to be held by a senior 'generalist' from each Member State's Ministry of Foreign Affairs.

Thirdly, it is interesting to note that Ireland has above-average numbers of diplomats and, consequently, below-average numbers of technicians in its permanent representation. This is obviously not accidental, but the reasons for the discrepancy are not clear. There may be a problem of recruitment — career diplomats generally have better language skills than officials from the line departments, but intensive language courses should have solved this problem by now. Line department officials may be more reluctant than diplomats to move to Brussels for a tour of duty, but younger officials at least are generally fairly mobile. It is much more likely that this paucity of Irish technicians in Brussels is a consequence of the smallness of the national administration and, perhaps to a lesser degree, what may be perceived as the relatively few areas of really vital national interest touched on by the EC; thus, the technical experts remain in Dublin and attend regular meetings in Brussels when necessary, leaving the day-to-day work to a small group of less specialized officials in the representation.

The facts and figures which emerge from this table emphasize a general characteristic of the work of the permanent representations which differentiates them from traditional diplomatic posts: protection of their nationals does not form part of the work of the permanent representations, and they have only a residual representational role. Instead, their task is the permanent negotiation of extremely technical dossiers. The resulting need for sectoral specialists from the technical ministries hints clearly at an infringement of the diplomats' traditional monopoly in dealing with international affairs.

The Permanent Representatives, as a general rule, are career diplomats, because of the high premium put on expertise and negotiation as essential qualities for this post. Many have gone on to senior posts in other international organizations or, where the national system allows it, to political office. Their nomination is usually the result of a 'political' decision,

[14]This is an on-going trend, although the relative proportions across the Community are subject to slight changes from year to year: 1986 — 46 diplomats and 54 technicians; 1987 — 37 diplomats and 63 technicians (i.e. an average of 3 less diplomats and 3 more technicians for each permanent representation between 1986 and 1987, and just over 1 extra diplomat and 1 less technician per representation between 1987 and 1988).

in both the partisan and high-level meanings of the word, although the balance between the two may differ from Member State to Member State. Thus, the decision on the appointment of a new Permanent Representative will be taken at the highest levels.

Sympathy with governmental policy seems to be more of a determining factor for nomination in Spain and France than is the case in Ireland. General de Gaulle placed 'dependable' men in Brussels in the 1950s and 1960s, who were sympathetic to his policy of creating an intergovernmental Community with France at the helm. Likewise, in January 1986, the French Permanent Representative, Luc de la Barre de Nanteuil, was recalled to Paris for having criticized certain governmental decisions in private and above all, for not being 'dependable' in the context of future *cohabitation* (*Le Monde*, 5–6/1/86). In Ireland, the appointment is not partisan — long-established habits of national administration and the fact that membership of the European Communities is not an issue which divides the political parties, means that the Ambassador is chosen in Dublin on the basis of merit rather than political affiliation.

A large part of the Ambassadors' time is spent at meetings of COREPER, the origins of which have already been mentioned. At the beginning of 1962, the committee was divided into two parts which have continued to co-exist — the Permanent Representives/Ambassadors (COREPER II) and the Deputies (COREPER I). The distribution of dossiers between the two parts is decided by the President of COREPER II, with the help of the Council Secretariat. At present,[15] the Ambassadors are responsible for the following dossiers: external relations; energy; relations with developing countries; nuclear questions (Euratom); economic and financial matters; political co-operation; the statute of Community personnel ('important questions'); trade union questions; regional policy and institutional questions.

The Deputy Permanent Representatives, who often have the rank of minister plenipotentiary, are not necessarily career diplomats. While they are in the case of each of the Member States studied here, the German Deputy, for example, traditionally comes from the Ministry of Economic Affairs. Like the Ambassadors, the Deputies have a heavy workload, as they are responsible for the administrative co-ordination of the permanent representation. In addition, they follow all the matters dealt with in COREPER I — i.e. the budget; social affairs; transport; education; fisheries; environment; replies to written questions from MEPs; the statute of Community personnel; harmonization of legislation; freedom of establishment; the internal market; procedural questions; and industrial affairs.

[15]At the beginning of the last (Greek) Presidency — i.e. in July 1988 — some dossiers on internal market topics were given to the Ambassadors, in an effort to reduce the workload of the Deputies.

The functions of the career diplomats are allotted according to the traditional hierarchical system of modern embassies. They normally prepare the work of the Permanent Representative and the Deputy, ensuring co-ordination of the dossiers before COREPER meetings. However, their tasks cannot be reduced to a single horizontal function of co-ordination. The diplomats are obliged to follow the activities of many specialized working groups of the Council. Most of them have held posts in the departments or divisions dealing with the European Communities in their Ministries of Foreign Affairs, before coming to Brussels, thereby gaining sometimes considerable expertise. Within diplomatic administrations, the Community specialists constitute a very specialized body, to the extent that a French diplomat was able to say:

> In the Quai d'Orsay, there are about twenty specialists in Community affairs who rotate between the *service de co-opération économique*, the permanent representation and the SGCI.[16] It is possible to guess who will be the next Deputy Permanent Representative a few years in advance by looking at the grade, age and length of service of the candidates. (Interview, Paris, 18/6/87)

The officials from the technical ministries are recruited in the national administration for their particular competence in the Community domain, and often remain in the representation longer than the diplomats (for whom the posting is, after all, just one of several during their careers). They are placed at the disposal of the Ministry of Foreign Affairs by their own ministry during their term of service in Brussels. In the case of Ireland, they are actually seconded to and paid by the Ministry of Foreign Affairs; the French officials continue to be paid by their ministry of origin, and the Spanish arrangements are a mixture of the two.[17] About 10 line departments delegate officials to each of the permanent representations: agriculture, social affairs, economics and finance, industry, energy, environment, telecommunications, transport, etc., although the number and mix may obviously vary over time and between Member States, depending on priorities and current dossiers. The Ministries of Economic Affairs, Finance and Trade are most heavily represented (Spain — 10, France — 8 and Ireland — 7).

Despite the importance of the Common Agricultural Policy (CAP), there are relatively few agricultural counsellors in the permanent representations

[16]The SGCI is the *Secrétariat général du comité interministériel pour les questions de co-operation économique européenne*. It is attached to the Prime Minister's office, and is responsible for the day-to-day co-ordination of the position to be negotiated in the EC and the OECD (the Organization for Economic Co-operation and Development).

[17]These administrative arrangements may have implications for the loyalty of officials to their ministry of origin, officials in which may put pressure on them to report back directly to them rather than going through the centralized channels which are the norm for most Member States.

(Spain — 5, France — 2 and Ireland — 2). Since the control of the Commission's management of the market organizations rests with the capitals, the Member States are represented in the Commission's Management Committees by officials from the national Ministries of Agriculture. The agricultural counsellors in the permanent representations are basically involved in preparing new legislation for adoption in the Council of Ministers. Such work is largely done in the Special Committee on Agriculture (SAC),[18] which reports directly to the Council of Ministers, using the same procedural rules as COREPER. The latter deals with a limited number of agricultural dossiers, particularly those with financial or political implications.[19]

As a Brussels-based auxiliary of national administrations, the permanent representations are veritable administrative melting-pots. Different ministerial origins do not appear to give rise to traditional rivalries; the interdependence of the dossiers necessitates a horizontal approach by the different counsellors. For example, in the framework of the Commission's programme 'Making a Success of the Single European Act' (Bulletin of the European Communities, Supplement 1/87), the 'reform of the structural funds' dossier, which is being dealt with in the Council's *ad hoc* Structural Funds Group, is followed by a diplomat in the French case, and by a counsellor from the Economics Ministry in the Irish and Spanish cases.

There is, nonetheless, a certain mistrust of the experts who come from the line ministries who are often regarded as being too involved in their own narrow portfolio to have a horizontal vision. Conversely, national experts claim that permanent representations are not always rigid enough, that diplomats, rather than push national interests, 'go native' and end up being more understanding of the positions of other Member States than of their own. As an official from the French Ministry of Social Affairs put it:

> Our diplomats tend to be more docile than the negotiators from the other Member States. . . . It is partly because of this that France did not succeed in making its point of view prevail during discussions on the Vredeling Directive (Interview, Paris, 19/11/87).[20]

This mutual dissatisfaction begs the question of what the main role of a mission to the EC should be: to plead national interests, to interpret the

[18]This body was created by a Decision on 12 March 1960, at the same time as the decision was taken to speed up the pace of achievement of the CAP — *Official Journal*, 1960, p. 1217. To our knowledge, no detailed study has been done on the functioning of the SAC, although it has been mentioned in more general studies.

[19]The other main area which is not treated by COREPER is external trade negotiations, which are dealt with by a body set up for the purpose — the Article 113 Committee.

[20]The Vredeling Directive contained proposals to institute a form of industrial democracy throughout the EC.

views of the host country — or those of the Commission and the other 11 Member States. It is a debate which will probably never be satisfactorily resolved, since both types of activity are needed.

THE ROLE OF THE PERMANENT REPRESENTATIONS IN EC DECISION-MAKING

As the major channels of information on EC matters, the officials in the permanent representations are in a prime position to influence the formulation of national policy towards the EC. They have a role to play at all stages of the Council decision-making process (i.e. at the level of working groups, COREPER, the various Councils of Ministers and the European Council), and fulfil a number of different functions.

Informing the Capital

The permanent representation keeps the national administration informed about most of the meetings which take place in the context of the Community organs. This information can be official — i.e. gained from a meeting, or provided by one of the other Community institutions; it can also be informal — i.e. provided by an authorized source which was not obliged to transmit it (e.g. the minutes of the weekly meeting of the Commissioners or their Chefs de Cabinet, which are regularly passed to the permanent representations). Comments on clarification and suggestions of alternative options are added to the texts before they are sent to the capitals. The permanent representation thus acts not only as a central post-box for all documentation and correspondence exchanged between the Community institutions and the Member States, but also as a type of benevolent censor.

Each of the Member States has its own system of inter-ministerial co-ordination for the formulation of its position in the Council of Ministers. In France, the co-ordination of the national position is the preserve of an inter-ministerial organism, under the tutelage of the Prime Minister — the SGCI (mentioned above; Lequesne, 1987). In Ireland, a European Communities Committee has existed since 1973; at first, it was chaired by the Secretary, and later a Deputy Secretary of the Ministry of Foreign Affairs (Burns and Salmon, 1977; Hayes, 1984), but since March 1987 it has become the responsibility of the Minister of State at the Ministry of the Taoiseach (Prime Minister). Since May 1988 there is also a Committee of Ministers and Secretaries, chaired by the Taoiseach, which deals with issues relating to the internal market and structural funds. In Spain, the co-ordination of the national position is under the jurisdiction of the State Secretariat for the European Communities, which is attached to the Ministry of Foreign Affairs (Mayor Lopez, 1987).

The actual degree of participation by the members of the permanent representation in inter-ministerial meetings varies, and is important for three main reasons. First, it is an indication of the perceived importance of such officials, whose job it is to defend the national position, not only during meetings, but in the course of all their contacts with colleagues from other Member States. Second, it provides them with a much more direct means of influencing governmental opinion in the capital than is the case from Brussels. Finally, the greater the involvement of the official from the permanent representation in the formulation of the national position, the easier it will be for him/her to negotiate in Brussels, in that they will have a clearer idea of the national problems and the margin of manoeuvre granted to them, whether implicitly or explicitly.

Thus, the French Ambassador sends his Deputy or a counsellor to the meetings of the SGCI, while he himself is received once a month by the Minister of Foreign Affairs and more regularly by the junior Minister for European Affairs. He takes part in the monthly meeting at the Quai d'Orsay under the chairmanship of the Minister of Foreign Affairs, which prepares the French position for the General Affairs Council. Similarly, the Irish Permanent Representative attends the monthly meeting of the European Communities Committee in Dublin, where the Irish position on forthcoming dossiers is decided upon. In Spain, participation of the Permanent Representative in co-ordination meetings in Madrid is not envisaged in a systematic fashion although, given the usefulness of the practice, this may change in time. However, the Ambassador can meet the Secretary of State for European Affairs regularly, as the latter usually spends about two days of every week in Brussels.

In the event of inter-ministerial disputes, or when there is a need for arbitration, the political authorities tend to consult the Permanent Representative in his capacity as chief negotiator. He is viewed as the expert who understands the possible as opposed to the desirable. His job is constantly to set the interest of the capital in the context of a potentially feasible negotiating strategy, a task in which he is helped by the other members of the permanent representation.

Interpretation of Instructions

The margin of manoeuvre granted to officials in the permanent representations is difficult to assess with any precision, and will probably differ from dossier to dossier, depending on the interest of the Member State in that particular issue. In France, as for all Member States, the margin is limited or non-existent for important decisions of principle. A certain number of taboo subjects exist, such as the reform of the Community institutions, on which France's position is not negotiable. On those questions which do not have major policy implications, the SGCI indicates the objective to be achieved, leaving the permanent representation free as to the means of attaining it.

In Ireland, the process is less centralized. The positions to be defended are indicated by the national expert responsible for the dossier simultaneously to the Ministry of Foreign Affairs and to the counsellor dealing with the matter in the permanent representation. Thus, there is direct contact between the official from the line department and the official in the mission in Brussels. The latter sends the dossier to the Permanent Representative, who is officially charged with the conduct of the negotiations. The margin of manoeuvre of the counsellor in the representation is wide; he often moulds the instructions in the interests of the consensus in COREPER. Because of the more limited number of Community issues which are perceived as being of direct and vital national interest, the instructions from Dublin are rarely dogmatic. Almost the only exception is agriculture: instructions here are much more strict, and a Brussels-based official deviates from them at his peril.

The instructions which come from Madrid do not appear to have been very constraining as yet 'because it is so soon since our accession', as one Spanish official remarked (Interview, Madrid, 5/1/87). This may change as familiarity with the Community system increases, although the problem of adaptation to the necessities of Community negotiation still appears to affect other new Member States.

Officially, the members of the permanent representations are supposed to receive instructions only from the organs responsible for inter-ministerial co-ordination. In practice, they are in informal contact — mainly by telephone — with all the ministries in their national administration. The tendency for certain ministries to try to circumvent inter-ministerial co-ordination by exerting direct pressure on the Brussels-based negotiators is a fact of Community life. It happens regularly, particularly on the part of the influential ministries (foreign affairs, agriculture and economic affairs). In the Spanish case, attempts at short-circuiting seemed to be especially frequent in the early stages of its membership, with many contradictions between the instructions from the State Secretariat for European Affairs and those provided for the officials directly by their ministry of origin, particularly by the Ministry of Agriculture (*El Pais*, 10/5/87). Under such circumstances, the position of the Permanent Representative becomes even more critical.

Defending the National Position

The process of ministerial adoption of a Commission proposal for a Regulation or a Directive can be slow and is always the subject of hierarchical treatment. Prior to arriving before the Council of Ministers, a Commission proposal will have been examined in detail by one or more working groups of experts on the subject, as well as by COREPER I or II, depending on the subject area. During this pre-Council phase, the role of the Brussels-based officials is decisive, since they are the true spokesmen of their governments at the negotiating table.

The Working Groups.[21] COREPER is assisted by a large number of subcommittees and working groups, whose job it is to make an initial technical examination of the Commission proposals; indeed, a large part of the day of most days of the week is spent by a majority of members of the permanent representations in working groups. These groups are composed of officials from the Member States and a representative from the Commission; they may be permanent or *ad hoc*. As the Council Secretariat does not have an official list of all these auxiliary bodies, it is difficult to record them precisely, but they number about 190 at present.

The experts from the capitals have an important position in these working groups. In the case of the three states studied, there is a tendency to use national experts if the problem on the agenda is too technical for the Brussels-based expert, or simply if the ministry insists that one of its officials be involved (Ciavarini Azzi in Jamar and Wessels, 1985: 99–104). This is particularly true for agricultural dossiers, because of the absence of sufficient experts in the permanent representations.

COREPER. After the Commission proposal has been examined, the subcommittees or working groups prepare a report in which are indicated points on which agreement has been reached ('Roman I points' or *Points I*) and all other points ('Roman II points' or *Points II*), which are to be discussed in COREPER I or II depending on the subject matter. COREPER will normally ratify the 'Roman I points' accepted at the level of the working group and debate the questions on which the working group has not been able to agree. The possibility of sending the proposal back to the working group for more detailed examination is always present, and is frequently used. The Permanent Representatives and their Deputies are accompanied to COREPER meetings by advisers, either from the capitals or the permanent representations.

No actual voting takes place in COREPER I or II, this right belonging solely to the Council, which cannot delegate it to the Permanent Representatives or their Deputies. In practice, however, the members of these committees indicate how their Ministers will vote, and a dossier will usually not be sent to Council unless the necessary majority or unanimity has been

[21]Detailed information on the working groups which operate in the Council hierarchy is not readily available, with the result that the importance attached to these groups by those involved must be emphasized rather than demonstrated, until such time as the necessary detailed analysis can be undertaken.

obtained at COREPER level. On the whole, an effort is made to reach a consensus among the national representatives on every point on the agenda.

The Council. The Permanent Representatives and their Deputies make a different but no less important contribution to the rather more political phases of the negotiation in the Council of Ministers and the European Council. While the officials from the permanent representations do not have a direct decision-making role at this stage, they provide essential expert support.

The dossiers which are agreed upon by the delegations are placed *en bloc* on the agenda of the next Council meeting for approval by the Ministers without discussion — i.e. as 'A points' (*points agrées* or agreed points).[22] They concern questions of substance, but are often not of major political importance. However, they must obtain the prior agreement of the group of jurist-linguists, who ensure that the definitive text is translated accurately into each of the nine official languages of the European Community.[23]

The dossiers on which the Permanent Representatives or their Deputies have not been able to agree are submitted to the Council under the heading of 'B points', by which means COREPER suggests debate and decision by the Ministers. Provision was also made for a 'written procedure',[24] but the widespread use of the A points procedure has largely done away with the need for this method of decision-making.

The Permanent Representatives and the Deputies attend Council sessions. The question of whether they are entitled to vote in Council meetings is of particular importance, because the Single European Act has reinforced the possibility of moving to a vote. Article 5 of the Council's new internal rules of procedure, adopted on 20 July 1987, lays down that, from now on, the President 'shall . . . be required to open voting procedures on the initiative of a member of the Council or of the Commission provided that a majority of the Council's members so decides.'

However, this article has not modified the conditions governing the delegation of powers. In theory, this is only admissable 'in favour of another member of the Council' — i.e. the absent Minister is supposed to be represented either by another member of his government or by a colleague from another delegation. In practice, it is normally the Ambassador or the Deputy Permanent Representative who replaces the Minister. They present and defend the position of their government and are authorized to indicate how their delegation will vote. The President and the Council Secretariat ensure the respect of the rules on quorum — i.e. the presence of at least six

[22] It is estimated by those involved that more than 75 per cent of 'Council' decisions can be attributed to COREPER I (i.e. the Deputies), by means of the A points procedure.

[23] These languages are: Danish, Dutch, English, French, German, Irish, Italian, Portuguese and Spanish.

[24] In Article 6 of the Council's internal rules of procedure.

Ministers in the room. Although it is not a question of a delegation of power in the legal sense of the term, the Permanent Representative and the Deputy fulfil the function of spokesmen of the delegation in the absence of the Minister.

The European Council. When summits were institutionalized in the form of the European Council in 1974, it was decided that only Heads of State or Government and Ministers of Foreign Affairs would attend, as well as the President and Vice-President of the Commission (Bo Bramsen, 1982: 624–45). The Permanent Representatives, who are physically present at all sessions of the Council of Ministers, do not attend these meetings (see Bulmer and Wessels, 1987; Bulmer, 1985: 98–104). This does not mean, however, that they have no role to play there. The types of issues which have featured on recent European Councils (e.g. the Delors Package and movement towards Economic and Monetary Union) have meant that the Heads of State or Government are increasingly being forced to enter more and more into the technical detail of dossiers, making access to expert advice indispensable. As a result, the national delegations charged with advising the Heads of State or Government consist of a large number of advisers from the ministerial cabinets and the permanent representations, and the Permanent Representative is often responsible for their co-ordination.

Since 1975, only one adviser from each permanent representation — the so-called 'Antici person' (Hayes, 1984: 183–4) — has had access to the European Council meeting in the capacity of liaison officer between the Heads of State or Government and the national delegations. These officials belong to the Antici Group,[25] whose main task is the preparation of the agenda of the Ambassadors' weekly meeting; the individual members also normally become Presidency Co-ordinator when their Member State holds the Presidency. In the three Member States studied, it is a diplomat from the permanent representation who fulfils the important liaison function during European Council meetings, acting as yet another transmission-belt between the political, negotiating sphere and the administrative, advisory sphere.

CONCLUSION

In his contribution to a study of the Presidency of the Communities, Philippe Moreau Defarges (O'Nuallain and Hoscheit, 1985: 135) remarked:

> The attitude of each national administration to the construction of Europe, be it German or Italian, British or Danish, Irish or French,

[25] The Group is named after the Italian Deputy Permanent Representative who was its first chairman when it was set up in 1975, during the Italian Presidency.

sums up, illustrates — sometimes to the point of caricature — its traditions and its idiosyncracies.

This study of the organization, functioning and status of the French, Irish and Spanish permanent representations to the EC only partly confirms this view. It cannot be denied that national traditions and idiosyncracies have repercussions on both the formal attributes and the behaviour of these missions (e.g. overall figures in the representation and the degree of participation in co-ordination meetings in the capital), but these can be at least partly accounted for by other factors, such as geography. However, it is just as obvious that there are more similarities than differences between them, and experience has shown that such minor differences as exist can be assimilated at no greater cost than occasional grumbling on the part of other Member States.

Given the high degree of centralization of decision-making on EC issues in Paris (Lequesne, 1987), the French permanent representation is relatively small, and is relieved of a large part of the necessary inter-ministerial co-ordination which Community dossiers require. The more negative effect of this arrangement is that its members appear to have less margin of manoeuvre than their colleagues in COREPER, giving the French the reputation of being predictable, if sometimes intransigent, in Brussels. This state of affairs requires a head of mission who is sympathetic to the instructions he receives, with the result that the post of Ambassador to the EC has become an overtly political appointment.

The limited number of personnel in the Irish representation is a direct result of the smallness of the national administration in both numerical and spatial terms. The number of officials involved in Community decision-making is small, and all of the main government ministries are situated at a few minutes' walking distance of each other in Dublin, making co-ordination relatively easy. The style of decision-making is relatively informal, as all those involved are known to each other, and this lack of formality spills over to the treatment of Community business in Brussels. Lack of personnel was a problem for the Irish in the early years of membership, because of the large number of dossiers to be covered, but co-ordination has improved and the Irish members of COREPER appear to have a greater margin of manoeuvre than many of their colleagues. The fact that Ireland has a relatively limited number of areas of perceived vital interest no doubt accounts for a large degree of this flexibility.

It is clear that Spain is still searching for a way of enabling its administration to follow dossiers quickly and efficienctly. The only way for it to attain a cruising-speed in the conduct of Community negotiations is through the benefit of experience and an objective evaluation of its internal politico-administrative pecularities, particularly the vertical constraint exerted on the decision-making process by the need for the association of the autonomous communities (see Associacion Espanola para el Estudio des Derecho Europeo, 1985; and Moderne, 1987: 137–55). The Spanish authorities must also assess the strengths and weaknesses of its model as opposed to those of its partners, in the knowledge that it is not always possible to transfer processes directly from one national context to another.

While it is generally true that the members of the permanent representations are the trustworthy executors of the instructions from their respective capitals, they also feel strongly united by a tie of solidarity which manifests itself in efforts to 'help' colleagues bound by difficult instructions. Within the Brussels microcosm they form an administrative elite with extremely personalized relations, due to their virtually constant attendance of meetings. Subject to similar constraints from their respective capitals, their attitude towards the negotiation process gradually becomes ambivalent; the necessity to defend national positions is accompanied by a constant desire to see the debate reach a successful conclusion. If this requires 'giving in' on one particular dossier, it is in the knowledge that help will be forthcoming in the negotiation of another, because of the propensity to take decisions by means of 'package deals'.

Throughout their time in Brussels, the members of the permanent representations are in a position constantly to 'educate' their governments about Community processes. Despite many years of experience with the EC, many Member States still have to be persuaded that insisting on short-term sectoral interests can block all future negotiations — an understandable problem, given the different timetables of the national and Community administrations. The officials in the permanent representations are also required to fulfil what one author has called an 'irreplaceable role of filter or bridge' (Dewost, 1982: 33) between two groups with largely different interests — i.e. the experts from the Commission and the Member States on the one hand, and the Commissioners and Ministers on the other. It is a vital role for the conduct of Community affairs and one which the members of the permanent representations have fulfilled admirably in their individual ways over the years.

REFERENCES

Associacion Espanola para el Estudio des Derecho Europeo (1985) *La integracion de Espana en las Communidades Europeas y las competencias de las Communidades Autonomas* (Barcelona: Generalidad de Catalunya).

Bo Bramsen, C. (1982) 'Le conseil européen: son fonctionnement et ses résultats de 1975 à 1981', *Revue du Marché Commun*, 262, 1982, pp. 624–45.

Bulmer, S. (1985) 'The European Council's First Decade: between interdependence and domestic politics', *Journal of Common Market Studies*, XXIV, 2, December, pp. 89–104.

Bulmer, S. and Wessels, W. (1987) *The European Council: Decision-making in European Politics* (London: Macmillan).

FIONA HAYES-RENSHAW, CHRISTIAN LEQUESNE AND PEDRO MAYOR LOPEZ 137

Burns, B. and Salmon, T. (1977) 'Policy-making Co-ordination in Ireland on European Community Issues', *Journal of Common Market Studies*, XV, 4, June, pp. 272–87.

Ciavarini Azzi, G. (1985) 'Les experts nationaux: chevaux de Trois ou partenaires indispensables?', in J. Jamar and W. Wessels eds., *L'administration communautaire à l'heure des choix* (Bruges: Collège d'Europe/de Tempel).

Coombes, D. ed., (1983) *Ireland and the European Communities* (Dublin: Gill and Macmillan).

De l'Ecotais, Y. (1975) 'Les ministres et les représentants français', in J. Rideau *et al.*, eds.: *La France et les Communautés européennes* (Paris: LGDJ).

Delhaye, R. (1971) *Le Comité des représentants permanents de la Communauté économique européenne*. Dissertation for a degree in political science (Louvain: UCL).

Dewost, J. L. (1982) 'Le processus de décision dans les Communautés européennes', *Administration* (Paris), 17, September, pp. 30–8.

Edwards, G. and Wallace, H. (1977) *The Council of Ministers of the European Community and the President-in-Office* (London: Federal Trust for Education and Research).

Hayes, F. (1984) 'The Role of COREPER in EEC Decision-making', *Administration* (Dublin: Institute of Public Administration), 32, 2, pp. 177–200.

Houben, P. H. (1964) *Les Conseils des Ministres des Communautés européennes* (Leyde: Sijthoff).

Lequesne, Ch. (1987) 'Coordonner la politique européenne de la France', *Projet*, 206, juillet-août, pp. 41–54.

Mayor Lopez, P. (1987) *Inter-ministerial Co-ordination for the Formulation of the Spanish Position on Community Policies*. Unpublished research paper (Bruges: College of Europe).

Moderne, F. (1987) 'L'administration espagnole et l'intégration européenne', *Annuaire Européen d'Administration Publique*, IX/1986 (Paris: CNRS) pp. 137–55.

O'Nuallain, C. and Hoscheit, J-M. eds., (1985) *The Presidency of the European Council of Ministers — Impacts and Implications for National Governments* (London: Croom Helm).

Virally, M., Gerbet, P. et Salmon, J. eds., (1971–6) (Dotation Carnegie pour la Paix Internationale dir.), *Les missions permanentes auprès des organisations internationales* (Bruxelles: Bruylant, 1971–6), 4 vols.

[13]

LEGAL APPROACHES TO EUROPEAN INTEGRATION: THE ROLE OF COURT AND LEGISLATOR IN THE COMPLETION OF THE EUROPEAN COMMON MARKET

Alex EASSON
Professor at Queen's University, Kingston

It is surely of some significance that the Commission's White Paper, *Completing the Internal Market*,[1] devotes only eight short paragraphs, out of a total of two hundred and twenty-two, to the "Application of Community Law" and that the Court of Justice is not even mentioned in those eight paragraphs. Indeed, only four references to the Court appear in the entire document and in each case the reference is to what the Court has achieved in the past: no specific role at all was perceived for the Court in the completion of the internal market by the 1992 target date. The Court fares somewhat better in the Single European Act,[2] which provides for the creation of a new court of first instance[3] to deal with certain types of cases. But this seems to have been in response to an already excessive work load rather than to any expectation that the Court would have an additional burden to bear on the road to 1992.

All this is somewhat surprising, since there is widespread consensus that the Court has played a major part in the progress towards European integration to date and has probably been the most successful of the institutions in that regard.[4] Why, then, has the Court not been cast in a starring role in Europe's new spectacular production of "1992 and All That"?

Two explanations, which are mutually reinforcing, have been provided by Judges Pescatore and Koopmans. In his farewell address to the Court[5] of

---

[1]White Paper from the Commission to the European Council, June 14, 1985; Doc. COM (85) 310 final.

[2]Single European Act of February 28, 1986 (O.J. 1987 L 169/1).

[3]Arts. 4, 11, 26.

[4]See, generally, M. CAPPELLETTI, M. SECCOMBE and J. WEILER (eds.), *Integration through Law* (European University Institute, 1986) and especially the contributions of the editors (Book 1, p. 51), of F. JACOBS and K. KARST (Book 1, p. 200), and of M. CAPPELLETTI and D. GOLAY (Book 2, p. 308).

[5]Reproduced in *European Law Review*, 11 (1986), p. 3.

Revue d'intégration européenne/Journal of European Integration, 1989, XII, nos. 2-3, Canada.

which he had been a distinguished member for 18 years, Judge Pescatore recalled three distinct phases in the history of the Court. The 1960s was a period of excitement and drama, in which the Court issued a series of famous judgments defining the fundamental characteristics of Community law. In the 1970s the Court "defined and refined the legislative system of the Community." But now, in the 1980s, issues have become infinitely more complex and "the great questions of principle are resolved," leaving the Court to deal with a thousand and one problems of a more technical nature. Judge Koopmans, too, identifies three phases[6]: institutionalism, instrumentalism and minimalism. During the first decade, the Community legal system was established as a legal order in its own right. The cases of the second phase, the 1970s, generally did not concern institutional problems but dealt rather with the way in which the law can contribute to realizing the general aims of the treaties. To quote Judge Koopmans, "the Europeans first discovered the importance of law and legal institutions, and then found out how many interesting things you could *do* with the law."[7] But this was followed by a breakdown of legal optimism and a realization that the courts cannot by themselves achieve European integration. As a consequence, the third phase, the 1980s, has been marked by a "return to minimalism," or what might perhaps be described as a period of consolidation, in which it is the legal craftsman who is needed more than the visionary or the missionary.

The era of the judge as lawmaker thus appears to be largely past. In part, this may reflect a gradual change in the Court's own perception of its role and a collective retreat from judicial activism: certainly, there have been a few decisions in recent years in which the Court has appeared rather more cautious than might have been the case ten or fifteen years earlier. But essentially, it is submitted, this change of role results from the fact that the great questions of principle have indeed been resolved. Community law has been established as a distinct legal system, enforceable by and against citizens in their own national courts, through a process of "constitutionalization" of the founding treaties. Provisions of the treaties have been interpreted by the Court in such a way as to establish enforceable rights and obligations: in so doing, the Court has explored the limits of those provisions—some would argue that it has frequently gone well beyond those limits[8]—and has as a consequence defined the parameters of the legislative function. Whilst it is not intended to suggest that no new interpretations of importance can be expected from the Court, it does seem that, with respect to most of the provisions of the EEC Treaty which relate to the completion of the internal market, the Court has pronounced sufficiently to indicate to the legislature where it may not tread, and where it must act if further

[6]T. KOOPMANS, The Role of Law in the next Stage of European Integration, *International and Comparative Law Quarterly*, 35 (1986), p. 925.

[7]Id., at p. 928.

[8]See H. RASMUSSEN, *On Law and Policy in the European Court of Justice* (Nijhoff, Dordrecht, 1986).

progress is to be achieved. The third phase, then, must be primarily the era of the legislator.

I. THE CONSTITUTIONALIZATION OF THE TREATIES

For a lawyer, and perhaps for a political scientist too, the most striking feature of the European Community and that which distinguishes it most clearly from other international groups or organizations of states, is the essentially federal nature of its legal system. What are in their initial conception multipartite treaties have been transformed into constitutional documents[9] and the Court of Justice has evolved into a constitutional court.[10] That this is so is almost entirely the doing of the Court itself, for the "constitutionalization" of the treaties rests principally upon the twin concepts which it has developed, of the direct effect and supremacy of Community law.[11]

A. Direct Effect

The literature on the concept of direct effect is extensive[12] and it is not intended here to examine the jurisprudence in detail, but in order to demonstrate its fundamental importance in the system of Community law it is appropriate to trace briefly the evolution of the concept. To do so, one must return to the famous *Van Gend en Loos* case,[13] arguably the single most important judgment ever delivered by the Court and one of the turning points in the history of the Community.

The facts of the case were very simple. The Dutch government had increased the customs duties on certain products, contrary to Article 12 of the EEC Treaty, which had imposed a standstill obligation on the member states. The question posed by a Dutch tax court to the Court of Justice, under the preliminary ruling procedure of Article 177, was whether Article 12 had direct

---

[9]M. CAPPELLETTI and D. GOLAY, *supra* no. 4, at p. 309. See also E. STEIN, Lawyers, Judges and the Making of a Transnational Constitution, *American Journal of International Law*, 75 (1981), p. 1.

[10]It is clearly viewed as such by one former justice of the Court: U. EVERLING, The Court of Justice as a Decision-Making Authority, *Michigan Law Review*, 82 (1984), p. 1294.

[11]J. WEILER, Community, Member States and European Integration: Is the Law Relevant?, *Journal of Common Market Studies* 21 (1982-83), at p. 42. See also the observations of another justice of the Court, LORD MACKENZIE STUART, *The European Communities and the Rule of Law* (Stevens, London, 1977), at p. 16 ff.

[12]For a comprehensive study, see M. MARESCEAU, *De Direkte Werking van het Europese Gemeenschapsrecht* (Kluwer, Deventer. 1978). More concisely, see G. BEBR, *Development of Judicial Control of the European Communities* (Nijhoff, The Hague. 1981), Chap. 13; P. PESCATORE, The Doctrine of "Direct Effect": An Infant Disease of Community Law, *European Law Review*, 8 (1983), p. 155.

[13]Case 26/62, *Van Gend en Loos* [1963] E.C.R. 1.

application, in the sense that nationals of member states could claim individual rights based thereon. The Dutch government, which was supported by the governments of Belgium and Germany, accepted that the Article imposed obligations on the national governments. Consequently, it submitted, failure to fulfill those obligations might lead to proceedings against the offending state, but until such time as the state rectified its breach the courts of that state would be obliged to apply the offending national law. The Court, however, rejected this view and ruled that the obligation which the Treaty clearly and unconditionally imposed upon the member states gave rise to corresponding rights enforceable by individual citizens. In effect, an individual could rely upon the Treaty against an attempt by national authorities to impose a charge which contravened the Treaty.

Now the Treaty itself nowhere states what is to be the effect of Community law within the member states. It can reasonably be assumed that its authors intended some effect, otherwise there would be little point in Article 177 allowing or requiring national courts to seek rulings as to its interpretation, but these effects might have been intended to be extremely limited: treaty provisions are applied, to a greater or lesser extent, in most countries even if this extends no further than a rule of interpretation that ambiguities in domestic legislation be resolved in a manner which is consistent with the state's international obligations. The Court of Justice was thus faced with a clear choice, between a literal approach—that the provision, being addressed only to states, was binding only upon them—thus observing the principle that transfers of sovereignty are to be interpreted narrowly, and a goal-oriented approach, seeking by interpretation to further social, economic and political integration.[14] In choosing the latter, the reasoning of the Court showed "that the judges had *une certain idée de l'Europe* of their own."[15]

The impact of *Van Gend en Loos* becomes obvious when one considers what the Community would have been like without the principle of direct effect. In similar circumstances, the importer might have complained to the Commission that customs duty was being improperly imposed, the Commission would have made representations to the offending government, leading eventually to an action under Article 169 if the state did not remedy the situation, the Court would have condemned the infraction and, in due course, which might well have been five or six years, the offending legislation would have been amended.

All this changes as a consequence of direct effect. Individuals have an immediate remedy, in their own national courts, against the defaulting state. Moreover, there is the immense advantage, from the point of view of the public

---

[14]See RASMUSSEN, *supra* no. 8, at p. 12.

[15]PESCATORE, *supra* no. 12, at p. 157.

perception, that Community law is seen to come to the assistance of private individuals. As the Court itself observed, in *Van Gend en Loos*,

> [t]he vigilance of individuals concerned to protect their rights amounts to an effective supervision in addition to the supervision entrusted by Articles 169 and 170 to the diligence of the Commission and of the member states.

Individuals are thus given an incentive to raise issues of Community law before their national courts, which in turn may request preliminary rulings from the Court of Justice under Article 177. This affords the Court further opportunity to interpret the treaties and the secondary legislation of the institutions, thereby further defining and refining the concepts of Community law.[16]

Over the years, the original concept has been broadened considerably so that the capacity to create direct effects is no longer regarded as something exceptional possessed by only a few special provisions of the Treaty. Rather, it is, in the words of Judge Pescatore, "the normal state of health of the law."[17] The Treaty forms part of the legal order of each member state, and an inherent characteristic of law is that it is applied by courts where it is possible to do so.[18]

Two additional developments, both entirely the product of the Court's jurisprudence, call for a brief comment. Firstly, it has been established that it is not only provisions of the Treaty which are capable of producing direct effects. Regulations, directives,[19] and decisions adopted by the Community institutions, and agreements entered into by the Community with other states, may also in appropriate circumstances give rise to rights enforceable by individuals in their national courts.

---

[16]By the end of 1987, the Court had delivered rulings in 1,317 cases under Art. 177, and had decided 243 cases under the direct procedures of Arts. 93, 169 and 171. Since a high proportion of the latter concerned failure to implement directives, it is probably fair to say that about 90 percent of rulings on the interpretation of the EEC Treaty and secondary legislation have been delivered in Art. 177 cases, and that very few of those references would have been made had it not been for the principle of direct effect.

[17]*Supra*, no. 12 at p. 155.

[18]There are, of course, provisions which, by their terms, cannot be applied directly. See, for example, Case 203/80, *Casati* [1981] E.C.R. 2595, concerning the free movement of capital.

[19]As PESCATORE points out, the Court has never actually said that directives have direct effect, rather that they may produce analogous effects; *supra* n. 12 at p. 167. What is important is that provisions contained in directives may, at least in certain circumstances, be relied upon by individuals.

The importance of this development can be appreciated when one considers the delays which commonly occur in the implementation of directives and the frequency with which member states are brought before the Court, under Article 169, for failure to implement directives.[20] The directive is the instrument prescribed by the Treaty for attaining many of the objectives of the common market, and especially for the harmonization of laws, and is thus of particular importance as a means of completing the internal market. The fact that, if member states are derelict in their duty to translate directives into provisions of domestic law within the time prescribed, individuals may rely upon the directive in legal proceedings against the state—for example, refusing to pay a tax which should have been abolished[21]—makes it a far more potent instrument of integration than it would otherwise have been.

Secondly, the court has developed the concept that has come to be known as "horizontal" direct effect. The *Van Gend en Loos* case, as we have seen, was concerned with the question whether or not an individual could rely upon the Treaty as against a member state which was in breach of the Treaty, and the same has been true of the great majority of subsequent cases referred to the Court under Article 177 by national courts. The actual consequence of the principle of direct effect has generally been the non-application of some national rule, at the instance of an individual and normally in proceedings in which the other party is the offending government. This is described as "vertical" direct effect. However, a further question arose as to whether provisions of Community law could also have a "horizontal" effect—that is to say, could they create rights which one individual could enforce against another individual?

It seems to have been assumed from the very beginning that the competition rules, or at least the provision in Article 85 making void certain agreements between undertakings, produced direct legal effects between individuals.[22] Subsequently, the Court has found that other provisions of the Treaty may also produced horizontal effects; thus, Article 30 may be relied upon to prevent an individual enforcing a patent or trademark right, where to do so would result in a partitioning of the market,[23] and Articles 48, 52 and 57, which forbid discrimination against workers and self-employed persons who are nationals of other member states, in relation to employment and the provision of

---

[20]Over a seven-year period, 1975-1981, the Commission initiated 1,001 infringement proceedings against member states, of which 66% were for non-implementation: S. KRISLOV, C-D EHLERMANN and J. WEILER, Community Policy-Making and Implementation Processes, in *Integration through Law*, *supra* n. 4, Book 2, at 69. Normally, proceedings are commenced only in the more egregious cases of delay.

[21]See Case 8/81, *Becker* [1982] E.C.R. 53.

[22]This assumption was implicit in the first reference made to the Court under Art. 177; Case 13/61, *Bosch* [1962] E.C.R. 45.

[23]Case 78/70, *Deutsche Grammophon* [1971] E.C.R. 487; Case 15/74, *Centrafarm* [1974] E.C.R. 1147.

services, are binding not only on states but also on employers, trade associations, professional bodies and the like.[24] And in *Defrenne*—perhaps the most controversial of all the Court's rulings[25]—horizontal effect was extended to Article 119, requiring the application of the principle that men and women should receive equal pay for equal work. The Court's ruling effectively conferred rights upon individuals, enforceable against their employers, which were not dependent upon the introduction of implementing legislation on the part of their national governments.[26] Recently, however, the Court has adopted a more cautious stance—perhaps reflecting its new "minimalist" role—in denying horizontal effects to directives.[27]

B. The Supremacy of Community Law

Direct effect ensures that Community law is operative within the legal order of the member states: it does not, of itself, establish the status of Community law within the hierarchy of applicable legal norms, for although the *Van Gend en Loos* case was essentially concerned with the question whether the new Dutch tariff prevailed over the Treaty, the supremacy of the Treaty—once it was established that it had direct effect—resulted from the provisions of the Dutch Constitution. The supremacy of Community law over conflicting national law was most clearly articulated in the famous decision, *Costa v. ENEL*,[28] which concerned the validity of Italian legislation adopted after the EEC Treaty had entered into force. The Italian *Corte Costituzionale* had taken the view that, although the provisions of the Treaty were effective, the earlier obligation must give way to the subsequent law in accordance with the principles governing the succession of laws in time; *lex posterior derogat legi priori*. The Court of Justice, however, ruled that the EEC Treaty had created its own legal order, whereby member states had restricted their sovereign rights, with the result that a subsequent unilateral law may not prevail if it is incompatible with the aims of the Community. This principle of supremacy was clearly reaffirmed in a subsequent reference from an Italian court,[29] in which it was ruled that the national courts are obliged to set aside any provision of national law that conflicts with Community law, whether prior to or subsequent to the Community rule, even where the national constitutional law permits only

---

[24]Case 36/74, *Walrave* [1974] E.C.R. 1405; Case 13/76, *Dona* [1976] E.C.R. 1333.

[25]Case 43/75, *Defrenne* [1976] E.C.R. 455.

[26]The consequences of the ruling were potentially so far-reaching that the Court took the exceptional step of restricting the temporal effect of its decision.

[27]Case 152/84, *Marshall* (decision of February 26, 1986).

[28]Case 6/64, *Costa* [1964] E.C.R. 585.

[29]Case 106/77, *Simmenthal* [1978] E.C.R. 629.

the Constitutional Court of that country to declare a law to be invalid. Community law thus prevails even over national constitutional law.

C. Preemption and Fundamental Rights

Although the principles of direct effect and supremacy are justly regarded as the cornerstones of the system of Community law, two further principles have been evolved and form important elements in the process of constitutionalization. The doctrine of preemption has been described as "the third hallmark of normative supranationalism,"[30] though its limits have yet to be fully circumscribed.[31] In its purest form, the doctrines of direct effect and of supremacy are taken a stage further; in relation to those areas in which the Community has been given or has assumed policy-making competence, the member states are not only precluded from enacting legislation conflicting with Community law but are preempted from taking any action at all. The jurisprudence of the Court provides support for this proposition, at least with respect to the external competence of the Community and of the member states;[32] in purely internal situations the position is less clear.[33] In some instances, national legislation has apparently been struck down because it has trespassed into a field already "occupied" by the Community; in others, on the narrower ground that it is incompatible with existing Community law or established policy.

Since the completion of the internal market does not seem to be dependent upon the existence of a principle of preemption—at least not in the same way that direct effect and supremacy are crucial—further discussion is not called for here. The same may be said of fundamental rights. Although the treaties are silent on the matter, the Court has, in a series of decisions,[34]

---

[30] J. WEILER, The Community System: the Dual Character of Supranationalism, *Yearbook of European Law* 1 (1981), at p. 277.

[31] For a penetrating analysis, see M. WAELBROECK, The Emergent Doctrine of Community Preemption—Consent and Re-Delegation, in T. SANDALOW and E. STEIN, *Courts and Free Markets* (Oxford, 1982), Book 2, at p. 548.

[32] Case 22/70, *Commission v. Council* [1971] E.C.R. 273; Case 41/76, *Donckerwolcks* [1976] E.C.R. 1921. See Further, R. BIEBER, On the European Communities and the National Legal Orders, *European Law Review* 13 (1988), p. 147; J. TEMPLE LANG, The *ERTA* Judgment and the Court's Case-Law on Competence and Conflict, *Yearbook of European Law* 6 (1986), p. 183.

[33] Contrast the decisions in Case 31/74, *Galli* [1975] E.C.R. 47; Case 50/76, *Amsterdam Bulb* [1977] E.C.R. 137.

[34] Case 29/69, *Stauder* [1969] E.C.R. 419; Case 11/70, *Internationale Handelsgesellschaft* [1970] E.C.R. 1125; Case 4/73, *Nold* [1974] E.C.R. 491. See further, J. WEILER, Eurocracy and Distrust, *Washington Law Review* 61 (1986), p. 1103; J. FROWEIN, S. SCHULHOFER and M. SHAPIRO, The Protection of Human Rights as a Vehicle of Integration, in *Integration Through Law, supra* no. 4, Book 3, p. 231.

imported into Community law the basic principles of the European Convention on Human Rights. This process, important as it is in the context of the constitutionalization of Community law, has relatively little impact upon the process of completion of the internal market.

D. The Role of National Courts in the Constitutionalization Process

The essential consequence of the constitutionalization of Community law is that it is in the national courts that Community law is applied. That is, after all, precisely what is meant by "direct effect." But to be effective, the process necessarily requires the collaboration of the national courts themselves—the principles articulated by the Court of Justice, especially the principle of supremacy, have to be accepted and applied by the courts of the member states. This has not been achieved without resistance in some cases,[35] but one should equally recall that the courts of other member states have played an active role in the process of constitutionalization.[36] And it is, of course, the national courts that must apply Community law, which can be enforced only by means of national procedures and the remedies that exist under national law.[37]

II. THE INTERPRETATIVE FUNCTION—DEFINING THE LEGISLATIVE PARAMETERS

Whilst the landmark decisions in *Van Gend en Loos* and *Costa* were handed down in the 1960s, the process of constitutionalization continued into the 1970s, with the confirmation of the direct effect of directives and the principle of horizontal direct effect. Meanwhile, the Court had embarked upon what Judge Koopmans has termed its "instrumental" phase.[38] During this period, the Court decided a number of cases that were not concerned with institutional problems, but rather with the way the courts could contribute to the realization of the general aims of the treaties.

---

[35] For example, the reluctance of French and German courts to accept the direct effect of directives.

[36] For example, the Belgian Cour d'Appel in *Fromagerie Le Ski* [1970] C.M.L.R. 219.

[37] See J. BRIDGE, Procedural Aspects of the Enforcement of European Community Law through the Legal Systems of Member States, *European Law Review* 9 (1984), p. 28; J. STEINER, How to Make the Action Suit the Case, *European Law Review* 12 (1987), p. 102.

[38] *Supra*, n. 6, at p. 927.

A. The Teleological Approach: Establishing the Four Freedoms

In establishing Community law as an independent legal order producing individually enforceable rights, the Court possessed *une certain idée de l'Europe*;[39] this vision seems equally to have guided the Court in its instrumental role in determining the precise contents of those rights. The EEC Treaty itself establishes the "four freedoms" which constitute the "foundations of the Community"—the free movement of goods, persons, services and capital; the Court, in its role as interpreter of the Treaty, determines the precise extent of those freedoms.

In performing this function, the Court has consistently adopted the principle of *l'effet utile*; the Treaty should be interpreted in such a way as to promote and attain its stated objectives.[40] A review of the jurisprudence would be superfluous here, but since the "four freedoms" are an essential part of the internal market, to be completed by the end of 1992, it scarcely needs to be observed that the definition of those freedoms is a matter of crucial importance.[41] One case, the famous ruling in *Cassis de Dijon*,[42] will suffice as an illustration.

The plaintiff in the original proceedings appealed against a refusal by the competent national authority to allow the marketing in Germany of a liqueur imported from France known as *Cassis de Dijon*. The refusal was on the basis of a statutory provision that fixed a minimum alcohol content for various categories of drinks. Cassis de Dijon had an alcohol content below the prescribed minimum. The importer alleged that this refusal, and the national legislation upon which it was based, contravened Article 30 of the EEC Treaty, and constituted a measure having an effect equivalent to a quantitative restriction on imports from other member states. The question referred to the Court of Justice by the *Finanzgericht* was whether legislation such as that fixing minimum alcohol contents for drinks, with the result that traditional products

---

[39] P. PESCATORE, *supra* n. 17.

[40] See further, F. DUMON, The Case Law of the Court of Justice: A Critical Examination of the Methods of Interpretation, and C. HAMSON, Methods of Interpretation: A Critical Assessment of Results, in the *Report of the Judicial and Academic Conference* (Luxembourg, 1976).

[41] On this, see P. VERLOREN VAN THEMAAT, The Contributions to the Establishment of the Internal Market by the Case-law of the Court of Justice of the European Communities, in R. BIEBER *et al.* (eds.), *1992: One European Market?* (European University Institute, 1988), at p. 109.

[42] Case 120/78, *Rewe-Zentrale AG* [1979] E.C.R. 649. Of the abundant literature on this case, see especially A. DASHWOOD, The Cassis de Dijon Line of Authority, in St. J. BATES *et al.* (eds.), *In Memoriam J.D.B. Mitchell* (Sweet & Maxwell, London, 1983).

from other member states could not lawfully be marketed, did indeed offend against Article 30.

The Court accepted that, in the absence of common rules on the production and marketing of alcohol, those were matters for the member states to regulate themselves. However, it ruled:

> Obstacles to movement within the Community resulting from disparities between the national laws relating to the marketing of the products in question must be accepted in so far as those provisions may be recognised as being necessary in order to satisfy mandatory requirements relating in particular to the effectiveness of fiscal supervision, the protection of public health, the fairness of commercial transactions and the defence of the consumer.

That is to say, where obstacles to trade are caused by national rules, those rules are inapplicable unless they can be justified and, for this to be so, those rules must serve a legitimate end and go no further than is necessary to attain that end. To quote Professor Dashwood:

> The Court was quite clearly talking about rules that do not discriminate between imports and domestic products but hinder the movement of goods simply because they differ from the relevant rules in the member state of export.[43]

Thus, it is not only rules which discriminate against the products of other member states that are prohibited.[44] In the absence of harmonization, national rules must be judged by a standard of reasonableness and will not be permitted unnecessarily to obstruct trade. Not only does this greatly expand the number of situations in which individuals may claim the protection of the Treaty but, as we shall see, it also has important implications for the Communities harmonization programme.

---

[43]*Supra*, n. 42 at pp. 146-47.

[44]Contrast this with the jurisprudence on freedom of establishment (Art. 52) and freedom to provide services (Art. 59). In the former case, the prohibition is against discrimination; see Case 221/85, *Commission v. Belgium* (decision of February 12, 1987). In the case of Art. 59, however, the Court has been more inclined to take the same broad view as with Art. 30, and to strike down unreasonable obstacles to the freedom to provide services even when these are not overtly discriminatory: see further VERLOREN VAN THEMAAT, *supra* n. 41 at p. 120.

B. The Relationship between Secondary Legislation and Directly Effective Treaty Provisions

In *Cassis de Dijon* the Court rejected the proposition that the prohibition contained in Article 30 should be restricted to those national rules which are discriminatory and, implicitly, that differences in national rules which interfere with the proper functioning of the common market may only be eliminated by way of the harmonization of laws. This was entirely consistent with its earlier ruling in *Reyners*.[45] There, the Court had ruled that the prohibition, in Article 52 of the EEC Treaty, against discrimination on the basis of nationality with respect to the freedom of establishment was an absolute one, once the transitional period provided for in the Treaty had expired, notwithstanding that the Treaty itself envisaged the adoption of directives to secure this freedom. According to the Court:

> The rule on equal treatment with nationals is one of the fundamental legal provisions of the Community. . . . In laying down that freedom of establishment shall be attained at the end of the transitional period, Article 52 thus imposes an obligation to attain a precise result, the fulfillment of which had to be made easier by, but not made dependent on, the implementation of a programme of progressive measures. The fact that this progression has not been adhered to leaves the obligation itself intact beyond the end of the period provided for its fulfillment. . . . After the expiry of the transitional period the directives provided for by the Chapter on the right of establishment have become superfluous with regard to implementing the rule on nationality, since it is henceforth sanctioned by the Treaty itself with direct effect.

One result of the decision was that the Commission scrapped a number of proposed directives, designed to secure the abolition of discrimination based on nationality, since these had become "superfluous." Henceforth, the task of the Community was seen as one of approximating those (legitimate) provisions of national law, where it was the differences between national rules, rather than the content of any particular rule, which impeded the freedom of establishment or the freedom to provide services.

The effects of the *Defrenne* judgment[46] were essentially similar. The direct effect of Article 119 meant that it was no longer necessary to try to produce Community legislation on equal pay; the focus consequently shifted to those areas beyond the reach of directly effective Treaty provisions, such as equal access to employment. And as a result of *Cassis de Dijon*, the Commission's

---

[45] Case 2/74, *Reyners* [1974] E.C.R. 631.

[46] *Supra*, n. 25.

entire strategy towards harmonization of technical standards was revised.[47] National laws which created obstacles to the free movement of goods, and which could not be justified according to the criteria laid down by the Court, had (in theory) become unenforceable; the Commission's work of harmonization would henceforth have to be directed mainly at those national laws impacting upon the common market which were not invalid by virtue of Article 30. Thus the scope given to Article 30, as interpreted by the Court, had impacted directly upon the role of secondary legislation to be adopted under Articles 100–102.[48]

Nor is the effect of the Court's rulings limited to rendering secondary legislation superfluous. It is axiomatic that provisions of the Treaty which have direct effect cannot be made to depend on a further contingency, such as the adoption of directives.[49] As a consequence, no derogation by any measure adopted by an institution of the Community will be permitted from a provision of the Treaty which is of a mandatory nature.[50] Secondary legislation adopted by the Council or Commission must be in conformity with the Treaty, with the result that Community regulations, decisions or directives may not sanction a violation of Community law on the part of a member state,[51] or otherwise modify the Treaty.[52]

The boundaries of legislative competence are thus effectively determined by the Court. On the one hand, through the exercise of its power to review and to rule upon the validity of Community acts,[53] the Court ensures that the acts of the institutions are in accordance with the Treaty. On the other hand, as we have seen, the interpretative rulings of the Court may have the effect of

---

[47]Communication from the Commission to the Council, published October 3, 1980; O.J. 1980, C256/2.

[48]See further, P. COLLINS and M. HUTCHINGS, Articles 101 and 102 of the EEC Treaty; Completing the Internal Market, *European Law Review* 11 (1986), p. 191; J. CURRALL, Some Aspects of the Relation between Articles 30-36 and Article 100 of the EEC Treaty, with a Closer Look at Optional Harmonization, *Yearbook of European Law* 4 (1984), p. 169.

[49]CURRALL, *supra* n. 48 at pp. 181, 185-87, and see Case 168/78, *Commission v. France* [1980] E.C.R. 347; Case 193/80, *Commission v. Italy* [1981] E.C.R. 3015.

[50]Case 15/81, *Gaston Schul* [1982] E.C.R. 1489. In cases of ambiguity the Court will consequently interpret a provision of a directive (or regulation) in a manner which is consistent with the Treaty, if this is possible.

[51]WAELBROECK, *supra* n. 31 at p. 571, and see Case 59/75, *Manghera* [1976] E.C.R. 91; Cases 80, 81/77, *Commissionaires Reunis and Ramel* [1978] E.C.R. 927.

[52]Case 12/74, *Commission v. Germany* [1975] E.C.R. 181; Case 24/75, *Petroni* [1975] E.C.R. 1149; Case 46/76, *Bauhuis* [1977] E.C.R. 5.

[53]Under Art. 173/EEC a direct challenge may be made as to the validity of acts of the institutions. Essentially the same issues may also be brought before the Court by way of requests for preliminary rulings on validity, under Art. 177.

precluding certain actions which the Community legislators might otherwise have considered taking.

III. COMPLETING THE INTERNAL MARKET: THE ROLE OF THE LEGISLATOR

The preceding sections of this paper have attempted to illustrate the extent to which the Court of Justice has been responsible for the promotion of integration within the Community. The treaties have been transformed into a constitution, which has become an essential part of the law applied by the courts in all of the member states, Provisions of the treaties have been interpreted in such a way as to create meaningful rights, enforceable by citizens in those courts. But there are limits to the extent to which the courts can contribute to the establishment of the internal market, and the courts cannot by themselves achieve full integration.[54] When these limits are reached, further progress must depend upon the legislators.

The limits, it appears, have for the most part already been reached. The Court is now widely perceived to be entering its minimalist phase, its main tasks completed, and the White Paper concentrates its attention upon the legislation which must be adopted in order to create a fully integrated market.[55] In the case of the free movement of goods, for example, it is thanks to the Court that national measures which discriminate against imported products, or which unreasonably restrict trade, have been eliminated;[56] but there are many cases in which it is the differences between national measures that obstruct the free flow of goods and cause partitioning of the market, without those measures being in any way contrary to Community law. In such cases, only harmonization can eliminate the remaining barriers. Similarly with the freedom of establishment and the freedom to provide services across frontiers. Discriminatory taxation, too, has largely been eliminated as a result of the Court's jurisprudence, but the elimination of fiscal frontiers requires not only the abolition of discrimination but also a relatively high degree of uniformity of tax systems and rates—something which can only be achieved by legislation at the Community level.

---

[54]KOOPMANS, *supra* n. 6 at p. 930; VERLOREN VAN THEMAAT, *supra* n. 41 at p. 123.

[55]*Supra* n. 1. The Annex sets out a timetable of well over 300 measures which must be adopted. For analysis of the programme, see especially, N. FORWOOD and M. CLOUGH, The Single European Act and Free Movement, *European Law Review* 11 (1986), p. 383; H. SCHMITT VON SYDOW, The Basic Strategies of the Commission's White Paper, in *1992: One European Market?*, *supra* n. 41, p. 79.

[56]That is not to say that such measures no longer exist; the number of infraction proceedings brought by the Commission against member states under Art. 169 is testimony to their persistence. But such measures can be challenged in the national courts and, if found to offend against Art. 30, may not be enforced.

The Court, in its role of interpreter of the treaties, defines the task of the legislator. It then rests with the legislator to choose the appropriate means of attaining the prescribed objective, subject to the proviso that those means must be consistent with the fundamental principles of Community law enunciated by the Court. Thus, for example, free movement of goods might be achieved in any of a number of ways:

(a) by the abolition of all restrictions upon importation and marketing of goods, or of certain categories of goods;

(b) by accepting the principle of mutual recognition—that is to say, each member state would prescribe its own standards (of health and safety regulations, consumer and environmental protection, etc.) but would permit the products of other member states which comply with the standards laid down in the state of exportation to be freely introduced into and marketed in its territory;

(c) by a modified form of mutual recognition, with the Community prescribing certain minimum standards to be applied in all member states, so that all goods produced in the Community would at least meet those standards and would be freely marketable;

(d) by adopting a uniform standard throughout the Community.[57]

Any of these approaches might be consistent with the principles of Community law.[58] It is for the Commission, the Parliament and, ultimately, the Council, as legislators, to determine which is the most appropriate and acceptable solution in the particular circumstance.

IV. THE RELATIONSHIP BETWEEN COURT AND LEGISLATOR IN THE PROCESS OF INTEGRATION

The importance of law in the process of integration is self-evident. As the editors of the monumental study, *Integration Through Law*, state:

---

[57] There are other possible solutions, which do not secure complete free movement but which nevertheless are probably not contrary to Art. 30/EEC; for example, separate national standards and a single Community standard could co-exist, with only those goods which meet the Community standard being in completely free circulation. For discussion of the various approaches, see R. LAUWAARS, The Model Directive on Technical Harmonization, in *1992: One European Market?*, *supra* n. 41, at p. 151.

[58] Art. 100A of the EEC Treaty, added by the Single European Act, Art. 18, now requires the *Commission*, in its proposals for harmonization concerning health, safety, environmental protection and consumer protection, to "take as a base a high level of protection." Whether this would permit the Court to strike down a *Council* directive, on the ground that it provided inadequate protection, is questionable.

> Integration is not a simple exercise in power sharing, but goes deeper and aims at a fundamental restructuring of society and of societal attitudes, and these changes are reflected in and promoted by the law.[59]

Law is not simply *an* instrument, but is *the* instrument, through which integration is achieved.

In this process, the legislator and the judge play complementary roles. Insofar as the function of the courts is to interpret and apply the laws promulgated by the legislator, the judiciary plays a supporting role; but in that the judiciary may ultimately possess the power to determine what the legislator may or may not do, the legislator may be perceived as an auxiliary, whose task it is to fill in the details in the grand scheme, outlined by the authors of the Treaty—or Constitution—as interpreted by the judges. Usually, the courts are more accustomed to playing the supporting role, and it is probably because the European Court has been perceived as so often playing the dominant role that it has attracted so much interest and attention.

To fully appreciate the respective roles of court and legislature, it is necessary to consider the dynamics of the Community. On the one hand are what may be termed the external dynamics—the relationship between the central, Community, competence and that of the peripheral member states. On the other are the internal dynamics—the interrelationship of the Community organs themselves.

Until comparatively recently, attention had largely been concentrated upon the Court's participation in the relationship between Community and member states. Inevitably, comparisons have been drawn with the role of supreme courts in other federal systems; two of the most influential compendia in recent years, *Courts and Common Markets*[60] and *Integration Through Law*,[61] have taken as their main theme such comparisons, and Professor Rasmussen's controversial study[62] also draws heavily upon comparative material. Invariably, such studies reveal the European Court to be unusually integrationist, or "federalist." Undoubtedly, this centrist bias derives in large measure from the Court's own vision of Europe, and for the most part it has secured the approbation of the critics, most of whom seem to share that vision. But this bias, it is suggested, may be justified on more objective grounds.

---

[59] *Integration Through Law*, *supra* n. 4, pp. 42-43.

[60] *Supra*, no. 31.

[61] *Supra*, no. 4.

[62] *Supra*, n. 8.

Generally, in federal systems, the supreme or constitutional court is required to hold the balance between central and regional interests. It must strive to preserve the union from disintegration, whilst protecting the constituent members from undue encroachment on the part of the central power. But in the European Community such encroachment is, or has been until the present, not a real danger. The power to legislate on behalf of the Community resides primarily with the Council of Ministers, that is to say with the representatives of the member states themselves, and since the so-called "Luxembourg Accord" of 1966 virtually all important decisions of the Council have in effect been taken unanimously.[63] For all practical purposes, therefore, any involuntary incursion upon the legislative territory of a member state is highly unlikely, if not impossible. In that sense, therefore, there is no balance for the Court to maintain. The only danger is that of disintegration and dissipation of the *acquis communautaire*, by the improper actions of the member states acting individually or in concert in the Council, and the Court is thus perforce cast in a centrist role. This is not to deny, of course, that it may play that role with greater or less vigor and conviction. In determining, for example, that Article 30 of the EEC Treaty prohibits not only those national measures which formally discriminate against the products of other member states, but also those which, while formerly neutral, have that effect, and that measures which incidentally have a discriminatory effect offend no less than those which are so designed, the Court made positive choices which displayed a centrist bias. Those choices, however, are largely perceived to have been legitimate ones.

More controversial, at least in recent years, has been the Court's internal, or institutional, role. In particular, as Rasmussen would allege,[64] the Court has become too deeply and too frequently involved in the political government of the Community and has, in effect, usurped the role of the legislator. As Rasmussen states,

> . . . the Court of Justice's lawmaking activities, defiant of much European tradition in that respect, were regularly preceded by deep involvements in making choices between competing public policies for which the available sources of law did not offer the Court judicially applicable guidelines.

---

[63]To what extent, if at all, this practice will be changed by virtue of the Single European Act remains to be seen; see further D. EDWARD, The Impact of the Single Act on the Institutions, *Common Market Law Review* 24 (1987), p. 19. If the practice does change, it will be interesting to see if this affects the centrist leaning of the Court.

[64]*Supra*, no. 8, at p. 508. For comprehensive critiques of Rasmussen's analysis, see M. CAPPELLETTI, Is the European Court of Justice "Running Wild"?, *European Law Review* 12 (1987), p. 3; J. WEILER, The Court of Justice on Trial, *Common Market Law Review* 24 (1987), p. 555.

Thus, in cases such as *Reyners*[65] and *Defrenne*,[66] the Treaty clearly envisaged action on the part of the legislature to secure the abolition of discrimination with regard to the freedom of establishment, and to promote equal pay for men and women; yet the Court was prepared to circumvent such action, or compensate for legislative inaction, by declaring Articles 52 and 119 to have direct effect. In the opinion of Rasmussen, these are cases of "blatant and unacceptable activism."[67]

Here again, however, the activism of the Court has to be viewed in the context of the institutional structure of the Community and the legislative paralysis which it engenders. Certainly, the Court has on many occasions assumed the role of legislator.[68] For example, Article 95 prohibits member states from taxing imported products more heavily than similar domestic products; if product A (imported) is taxed more heavily than product B (domestic), infraction of the Treaty can be remedied by:

(a) reducing the tax on A to the level of that on B,

(b) increasing the tax on B to the level of that on A,

(c) altering the taxes on both A and B so that they are now the same, or

(d) abolishing the taxes on both products.

Since any one of these methods would accord with the Treaty, it ought to be left to the legislature, exercising its power to issue directives for the harmonization of taxes under Article 99, to select the most appropriate or acceptable method. In that sense, for the Court to choose any one method is to usurp the role of legislator. Yet faced with inactivity on the part of the legislature, method (a) is the only practicable choice to secure compliance with the Treaty.[69] In other

---

[65] *Supra*, no. 45.

[66] *Supra*, n. 25.

[67] *Supra*, no. 8, at p. 29.

[68] Professor Cappelletti would prefer to describe the judges as "lawmakers," rather than as "legislators"; M. CAPPELLETTI, The Law-making Power of the Judge and Its Limits: A Comparative Analysis, *Monash University Law Review* 8 (1981), at p. 42. That is to say, legislatures and judges both have a part in the creation of the law. But in a real sense, Professor Rasmussen's charge, that the Court of Justice has acted as legislator, seems justified.

[69] That is so at any rate in the context of proceedings for a preliminary ruling under Art. 177. In such a case an individual will normally have contested, in a national court, a demand for tax on an imported item and will allege that the tax is contrary to Art. 95. Realistically, the national court can secure compliance only by reducing the tax to the same level as that imposed on similar domestic products or by dismissing the claim to tax entirely. It is different where the proceedings are brought by the Commission under Art. 169 against the member state. There, the Court can simply order the state to remedy the infraction, leaving it the choice of any one of the four methods.

words, of the range of options open to the legislator only some are available to the courts; a court can order that a tax assessed on a particular product be reduced, but cannot impose an increase of tax on other products.

As a result of this limited range of option, solutions prescribed by the Court are not always entirely satisfactory. Sometimes, indeed, they may be the direct cause of legal uncertainty which, in turn, can only be remedied by legislative action.[70] But if such uncertainty is to be deplored, it is not so much because the Court has usurped the proper function of the legislator, but rather because the legislator has failed to act where action has been necessary and required by the Treaty. If the Court has become too deeply involved in making choices between competing policies, it is primarily because the Council has been unable or unwilling to make those choices. In the great majority of cases in which the Court has assumed the role of legislator, the alternatives have not been action by the Court or action by the Council, but rather action by the Court, sometimes in circumstances where such action is contrary to the intentions of the authors of the Treaty, or where the Court lacks the means to secure an entirely satisfactory result, and the non-observance of the Treaty itself, bringing into disrepute the entire fabric of Community law. The Court would thus have been in dereliction of its duty to ensure that in the interpretation and application of the Treaty the law is observed.[71] In such circumstances, usurpation is to be preferred to disintegration.

---

[70]The most notable example of this was probably the decision in Case 57/65, *Lutticke* [1966] E.C.R. 205, which made the adoption of the common system of value added tax inevitable. In the same way, the *Cassis de Dijon* ruling, *supra* n. 42, can be said to have resulted in a state of uncertainty which can be remedied only by the adoption of directives for the harmonization of laws.

[71]Art. 164/EEC.

[14]

Between Self-Restraint and Activism: A Judicial Policy for the European Court

By Hjalte Rasmussen*

Associate Professor of Law, Copenhagen School of Commerce and Business Administration; External Professor, College of Europe, Bruges; and the European Institute of Public Administration, Maastricht

On court ideology and this paper's themes

The thrust of the social task of courts is to render essentially predictable judgments. According to most accumulated scholarship predictability flows from the availability of the following main characteristics of judges' adjudicative work. It is that from some "applicable," basically pre-existing and ideally neutral and principled norm, and following an adversary process, the independent judge, by utilising a reasoning dictated by pre-established thought-techniques—amongst which logic is of pre-eminence—arrives at a normally inescapable "winner-take-all" verdict which—except for a possible appeal—definitively settles the case and conflict brought before this court.[1]

This portrait is not solely descriptive. Instead, it is loaded with ideology. The ideal is that judicial authority and legitimacy flows from courts' simultaneous realisation of all the above-mentioned five core elements of the judicial task. In this perception, the more completely the ideal is translated into judicial reality, the richer is judicial authority and legitimacy believed to be. Inversely, without authority and legitimacy there will be no "court" in the ordinary sense of this word. Therefore, judges *ought to* live up to the ideal. The portrait has ceased to be solely factual and has entered the realm of deontology and metaphysics.

The underlying sociological rationale of the need for an ideal-type performance is, in Professor Dawson's words, that it meets society's "deeply felt and constant need for trustworthy neutrals." From an ideal-type performance, Dawson says, follows courts "peculiar power to enlist obedience and impose control." And he continues, "Neutrality and trust were not necessarily forfeited when judges made up the rules as they went along; as in medieval England . . . ." On the other hand the experience of France reveals that:

> "there are limits to the allegiance that judges can inspire. . . . The judges of pre-revolutionary France became partisans in political strife for a reason that seemed to them persuasive—that other political agencies had failed as restraints on royal absolutism. In their attempt to fill a great gap in French political institutions they brought disaster on themselves and caused a last-

* The following is the reworked text of a lecture which I gave at a conference organised by the Law Department of the University of Leicester on July 11, 1987.

[1] Martin Shapiro, *Courts* (The University of Chicago Press, 1981) offers an interesting analysis hereof.

ing impairment of their own function whose effects in France are not yet spent."[2]

This paper deals with the potentiality for *the emergence of an analogous "disaster"-problem* in Community law and society, that is one generated by the European Court's activist rôle-performance. The paper's focal points of attention are in this respect mainly on questions of methodologies of judicial (activism) research and on jurisprudence; it much less represents an attempt to offer a definitive reply to the question whether "disaster" resulted or not.

The European Community's politico-constitutional framework of the present enquiry is (at least) twofold. It is, on the one hand, commonplace that the political arms of the Community's governmental structure soon after their inception submerged in a bog of visionless quarrels about the administration of short term, adverse, mostly economic interests. In this process decisional supranationalism was wrecked in the face of powerful forces of centrifugalism and protection of States' rights.

Nor is there, on the other, any need to dwell at length here before the fact that the European Court in the meantime laboured strenuously to ensure that, despite legislative inertia, the Founding Fathers' visions about the emergence of an ever closer legal and political union on Western European soil become real. The European Court in the 1960s invented and distributed normative supranationalism[3] in an endeavour that peaked during the latter half of the 1970s. The European Court's pro-Community policy-making by and large has been a success-story in the sense that the European Court did achieve its main policy-objectives while not forfeiting, in many people's perceptions, neutrality and trustworthiness. The European Court probably even recruited some non-negligible political support for the Community régime. The success was less than a complete one, though. That lack of completeness merits academic attention and study, I submit.[4] Yet, at a place like the present space-constraints dictate that topical choices be made, sometimes hard but inevitable. Therefore, merely five themes *have* been retained for treatment below.

The themes on which I shall focus are: the thrust of judicial activism research; the proper rôle of the preamble and of judges' philosophy in judicial policymaking; the fact that a normative theory of interpretation of Community law is not a precondition for discussing meaningfully judicial excess of power; the advantages and disadvantages of a sociological method of measuring judicial border transgressions; and last, but not least, whether there has been actual unwarranted activism by the European Court?

Four fundamental premises of judicial activism research

Four fundamental premises underlie any judicial-activism research. The first is, as Professor Schermers has rightly emphasised, that "The Court's consti-

[2] The quotes are from J.P. Dawson, *Oracles of the Law* University of Michigan, Ann Arbor, Thomas Cooley Lectures, 1968.

[3] Joseph H.H. Weiler, "The Community System: the Dual Character of Supranationalism," in *Yearbook of European Law* (1981, I) on pp. 273–306.

[4] Hjalte Rasmussen, *On Law and Policy in the European Court of Justice. A Comparative Study in Judicial Policymaking* (Martinus Nijhoff, 1986) (cited in this paper as "Rasmussen") with further references. See also Mauro Cappelletti, "Is the European Court of Justice 'Running Wild?' " in (1987) 12 E.L.R. 3.

tutional rôle is enormous."[5] The second is intimately interconnected. That constitutional rôle is, nonetheless, not boundary-free. The European Court's judges should not be considered "a unique body of impervious legal technicians above and beyond the political struggle."[6] Yet, if a boundary does exist, there resides an interest in locating it. At the very least, its approximate location must be determined or understood by those involved in making judicial decisions or in commenting on their rôle in political integration. Judicial research has as yet only paid a limited attention to this problem.[7]

A comparative perspective constitutes the third premise. Indeed, as is well known, during the formative years of the American Union, the United States Supreme Court's constant *leitmotif* in adjudication of the nation's federalism conflicts was the Constitution's "more-perfect-union" declaration. The parallel between the American Court's endeavours then, and the centralising tendencies of the European Court's "ever-closer-union"-inspired case law some 150 years later, is self-evident. This is of considerable interest, because experience informs us that early Supreme Court's activism triggered widespread and often violent accusations that the Court was violating the Constitution's presumed balance of powers between the central and the local governments by steadily carving out State powers, thereby infringing on the States' rights. In so doing, the Supreme Court was believed to usurp constitution-making powers.

American constitutional history also informs us that several other confrontations between the Supreme Court and the political arms of government occurred at later points of time, following the Court's promotion of values that powerful segments of the body politic did not fully share.[8] At stake in each of these confrontations was the United States Supreme Court's authority and legitimacy. The fourth premise may be thus formulated: With hindsight we know that the American Court has survived all attacks. Today its prestige in American society is enormous and its authority is largely unchallenged.

In the European Community, no similar hindsight provides us with a similarly comfortable assurance that the European Court will emerge unweakened from similar confrontations with *its* countervailing powers, be they Community institutions or State-associated agencies or interests. No régime is likely to accept important political powers wielded by an isolated judicial corps free of political restraints. Indeed, if the European Court were to be seen to overstep the boundaries to its function and if court-curbing or court-destroying initiatives were launched accordingly, the European Court might well come out ruined in its authority and legitimacy. A day-to-day erosion of the European Court's authority and legitimacy would be ruinous too. Such outcomes would not be catastrophic solely for the European Court but for the entire Community experience, precisely because the European Court has been in the past an important source of Community regulatory legitimacy—a source which the Community could not afford to witness drying out under the weight of an uncon-

[5] Henry G. Schermers in preface to *On Law and Policy in the European Court of Justice*, cited in note 4 above (at p. XIV).

[6] Martin Shapiro *On Law and Politics in the Supreme Court* (Free Press of Glencoe, 1964).

[7] For a survey and analysis of most existing European literature on this subject, see Rasmussen Chap. 6.

[8] This comparative perspective is dealt with in more detail in Rasmussen especially Chap. 5.

trolled pro-Community activism. It is likely, I submit, that the Community also in the future will remain uniquely dependent on the Court for much of its integrational progress.

The thrust of the EC activism discussion

The entire activism discussion thus in a manner deals with the protection/destruction issue in relation to the European Court's original and accumulated authority and legitimacy. The paradox is probably unavoidable. At stake in any powerful promotion of political integration by judicial decision is always the court's unfettered ability to continue to promote precisely political integration. This is inevitably so because the European Court has to invent legal constructions to the political problems under adjudication with which enforcement agencies on Community and national level will comply; and because non-compliance and defiance is likely to flow from a perception of the European court as a usurper of political power.

On the limits to judicial law

An old English maxim says that society should be governed by law, not by man. Mechanical jurisprudence more than anything has paid tribute to that ideal. Yet few will dispute or regret that, today, mechanical jurisprudence is defunct. Closer to present-day understandings of courts, Lord Diplock observes that "Courts by the very nature of their function are compelled to act as legislators."[9]

What is, however, the scope of judicial discretion? It is not, and Lord Diplock does not suggest it to be, as limitless as our political lawmaking institutions' discretion to invent new public policies or to modify existing policies or to change hitherto established priorities between competing public policies and to embed them in law.[10]

Where lies the boundary and how may it be located? One inherited wisdom merits particular attention here. Indeed, we have both by judges and jurisprudential writers been told that a presumably fairly neutral and objective operation of a variety of methods of interpretation function to limit the judge's discretion. These arguably enlighten his choice in each individual case of the "correct" way to proceed to interpret the provision in dispute. Although not empirically verifiable—they are part and parcel of the realm of metaphysics—the methods of interpretation are believed to be more of the judge's masters than he, more realistically viewed, masters the concrete choice of method in a given case.

Since, however, we do not have reliable data about how the judge's mind interacts with the directives of the methods of interpretation, it is useful to turn

[9] Lord (then Sir Kenneth) Diplock "The Courts as Legislators," in *The Lawyer and Justice* B.W. Harvey (ed.), Sweet and Maxwell, 1978) on p. 266.

[10] Mauro Cappelletti, "The Lawmaking Power of the Judge and its Limits," in (1981) 8 Monash L. Rev. on p. 15, with further references. In passing we might add that in his habitual colourful language the famous Danish Realist Alf Ross has coined these somewhat trivial truths in these words: "The judge shall not be like the Homeric king who received his themistes from Zeus; nor like the Oriential Cadi who makes his decision out of an esoteric wisdom," *On Law and Justice* (Stevens, 1958 and University of California Press, 1959) on p. 281.

our attention to the verifiable elements of the judicial process of value-conversion, in this case to judicial outcomes. From analysis and comparison of a great many judgments of the European Court we have learned that the method of teleological interpretation and its progeny—all closely associated with the "ever-closer-union" *leitmotif*—dominate adjudicative choices between competing public policies. Is that domination following a judicially perceived duty to act, a duty decreed by the methods of interpretation? Hardly, I should assume. A postulate to that effect will, in any event, not be empirically verifiable.[11]

Some remarks on the rôle of judicial philosophies

Today, the proposition that with a different staffing of the European bench a radically different judicial output might have emerged would hardly become subject to real dispute. Yet, to realise the importance of the human element means to ride on collision course with the above-cited maxim about rule by law and not by men. This is not, however, a good reason for denying the crucial rôle of the individual judge's personal philosophy—nor for trying to conceal its impact on judicial outcome. Judge, now Professor Pescatore has put this point quite nicely when he wrote that the European Court and its judges have "*une certaine idée de l'Europe*" of their own. In crucial situations of choice this idea, he says, was made decisive "and not arguments based on the legal technicalities of the matter."[12]

More radically, some American realists have suggested that, in order to predict judicial outcome, it would be of far greater importance to know judicial philosophy than established case-law and precedent. Albeit this view hardly holds completely true for Community case law, both Pescatore's above cited observation and the words by Judge Koopmans, which I quote below,[13] can be viewed as insiders' guidance about the prevailing judicial philosophy-orientations, published for the benefit of the outside world's interest in predicting outcomes of the European Court's process of value conversion. Such guidance is indeed extremely helpful even for those who happen to know the legal directives embedded in precedent.

There is another interesting perspective on the importance of judicial philosophies. It is that attention is regularly not paid to them as long as the values protected by the majority on the studied bench coincide with the values which, according to a societal consensus, merit protection. In itself this observation is quite trivial but it is noteworthy that in some societies a discrepancy between judicial and societal values never developed and in some others it did. For example, to the best I know an unbridgeable discrepancy never developed in England. Denmark represents another case of substantial harmony.

In the Community such a discrepancy was hardly avoided, however. Also pre-

[11] The observations over this footnote encapsulate the essence of the analysis which I have published in detail elsewhere, see notably the source mentioned in note 4 above.

[12] Pierre Pescatore "The Doctrine of Direct Effect: An Infant Disease of Community Law," in (1983) 8 E.L.Rev. on p. 157. One might here suitably recall J. A. G. Griffith's warning: "When judges get carried away by their personal convictions (. . .) they create uncertainty. If those convictions are held on issues which are political (. . .) then they will arouse animosity as well as support, and if these issues are serious and large (. . .) judicial pronouncements begin to lose their authority and legitimacy." The quote is from *The Politics of the Judiciary* (Fontana Paperbacks, 2nd ed.) 1981, on p. 205.

[13] Over note 28, below.

revolutionary France experienced one.[14] End of nineteenth century Norway features a rather shortlived but violent clash between a majority on that nation's Supreme Court and the political elites.[15] The clash evolved although Norway—like Denmark—is a fairly small and homogeneous country featuring a comparable constitutional history.[16] The history of Canadian constitutionalism likewise informs us about an important discrepancy between the federalism case law handed down by the Queen's Privy Councillors and the national aspirations of most Canadians. To end this shortlived and deliberately arbitrary list with the self-evident: in the United States clashes periodically broke out between the Supreme Court and the co-ordinate branches of government or with other power-elites.[17]

Despite the issue's apparent and even compelling interest, by investigating the impact of individual judicial philosophies we have only come slightly nearer the point where we shall be able to close the unwarranted-activism dossier with a determination of "excess"—or "no excess." Although, it does not offer us an operational activism-test, the great intrinsic merit, in my view, of focusing on the judicial philosophies is that it lays bare the rôle of human flesh, a rôle that is probably more predominant in constitutional adjudication than in judicial involvement in politically less contagious areas of public policy.

An intermediate conclusion

We may therefore conclude this first part of our analysis and its discussion of accumulated scholarship by stating that this paper's fundamental question has escaped complete encapsulation and, for that reason probably, resolution also.

Using the method-of-interpretation language we may though now rephrase that question in the following manner: how liberally may the Community judge, following his perception of the (correct) policy-orientation, which ought to prevail in judicial decision, give preference to teleology over text; to some nebulous *effet nécessaire* over Treaty-provisions which do not ordain such effect; or give preference to systematic construction in order to incorporate visions of the Founders into operational constitutional law; over society's apparently changing taste for more integration, at least if it is judicially decreed at high speed?

There should, despite the observations which I have made in the preceding paragraphs, exist no doubt that the preamble *self-evidently* offers interpretative guidance to the European judges. And as the Community experience went on, some evidence is also supportive of the proposition that the judges' frequent use of the "ever-closer-union" *leitmotif* was tolerated as warranted; in some quarters it drew even applause.[18] This is merely one side of the coin, however.[19]

Indeed, students of courts in general and of the European Court in particular

---

[14] See *op. cit.*, in note 2 above.

[15] Ulf Torgersen, "The Role of the Supreme Court in the Norwegian Political System," in *Judicial Decision-making*, G. Schubert (ed.), (London 1963) on pp. 221–233.

[16] See about Denmark, Rassmussen pp. 56 *et seq.*

[17] For a survey of Canadian Constitutional history, see Rasmussen pp. 102 *et seq.*, and for that of the United States Chap. 5.

[18] See Rasmussen *e.g.* on pp. 32, 63 and 71. Professor Mauro Cappelletti does not seem to have understood this, see his *op. cit.* in note 4, especially pp. 5 *et seq.* The seen depends on the eyes of the beholder.

[19] There were important negative reactions as well; see texts over notes 25, 26 and 27 *infra*, with references.

will not be strangers to the proposition that any court has to calculate its activism nicely because miscalculation is likely to provoke clashes with other organs of government. Careful calculation becomes a complicated matter, however, if only because activism feeds on itself. Once begun, the activist course often must not only continue, it must also intensify. If it does not, litigants' deceived expectations are ultimately at a risk of turning other future client-litigants away from the court-rooms where the particular offered, respectively demanded, value-promotion used to be available. Yet, our experience seems to confirm that late arriving litigants will become increasingly demanding. They will arrive in court with high hopes that new (pro-community) terrain is likely to be taken under the judicial plough, merely for the asking. Whence: not only continuation but intensification.

Be this as it may, the question about how calculation is technically made remains unanswered. If a normative theory of Community Law interpretation were available the answer could be given. Indeed, activism would be excessive (miscalculated) above or beyond these interpretative results warranted by the theory. Above and beyond that limit clashes with the other organs of government would develop. Yet a normative theory does not exist.

No normative theory of interpretation of community law

Is the formulation of a normative theory of interpretation of Community law (hereinafter referred to as a "normative theory") feasible? I submit that at the present stage of development of the Community and of its law this question should be answered by the negative. I shall here explain why, but, first, outline the circumstances of which a normative theory would have to take full account.

The peculiarities of Community law interpretation, include:

(1) that the Community was created by a covenant between fully sovereign States;

(2) that, neither at the moment of creation nor at any subsequent point of time, have the political circumstances normally believed to condition a successful federalisation of independent states been present;

(3) that the *travaux préparatoires* have remained and probably will remain inaccessible for the purpose of interpretation of Community law;

(4) that the Treaty-draftsmen's legacy, the Treaties, are documents frequently displaying widely incompatible declarations of intent (incompatibility most notably emerges between the Preamble (plus the opening Articles) and many of the operational Articles) and

(5) that since the inception of the Community merely 30 years ago, the number of component parts has risen at a quick pace from six via nine and 10, to 12.

The claimed impossibility of construction of a normative theory, pretending to represent anything but an academic interest, follows if one considers the seventh but crucial analytical component of such a theory: the availability of some sort of a consensus in relation to the integration/co-operation experiment's fundamental values. Indeed, if a genuine consensus about the basic supranationalism/integration-value ever existed, intervening changes in the value-priorities of the Community's body politic may have triggered changes in the substantive ingredients of that consensus and in the conjecture in which it operates.

This is the stumbling block. Indeed, as long as nothing remotely resembling a consensus in that respect is not at hand—and I submit that it is not and that it will hardly develop in any foreseeable future—any attempt to formulate a normative interpretative theory is doomed to failure.

In my view this conclusion is compelling since the necessary balancing of the relative weight of the six core elements of any normative theory enumerated above must—and can only—be accomplished if the seventh ingredient, the consensus-element, is a known variable. As long as that consensus is still, at best, in the making, to construe a theory about judicial decision's possible contribution to political integration/co-operation—or its future potentiality for relieving society of the freezing effects of political inertia—remains a nonsensical enterprise—or, perhaps more precisely put, an enterprise of almost exclusive academic interest. Be this even as it may, no-one else has as yet (to my knowledge) successfully tried out his inventive skills in establishing such a theory.[20]

Finally, needless to say, it is not possible to turn to the European Court for an authoritative answer to our question about a normative theory. This follows because it is precisely the European Court's interpretative handling of its business that has led to our present activism-investigations. To turn to the European Court would, indeed, amount to little more than to entrust the guardianship of cabbage to goats.

In the real world, not one ideology but a *multitude* of ideologies and theories of interpretation of Community law are in current circulation, simply because many lawyers and some laymen alike do have some yardstick of that sort of their own making. These yardsticks will usually be on a fairly unsophisticated level, but, most importantly, they will bear the inevitable imprint of the characteristics of the legal-cultural background of the many persons in question. One of the real problems in connection with the activism-discussion in the Community context is precisely that, without using a common standard or test, and often only by intuition, most of us believe that we will recognise an "excessive" activism when we see it in operation. It may be regrettable but it is inescapable that for reasons set out above, no single one of this multitude of activism-tests, or a suitable mix of elements of some of them, may at the present stage of development of Community law, be fused or elevated to normative prominence.

An alternative, sociological yardstick

If the construction of a normative theory is not a viable tool for our activism-analysis, another measuring rod may be made available. Indeed, beyond the subjective I-know-it-when-I-see-it tests, a second *more* objective level of activism analysis may be identified. I have elsewhere in great detail demonstrated what this consists of and how the new test can be operated.[21] Here it will suffice to say that the proposed second-level test is legal-sociological in nature. It oper-

[20] Clarence J. Mann deals with numerous aspects of this problem in his seminal study entitled: *The Function of Judicial Decision in European Economic Integration* (Martinus Nijhoff, 1972). There, he worked out a subtle and comprehensive theory about the relationship between legal interpretation, judicial decision and the political integration progress. The relative silence surrounding, however, that theoretically thorough work suggests in its own way that his theories had little to offer for interpretative and political reality. Joseph H. H. Weiler seeks to regenerate some academic interest in this problem in "The Court of Justice on Trial, A Review Essay," in (1987) 24 C.M.L.Rev. 555.

[21] Chaps. 3 and 10 through 12.

ates by way of a careful and comprehensive collection of the known reactions to the European Court's jurisprudence given by society's countervailing powers. Such case law data represents the positive and the negative policy-signals or policy-inputs relevant to the rôle of judicial decision in European political integration.

The countervailing powers range from the co-ordinate arms of the Community's own government to courts, parliaments, administrations, legal commentators, press, etc. of the various Member States. Hence, indirectly this test builds on the myriad of level-one evaluations of the European court's case law. The quintessence and merits of the proposed policy-input study is that it avails the Members of the European Court as well as commentators of its case law with the same, basic data to be used as a measuring rod for identifying the limits to activism. Methodologically and factually synchronised, a meaningful if not agreeable, discussion of the existence or not of the conflict-laden phenomenon of judicial activism may take off on the basis of those data.

As it has already appeared the proposed test is only *more* objective. It is not ideal objectivity.[22] It is therefore still quite possible that two or more evaluations arrive at different conclusions. However regrettable, this circumstance does not, I submit, ruin the test's validity or viability which resides in that an interpersonal control has been made possible. If misunderstood the proposed acceptability-of-activism test might be taken to suggest that the judge's registration of the surrounding society's favourable or critical reception of his case law aims at making him subservient to the fluctuating whims and policy preferences of the power élites of the moment.[23] This is not so, however, although it is true that he should collect the policy-inputs in order to decide whether his case-law is acceptable or unacceptable and whether it, if unacceptable ought to be modified or not. Far from urging the judge to seek to please the bastions of political power, I want to emphasise that it is one of the most important virtues of the judge's function generally, and especially of judicial review (in the Community and elsewhere), not to be strictly bound to the environment's powers and pressures.

The European judges are merely bound to ensure "that in the interpretation and application of the Treaty the law is observed": EEC Article 164. Article 164 does not, however, help the judge whose case law triggers protest, evasion or/ and defiance. Article 164 does not inform him where that Article's solemn obligation must give in to another, as fundamental prerequisite of supreme constitutional umpiring and judicial policy-involvement. This is that in the long run, "given adamant public demand, a constitutional court ultimately must defer to

[22] Mauro Cappelletti *op. cit.* in note 4) seems not to have read my book carefully on this point either. I do not lay down any claim on "objectivity" or just on "approximating objectivity" (*Cappelletti, op. cit.* note 4 on p. 4). I repeatedly, and much more modestly say that the aim of the "policy input study" is to "enable (the researcher) to draw conclusions (about judicial activism) with greater authority than those afforded by his personal judgment" (*op. cit.* note 3 on p. 31); or "One may say that the study of the body politic's positive and negative policy inputs provides the necessary framework for elevating the activism discussion from a purely subjective level of speculations and contentions to the best available level of objective discussion" (*op. cit.* note 4, on p. 261); see further *op. cit.* on pp. 44, 53, 170 and 263.

[23] Mauro Cappelletti *op. cit.* note 4 on p. 7, erroneously draws that conclusion. Claus Gulmann, on the contrary (in Anmeldelse (Book-review of Rasmussen) in Ugeskrift for Retsvæsen, (1987) B p. 189) specifies that the acceptability-test is well suited to the kind of analysis it was designed as a tool for making.

the people's choice."[24] In other words, the judge will have to conform his decisional output to election-day results. This criterion implies that, although a judge should never act as the red-robed puppet of the powerful, it is equally indisputable that judicial authority and legitimacy will erode if, for lengthy periods of time, the judge pursues policies which fly in the face of some prevailing value-consensus in society. The critical hours of confrontation between the Hughes Court and American Society led by President Roosevelt in 1936, a confrontation which ended with judicial submission, illustrates well this point.[25]

Concluding remarks

Let me conclude by repeating what I consider to be the thrust of any activism-discussion: it is the protection/destruction issue in relation to judicial authority and legitimacy. I have elsewhere in detail argued that in its endeavour to "make Europe" the European Court went too far too often. In defiance of much European tradition, the European Court engaged in a teleological, pro-Community crusade, the banner of which featured a deep involvement which led it to give primacy to pro-integrationist public policies over competing ones that were often, even outside of the ring of losing litigants, considered as meriting some protection. Moreover, this engagement seemed to increase throughout the 1970s despite the emergence of numerous warning signs indicating that society was in the process of undergoing change away from the immediate post World War II ideologies so favourable to the inception of the European Communities with their professed supranational aspirations.

Although subject to much admiration and applause from many sides, including that of most Community law specialists, irritation, dismay and wrath accumulated in other quarters. And although the European Court's co-operation with national courts under Article 177 is telling about confidence and mutual trust, pathological cases do come out of some court-rooms.[26] Should one dismiss the few pathological cases as irrelevant in the face of the numerically far more important success-stories? I would warn against such complacency. Continuing the medical metaphor few cancer-cells are, indeed, under favourable growth-conditions, able to ruin completely the healthiest body.

In my evaluation, the negative policy-inputs were suggestive of a perception of the European Court, shared by powerful countervailing powers, that it had transgressed into functions constitutionally vested in the political arms of government. Clearly, the increasing implementation back-logs from which many of the European Court's Article 169 rulings are conspicuously suffering in recent years in the hands of several national governments, are also inducive of concern of this kind. Unless otherwise proven, I submit, suspicion that a linkage between the ailing will to comply diligently with the European Court's condemning rulings and the perception of the European Court as a not fully trustworthy neutral

[24] Clarence J. Mann *op. cit.* note 20 above, on p. 92.

[25] For accounts and discussions of this event, see, *e.g.* Lawrence Tribe *American Constitutional Law* (The Foundation Press 1978), on p. 235; John Ely Hart *Democracy and Distrust* (Harvard University Press, 1980) on p. 46; and Rasmussen on pp. 43 and 137 *et seq.*

[26] A computerised research work, conducted by a multinational team of researchers under the auspices of the European University Institute in Florence (European Policy Unit, Joseph H.H. Weiler—which is under publication—is supportive of these conclusions.

arbiter might exist, should not be dismissed easily as sheer fantasy. I then concluded that the situation was threatening with possible court-curbing or even court-destroying counter-measures. I consequently recommended the European Court to act with greater care.[27]

I may prove to be wrong in my evaluation. I may, indeed, prove to have been too prudent and cautious. Be this as it may, there are in fact indications that some members of the European Court may feel the same way. To illustrate this point, I shall quote from a recent article written by Judge T. Koopmans:

> "Maybe we ought to go back to the second role (of judicial function): a *minimal* role. It seems that American case law is heading for that result. It is, more than formerly, based on the essential peace-making function of the law and is being stripped of its more daring and activist sidelines . . . . A similar evolution may be taking shape in the European Communities, especially in the case law of the European Court . . . . If this trend exists, and if it continues, it will make life more difficult for the Community's political institutions especially the Commission. In the past, the Commission often thought it could rely on the Court's help when its case was likely to strengthen European integration. In the future, perhaps it will only be able to do so when it can show a solid legal basis, as the Court's willingness to construct such a basis on its own initiative may diminish."[28]

[27] See notably Chaps. 11, 13 and 14 of the book cited in note 4, above.

[28] T. Koopmans "The Rôle of Law in the Next Stage of European Integration," in (1986) 35 I.C.L.Q. 925.

Part IV
Rules and Processes

[15]

5. THE COMMON MARKET

Quantitative restrictions and measures having equivalent effect

Laurence Gormley

Cassis de Dijon and the Communication from the Commission *

There have been various notes on *Cassis de Dijon* [1] in recent issues of this *Review*. The purpose of this article is to examine the Commission's Communication [2] on the consequences of the *Cassis de Dijon* Judgment.

The Judgments in the *Cassis de Dijon* case and the cases which followed it have had the effect of allowing the Commission to reappraise its priorities and methods of attack in the field of harmonisation. Bearing in mind that the Commission's aim in this field is "not to accumulate directives but to remove hindrances to trade" [3] the realisation that Article 30 may be used as a major means of challenging technical barriers to trade which already exist and, indeed, to prevent the erection of new barriers must be most welcome. However the Commission has taken the case law of the Court [4] not merely as an opportunity to redirect its harmonisation activities under Article 100 but also as the pace-maker for the abolition of marketing restrictions on the free movement of goods within the Community. It remains to be seen, though, whether the Commission will in fact keep current and proposed national provisions under constant review, perhaps in a manner analogous to that provided for in Article 93 EEC.[5]

Although the Judgments in the *Cassis de Dijon* case and in *Gilli & Andres* [6] and *Fietje* [7] are by no means revolutionary [8] (for they do not substantially modify Community law) they have significantly developed the interpretation of Community law to enable it to cope with new situations. Thus it was that the Commission took the initiative and addressed its Communication to the Member States.[9]

The background to the Communication

It will be remembered that the Commission on November 6, 1978, had addressed letters to the Member States (before, of course, the Judgment in

* I am indebted to C. J. Hudson LL.B. (Liverpool) for invaluable discussions and research in the preparatory stages of this paper and also to the Commission's information office in London for the use of its materials. The article in (1981) 18 C.M.L.Rev. 271 by Barents was published after this note was prepared but some of his points have been taken into account at proof stage.

[1] Case 120/78, *Rewe-Zentral AG* v. *Bundesmonopolverwaltung für Branntwein* [1979] E.C.R. 649, [1979] 3 C.M.L.R. 494 and other cases, noted by Wyatt (1981) 6 E.L.Rev. 185. See also Dashwood (1981) 6 E.L.Rev. 241.

[2] O.J. 1980 C256/2.

[3] *Removal of Technical Barriers to Trade*, January 24, 1980: COM (80) 30 final (Communication to the European Parliament) Point III.

[4] The Judgment of the Court in *Cassis de Dijon* has now been confirmed and even strengthened so much that it cannot be dismissed as a mere bagatelle of the Second Chamber. (*Cf.* State Secretary Grüner in answer to a question in the Bundestag : 16290 *Deutscher Bundestag—8. Wahlperiode—203. Sitzung*. Source Meier, (1981) Eu.R. 43 at p. 46).

[5] The Member States would have to co-operate with such a review by virtue of the provisions of Art. 5 of the Treaty (Meier, *op. cit.* at p. 47).

[6] Case 788/79, [1980] E.C.R. 2071.

[7] Case 27/80 [1980] E.C.R. 3839.

[8] In the same sense, Mattera (1980) R.M.C. 505 at p. 513 (No. 241) and Barents, *op. cit.* at p. 295. It is reported that Dr. Mattera rejoices in the title of "Dr. Cassis" in Brussels, see *Eurobrief* No. 4 (June 1981) at p. 5.

[9] The European Parliament and the Council were also notified of its contents.

Cassis de Dijon) in which it outlined typical examples of barriers to trade which were under investigation.[10] It furthermore stated that it would "call upon national Governments to take all necessary measures to ensure the correct and effective fulfilment of the obligations arising out of Community law and to support the action taken by the Commission to safeguard the free movement of goods within the Community." [11] Pressed on by questions in the European Parliament,[12] the Commission declared that it would "make use of the interpretative guidelines established by the Court . . . in order to ensure that the rules of the EEC Treaty are more strictly and more effectively applied and to achieve thereby wider and more effective liberalisation of trade within the Community, also in those fields in which it has not yet been possible to obtain harmonisation at Community level." [13] Already in the Interim Report on the removal of technical barriers to trade within the Community (which was drawn up on behalf of the Economic and Monetary Affairs Committee [14]) it was recognised that the Commission had recently made greater use of Articles 30 *et seq.* against the erection of new barriers to trade. However it was also recognised that where existing barriers to trade were "justified" (be it under Art. 36 or any of the analogous interests which have been deemed worthy of protection) the only method of dismantling them lay in harmonisation directives.[15] It was, in effect, common ground between the Commission and the Parliament that the Commission should be given extra delegated powers under Article 155 EEC to obviate the necessity of directives implementing a framework directive having themselves to go through the procedure of Article 100 EEC.[16] Thus the Commission had, for some time, been preparing to increase its attacks on barriers to trade within the Community and the Communication to the Member States represents the warning as to its future activities.

The contents of the Communication

The Commission commenced by referring to its earlier letters [17] and to the Court's definition of barriers to free trade which are prohibited under Articles 30–34 of the Treaty. These include "any national measure capable of hindering, directly or indirectly, actually or potentially, intra-Community trade," which is, of course, effectively a restatement of the basic principle in Dassonville.[18] One of the results of this was, naturally enough, that "any product lawfully produced and marketed in one Member State must, in principle, be admitted to the market

[10] Not published as such but communicated to the Parliament and the Council as well (*Safeguarding freedom of trade within the Community*—November 10, 1978).

[11] Page 4 of the Communication of November 10, 1978 (see note 10, *supra*).

[12] Such as those of Mr. Glinne (Written Question No. 670/79, O.J. 1979 C310/29), Mrs. Boot (Written Question No. 835/79, O.J. 1980 C105/7) and Messrs. de Ferranti, Gavazzi, Leonardi and Petronis (Written Question No. 243/80, O.J. 1980 C183/57). Also of interest is the debate in the European Parliament on the free movement of goods, with the reply by Davignon (October 22, 1979).

[13] Reply to Mrs. Boot's question (see note 12, *supra*).

[14] E.P. Working Docs. 1980–81 : Doc 1–440/80.

[15] *Ibid.* See also Faure (1980) R.M.C. 443 (No. 240).

[16] COM (80) 30 final, point IV (1) and (2) (see note 3, *supra*) and E.P. Working Document (see note 14, *supra*). Although the Commission did point out that as long as reference to agreed standards (for example, in the construction industry to those of CEN and CENELEC—see note 33, *infra*) is as difficult as it is now, tedious and time-consuming consultations would still stand in the way of speedy progress.

[17] To the Member States, see note 10, *supra*.

[18] [1974] E.C.R. 837 at p. 852, [1974] 2 C.M.L.R. 436.

of any other Member State." This is the basic principle of the mutual acceptance of goods and forms the basis of the first guideline which the Commission gives in the Communication.[19] This, though, is followed by the important qualification which was described by Slot as something resembling an inverted rule of reason.[20] This, however, is not an entirely convincing label for the phrasing adopted by the Commission. The wording used is significant. "Technical and commercial rules, even those equally applicable to national and imported products, may create barriers to trade only where those rules are necessary to satisfy mandatory requirements and to serve a purpose which is in the general interest and for which they are an essential guarantee. This purpose must be such as to take precedence over the requirements of the free movement of goods, which constitutes one of the fundamental rules of the Community."

Several observations may be made about this statement. First of all, it, like the rule of reason in *Dassonville*, recognises that there are interests (which the Member States may protect) which are sufficiently important to override the basic principle of the free movement of goods. This recognition is, of course, enshrined in such famous cases as Cases 3, 4 & 6/76 *Cornelius Kramer et al.*[21] Far from being an inverted rule of reason it is a recognition of the necessity and purpose of that rule. Secondly, even though it is clear that equally applicable measures creating technical and commercial barriers may well be justified where they are "necessary to satisfy mandatory[22] requirements" they will still be subject to the second sentence of Article 36.[23] Thirdly, the statement has raised a certain amount of controversy as to whether the Commission's views on equally applicable measures has changed.[24] It will be remembered that the Commission had stated that it felt that measures applicable equally to imports and domestic products did not *in principle* fall within the prohibition of Article 30 of the Treaty. It was becoming steadily more of an artificial contention as the

[19] Slot in (1981) 29 S.E.W. 174 at pp. 177–178 criticises the Commission for its juxtaposition of the basic mutual acceptance principle and the restriction following it (which he saw as effectively incompatible with it). However for the contrary (and, it is submitted, better view) see Timmermans, (1981) 29 S.E.W. 381 at p. 382. Slot challenges whether a positive mutual acceptance principle can be read into para. 15 of the *Cassis de Dijon* Judgment [1979] E.C.R. 649 at p. 664 ("where the importation of alcoholic beverages lawfully produced and marketed in another Member State is concerned.") but it is felt that the principle of the mutual acceptance of goods is so well enshrined in Community law that this objection may be set aside. See also Case 27/80, *Fietje* which follows the Commission's explanation of the *Cassis de Dijon* Judgment.

[20] An inversion of the rule of reason in *Dassonville* (see note 15, *supra*) in which, it will be remembered, the Court stated: "In the absence of a Community system guaranteeing for consumers the authenticity of a product's designation of origin, if a Member State takes measures to prevent unfair practices in this connection, it is, however, subject to the condition that these measures should be reasonable and that the means of proof required should not act as a hindrance to trade between Member States, and should, in consequence, be accessible to all Community nationals." [1974] E.C.R. 837 at p. 852.

[21] [1976] E.C.R. 1279, [1976] 2 C.M.L.R. 440 (environmental and consumer protection).

[22] *Cassis de Dijon* [1979] E.C.R. 649 at p. 662. In *Gilli & Andres* (note 6, *supra*) the Court said 'imperative" [1980] E.C.R. 2071 at p. 2078.

[23] Which might prove to be fatal to the new British turkey and chicken health regulations, bearing in mind the press gloating over the use of a health requirement as a disincentive to imports.

[24] The view was expressed in Dir. 70/50 (O.J. 1970 113/29, O.J. English Special Edition 1970 (I) 17. Slot, *op. cit.* at p. 178 considers that the Commission has now reversed its view of equally applicable measures. It is submitted, however, that such a proposition is by no means clear cut. In the same sense: Barents, *op. cit.* at p. 299. For an alternative viewpoint to that of Slot, see Mattera, *op. cit.*

Court proceeded to look to the effects of particular measures rather than to whether they formally applied without drawing a distinction domestic and imported products. This became particularly apparent in the cases concerning price-regulatory measures.[25]

The Commission then proceeded to set out certain policy conclusions based on the case law of the Court. The first of these is straightforward enough,[26] dealing with the competence of the Member States to regulate the terms of marketing of products produced in their own territory (in the absence of any relevant Community measures). The second conclusion lays down the principle of mutual acceptance, *i.e* that goods lawfully produced and marketed in one Member State should *in principle* be admitted to the other Member States.

The somewhat unfortunate result is that whilst national products may have to comply with certain rules the equivalent products from other Member States will be advantaged because the rules concerned cannot be enforced against them unless, of cource, they fall within the permitted exceptions to the basic rule of the free movement of goods.[27] In the Commission's view it would therefore be necessary for Member States to give "consideration to the legitimate requirements of the other Member States," when drawing up technical or commercial rules liable to affect the free movement of goods.[28] The Commission's expression of the conditions under which the Court will accept exceptions to the basic principle of the free movement of goods (the mutual acceptance principle) is remarkable for the fact that it contains no reference to the second sentence of Article 36, to which, as has already been submitted, any permitted or tolerated exceptions must be subject. The expression of the exceptions details the restriction on the mutual acceptance principle which has already been mentioned above. It will be apparent, though, that these exceptions are much wider in their scope than the exceptions provided for in the first sentence of Article 36 (or, for that matter, in the rule of reason as originally enunciated in *Dassonville*). This is, though, scarcely surprising given the developments in earlier case law, and the formulation adopted accord with the authorities.[29]

After having stated its policy conclusions the Commission set out a number of guidelines, most of which concern the future direction of its harmonisation activities. The first guideline, though, repeats, in effect, the mutual acceptance principle. Thus a product lawfully produced and marketed in accordance with the technical or quality requirements of Member State A in that Member State must be admitted to Member State B (and be permitted to be sold there) even though the domestic products of Member State B have to fulfil different standards. Provided that the imported product "suitably and satisfactorily" fulfills the legitimate objective of Member State B's rules, Member State B may not attempt to justify prohibiting the sale of the product on the ground that it does not fulfil the objective in *precisely* the same way as domestic products do. In other words, if a product already meets standards adopted in pursuance of an

[25] See, for example, Case 13/77, *NV GB-INNO BM* v. *Vereniging van de Kleinhandelaars in Tabaak* [1977] E.C.R. 2115.

[26] Slot, *op. cit.* at p. 178, viewed this as an exception to the rule of reason in *Dassonville*.

[27] In the same sense, Slot, *op. cit.* at p. 178, and Mattera, *op. cit.* at pp. 509 and 513.

[28] Slot, *op. cit.* at p. 178 feels that this statement may well be a development of Art. 5 of the Treaty and wonders whether the agreement of the Representatives of the Member States meeting within the Council (of May 28, 1969 on the programme for the removal of technical barriers to trade) amounts to some such obligation. See also notes 5 and 11, *supra* and text thereto.

[29] See further, *Encyclopedia of European Community Law*, Vol. B (ed. Simmonds), paras. B 10–070/1 *et seq.* (Gormley) especially at para. B 10–072.

acceptable policy (be it the protection of the consumer or the environment or public health, etc.) in its original Member State then it must be treated as if it met the standards applicable in the Member State into which it is imported, for any attempt to prevent the sale of the product absolutely would not fall within the concept of an essential guarantee as developed by the Court. It would not be necessary in order to satisfy an overriding requirement. Yet, as Slot has pointed out, the existence of the rules in Member State A at least raises a presumption that compliance with the rules of Member State B is unnecessary.[30] However, as *Denkavit*[31] shows, it may be unwise to expect that such a presumption will be automatically recognised. It may well be that the idea of a product meeting one country's standards being allowed free access to other markets in the Community might lead to products' standards falling—as the German Government claimed in its submissions in the *Cassis de Dijon* case—through the eventual acceptance of a lowest common denominator. But against this it must be said that if the standards with which the product complies do not "suitably and satisfactorily" fulfil the objective of the rules of the importing Member State then that Member State will be justified in applying its national rules (subject, of course, to any applicability of the second sentence of Art. 36). In any event this sort of problem is precisely that which the Commission is now seeking to remove by harmonising those national laws which create barriers which have been deemed acceptable!

It is clear, then, that if any product is lawfully produced and marketed in Member State A it must be admitted to Member State B unless its prohibition can be justified under Article 36 (or the extended rule of reason). However the application of a rule justified under Article 36 to such a product will still be illegal if the rules of Member State A with which it complies are comparable with those of Member State B and afford protection similar to that afforded by Member State B's rules. The principle put simply is this: If the aim of the importing Member State's rules has been complied with then that is sufficient, there is no longer any interest to be served in requiring the aim to be met a second time in a different manner. Of course if the aim has not been complied with at all then there is no reason to prevent the importing Member State from enforcing its rules.[32]

Thus it is against this background that the Commission concluded its Communication with a summary of its main aims in the field of harmonisation from now on. It will, of course, concentrate on the removal, by harmonisation directives, of such national barriers as are still permitted under the case law of the Court, concentrating most of all on those barriers which exist in sectors economically relevant to the creation of a single internal market. It is intended to transform CEN and CENELEC[33] into effective bodies, but this will require the wholehearted commitment of the Member States to these bodies. Also of significance for the removal of technical barriers to trade, of course, is the contribution which the Community is making to the various bodies working for international standardisation.[34] It is perhaps useful to recall the view expressed in the European Parliament Working Document:[35] "One should always remember

---

[30] Slot, *op. cit.* at p. 180.

[31] Case 251/78, *Firma Denkavit Futtermittel GmbH* v. *Minister für Ernährung, Landwirtschaft und Forsten des Landes Nordrhein-Westfalen* [1979] E.C.R. 2269.

[32] See Timmermans, *op. cit.* at p. 383.

[33] European Committee for Standardisation and European Commission for Electrotechnical Standardisation respectively. See further COM (80) 30 (*cf.* note 3, *supra*).

[34] See COM (80) 30 at p. 13, *cf.* note 3, *supra*.

[35] See note 14, *supra*.

that harmonisation is not carried out for its own sake but that its purpose is [36] to open the markets of one member country to another." [37] Furthermore, "If a manufacturer does not intend to make use of this opportunity to market his products throughout Europe, there is no justification for compelling him to adjust his production in line with European directives." [38]

Conclusion

It remains to be seen, of course, just how far the Commission will be successful in its newly-redirected activities. It is also not yet totally clear to what extent the Commission's aims will have to be achieved by total harmonisation (that is the requirement of production to a European Standard) as opposed to optional harmonisation (which would allow domestic production to national standards to continue). Mattera,[39] however, feels that the death-blow has been administered to notions such as "Eurobeer" and other "Europroducts." Thus he feels that the common market should not become a melting pot in which national or regional specialities would disappear. Thus he expresses the view that the consumer will be better protected if he can have a wide variety of choice, giving full freedom to products "lawfully manufactured and sold" in their country of origin. Accordingly the Judgment in *Cassis de Dijon* should be seen as a triumph for regional and national specialities and a blow to those who would standardise purely for standardisation's sake.[40]

Whatever doubts the Member States may entertain about the direction in which the case law of the Court is taking and the interpretation of that case law by the Commission they would do well to bear in mind the words of Ehlermann, "Es dürfte niemandem schwerfallen, dem Gerichtshof zu folgen." [41]

[36] "it" in the Working Document (obviously a printing error).

[37] At p. 9 of the Working Document (see note 12, *supra*).

[38] *Ibid.*

[39] *Op. cit.* at p. 513.

[40] Mattera, *op. cit.* at p. 510, disagrees with those who conclude that the new case law of the Court would bring virtually all harmonisation activity within the scope of Art. 30 *et seq.* "Certes il est vrai que les nouvelles orientations de la Cour limitent l'éntendue du champ d'application de l'article 100 mais il est tout aussi indubitable qu'elles permettront de valoriser davantage la capacité opérationelle de cet instrument et récompenseront bien plus que dans le passé les efforts et les moyens déployés par la Communauté en la matière."

[41] C.-D. Ehlermann, *Das Verbot der Massnahmen gleicher Wirkung in der Rechtsprechung des Gerichtshofes* in *Hamburg, Deutschland, Europa* (Eds. Stödter & Thieme) (Tübingen 1977), *Festschrift* for Ipsen. This also contains the valuable contribution "*Die Verantwortung der Mitgliedstaaten für den freien Warenverkehr im Gemeinsamen Markt*" by Matthies.

[1] Case 152/73, [1974] E.C.R. 153.

[16]

THE JOINT-DECISION TRAP: LESSONS FROM GERMAN FEDERALISM AND EUROPEAN INTEGRATION

FRITZ W. SCHARPF

Compared to early expectations, the process of European integration has resulted in a paradox: frustration without disintegration and resilience without progress. The article attempts to develop an institutional explanation for this paradox by exploring the similarities between joint decision making ('Politikverflechtung') in German federalism and decision making in the European Community. In both cases, it is argued, the fact that member governments are directly participating in central decisions, and that there is a *de facto* requirement of unanimous decisions, will systematically generate sub-optimal policy outcomes unless a 'problem-solving' (as opposed to a 'bargaining') style of decision making can be maintained. In fact, the 'bargaining' style has prevailed in both cases. The resulting pathologies of public policy have, however, not resulted either in successful strategies for the further Europeanization of policy responsibilities or in the disintegration of unsatisfactory joint-decision systems. This 'joint-decision trap' is explained by reference to the utility functions of member governments for whom present institutional arrangements, in spite of their sub-optimal policy output, seem to represent local optima when compared to either greater centralization or disintegration.

INTRODUCTION

In political philosophy government is justified, in comparison to anarchy, as an arrangement for improving the chances of purposive fate control through the *collective* achievement of goals (including protection against threats) which would be beyond the reach of *individual* action. The same logic of effectiveness would justify enlarging the scale of government whenever the achievement of goals, or the defence against threats, would be aided by the larger action space and resources of larger units. The countervailing logic of democratic legitimacy, however, would favour smaller units of government in which a greater homogeneity of preferences would allow collective choices to approximate aggregate individual choices. It is also

Fritz W. Scharpf is Director at the Max-Planck-Institut für Gesellschaftsforschung, Cologne. Manuscript completed in 1988. Shorter versions (1986) have appeared under the title 'Die Politikverflechtungsfalle: Europäische Integration und deutscher Föderalismus im Vergleich' in: *Politische Vierteljahresschrift* 26: 323–56 (Dezember 1985) and under the title 'La trapolla della decisione congiunta: federalismo tedesco e integrazione europea' in *Stato e Mercato* 17: 175–216 (Agosto 1986).

Public Administration Vol. 66 Autumn 1988 (239–278)
 ISSN 0033–3298 $3.00

claimed that a world of small government units would not, in the first place, produce most of the threats to security that large units of government are needed to provide protection against (Kohr 1978).

The search for the optimal scale of government, in the light of apparent trade-offs between the greater effectiveness of larger and the greater legitimacy of smaller units, is the subject of sophisticated speculation in the fields of public choice, fiscal federalism and political science (Breton and Scott 1978; Kirsch 1977; Mueller 1979; Oates 1972; Olson 1969; E. Ostrom 1984; Rothenberg 1970; Tullock 1969; Ylvisaker 1959). Historically, of course, it was the nation state which, during the nineteenth and early twentieth centuries, seemed to provide the most attractive balance: sufficiently large and resource-rich to cope with most external threats, it was also internally homogeneous enough to facilitate the acceptance of collective choices. Indeed, the history of national unification in the nineteenth century, as well as of the disintegration of multi-national empires in the twentieth century, suggest that national 'identity' was a more powerful determinant of the prevailing scale of government authority than either the greater internal homogeneity of sub-national communities or the greater power resources of supra-national political units (Sharpe 1985).

In the post-1945 period, however, political authority on the scale of the nation state seemed to have lost much of its claim to optimality. Having been rescued from military disaster by the United States for the second time, most European nation states chose to renounce their claims to military self-sufficiency in favour of an American-led alliance. At the same time, European recovery, not only from war damages but also from the pre-war disintegration of the international economy, seemed to require the creation of a larger 'common market' at least within Western Europe. For the committed 'Europeanists', of course, this was only a beginning. They hoped, and worked, for a politically united Western Europe which would again be able to hold its own in a world dominated by military and economic 'super powers'. In these hopes they were encouraged by integration theories in the social sciences, expecting closer communications among member countries, and the 'forward spill overs' of functionally specific European institutions, to generate the political momentum for an ever deeper and wider social and political integration (Deutsch 1957; Haas 1958). Thus, NATO and the EEC were seen as only the first steps on the road to 'a more complete union' modelled after the federal system of the United States of America.

Thirty years later, NATO is still no more than a defence alliance under the undisputed hegemony of the United States, but as such it has been remarkably successful by its own standards. The European Community, on the other hand, has increased its territorial scale from the original six to twelve member states, and it has also broadened its functional responsibilities beyond the specific mandates of the original treaty. Indeed, there is considerable pressure for further functional expansion in such areas as industrial policy, technology policy, communications policy and monetary policy, where the Community is urged to assume governing responsibilities for which the nation state has become too small.

Nevertheless it is fair to say that the Community, unlike NATO, is not characterized by the self-satisfaction of secure accomplishments but, rather, by a pervasive sense of disappointment, frustration and general malaise. The 'Common Market', to be sure, is functioning more or less effectively as a customs union in the industrial sector, constraining the protectionist tendencies of member countries in exchange for the growing protectionism of the Community itself. In industrial policy, however, the relative success of common ventures in aerospace resulted mainly from collaboration outside of Community institutions, while Community efforts to cushion the decline of old industries are severely criticized as economically inefficient. Some beneficial programmes, such as the Regional Fund and the Social Fund, are ridiculously under-financed in relation to the problems they are supposed to attack, while in other areas the transfer of regulatory powers to the European level has mainly had the effect of frustrating more aggressive initiatives for pollution control or consumer protection at the national level. Most important, however, the centrepiece of European economic integration, Common Agricultural Policy, is now almost universally considered a grandiose failure. CAP has managed to generate huge agricultural surpluses, at the expense of European consumers and taxpayers who have to pay twice, for food prices far above the world-market level as well as for enormous subsidies for the purchase, storage and disposal of surplus production. And in spite of it all, CAP has neither been able to assure acceptable family incomes for small European peasants, nor has it maintained its major original achievement of common prices in a common European market for agricultural goods.

Thus, if there should be any 'spill overs' at all from functional integration, they are more likely to be negative. Indeed, the controversies over British contributions, which almost wrecked the Community in 1984, were closely related to the perversities of CAP, and so are the budgetary conflicts with the European Parliament. Open conflict, it is true, might help to politicize European issues and thus, ultimately, further political integration (Schmitter 1969). But it is hard to believe that extremely low voter participation at European elections should be understood as the expression of vigorous political demands for more integration, rather than as a vote of non-confidence for the Community.

At the same time, however, the European Community is not only just 'hanging on'. Direct elections for the European Parliament, which were finally accepted in the 1970s, may not have achieved the political mobilization that had been hoped for, but they are still a symbol of institutional consolidation. In spite of acute conflicts of interest, Britain is still within the Community, and Spain and Portugal have finally been admitted. The European Monetary System did not only survive against many odds, but it is now promoted as the nucleus of a future European Monetary Union with a common currency and a unified monetary policy.

In short, the history of the European Community has not confirmed the hopes, of 'Europeanist' politicians and 'neo-functional' theorists alike, for dynamic processes of deepening and widening functional integration, culminating in the creation of a full-fledged federal state; but the European enterprise has proven much more resilient than the 'realist' school of international relations and the political and scholarly promoters of an *Europe des patries* would have predicted. Paradoxically, the European Community seems to have become just that 'stable middle ground between the cooperation of existing nations and the breaking in of a new one' which Stanley Hoffmann (1966, p. 910) thought impossible.

It is tempting to ascribe the paradox of European integration – frustration without disintegration and resilience without progress – to historical accidents or to the interventions of certain powerful individuals. Instead, I will try to argue in this paper that the European malaise may be systematically explained as the consequence of a characteristic pattern of policy choices under certain institutional conditions. This pattern, the 'joint-decision trap', was first identified in the institutional setting of federal-*Länder* relations in West Germany. It can be shown that similar institutional conditions are producing similar decision patterns in the European Community.

TWO MODELS OF FEDERALISM

When 'Europeanist' politicians and social scientists were considering processes of integration that might lead to a 'United Europe', what they had in mind was a federal system fashioned after the American model. What was created, however, were institutional arrangements corresponding more closely to the tradition of German federalism. The fundamental difference between the two models is often misunderstood in Anglo-American treatises on federalism which tend to dismiss the German variant as little more than a camouflage for *de facto* centralization (Wheare 1960). Even William Riker (1964, p. 123), who recognized the unique characteristics of the German model, finds it hard to fit into his conceptual scheme which classifies federal systems according to the relative weights of the spheres of *independent* authority of central and constituent governments, respectively. What is missed is the possibility that authority might not be allocated, in zero-sum fashion, to either one or the other level of government, but that it might be *shared* by both (Johnson 1973). This is what distinguishes the German model from American federalism. Of course, a good deal of sharing, 'marble-cake' or 'picket-fence' like, is going on in the United States as well (Riker 1975), but differences at the constitutional level are nevertheless important.

In both models, the powers of the central government are limited, and constituent governments (the 'states' or the *Länder*) continue to exercise original governing powers legitimated by democratic elections. In the American model, however, the central government's authority is derived entirely from direct elections of the President and of both houses of Congress, and the federal government is able to rely upon its own administrative infrastructure at regional and local levels whenever it so chooses. In other words, the exercise of federal government functions is formally independent of the governments of the American states, and those functions that have been taken over by the federal government are effectively nationalized. Whatever sharing of functions is going on, is voluntarily granted, and may be withdrawn again by the federal government, as is illustrated by successive waves of the 'New Federalism'.

In the German model, by contrast, only one house of the federal legislature (the

Bundestag) is based upon direct, popular elections, while the other one (the *Bundesrat*) provides for the representation of *Länder* governments. In practice, all important federal legislation does require concurrent majorities in the *Bundestag* and the *Bundesrat* and does depend, therefore, upon the agreement of *Länder* governments. In addition, the federal government is severely limited in its executive powers, having to rely upon the administrative services of the *Länder* for the implementation of most federal legislation. On the other hand, the revenue of both, the federal government and the *Länder*, is generally determined by federal tax legislation which imposes severe constraints upon the financial freedom of action of *Länder* and local governments. In short: the exercise of most governing functions is shared between the federal government and the *Länder* governments in West Germany. More specifically, for my present purposes, *Länder* governments have a significant share in the exercise of many of the important functions of the federal government. It is in this regard that German federalism is most comparable to the European Community.

It is probably fair to say that, even in the heyday of political enthusiasm for European integration in the 1950s, a European union along the lines of the American model of federalism was never a realistic possibility. The Community was created by the action of national governments at a time when their own continuing viability was no longer considered precarious (as it had been immediately after the war). The potentially most powerful motive for federation, common defence, was satisfied by the separate organization of the NATO alliance under US hegemony. What remained was the opportunity pull of economic integration (Scitovsky 1958; Balassa 1962) whose attraction was certainly not sufficient to persuade national governments of the need to commit institutional suicide. While recognizing the advantages of a common European market, they also had every interest in retaining as much control as possible over the substance, direction and speed of future steps towards political integration.

The primacy of national control is reflected in the limited authority of the European Parliament, even though it is now elected directly, and in the fact that the European Commission, the executive body of the Community, does not derive its authority from either the Parliament or from direct elections. Instead, the centre of power has remained in the Council of Ministers, representing national governments, and in the periodic summit meetings of the European Council. In both bodies, the principle of unanimous agreement has prevailed in important matters, providing each member government with an effective veto over European policy decisions affecting its own vital interests. Furthermore, the European Community is without administrative agencies of its own at the regional and local level; it must rely entirely upon member governments to execute its policies. And, of course, the Community has not been invested with its own powers of taxation, depending primarily upon import levies and upon contributions from the revenues of the member states (v.d. Groeben and Mestmäcker 1974; Wallace, Wallace and Webb 1977).

This is not to suggest that there are no significant differences between European institutions and German federalism. In fact, the European Community is much weaker in relation to its member governments than the German federal government is in relation to the *Länder*. Nevertheless, institutional arrangements are sufficiently similar to suggest that the difficulties of European integration might be illuminated by reference to some of the problems of German federalism which have been studied more systematically. The parallelism between European and German institutions appears to be particularly close in those areas of joint policy making which were added rather late (in 1969) to the existing structure of the German federal constitution. In these areas, which have been the subject of empirical and theoretical studies under the label of '*Politikverflechtung*' (Scharpf, Reissert and Schnabel 1976, 1977, 1978; Hesse 1978; Schultze 1982; Benz 1985) federal policy making is operating under the same requirement of unanimous consent which prevails at the European level. It is here that the 'joint-decision trap' was first identified.

JOINT POLICY MAKING IN WEST GERMANY

Under the original scheme of the German federal constitution, most important legislative functions are exercised at the federal level (with the agreement of the *Bundesrat*), while administrative functions are, with few exceptions, reserved to the *Länder*. Similarly, in the area of public finance, taxation is almost entirely governed by federal legislation, but tax revenues are shared by *Länder* and local governments. Even more significantly, the federal share of total public investment expenditures has always remained below 20 per cent.

In the early post-war period, political pressures focusing upon fiscal inequalities between rich and poor *Länder* gave rise to a formalized system of horizontal and vertical fiscal equalization payments and to a number of extra-constitutional federal grant programmes in such areas as housing and subsidies to agriculture and industry in depressed areas. In the 1960s, these programmes were increased in scope and volume even though their immediate post-war justifications had become less compelling. Instead, it had become clear that some of the important responsibilities of the modern state depended more upon the planning and financing of public infrastructure and public services than upon legislation. To that extent, the relative importance of the governing functions reserved to the *Länder* was seen to increase, while the legislative powers of the federal government appeared to lose some of their political salience.

At the same time, however, it was widely felt that the action space, and the action perspectives, of *Länder* governments were too narrowly circumscribed to deal effectively with some of the problems that had become major political issues in the 'reformist' political climate of the mid-1960s. Foremost among these was the perceived need to deal with the 'education gap' (or, even more dramatically, the *Bildungskatastrophe*) when participation rates in secondary and university-level education were seen to be far lower in West Germany than in other modern countries. Similar needs were perceived in some areas of large-scale public infrastructure, such as urban and inter-urban mass transport, urban renewal or the modernization of the hospital system. Furthermore, German peasants were about to be exposed to the direct competition of their European neighbours which they could only survive, or so it was thought, if the modernization of their farms and of agricultural infrastructure was heavily subsidized. By the same token, it seemed necessary to accelerate and subsidize industrial development in those rural and peripheral areas where agricultural employment was about to decline. In addition, the late conversion of German economic policy makers to the Keynesian philosophy of anti-cyclical demand management emphasized the importance, for economic stabilization, of national controls over the volume and the timing of public-infrastructure expenditures.

What is important is that these were all policy areas under the dominant influence of the *Länder*, but that 'enlightened public opinion' was highly sceptical of their willingness, or ability, to provide acceptable solutions. Such scepticism was sometimes, as in education, based upon a preference for nationally uniform solutions over the ideological and religious pluralism of *Länder* policies. In other areas, such as university or hospital construction, it was thought that the positive externalities of large, central institutions might be ignored by the policy choices of smaller *Länder*, or that their resource base would be inadequate for projects that could take advantage of important economies of scale. The resource constraints of small or relatively poor *Länder* were also regarded as obstacles for efficient policy solutions in urban mass transportation, urban renewal and in agriculture (where the problems of small peasant holdings are concentrated regionally). In regional industrial policy, finally, criticism focused mainly upon the undesirable consequences of 'ruinous competition' between *Länder* which were forced to attract new industrial settlements through ever larger offers of subsidies. What was needed, in short, were joint federal-*Länder* efforts to mobilize the common resource base, and to exploit the combined action space, of both levels of government for the achievement of common, national goals.

The federal government had, of course, tried to deal with some of these problems through its grant programmes which attempted to provide a degree of co-ordination between *Länder* policies, to impose some uniform standards, and to equalize some disparities of *Länder* resources. It was constrained, however, by unresolved doubts about the constitutionality of conditional federal grants in areas within *Länder* jurisdiction. The whole range of issues was, therefore, entrusted to an expert commission whose final report recommended far-reaching changes in the constitutional arrangements of fiscal federalism (Kommission für die Finanzreform 1966). In the general spirit of 'reform politics' and under the aspects of a 'Grand Coalition', such changes had indeed become politically feasible.

But constitutional change under the West German 'Basic Law' does require two-thirds majorities in the *Bundesrat* as well as in the *Bundestag*. As a consequence, the constitutional reforms of 1969 had all the characteristics of a negotiated settlement among independent, sovereign parties. To that extent, they represent an even closer approximation to the decision structures of the European Community than does the original constitution of the Federal Republic. Briefly, agreement was reached on three new areas of joint policy making, each involving the federal government and all the *Länder*:

- 'Community tasks' requiring joint planning and joint financing in the areas of university construction, regional industrial policy, and agricultural structural policy (Article 91a, Basic Law);
- federal subsidies to *Länder* investment programmes in such policy areas as housing, urban renewal, urban transportation or hospitals, and in short-term economic stabilization (Article 104a IV, Basic Law); and
- federal-*Länder* agreements to collaborate in the planning of primary and secondary education and in research financing (Article 91b, Basic Law).

Of these, primary and secondary education turned out to be the ideologically most controversial policy area. As there was very little federal money at stake (apart from federally financed 'model experiments'), 'progressive' and 'conservative' *Länder* felt free to engage in all-out conflict over their educational philosophies. For once, the Social-Liberal federal government was also willing to take a clear cut partisan position, so that the first drafts of the 'integrated education plan' turned out to be remarkably progressive documents. Unfortunately, however, they could not be adopted at the level of the heads of government, where the agreement of nine (out of eleven) *Länder* prime ministers was formally required. As a consequence, existing educational policies remained unchanged while efforts continued to reach agreement over ever more watered-down versions of the educational plan. In the meantime, public enthusiasm and political support for educational reforms began to erode, and so did financial resources for education at the onset of the economic and fiscal crisis after 1974. Predictably, the difficulties of reaching agreement in the face of acute political conflicts led to outcomes which frustrated not only the qualitative goals of progressive educational reformers, but also the quantitative goals shared by both the progressive and the conservative members of the education establishment (see Heidenheimer, Heclo and Teich-Adams 1975, 1983). In the end, the whole enterprise was abandoned in 1982 (BMBW 1982).

The lesson was not lost on others, and the internecine ideological battles of the educationists were not repeated elsewhere. Realizing the importance of presenting a united front toward an outside world of political 'generalists' in chancelleries, finance ministries and parliamentary budget committees, agreement became the primary goal itself. Thus, the specialist ministries responsible for federal-*Länder* negotiations at both levels developed decision rules approaching unanimity even in areas where, by law, majority decisions would have been possible. Perhaps still more important was a perception of common interest which prevented even those *Länder* that would have benefited in the particular case, from voting with the federal government as long as there was no nearly unanimous agreement among all of them.

Länder solidarity thus prevented the federal government from playing off the interests of some *Länder* against others in forming the 'minimum winning coalitions' which coalition theory would have predicted under such circumstances (Riker 1962). In fact, the 'cartelization' of *Länder* interests has been observed even in the field of research policy, where independent action by the federal government and individual *Länder* would have been entirely feasible and probably more effective (Bentele 1979), or in the planning of federal highways, where the federal government is legally empowered to decide unilaterally, but is in fact dependent upon the expertise of highway administrations at the *Land* level (Garlichs 1980). If even such weak linkages could bring about the application of *de facto* unanimity rules, the underlying mechanisms must be powerful indeed, and they have been operative long before the federal constitutional court did write the unanimity requirement into law for some of the joint-programme areas (BVerfGE 1975, p. 96). Perhaps this might give pause to those who tend to regard unanimity in the European Community as a merely technical problem which could be solved by a more authentic interpretation of the Treaty of Rome.

The substantive outcomes of joint decision making in West Germany may be roughly described as follows. During the early 1970s, joint programmes were remarkably successful in increasing the financial resources available for their respective policy areas, and in defending their expenditure levels even after 1975, when many other programmes were severely curtailed in response to the fiscal crisis arising from the economic recession. As a matter of fact, the share of joint programmes among total federal expenditures increased from 6.8 per cent in 1970 to 9.5 per cent in 1974 and 11.2 per cent in 1977 (BMF 1985, tables 1 and 6). In the following years, however, the hopes associating joint decisions with new opportunities for more effective public policy making gave way to a growing sense of disappointment and frustration, first among political and bureaucratic insiders (Scharpf, Reissert and Schnabel 1977), but then among the wider public as well. Instead of utilizing the joint action spaces of the federal government and the *Länder* for the purpose of more active and creative problem solving, joint programmes were increasingly seen as being either inefficient, or inflexible, or unnecessary and, in any case, quite undemocratic.

On the basis of our detailed studies of decision processes and outcomes in the various joint-policy areas, we tend to agree with these criticisms and, indeed, we may have contributed something to their overall thrust and credibility. Obviously, a satisfactory restatement of our findings would be beyond the scope of this article, but the gist of our analyses might still be conveyed through a few illustrative examples.

As far as the alleged *inefficiency* is concerned, it is claimed that joint programmes tend toward 'overspending' even by their own narrow criteria of optimality, and that the inter-regional distribution of funds tends to violate even their own criteria of allocative efficiency. The first claim is, perhaps, best illustrated by the joint programme to finance capital investments in the hospital sector. As German health insurance regulations allow hospitals to charge their full operating costs to the insurance system, hospitals had every incentive to increase their capital expenditures, once the joint programme provided for the full reimbursement of investment costs. The *Länder*, on their part, did not wish to forfeit their allotted share (determined by a per capita formula) of the available federal funds – with the predictable outcome of rapidly increasing investments even in areas where hospital services were fully adequate. As a result, there are now considerable excess capacities in the hospial sector (and rapidly escalating deficits of the health insurance system). Apparently, the joint programme had eliminated existing financial constraints without being able to introduce functionally equivalent mechanisms of rational planning and efficient allocation (Schnabel 1980).

The per-capita formula for distributing federal funds among the *Länder*, which prevails not only in hospital finance but in most other joint-programme areas as well, is obviously also a source of allocative inefficiency whenever there should be significant inter-regional differences in the need for, or the existing supply of, particular public services. A glaring example was agricultural investment subsidies. There the established distribution of federal funds, favouring the big-farm regions of Northern Germany, was found to be grossly unresponsive to criteria of actual need and programme effectiveness by a programme planning and evaluation group set up by the ministers of agriculture themselves. Nevertheless, redistribution in favour of the disadvantaged small-farm and hill regions in Southern Germany proved impossible under the conditions of joint decision making.

The example of agricultural subsidies might also be used to illustrate the alleged *inflexibility* of joint decision making. Even more to the point, however, would be the case of regional industrial policy. Evolving from a tradition of *ad hoc* federal subsidies to depressed areas in the early post-war period, this had become the joint-policy area with the greatest claim to substantive and procedural rationality by the early 1970s. Far from distributing federal funds evenly among the *Länder*, or according to some arbitrary or traditional formula, regional policy managed to achieve agreement on economic criteria for subsidization and on the use of sophisticated econometric analyses for the designation of assistance areas. In the main, these were located along the eastern boundaries of the Federal Republic and in certain under-industrialized areas throughout the country.

The reputation for allocative efficiency suffered a severe blow, however, when regional industrial policy was unable to respond to the economic recession after 1974. Its impact was most severe in some of the old industrial regions, which in the past had been too prosperous to be included among the assistance areas. Now that their unemployment rates became much worse than those of many rural areas which were traditionally subsidized, agreement on an inter-regional redistribution of funds could not be reached. The best that the federal government could achieve was acquiescence of the beneficiaries of the status quo when *additional* federal funds were temporarily made available to some regions dominated by the newly depressed automobile industry. In the following years, similar *ad hoc* programmes were introduced for the Saar region, for regions dominated by the steel industry generally, and for the Bremen area suffering from the simultaneous decline of steel and ship building. Thus, regional policy is still aimed at under-industrialized peripheral areas while a growing number of special assistance programmes are used to subsidize declining industrial regions without curbing subsidies to peripheral regions. Instead of the necessary reorientation of assistance criteria in response to fundamentally changing economic circumstances, the result has been a cumulation of conceptually contradictory assistance programmes, reintroducing just that pattern of inter-regional competition for the subsidization of mobile firms which the original programme had been designed to eliminate.

The claim that some joint programmes may in fact be, or have become, *unnecessary*, is derived from a normative analysis of the type of problems that might justify joint federal-*Länder* action in the first place. Some of these justifications, such as the existence of significant inter-jurisdictional externalities, of economies of scale, or of redistributive goals (Oates and Wallace 1972; Breton and Scott 1978) seem to be as applicable now as they were when federal grant programmes originated in the early post-war period. In other areas, however, such as housing or urban renewal or, perhaps, local road construction, we have argued that the objective need for any federal involvement had disappeared over time. At least after the mid-1960s, aggregate disparities between the *Länder* had been sufficiently equalized to eliminate the need for federal intervention (and the fact that in these areas federal money is allocated to the *Länder* on a per-capita basis tends to confirm our judgement). At the same time, some of the joint programmes, in such areas as university construction, hospital investments and urban mass transport, seem to have achieved most of their original goals, so that the remaining externalities and economies of scale could be handled within *Länder* jurisdictions. In many areas, therefore, it has become difficult to identify any purposes of federal involvement which could not be equally well pursued at the *Länder* level. On the other hand, the degree of red tape generated by the cumulation of regulations in jointly financed programmes seems to be so high that the costs of delays and inefficiencies of programme implementation have themselves become a major source of irritation (Lehner 1979, 1979a; Zeh 1979; Borell 1981).

In addition to being allegedly inefficient, inflexible and, sometimes, unnecessary, joint programmes are also often criticized for their *undemocratic* character, confronting parliaments with the *faits accomplis* of bureaucratic negotiations between the two levels of government (Klatt 1979). To some extent, this criticism seems trivial, as some loss of parliamentary control is necessarily involved in all forms of intergovernmental bargaining. Parliaments may ratify or reject the outcome, but they will rarely be able to exercise direct control over the negotiation process itself – except by Carl Friedrich's 'rule of anticipated reaction'. To some extent, it may also express unhappiness with the political conditions of German federalism, combining party-political confrontation in the *Bundestag* with the need to reach all-party agreement in the *Bundesrat*, at least until 1982 (Lehmbruch 1976). But the criticism may also cut deeper. The fact that certain programmes are jointly financed by two (or sometimes three) levels of government reduces their opportunity costs at each level. In comparison to competing programmes which would have to be financed entirely from one source, joint programmes thus seem to have an 'unfair' advantage at each level. One of the consequences is the tendency to 'overspend' on joint programmes, which was discussed above as one of the sources of inefficiency. Another is the distortion of 'real' political preferences at the local and *Land* levels whenever some programmes, but not all, are heavily subsidized by the federal government. Under such conditions, joint programmes may indeed become offers which a *Land* or a city 'cannot afford to reject', and, thus, a serious constraint upon local and regional democratic control (Späth *et al.* 1979). Finally, the role of *Länder* governments in federal legislation has tended to increase the salience of 'federal' issues in Länder elections at the expense of regional issues (Heidenheimer 1958; Hesse 1962; Lehmbruch 1976; Fabritius 1978; Abromeit 1982).

Taken together, these four lines of critical attack have seriously weakened the political attractiveness of joint programmes in West Germany since the mid-1970s (Schmidt 1980; BMF 1982). In addition, there have been specific reasons for disenchantment at each level. The federal government, for instance, found itself frustrated by the inflexibility of joint programmes when it tried to respond to the economic recession through fiscal redistribution. Instead of adjusting existing programmes as needed, it was forced to pay for additional programmes in regional industrial policy as well as in the field of public infrastructure investments (Nöllig 1977, p. 391). Furthermore, empirical research has demonstrated that increases in the volume of joint programmes were relatively ineffective as an instrument of anti-cyclical fiscal policy (Knott 1981). The *Länder* and, even more so local governments, tended to shift expenditures from one sector to another rather than to increase the overall level of their own spending as the federal government increased the volume of its grants (Reissert 1984). Thus, the federal government has again reduced its financial commitment to joint programmes from 11.2 per cent of total expenditure in 1977 to 8.2 per cent in 1980 and 7.4 per cent in 1983 (BMF 1985). One area, hospital finance, was even taken out of joint-finance arrangements altogether in 1984 (BMF 1985, pp. 43–4).

Resistance of the *Länder* against such cutbacks has been remarkably muted. It seems that some of the 'rich' *Länder* have by now concluded that joint programmes had been a bad idea to begin with, and that they would be better off regaining their freedom of independent action. Poor *Länder*, on the other hand, have been disappointed by the absence of significant redistributive effects (because of the per capita allocation of federal funds in most programmes). Furthermore, the standard of equal treatment in all programmes implied that rich and poor *Länder* had to comply with the same matching requirements, which meant that some of the poorest *Länder* were in fact unable to claim their allotted share of federal funds during the recession. They, surely, would have been better off if the earlier practice of bilaterally negotiated federal grants would have continued.

What has been described is, however, mainly the response of 'policy generalists' in the federal and *Länder* chancellories, ministries of finance and parliamentary budget committees. They seem now committed to resist all suggestions for establishing new joint programmes. But such suggestions are still forthcoming from the vertical alliances of 'policy specialists' who are pushed toward federal-*Länder* arrangements by the original logic of a constitution under which the fragmentation of functions can only be overcome through the sharing of responsibilities. In a period of general disenchantment with activist philosophies of state intervention, such pressures may be resisted. But the underlying logic is still powerful enough to prevent the wholesale dismantling of existing joint programmes.

JOINT POLICY MAKING IN THE EUROPEAN COMMUNITY

In some areas, the similarities between European policy making and joint policy making in Germany are so obvious as to be trivial. When small European programmes are simply 'tacked on' to ongoing national programmes, they will add to the bureaucratic and political costs of vertical co-ordination (Hrbek 1979) without being able to change national policy priorities very much. The only interesting question is whether European funds will add to, or substitute for, national expenditures, but the ability of national dogs to wag the European tail is not really in doubt. Thus, it is not at all surprising that decision patterns corresponding closely to the model of joint programmes in Germany have been identified in studies of the European Regional Fund (Bruder 1983; Noé 1983; Martins and Mawson 1982) and of the Social Fund (Laffan 1983), and that they also seem to govern the regional allocation of European R&D funds (Steinle and Stroetmann 1983).

The more interesting question is whether such similarities can also be found in Common Agricultural Policy which, by common consent, is the one area in which the European Community is approaching the full powers of a federal government. At least in the field of market and price regulations, CAP is not 'add on' but has replaced national programmes altogether, and its financial volume of 16.5 billion ECU in 1984 (amounting to 65 per cent of Community expenditure) is anything but trivial. Here, if nowhere else, we surely have a genuine European dog.

At the same time, CAP is formulated in a decision structure that is strikingly similar to that of joint programmes in West Germany. In both cases, important policy functions were moved up to the next-higher level of government, while their exercise remained dependent upon the unanimous agreement of member governments (Feld 1980). As in the German case, CAP was originally praised as a successful solution to the obvious co-ordination problems of national agricultural policies in an internationalized market for agricultural products, and it is now increasingly criticized for being outrageously wasteful as well as ineffective in terms of its own original goals. Most of the criticism is levelled at agricultural market policy (as distinguished from agricultural structure policy): it has burdened European consumers with food prices far above the world market; it has burdened European tax payers with a rapidly rising volume of subsidies; it is responsible for growing surpluses of agricultural production in Europe which must either be destroyed or dumped on the world market at enormous losses; and despite all these exertions, CAP was not successful in achieving its primary goals, a truly common market for agricultural products in Europe and adequate standards of living for low-income farmers (Body 1982; Rodemer 1980).

The alleged failures of CAP are directly related to its basic policy choices. At bottom, they can all be derived from the decision to protect and raise the income of European farmers through a system of price supports, rather than through direct income transfers. Once this choice had been made (which was probably inevitable in the light of the traditional agricultural protectionism of the founding members of the community), the further characteristics of CAP could be derived from the underlying structure of national interests (German and French, in particular) within the logic of unanimous decision making.

Compared to Germany, France had a much larger and, on average, more productive agricultural sector and significantly lower food prices. As a food-exporting country, France was vitally interested in free access to the larger European market, especially as she was likely to suffer from the German strength in industrial exports. German peasants, on the other hand, had little to gain and much to fear from a common European market for agricultural products, unless it was possible to maintain the high price levels prevailing in Germany for the typical products of German agriculture (mainly dairy products, meat, grains and sugar). The compromises which were reached after protracted negotiations, and dramatic Franco-German confrontations, predictably managed to accommodate both positions: the European market was to be opened to French producers (which precluded the general introduction of a system of production quotas), but prices were to be maintained at levels close to those prevailing in West Germany through a system of import levies and minimum prices (at which the 'European Agricultural Guidance and Guarantee Fund' has to purchase farm products that cannot be sold on the open market). As these 'intervention prices' were fixed far above the world market, and also far above production costs in the more productive agricultural regions in Europe, increasing agricultural surpluses were inevitable. The results were escalating guarantee payments which rapidly exceeded the revenue obtained through import levies. Far from being self-financing, the guarantee fund did require enormous subsidies, rising to more than 6 billion ECU (or about 75 per cent of the total community budget) by 1976, to almost 12 billion ECU in 1980 and to 16.5 billion ECU in 1984 (DIW 1984).

But even at that price, an effectively unified agricultural market could not be realized because of divergent national interests in the face of continuing variations in the exchange values of national currencies. When the French franc was devalued by 11 per cent in 1968, France was not willing to let food prices rise accordingly. Instead, food imports were subsidized and French agricultural exports penalized at the border. And when Germany revalued the Deutschmark later in the same year, the precedent was invoked to avoid price reductions for German farmers. A similar pattern was followed on many later occasions. The border levies on imports from low-value currency countries, and the border subsidies paid to exports from high-value currency countries, produced a 'green exchange rate' differing more and more from the official exchange rates among the currencies of member countries. As a consequence, the internal price level for agricultural products was relatively higher in the high-value currency countries such as Germany or the Netherlands, and so was the amount of EC subsidies flowing into these countries. Thus, the incentives for agricultural overproduction, which originally were the largest in France, have later tended to favour German and Dutch producers (Feld 1980).

At the same time, CAP was also unable to achieve the income goals for which it had been instituted. Price support for agricultural products meant that fewer people were leaving the farms than had been expected, so that per capita farm incomes still were not able to catch up with average earnings. Furthermore, while large and productive farms did extremely well at CAP prices, price support alone could not significantly reduce the economic plight of small peasants in agriculturally disadvantaged areas where industrial jobs are also scarce (Balz *et al.*, 1982). A special subsidy programme for hill farmers does provide some income support, but its volume is minimal compared to the expenditures on price support.

As in the German example, the growing disappointment and frustration over CAP is beginning to have an effect. The United Kingdom and, to a lesser extent, the Federal Republic, as the two large net contributors to the Community budget, have been trying to apply financial brakes to the vicious cycle of agricultural subsidies and surpluses. The formal opportunity to do so was provided by the growing budget deficit of the Community requiring an increase of the VAT levy (which also required unanimous agreement). For several years, CAP barely managed to squeeze by without re-examination because rising prices in the world market for agricultural products had unexpectedly reduced the need for subsidies. But in the spring of 1984, some adjustment had become inevitable. It took the form of a relatively permissive quota system for milk production and a more decisive effort to eliminate border equalization subsidies and levies in order to bring the 'green exchange rate' more into line with official exchange rates (Jürgensen and Schmitz 1984). Obviously, this last measure would hurt producers in high-value currency countries, such as West Germany, and it is perhaps not surprising that the immediate German response (accepted by the Community) was to provide national subsidies to make up for these losses (DIW 1984a). Thus, the Community had eased its budgetary problems somewhat, but at the sacrifice of one of the most cherished principles of European integration – the elimination of national farm subsidies and their replacement by what should have been a *common* agricultural policy.

But even with the 1984 compromise, the future of CAP is far from assured. Incentives for overproduction have not been eliminated, quota systems have not worked well in other areas, and the spill-overs from exchange rate fluctuations are likely to disturb the regulated markets for agricultural products in the future again. Furthermore, the entry of Spain and Portugal, with large agricultural surpluses of their own, will upset the precarious equilibrium of the Community budget even though their major products are not as heavily subsidized as the 'Northern' products that were the subject of the original Franco-German compromise.

Nevertheless, judging by the past record as well as by the current 'revealed preferences' of national governments, it is more likely that CAP will hang on, even if its original logic and purpose should be distorted beyond recognition, rather than that it will be either scrapped or reorganized into a more defensible policy system. In the following sections, I will attempt to develop an analytical argument that might explain both the substantive deficiencies and the persistence of joint policy making in the Federal Republic and in the European Community.

JOINT DECISIONS AND THE PATHOLOGY OF PUBLIC POLICY

The contribution of institutional arrangements to the substantive deficiencies of joint policy making in West Germany and in the European Community are related to two simple and powerful conditions:

— that central government decisions are directly dependent upon the agreement of constituent governments; and

— that the agreement of constituent governments must be unanimous or nearly unanimous.

The German experience further suggests that the first condition may imply the second one, and that unanimity will evolve even in the absence of formal requirements. This might not be so if the number of constituent governments were very large (raising the transaction costs of unanimous agreement) or if the central government were allowed to negotiate bilateral agreements with each of the member governments separately. But in multilateral negotiations among a small group of governments over uniform regulations which will apply to all of them, unanimity seems a rational rule to follow for risk-averse participants even if they might benefit from majority decisions in the individual case (Everling 1980, p. 221). Nevertheless, it is useful to distinguish between the two aspects of 'joint decisions', their inter-governmental character, and the unanimity rule.

The importance of the *inter-governmental* aspect becomes clear when one compares the representation or regional interests in the US Senate and in the German *Bundesrat*. In both cases, the territorial distribution of societal interests is emphasized at the expense of other dimensions of multi-dimensional interests (and at the expense of the Rousseauean ideal of the 'general interest'). But while US Senators, ideally, represent only the interests of their constituents (mediated through their own interest in re-election), the *Bundesrat* also (or, rather, primarily) represents the institutional self-interests of *Länder* governments. Thus, Claus Offe's '*Interesse des Staates an sich selbst*' (1975, p. 13) will be introduced twice, as 'withinput' and as 'input' in Eastonian language (Easton 1965, p. 54), into the political processes of the central government. One might expect, therefore, that the policy output of joint decision systems, when compared with unitary governments or the American model of federalism, will be less responsive to constituency interests and more oriented toward the institutional self-interests of governments and their 'bureaucratic convenience' (Tullock 1965; Niskanen 1971). More important, however, is the fact that these governmental interests are not, in the strict sense, 'represented' at all. Instead, they are direct participants in central decision processes. In that regard, what we have is a system of direct, 'participatory' democracy without any of the safeguards for detached reflection on the general interest, by non-instructed delegates, which has been emphasized by theorists of representative government ever since Edmund Burke (Scharpf 1970). Also, as far as member states are concerned, there is none of the 'generalization of support' which Talcott Parsons (1967, pp. 231–4) thought necessary for the maintenance of effective government in a democracy. In joint-decision systems, the central government is not free to respond creatively to external demands, or to anticipate future consensus; its actions are determined directly by the immediate self-interests of member governments.

Nevertheless, differences are important. While decisions of the European Community are completely determined by the outcome of negotiations among member governments, the German federal government has a political identity, resources and strategic and tactical capabilities of its own. It cannot adopt and implement effective public policy without *Länder* agreement, but it can design and pursue bargaining strategies against the *Bundesrat* which the European Commission cannot similarly pursue against the Council of Ministers or the European Council.

But the German federal government is also paying a price for its greater strategic autonomy: being able to bargain with the *Länder* over policies which it considers essential to the national interest (or to its own political survival), it still must obtain their agreement. Sometimes it may be possible to design 'win-win solutions' which are intrinsically attractive to the *Länder* as well. More often, its original policy proposals were watered down in substantive compromises. And if the federal government insisted upon its objectives, it often had to buy support for national policies at the expense of permanent improvements of the institutional and financial position of the *Länder*. Thus, just as the emperors of the Holy Roman Empire were forced to expend their dynastic possessions and, finally, the imperial prerogatives, in order to maintain the loyalty of their vassal princes, so the German federal government has seen its share of total revenue reduced from 53 per cent in 1970 to 48 per cent in 1983 (BMF 1985, Table 2). As there was, of course no corresponding reduction of federal responsibilities, the total volume of the federal debt increased from 54 per cent of expenditures in 1970 to 105 per cent in 1980, while *Länder* debts increased only from 62 per cent to 76 per cent of expenditure during the same period (Simmert and Wagner 1981, p. 455). Being entirely the creature of member governments, the European Community could not, of course, be similarly exploited by them.

But what are the implications of inter-governmentalism for the substance of public policy? The most clear-cut connection seems to exist with the alleged tendency of joint programmes to increase expenditures beyond the level that would be politically acceptable within a unitary government. This tendency seems to follow directly from 'rational' calculations of financial costs and political benefits at each level of government. If we assume that elected officials are sensitive to interest group pressure at all levels of government, and that interest groups are capable of presenting demands and exerting pressure at each level as well, then the political benefits associated with positive responses to interest group demands will be fully realized at each level, even if the response is delivered by a joint programme. On the other hand, if the joint programme is also jointly financed, its costs will be reduced accordingly for each level of government. Compared to single-government decisions, therefore, joint decisions have politically more attractive cost-benefit ratios. To put it crudely, more votes can be bought for less money at each level.

The conditions assumed in this model are closely approximated in West Germany, where governments at the local, regional and federal levels are dependent upon direct elections, where interest groups are active at all levels, and where joint programmes have matching requirements involving at least two, and usually three, levels of government in their financing. Under such conditions, the separate calculation of costs and benefits at each level will indeed suggest a relative increase of expenditures on joint programmes at the expense of programmes which have to be financed entirely by a single level of government. Our interviews in Germany have shown that active participants in policy processes are fully aware of these mechanisms – which explains why the vertical coalitions of interest groups, politicians and bureaucrats specialized in a certain field, are completely unanimous, in spite of all other internal disagreements, in defending the privileged status of their policy field as one of the joint programmes. But what about CAP, where at least two of the conditions assumed above seem to be missing? First, there are no matching requirements in the core areas of price subsidies, so that expenditures are all on the European level. Second, even though there are now direct elections to the European Parliament, it is obviously impossible to interpret CAP as the response of vote-maximizing politicians at the European level. By contrast to the German model, where all levels of government are profiting from joint programmes, it seems that the European Community has to bear the full costs without capturing any of the political benefits associated with CAP.

But, of course, it is national, rather than European, politicians who are determining CAP choices. And their cost-benefit calculations are obviously quite different. If we differentiate, for the sake of clarification, between the calculations of policy specialists and of generalists (say, national ministers of agriculture and national ministers of finance), the former must see CAP as an entirely free good whose production they have every incentive to maximize. For the finance ministers, on the other hand, a self-interested response would seem to depend mainly on the net position of their country with regard to the EC budget. Net beneficiaries would surely have less reason to object to the cancerous growth of CAP than net contributors. Thus it must be the acquiescence, or resistance, of net-contributing countries, the Federal Republic and the United Kingdom in particular, which explains the growth of the CAP.

For most of the period since the commencement of CAP in the middle of the 1960s, it has been acquiescence. The Germans were, and are still (Höhnen 1984) aware of the fact that they had to buy CAP in exchange for the common market for industrial products which favoured German exports. And they also know that the high price levels prevailing under CAP, which are the cause of overproduction and, hence, of rising subsidies, were adopted at their own insistence to protect the prevailing income levels of German farmers. Thus, the one country that should have had a financial interest in limiting CAP was among its original supporters for reasons unrelated to the specific incentives and constraints of its decision structure.

Of course it is true that the Germans, like everybody else, had vastly underestimated the dynamics of price support, overproduction and escalating subsidies in European agriculture – but when they found out, they were already caught in the rigidities of an ongoing decision system based upon the principle of unanimous agreement. *Unanimity* is generally considered as the decision rule which is most in conformity with the methodological individualism of public choice theory. If collective decisions depend upon the voluntary agreement of all members of the community, they are also likely to meet the welfare-theoretical criterion of Pareto optimality (Buchanan and Tullock 1962). Difficulties are likely to arise from increasing transaction costs in large communities and from the disruptive consequences of 'strategic voting', when members are tempted to conceal their true preferences for public goods in order to exact concessions in the allocation of costs (Buchanan 1975, p. 41). Given the small number of member governments, and the transparency of their (institutional and constituency) interests, neither problem should be of great importance in German federalism or in the European community.

What public-choice theorists have generally neglected, however, is the importance of the 'default condition' or 'reversion rule', which was recently pointed out by Elinor Ostrom (1984). The implications of unanimity (or of any other decision rule) are crucially dependent upon what will be the case if agreement is not achieved. The implicit assumption is usually that in the absence of an agreed decision there will be no collective rule at all, and that individuals will remain free to pursue their own goals with their own means. Unfortunately, these benign assumptions are applicable to joint decision systems only at the formative stage of the 'constitutional contract', when the system is first established. Here, indeed, agreement is unlikely unless each of the parties involved expects joint solutions to be more advantageous than the status quo of separate decisions. Parties with no interest in joint decisons will either opt out or will have to be bribed with side payments. Thus, the original agreement is indeed likely to be in everybody's interest, which may explain the general sense of satisfaction, enthusiasm and optimism associated with the early years of both European integration and joint policy-making in West Germany.

The 'default condition' changes, however, when we move from single-shot decisions to an ongoing joint-decision system in which the exit option is foreclosed. Now non-agreement is likely to assure the *continuation* of existing common policies, rather than reversion to the 'zero base' of individual action. In a dynamic environment, the implications for the substantive quality of public policy are obvious: when circumstances change, existing policies are likely to become sub-optimal even by their own original criteria. Under the unanimity rule, however, they cannot be abolished or changed as long as they are still preferred by even a single member. Thus, the association of unanimity and Pareto optimality emphasized by public-choice theorists seems to be restricted to single-shot decisions. In ongoing decision systems, by contrast, unanimity is likely to be associated with a systematic deterioration of the 'goodness of fit' between public policy and the relevant policy environment – unless there should be very powerful mechanisms of consensus formation.

The problem is even more serious when the freedom of individual action is entirely eliminated even in areas where there is no prior agreed-on policy at all.

Obviously, this is not a necessary characteristic of joint-decision systems: Federal constitutions usually allow for the 'concurrent jurisdiction' of member governments as long as federal legislation has not 'pre-empted the field'. But if joint-decision systems are specifically set up to regulate externalities of member-government policies, or to establish a truly common market, then the field must be pre-empted (Weiler 1982). That also means, however, that member governments will be precluded from dealing individually with pressing problems even if the Community cannot agree on an effective solution.

In short, joint-decision systems are doubly vulnerable to the consequences of non-agreement: they may be incapable of reaching effective agreement, and they may lose the independent capabilities for action of their member governments. As a consequence, their overall problem-solving capacity may decline – certainly in comparison to a unitary state of similar size and resources, but possibly also in comparison to smaller states, with less resources but an unfettered ability to act individually. Everything depends, therefore, upon the capacity of ongoing joint-decision systems to generate, maintain and adjust agreement on joint policies in the face of inevitably differing interests, goals and perceptions, and in the face of inevitably changing circumstances.

'PROBLEM SOLVING' AND 'BARGAINING' IN JOINT DECISIONS

Obviously, effective agreement is problematical under all conditions (even Robinson Crusoe had difficulty in making up his mind). But in decision theory it is increasingly recognized that the nature of the problem, and its inherent difficulty, varies systematically with the modalities under which effective agreement must be achieved. One dimension of these modalities is defined by the applicable decision rules (unanimous, majority or unilateral/hierarchical decisions). The other dimension is defined by the prevailing orientation of participants, and by the strategies which they are expected to employ in order to influence the outcome. There is, as yet, no agreement on terminology: March and Simon (1958) discuss different 'processes of conflict resolution', Richardson (1982) refers to different 'styles of decision-making', while Boboma (1976) proposes to distinguish among different 'power systems'. But substantive agreement on the distinctions actually subsumed under these different labels seems to be remarkably high: March and Simon's (1958, p. 129) four-fold classification of 'problem-solving', 'persuasion', 'bargaining' and 'politics' is overlapping with Olsen's 'problem solving', 'bargaining', 'mobilization' and 'confrontation' (Olsen *et al.* 1982). And it also seems possible to relate Bonoma's (1976) discussion of 'bilateral', 'mixed' and 'unilateral power systems' and Bühl's (1984) emphasis upon dominant orientations toward 'values', 'interests' or 'power' to these more process-oriented classifications of decision making.

For present purposes I will adopt Richardson's generic label of 'decision styles' and a three-fold distinction between 'problem solving', 'bargaining' and 'confrontation'. At the most general level, each of these 'styles' may be characterized by specific value orientations and sanctioning strategies: 'problem solving' by the appeal to common ('solidaristic') values and by resort to ostracism and exclusion as the ultimate collective sanction; 'bargaining' by the appeal to the individual self-interests of all (necessary) participants and by resort to incentives; and 'confrontation' by the appeal to the interests of the dominant individual or coalition and by resort to power and coercion as the ultimate sanction. While these definitions are logically independent from the applicable rules of decision (prescribing 'unanimous', 'majority' or 'unilateral/hierarchical' assent for effective decisions), that does not preclude substantive interdependence. Obviously, 'confrontation' under majority rules means something different from 'confrontation' under the unanimity rule. In each case, therefore, it is the specific combination of a decision style with a decision rule which will determine the characteristic capacity of the decision system to reach effective agreement on collective policy choices.

Returning, after this exercise in conceptual clarification, to the problems of conflict resolution and consensus formation in joint-decision systems operating under the unanimity rule, one might consider 'confrontation' as the least promising style of decision. As German education reformers had to learn the hard way, there is no sense in trying to push people around if you are dependent upon their agreement in the end. Indeed, Gerhard Lehmbruch (1976) has based his incisive analysis of the political dynamics of German federalism during the period of the Social-Liberal coalition squarely upon the idea that there was a fundamental contradiction between the confrontation politics staged by the federal government against the parliamentary opposition, and the manifest need to obtain all-party agreement in the *Bundesrat* for all major policy initiatives. But, of course, confrontation under the unanimity rule is a highly asymmetric game, and there is no reason to assume that the opposition parties should have been equally unhappy about its outcomes.

More generally, 'confrontation' under the unanimity rule seems highly serviceable for participants interested in preserving the status quo (or in exacting maximum concessions for their agreement to policy changes). It is the proponents of policy change who depend upon agreement, and who are likely to suffer defeat when a confrontational decision style prevails. And even here there are differences, depending upon whether the exit option is available, and whether it can be employed as a credible threat. In German federalism, exit is generally foreclosed in regulatory programmes, but individual *Länder* might opt out of matching-grants programmes. In the European Community, however, 'secession' also continues to be a live political option which may be invoked in confrontation strategies. Both Charles DeGaulle and Margaret Thatcher, have been able to achieve significant policy changes in this fashion. But, of course, secession might not have quite the same threat value for all member countries, and its credibility might be quite low in the case of countries whose economic stake in, and political attachment to, the Community is known to be very high. On the whole, therefore 'confrontation' is indeed the least promising decision style for policy changes and institutional reforms in joint-decision systems. If progress is to be achieved at all, it must be achieved within a 'bargaining' or 'problem-solving' framework in which it is not possible to short-circuit the requirement of unanimous agreement, and to impose solutions unilaterally.

Of these 'bargaining' seems to be the less demanding and, hence, more robust decision style. It is premised upon the assumption that participants will pursue their individual self-interest, and that agreement can only be obtained if its anticipated utility is at least as high for each participant as the anticipated utility of no co-operation (Nash 1950). 'Problem solving' in its pure form, on the other hand, is premised upon the existence of a common utility function and the irrelevance of individual self-interest for the decision at hand – either because individual interests are submerged in the common interest, or because they are effectively neutralized through institutional arrangements separating the pursuit of common goals from the distribution of costs and benefits. Furthermore, while disagreement may be an entirely acceptable outcome in 'bargaining', it is not so in 'problem solving', where the common commitment to the common goal would de-legitimate open non-co-operation. But that does not mean that agreement should be more easily obtained: battles over the proper definition of the common goal, or over appropriate strategies, might indeed be more bitter and divisive than the search for mutually agreeable compromises at the 'bargaining' table (Bonoma 1976).

Two further points need to be emphasized. First, the distinction between 'bargaining' and 'problem solving' is not logically related to the difference between zero-sum and non-zero-sum games. Indeed, in the prototypical exchange situation analyzed by Nash (1950), bargains will only be struck if individual valuations of tradeable goods are sufficiently different to allow *both* parties to increase their respective utilities. Conversely, zero-sum conflicts over the distribution of limited resources are perhaps better resolved in the 'problem-solving' style by recourse to common norms and values and, perhaps, to adjudication, rather than by pure 'bargaining', where the have-nots are without recourse against the distribution of original 'endowments'.

Second, just as 'mixed-motive games', combining elements of zero-sum and positive-sum situations, are more important in real-world situations than either of the pure game forms (Bacharach and Lawler 1980), so is there also a wide overlap between 'bargaining' and 'problem solving' in real decision processes. The empirical distribution may be highly asymmetrical, however. While pure 'bargaining' seems to be quite frequent in practice, it is unlikely that there will be many 'problem-solving' interactions without an admixture of 'bargaining' behaviour. Thus, decision styles may evolve and change over time in real-world decision systems, but it is possible that their dynamics will have only one stable resting point at the 'bargaining' end of the continuum.

In discussing this hypothesis, it seems useful to distinguish the pursuit of common interests from that of a class of individual interests whose realization does depend upon co-operation. In the case of jointly produced private goods it is indeed likely that purely self-interested exchange relationships may develop into stable networks of mutual dependence in which participants will anticipate, and respect, the self-interest of their partners (Scharpf 1978). But that will not, by itself, move interactions out of the 'bargaining' mode. The same is true of that 'cooperation among egoists' which Axelrod (1981) discovered in computer-simulated iterations of the Prisoners' Dilemma and in similarly structured real-world situations (Axelrod 1984). The Prisoners' Dilemma is, after all, one of the 'paradoxes of rationality' (Howard

1971) in which narrowly selfish calculations will lead to sub-optimal outcomes in terms of individual self-interest. What has been discovered, following theoretical work in biological evolution (Trivers 1971; Dawkins 1976), is a certain strategy ('Tit-for-Tat') which is co-operative but non-exploitable, and which does so well in long iterations of the game that it tends to drive other strategies out of competition. Thus, co-operation eliminates the 'paradox' and allows participants to return to the rational pursuit of their individual self-interests.

By contrast, what is necessary for the 'problem-solving' style to emerge is an orientation towards *common* interests, values or norms which are distinct from the individual self-interest of participants (Bonoma 1976, p. 507) and which, therefore, may facilitate voluntary agreement even when sacrifices in terms of individual self-interest are necessary and cannot be immediately compensated through 'side payments' or 'package deals'. Only when this is possible is there a good chance that ongoing decision systems operating under the unanimity rule might be able to avoid the 'joint-decision trap'.

The emergence of such common orientations may be rooted in genuine altruism – a human motive whose possibility is certainly not ruled out by methodological individualism (Sen 1970; Elster 1979, p. 141) but which, nevertheless, is unlikely to play much of a role in interactions among governments, rather than among individuals. More pertinent may be the perception of a common 'identity' defined in terms of an ethnic or cultural homogeneity or a 'community of fate' derived from shared perceptions of a common history, of a common 'manifest destiny' (or common ideological goals), or of a common vulnerability. As Peter Katzenstein (1984, 1985) has pointed out, it is the latter characteristic which helps to explain the greater ability to achieve policy consensus of the smaller European states, as compared to the larger ones. And it is worth emphasizing that the perception of a common vulnerability may be derived not only from the exposure to external military or economic threats, but also from the living memory of fratricidal internal conflicts, as in the cases of Austria and Finland – which may also explain the rapid evolution of neo-corporatist arrangements in post-Franco Spain (Pérez-Diaz 1985).

Unfortunately, neither German federalism nor the European Community have been able to profit much from such perceptions of common identity or common fate during the last decade or so. In Germany, the post-war ideology of 'social partnership' is eroding under the impact of the world-wide recession (Vobruba 1983) and party-political confrontation during the period of the Social-Liberal coalition did reinforce ideological divisions in the political arena. Europe, on the other hand, has certainly profited from the traumatic memories of two world wars. But once the European Defence Community had failed, the overriding problems of common European vulnerability, protection against Germany and protection against the Soviet Union, were institutionally entrusted to NATO (and substantively to the United States), rather than to the Community. In most other regards, of course, the present European condition is one which tends to emphasize historic, ethnic, cultural, ideological and economic diversity, rather than identity, at least when compared to the smaller European states which, in some cases, are doing very well under the near-unanimity rules of consociational democracies (Lehmbruch 1967; Lijphart 1975; Katzenstein 1984).

The question is, therefore, whether 'problem solving' does have any chance at all in joint-decision systems which do not have the benefit of a traditional sense of common identity or an overriding perception of common vulnerability? There is a certain parallel here to early sociological discussions of *Gemeinschaft* and *Gesellschaft*, and to the pessimistic hypothesis, entertained by Tönnies (1963) and Freyer (1964, p. 182), of an unidirectional erosion of the traditional motivational resources of *Gemeinschaft*. But, of course, at the interpersonal level, *Gemeinschaften* are newly created all the time, and the same is true in modern industries, where they have been rediscovered under the new label of 'clans' or the old one of 'communities' (Ouchi 1980; Streeck and Schmitter 1984; Hollingsworth and Lindberg 1985). But it is also true that the evolution of 'communal' or 'solidaristic' norms among egotistic actors (who are not part of a traditional community, or shocked into solidarity by the awareness of their fatal vulnerability to internal conflict) must be a fragile process which is easily reversed.

This is true even under the best of circumstances, when the non-negative-sum character of the common enterprise is fully recognized by all participants. The willingness to accept unilateral sacrifices, on the understanding that they will not be exploited but reciprocated by others when the occasion arises, presupposes a high degree of mutual trust. If that is not yet established, but needs to be built into the process itself, the most fatal risk is bona fide disagreement over the purpose and direction of the common enterprise, which is easily misinterpreted as defection from the common endeavour. When that happens, any unilateral retaliation is likely to provoke more suspicion and even harder retaliation, setting in motion that downward spiral of 'sacrilege' and 'just retribution' which Victor Pérez-Diaz (1985) found in the Basque conflict. Thus, the absence of any strong moral, ideological or idealistic commitment on all sides is almost a necessary precondition for the *gradual* evolution of communal norms. But in the absence of such non-egotistic commitments it is also hard to see how community interactions might rise above the calculus of individual self-interest.

The best hope of avoiding this 'double bind' exists, of course, under conditions of continuous economic growth, when the common enterprise is clearly a positive-sum game from which all are profiting. And if it is possible to establish agreement on common criteria for the distribution of benefits and contributions under these benign circumstances, there is at least a chance that the agreement might hold even when the nature of the game changes to zero-sum or negative-sum.

On theoretical grounds, there is indeed reason to assume that commonly accepted 'rules of fairness' may evolve from the interaction of purely egotistical participants (Baumol 1982; Runge 1984). Similar processes of rule generation must have been going on in German federalism and in the European Community as well, or else even the limited degree of mutual accommodation and adaptation to changing circumstances, which they have in fact achieved, would have been impossible. But given the absence of a more fundamental ideological agreement on common values, purposes and strategies, one would also expect such rules to be relatively simple and 'obvious' in the sense defined by Schelling (1960) and, hence, quite rigid in the face of changing circumstances.

In our studies of joint decisions in German federalism, we have indeed discovered a number of such rules which all seem to follow from a common logic of conflict avoidance or conflict minimization under conditions of continuing goal dissensus (Scharpf, Reissert and Schnabel 1976, pp. 62, 218–35; 1978). The most important one, governing institutional change, will be discussed in the next section. More pertinent to the present discussion are two rules governing the distribution of federal funds among the *Länder*. According to the first, all *Länder* must be allowed to benefit *equally*, according to some simple and straightforward formula, such as the number of inhabitants or, perhaps, the number of registered automobiles for the allocation of road-building funds. But if equality cannot be maintained, the fall-back rule seems to require that the losers in relative terms must at least receive their past share in absolute terms.

The fall-back rule is, of course, what one would expect from individualistic bargaining, with status quo policy as the base line for everyone, while the first rule has some claims to greater dignity. In jurisprudence and philosophy, formal equality is justified as the measure of distributive justice which should be applied in the absence of more compelling criteria based upon either unequal needs or unequal contributions (Noll 1984; Rawls 1971). As it is difficult, under conditions of party-political competition, ideological heterogeneity and significant differences in size, wealth and economic conditions, for the German *Länder* to agree upon substantive criteria of unequal need and merit, it is perhaps not surprising that formal equality, in the form of uniform conditions and per capita formulas, prevailed in most of the joint programmes in West Germany. But the rule obviously does not explain the highly unequal allocation of contributions and benefits among the member countries of the European Community, or in German regional assistance.

In both cases there was, at least originally, a rough agreement on the recognition of unequal needs and deserts which, in the EC, was presumably based upon the perception of a fundamental asymmetry of interests between West Germany and the rest of the Community. If the Germans were seen as the major beneficiaries of a common market for industrial goods, it was only fair that they should bear the major burden of EC financial contributions, and that they should benefit less from Community programmes. A slightly different justification could point out that the Community lacks the mechanism of horizontal transfer payments which were used to reduce fiscal inequalities among the German *Länder* long before the invention of joint programmes (Franzmeyer and Seidel 1976). Some EC programmes, such as the Regional Fund and the Social Fund, should thus be regarded as functional equivalents to fiscal equalization (Reissert 1979) which, of course, would preclude reference to formal equality as the relevant criterion of justice.

When the same contribution rules were applied to the United Kingdom, however (or now to Portugal), they had distributive consequences which certainly the British did not consider fair. Yet, under the unanimity requirement, the Community was unable to agree on new rules which would have redefined the criterion of fairness in the light of the new situation. Instead, the decision style changed from a search for just solutions to 'bloody-minded' bargaining and even confrontation, and it took the combined threats of British exit and of the bankruptcy of CAP to achieve even the *ad hoc* adjustments of 1984. Apparently, rules of fairness that depart from formal equality are less 'obvious' in the sense defined by Schelling (1960) and, therefore, more difficult to redefine consensually in the face of changing circumstances. If they are challenged, the joint-decision system is more likely to revert to the calculus of pure individual self-interest than to adjust its standards of fairness.

This does not mean that consensus is now impossible, and that joint-decision systems will necessarily destroy themselves through self-blockage. In an ongoing system without exit, and with 'pre-emption', pressures to reach some kind of agreement are very powerful, indeed (Weiler 1982, p. 49). But the terms of agreement are likely to be defined by a 'bargaining' logic in which the benefits received under the present policy become the base line below which nobody will settle. In the case of regional assistance in Germany, additional federal funds were required for add-on programmes dealing with the new problems of declining industrial areas. In the absence of a federal government with independent resources, or of an 'hegemony' that could be exploited (Olson and Zeckhauser 1966), 'log rolling', 'package deals' and 'side payments' are the typical modes of conflict resolution in decision systems confronted with a plurality of veto positions (Taylor 1980).

Given the claims to a substantive 'intelligence of democracy' associated with seemingly similar patterns of bargaining in American pluralism (Lindblom 1965; Dahl 1967), it is perhaps necessary to spell out more precisely what I consider the deficiencies of 'bargaining' in joint-decision systems. They are not primarily related to the difference between 'disjointed incrementalism' and an over-ambitious concept of 'synoptic problem solving' (Braybrooke and Lindblom 1963). What is important, instead, is whether analyses (and disagreements) relating to the best way of achieving *common* goals can, or cannot, be effectively separated from disagreement over the *individual* distribution of costs and benefits. If members distrust the fairness of distribution rules, they will be tempted, or even forced, to link substantive and distributive issues. Using their veto on substantive choices in order to improve their distributive position, they must contribute to the interminable haggling over package deals and side payments that are characteristic of all EC decisions. But, of course, distributive issues are legitimate even in a *Gemeinschaft*, and if they cannot be neutralized by agreed-upon rules of fairness, they must somehow be settled in negotiations.

There are, however, many decision situations in which adequate compensation is impossible – either because the losses involved would be of a non-quantifiable, qualitative nature, or because of uncertainty over their future incidence and magnitude, or finally because of the negative-sum character of the decision situation itself. The first case is of considerable importance not only under conditions of ideological disagreement, but even more so when considerations of national 'sovereignty', or *Länder* 'autonomy', or interference with established bureaucratic routines and networks of interaction, come to play a significant role. It is under such conditions that the imperatives of 'conflict avoidance' and 'non intervention' have their strongest impact upon the substance of joint decisions in Germany, and the same mechanisms seem to restrict the directive effectiveness of Community policies and of their implementation (Laffan 1983). The second case seems to be particularly damaging under conditions, labelled the 'interdependence trap' by Paul Taylor (1980, p. 374), when the costs of an advantageous policy proposal are well defined and certain, while the benefits are more diffuse and uncertain. In the third case, finally, the negative-sum character of the overall situation may not be generally appreciated while participants are bargaining over the avoidance of individual losses. It is plausible that these difficulties became more acute when the world economic environment changed from benign to hostile in the 1970s (Ziebura 1982).

In all three cases, however, the outcome is similar: Individual losses expected from a policy option which would be collectively optimal, cannot be adequately compensated through side payments. Under such conditions, therefore, 'bargaining' is likely to lead to solutions which are unable to achieve realizable common gains or to prevent avoidable common losses.

To summarize a perhaps overly involved line of argument, unanimity is a decision rule which can claim welfare-theoretic optimality, most plausibly, for single-shot decisions. In ongoing joint-decision systems, from which exit is precluded or very costly, non-agreement would imply the self-defeating continuation of past policies in the face of a changing policy environment. Thus, pressures to reach agreement will be great. The substance of agreement will be affected, however, by the prevailing style of decision-making. In its ability to achieve effective responses to a changing policy environment, the 'bargaining' style is clearly inferior to the 'problem-solving' style. But the preconditions of 'problem-solving' – the orientation towards common goals, values and norms – are difficult to create, and they are easily eroded in cases of ideological conflict, mutual distrust or disagreement over the fairness of distribution rules. Thus, reversion to a 'bargaining' style of decision making was characteristic of German federalism during the 1970s, and it seems to have been characteristic of the European Community ever since the great confrontations of the mid-1960s. The price to be paid is not simply a prevalence of distributive conflicts complicating all substantive decisions, but a systematic tendency towards sub-optimal substantive solutions. In short, it is the combination of the unanimity rule and a bargaining style which explains the pathologies of public policy associated with joint decisions in Germany and in Europe.

JOINT DECISIONS AND THE DYNAMICS OF EUROPEAN INTEGRATION

At this point, we can return to the concerns raised in the introduction. Why is it that real developments since the mid-1960s – the frustration without disintegration and resilience without progress – have disappointed hopes for a dynamic deepening and widening of European integration and invalidated predictions of an inevitable return to the intergovernmental relations of sovereign nation states? An explanation has been derived from the decision logic inherent in the particular institutional arrangements of the European community. Relating these findings to both the optimistic and pessimistic prognoses of the future course of European integration, the following conclusions appear to be warranted.

First, the early optimism of neo-functional integration theorists was based upon the expectation that a 'new political community, superimposed over the pre-existing ones' would emerge through the gradual shifting of the loyalties, expectations and activities of political elites toward the new European arena (Haas 1958, p. 16). The basic mechanism driving the process of political integration was identified by Ernst Haas in the concept of 'spill over' which, essentially, meant that narrowly defined European decision functions would have lateral effects on other interests which, in turn, would redirect their demands, expectations and, eventually, loyalties to the European political process. As a consequence, the support for European integration among interest groups and political parties would grow, and governments would realize that further sabotage or evasions were politically unprofitable. Hence, the powers of European institutions would be enlarged, with the consequence of further spill overs eventually bringing about a genuine political community and the acceptance of a full-fledged federal authority (Haas 1958, pp. XXXIII/IV, 3–31, 283–317).

While later interpretations by neo-functionalists, including Ernst Haas himself, have been more cautious, differentiating and, ultimately, even agnostic in their predictions (Haas 1964; 1971; Haas and Schmitter 1964; Lindberg 1963; Lindberg and Scheingold 1970; Schmitter 1969; 1970; Scheingold 1970), they have continued to place their primary emphasis upon the interaction between European decisions and the interests, expectations, activities and loyalties of interest groups, political parties, politicians and bureaucrats, in short: upon the perspectives and actions of a plurality of political elites, rather than upon the institutional self-interests of national governments operating within the constraints of particular institutional arrangements at the European level (Bulmer 1983, p. 353). As William Wallace (1982, p. 64–5) has put it: 'The success of the neo-functional approach depended upon national governments not noticing – in effect – the gradual draining away of their lifeblood to Brussels.'

The tendency to treat institutional arrangements not as a powerful independent variable, but merely as the resultant of economic, social and political interactions, was even more characteristic of the older, 'functionalist' school of international organization, as illustrated by David Mitrany's dictum (1975, p. 27) that 'in the last resort, the form of government and its laws and institutions are shaped and reshaped by the restless flux of the community's social pressures.' And the same non-institutional perspective is, of course also characteristic of the 'communications' approach to political integration developed by Karl Deutsch (1953) and his collaborators (Deutsch *et al.* 1957; 1964; Merrit and Russett 1981).

The re-emergence of 'inter-governmentalism' in the European Community after 1966 (Wallace, Wallace and Webb 1977, pp. 24–5; Taylor 1983, pp. 60–92) came as a disappointment to all such theories of political integration, giving rise to several varieties of *ad hoc* explanations emphasizing either changes in 'background' variables external to the theory, or the historical uniqueness of DeGaulle and his personal intervention. By contrast, and with the benefit of hindsight, my explanations assume explicitly that 'institutions do matter'.

Given this premise, the two most powerful institutional conditions affecting the processes of European integration are, first, the fact that national governments are making European decisions and, second, the fact that these decisions have to be unanimous. The 'joint-decision trap' set up by these two conditions is responsible for the pathologies of substantive public policy described and analysed above.

But joint-decision systems are a 'trap' in yet another, and more important sense. They are able to block their own further institutional evolution. This possibility has been overlooked by functionalist and neo-functionalist writers, and even William Riker, the most agnostic student of federalism (1966), had assumed that in any federal arrangement one of two tendencies, 'centralizing' or 'peripheralizing', must eventually win out (1964, p. 6), with the 'structure of the party system' as the controlling variable (1964, pp. 129–36). While peripheralized federalisms will gradually fall apart, centralized federalisms will 'become more like unitary or imperial governments in time' (1964, p. 7). But neither outcome is happening in either the EC or Germany. The institutional arrangements of German federalism are quite stable, and the European Community seems to be securely 'stuck between sovereignty and integration' (Wallace 1982, p. 67). Our studies of joint decisions in German federalism have discovered a mechanism that preserves the institutional status quo: it is the political priority of substantive solutions over institutional reforms.

All through the 1970s, the German federal government was confronted with urgent problems of unemployment and inflation that seemed to require vigorous action at the national level which, however, depended upon the collaboration of the *Länder*. Even though the majority of the *Bundesrat* consisted of *Länder* governments controlled by parties in opposition to the Social-Liberal federal government, collaboration was never flatly refused. If that had been the case, the legitimacy of the *veto* position of the *Bundesrat* could have become a major political issue which might have strengthened centralist forces. As it was, the *Länder* were always willing to compromise on substantive policy, and the federal government was too hard pressed politically to refuse the compromises which were offered. In the process, however, the institutional position of the *Länder* was continuously improved. Fiscal resources were shifted from the federal level to the *Länder*, precisely during the decade when the federal government was more activist and interventionist than ever before. During the same period, the *Länder* have time and again consented to enlarge the substantive responsibilities of the federal government, but they have also increased their own control over the exercise of these responsibilities. In order to avoid this gradual erosion of its institutional position, the federal government would have had to provoke the direct confrontation of the *Länder* over institutional issues. But under the pressure of urgent substantive problems, it was never willing to risk the complete blockage of joint-decision processes in the (uncertain) hope of improving its position in the longer run. Acting as a 'locally maximizing machine' (Elster 1979, p. 4), the federal government contributed to the tightening of the ropes that reduced its own ability to act.

The situation is even more one-sided in the European Community. In the absence of a European government with a popular political base of its own, all possibilities of institutional transformation are entirely determined by the self-interests of national governments. And even those among them which most vigorously support activist and expansionary European policies are likely to hedge their bets when it comes to relinquishing their veto powers. Conversely, the 'reluctant Europeans' among member governments have been much more willing to accept disagreeable compromises on substantive policy than to weaken their own institutional control over the substance of future decisions. As a consequence, the jurisdiction of the Community has expanded, and Community law has achieved the effectiveness of the legal order of a federal state – but the price has been 'an ever closer national control exercised in the decision processes' (Weiler 1982, pp. 46–7).

Thus, the establishment of the European Council should be interpreted as a symbol of the increasing importance of European policy choices and as an attempt to assert the control of national policy generalists over the vertical alliances of policy specialists dominating the Council of Ministers as well as the European Commission. But that only means that it is national heads of government, rather than national ministers, who are likely to tighten their grip in European policy making (Bulmer, 1983). Nor are these conclusions controverted by the packages of compromises and reforms culminating in the 'Single European Act' of 28 February 1986 which seems to have ended the long period of confrontations and deadlock of the 1970s and early 1980s. Spain and Portugal were finally admitted and interim settlements for the budget issues were found. Even more spectacularly, governments committed themselves to complete the 'internal market' – 'an area without internal frontiers in which the free movement of goods, persons, services and capital is assured' – by the end of 1992 (article 13), and they also renewed their aspirations toward an 'Economic and Monetary Union' requiring the convergence of national economic and monetary policies (article 20).

Compared to these substantive commitments, whose implementation continues to depend upon the agreement of national governments, the institutional changes which were adopted seem to fall far short of the visionary goals of achieving 'genuine political unity' through the creation of 'effective democratic institutions' that had been asserted only a year before (Report of the Dooge Committee 1984). To be sure, on a long list of routine decisions, qualified-majority voting in the Council (which always would have been possible) is now explicitly provided for in the Treaty – and it is apparently practised quite frequently, with governments preferring to be outvoted, rather than having to agree formally to an inevitable but unpopular Council decision. It remains to be seen whether the weakening of the pressures toward consensus will be outweighed by the lower threshold of agreement. At any rate, a long list of more important decisions, and all further evolutions of the Treaty structure, are explicitly reserved for unanimous voting, and the general principle under which all members may exercise a veto in matters affecting their vital national interests remains unchallenged. Ironically, the very limited efforts to strengthen the powers of the European Parliament not only have taken the form of adding another institutional hurdle to European decision making, but have reinforced the practical significance of unanimity within the Council (where it is necessary to override objections or amendments of the Parliament).

On the basis of German experience, one would expect that even the formal relaxation of the unanimity rule may not make much of a difference in practice. As long as it is still national governments that are making European decisions, their common interest in preserving their institutional veto is likely to prevail as well (Everling 1980). In that regard, all neo-functionalist hopes that learning processes would lead to an institutional transformation seem to have been misplaced. The 'transformation group' (Piaget 1973, p. 14; Deutsch 1977, p. 23) of a joint-decision system does not seem to include the self-transformation into a simpler system based upon binding majority decisions. Or, as Helmut Schmidt once remarked with a view to German federalism: 'Any attempt to reform a complex constitution can only increase its complexity.'

If that is so, two of the crucial spill-over mechanisms, which neo-functionalist theory expected to create external political pressures for more integration, seem to be blocked or seriously weakened. First, the reorientation of economic, social and political interests toward the European level remains incomplete. As long as European decisions continue to be made by national governments, the interests affected by them will be mediated by national governments as well. Of course, interest groups will also operate at the European level, but ultimately it is still national governments which they will have to persuade. As a consequence, nationally specific definitions of group interests, and of party-political ideologies, will be maintained and reinforced, rather than amalgamated into European interest associations (Averyt 1976) and European political parties. In that regard, the tendencies toward the segregation of interests and ideologies inherent in federal, as compared to unitary, states are even more pronounced among the member states of the Community (Kirsch 1984, p. 122). By the same token, there is less reason to expect a transfer of the demands, expectations and loyalties of political elites from the national to the European level.

Second, there is much less reason to expect that 'goal frustration' should lead to 'politicization' and, ultimately, to a redefinition of goals and the 'transcendence' to a higher level of political integration (Schmitter 1969, p. 164). If the iron grip of national governments cannot be broken, the decision logic of European institutions will continue to reproduce the substantive pathologies discussed above. Beyond a certain point, surely, political frustration and exasperation over the inefficiency and inflexibility of European policy making, and over its structural inability to respond to crises creatively, may not lead to renewed demands for 'a more perfect union' but, rather, to cynicism and indifference or to a renewed search for national remedies, however imperfect and limited, for the problems which the Community seems to handle so poorly. As was the case with joint policies in West Germany, the dynamic movement toward greater European integration may have been retarded and, perhaps, reversed, not by the ideological strength of nationalism or by the obstructions of a Charles DeGaulle or a Margaret Thatcher, but by the pathological decision logic inherent in its basic institutional arrangements.

But why is it, then, that the Community didn't disintegrate long ago? As in the case of German federalism, an adequate explanation of its continuing resilience needs to consider two levels of interest, functional and institutional. At the functional level, it is clear that at least some of the benefits predicted by the economic theories of integration have in fact been realized. This tends to be more true for the benefits of 'market integration' than of 'policy integration' (Pelkmans 1980) or of 'negative', rather than 'positive', integration (Taylor 1980, pp. 384–5). But as it is uncertain, even in the industrial sector, whether the common market could be maintained in the absence of a substantial commitment to common (and compensatory) policy measures in such areas as the Social Fund, the Regional Fund and Industrial Policy, one probably could not have the one without the other. In other words, to the extent that joint policies are addressing, however inadequately, real problems which could not be handled at the level of member governments, these problems would simply reassert themselves if the joint-policy system were to be dismantled.

The functional argument is not controverted by the fact that not all economic-policy problems can be handled at the Community level (Ziebura 1982), or that some of the smaller European countries outside of the Community (Switzerland, Austria, Finland, Sweden and Norway) have, on the whole, done better during the world-wide recession of the 1970s than similar countries within the Community (Denmark, the Netherlands, Belgium and Ireland). As all of the successful outsiders are dependent upon industrial exports to the Community, they may simply have been free riders profiting from the creation of the common market and from the Community's relatively liberal trade policies in the industrial sector. Exporters of agricultural goods, on the other hand, like Denmark, Ireland, Greece, Spain and Portugal, had every incentive to join the Community in order to evade CAP's prohibitively high protective barriers. Thus, the appeal of economic integration remains alive, and it is even reinforced, at least for the European Left, by the realization that the internationalization of capital markets has destroyed any hopes for Keynesian full employment policies at the national level (Pelkmanns 1980, pp. 344–5; Scharpf 1987, chs. 11–12). Unfortunately, if my understanding of the 'joint-decision trap' is correct, hopes for an effective 'European Keynesianism' are likely to be futile as well.

At the institutional level, the Community is unequivocally supported by the self-interest of the vertical alliances of policy specialists – interest associations, national ministries and parliamentary committees, and the large contingents of specialized lobbyists, bureaucrats and politicians operating at the European level. They all profit from the availability of additional resources, and of additional points of access to political decision processes, providing additional opportunities for playing the game of influence and obstruction which is their *raison d'être*. Of course, they also must cope with the political frustration, among their clienteles or electorates, over the impact of sub-optimal or even counter-productive European policies. But, as in German federalism, the political effect of voter frustration is largely neutralized by the very diffusion of responsibility and accountability which is characteristic of joint-decision systems (Scharpf, Reissert and Schnabel 1976, p. 236).

Similar cost-benefit calculations tend to stabilize the Community from the perspective of national policy generalists – heads of government, finance ministers and parliamentary budget committees – if their countries are among the net beneficiaries of the Community budget. Net contributors, on the other hand, find themselves locked into an ongoing decision system whose direction they could only hope to change significantly by either assuming the burdens and costs of hegemonic leadership or by threatening to leave the Community altogether. As it is, the only pretender to hegemonic status, West Germany, is too weak or too egoistical to assume the burdens of leadership, while confrontation strategies are unlikely to work for countries whose interest in, and attachment to, the Community is known to be very great. Thus, the Community is likely to remain secure as long as care is taken to concentrate net contributions to the Community budget upon those countries which would have most to lose economically and politically by its dissolution and, in particular, by the disintegration of the common market.

By way of summary, it is now possible to define the 'joint-decision trap' more precisely. It is an institutional arrangement whose policy outcomes have an inherent (non-accidental) tendency to be sub-optimal – certainly when compared to the policy potential of unitary governments of similar size and resources. Nevertheless, the arrangement represents a 'local optimum' in the cost-benefit calculations of all participants that might have the power to change it. If that is so, there is no 'gradualist' way in which joint-decision systems might transform themselves into an institutional arrangement of greater policy potential. In order to be effective, institutional change would have to be large-scale, implying the acceptance of short-term losses for many, or all, participants. That is unlikely, but not impossible (Elster 1979). And, of course, the system might be jolted out of its present equilibrium by external intervention or by a dramatic deterioration of its performance which would undermine even its 'local optimality' for crucial participants. Thus, I have not described a deterministic world, even though the logic of the 'joint-decision trap' may provide as close an approximation to structural determinism as one is likely to encounter in the social sciences.

SOME TENTATIVE EXTENSIONS

Our analyses of '*Politikverflechtung*' pose the question of whether or not the findings can be generalized. We tended to emphasize the specificity of the historical case from which the conclusions were derived (Scharpf 1978a) but nevertheless we attempted to formulate the findings in the language of universalistic propositions. The present essay claims that these propositions also help to explain the European experience. In effect, these cases may be instances of a universal decision logic inherent in particular 'patterns', in the sense discussed by von Hayek (1967), of institutional arrangements. This conclusion offers a few speculative suggestions about other areas of potential application.

Clearly, the 'joint-decision trap' is not inherent in all forms of *de facto* unanimous decision making, even if we exclude (as one should) single-shot encounters. By the same logic, one should probably also exclude all forms of ongoing associations from which exit is very easy, either because their benefits are of marginal value to members, or because they could easily be substituted from another source. Furthermore, it seems also appropriate to exclude associations in which the tension between common and individual interests could not arise because member interests are complementary, and costs low in comparison to the benefits of associaton. Cliques, clubs and business consortia might fall into that class. More doubtful candidates for either inclusion or exclusion are organizations with member interests that are partly complementary and partly competitive, but where members are not expecting each other to pursue anything but their own, individual self-interest. Many forms of long-standing vertical relationships between suppliers and customers fall into that category, but also horizontal cartels and 'free collective bargaining' between employers and trade unions. I would also include here the 'co-operation among egoists' in long sequences of the Prisoners' Dilemma and similar real-world situations. In my view, cases in this category would not provide valid tests for the 'joint-decision trap' hypothesis. While an outside observer might perceive potential 'common' interests and, hence, benefits from 'problem solving', participants may have good reasons to define their mutual relations purely in 'bargaining' terms. Being where they want to be, they are not in any meaningful sense in a 'trap'.

But even if we limit the discussion to ongoing joint-decision systems without exit, in which 'common' interests have a normative validity that is separate from, but not necessarily superior to, the individual self-interest of participants, and in which 'problem solving' would be the more efficient style of decision making, we would still cast the net too wide. 'Problem solving' is, after all, a style of decision making that is frequently encountered in decision situations which are formally operating under hierarchical or majority decisions rules, even though there may be *de facto* unanimity for most practical purposes. Indeed, that may be the secret of their success: 'participative management' (as distinguished from '*laissez-faire* management') is likely to profit from the creativity and intelligence of employees precisely because disintegrative tendencies are held in check by a hierarchical authority that has abdicated some, but not all, of its functions. Conversely, formally egalitarian decision situations might profit from the *de facto* hierarchical role of one hegemonic member – as exemplified by the powerfully integrative role of Prussia in Bismarck's Germany. Similarly, one might suspect that 'consociational democracies' and even American-style 'pluralism' would not work quite as well if obstinate minorities did not have to reckon with the possibility that the formal rule of majority decision might still be invoked against them. The precarious stability of 'problem solving', and the tendency to revert to the 'bargaining' style is, thus, likely to manifest itself most clearly in joint-decision systems in which *de facto* unanimity is not backed up by the formal possibility of unilateral or majority decisions or by the clear preponderance of power of a hegemonic member.

Even within these definitional constraints, however, there seems to be a wide range of institutions to which the logic of the 'joint-decision trap' might plausibly apply. Faculty self-government (in the absence of a powerful president or dean) might be one example. Legalized communes of squatters in West Berlin (tied to their houses by the sunk costs of rebuilding them) could be another. Further candidates could be connubia, business partnerships and joint ventures, political coalitions, military alliances, 'neo-corporatist' arrangements and a wide variety of permanent inter-organizational networks. They are all likely to be confronted with tensions between a recognized common interest and the individual self-interest of participants; they all would profit from a 'problem-solving' style of decision making, if only distributive conflicts could, somehow, be neutralized; and they all should be exposed to the entropic push toward 'bargaining'. At the same time, they all should have difficulties in adopting a decision rule (majority or hierarchy) that could avoid reversion to the bargaining style at the expense of membership control over the substance of decisions.

Thus, it should be possible to test the 'joint-decision-trap' hypothesis under an extremely wide variety of institutional conditions. More interesting, from my point of view, would be the opportunity provided by such empirical studies to identify more precisely those factors that are able to influence the changes of decision styles, from 'bargaining' to 'problem solving' and vice versa, in joint-decision systems. Given an increasingly interdependent world, all mechanisms and strategies that might help to avoid the 'joint-decision trap' ought to be of very considerable scholarly and practical interest.

REFERENCES

Abromeit, Heidrun. 1982. 'Die Funktion des Bundesrats und der Streit um seine Politisierung', *Zeitschrift für Parlamentsfragen* 13, 462–72.

Averyt, William F. jr. 1976. *Agricultural interest groups in the European Community: the Commité des Organisations Professionelles Agricoles.* Ph.D. Yale University, May.

Axelrod, Robert. 1981. 'The emergence of cooperation among egoists', *American Political Science Review* 75, 306–18.

Axelrod, Robert. 1984. *The evolution of cooperation.* New York: Basic Books.

Bacharach, S. B. and E. J. Lawler. 1980. *Power and politics in organizations.* London: Jossey-Bass.

Balassa, Bela. 1962. *The theory of economic integration.* London: George Allen and Unwin.

Balz, M., R. Meimberg and M. Schöpe. 1982. 'Agrarstrukturpolitik in der EG – Regionale Entwicklungsstrategien erforderlich', *Ifo Schnelldienst* 32/82, 10–20.

Baumol, William J. 1982. 'Applied fairness theory and rationing policy', *American Economic Review* September, 639–51.

Bentele, Karlheinz. 1979. *Kartellbildung in der allgemeinen Forschungsförderung.* Königstein: Anton Hain.

Benz, Arthur. 1985. *Föderalismus als dynamisches System.* Opladen: Westdeutscher Verlag.

BMBW. 1982. *Informationen/Bildung/Wissenschaft des Bundesministers für Bildung und Wissenschaft.* Nr. 4/82. Bonn: 22 April.

BMF. 1985. Bundesministerium der Finanzen. *Die finanzwirtschaftliche Entwicklung von Bund, Ländern und Gemeinden seit 1970.* Dokumentation 2/85. Bonn: 31 January 1985.

BMF. 1982. Bundesministerium der Finanzen. *Die Finanzbeziehungen zwischen Bund, Ländern und Gemeinden aus finanzverfassungsrechtlicher und finanzwirtschaftlicher Sicht.* Bonn.

Body, Richard. 1982. *Agriculture: the triumph and the shame.* London: Temple Smith.

Bonoma, Thomas V. 1976. 'Conflict, cooperation and trust in three power systems', *Behavioral Science* 21, 499–514.

Borell, R. 1981. *Mischfinanzierungen. Darstellung, Kritik, Reformüberlegungen.* Wiesbaden: Karl-Bräuer-Institut.

Braybrooke, David and Charles E. Lindblom. 1963. *A strategy of decision. Policy evaluation as a social process.* New York: The Free Press.

Breton, Albert and Anthony Scott. 1978. *The economic constitution of federal states.* Toronto: University of Toronto Press.

Bruder, Wolfgang. 1983. *The regional policy of the European Community: problems and perspectives.* MS. Universität Konstanz.

Buchanan, James M. and Gordon Tullock. 1962. *The calculus of consent. Logical foundations of constitutional democracy.* Ann Arbor, Michigan: University of Michigan Press.

Buchanan, James M. 1975. *The limits of liberty. Between anarchy and Leviathan*. Chicago: University of Chicago Press.

Bühl, Walter L. 1984. 'Die Dynamik sozialer Konflikte in katastrophentheoretischer Darstellung', *Kölner Zeitschrift für Soziologie und Sozialpsychologie*, 641–66.

Bulletin der Europäischen Gemeinschaften. Nr. 11, 1984.

Bulmer, Simon. 1983. 'Domestic politics and European Community policy making', *Journal of Common Market Studies* 21, 349–63.

BVerfGE. 1975. Entscheidungen des Bundesverfassungsgerichts. Band 39.

Dahl, Robert H. 1967. *Pluralist democracy in the United States: conflict and consent*. Chicago: Rand McNally.

Dawkins, Richard. 1976. *The selfish gene*. Oxford: Oxford University Press.

Deutsch, Karl. 1953. *Nationalism and social communication: an inquiry into the foundations of nationality*. Cambridge, Mass.: MIT Press.

Deutsch, Karl (with S. A. Burell, R. A. Kann, M. Lee, M. Lichtermann and R. W. van Wagenen). 1957. *Political community and the North Atlantic area*. Princeton: Princeton University Press.

Deutsch, Karl (with P. E. Jacob, H. Teune, J. V. Toscano and W. L. C. Wheaton). 1964. *The integration of political communities*. Philadelphia: Lippincott.

Deutsch, Karl. 1977. 'National integration. Some concepts and research approaches', *Jerusalem Journal of International Relations* 2, 1–29.

DIW. 1984. Deutsches Institut für Wirtschaftsforschung. EG-Haushalt und -Agrarpolitik. DIW Wochenbericht 40/84, 497–501.

DIW. 1984a. Deutsches Institut für Wirtschaftsforschung. *Statt Subventionsabbau neue Hilfen für die Landwirtschaft*. DIW Wochenbericht 25/84, 297–302.

Downs, Anthony. 1957. *An economic theory of democracy*. New York: Harper and Row.

Dunsire, A. 1978. *Implementation in a bureaucracy*. Oxford: Martin Robertson.

Easton, David. 1965. *A systems analysis of political life*. New York: John Wiley.

Elster, Jon. 1979. *Ulysses and the Sirens. Studies of rationality and irrationality*. Cambridge: Cambridge University Press.

Everling, Ulrich. 1980. 'Possibilities and limits of European integration', *Journal of Common Market Studies* 18, 217–28.

Fabritius, Georg. 1978. *Wechselwirkungen zwischen Landtagswahlen und Bundespolitik*. Meisenheim: Anton Hain.

Feld, Werner J. 1980. 'Two-tier policy making in the EC: the Common Agricultural Policy', in Leon Hurwitz (ed.), *Contemporary perspectives on European integration*. London: Aldwich Press.

Franzmeyer, Fritz and Bernhard Seidel. 1976. *Überstaatlicher Finanzausgleich und Europäische Integration*. Bonn: Europa Union Verlag.

Frey, Bruno S. 1977. *Moderne Politische Ökonomie*. München: Piper.

Freyer, Hans. 1964. *Soziologie als Wirklichkeitswissenschaft*. Stuttgart: Teubner (First Edition 1930).

Garlichs, Dietrich. 1980. *Grenzen staatlicher Infrastrukturpolitik. Bund/Länder-Kooperation in der Fernstraßenplanung*. Königstein: Anton Hain.

v. d. Groeben, Hans and Ernst-Joachim Mestmäcker. (Hrsg.). 1974. *Verfassung oder Technokratie für Europa*. Frankfurt/M.: Athenäum Fischer.

Haas, Ernst B. 1958. *The uniting of Europe. Political, social and economic forces 1950–1957*. London: Stevens and Sons (1968 edition by Stanford University Press).

——. 1964. *Beyond the nation state. Functionalism and international organization*. Stanford: Stanford University Press.

Haas, Ernst B. and Philippe C. Schmitter. 1964. 'Economics and differential patterns of political integration: projections about unity in Latin America', *International Organization* 18, 705–37.

Haas, Ernst B. 1971. 'The study of regional integration: reflections on the joy and anguish of pretheorizing', in L. N. Lindberg and S. A. Scheingold (eds.), *Regional integration, theory and research*. Cambridge, Mass.: Harvard University Press, 3–42.

Harrison, Reginald J. 1974. *Europe in question: Theories of regional international integration*. London: George Allen and Unwin.

von Hayek, F. A. 1967. 'The theory of complex phenomena', in F. A. von Hayek, *Studies in philosophy, politics and economics*. London: University of Chicago Press.

Heidenheimer, Arnold. 1958. 'Federalism and the party system – the case of West Germany', *American Political Science Review*. September.

Heidenheimer, Arnold J., Hugh Heclo and Carolyn Teich-Adams. 1975. *Comparative public policy*. New York: St. Martin's Press.

——. 1983. *Comparative public policy. The politics of social choice in Europe and America*. Second Edition, London: Macmillan.

Hesse, Konrad. 1962. *Der unitarische Bundesstaat*. Karlsruhe: Müller.

Hesse, Joachim Jens, (Hrsg.), 1978. *Politikverflechtung im föderativen Staat*. Baden-Baden: Nomos.

Höhne, Wilfrid and Günther Horzetzky. 1984. 'Europäische Agrarpolitik: Probleme und Reformansätze', *Gewerkschaftliche Monatshefte* 35, 310–22.

Hoffman, Stanley. 1966. 'Obstinate or obsolete? the fate of the nation-state and the case of Western Europe', *Daedalus* Summer 1966, 862–915.

Hollingsworth, J. Rogers and Leon N. Lindberg. 1985. *The government of the American economy: the role of markets, clans, hierarchies and associative behavior*. MS University of Wisconsin.

Howard, Nigel. 1971. *Paradoxes of rationality: theory of metagames and political behavior*. Cambridge, Mass.: MIT Press.

Hrbek, Rudolf. 1979. 'Politikverflechtung macht an den Grenzen nicht halt. Auswirkungen der EG-Mitgliedschaft auf die föderative Ordnung der Bundesrepublik Deutschland', *Der Bürger im Staat* 29, Jahrgang, Heft 1, 38–43.

Hrbek, Rudolf and Wolfgang Wessels (Hrsg.). 1984. *EG-Mitgliedschaft: ein vitales Interesse der Bundesrepublik Deutschland?* Bonn: Europa Union Verlag.

Johnson, Nevil. 1973. *Government in the Federal Republic of Germany. The executive at work*. Oxford: Pergamon Press.

Jürgensen, Stephan and Schmitz, Peter M. 1984. 'EG Agrarpolitik: Der Streit um den Grenzausgleich', *Wirtschaftsdienst* IV/84, 192–6.

Katzenstein, Peter. 1984. *Corporatism and change. Austria, Switzerland and the politics of industry*. Ithaca: Cornell University Press.

——. 1985. *Small nations as experiments? Experiences from Europe (and other places)*. MS Ithaca, February.

Kirsch, Guy (Hrsg.). 1977. *Föderalismus*. Stuttgart: Gustav Fischer.

Kirsch, Guy. 1984. 'Fiscal federalism', *Wirtschaftswissenschaftliches Studium*, März, 118.

Klatt, Hartmut. 1979. 'Die Länderparlamente müssen sich wehren. Möglichkeiten und Ansätze einer Reform des Länderparlamentarismus', *Der Bürger im Staat* 21, Heft 1, 1979, 20–8.

Knott, Jack H. 1981. *Managing the German economy. Budgetary politics in a federal state*. Lexington, Mass.: Lexington Books.

Kohr, Leopold. 1978. *The breakdown of nations*. New York: Dutton.

Kommission für die Finanzreform. 1966. *Gutachten über die Finanzreform in der Bundesrepublik Deutschland*. Stuttgart: Kohlhammer.

Laffan, Brigid. 1983. 'Policy implementation in the European Community: the European Social Fund as a case study', *Journal of Common Market Studies* 21, 389–408.

Lehmbruch, Gerhard. 1967. *Proporzdemokratie: Politisches System und politische Kultur in der Schweiz und Österreich*. Tübingen: J. C. B. Mohr.

——. 1976. *Parteienwettbewerb im Bundesstaat*. Stuttgart: Kohlhammer.

Lehner, Franz. 1979. 'Politikverflechtung: Institutionelle Eigendynamik und politische Kontrolle' in Joachim Matthes (Hrsg.), *Sozialer Wandel in Westeuropa. Verhandlungen des 19. Deutschen Soziologentages*. Frankfurt: Campus, 611–25.

——. 1979a. 'Politikverflechtung – Föderalismus ohne Transparenz', *Der Bürger im Staat* 129, Heft 1, 3–8.

Lijphart, Arend. 1975. *The politics of accommodation. Pluralism and democracy in the Netherlands*. Second Edition, Berkeley: University of California Press.

Lindberg, Leon N. 1963. *The political dynamics of European integration*. Stanford: Stanford University Press.

Lindberg, Leon N. and Stuart A. Scheingold. 1970. *Europe's would-be polity. Patterns of change in the European Community*. Englewood Cliffs: Prentice-Hall.

Lindblom, Charles E. 1965. *The intelligence of democracy*. New York: The Free Press.

March, James G. and Herbert A. Simon. 1958. *Organizations*. New York: John Wiley.

Martins, Mario R. and John Mawson. 1982. 'The programming of regional development in the EC: Supra-national or international decision-making?' *Journal of Common Market Studies* 20, 229–44.

Merrit, Richard L. and Bruce C. Russett. (eds.). 1981. *From national development to global community*. London: George Allen and Unwin.

Mitrany, David. 1975. 'A political theory for the new society', in: A. J. R. Groom and Paul Taylor (eds.), *Functionalism. theory and practice in international relations*. London: University of London Press, 25–37.

Mueller, Dennis C. 1979. *Public choice*. Cambridge: Cambridge University Press.

Nash, John F. jr. 1950. 'The bargaining problem', *Econometrica*, 18, 155–162.

Niskanen, William A. 1971. *Bureaucracy and representative government*. Chicago: Aldine-Atherton.

Noé, Claus. 1983. 'Wo sind 19,5 Milliarden DM geblieben? Bemerkungen zu Zielen, Mitteln und Wirkungsweise regionalpolitischer Versuche der Europäischen Gemeinschaft', *Raumforschung und Raumordnung*, 15–20.

Nölling, Wilhelm. 1977. 'Das Programm für Zukunftsinvestitionen', *Wirtschaftsdienst* VIII, 391.

Noll, Peter. 1984. *Diktate über Sterben und Tod*. Zürich: Pendo.

Oates, Wallace E. 1972. *Fiscal federalism*. New York: Harcourt Brace Jovanovich.

Offe, Claus. 1975. *Berufsbildungsreform. Eine Fallstudie über Reformpolitik*. Frankfurt: Suhrkamp.

Olsen, Johan, Paul Roness and Harald Saetren. 1982. 'Norway: still peaceful coexistence and revolution in slow motion?', in Richardson, J. (ed.), *Policy Styles in Western Europe*. London, 47–9.

Olson, Mancur and Richard Zeckhauser. 1966. 'An Economic Theory of Alliances', *Review of Economics and Statistics* 48, 266–79.

Olson, Mancur. 1969. 'The principle of fiscal equivalence: the division of responsibilities among different levels of government', *American Economic Review* May Supplement, 479.

Ostrom, Elinor. 1984. *Multiorganizational arrangements and coordination: an application of institutional analysis*. MS. Workshop in Political Theory and Policy Analysis. Bloomington, Indiana: Indiana University.

Ostrom, Vincent. 1984. *The political theory of a compound republic*. Revised Edition, Bloomington, Indiana: Indiana University.

Ouchi, William G. 1980. 'Markets, bureaucracies and clans', *Administrative Science Quarterly* 25, 129–41.

Parsons, Talcott. 1967. 'Voting and the equilibrium of the American political system', in T. Parsons, *Sociological theory and modern society*. New York: Free Press, 223–63.

Pelkmans, Jacques. 1980. 'Economic theories of integration revisited', *Journal of Common Market Studies* 18, 333–54.

Pentland, Charles. 1973. *International theory and European integration*. London: Faber and Faber.

Pérez-Diaz, Victor M. 1985. *Governability and mesogovernments: regional autonomies and neo-corporatism in Spain*. MS Madrid, February 1985.

Piaget, Jean. 1973. *Der Strukturalismus*. Olten und Freiburg i. Br.: Walter Verlag.

Rawls, John. 1971. *A theory of justice*. Cambridge, Mass.: Harvard University Press.

Reissert, Bernd. 1979. *'Politikverflechtung' in der Europäischen Gemeinschaft*. MS. Wissenschaftszentrum Berlin.

——. 1984. *Staatliche Zuweisungen und kommunale Investitionspolitik (Politikverflechtung VI)*. MS. Wissenschaftszentrum Berlin.

Richardson, Jeremy (ed.). 1982. *Policy styles in Western Europe*. London: George Allen and Unwin.

Riker, William H. 1962. *The theory of political coalitions*. New Haven: Yale University Press.

——. 1964. *Federalism: origin, operation, maintenance*. Boston: Little Brown.

——. 1969. 'Six books in search of a subject or does federalism exist and does it matter?' *Comparative Politics* October, 135.

Riker, William H. 1975. 'Federalism', in F. I. Greenstein and N. W. Polsby (eds.), *Governmental institutions and processes*. Handbook of Political Science, Vol. 5. Redding, Mass.: Addison-Wesley, 93–172.

Rodemer, Horst. 1980. *Die EG-Agrarpolitik, Ziele, Wirkungen, Alternativen*. Tübingen.

Rothenberg, Jerome. 1970. 'Local decentralization and the theory of optimal government', in Julius Margolis (ed.), *The analysis of public output*. New York: Columbia University Press, 31–64.

Runge, Charles F. 1984. 'Institutions and the free rider: the assurance problem in collective action', *Journal of Politics* 46, 154–81.

Scharpf, Fritz W. 1970. *Demokratietheorie zwischen Utopie und Anpassung*; Kronberg: Scriptor (Nachdruck 1975).

——. 1972. 'Komplexität als Schranke der politischen Planung', *Politische Vierteljahresschrift* 13, Sonderheft 4, 168–92.

Scharpf, Fritz W., Bernd Reissert, and Fritz Schnabel. 1976. *Politikverflechtung. Theorie und Empirie des kooperativen Föderalismus in der Bundesrepublik*. Kronberg: Scriptor 1976.

Scharpf, Fritz W., Bernd Reissert, and Fritz Schnabel (Hrsg.). 1977. *Politikverflechtung II. Kritik und Berichte aus der Praxis*. Kronberg: Athenäum.

Scharpf, Fritz W. 1977. 'Public organization and the waning of the welfare state', *European Journal of Political Research* December, 339.
——. 1978a. 'Die Theorie der Politikverflechtung: Ein kurzgefaßter Leitfaden', in Joachim Jens Hesse (Hrsg.), *Politikverflechtung im föderativen Staat*. Baden-Baden: Nomos.
——. 1978. 'Interorganizational policy studies: issues, concepts and perspectives', in K. Hanf and F. W. Scharpf (eds.), *Interorganizational policy making. Limits to coordination and central control*. London: Sage, 345–70.
——. 1985. 'Beschäftigungspolitische Strategien in der Krise', *Leviathan* 1, 1–22.
Scharpf, Fritz W., Bernd Reissert, and Fritz Schnabel. 1978. 'Policy effectiveness and conflict avoidance in intergovernmental policy formation', in K. Hanf and F. W. Scharpf (eds.), *Interorganizational Policy Making*. London: Sage, 57–112.
Schelling, Thomas C. 1960. *The strategy of conflict*. Cambridge, Mass.: Harvard University Press.
Scheingold, Stuart A. 1970. 'Domestic and international consequences of regional integration', *International Organization*, 978.
Schmidt, Helmut. 1980. 'Ansprache des Bundeskanzlers in der 494. Sitzung des Bundesrates am 12.12.1980', *Stenographische Berichte des Bundesrats, von der 482. bis zur 494. Sitzung*, Bonn, 431–5.
Schmitter, Philippe C. 1969. 'Three neo-functional hypotheses about international integration', *International Organization* 23, Winter, 161–6.
——. 1970. 'A revised theory of regional integration', *International Organization* 24, 836–68.
Schnabel, Fritz, 1980. *Politischer und administrativer Vollzug des Krankenhausfinanzierungsgesetzes*. MS. Wissenschaftszentrum Berlin.
Schultze, Rainer-Olaf. 1982. 'Politikverflechtung und konföderaler Föderalismus: Entwicklungslinien und Strukturprobleme im bundesrepublikanischen und kanadischen Föderalismus', *Zeitschrift der Gesellschaft für Kanada-Studien* 2, 113–44.
Scitovsky, Tibor. 1958. *Economic theory and Western European integration*: London: George Allen and Unwin.
Sen, Amartya K. 1970. *Collective choice and social welfare*. Edinburgh: Oliver and Boyd.
——. 1977. 'Rational fools: a critique of the behavioral foundations of economic theory', *Philosophy and Public Affairs* 6, 317–44.
Sharpe, L. J. 1985. *Territoriality and the European state system*. MS Oxford, March.
Simmert, Diethard B. and Kurt-Dieter Wagner (Hrsg.). 1981. *Staatsverschuldung kontrovers*. Bonn: Bundeszentrale für Politische Bildung.
Slater, Martin. 1982. 'Political elite, popular indifference and community building', *Journal of Common Market Studies* 21, 69–86.
Späth, L., E. Teufel, E. Eppler, and J. Morlock. 1979. 'Föderalismus heute. Regierung und Landtagsfraktionen nehmen Stellung', *Politikverflechtung oder Föderalismus heute. Der Bürger im Staat* 29, Heft 1, 52–8.
Steinle, Wolfgang J. and Karl A. Stroetmann. 1983. 'Gemeinschaftliche Forschungs- und Technologiepolitik als Beitrag zur regionalen Entwicklung Europas', *Raumforschung und Raumordnung* 1983, 57–62.
Streeck, Wolfgang and Philippe C. Schmitter. 1984. *Community, market, state and associations: the prospective contribution of interest governments to social order*. Florence: European University Institute Working Paper 94.
Strohe, Franz-Josef. 1982. 'Zusammenwirken von Bund und Ländern bei der Bildungsplanung', BMF, 1982, 561–80.
Taylor, Paul. 1980. 'Interdependence and autonomy in the European Communities: the case of the European monetary system', *Journal of Common Market Studies* 18, 370–87.
——. 1983. *The limits of European integration*. London: Croom Helm.
Tönnies, Ferdinand. 1963. *Gemeinschaft und Gesellschaft*. Darmstadt: Wissenschaftliche Buchgesellschaft (First Edition 1887).
Trivers, Robert L. 1971. 'The evolution of reciprocal altruism', *Quarterly Review of Biology* 46, 35–57.
Tullock, Gordon. 1965. *The politics of bureaucracy*. Washington, D.C.: Public Affairs Press.
——. 1969. 'Federalism: problems of scale', *Public Choice*, 19–29.
Vobruba, Georg (ed.). 1983. *'Wir sitzen alle in einem Boot'. Gemeinschaftsrhetorik in der Krise*. Frankfurt.
Wallace, Helen, William Wallace, and Carole Webb (eds.). 1977. *Policy making in the European communities*. London: John Wiley.
Wallace, William. 1982. 'Europe as a confederation: the Community and the nation state', *Journal of Common Market Studies* 21, 57–68.

Weiler, Joseph. 1982. 'Community member states and European integration. Is the law relevant?' *Journal of Common Market Studies* 21, 39–56.
Wheare, K. C. 1960. *Federal government*. 4th Edition, Oxford: Oxford University Press.
Ylvisaker, Paul. 1959. 'Some criteria for a "proper" areal division of governmental powers', in: Arthur Maass, (ed.), *Area and power. A theory of local government*. Glencoe, Ill.: The Free Press.
Zeh, Wolfgang. 1979. 'Musterfall Gemeinschaftsaufgaben. Erscheinungsformen, Willensbildungsmuster und Ursachen der Politikverflechtung', *Der Bürger im Staat* Heft 1, 15–19.
Ziebura, Gilbert. 1982. 'Internationalization of capital, international division of labour and the role of the European Community', *Journal of Common Market Studies* 21, 127–40.

[17]

Common Market Law Review **27**: 709–739, 1990.

DIRECTIVES: THE EFFECTIVENESS OF JUDICIAL PROTECTION OF INDIVIDUAL RIGHTS

DEIRDRE CURTIN*

1. Introduction

The speeding up of the decision-making process for giving effect to the White Paper on the completion of the internal market[1] has meant that the Community instruments adopted in this connection have been coming into force faster: of the 151 measures definitively adopted, 103 came into force in 1989 and 84 of these require national incorporating or implementing measures.[2] While hitherto the Commission in its political statements had been stressing the need to make the new decision-making mechanism set up by the Single Act fully credible, it is now endeavouring to make the Member States aware of the need to give effect, within the time limits set, to the directives, decisions and regulations adopted to establish the single market.[3] This entails ensuring that the conditions permitting the implementation of such measures are created and in particular that the measures incorporating the Directives into national law are completed on schedule.[4] The need for such active monitoring by the Commission is immediately apparent upon examination of the figures. Among those instruments relating to the single market which were already in force in 1989, deadlines were not respected in

*. Legal Secretary, Court of Justice of the European Communities. The author wishes to thank Onno Brouwer and Anthony Collins for their helpful comments on an earlier draft. The views expressed are purely personal.

1. COM (85) 310, 14 June 1985.

2. *Seventh annual report to the European Parliament on Commission monitoring of the application of Community law – 1989*, O.J. 1990, C 232/1.

3. *Seventh report*, 6.

4. Communication from the Commission on Implementation of the legal acts required to build the Single Market, COM (89) final.

some 45% of cases;[5] in 1988 the figures were even more striking, very few of the Directives adopted pursuant to the single market programme having been implemented in all the Member States.[6]

Given this very high instance of Member States failing to implement Directives in time in breach of their clear obligations, the Commission initiated a debate at the political level on the application of the instruments for establishing the single market by presenting a communication to the Council,[7] analysing the situation and proposing a number of concrete measures, some of which have been given effect.[8] In addition to this political approach, the Commission has stepped up its judicial activity against errant Member States. In 1989 alone 664 letters of formal notice were sent, 180 reasoned opinions and 96 Article 169 infringement proceedings were commenced before the Court of Justice.[9] From my examination of all the judgments given by the Court in the context of infringement proceedings over the course of the last three years, ending in 1990, it emerges that more than half of these cases concerned failures by Member States to implement directives into national law. Of those infringement proceedings currently pending before the Court there are significantly more cases concerning the failure by Member States to implement directives than alleged infringements on other grounds.[10] However even these fairly dramatic statistics do not necessarily equate with the totality of the dilemma since it is fairly undisputed that the Commission may sometimes be motivated by political considerations in failing to initiate legal proceedings even where the violation of Community law is apparent.[11] Moreover, the systematic monitoring by the Commission of the incorporation of directives into national law

5. See, *Seventh Report*, op. cit. at 2.
6. See, *Sixth annual report to the European Parliament on Commission monitoring of the application of Community law – 1988*, O.J. 1989, C 330/1, at V.
7. *Supra*, note 4.
8. *Seventh report*, op. cit. at 6.
9. See, *Seventh report*, op. cit. at Table 1, page 31.
10. In October 1990 a total of 79 Article 169 actions pending before the Court related to failure by Member States to implement directives into national law as compared to 59 infringements on other grounds.
11. Ehlermann, "Ein Pladoyer für die dezentrale Kontrolle der Anwendung des Gemeinschaftsrechts durch die Mitgliedstaaten" in *Liber Amicorum Pierre Pescatore* 205, 207; Barents, "Een klacht bij de Commissie", (1990) *Advocatenblad* 646.

resulting in the immediate initiation of infringement procedures as soon as deadlines are reached[12] is superficial in the sense that it does not reach the substantive content of implementing measures. This strategy must also be viewed in the light of the reality that such a judicial strategy is not as successful in compliance terms as the Commission would no doubt wish. The number of Court judgments which were not complied with in 1989 remained at approximately the same high level as the previous year (82 compared with 88 in 1988).[13] The Commission had responded to this stalemate by employing the only remaining weapon in its legal armoury, Article 171 of the EEC Treaty, and has initiated an unprecedented 26 new procedures in 1989 seeking compliance with a previous Court judgment under Article 169.[14] Sadly, the effectiveness of the Article 171 procedure is probably minimal given that a deliberately disobedient Member State can simply refuse, once again, to implement a judgment given on the basis of Article 171. The fact that the Court cannot impose a dissuasive penalty on such an errant State gives directives a dangerously elastic quality: Italy, Greece or Belgium (the most frequent culprits) may, for example, agree to accept the enactment of a directive with which it is uncomfortable knowing that the price to pay for possible failure to transpose is non-existent or minimal.[15]

This unhappy impasse with regard to the *direct* enforcement of Community law clearly jeopardizes the fundamental principle of a Community based on the rule of law[16] and risks developing into a credibility problem for the Community. Indeed, as one eminent author has convincingly argued: "if a Court is forced to condone the wholesale viola-

12. *Seventh report*, op. cit. at 6.

13. *Seventh report*, op. cit. at 5.

14. Of those 8 Article 171 proceedings which are still pending before the Court in Oct. 1990, only 2 concern Member State infringements other than failure to implement directives into national law.

15. Mancini, "The making of a Constitution for Europe" 26 CML Rev (1989) 596, 602.

16. See, in particular, in this respect Case 294/83, *Les Verts* v. *European Parliament*, [1986] ECR 1357; Case C-2/88 Imm., *Zwartveld*, Order of 13 July 1990, not yet reported.

tion of a norm, that norm can no longer be termed law".[17] It has given rise to renewed calls, in the context of the intergovernmental conference, that the means of enforcing obligations with which Member States fail to comply be strengthened.[18] In particular, proposals of financial penalties on recalcitrant Member States are once more being mooted.[19] I do not intend to elaborate on this strategy, which has been discussed for some time now, other than to highlight its probable lack of acceptability to certain Member States, particularly those who are hauled most frequently before the Court for defaulting on their implementation obligations.[20]

An alternative which does not require any Treaty amendment whatsoever lies in the hands of vigilant individuals and enables them to *indirectly* enforce Community law[21] and in particular the provisions of directives before their national courts. The active utilization of this option by individuals entails a qualitatively better guarantee of Member State compliance since it will in practice be much more difficult for Member States to disregard a decision of their own courts concerning their liability to individuals for damage caused by their failure to comply with the provisions of a directive than it is to disregard the decision of the more remote Court of Justice. Moreover the benefit to the individual concerned whose rights are effectively protected in this manner invests the notion of Community citizenship with concrete meaning[22]

17. Cappelletti, Seccombe and Weiler, "A general introduction" in *Integration through law*, Vol. 1, Book 1 (1986), 38.

18. See, in particular, Memorandum from the Danish government, Agence Europe, 17 Oct. 1990.

19. See, Resolution of European Parliament of 22 Nov. 1990 relating to the intergovernmental conferences, in particular the suggested amendment to Article 171 of the Treaty. See also, the Parliament's earlier Draft Treaty on European Union, article 44.

20. Italy, for example. The Commission has, however, expressed optimism with regard to the backlog in the implementation of directives into Italian law as a result of the entry into force of the *La Pergola Act* (see, *Seventh report*, op. cit. at p. 6). See, Tizzano, "La nouvelle loi italienne pour l'execution des obligations communautaires" 339 RMC (1990) 532.

21. To use the Court's terminology, first employed in Case 26/62, *van Gend en Loos*, [1963] ECR 3.

22. Dashwood, "The principle of direct effect in European Community law" (1977) JCMS, 229, 244.

and provides an efficient and effective paradigm of the much acclaimed principle of subsidiarity.

This article starts from the premise that in order to evaluate correctly the effects of directives on individual rights account must be taken both of the necessity that they be implemented by Member States as well as the fact that certain provisions may confer directly effective rights on individuals. This article will therefore commence with a brief look at the manner in which the Court has fine-tuned the margin of discretion conferred on Member States under Article 189(3) of the Treaty. This will be followed by an examination of the legal effects of unimplemented Directives (by which is meant both non-implementation and putative implementation which is faulty) from the perspective of an individual seeking to enforce before his national court rights conferred by Community law. The anomalies inherent upon the Court's denial of horizontal direct effect to provisions of directives in *Marshall* v. *Southampton and South West Hampshire Area Health Authority*[23] will not be elaborated upon as they have been extensively discussed elsewhere.[24] Finally, it will be argued that the discretion which the national judge putatively enjoys with regard to the choice of national remedies for the application of an individual right stemming from Community law has been significantly limited by the Community law principle of the effectiveness of the judicial protection of individual rights, as most recently reiterated by the Court in *Regina* v. *Factortame*.[25] The proposition will, *inter alia*, be mooted that Article 5 of the Treaty, together with the general principles of Community law, oblige the Member States to provide for a system of compensation for private individuals in cases where those Member States are responsible for damages caused

23. Case 152/84. [1986] ECR 723.

24. See, in particular, Prechal, "Remedies after *Marshall* 27 CML Rev. (1990) 451; Curtin, "The province of government: delimiting the direct effect of directives in the common law context" EL Rev. (1990) 195 and annotation by Szyszczak of Case C-188/89, *Foster and Others* v. *British Gas plc.*, judgment of 12 July 1990, not yet reported, below, 859–871.

25. Case C-213/89, *The Queen* v. *Secretary of State for Transport, ex parte Factortame Ltd. and others*, judgment of 19 June 1990, not yet reported, annotated by Toth in this Review, 27 CML Rev. (1990), 573–587. See also the interesting conclusions on the same case of Advocate General Tesauro of 17 May 1990.

to them in violation of their individual rights conferred by Community law. The importance of the availability of such indirect control by individuals lies not simply in its deterrent and penalty value towards a recalcitrant Member State but also because the effective protection of individual rights conferred by Community law *ex post facto* arguably entails ensuring, subject to the procedural rights of the national forum, the payment of compensation in respect of the period between the commission of the wrong by the State and its rectification, thereby placing the individual in the position he would have been in had the wrong not been committed.

2. Article 189: The limits of Member State discretion

The primary legal obligation of a directive is to impose upon the addressee Member States what in the Community jargon is known as an obligation of result,[26] namely an obligation to take such measures as are necessary to incorporate its provisions into national law.[27] This obligation of result extends to all organs of the administration, including decentralized authorities such as municipalities.[28] The duty to implement Directives is absolute: no excuses such as the slowness of the legislative process, governmental crisis etc. are brooked by the Court of Justice as potential justification for failure to do so.[29] Indeed, non-implementation is a breach not only of the specific provisions of Article 189 of the Treaty but also of the duty of Community "solidarity" as enshrined in

26. Pescatore, "L'effet des directives communautaires. Essai de demystification", (Dalloz, 1980) *Chronique*, p. 171.

27. As the French *Conseil d'Etat* insisted in a recent judgment, the pertinent national authorities cannot, after the expiry of the implementation time limit, lawfully permit the continued existence of national rules, which would be incompatible with the objectives laid down in the Directive or issue rules which would be contrary to it: *Compagnie Alitalia* [1990] 1 CMLR 248.

28. Case 103/88, *Fratelli Costanzo S.p.A.* v. *Commune di Milano*, judgment of 22 June 1989, not yet reported.

29. Case 52/75, [1976] ECR 277; Case 10/76, [1976] ECR 1359; Case 163/78, [1979] ECR 771; Case 42/80, [1980] ECR 3635 and Case 43/80, [1980] ECR 3643 – *Commission* v. *Italy* in all cases. Case 100/81, *Commission* v. *The Netherlands*, [1982] ECR 1837.

Article 5 of the Treaty, this coupling adding gravity to the breach inherent in non-implementation.[30] Central to this notion of solidarity is the protection of individual rights since the non-implementation by a Member State may prejudice the legal position of the individual who finds himself subject to two sets of contradictory rules.[31] This duty of solidarity is reinforced by the doctrine of the supremacy of Community law which has as a logical corollary the requirement that Member States must do all in their powers to make effective the fundamental principles of Community law.

Article 189 nevertheless confers upon a Member State a discretion as to the "choice of form and methods" with which it transposes a Directive into national law. Thus the Member States have apparently been given the widest possible choice of possibilities as far as the implementation of Directives at national level is concerned. However this margin of discretion has been fettered in several distinct ways. First, "guidelines" gleaned from the text of the Directive may indicate, expressly or implicitly, a particular mode of implementation,[32] in the sense that the national implementation measures must be of equivalent legal effect to those existant in the Member State in question for the pertinent subject-matter. Second, Member States are apparently under an obligation to adopt "within the framework of their national legal systems, all the measures necessary to ensure that the directive is fully *effective*, in accordance with the objectives which it pursues".[33] It is in this context that the Court has held that collective agreements, even if widespread

30. Green, "Directives, equity and the protection of individual rights," (1984) EL Rev 295, 296. See, on the duties imposed by Art. 5, Temple Lang "Community constitutional law: Article 5 EEC Treaty."

31. Case 39/72, *Commission* v. *Italy*, [1973] ECR 101, 116. This point is vividly illustrated by the facts in Case C-208/90, *Emmott*, still pending, where the administrative literature distributed by the errant Member State, Ireland, to inform a particularly disadvantaged section of the community (social welfare recipients) about their rights only referred to the unaltered national legislation which some years later (and after the expiry of the pertinent time-limits) was found to be incompatible with directly effective Community law.

32. Case 102/79, *Commission* v. *Belgium*, [1980] ECR 1473; Case 291/84, *Commission* v. *The Netherlands*, [1987] ECR 3483. See also the opinion of Advocate General van Gerven in Case C-131/88, *Commission* v. *Germany*, 25 Sept. 1990, not yet reported.

33. Case 14/83, *von Colson and Kamann* v. *Land Nordrhein Westfalen*, [1984] ECR 1891, at para. 15.

and important, do not represent adequate means for *fully* implementing a directive when they concern only some sectors and impose obligations only between the members of the trade unions and the employers bound by the agreement.[34] In addition the most *appropriate* form and method to fully implement directives must be chosen in order to ensure their effective functioning within the national legal systems.[35]

The Court, motivated by a strong desire to safeguard the interests of potentially affected parties by affording them a genuine opportunity to seek redress in the national courts, has sought to maximize the effectiveness of directives in Community law. This would seem to be one of the main reasons why the Court has been so adamant in condemning the still prevalent practice of implementing a Directive by an administrative circular.[36] The main objections to this type of "form and methods" would seem to be that, in addition to the fact that such circulars may be changed as the authorities please and hence lack legal force[37] such circulars may not be readily available, in particular to interested nationals of other Member States or their legal advisers, and may not, depending on the pertinent system of administrative law, provide interested parties with an adequate opportunity to seek redress in the national courts.[38] In other words the danger is that the very inaccessibility of such circulars in practice occasions a breach of natural justice.

The question whether or not a Member State has adequately implemented a directive is essentially one of Community law, although it can only be answered by first determining, according to the relevant

34. Case 235/84, *Commission* v. *Italy*, [1986] ECR 2291. See further, on this point, Adinolfi, "The implementation of social policy directives through collective agreements", (1988) CML Rev. 291. With regard to the criteria of adequacy see Case 102/79, *Commission* v. *Belgium*, [1980] ECR 1473.

35. See, Case 48/75, *Royer*, [1976] ECR 497; Case 38/77, *ENKA*, [1977] ECR 2203.

36. Case 102/79, *Commission* v. *Belgium*, [1980] ECR 1473; Case 96/81, *Commission* v. *The Netherlands*, [1982] ECR 1791; Case 97/81, *Commission* v. *The Netherlands*, [1982] ECR 1819; Case 300/81, *Commission* v. *Italy*, [1983] ECR 449; Case 145/82, *Commission* v. *Italy*, [1983] ECR 711; Case 168/85, *Commission* v. *Italy*, [1986] ECR 2945; Cae 239/85, *Commission* v. *Belgium*, [1986] ECR 3645; Case 236/85, *Commission* v. *The Netherlands*, [1987] ECR 3989.

37. See in particular Case 29/84, *Commission* v. *Germany*, [1985] ECR 1661. Case 1661. Case 96/81, *Commission* v. *The Netherlands*, [1982] 1791.

38. See further, Kovar, "Observations sur l'intensité normative des directives" in *Liber Amicorum Pierre Pescatore* 359, 367.

principles of national law what are the relevant effects of the measures which purport to implement the directive[39] or if there are no such measures whether the general legal context is adequate.[40] What constitutes proper implementation of a directive therefore involves both questions of national and Community law. The Commission's strategy in challenging Member States' choice of inadequate "forms and methods" seems to bear witness to a regrettable lack of consistency. Whilst, for example, it has vigorously contested the *German* and *French* implementation of certain directives on atmospheric pollution by administrative circulars, which it maintains do not have the force of law and the requisite transparency and justiciability,[41] the Commission continues to turn a blind eye to the fact that many Directives are purportedly implemented into *Irish* law by administrative circulars.[42] And yet the same doubts prevail under Irish law as under German law as regards their legal effect, a matter which as yet awaits definitive judicial clarification.[43] The validity of the Commission's ostrich-like approach to the Irish situation may be questioned further since the decision in *Greene* v. *Minister for Agriculture*[44] where the national judge ducked the issue of the validity of the practice of implementing directives by circular[45] despite the fact that such implementation seemed to fly in the face of the well-established case law of the Court.

It seems that if the "results" to be achieved in order to comply with a

39. As, for example, is the issue in Cases C-361/88 and C-59/89, *Commission* v. *Germany*, still pending.

40. Case 363/85, *Commission* v. *Italy*, [1987] ECR 1733. See also, Case C-106/89, *Marleasing S.A.* v. *La Commercial Internacional de Alimentacion S.A.*, judgment of 13 Nov. 1990, not yet reported.

41. Cases 361/88 and 59/89, *Commission* v. *Germany*, still pending, concerning respectively incorrect "forms and methods" of implementing Directive 80/779, of 15 July 1980, O.J. L 229/30 and Directive 82/884, of 3 Dec. 1982, O.J. L 378/15 into German law. Cases 13/90 and 14/90, *Commission* v. *France*, concerning respectively Directive 82/884 and Directive 85/203, of 7 March 1985, O.J. L 87/1.

42. See, in particular, Hogan, "The legal status of administrative rules and circulars" (1987) *Irish Jurist* (n.s.) 194 and Robinson, "Application in Ireland of the directives on public procurement" in *L'application dans les Etats membres des directives sur les marches publics*, Fourteenth Congress of FIDE (Madrid, 1990), 169, at 175–176.

43. Hogan, ibid.

44. [1989] 3 CMLR 830.

45. [1989] CMLR 830. See, however, *Browne* v. *An Bord Pleanala* [1989] I.L.R.M. 865 where another High Court judge stressed that a Member State must choose a method of implementing a directive which has the force of law in that State and concluded that a circular letter does not enjoy the requisite force of law in Ireland.

Community directive have already been attained in the national legal orders, there appears to be no need to adopt special implementing measures.[46] This is subject to the proviso however that where the directive is intended to create rights for individuals, the legal position arising from these principles is sufficiently precise, clear and transparent and where appropriate those individuals are afforded the possibility of relying on their enforceable rights before the national courts.[47] This requirement of an adequate and transparent system of judicial control applies with the same force to national implementing legislation.[48] If the national legal situation remains ambiguous despite the enactment of specific implementing legislation then the Member State in question will be considered to have incorrectly implemented the directive in question into national law.[49] It would thus seem to follow that the mere existence of a specific national law or rule which is contrary to a more general piece of national legislation implementing the terms of a directive into national law constitutes *per se* an incorrect transposition of the directive in question into national law.[50] Such an ambiguous legal context is incompatible with the Member States obligation of result since it jeopardizes the justiciability of directives and dilutes their normative force.

3. Unimplemented directives as a source of individual rights

Flowing from the Member States' legal obligation to implement a directive into national law is a phenomenon which arises when a Member

46. Case 363/85, *Commission* v. *Italy*, [1987] ECR 1733.
47. Case 29/84, *Commission* v. *Germany*, [1985] ECR 1662.
48. Specifically with regard to those situations where national implementing legislation will be adopted, the Council has recently approved a standard form of wording to be included in the text of all future directives: "when Member States adopt [the measures necessary to comply with the Directive], they shall contain a reference to this Directive or shall be accompanied by such reference on the occasion of their official publication. The methods of making such reference shall be laid down by the Member States." See further, *Agence Europe*, 28 Nov. 1990, at 14.
49. Case 167/83, *Commission* v. *France*, [1974] ECR 359. Case 168/85, *Commission* v. *Italy*, [1986] ECR 2945. See, Commission's observations in Case 177/88, *Dekker* v. *Stichting Vormingscentrum voor Jong Volwassenen*, judgment of 8 Nov. 1990, not yet reported. See also conclusion of Advocate General Darmon in *Dekker* at p. 4 of the mimeographed version of the text.
50. See, Advocate General Darmon in *Dekker supra* note 49, at p. 5.

State acts in breach of that obligation, thereby failing to confer on a private person a right enforceable in its own courts. This phenomenon which constitutes a minimum guarantee[51] is known by the term of art "direct effect" and is usually described as the existence of subjective rights enforceable by individuals before their national courts. It has been referred to as the most significant single development in the evolution of Community law.[52] The concept of direct effect is a product of the jurisprudence of the Court and in the context of directives it has been elaborated, at least in recent years, in terms of a reflex or ricochet effect rather in the nature of estoppel[53] – it only occurs when a Member State has failed to perform its obligations, and this cannot be the case until the time limit for the performance of those obligations has expired.[54] The doctrine of estoppel in Community law is thus essentially employed as a defensive mechanism used by the courts to cope with the fact that implementation has not taken place.[55] The side-effect is that even though a Directive has not been implemented at all – or it has been imperfectly implemented – it may create rigths and obligations (in the legal relationships between Member States and individuals) which are enforceable in the national courts. In particular a Member State which has not taken measures to implement a Directive within the time-limits may not rely on its wrong by pleading its own failure to perform its obligations under the Directive against individuals. The doctrine of

51. Case 168/85, *Commission* v. *Italy*, [1986] ECR 2945.

52. Easson, "The 'direct effect' of EEC directives", 28 ICLQ (1979) 319.

53. See, Green, op. cit. at 306. See further with regard to the changing theoretical basis underpinning the concept of direct effect of directives: Prechal, op. cit. at 452–3 and Curtin, op. cit. at 196–7.

54. This does not mean that a directive is deprived of all legal effect before the deadline for implementation has expired: Case 80/86, *Criminal proceedings against Kolpinghuis Nijmegen B.V.*, [1987] ECR 3969. The duty imposed on national courts to construe domestic legislation in accordance with any relevant directive arises as soon as the directive has been adopted, subject to the principles of legal certainty and non-retroactivity. See further, *infra*.

55. The theoretical underpinning of the doctrine of direct effect of directives on the principle of estoppel must have gone a considerable way towards alleviating the fears expressed by the House of Lords Select Committee on the European Communities in its famous *Tenth Report* of the 1974–1975 Session which regarded *van Duyn*, [1974] ECR 1337, as holding that provisions of directives may be "directly applicable" like regulations.

direct effect can thus act as a powerful countercheck to the non-implementation of directives in the sense that individuals are thereby given a legal tool to assist them in the process of squeezing effects from unimplemented directives in the national legal context.

The classic tests posited by the Court for assessing whether a particular Community provision was capable of enjoying the quality of direct effect and thus enabling an individual to invoke it before a national court were that it must be clear and precise, unconditional and not subject to any discretion on the part of the Member States or Community institutions.[56] With regard to directives these tests were applied relatively flexibly, due regard being paid to the very nature of a directive where Member States inevitably enjoy a measure of discretion in implementing according to the very terms of Article 189.[57] Thus the fact that Member States are required to take further acts for implementation does not in itself prevent direct effect, provided no substantive discretion has been allowed for this implementation. However for a long time it seemed that where a real option or faculty to choose between various solutions is allowed, the provision of the directive in question could have no direct effect. This belief was explicitly refuted by the Court in *McDermott and Cotter* v. *The Minister for Social Welfare*[58] where, in spite of the fact that Member States were left with (considerable) discretion as to how they should implement the principle of equal treatment in their national systems of social security, the Court seemingly had little trouble in concluding that such discretion as to "form and methods" does not operate so as to deprive the pertinent provision of direct effect. A discretion as to means can therefore not be allowed to spill over so as to also affect the end of ensuring that Member States do not in any way restrict or place conditions on the application of the directly effec-

56. See, for example, Case 26/62, *van Gend en Loos* v. *Nederlandse Administratie der Belastingen*, [1963] ECR 1; Case 33/68, *Salgoil* v. *Italian Minister for Foreign Trade*, [1968] ECR 453; see generally, Pescatore, "The doctrine of 'direct effect': an infant disease of Community law" (1983) EL Rev. 155.

57. See Advocate General Warner in Case 131/79, *Santillo*, [1980] ECR 1585. See also Maresceau, *De directe werking van het Europese Gemeenschapsrecht*, (Deventer, 1978) at pp. 69, 86 and 95, and Timmermans "Directives: their effect within the national legal systems" 16 CML Rev. (1979) 533, 539.

58. Case 286/85, [1987] ECR 1453.

tive right in its particular area of application.[59] In this manner individuals can invoke the limits set to the exercise of the discretion at issue by the Member States.

Building on the logic of this reasoning the Court went much further than it had ever gone before and dictated to the national court in *McDermott and Cotter* the substantive test it had to apply in enforcing the rights enjoyed by individuals as a result of Ireland's failure to implement the Directive at issue on time. Two points are of importance. First, it applied the most favorable option possible to the individuals in question (in the jargon, a "levelling-up" solution) until the Member State acted to implement the provisions of the Directive correctly, namely that "women are entitled to be treated in the same manner, and have the same rules applied to them, as men who are in the same position, since, where the Directive has not been implemented correctly, those rules remain the only valid point of reference".[60] This constituted a "default" option which would take effect if not otherwise transposed by a Member State. Second the Court implicitly ruled that a Member State, when it finally did adopt the requisite implementing legislation, could not retroactively exercise its discretion in a manner in which the substance of the directly effective rights would be reduced in the interim period. In quite a concrete manner therefore involving the application of the directly effective provision as a rule of law by a national court the Court penalized the errant Member State for its failure to fulfill its Treaty obligations by not implementing the Directive in time.[61] In practical terms this evolution in the Courts' case law is profound. It

59. This reasoning holds good where a Member State has been given the option to derogate from certain provisions of a Directive in certain defined circumstances. In the United Kingdom, the Court of Appeal has energetically asserted a right to decide whether any purported exercise of such option conferred by a provision of a Directive falls within the ambit of the authority conferred by the provision in question and in particular within the principle of proportionality: *Secretary of State for Social Security* v. *Thomas et al.*, 31 July 1990, unreported.

60. [1987] ECR at 1468. See also the very concrete application of this principle in Case 384/85, *Borrie-Clarke* v. *Chief Adjudication Officer*, [1987] ECR 2865.

61. The national courts in this particular case have experienced considerable difficulty in fleshing out the practical application of the principle of direct effect as elaborated by the Court and in determining which social welfare benefits had to be paid out to the claimants and as and from what date. See further *infra*.

means that a Member State's own citizens can force a Member State, which has not fulfilled its duty under Article 189 and Article 5 of the EEC Treaty to implement, to effectively "level up", granting them specific benefits under unamended national law pending adequate implementation.[62]

Many Directives, for example in the field of company and employment law, environment and consumer law, product liability and trade mark law contain obligations for both the State and either individuals or natural persons. A good example is the Directive introducing the principle of equal treatment into occupational social security schemes.[63] Two types of obligations are imposed by the terms of the Directives: one on the Member States to introduce legislation by 30 July 1990 (Article 12) and one, implicitly, on the occupational pension funds themselves to adapt their existing arrangements to take account fully of the principle of equal treatment (Article 5). Article 5 of this directive defines and outlines the scope *ratione materia* of the principle of equal treatment and is phrased in identical terms to Article 4 of the earlier Directive 79/7 introducing the principle of equal treatment into *statutory* social security schemes.[64] According to orthodox wisdom "direct effect" attaches solely to those legislative instruments which satisfy the pre-conditions of legal certainty: clarity, precision and unconditionality. Applying these criteria to Article 4 of the latter directive, Directive 79/7, the Court in *McDermott and Cotter* had no difficulty in concluding that it was directly effective. On this analysis there should be no difficulty in reaching the same conclusion with regard to Article 5 of the later (occupational) directive. However the critical difference between the two Directives is that the former is "vertical" concerning as it does *statutory* social security schemes, claims against which will by their very nature always be enforced against the State and the latter Directive is a "horizontal" one concerning *occupational* schemes. According to the by now well-established case law of the Court,[65] an individual injured

62. See, in particular, the Court's judgment in *Borrie-Clarke*, supra.

63. Directive 86/378, of 24 July 1986, O.J. 1986 L 225/40; see also corrigendum to Art. 2(2), O.J. 1986 L 283/27.

64. Directive 79/7, of 19 Dec. 1978, O.J. 1978 L 6/24.

65. Case 152/84, *Marshall* v. *Southhampton and South-West Hampshire Area*

by the failure of, for example, a particular occupational pension fund to comply with the mandate of equal treatment cannot enforce that obligation as against the pension fund in legal proceedings before its national court in the absence of implementing legislation. The reason for this is that the obligations or rights imposed by directives can never be enforced against private parties as opposed to "the State", as broadly construed.[66] As a result, the notion of direct effect is not homogeneous and objective. Moreover it can be argued that the denial of horizontal direct effect in circumstances such as those outlined above constitutes a denial of the primacy of Community law, since incompatible national legislation may validly continue to be applied to individuals in the absence of adequate national implementing legislation.[67] The significance and anomalous nature of this ruling is exacerbated by the increasing trend towards privatization in a number of Member States.

In order to guarantee nevertheless the effectiveness of the individuals' rights even in a horizontal relationship the Court of Justice has developed a parallel obligation, imposed on national courts, to interpret their national laws in the light of the objective and wording of any pertinent Community directives.[68] It emerges from a recent judgment in *Marleasing S.A.* v. *La Commercial Internacional de Alimentacion S.A.*[69] just how extensive and farreaching that obligation can be. This case concerned the attempt by Marleasing S.A. to obtain a declaration of the nullity of La Commercial Internacional de Alimentacion S.A.

Health Authority (Teaching), [1986] ECR 723; Case 80/86, *Criminal Proceedings against Kolpinghuis Nijmegen*, [1987] ECR 3969; C-221/88, *ECSC* v. *Busseni*, judgment of 22 Feb. 1990, not yet reported; Case C-106/89, *Marleasing S.A.* v. *La Commercial Internacional de Alimentacion S.A.*, judgment of 13 Nov. 1990, not yet reported.

66. See, C-188/89, *Foster and others* v. *British Gas*, judgment of 12 July 1990. See annotation by Szyszczak below, 859–871.

67. See however the Court's complementary jurisprudence on the so-called "indirect" effect of directives, see further, *infra*.

68. Case 14/83, *von Colson and Kamann* v. *Land Nordrhein Westfalen*, [1984] ECR 1891 at para. 26; Case 79/83, *Harz* v. *Deutsche Tradex*, [1984] ECR 1921 at para. 26; Case 222/84, *Johnston* v. *Chief Constable of the Royal Ulster Constabulary*, [1986] ECR 1651 at para. 53; Case 80/86, *Criminal Proceedings against Kolpinghuis Nijmegen*, [1987] ECR 3969 at para. 12; Case 31/87, *Gebroeders Beentjes* v. *The Netherlands*, [1988] ECR 4635 at para. 39; Case 125/88, *Nijman*, judgment of 7 Nov. 1989, not yet reported at para. 6; and Case C-106/89, *Marleasing S.A.* v. *La Commercial Internacional de Alimentacion S.A.*, judgment of 13 Nov. 1990, not yet reported, at para. 8.

69. Case C-106/89, *supra*.

from a Spanish tribunal on the ground that it was vitiated by the lack of (lawful) consideration in violation of Articles 1261 and 1275 of the Spanish Civil Code. In its defence, La Commercial relied on Article 11 of the first Company law Directive[70] which lists exhaustively the cases in which the nullity of a company may be declared, not including the lack of (lawful) consideration, which had not been implemented at that point in time into Spanish law. The national tribunal before whom this case arose considered that it raised the problem of the direct effect of a directive which had not been transposed into national law and accordingly it asked the Court of Justice whether Article 11 of the Directive in question could be considered as directly effective. In view of the fact that this question was raised in a *horizontal context*, the established case law of the Court since *Marshall* would dictate a negative response. The Court, however, in its reply to the national tribunal, neatly side-stepped this response by re-wording the question asked in terms of the existence or otherwise of an obligation to interpret national law in conformity with the provisions of a directive. By so doing the Court was able to inform the national court that it was obliged to interpret its national law, irrespective of whether it pre-dated or post-dated the pertinent directive, in the light of the terms of the directive.

In *Marleasing* the end result was that the Spanish tribunal was obliged to interpret the provisions of the Spanish Civil Code in a manner so as to preclude a declaration of nullity of a public limited company based on a ground different from those set out in Article 11 of the (unimplemented) first Company Directive. This means in effect that the obligation contained in a directive is placed on *private parties*, albeit after having been transformed, via judicial interpretation, into one of national law.[71] In practice, this clever judicial strategy achieves, where the national law is at all open to interpretation,[72] the same result as if

70. Council Directive 68/151 of 9 March 1968 on coordination of safeguards which, for the protection of the interests of members and others, are required by Member States of companies within the meaning of the second para. of Art. 58 of the Treaty, with a view to making such safeguards equivalent throughout the Community (O.J. English Special Edition 1968 (1), p. 41.

71. Steiner, "EEC directives: a new route to enforcement?" 101 LQR (1985) 491, 495.

72. See, the rider added in this respect in case C-106/89, *Marleasing, supra* note 68, regarding the extent to which the national norm is open to interpretation (paragraph 8:

a particular provision of that directive could be recognized as enjoying horizontal direct effects.[73] In this manner "horizontal" rights which are enshrined in directives can have the force of law as between individuals without a specific domestic legislative process[74] and the primacy of Community law is assured.

The question whether an interpretation is in conformity with the provisions of a directive will normally arise in relation to provisions of national law which are specifically intended to implement the directive concerned.[75] However in *Marleasing* the Court resolved an important controversy by extending the requirement that national judges give an interpretation in conformity with a directive to all national provisions in an area covered by a directive irrespective of whether they predate the directive in question and were therefore clearly not enacted for its implementation.[76] In addition, as a result of the express wording used by the Court in *Marleasing* should a national parliament expressly repudiate a particular obligation, national courts would nevertheless be obliged to interpret their domestic law to comply with the obligation contained in the EEC directive. This was implicitly accepted by the French *Conseil*

"dans toute la mesure du possible"). Compare with the terminology used in the earlier cases cited in note 68. Presumably this consistency between the Community norm and the national norm must be sought no matter how wide a departure from the *prima facie* meaning of the language used might be needed to achieve consistency. See also, Lord Diplock in *Garland* v. *British Rail Engineering Ltd.* [1983] 2 AC 751.

73. See, for example, the similar approach taken by the German Federal Court in its judgment of 14 March 1989, NJW (1990), 65.

74. See, the views expressed in this regard by Advocate General Darmon in Cases C-177/88, *Dekker* and C-179/88, *Hertz*, in his Opinion of 14 Nov. 1989 (para. 15 of the mimeographed text), judgment of 8 Nov. 1990, not yet reported, and by Advocate General van Gerven in his Opinion of 12 July 1990 in Case C-106/89, *Marleasing S.A.*, *supra* note 68.

75. This has in fact been the case in most of the cases which have come before the Court cited *supra* note 68, with the notable exception of Case C-106/89, *Marleasing*.

76. This point was in particular controversial in the United Kingdom where the House of Lords some years previously in *Duke* v. *Reliance Systems Ltd.* [1988] Q.B. 108 had refused to interpret the Sex Discrimination Act 1970 (as amended) to comply with the subsequent Equal Treatment Directive as interpreted by the Court in *Marshall*, *supra*. The result of this finding was that where a person sought to enforce a directive against an individual, British courts were not obliged to interpret preexisting national law to comply with the terms of the Directive. See the similar decision of the House of Lords with regard to the Sex Discrimination (Northern Ireland) Order 1976 (even though the Order was issued some five months *after* the pertinent Directive) in *Finnegan* v. *Clowney Youth Training Programme Ltd*, [1990] 2 CMLR 859.

d'Etat in *Rassemblement des opposants a la chasse and others*,[77] annulling a Ministerial Order which had laid down legislative requirements in blatant disregard of the objectives enshrined in Directive 79/409 on the conservation of wild birds.[78]

4. The hurdle of national procedural rules

The orthodox understanding is that Community law requires no more than that national courts and tribunals must ensure that individual rights conferred by it are indeed effectively protected, leaving it to those courts and tribunals to apply whichever they consider to be the most *appropriate* of the various remedies and procedures available under national law for that purpose.[79] Whereas this presupposes that national law must provide procedures for the protection of rights arising from Community rules,[80] it at the same time subjects directly effective rights to the vicissitudes of national procedural and remedial law, a reality which can only jeopardize the attainment of the objective of the uniform application of Community law. Thus, it is for the national legal system to determine which court or tribunal has jurisdiction to hear actions for the enforcement of directly effective Community rights and, for this purpose, to decide how the individual position thus protected is to be classified[81] as well as laying down the related procedural rights. In addition procedural points such as periods of limitation, rights of set-off, the extent of rights of reimbursement of improper charges, payment of interest and so on are matters to be regulated by the domestic law of the Member State in whose courts the individual right-holder seeks to proceed.

The disintegrating effect of national procedural differences has been countered by Community legislation harmonizing national procedures

77. [1990] CMLR 831.
78. O.J. L 1979 103/1.
79. Case 34/67, *Luck*, [1968] ECR 245.
80. The existence of such an obligation was confirmed by the Court in Case 13/68, *Salgoil*, [1968] ECR 453.
81. Case 13/68, *Salgoil*, [1968] ECR 453, 462–3.

and remedies relating to actions based on Community rights only to a very limited extent.[82] The absence of such Community rules undermines the uniformity of Community law. Only *minimum* requirements have been imposed by the Court, namely, first that the national rules of procedure must not make it impossible in practice to exercise such rights and second, the national rules of procedure may not be less favorable than those governing the same right of action on an internal matter.[83] However this insistence on equal treatment for Community cases and analogous national cases in the context of the legal system of each Member State virtually guarantees the provision of unequal remedies and procedures over the Community as a whole.[84] In *Rewe-Zentralfinanz eG and Rewe-Zentral AG* v. *Landwirtschaftskammer für das Saarland*[85] the applicable period of limitation within which an action must be brought against an incompatible national measure was one month or, in certain circumstances, one year. In an identical Dutch case,[86] in which a preliminary ruling was sought at the same time, the applicable Dutch statute on administrative jurisdiction over trade organizations prescribed a period of limitation of 30 days. These parallel cases provide cogent examples of the scope for inequality of treatment of nationals of different Member States by virtue of the Community's reliance on national procedural rules.[87] This, in turn, is likely to result

82. See, in general, Mertens de Wilmars "L'efficacité des différents techniques nationales de protection juridique contre les violations du droit communautaire par les autorités nationales et les particuliers" CDE (1981) 379; Bridge "Procedural aspects of the enforcement of European Community law through the legal systems of the Member States" EL Rev. (1985) 28; and Oliver, "Enforcing Community rights in the English courts", 50 MLR (1987), 881.

83. See Case 45/76, *Comet BV* v. *Produktschap voor Siergewassen*, [1976] ECR 2043; Case 177/78, *Pigs and Bacon Commission* v. *McCarren and Company Ltd.*, [1979] ECR 2161: Case 68/79, *Hans Just I/S* v. *Ministère danois des impôts et accises*, [1980] ECR 501; Case 199/82, *Amministrazione delle Finanze dello Stato* v. *San Giorgio*, [1983] ECR 3595. See further, Hubeau, "La répétition de l'indu en droit communautaire", RTDE (1981), 442; Barav, "La répétition de l'indu dans la jurisprudence de la Cour de Justice des Communautés européennes", CDE (1982), 507. See also, Case 309/85, *Barra* v. *Belgium*, [1988] ECR 355.

84. Bridge, op. cit. at 40.

85. Case 33/76, [1976] ECR 1989.

86. 45/76, *Comet*, supra.

87. It is clear that national procedural rules can only be held applicable to the enforcement of Community rights where no relevant procedural rules have been adopted

in unfairness and selectivity in the protection of individual rights conferred by Community law.

The national judge's duty to ensure the effectiveness (*effet utile*) of directly effective Community law entails the faithful application hand in glove of the paramount doctrines of direct effect and supremacy of Community law. These two principles reached their zenith in *Simmenthal*,[88] subsequently confirmed in *Factortame*,[89] where it was made quite clear that national courts are under a duty to disregard any inconsistent provision of national law of whatever nature, whether prior or subsequent to the Community rule. However, what does this mandate mean in practice for the application of Community law? It almost certainly entails the disapplication by a national judge of a rule or judicial mechanism of national law which would prevent the directly effective right from being fully applied.[90] However, what of the situation where a Member State has not legislated to implement a directive into national law at all and it is only after lengthy court proceedings, including a reference to the Court, that it is finally established that the pertinent provision of a directive enjoys direct effect: can the Member State in default rely on a national procedural rule relating to time limits to defeat the claims of all other potential claimants except those who had instigated legal proceedings within the relevant (short) time limit?[91] Where the national judge is given a discretion under the relevant national procedural rule to extend this time limit if he considers that the reason for the delay in the bringing of the action warrants doing so, does the principle of the effectiveness of Community law require the national judge to exercise this discretion in favour of the applicant where it was

on the Community level. See, Case C-34/90, *Plapied and Gallez* v. *The Catholic University of Louvain*, still pending.

88. Case 106/77, supra at 644.

89. Case C-213/89, supra.

90. A good example is provided by the acceptance by the Irish High Court of the argument that a national law principle of "equity" (or prohibiting unjust enrichment) could operate so as to modify the effect in national law of a directly effective provision of a directive. On appeal to the Supreme Court preliminary questions were referred on this matter to the Court: Case C-377/89, *Cotter and McDermott*, Opinion of Advocate General Mischo of 29 Nov. 1990, still pending.

91. See the analogous issues raised in Case C-208/90, *Emmott* v. *The Minister for Social Welfare*, a reference from the Irish High Court, still pending.

reasonable in the circumstances for the applicant to be unaware of the existence of the Community right? Or must the Member State in any event be considered as estopped from relying on such a procedural rule where the result would be to allow the Member State in question to benefit from its own wrong, namely its failure to fulfill the Community law obligation of implementing the terms of a directive into national law on time? The determination of questions such as these, on which the Court has to date given little substantive guidance, can be considered as essential for the purpose of determining the actual content and scope of the judicial protection the national courts are required to apply in the context of individuals seeking to enforce directly effective rights.

5. Remedies: The national cause of action for damages against the State

The availability of adequate judicial remedies for the effective protection of individuals in the national courts in relation to enforceable Community rights may be described as an essential requirement of Community law.[92] Indeed, it seems that the principle of the effectiveness of the remedy proffered may be developing into a general principle of Community law.[93] Thus, in *Johnston* v. *Chief Constable of the Royal Ulster Constabulary*[94] the Court linked the requirement of effective judicial control to a general principle of law which underlines the constitutional traditions common to the Member States. In addition, that principle is also laid down in Articles 6 and 13 of the European Convention of Human Rights and Fundamental Freedoms, an element which is taken into consideration in Community law.[95] In *Heylens* v. *UNECTEF*[96] the Court stressed that all individuals have the right to

92. Barav, "Enforcement of Community rights in the national courts: the case for jurisdiction to grant an interim relief" 26 CML Rev. (1989), 369.
93. See, in this sense, Dubois, "A propos de deux principes generaux du droit communautaire", Rev. fr. Droit adm. (1988), 691.
94. Case 222/84, [1986] ECR 1651.
95. See, *Johnston*, *supra* note 94.
96. Case 22/86, [1987] ECR 4097; see also, albeit in a different context, Joined Cases C-143/88, *Suderdithmarschen* v. *Hauptzollamt Itzehoe* and C-92/89, *Zuckerfabrik Soest* v. *Hauptzollamt Paderborn*, still pending.

obtain an effective remedy in a competent national court against national measures which they consider to be contrary to Community law. This general principle of the effectiveness of judicial protection has been encapsulated in legislative form in two notable areas. First, in the directives relating to the equal treatment of male and female workers, Member States are required to adopt measures which are sufficiently effective to achieve the objective of the Directive.[97] Second, with regard to public procurement, the recently published draft "Compliance Directive" relating to the application of Community rules on procedures for the award of contracts in the fields of water, energy, transport and telecommunications ("excluded sectors")[98] makes reference to the obligation on Member States to provide effective legal means of recourse with the view to setting aside decisions violating Community legislation and national implementing legislation[99] as well as to provide for the compensation of injured tenderers.[100]

The principle of effective protection of individual rights in Community law[101] involves an obligation on national authorities to ensure that national legal provisions, including provisions in collective agreements,[102] which are inconsistent with those Community rights do not have effect. However, the fact that a Community law provision can be considered as directly effective does not of itself determine whether the right created in the individual is to be categorized by the national law as a private law right to be protected by such remedies as the national legal system provides for such a right, or as a right to have the public law enforced, to which are attached the remedies appropriate for such

97. Case 14/83, *von Colson, supra* with regard to Article 6 of Directive 76/207, O.J. 1976 L 39/40. See also, Case 177/88, *Dekker, supra* para. 23.

98. COM(90) 297 final, O.J. 1990 C 216/8.

99. Art. 1(1). See also, Proposal for a Council Directive co-ordinating the laws, regulations and administrative provisions relating to the application of Community rules on procedures for the award of Public Supply and Public Works contracts, COM (87) 134 final, 1 July 1987, Art. 1. The revised Directive was adopted on 22 March 1988, the compliance provision having been dropped: O.J. 1988 L.

100. Article 2(1) (c).

101. Case 179/84, *Bozzetti*, [1985] ECR 2301.

102. See, Case C-33/89, *Kowalska* v. *Frei und Hansestadt Hamburg*, judgment of 27 June 1990, not yet reported and Case C-184/89, *Nimz* v. *Frei und Hansestadt Hamburg*, judgment of 7 Feb. 1991.

enforcement. Nevertheless, in as much as it is for the national court to give effect to Community rights, the remedies offered must be effective; this obligation would seem to imply that the remedies provided be *dissuasive* of breaches of individual rights.[103] Following from this analysis, Community law may require national courts to make available, pursuant to the failure by a Member State to implement a directive into national law, a remedy in damages (as opposed to a mere declaratory order) vested in those individuals injured by the national public authorities' violation of Community law.[104]

Enforceable Community rights are created by the actual provisions of Community law having direct effect in the Member States internal order and not as a result of a judgment given by the Court against a Member State in the context of proceedings instituted by the Commission under Articles 169 to 171 of the Treaty.[105] National courts are therefore not permitted to make the availability of remedies to enforce such Community rights dependent upon a prior judgment by the Court but are obliged to apply them if necessary of their own motion and availing where appropriate of the consultation procedure laid down in Article 177 of the Treaty. There is however some authority in the case law of the Court for the proposition that the interest of having a judgment by the Court in the context of proceedings under Article 169 of the Treaty is that it may establish the basis of the *liability* the State may incur, in particular towards individuals as a result of the breach of its obligations.[106] This statement has been recently reiterated by the Court in the context of an action concerning a Member States' failure to correctly transpose a Directive into national law.[107]

103. See, Case 14/83, *von Colson and Kamann*, [1984] ECR 1891, para. 23. See also the judgments of the *Bundesarbeitsgericht* of 14 March 1989 in 8 AZR 447/87 and 8 AZR 351/86, annotated in 4 EuR (1990) 362 and 368. See, however, the EAT in *Southampton and South West Hampshire Health Authority* v. *Marshall*, [1989] 3 CMLR 771 where it was held that the remedies are a matter of discretion for the State subject only to the principle of *de minimis*.

104. See, in the same sense, Prechal, op. cit. at 466.

105. Joined cases 314 to 316/81 and 83/82, *Waterkeyn and Cayard*, [1982] ECR 4337, 4361.

106. Case 39/72, *Commission* v. *Italy*, [1973] ECR 101; Case 309/84, *Commission* v. *Italy*, [1986] ECR 599; Case 103/84, *Commission* v. *Italy*, [1986] ECR 1759; Case 154/85, *Commission* v. *Italy*, [1987] ECR 2717.

107. Case C-287/87, *Commission* v. *Greece*, judgment of 18 Jan. 1990, not yet reported.

The proposition that damages should be awarded under national law to those individuals who suffer loss as a result of a Member State's breach of Community law received some support in *Russo* v. *AIMA*.[108] After holding that producers of durum wheat were entitled to sell their products at a price approximating the target price (and in any event no lower than the intervention price) determined by a Council regulation, and that those who were precluded from doing so were entitled to claim that they had suffered damage, the Court held that: "It is for the national court to decide on the basis of the facts of each case whether an individual producer has suffered such damage. If such damage has been caused through an infringement of Community law the State is liable to the injured party of the consequences in the context of the provisions of national law on the liability of the State."

It can therefore be argued on the basis of this judgment that the Court has acknowledged the right to damages in the event of loss sustained as a result of a breach by the national public authorities, albeit in the context "of the provisions of national law on the liability of the State". It is not thereby authorizing a system of national law to deny all liability of the State but rather placing the Community right in the context of such liability.[109] In the absence of any Community harmonization the arrangements for the compensation of individuals injured by an unlawful act of a public authority is still governed by the national legal systems with the corollary that the systems both of evidence and of estoppel prevailing in the separate Member States will apply, thereby jeopardizing any hope of attaining a uniform system of rules. Nevertheless, the principle that the State is liable is acknowledged in all the Member States provided that the damage was caused by the public authority in the exercise of their functions.[110] Under no national legal system is

108. Case 60/75, [1976] ECR 45. See also, 6/60, *Humblet* v. *Belgian State*, [1960] ECR 559, albeit in the context of the Coal and Steel Treaty. See Green and Barav, "Damages in the national courts for breach of Community law", (1987) *Yearbook of European law*, 55, 60.

109. Durand, "Enforceable Community rights and national remedies" (1987) *Denning Law Journal* 43, 59.

110. For a general overview of the regimes of public authority liability in the various Member States see Schockweiler, "La régime de la responsibilité du fait d'actes juridiques dans la Communauté européenne", 26 RTDE (1990), 27.

liability arising from acts in the nature of secondary legislation automatically excluded.[111] In a majority of Member States *fault* by a public authority has to be demonstrated[112] whereas in others an unlawful act by an authority is virtually equivalent to a fault.[113] In common law terms, it is probably correct to draw an analogy between the tort a Member State commits in failing to implement the provisions of a directive into national law in time, if the Directive provides for the protection of individual rights, and the cause of action arising out of a breach of a public duty under a statute[114] or under the Irish Constitution for which the Crown or the State, respectively, owes a duty to individual subjects or citizens.[115]

Despite this diverging content of national law the national court is, in any event, as regards its national legal order, obliged on the basis of the general obligations imposed upon Member States in Article 5 of the Treaty, to draw the consequences flowing from their State's membership of the Community. This means that it must determine the extent of the protection national law offers individuals affected by any breach of provisions of Community law, which establish individual rights, in

111. See, Answer given by Mr. Delors to Written Question No. 2423/88, O.J. 1989 C 276/24.

112. Denmark, Germany, Ireland, Luxembourg, the Netherlands, Portugal and the United Kingdom: see further, Schockweiler, op. cit. See also *Bourgoin, infra* note 120; *Roussel Laboratories BV* v. *The Netherlands*, judgment of 18 July 1984 by the Hague District Court; *Moyne* v. *Londonderry Port and Harbour Commissioners* [1986] *Irish Reports* 299, *Pine Valley Developments Limited* v. *The Minister for the Environment* [1987] *Irish Reports* 23, judgments by the Irish Superior Courts.

113. Belgium, France and Luxembourg: see Schockweiler, op. cit. In *Alivar* v. *Ministre du commerce exterieur* (23 March 1984), AJDA (1984) 396 the French *Conseil d'Etat* held that the French authorities were liable to pay damages to the plaintiff whose claim arose from certain French export restrictions which were in violation of Community law (Case 68/76, *Commission* v. *France*, [1977] ECR 515) on the basis of liability without fault provided that the plaintiff could show abnormal and special harm attributable to the intervention of the French administration. See further, Green and Barav, op. cit. at 72 *et seq.*

114. See, *Garden Cottage Foods* v. *Milk Marketing Board* [1983] 2 All ER 770 where the House of Lords (per Lord Diplock in an *obiter dicta*) categorized a breach of Art. 86 in English law as "a breach of a statutory duty that is imposed not only for the purpose of promoting the general economic prosperity of the Common Market but also for the benefit of private individuals to whom loss or damage is caused by a breach of that duty".

115. See, in particular, *Pine Valley Developments* v. *The Minister for the Environment* [1987] *Irish Reports* 23.

accordance with the Community law principles of effectiveness and appropriateness. Advocate General Reischl expressed this idea in crystal clear terms in *Russo*.[116] He stressed that "the liability of a Member State for the consequences flowing from an infringement of Community law also arises out of the obligation to provide *effective protection* of these rights provided that the other prerequisites under national law are present".[117]

The importance of the enforcement of Community law from the inception was forcefully stressed by Advocate General Reischl in his opinion in *Simmenthal* when he concluded that the protection afforded to directly effective rights must apply in a *total* fashion. Thus it would be inadequate for remedies to focus only on curtailing unlawful behaviour and thereby ensuring future compliance. The requisite remedies must therefore also look *backwards* to the period of rectification by a court.[118] Community law must prevail as far as possible *ex post facto* in the sense that the necessary compensation for its temporary non-application must be available.[119] To deny any remedy for any breaches which have taken place before determination of the illegality of the act complained of would infringe the principle of complete and effective judicial protection. The type of remedy which seems to be envisaged by Community law is analogous to a *private law* remedy available for breach of a duty, be it statutory or constitutional, owed specifically to the claimant and clearly involves the payment of compensation or damages in respect of the period between the commission of the wrong and its rectification.

It follows from the fact that a right to recover damages can be regarded as an adjunct to the individual right to have the provisions of the EEC Treaty observed that national courts no longer retain the discretion under national law to apply purely *public law* remedies where that would result only in a declaration of illegality for the future.[120] This

116. [1976] ECR 45, 58.
117. [1976] ECR 45, 63. Author's emphasis.
118. Green and Barav, op. cit. at 60.
119. See, the conclusions of Advocate General Reischl in Case 106/77, *Simmenthal* [1978] ECR 629, at 656.
120. See Lord Diplock in *Garden Cottage Foods* v. *Milk Marketing Board* [1982] 2 CMLR 584. See further, Green and Barav, op. cit., at 63 and Durand, "Enforceable

does not mean in my submission that national courts are obliged to formally classify directly effective Community rights as falling under domestic private law; they still retain the discretion to classify these rights in the national legal context as they see fit according to the precepts of national law,[121] provided however that they ensure that in enforcing such Community rights that they apply the principle of effectiveness.[122]

The Court of Justice has denied that national courts are under a duty to create *new* remedies for the application of Community law but has insisted that it must be possible for every type of action provided for by national law to be available for the purpose of ensuring observance of Community provisions having direct effect.[123] However, some recent case law bears witness to a tendency for Community substantive law to exert an influence on the form and availability of national remedies.[124] In particular it can be argued that it follows from the Court's judgment in *Factortame* that Community law requires that the remedy of interim injunctive relief be available against the Crown in order to ensure the effectiveness of the judicial protection offered to individuals before their national courts when seeking to rely on putative directly effective

Community rights and national remedies" (1987) *Denning Law Journal*, 43. It follows from this proposition that the English Court of Appeal may be criticised for its holding in *Bourgoin SA and others* v. *Ministry of Agriculture, Fisheries and Food* [1985] 3 All ER 585 that breach by the United Kingdom government of the plaintiffs rights under Article 30 did not give rise to an action for breach of statutory duty sounding in damages, but to a public law action for judicial review. Such an action could only result in a declaration that the government's act was *ultra vires* and invalid. See, *contra*. the interesting dissenting judgment of Oliver L.J.

121. For the problems which may be experienced by the national judge in this context see, Steiner, "How to make the action suit the case: Domestic remedies for breach of Community law" (1986) EL Rev., 102; Green and Barav, op. cit.; Barav, "Damages in the domestic courts for breach of Community law by national public authorities" in *Non-Contractual Liability of the European Communities* (eds. Schermers, Heukels, Mead), 1988, 149.

122. Case 68/88, *Commission* v. *Greece*, 21 Sept. 1989, not yet published in which the Court reaffirms that "Article 5 of the Treaty requires Member States to take all measures appropriate to ensure the application and effectiveness of Community law". See also, Case C-2/88 Imm., *Zwartveld*, order of 13 July 1990, not yet reported, at consideration 17.

123. Case 158/80, *Rewe-Zentralfinanz*, *supra*.

124. See, Wyatt, "Enforcing EEC social rights in the United Kingdom", (1989) ILJ, 197, 206.

rights, even though that same remedy would not be available under purely national law.[125] What is this if not the imposition of a "new" remedy in a Community law context? In concrete terms it is submitted that the principle of the effectiveness of Community law entails the making available by a national court "of its own motion"[126] of a remedy in damages where no other remedy is available under national law which effectively compensates for the past, i.e. prior to the judicial establishment of the right. A court which would grant a remedy in damages if it were not for a contrary rule of national law is obliged to set aside or disapply the rule. However, where national law does not contain a *positive* rule preventing the courts from granting damages but simply does not provide the *jurisdiction* to do so, the national court is probably obliged to create a jurisdiction where none existed before,[127] a reality which goes considerably further than the phenomenon of "dis-application" propounded by the Court in *Simmenthal.*

It is submitted that at the substantive level Community law envisages a type of strict liability. It may be argued that where a Member State acts in breach of the directly effective provisions of Community law, any loss or damage suffered by an individual as a consequence sounds in damages.[128] The failure by a Member State to implement the directly effective provisions of, in the event, a directive into national law occa-

125. Compare the position under Irish law where such relief is readily granted: *Pesca Valentia* v. *Minister for Fisheries* [1986] *Irish Reports* 68. See Annotation of *Factortame* by Toth, in this Review, *supra* note 25.

126. Simmenthal *supra*, para. 24.

127. Support for this proposition can be gleaned from *Factortame* where the real problem at issue in that case was that under British law there was no positive rule preventing the national courts from granting interim relief against the Crown: the courts simply enjoyed no jurisdiction in that regard. See further, Toth, cited at note 25 *supra*; Simon and Barav, "Le droit communautaire et la suspension provisoire des mesures nationales. Les enjeux de l'affaire *Factortame*", 340 RMC (1990), 591. See also, Oliver L.J. in *Bourgoin, supra*.

128. Unlike their English counterparts (see case cited in note 129), it seems, on the basis of their existing case law dealing both with breach of statutory duty as well as breach of constitutional rights, that the Irish courts would have little difficulty in granting damages in these circumstances: see, in particular, *Moyne* v. *The Londonderry Port and Harbour Commissioners* [1986] *Irish Reports* 299; *Pine Valley Developments Limited* v. *The Minister for the Environment* [1987] *Irish Law Reports Monthly* 23; *Meskell* v. *Coras Iompair Eireann* [1973] *Irish Reports* 121; *Kennedy, Arnold and Arnold* v. *Ireland* [1988] *Irish Law Reports Monthly* 472.

sions the breach of individual rights which are deemed to be absolute and which lead to an action in damages. According to this analysis it would be incompatible with Community law for a national court to subject an injured individual's right to obtain damages from the State for violation of a directly effective right to the further restrictive proof of an abuse of power by the Member State.[129] A nascent tendency in Community law may be detected involving some dictation of the substantive content of the remedies which national law must obligatorily provide for the effective protection of directly effective Community rights. For example, in *Dekker* v. *Stichting Vormingscentrum voor Jong Volwassenen* (*VJV Centrum*) *Plus*[130] the Court emphasized, with regard to sanctions provided under national law for the breach of an individual's right to receive equal treatment in employment, that the mere breach of this fundamental principle of equal treatment must result in the strict liability of the employer in question to compensate the victim for that violation and that national law may not subject the employer's liability to the proof of fault on the part of the employee or to the absence of any justification.[131]

6. Conclusion

A genuine rule of law in the European context implies binding rules which apply uniformly and which protect individual rights.[132] A lacu-

129. Actionable under the tort of misfeasance in public office: per Parker L.J. (for the majority) in *Bourgoin*, *supra* note 120 at 629. The majority of the Court of Appeal reasoned that the violation *simpliciter* of a directly effective right by a Member State does not suffice to render the State liable to individuals in damages but, by analogy with the Court's restrictive requirements imposed on the public tort liability of the Communities under Article 215 of the Treaty, it required proof of misuse of power in addition. See with regard to Art. 215: Joined Cases 83 and 94/76, 4, 15 and 40/77, *Bayerische HNL* v. *Council and Commission*, [1978] ECR 1209; Case 238/78, *Ireks-Arkady* v. *Council and Commission*, [1979] ECR 2955. See further, Barav, "Damages in the national courts for breach of Community law by national public authorities", *supra* note 121.

130. Case C-177/88, judgment of 8 Nov. 1990, not yet reported.

131. Case C-177/88, *Dekker*, *supra*. paras. 24 and 25.

132. Suggestions of the Court of Justice on European Union in *Bulletin of the European Communities*, Supplement 9/75 at 17.

na in the Treaty of Rome is that it does not provide for any effective sanction against a State which fails to fulfil its obligations to the detriment of those who do. Whereas the principle of direct effect has given individuals a powerful tool which can be wielded to great effect before their national courts, the utility of this uniquely Community law tool has been stunted by the Court's denial of horizontal direct effect to the provisions of directives. Nevertheless the repeated reiteration by the Court in recent years of the duty of solidarity imposed on national courts by Article 5 of the Treaty has meant that these courts are clearly obliged not only to interpret both earlier and later national legislation in the light of Community directives, despite that facts that such "construction" may involve considerable straining of language, but also that national courts are obliged to ensure the effective protection of individuals' Community rights.

The latter mandate in particular means that the national courts are obliged to ensure that these rights are not abridged but are capable of being actually enforced in the remedial and procedural sense. Individuals must therefore be capable of being placed in the same position as if the right had not been broken. However, it is probably only when the breach of the Member States' "public" duty under Article 189 inflicts loss or damage on the individual that the individual has a "private" cause of action in damages under national law and that the national courts duty to protect fully and immediately rights granted by Community law comes into play.[133] An important question in this respect is whether private individuals who have been adversely affected by the failure of a Member State to implement the terms of a directive into national law should be able to claim compensation against the State for

133. This analysis can be supported by a close reading of Case 158/80, *Rewe* v. *Hauptzollamt Kiel* ("butter-buying cruises"), [1981] ECR 1805, in particular Advocate General Capotorti's distinction between those individuals with directly effective rights under Community law, a defined class and those who might have an *interest* in the correct application of the law, a potentially much larger class where there can be no question of its members enjoying "individual" rights as such and whose remedy, if any, will lie in public law as opposed to the private law domain of damages. He entirely rejected the proposition that the doctrine of direct effect had created some kind of popular action so that anyone with an interest in the correct application of Community law could seek a review of the application of Community law by the State.

damage sustained as a result, even in relation to provisions of the directive which do not enjoy direct effect in the formal sense.[134] It can be argued that it would be incompatible with the binding effect attributed to a Directive by Article 189 of the Treaty to exclude, in principle, the possibility that the obligation which it imposes may be invoked by those individuals whose rights have been directly or indirectly adversely affected by the Member State's failure to implement correctly or on time, even where the norm in question may not enjoy direct effect as such.[135] It must be recognized that the existence of such effect would constitute an important additional weapon in the legal armoury of vigilant individuals affected by a Member State's failure to correctly, and in good time, transpose the provisions of a Directive into national law. Such reinforced "internalization" of Community law[136] could only serve to significantly optimize the applicability of directives in the national legal orders. However the recognition that Community law requires such a remedy in damages to be available at the national level should ideally go hand in glove with the elaboration by the Community legislator of legislation purporting to harmonize the procedural arrangements accompanying the remedy as well as detailing its substance.

134. This issue has been squarely raised before the Court for the first time in two references from Italy: Joined Cases 6 and 9/90, *Francovich and Bonifaci* v. *Italy*, still pending, where the respective national jurisdictions seek the guidance of the Court on whether there is a Community law requirement that a private individual who has suffered loss in consequence of a Member State's failure to implement the terms of a Directive into national law must be enabled to claim damages against the State, even where the pertinent terms of the Directive are not directly effective. Interestingly, the same submission seems to have been raised as an alternative to direct effect before the Irish courts, but was not dealt with: Case C-377/89, *Cotter and McDermott* and Case C-208/90, *Emmott*, both cited *supra*.

135. This type of rationale is much broader than the objective conditions required by the Court to establish Community liability in the context of Art. 215 of the Treaty (which in turn borrows heavily from the German *Schutznormtheorie*).

136. See, Pescatore, *The law of integration, emergence of a new phenomenon in international relations based on the experience of the European Communities* (1974), at 104.

[18]

A European Budget made in Strasbourg and unmade in Luxembourg*

Helen Wallace

Introduction

Putting its budgetary house in order remains an elusive goal for the European Community. No democratic government finds making budgets an easy task. In any political system where powers are divided between different levels of government, there are particular and intrinsic obstacles to the development and maintenance of budgetary coherence and consensus. One has only to examine the problems of the Federal Government of the United States in this field to illustrate the point, or to observe the complexities, contortions and contentiousness of public finance between local and central government within a country such as the United Kingdom. Add the complication of a climate of austerity and it is no surprise that the raising of revenue and allocation of public expenditure should generate great arguments.

The Community has additional fragility.[1] Community-level decision-making is dependent on the striking of bargains among governments and the domestic interests which lie behind them. Whoever pays the piper, and the answer to that question is not clear, no one in the Community is in a position to call the budgetary tune. Agreement depends instead on the marshalling of shifting and often unpredictable coalitions of interests. The democratic checks and balances of accountability operate in a very curious way. The European Parliament has some powers over expenditure, but no responsibility for revenue raising; for the rest, the line of accountability runs indirectly and opaquely via member governments back to national parliaments. Key issues about policy and therefore spending priorities lurk beneath the financial arguments, but again skewed by the historical accidents and political bargains which were responsible for the revenue dowry and expenditure instruments that currently comprise the Com-

Dr Wallace is a Research Fellow at the Royal Institute of International Affairs, London, and Director of its West European programme. This study arises from work funded by the Gatsby Charitable Foundation.

[1] For general background on the budget process see Guy Isaac (ed), *Les ressources financières de la communauté européenne* (Paris, Economica 1986), J. Ørstrøm Møller, 'Financing European integration: the European Communities and the proposed European Union' in *An Ever Closer Union*, European Perspectives (Brussels 1985) 73–102, and Daniel Strasser, *The Finances of Europe*, European Perspectives (Brussels 1984).

munity budget. Furthermore, the partly formed character of the European Community as a political system has the consequence that debates over the rather significant budgetary role of the Community are often encoded versions of a much broader debate about the process of European construction as a whole.[2]

Events over the last twelve months have well illustrated the interplay of conflicting interests engaged in efforts to establish political boundaries.[3] The Community entered the new fiscal year of 1986 with a budget adopted by the European Parliament, but contested by the Council before the European Court of Justice. It ends the year with the revised version of the 1986 budget overtaken by higher expenditure and falling revenue. It faces the next fiscal year with the prospect of reaching the constitutionally defined revenue ceiling, without having in the meantime reduced the drain of expenditure on agricultural guarantee under the Common Agricultural Policy (CAP). It is no new experience for the Community to have had to deal with a budget contested between the European Parliament and the Council of Ministers. The difference in 1986 was that instead of simply complaining, both the Council of Ministers and several member governments chose to put the issues to the European Court of Justice (ECJ) and to pursue the case. It is the purpose of this article to set this story and result of the ECJ case in context and to explore the political implications of the judgment for the budgetary process.

The pre-history

Members of the European Parliament (MEPs) have often exploited their powers under the EC Treaties to harass budget Ministers. They have done this for a mixture of reasons. First, it has been and remains a symbolic exercise of limited constitutional power. Without hard influence on Community legislation and with only blunt instruments with which to rein the Commission, still less the Council, it is a natural parliamentary reaction to exploit budgetary powers. Secondly, MEPs to some extent have seen themselves as the conscience of the European Community on budgetary matters, with a duty to raise some of the uncomfortable dimensions of Community expenditure which are squeezed out by the bargaining amongst governments. Thus, they have persistently focused on the problems of own resources. Thirdly, MEPs have had views about policy substance which they have wished to see reflected in budgetary appropriations. Their recurrent concerns have been the structural funds and overseas develop-

[2] See Helen Wallace, 'Distributional Politics: Dividing up the Community Cake' in Helen Wallace, William Wallace and Carole Webb, *Policy-Making in the European Community* (John Wiley, Chichester 1983) 81–113.

[3] The House of Lords, Select Committee on the European Communities, *Community Budget 1986–1987* Session 1985–86 HL 239 (London, July 1986) and William Nichol, 'From Rejection to Repudiation: EC Budgetary Affairs' 25 *JCMS* No. 1, 31–49 (1986).

ment assistance, and currently research and development for technological industries.

But from the perspective of some other actors on this particular stage the consequences have been to cause turbulence. This reflects structural features of the budgetary process. It is a typical trait of democratic politics that there should be tensions between parliament and executive, especially where there is a separation of powers. In the Community case, the tensions are compounded by the total absence of responsibility (in a formal sense) by the European Parliament for the revenue consequences of their expenditure preferences. There is, however, a further and important factor. Over the years the different Community institutions have groped uneasily towards the establishment of rules, procedures and processes which would provide workable parameters for difficult budgetary decisions.

Previous stalled and contested budgets had focused attention on three difficulties. First, the Treaties laid down rules about the scope of parliamentary influence on expenditure appropriations in the form of a 'maximum rate' of budgetary growth for non-obligatory expenditure and a 'margin of manoeuvre' linked to it. The European Parliament was granted the power to increase certain items of 'non-obligatory' expenditure, but not beyond the 'margin of manoeuvre' extrapolated from the maximum rate by the Commission at the beginning of the budgetary procedure. Thus, the overall size of the budget was to be constrained annually in advance of final decisions about appropriations. Those rules had repeatedly been subject to conflicting interpretations.

Second, in cases of persistent disagreement between the Council and the Parliament the procedures for securing a negotiated settlement had proved inadequate. As a result, the 'triloque' procedure was established following a previous budget crisis in June 1982 to facilitate negotiation and to bring in the Commission through the involvement of the Presidents of the three political Institutions. Third, and more difficult to pin down, there was a growing impatience in the Council of Ministers, articulated more vigorously by some member governments than others, at the apparent willingness of some MEPs to play politics rather than recognise financial realities. Supporters of this view tended to argue that some clarification of the budgetary rules and procedures was necessary to reduce the scope for irresponsible and potentially unconstitutional behaviour by the European Parliament. The Council's conclusions on budgetary discipline, adopted in December 1984, indicated its own concern to constrain the growth of expenditure.

Behind this aggravation over the precise import of the Treaty articles lay two wider issues, one constitutional and the other financial. The row over the 1986 budget erupted during the closing stages of the Intergovernmental Conference on Treaty reforms. One of the questions on the table was whether and how the powers of the European Parliament might be extended. Many MEPs felt that their initiative—the Draft Treaty on

European Union—was being whittled away by the excessive caution of some member governments. A robust position on the 1986 budget was a means of reminding the Council of Ministers that the European Parliament was a force to be reckoned with. On the other side, member governments in the Council could see the implications of action by the Parliament which might extend their constitutional powers. Already the Council had signalled its discontent at the Parliament's inclusion in the 1985 budget of a smaller amount of expenditure beyond their clearly legal entitlement. Those governments which did not like what they saw had an interest in checking on the precise constitutionality of the European Parliament's action not only for budgetary reasons, but also to define the context in which the Parliament's new legislative role would emerge following ratification of the Single European Act. Already on two occasions the European Parliament had been threatened with an action by the European Court of Justice: in 1981, when three governments tabled but did not prosecute their case; and in 1982, when a settlement rendered the Council's intended action redundant.

In this context, we should note the discrepancy between rhetoric and practice. No member government wishes too publicly or too explicitly to castigate the European Parliament, a fact reflected in the language of encouragement found in formal statements. But privately attitudes are much more circumspect and thus often amenable to steps which might constrain the European Parliament's greater ambitions.

The other broad issue behind the debates and disagreements over the 1986 Community budget has to do with the general development of EC finances. Some fifteen years previously, the Community had set itself on course to raise its own direct revenue and to establish a wide range of spending programmes. The budgetary procedures were altered to underpin this and revised subsequently to consolidate the arrangements. Yet repeatedly the budget has become the focus of controversy, with arguments about substance and procedure continually intermingled. The 1984 and 1985 budgets had run into difficulties. The Community was reaching and eventually exceeding the 1 per cent VAT revenue ceiling in advance of final ratification by all Member States of the new 1.4 per cent ceiling. The European Parliament had on these grounds rejected the Council's version of the 1985 budget, leaving the Community to operate until June 1985 the 'provisional twelfths' system, whereby expenditure appropriations are limited month by month to the levels of the previous year. Intergovernmental Agreements in October 1984 and April 1985 had resolved the revenue shortfall by Member States agreeing to make one-off national exchequer payments, in the form of non-refundable advances.[4] But disputed territory remained between the Parliament and the Council, with MEPs claiming that it was irresponsible of governments to propose a budget that could not be covered by the normal flow of Community revenue. And all this against a

[4] (EC) *Bulletin* No. 4 (1985) 56.

backcloth of an attempt to resolve the revenue problems of the Community by increasing the VAT limit from 1 per cent to 1.4 per cent from 1 January 1986, headroom which vanished almost as soon as it appeared.

Hardly anyone involved finds the consequences of these disputes and their procedural handling satisfactory, from whichever perspective the issues are appraised. The option of devising budgetary arrangements *de novo* is almost certainly not available. But the prospect of continuing to work with unsatisfactory arrangements is not attractive to any of the participants, especially with the attendant risk that lurching and contradictory incrementalism may be the outcome. One result of this frustration has been the concern to go for greater precision in determining some of the reference points rather than to rely on negotiated understandings which may prove to be not such gentlemanly agreements in practice.

The 1986 budget

None the less, in mid-1985 there was some optimism in Community circles that the deliberations over the 1986 budget would be much less tense than in previous years. Two major issues had apparently been removed from the table. The UK rebate, so often a source of controversy, had been broadly resolved by the Fontainebleau settlement of June 1984, leaving only the details of the calculations to be fixed, that is, a problem of practice not principle.[5] Farm spending looked less worrying in that forecast appropriations were restrained in line with the agricultural guideline set by Finance Ministers to develop 'budgetary discipline', an assumption resting on misplaced optimism, as subsequent developments demonstrated. In their place, two different issues had emerged: one was the financial consequences of Iberian enlargement on 1 January 1986; the other the extent of appropriations for the structural (i.e. mainly regional and social) funds. In the background were a number of smaller issues over items such as food aid.

On enlargement, the Spanish Government was understandably at pains to insist on its concern to avoid any result less than neutral for its financial transfers to and from the Community budget, while the Portuguese expected to be modest net beneficiaries. The Council of Ministers argued that this need not be a problem, but that in any case the inevitable imprecision of forecasting meant that the precise consequences for Portugal and Spain would have to be dealt with later. At that stage, the Portuguese and Spanish Governments had only observer status. MEPs had already signalled their concern that allowance for this should be built into the 1986 general budget at the outset rather than deferred to a supplementary budget.

The other issue on the structural funds became the *cause célèbre* of the year, encoded as the 'cost of the past'. A recurrent difficulty in Community

[5] (EC) *Bulletin* No. 6 (1985) 7–12.

budgeting is managing the flow of expenditure to an anticipated timetable. The division of the budget into two sections—one for *payments* in the given fiscal year and the other for *commitments* authorising future contracts linked to multi-annual estimates—was designed to facilitate financial management. The difficulty arises with the scheduling of commitments which are, in turn, dependent on implementation in and co-financing by the Member States, typically the case for social and regional expenditure. Efforts had been made to tighten up programme management in order to prevent the accumulation of commitments. The revenue shortfalls of 1984 and 1985 had resulted in the deferring of some expenditures to enable the books to balance. The net result was that the Commission estimated that a spending increase would be needed in 1986 to deal with this 'cost of the past' for outstanding and contracted commitments. There is a further element of budgetary overhang, in the form of accumulated intervention stocks under CAP product regimes. Another complication stems from the historical encroachment of obligatory agricultural expenditure which is not cash-limited in the budget. These add to the inherited expenditure obligations of the Community, and complicate the problems of shifting the proportions of total expenditure away from agriculture.

When the Budget Council met on 18 September 1985, it began to be clear that the circles would not easily be squared. The combination of claims for non-obligatory expenditure could not be met within the 7.1 per cent 'maximum rate' for budgetary growth set earlier in the year. After nineteen hours of vigorous deliberation, Ministers decided to postpone decisions on both the Iberian Governments' claims and the accumulation of inherited commitments on the structural funds, together with several smaller cut-backs of expenditure thus remaining within the maximum rate limit. The decision, taken by qualified majority vote, as is usual in the Budget Council, left three member governments—Greece, Ireland and Italy—dissatisfied, but unable numerically to block this outcome.

The reaction of the European Parliament in November 1985 was to contest vigorously the Council's version of the budget. It sought to insert appropriations by way of its amending powers which went well beyond its legal margin of manoeuvre—well over 2 billion ECU rather than the 217 million ECU—to cover the impact of enlargement, the 'cost of the past' (both carry-overs from 1985 and accumulated commitments) and food aid, with approximately the legal margin of manoeuvre dedicated to new policies, technology, energy and environment. MEPs were well aware of the discrepancy between the legal limit and their own proposals, but argued that they had just cause, in so far as the Budget Council had not fulfilled its own responsibilities to honour established spending obligations. In other words, the Parliament wittingly challenged the Council's majority decision, presumably in the hope that the Council would have second thoughts.

The Parliament's gamble almost paid off. When the Budget Council met in November 1985, a majority emerged for a partial inclusion of the disputed appropriations, enough, they hoped, to satisfy their critics in Strasbourg, but without reneging on their intention to maintain a prudent financial posture. The precise form of the package was a result of the complex bargaining processes of the Council. To palliate the concern over enlargement, Ministers inserted a special contingency reserve of 250 million ECU and to respond to the arguments over the 'cost of the past' they included 400 million ECUs. But they held to the freeze on social and regional expenditure in the existing Member States. Ministers also reduced to 100 million ECUs (as against 217 million) the Parliament's appropriations for new policies within the legal 'margin of manoeuvre', hoping to force MEPs to contribute the remaining amount towards the burden of Iberian enlargement.

Two governments out of the Ten voted against the package: the Irish, because of the freeze on regional and social programmes, and the British, because of the weakened commitment to budgetary discipline. Again, it must be remembered that Portugal and Spain still had observer status, though both governments added voices if not votes of protest. Behind these overt signs of dissent it was evident that member governments were beginning to align themselves in different camps. On the one hand, there was an emergent 'austerity' caucus, consisting of France, the Federal Republic of Germany, the Netherlands and the United Kingdom with some support from Belgium. Their alignment of attitudes reflected a mix of factors, partly the concern of the net payers to limit their financial burdens and partly (and to an extent overlapping) a less parochial determination to practice financial prudence and discipline at a period of necessarily (for some desirably) low growth in national budgets. The other caucus comprised the spenders, that is, those governments which argued the necessity of maintaining and even reinforcing spending programmes. This group also combined different objectives: for some, it reflected a straightforward preoccupation with their own level of financial return, although with varying policy priorities; for others, it was also a matter of principle to retain a dynamic and growing Community budget. The Commission was keen to ensure a budget large enough to cover contractual expenditure obligations, including both the 'cost of the past' and Iberian enlargement, but it did not argue hard for budget growth in general.

The formal position of the Budget Council and the complex motivations expressed by governments presented MEPs with a difficult choice, when set against the heady ambitions expressed by the European Parliament in November. Some MEPs argued strongly the case for continuing to challenge the Council; this was the preponderant view of the Socialist Group. The Liberals with a few other supporters were the most willing to lower their sights to modest increases which the Council might fairly readily accept, while the Christian Democrats and Gaullists pitched for an intermediate level of increase. Significantly, despite a special third Budget Council held during the Parliament's plenary session in December, the procedures for conciliating the differences between the Council and Parliament and with the Commission failed to generate a mutually agreeable solution. While this might appear as a failure of procedure, the reality was different. Both Council and Parliament had been pushed to the bottom lines of their negotiating positions, given the divergences of view inside both institutions. The problem was that the bottom lines did not meet.

Interestingly, from November onwards to the eventual budget crisis the Commission remained relatively quiet, choosing on this occasion to leave the other two institutions to fight it out among themselves. The point is noteworthy, given that in previous budgetary arguments the Commission had often opted for a higher profile with regard to expenditure. Its reticence demonstrated a qualitative change towards acute concern for balancing the budget in recognition of, first, the serious constraints on revenue raising, secondly, the risks of subsequent over-spending emerging during the fiscal year and, thirdly, the management problems of a protracted crisis. The Commission also anticipated that any budget adopted by the Parliament in excess of the maximum rate would breach Treaty rules, unless the Council had concurred.

In the event, the European Parliament voted on 12 December 1985 for the adoption of a budget some 629 million ECU in total higher than the Council's package. The Council President, Mr Juncker from Luxembourg, immediately attacked the outcome as illegal and thus actionable before the European Court of Justice, although the Greek, Irish and Italian Governments were broadly prepared to accept the result. Mr Christophersen, the Budget Commissioner, quickly pointed out that the dispute would create huge practical problems. The sums of money eventually at the centre of the dispute—only about 1 per cent higher than the Council was ready to concede—were not large, but they became symbols for the protagonists of statements of positions which they were not prepared to alter. In spite of the financial difficulties and legal challenge which were bound to follow, on 18 December M. Pflimlin, President of the European Parliament, signed the disputed budget as adopted.

Governments individually, the Council of Ministers collectively and the Commission had all then to determine how to respond. The Commission held the responsibility for implementing the budget and had to decide whether to do so or not. The Council had to choose whether to wage a united campaign against the Parliament and if so how. Individual governments had to establish whether or not to prosecute the Parliament and if so on what grounds, and also whether or not to make payments into a contested budget. In 1981 the French and German Governments had decided, in different circumstances, to withhold payments through national exchequers until the overall dispute was resolved.

Positions began to take shape quite rapidly. The British, Dutch, French, German and Luxembourg Governments openly favoured a case before the European Court of Justice against the European Parliament, a decision on which six Member States, i.e. a majority, had to agree to permit the action to be brought by the Council itself. The Greek, Irish and Italian Governments preferred not to move, while the Belgians and Danes asked for thinking time. The Belgians joined the legal retaliation group, to be followed by the Danes. On the back of this majority support the Council decided to prosecute the European Parliament before the Court for having agreed an illegal budget. The Commission decided to implement the budget as adopted by the Parliament, until a decision emerged on the legality of the budget as adopted. Thus, from January 1986, the Commission's services began to plan and authorise expenditures and, in some cases, for special reasons, in such a way that particular small budget lines were immediately allocated for much or most of the fiscal year.

Preparing the legal ground

The sequence and character of events in the ensuing months turned out to be more interesting for their political content than for revelations of fine points of Community law. Some significant legal issues needed to be and were eventually clarified, as Hendrik van Lier demonstrates, but these were narrow compared with the political and financial dimensions.[6] The case against the European Parliament was prosecuted both by the Council and by several Member States individually. Of the latter, the British Government was by far the most active in practice. On face value the explanation was obvious. British Ministers and officials had made it plain throughout the autumn of 1985 that the Council should not give way to pressure from MEPs, since more important issues of budgetary discipline were at stake.[7] They had not wavered from opposing Council concessions and had voted against the Council package in November as being too lenient. Domestic opinion in the UK was largely in tune with the Government's approach.

Yet the step from that position to playing the role of leading prosecutor was a large one. The British were still not entirely at home with the system of Community law, fearing that at the end of the day the cards might be stacked against them, not least because of the past inclinations of European judges to lean towards decisions which reinforced rather than eroded the impact of the Treaties and Community legislation. Though seven Member States had backed the proposal for a case against the Parliament, the legal arguments were not unambiguous. A plausible legal case could be made for the Parliament's contention that the Council had been legally delinquent in not honouring contractual obligations for some of the payments which the

[6] Hendrik van Lier, 'L'autorité budgétaire devant ses juges: l'affaire 34/86' *RMC* No. 301 (1986) 513–26.

[7] For background see House of Commons, Treasury and Civil Service Committee, *Budgetary Discipline in the European Community* Session 1985–86 (London, April 1986).

Parliament had reinstated. The willingness of the British Government to lead off was paradoxically an indication of a coming of age as a Community Member State. The Government put its trust in the due processes of Community law, in effect accepting the risk of an unpalatable outcome, while hoping to demonstrate that the law was there to offer protection against abuse. Another factor was British irritation at past difficulties with the Parliament over budget rebate. The Fontainebleau settlement of June 1984 made it easier and more attractive for the United Kingdom to embark on litigation, just as it removed from the French Government an inhibition against legal action.

Moreover, the British Government prepared its position with great attention not only to the legal details but also to its political profile. It chose not to withhold payments to the disputed 1986 budget, though in 1981 the French and German Governments had withheld payments until the 1981 dispute was resolved. British Ministers were willing to defend this position robustly to a puzzled House of Commons, where many members attacked what they thought to be an illogical position and showed scepticism about the likely political neutrality of the European Court.

One of the difficulties to be faced was the length of time normally needed for the ECJ to deliberate on a case. Again the British Government made a tactical move by asking the Court in February to block temporarily the contested extra payments until the case as a whole was heard and resolved and to refund the relevant revenue contributions already transferred by Member States. The British asked the Court to order the Commission not to make payments on the disputed parts of the budget. The objective was clear—not all of the budget was in dispute, only those payments which exceeded the budget as defined at the Council's second reading. The British Government thus signalled a clear willingness to separate the disputed issues, partly to show political sensitivity and partly to focus the legal arguments. No other government joined in pressing for interim measures: the Dutch were inhibited by the Presidency, the French by their national elections, the Danes by their referendum on the Single European Act, the Germans by their reflex to defer to the European Parliament.

On the main issues, the British Government, joined by the Dutch, French, German and Luxembourg Governments, made individual cases alongside the central case of the Council. No Member State actively supported the European Parliament. The first hearing was held on 10 March, at which the British sought interim measures and the Parliament retorted with its counter-arguments of the Council's dereliction of its legal duty. That hearing served to some extent as a dress rehearsal for the main hearing on 30 April where the Council and the French and German Governments also took part. The Commission studiously avoided taking legal sides, but explained that, in any case, expenditure was likely to be higher than even the upper level of Parliament-inspired appropriations. Agricultural spending was already rising above estimate. Surrounding empirical evidence aggravated the situation in practical terms. So, for instance, statements from the Court of Auditors reinforced the point by highlighting the persistent shortfall of revenue to meet expenditure targets—itself a source of legal debate, given that Treaty provisions also stipulate that the budget must balance. Meanwhile, unhelpfully, the value of the dollar was falling, thus simultaneously reducing Community revenue for levies and duties and increasing the potential expenditure on agricultural guarantee, especially for export restitutions.

Some attention is due to the positions of other key players in the Community game. The net payers in the Community by the time of the 1986 budget dispute were Britain, the Federal Republic of Germany and France. Furthermore, revenue rebates to the UK had to be met by other Member States digging deeper into their pockets. The German Government, or at least the Finance Minister, Herr Stoltenberg, purported to be as determined as the British to instil a sense of financial responsibility. The 1986 budget as adopted by the European Parliament implied a VAT rate of 1.26 per cent for most Member States (1.15 per cent average) as against the Council's implied rate of 1.22 per cent (1.11 per cent average). Commission estimates suggested by March 1986 that expenditure would require a still larger VAT precept and, by implication, that the guideline to control the growth of agricultural guarantee expenditure had failed to bite. Herr Stoltenberg went on record arguing that there was no question of exceeding the 1.4 per cent ceiling, a position echoed by the French Government albeit with less public show.

The legal pronouncements

On 17 March 1986, the President of the European Court of Justice made an interim ruling on the more technical British case for freezing the disputed appropriations.[8] He accepted without prejudice to the ultimate judgment that Britain had a prima facie case in its objections to the disputed appropriations, accepted for the purposes of interim measures the admissibility of the case against the Parliament, and granted to the UK the injunction it had sought. This required the Commission to restore to the UK, and by implication to other Member States, the revenue called in to finance the disputed appropriations. Thus, until the final judgment emerged, the Commission was to behave as if the 1986 budget was the Council version instead of the adopted Parliament version. The consequent confusion for budgetary management on the disputed appropriations should not be underestimated. The Commission services, three months into the fiscal year, had to reappraise the flow of allocations and thus their whole planning horizon. Prudence required them to work on the assumption that

[8] Case 23/86 R *United Kingdom* v *European Parliament* [1986] 3 CMLR 82; OJ 1986 C63.

the Parliament could lose the case. Therefore, they had immediately to trim their estimates of cash flow and, in cases where particular budget lines had been exhausted, to look for compensating savings elsewhere. While in global terms the sums involved were small, their impact on recipients was much larger.

On 2 June 1986, Signor Federico Mancini, one of the Advocates General of the ECJ, produced his Opinion on the main case.[9] He argued robustly both that the European Parliament had exceeded its legal powers and that the Council of Ministers had acted unlawfully in not meeting legally incurred commitments and deviously by attempting to preempt the Parliament's 'margin of manoeuvre'. The Advocate General also held that it was a question of the validity of the act adopting the 1986 budget, thus undermining the legality of the budget as a whole and not just the specifically disputed appropriations. But operations from the 1986 budget as it had been adopted had given rise to legal effects, which would have to be recognised. On 3 July 1986, the Court in essence followed the Advocate General's Opinion but was more cautious and more narrow in focus.[10] The ECJ declared the whole budget unconstitutional in so far as President Pflimlin's signature to adopt the budget was invalid, thus discarding the option of endorsing the budget as set out in the Council's second reading. It refused to be drawn into the political battle between Council and Parliament, and criticised both for failing to resolve their differences by political agreement. To alleviate the problems of the budget managers and in recognition of their legal effects, the Court declared that spending on obligations already under the now illegal 1986 budget should be regarded as valid. The institutions were required to pick up the budget at the stage where they had left off, that is, after the Parliament's second reading. We should also note how quickly the ECJ process was completed, much more rapidly than had generally been thought possible.

What, then, was the Court doing in reaching these conclusions? The pronouncements held that legally both Council and Parliament had been remiss, but that it was not the Court's task to settle the political (as distinct from constitutional) arguments. The Court endorsed the Treaty provisions on the 'maximum rate' and the 'margin of manoeuvre'. In essence, therefore, the Court accepted that there was an effective legal ceiling on the Parliament's room for manoeuvre and an upward revision needed both Council and Parliament to agree. But the responsibility could not and should not be shifted to the Court where the point at issue was political. The judges thus sat pat upon the Treaties and would not entertain any redefinition of the rules. They all but accused the Parliament and the Council of wasting the Court's time as a result of a political failure of negotiation. The Court chose not to make a categorical statement on the issue of how firm a contractual obligation the budgetary authorities had on the accumulated

[9] Case 34/86 *Council* v *European Parliament* [1986] 3 CMLR 94, 103.

[10] Case 34/86 OJ 1986 C200, [1986] 3 CMLR 94, 142.

'cost of the past', nor to venture into the thorny and disputed issue of the precise classification of obligatory and non-obligatory expenditure.

A new budget for 1986

The European Community thus found itself halfway through the fiscal year without a lawful budget and about to embark on the budget procedure for 1987. This produced a remarkable concentration of minds. The British Government carefully avoided appearing triumphant so as not to antagonise the Parliament, stating simply that the Court had confirmed and clarified the Treaty. Within a week, the Commission presented a revised 1986 budget which had to take into account the evolution of the financial parameters since the previous autumn, in particular a sharp rise in projected farm spending and the anticipated shortfall in revenue. The Commission had already taken the precaution in May of introducing a supplementary draft budget. The consolidated proposal was for a total budget of 35.1 billion ECU as against the Council's initial preference for 32.7 billion and the Parliament's invalid budget of 33.3 billion, an ironic outcome in view of the arguments of substance made in the closing weeks of 1985.

Finance Ministers, in seeking to clarify the frame of reference for the detailed work by budget Ministers, accepted the impact of the falling value of the dollar while labelling it as an 'abnormally large depreciation' and therefore a 'special circumstance'. This was an attempt to deal with the specific problem without conceding the importance of budgetary discipline and the agricultural guideline. By mid-1986 they also had to acknowledge the need to build in obligations to Portugal and Spain and some provision for the 'cost of the past'. After some inevitable shadow-boxing the Council and Parliament agreed the Commission's draft with only marginal changes on 10 July. The outcome pledged Community revenue in effect up to the new maximum VAT ceiling of 1.4 per cent.

The 1987 budget

Immediately the Community institutions then turned their attention to consideration of the 1987 budget, with the first Budget Council meeting on 21 July. As they faced this new task, it was evident that yet again they would have to contend with more claims than could be satisfied within the revenue ceiling. Agricultural expenditure could not be quickly reduced with a still falling dollar. Spain and Portugal were now full participants in the process, a fact which rendered impossible the deferring of some of the awkward questions arising over appropriations from the structural funds. Meanwhile, the Community had undertaken in the context of the Single European Act (though not yet fully ratified) to establish a new multi-annual spending programme on research and development by the end of 1986. And all of this had to be settled with the British Government occupying the presidential chair and thus charged with the responsibility for orchestrating an agreement.

As the Budget Council embarked on its early negotiations in July and September 1986, the extent of their difficulties began to be revealed. They now had to work as a fully fledged Community of Twelve, a fact which was radically to alter the bargaining patterns in the Council. The continuing weakness of the dollar made modest forecasts of expenditure and generous forecasts of revenue implausible. It is a profound irony that what may be good for the international economy and Community inflation levels can be very detrimental to the Community budget. Whatever the formal statements it became increasingly unrealistic to envisage the 1987 fiscal year ending without the revenue ceiling being hit. Although proposals abounded for reform of the CAP, none was likely to bite hard enough to reduce the pressures on spending on agricultural guarantee in time to help the 1987 budget. Awareness of these problems was crystallising the issues and focusing minds, but it was still a big jump from there to their political resolution, in spite of the great skill of Peter Brooke, the British Treasury Minister presiding over the Budget Council. And at the same time, Ministers were supposed to be agreeing new expenditure programmes, especially on technological research and development.

In the first round of negotiations, two linked problems predominated. Without question the crucial one was the emerging 'North–South' split. A survey of European press commentaries at the time shows a striking consensus of views on this new phenomenon and its far-reaching implication.[11] The simple fact of life in the Budget Council since Iberian enlargement is that it has become much easier to establish blocking minorities which stall changes from the status quo.[12] However powerful the opposing camp (comprising Denmark, France, Germany, the Netherlands and Britain, sometimes supported by Belgium and Luxembourg), they cannot win the vote on any budget line, unless they can cajole others to join their side. An effective majority also requires an alignment of policy, difficult in practice in the core area of expenditure on agricultural guarantee. The second, closely related, issue concerned the distribution of expenditure between agricultural and non-agricultural heads. The Dutch, French and German Governments were keen to include in the 1987 budget a serious contingency reserve for possible or probable increases in CAP expenditure, a point agreed by the Council to the tune of 665 million ECUs. The

[11] See for example 'Désaccord entre les Douze', *Le Monde* 24 July 1986, 'Europäisches Trauerspiel', *Frankfurter Allgemeine Zeitung* 1 August 1986 (which coins the expression 'die neuen Neinsager') and 'Tomato ketchup in the budget works', *Financial Times* 4 August 1986.

[12] Since 1 January 1986 weighted votes are: Germany, France, Italy and UK—10 each; Spain—8; Belgium, Greece, Netherlands and Portugal—5 each; Denmark and Ireland—3 each; and Luxembourg—2; a total of 76, out of which 54 constitute a qualified majority and 23 a blocking minority (Art 148 EEC).

Mediterranean Governments fought hard to prevent the erosion of expenditure on the structural funds. And both groups could reasonably anticipate that, on past performance, the European Parliament was likely to resist swinging cuts to non-agricultural expenditure, now in alliance with the blocking minority of Southern Member States.

By early September 1986, the nature of the argument had changed. The Commission presented its revised estimates of revenue, showing a shortfall of 776 million ECUs for 1986 and implying a stagnant or declining revenue base for 1987. This should not have been a surprise, but it was now unambiguous. The 'austerity' group of Member States increased their resolve to propose modest (around 4 per cent) increases for non-obligatory expenditure (i.e. structural funds and R and D), in the expectation that the Parliament would use its margin of manoeuvre to the full (but this time not more) and thus stay within the 8.1 per cent maximum rate. The Mediterranean Governments preferred a higher Council provision, no doubt also expecting the European Parliament to match their bid. In bargaining terms, a key issue was therefore the solidity of the two groups, with various efforts being made by the 'austerity' groups to split the spenders. On 9 September this had apparently been achieved, with Greece and Spain joining the austerity camp, leaving Ireland and Portugal opposing and Italy abstaining. The British Presidency facilitated this compromise by agreeing that part of its abatement claim, due at the latest from the 1988 budget, would not be claimed earlier.

In the following weeks, the gloomy prognoses continued about the revenue yield and likely claims on agricultural guarantee. Anxieties increased that a protracted financial crisis would not only be damaging in itself, but infect many other areas of Community debate. Interestingly the mood in the European Parliament was showing signs of changing towards far more vigorous strictures at the continued excesses of the CAP. On 16 October the Budget Committee of the European Parliament revealed its approach, based on the Report drawn up by David Curry, a European Democrat from the UK. They recommended respect, albeit sorrowful, for keeping the 1987 budget within the 1.4 per cent VAT limit. They also signalled a recommendation for restoring appropriations for research and development in industry and for overseas development and noted that the Community's structural funds should not be victim to reductions. At the plenary sessions of the Parliament in October and November some MEPs in addition expressed scepticism as to the realism of expenditure projections on CAP guarantee and the accuracy of assertions from the Commission and the Council that the 'cost of the past' was virtually resolved. Parliamentarians also showed some dissatisfaction at the implementation of the 1986 budget, suggesting that credits inserted by the Parliament were not being properly or sufficiently mobilised. Meanwhile the Commission was reflecting on the proposals it would have to make on the longer-term financing of the Community budget beyond the 1.4 per cent ceiling and the review of the structural funds. Mindful of the ECJ judgment, the President of the Parliament refused in December to sign a still disputed budget.

The outlook for the future

The outcome of the European Court of Justice case on the 1986 budget served as a sharp reminder to all those involved in the budgetary procedure of the Community that they had to work within the Treaty rules and to fulfil their political responsibilities. In the light of previous disagreements over parts of the budget, a delay for the second year running in achieving a fully agreed and authorised budget made the financial managers acutely conscious of the practical consequences of disputed budgets. But the Court's judgment did not in essence redefine the legal parameters or alter interpretations of the budget procedure. Its value was to remind people that litigation was possible and could succeed within a practicable timetable.

The Treaty rules as amended in 1970 and 1975 hold, but lacunae remain. We are no wiser as to the precise contractual status of commitment appropriations for unspecified future dates. Article 203.9 of the EEC Treaty refers to the possibility of revising the maximum rate for budgetary growth, and the Court has insisted that both Council and Parliament must concur. But the Council and Parliament continue to use different definitions of the precise basis of classification of obligatory and non-obligatory expenditure, from which the Parliament's margin of manoeuvre should be calculated. The Court held back from commenting on the Parliament's contention that the Council could not propose a budget which could not realistically cover likely expenditure. This problem may well recur, given the limits on VAT revenue and the volatility of receipts from levies and duties. Nor did the Court express a view about the creative accounting techniques which have been used now for several years in succession. The short answer to the puzzled observer is that legal rules do not, in the end, suffice to permit resolution of these issues. The European Parliament may have benefited from the legal void, which had previously existed, but it can now insist on the need to negotiate. As the European judges made clear, here we enter the world of political and financial responsibilities. Clarification of and respect for the legal parameters is very important, but no substitute for political agreement.

Such an admission should not astonish anyone—it is par for the course in a budgetary process where powers are divided and the authority at the centre weak. The key issues which remain are: the composition of the policy repertoire which gives rise to Community expenditure; efforts at imposing budgetary discipline; the complications of financial management; the assigning of political responsibilities; and the bargaining process. These issues are familiar to budget-makers in many other contexts.

The policies of the Community have been distorted by the accident of history which led to the establishment of the CAP in a particular form. Without the pressures of CAP guarantee the own resources system would not have been agreed in 1970 with the core principle of 'financial solidarity' or common financing. Consequently, the whole budgetary system—both revenue (the levies and duties elements) and expenditure—is especially vulnerable to exchange-rate fluctuations and guarantee expenditure, especially for export restitutions, on the currently prevailing rules cannot be cash-limited. Such phenomena arise in national budgets, as British governments have discovered to their discomfort with, for example, social security expenditure.

Three particular problems follow. First, the chicken-and-egg problem of which comes first, CAP reform or budgetary order, is a conundrum which has so far eluded resolution. Secondly, in the absence of a vision on the road to Brussels, can budgetary gadgets be devised which insulate the Community budget as a whole from the financial fluctuations endemic in the current form of the CAP? Or, more concretely, is it inevitable that hand-to-mouth budgetary arrangements will emerge incrementally to deal with the difficulties? In this context, prognoses and propositions abound. The tenor of most is that some parts of the CAP currently funded from the European Agricultural Guidance and Guarantee Fund are likely to be, for some should be, funded not collectively but directly by member governments. The difficulty is that the economically sensible and the politically expedient do not easily coincide. And, in any case, to relieve the Community budget burden is to add to national budget burdens for some, if not all, Member States. In this regard it is probably something of an illusion to imagine that the displacing of the burden will engender heady generosity for supporting the growth of the Community budget for other policy purposes.

This leads to the third policy problem, namely claims for expanding expenditure on other sectors. Here arise issues of principle and of priority, both as to the general desirability of increasing the budgetary impact of the Community and as regards the appropriate spending priorities. On these complex questions suffice it to note that the debates of the last twelve months show little sign of an emerging consensus either among governments or among the Community institutions. The two strongest candidates for further expenditure—industrial R and D and the structural funds—have both supporters and critics, and in neither case is it easy to demonstrate 'value for money' from modest and constrained investments by the Community.

Budgetary discipline has become Community shorthand for a bundle of related issues. One dimension is the continuing climate of slow economic growth and financial austerity in general, fostered by the doctrinal preference of several Member States for reducing the role of the public purse. An underlying issue for some is the need to establish definitively that the Community budget should be revenue- not expenditure-based. The last three years have seen a distinct shift in all Community institutions towards greater revenue consciousness. But this has not yet produced a universal reflex to give primacy to considerations of revenue. In the case of the European Parliament, debate is distorted by the absence of revenue responsibility to counter-balance its powers to alter, and usually increase, appropriations. The other interpretation of the prevailing concern with budgetary discipline narrows down to an approach aimed at limiting or reducing agricultural expenditure. It did not work in 1986 for what the Council called 'abnormal' reasons to do with the speed and rate of dollar depreciation. The agricultural guideline proved indicative but not enforceable. Further thought is being given inside and outside the Community institutions to the devising of more effective solutions.

The consequences of budget disputes for financial management are huge. For three successive years now the planning basis of the Commission has been seriously disturbed by extraneous events. These compound some of the inherent difficulties within the Commission's own approach to financial management. The results, to express them in very practical terms, include a tremendous amount of staff time spent on working and reworking figures. They produce unintended results in terms of which credits are used in what way, leaving the Commission vulnerable to criticisms of different kinds from governments, the recipients of Community money, the European Parliament and the Court of Auditors. This could well build up problems over the post facto authorisation of the accounts and the discharge process of the European Parliament. It also opens up a further can of worms, not discussed in this paper, about methods of altering the budget projections during the fiscal year by way of rectifying letters and supplementary budgets, which require endorsement by the Council and the Parliament.

The European Court of Justice in its judgment pointedly reminded the Community institutions of their political responsibilities. At one level this is an apparently straightforward question, at least in theory, of the responsibilities which flow from the Treaty rules on the budget. The problem, however, is that the budget does not exist in a vacuum, but encapsulates a far wider range of political interests and preferences. The Parliament, mindful of the ECJ case, may be more judicious in the future as regards compliance with the Treaty rules, as its stance on the 1987 budget suggests. But it is not likely to cease to harass the Council or to abandon its self-appointed role of Community conscience, though differences of view within the Parliament should not be underestimated. Inter-institutional tensions are endemic and fuelled by the separation of revenue raising from expenditure powers. There is a fair amount of evidence from working cases of fiscal federalism that this situation is inherently unstable. But the short-term scenarios do not realistically include access by the European Parliament to revenue powers or its abnegation of expenditure powers. The Council of Ministers will have to live with the consequences of the preference of Member States for freezing the distribution of powers in this way.

The Council itself lacks the coherence readily to exercise its own political responsibilities systematically and consistently. Its schizophrenic personality as part collective organ and part a conglomeration of Member States is an impediment. It is rather like asking a consortium of local authorities to govern collectively the United Kingdom. The division between Councils responsible for different areas of policy and for the budget does not make for effective concerted action. Over the last couple of years efforts have been made to establish new ground rules, especially for the agriculture/budget nexus, but they have borne sparse fruit. There is a long way still to go in terms of both Community and national decision-making to achieve coherence of policy priorities and expendiure instruments within the revenue capacity of the Community.

The Commission, too, has contrary inclinations in pursuing its budgetary responsibilities. As financial manager, it bears the responsibility for the consequences of imperfections in the current budgetary arrangements and the lack of agreed and deliverable budgetary guidelines. It has also to improve its own procedures for financial management. Yet, it also falls to the Commission to draft new proposals for improvements across the range of new 'own resources', current expenditure policies and new spending programmes. In December 1986, the Commission had to formulate proposals on some of these, while continuing to worry over ways of dealing with CAP expenditure. It is an unenviable task, given the obstacles to agreement in the Council and between the Council and Parliament.

At several points in this article, stress has been put on the characteristics of the bargaining process through which Community budgets are made and sometimes unmade. Enthusiasts for the strengthening of Community powers have mostly attached great weight to the value of majority voting in the Council as a means of cutting through disagreements. Observation of the budgetary process suggests that majority voting on the current rules and numbers is not an undisguised benefit. Blocking minorities are fairly easy to assemble in both theory and practice, especially since Iberian enlargement. A further complication arises from the scope for linking blocking minorities in the Council to majorities in the European Parliament. The fragmentation of the debate by budget head in the Council in some ways promotes blocking minorities on specific spending programmes. The bargaining mode more readily facilitates the freezing of the status quo than change, in the sense of encouraging inherited patterns of behaviour and inhibiting reorientation away from entrenched interests.

There is a growing literature in political science and economics on the interaction of decision rules and policy outcomes.[13] Though specific analyses differ, most emphasise the difficulties of accommodating

[13] See as examples of a much richer literature R. O. Keohane, 'Reciprocity in International Relations' 40 *International Organisation* No. 1, 1–27 (1986), C. F. Runge and H. von Witzke, *Institutional Change in the Common Agricultural Policy of the European Community* (Vauk Verlag, Kiel 1986) and F. W. Scharpf, *The Joint Decision-Trap: Lessons from German Federalism and European Integration* (International Institute for Management, Berlin 1986).

economic rationality and political feasibility. Sub-optimal ('satisficing') outcomes are more likely. Most analysts also stress the crucial importance of a bargaining system in which a variety of issues can be aggregated to permit reciprocal understandings. If these analyses are correct, then propositions for reform which seek to segment or fragment the individual elements of the budgetary nexus may either not work or compound the problems.[14] A real challenge confronts the Community in its search for a budget-making process which will resolve the substantive problems through effective decision rules. Events over the last year may have clarified some of the parameters and improved the diagnostic skills of the participants. But there is still no candidate for a prize for budgetary invention.

[14] See the proposal for 'segmentation' of agricultural expenditure in L. Spaventa et al, *The Future of Community Finance* CEPS Papers No. 30 (Centre for European Policy Studies, Brussels 1986).

[19]

Renaud Dehousse*

1992 AND BEYOND: THE INSTITUTIONAL DIMENSION OF THE INTERNAL MARKET PROGRAMME

'Non é cosa più difficile trattare, né più dubia a riuscire, ne più pericolosa a maneggiare, che farsi capo ad introdurre nuovi ordini. Perché lo introduttore ha per nimici tutti quelli che delli ordini vecchi fanno bene, e ha tiepidi defensori tutti quelli che delli ordini nuovi farebbeno bene.'

Machiavelli, *Il Principe*

I. THE OBJECTIVE

When the Delors Commission decided to make the internal market the first priority of its term, this choice met with some surprise in Community circles. The aim itself, as endorsed by the Brussels European Council in 1985 – 'to achieve a single market by 1992' – appeared extremely modest, especially when compared with the grand designs for relaunching European integration which were still under discussion. At a time when people were debating major issues like the reform of Community decision-making processes, the establishment of European Union, or the necessity to safeguard Europe's position *vis-à-vis* Japan and the United States, such an objective did not seem likely to arouse a renewed interest for integration matters amongst Community citizens. It could even be argued that the abolition of internal frontiers fell short of the goal set by the EEC Treaty almost three decades earlier: the creation of a common market in all factors of production.[1]

* Dr. Renaud Dehousse is Research Fellow and Executive Coordinator of the European Policy Unit, European University Institute, Florence, Italy.

1. See for instance the reflexions on the meaning of 'internal market', as opposed to that of a 'common market' referred to in the EEC Treaty, in Pescatore, 'Observations critiques sur

This apparent lack of ambition was sometimes perceived as a sign of weakness: if after thirty years of Community activities it proved still necessary to concentrate on that kind of problem, how could one reasonably believe that it would be possible to do away with national barriers to free movement by the end of 1992, unless the efficiency of Community institutions were reinforced? And, the promotors of the Parliament's Draft Treaty on the European Union added, this could not conceivably be done without at the same time improving the democratic character of Community decision making. Institutional reform was therefore regarded by many as a prerequisite for any new Community initiative.

Yet was there any choice? The work of the Dooge committee had confirmed that several Member States were not prepared to follow the Parliament's ambitions proposals. On none of the fields mentioned as possible new areas to be opened up to European integration – monetary policy, defence, or even culture – was there a consensus to give the Community a new role. At the same time, the situation on the internal market front was far from satisfactory. True, quotas and customs duties had been abolished; but practice had amply demonstrated that the existence different fiscal and regulatory regimes at national level seriously hampered intra-Community trade. Furthermore, under the impact of the economic recession of the 70s, the protectionist armoury had grown considerably. National provisions regulating the production and marking of goods could be used – and were actually used – in order to prevent access to national markets by goods originating from other Member States.[2] The Court of Justice had greatly contributed to the fight against this kind of practice, *inter alia* by giving a broad definition to the concept of 'measures having equivalent effect' to quantitative restrictions[3] referred to in Article 30 of the EEC Treaty, but repressive action was clearly not sufficient to eliminate non-tariff barriers. The only possibility envisaged by the Treaty in this respect was the harmonisation of national provisions. However, the unanimous consent of the Member States required by Article 100 did not facilitate the adoption of Community provisions: even where no major political difficulty was at stake, or if the issue at hand involved no major economic interest, national administrations could endlessly insist that their standard should be adopted at the European level. Finally, it had become apparent that the adoption of Community provisions was not the end of the story, but rather the beginning of a new chapter. For the amount of complaints received by the Commission

l'Acte unique européen', in: *L'Acte unique européen*, Brussels, Institut d'études européennes, 1986, at pp. 40–46, and VerLoren van Themaat, 'The contributions to the Establishment of the Internal Market by the Case-Law of the Court of Justice of the European Communities', in: Bieber, Dehousse, Pinder and Weiler (eds.), *1992: One European Market?*, Baden-Baden, Nomos, 1988, at pp. 110–111.

2. For an overview off all these protectionist practices, see A. Mattera, 'Les nouvelles formes du protectionisme économique et les articles 30 et suivants du traité C.E.E.', *RMC* (1983), pp. 252–272.
3. In particular in cases 8/74, *Dassonville*, (1974) E.C.R. 837, and 120/78, *Rewe-Zentrale* v. *Bundesmonopolverwaltung für Branntwein* (the famous 'Cassis de Dijon' case), (1979) E.C.R. 649.

reveal, and many studies confirm, that the problems are as manifold and as complex at the implementation stage as at the decision-making level: countless directives are not transposed into national law or simply not applied by national administrations.[4]

Seen against this background, the Commission's decision to focus on completion of the internal market is rather striking for its ambition. At the same time, given most Member State's confirmed dislike for 'grand designs', it was probably one of the few fields in which a consensus for more intensive Community actions was likely to emerge, as the Single European Act negotiations later confirmed. There was, however, a price to be paid for this pragmatism: how could the objective be attained without vesting in Community institutions competences the Member States were not prepared to relinquish, and without altering the decision making process based on consensus which characterises the Community? In theory, the answer would be: if you cannot change the rules of the game, adapt your tactics to those rules. Thus, the way to follow was to tailor the programme in such a way that Community intervention would be restricted to a minimum, which would by the same token considerably restrict resort to consensus. At the same time, it was clear that even the feasability of such a minimalist programme would be considerably reduced if the decision-making process was not somewhat simplified. No matter what their reluctance towards institutional reform might be, it was therefore necessary to secure from Member States the means that were indispensable in order to carry out the mandate received from the Brussels European Council.

II. THE STRATEGY: A NEW DIVISION OF TASKS BETWEEN THE COMMUNITY AND ITS MEMBER STATES

It is of course much more complex to implement this kind of general guidelines than to define them. For two decades, Community institutions had acted on the assumption that harmonisation was the only possible way to tackle the problems arising due to the existence of different regulatory systems in each Member State. Experience has demonstrated that this was no easy way. National administrations did not necessarily object to the principle of harmonisation, but they very often insisted that their own regulatory approach be adopted on a Community-wide basis. Even when agreement could be reached on harmonisation directives, their adaptation to technical progress remained a very cumbersome process.[5] Moreover, harmonisation

4. The Commission's Annual Report to the European Parliament on the Application of Community Law gives a good idea of the importance of this problem. See the fourth report, covering the year 1986, COM (87) 250 final, or OJ C 338 of 12 Dec. 1987.

5. This kind of problem is by no means limited to the Community; it is rather a common characteristic of all decision-making systems in which a plurality of actors are involved. See G. Calabresi, *Incentives, Regulations and the Problem of Legal Obsolescence*, in: M. Cappelletti (ed.), *New Perspectives for a Common Law of Europe*, Florence, 1978, pp. 291–307.

attempts necessarily imply a search for uniformity and an interference in the regulatory capacity of Member States. Some of them reacted fiercely against what they perceived as attempts at promoting 'Euro-products', and invited th Community to limit its activities to matters that directly affect economic processes.[6]

By the extension it gave to the scope of Article 30 in *Cassis de Dijon* and in subsequent rulings, the Court of Justice has opened new perspectives for Community institutions. As is known, the Court has assigned clear limits to Member States' capacity to regulate the production and marketing of goods by stating that they may not in principle prohibit the sale in their territory of goods lawfully produced and marketed in another Member State, even if the technical requirements that this product meets differ from those imposed on national goods. National regulations can take precedence over the fundamental principle of free movement only if, and to the extent that, they are necessary to satisfy 'mandatory requirements' such as those referred to in *Cass de Dijon*: effectiveness of fiscal supervision, protection of public health, fairness of commercial transactions and protection of the consumer.[7]

This new line of thought was to prove of considerable importance, for it stressed that in many years, the removal of barriers to free movement could be achieved even in the absence of harmonisation provisions. The Commission was very prompt to draw the political consequences of this case-law. In 1980 it outlined what would become the keystone of its new strategy: the concept of mutual recognition of national legislations.[8] This new approach rests on the same premise as *Cassis de Dijon* and the ensuing case-law, namely the fact that the objectives sanctioned in national regulations are basically equivalent.[9] The *White Paper* makes this very clear:

> 'Indeed, the objectives of national legislation, such as the protection of human health and life or the environment, are more often than not identical. It follows that the rules and controls developed to achieve these objectives, although they may take different forms, come down to

6. For an overview of the reactions met by the earlier approach to harmonisation, see G. Close, 'Harmonisation of Laws: Use or Abuse of the Powers under the E.E.C. Treaty', 3 E.L.Rev. (1978), pp. 461–468; D. Welch, 'From "Euro-Beer" to "Newcastle Brown"'. A Review of Community Action to Dismantle 'Divergent' Food Laws, XXII *Journal of Common Market Studies* (1983), pp. 47–70. See also the Report of the House of Lords Select Committee on the European Communities, *Internal Market – The Movement of Manufactured Goods within the EEC*, Session 1981–82, London, HMSO 1982.
7. The literature on this question is considerable. See for instance A. Dashwood, 'The Cassis de Dijon Line of Authority', in: *In Memoriam J.D.B. Mitchell*, London, Sweet and Maxwell, 1983, pp. 145–161; L. Gormley, *Prohibiting Restrictions to Trade within the EEC*, Amsterdam/New York/Oxford, North Holland, 1985; P. Oliver, 'Measures of Equivalent Effect: A Reappraisal', 19 *C.M.L.Rev.* (1982), pp. 217–224; C. Timmermans, 'The Free Movement of Goods', in: *Thirty Years of Community Law*, Luxembourg, 1983, pp. 237–285; P. VerLoren Van Themaat, *supra* note 1.
8. *Removal of Technical Barriers to Trade*, COM (80) 30 final of 24 Jan. 1980.
9. This idea was later made explicit by the Council in its conclusions on standardisation of 16 July 1984, published as an annex to the Council resolution of 7 May 1985. See OJ C 136 of 4 June 1985, p. 2.

the same thing, and so should normally be accorded recognition in all Member States.'[10]

The White Paper therefore proposed to distinguish between the areas where mutual recognition of national regulations could be sufficient, and those where harmonisation was essential. Conceived for the free movement of goods, where it stems from the interpretation given by the Court of Justice to Articles 30 to 36, this new approach was later extended to other fields. It now forms the basis of the Commission's strategy in fields like financial services,[11] University degrees[12] and vocational training. One can even note its influence in the Commission's proposals on indirect taxation: abandoning the idea of complete harmonisation, it now suggests a mere 'approximation' of tax rates. In the case of VAT, for instance, approximation would be limited to the fixing of two bands within which Member States would be free to choose, and to change, their own rate. Cross-border operations would not be affected by the existence of varying rates, for each operator would be allowed to deduct the tax paid by his supplier (which will of course require the establishment of a clearing house between Member States).[13]

I have argued elsewhere[14] that, although it was rather dictated by practical considerations and a concern for efficiency, this approach corresponds to the principle of subsidiarity which governs the sharing of competences in many federal systems: the higher level of government should only intervene when it can do something that lower levels cannot. As far as principles are concerned, the reasons to follow this line are probably even stronger as regards the Community than as regards most federal systems, given the great diversity – be it in terms of culture or in terms of economic development – which exists among its twelve Member States. Clearly, in the current situation, it is also the most adequate way to pursue the aims which are to be reached at Community level, since the Community system is essentially, and is likely to remain in the predictable future, based on consensus. The single market was no exception to the rule: reasons of principle and efficiency requirements both lead to the conclusion that Community action ought to be restricted to the measures which are necessary to reach the objective of market integration enshrined in the Treaty.

The pragmatic line adopted by the Commission probably accounts for a

10. *Completing the Internal Market*, White Paper from the Commission to the European Council, COM (85) 310 final of 14 June 1985, point 58.

11. Proposal for a second banking coordination directive, COM (715) final of 16 Feb. 1988.

12. See the proposed directive on mutual recognition of diplomas in higher education, COM (85) 355 final of 9 July 1985.

13. *Approxmation of Tax Rates and Harmonization of Indirect Tax Structure*, COM (87) 320 of 26 Aug. 1987. Some, however, argue that the removal of fiscal frontiers could be reached by adopting a system that permits the operation of VAG and excise duties without frontier documents. Approximation of rates would be needed only to control cross-border shopping, which could be done by setting a floor to the tax rates. See C. Lee, M. Pearson and S. Smith, 'Fiscal Harmonisation: An Analysis of the European Commission's Proposals', *IFS Report Series* 28, 1988.

14. 'Completing the Internal Market: Institutional Constraints and Challenges', in: Bieber, Dehousse, Pinder and Weiler, *1992: One European Market*, *supra* n. 1 at pp. 311–336.

large part of the positive response of most national capitals, and indeed of large segments of public opinion, to the ideas put forward in the White Paper. On the governments' side, this favourable reaction stemmed at least in part from the fact that, ambitious as it was, the White Paper did not involve any transfer of new competences to the Community, nor any significant increase in its spending. Pragmatism also made the presentation of the programme easier: wisely avoiding any discussion of objectives and priorities, the White Paper was able to focus on the operational part of the problem, *i.e.* the 300 or so measures needed to achieve the complete removal of internal borders and the timetable envisaged for the adoption. All this would not have been possible had it been necessary to define *a priori* the adequate level of regulation in fields like product safety or the protection of health. Furthermore, the 'competition between rules' implied by the new strategy offered a possibility to preserve national or regional diversities. No doubt, too, the reaction to the entire programme would have been less favourable if complete harmonisation of, say, educational or fiscal policies had been requested.

However, it must be stressed here that this division of labour between the Community and its Member States by no means implies that the latter still enjoy full discretion in fields which are not regulated at Community level.[15] On the contrary: though Member States retain their competence as regards societal values like health and safety or the environment,[16] their regulatory policies must take into account the general Community framework in which they take place. Besides, several types of Community intervention are necessary in order to make mutual recognition possible. A measure of harmonisation – variable according to each other – will be necessary to ensure a basic equivalence of national regulations. As regards the free movement of goods, for instance, it will be necessary to reach a common definition of the basic interests which can be regarded as 'justified' under Article 36 or as 'mandatory requirements' such as those referred to in *Cassis de Dijon*. The Court will of course scrutinise national regulatory policies, which remain subject to the interdiction contained in Article 30. But, since national regulatory regimes are to remain in force in a large number of fields, and given several Member States' poor record as regards the implementation of Community law, a middleway between harmonisation and repressive action is necessary if one wants to make sure that recognition of other Member States' rules is integrated into national law.

Council directive 83/189/EEC[17] – the so-called 'mutual information'

15. The Court of Justice has made this very clear as regards free movements of good: 'Article 36 is not designed to reserve certain matters to the exclusive jurisdiction of the Member States but permits national laws to derogate from the principle of free movements of goods to the extent to which such derogation is and continues to be justified for the attainment of the objectives referred to in that Article.' Case 35/76, *Simmenthal*, (1976) E.C.R. 1871, at p. 1886.

16. It is interesting to note in this respect that Art. 136R, para. 4 of the EEC Treaty now gives legal value to the subsidiary principle, by stating that Community intervention must be restricted to the fields where the Community can achieve more efficient results than the Member States taken separately.

17. OJ L 109 of 26 April 1983.

directive – provides an interesting intermediate stage. It imposes on Member States an obligation to notify to the Commission drafts of new technical regulations they intend to adopt.[18] The draft is then communicated by the Commission to the other Member States, which are given a chance to react if they deem that it contains elements likely to create new barriers to trade. This examination phase may last from three months to one year, depending on the reactions brought about by the draft, which may not be implemented during that period. If either the Commission or the Member States think that the proposed regulation will create new barriers to trade, they may request the introduction of amendments aiming at rendering it compatible with Article 30 and the principle of mutual recognition.[19] The Commission may also indicate that it envisages submitting a proposal to the Council on the problem at hand,[20] it will normally do so when the barriers created by the proposed regulation could appear as justified on the basis of Article 36 or by the Court's case-law.

The interest of this new procedure is twofold. First, the Commission and all Member States are offered an opportunity to be informed of new developments in national regulatory policies. The 'horizontal' dimension of this transparency process is essential, for Member States are more likely to give legal value to the principle of mutual recognition if they are aware of the legal requirements and of the procedures existing in other Member States. Second, Directive 83/189 also makes it possible to prevent the adoption of national provisions which would not be compatible with Community law. On more than one occasion, the Commission has been in a position to insist that the proposed legislation should allow market access to goods meeting the requirements of technical specifications in force in other Member States or that they should follow the proportionality principle brought out by the Court of Justice.[21] It can therefore exert a real guidance role, making sure that the regulatory policies pursued by the Member States take due account of their Community obligations. In this way, Community intervention through harmonisation can be restricted to areas where it is indispensable, without at the same time compromising the attainment of the objectives set out in the White Paper.

In more general terms, I would suggest that the development of this kind of 'cooperative federalism' device is necessary in order to reconcile the substantive objectives pursued at Community level (in this case, completion of the internal market) with institutional requirements such as the subsidiary

18. Initially, this system existed only for industrial products. The notification obligation has since been extended to high technology drugs by Dir. 87/22/EEC of 22 Dec. 1986 (OJ L 15/38 of 17 Jan. 1988), then to all agricultural products by Council dir. of 22 March 1988 amending directive 83/189/EEC (OJ L 81 of 26 March 1988).

19. Art. 9 para. 1.

20. Art. 9 para. 2. Since its modification in March 1988, Dir. 83/189 also imposes a standstill obligation of twelve months if a proposal is already being discussed in the Council.

21. For an overview of the functioning of the entire system and examples of the changes introduced in the drafts at the Commission's request, see S. Lecrenier, 'Vers l'achèvement du marché intérieur: l'évolution des procédures de contrôle prévues par la directive 83/189/CEE depuis quatre ans', *RMC* (1988), pp. 121–139.

principle. It may be worth pointing out in this connection that even federal states more and more often feel similar need for coordinated action by the component units and the federal government, each in its own sphere of competence, to reach certain ends without at the same time compromising the units' autonomy. Indeed, this development is seen by many leading experts as one of the most characteristic features of modern federalism.[22]

III. PROGRESS OR DELUSION? THE SINGLE EUROPEAN ACT AND THE INTERNAL MARKET

Needed as it may have been, the pragmatic line followed in the White Paper would probably not have been sufficient to reach a complete elimination of internal borders. Post experience clearly indicated that in a Community of twelve Member States with important differences in economic development, and interests which diverge sometimes to a considerable extent, decision-making was bound to be a difficult exercise – much more so when a consensus is needed. It was therefore necessary to modify the rules of the game to the extent necessary for the implementation of the White Paper programme. Most proposals put forward by the Commission at the time the intergovernmental conference was drafting the Single Act aimed at this simplification.[23]

A. VOTING PROCEDURES

The most ambitious proposal doubtless regarded voting procedures: the Commission suggested no less than a shift to majority voting for all measures necessary for the completion of the internal market.[24] It was followed only in part: voting by qualified majority was accepted on an *ad hoc* basis only.[25] The most important change is probably contained in the new Article 100A, which introduces majority voting for the approximation of national provisions. The wording of this latter provision is fairly broad, since it covers all

22. See for instance Morton Grodzins, *The American Federal System: A New View of Government in the United States*, ed. by D.J. Elazar, Chicago, Rand Mc Nally, 1966; Geoffrey Sawer, *Modern Federalism*, Carlton, Pitman, 1976.
23. On the legislative history of the Single Act, see J. De Ruyt, *L'Acte unique européen*, Brussels, Institut d'études européennes, 1987; C.-D. Ehlermann, 'The Internal Market following the Single European Act', 24 C.M.L.Rev. (1987), pp. 361–409; J.-P. Jacqué, 'L'Acte unique européen', R.T.D.E. (1986), pp. 575–612; J. Lodge, 'The Single European Act: Towards a New Euro-Dynasism?', XXIV, J. Com. Mark. Studies (1986), pp. 203–223.
24. See Art. of the Commission's working paper on the internal market of 16 Dec. This paper has been published as an annex to Ehlermann *supra* n. 23 at p. 405.
25. In fields like the liberalisation of capital movements with third countries (Art. 70), air and sea transport (Art. 84), the freedom to provide services for nationals of non-member countries established in the Community (Art. 59) or for the adoption of norms on the protection of working conditions (Art. 118A).

measures which are necessary in order to achieve 'the objectives set out in Article 8A', *i.e.* the creation of the single market. In total, two thirds of the proposals set out in the White Paper could now be adopted by majority vote.

Although it fell short of the Commission's proposals, such a radical departure from previous practice surprised more than one observer of the Community scene. Since the Luxembourg compromise, instances of majority voting were exceptional and regarded as such: it was generally thought that systematic resort to voting would involve a risk that Community decisions might not be applied by Member States which had been overruled.[26] After the 1982 vote on the fixing of agricultural prices, some attempts had been made to determine with greater precision in what circumstances one Member State could invoke 'essential interests' to prevent the Council from voting,[27] but it was not possible to reconcile Member States' views on this most delicate issue. At the time the Dooge Committee submitted its report, the United Kingdom, Denmark and Greece insisted that when a Member State considered that important national interests were at stake, negotiations should continue until unanimous agreement could be reached.[28]

How then was it possible to reach agreement to an extension of majority voting? The answer probably lies in a mixture of tactical and structural elements. On the tactical side, the achievement of a unified European market certainly represented a seductive objective for most Member States. In particular, the pragmatic line suggested in the White Paper, not least because of its strong de-regulatory bias, did appeal to the British government, and Britain was probably the key Member State among those showing reluctance about more intensive resort to voting. Given the general acceptance of the objective, it might be taken that no vital interest was likely to be harmed in the fields where a majority vote was made possible. This is in a way confirmed by the fact that unanimity remains the rule in sensitive sectors like the harmonisation of indirect taxation, or in fields where no basic agreement existed as to the objectives to be pursued at the Community level, as was the case for the rights of employed persons or the free movements of persons.[29] All it was possible to get in this latter case was a general commitment from Member States 'to cooperate, without prejudice to the powers of the Community'.[30]

26. Reactions after the 1982 vote on agricultural prices well illustrate this point: see 'Editorial Comments – The Vote on the Agricultural Prices: A New Departure?', 19 C.M.L.Rev. (1982), p. 371. See also J.-L. Dewost, 'Les relations entre le Conseil et la Commission dans le processus décisionnel communautaire', in: *Nature et évolution des institutions de la Communauté européenne*, Paris, Presses universitaires de France, 1981, at pp. 21–22.
27. See Jacqué, 'L'évolution du triangle institutionnel communautaire depuis l'élection du Parlement européen au suffrage universel direct', *Mélanges Teitgen*, Paris, Pédone, 1984, pp. 183–208.
28. See the reservations entered by their representatives as regards voting procedures. The report has been published as an annex to Bieber, Jacqué and Weiler (eds.), *An Ever Closer Union: A Critical Analysis of the Draft Treaty establishing the European Union*, Luxembourg, Office for Official Publications of the EC, 1985, pp. 330–342.
29. Art. 100A para. 2.
30. See the declaration adopted by the intergovernmental conference after the Single Act in EC Bull., supplement 2/86.

Another reason why majority voting could be accepted is to be found in the many clauses which were inserted in the Single Act to guarantee Member States that their interests would be adequately protected. Actually, two large groups of States felt that the completion of the internal market might involve certain risks. The less developed countries feared that the removal of border controls could threaten the position of their less competitive economies, thereby leading to increased regional discrepancies. Conversely, other Member States were concerned about a possible levelling down of their higher standards of environmental or consumer protection. To these two groups, majority voting was no purely institutional issue; the possibility of being overruled had concrete implications. It is in the sectors where they most feared this possibility that they insisted on retaining some kind of guarantee.[31] The antagonistic character of these two kinds of concern – the less developed countries being generally less concerned about environment or consumer protection – may explain why they were handled in a parallel fashion in the Single Act.

The guarantees offered to each group are of several types. At a 'macro-political' level, general considerations on the orientation of Community activities have been inserted in the Single Act. Both the search for economic and social cohesion and the protection of the environment have been raised to the level of fully-fledged Community policies. It was thereby formally recognised that some sort of Community action was needed in these two fields. However, the change was above all of a symbolic nature, since the Community had in the past resorted to Article 235 for the same purpose. Formal recognition was also given to the fact that these two kinds of concerns must be taken into account in the making of other Community policies.[32] Lastly, the Commission, as guardian of the minority interests, has been given programmatic guidelines. It has been required, when drawing up its proposals aimed at completing the internal market, to give consideration to 'the extent of the effort that certain economies showing differences in development will have to sustain'.[33] At the same time, it has also been invited to take as a base 'a high level of protection' in its proposals concerning health, safety, the environment and consumer protection.[34] Read in connection with Article 149, these provisions appear as guarantees that a Commission proposal which meets a specific concern of some Member States cannot be modified without their consent. One may, however, wonder whether the Commission will not sometimes find itself in a difficult situation, given the potentially contradictory character of these guidelines. Leaving that question aside, these provisions do not give rise to major institutional problems since,

31. During the negotiation of the Single Act, Germany insisted that the Member States with higher standards of environmental protection should get a kind of veto on measures to be adopted in that field (Jacqué, *supra* n. 23, at p. 608). Greece, Ireland and Portugal have stressed in declarations attached to the Single Act that majority voting could imply a threat in certain areas and insisted that the development of Community action should take place 'in such a way as not to harm sensitive sectors of Member States' economies'.

32. See Art. 130B and Art. 130R.

33. Art. 8C.

34. Art. 100A para. 2.

legally speaking, they treat all harmonisation in the same manner, without involving great threats to the objective of market unity.

The same cannot, however, be said about the other protective clauses integrated in the Single Act. These are rather of a 'micro-political' nature, in that their main effect is to authorise Member States facing specific problems to remain temporarily insulated from the larger market which will be created. Article 8C provides that derogations may be inserted into Community economies, but it adds that those derogations must be of a temporary nature and cause the 'least possible disturbance to the functioning of the internal market'. Likewise, Article 100A para. 4 envisages the inclusion in harmonisation measures adopted by a majority vote of safeguard clauses authorising Member States to take provisional measures 'for one or more of the non-economic reasons referred to in Article 36'.

These provisions do not significantly differ from existing Community practice, which already provided many examples of similar clauses.[35] Following the indications given by the Court of Justice, derogations will have to rest on criteria of an objective nature,[36] but this necessity seems to have been foreseen at least in part.[37] Derogations must also be of a temporary nature, given the existence of a general objective of market integration.[38] The political interest of these provisions lies in the fact that they allow Member States which face certain difficulties to stagger the implementation of Community rules over a period of time. True, they make possible the survival of internal barriers, and might therefore slow down the implementation of the entire programme. But the problem should also be seen from the opposite viewpoint: Member States will find it easier to agree on a proposal if they have the opportunity to adapt gradually to Community requirements. To take one concrete example, it is doubtful that agreement could have been reached on capital movements if the economically weaker

35. H.J. Glaesner, 'L'Acte unique européen', *RNC* (1986), pp. 307–321. For an overview of this practice, see C.D. Ehlermann, 'How Flexible is Community Law? An Unusual Approach to the Concept of Two Speeds', 82 *Michigan Law Review* (1983–84), pp. 1275–1293.
36. See case 153/73, *Holz & Willemsen* v. *Council and Commission*. (1974) E.C.R. 675 at p. 695.
37. The reference to 'economies showing differences of development' in Art. 8C even led Glaesner to conclude that derogations should apply to specific regions or sectors rather than to Member States as such (*supra* n. 35 at p. 313). However, this suggestion was not followed: Council dir. 88/361 of 24 June 1988 on capital movements (OJ L 178 of 8 July 1988) establishes a temporary derogation for several Member States on the basis of this provision.
38. It has been suggested that the reference to the end of 1992 in Art. 8A implies that derogations based on Art. 8C would not be applicable after this date. See N. Forwood and M. Clough, 'The Single European Act and Free Movement – Legal Implications of the Provisions for the Completion of the Internal Market', E.L.Rev. (1986), pp. 383–408, at p. 307. This interpretation might be too strict. As Ehlermann rightly suggested, time limits must take into account different factors, among them the type of situation which justifies the differentiation and the kind of general objective with which such differentiation might be in conflict (*supra* note 35 at pp. 1291–92). Given the great variety of economic situations within the Community, a general criterion might therefore not be possible, but it is clear that the establishment of a sinlge market is so much at the core of Community activities that the answer must rather lean on the side of a short adaptation period.

Member States had not been given more time to implement provisions adopted at Community level.[39]

However, the Single Act went one step further by authorising Member States to apply national rules after the adoption of harmonisation measures by majority vote, provided that the rules concerned be 'based on grounds of major needs referred to in Article 36 or relating to the protection of the environment or the working environment'.[40] True, this possibility is subject to strict Commission control, and other Member States are given the power to refer the matter directly to the Court of Justice, without resorting to the procedure established by Article 169. Nonetheless, this mechanism has been severely criticised,[41] *inter alia* for allowing Article 36 to be invoked in order to avoid the implementation of harmonisation provisions, a possibility which had been ruled out by the Court of Justice.[42] The negative impression generated by this setback was reinforced by the many uncertainties introduced by this provision.[43]

All these negative differentiation clauses are inspired by the need to provide Member States with a guarantee that Community rules to be adoptepd by majority vote will not be made enforceable to them against their wish. They can either insist on the adoption of derogation clauses based on Article 8C or on Article 100A para. 5, or invoke the escape clause contained in para. 4 of the same provision, provided of course that the kind of regulatory scheme they intend to maintain is not in contradiction with Court's case-law on Article 30 and following. The best way to prevent the use of this latter possibility would be to reach a unanimous decision, since unilateral derogations are possible only in case of a majority vote.

It does not automatically follow that this nullifies all hopes of one day realising a completely integrated market. The use of escape clauses will be restricted to specific situations and subject to a strict monitoring by the Court of Justice, which will of course apply the principles brought out by its case-law, and in particular the principle of proportionality. It would there-

39. Art. 6 of Council Dir. of 24 June 1988, *supra* n. 37, provides that the measures necessary to comply with the dir. must be taken by 1 July 1990, except for Spain, Portugal, Greece and Ireland, which may apply restrictions until the end of 1992.
40. Art. 100A para. 4.
41. The most radical criticism is to be found in P. Pescatore, 'Observations sur l'Acte unique européen', in *L'Acte unique européen*, Brussels, Institut d'études européennes, 1986, pp. 39–66 at pp. 40–46.
42. Cases 148/78, *Ratti*, (1979) E.C.R. 1629 at p. 1644; 251/78, *Denkavit*, (1979) E.C.R. p. 3369.
43. To mention but one: can this safeguard clause still be used if a general provision based on para. 4 of Art. 100A has been included in some harmonisation provision? It has been suggested that it could not (Glaesner, *supra*, n. 35 at p. 314) but this interpretation would restrict the guarantee offered to Member States by para. 4, since derogations adopted on the basis of para. 5 must be adopted by a majority vote: thus, a Member State which had been in the minority at the time of voting would be deprived of any safeguard (see Jacqué *supra* n. 23 at p. 600). For a detailed analysis, see Forwood and Clough, *supra* n. 38 at pp. 399–400.

fore be wrong to believe that Member States will enjoy a complete freedom of action. Secondly, and more importantly, it is clear that the very possibility of derogations should render more frequent use of voting procedures possible in the Council, since Member States know that in any event Community action will not be detrimental to their economic interests or to societal values they deem important. Instead of preventing a decision whenever they feel threatened, they can now make use of the escape clauses offered to them.[44] This will of course imply the persistance of some internal borders for a while, but market integration is less likely to suffer from temporary derogations than from a persistent stalemate.

All this makes it clear unlikely that a Member State could successfully invoke the Luxembourg compromise against measures which are part of the internal market programme.[45] Although the Single Act did not explicitly rule out that possibility, it created the conditions for its disappearance: it will now be harder for one Member State to convince its partners that its vital interests are being threatened by a proposal, if it can benefit from a derogation or retain its own legal rules. Significantly, whereas in the Dooge report several Member States had stressed the fundamental character of the compromise, none of them did so in the unilateral declarations presented at the moment of signing the Single Act. Some of them did, however, insist on the need for adequate protection through safeguard clauses, which demonstrates the close link they see between these two points.

That Member States could agree on a change in the Council's rules of procedure is emblematic of the new spirit that prevails at Community level. The new rules provide that the voting procedure must be initiated at the request of one Member State or of the Commission, provided a simple majority of the Council agrees,[46] and the Commission has indicated that it would press for a vote each time this is possible.[47] One can already note a clear shift away from unanimity in the Council's practice: instances of majority voting are now much more frequent than they were five years ago. Better than any elaborate legal or political reasoning, this would seem to demonstrate that the shadow of Luxembourg, which so often discouraged voting in the past, is no longer a strong obstacle on the way towards the completion of the internal market.

44. Incidentally, the mere existence of this possibility will also make it possible for Member States to insist that their specific interests be taken into account by the Commission when drafting its proposals.

45. But the Luxembourg compromise probably remains alive as regards other sectors of Community activities. True, those Member States which insisted on the need for full discretion in determining when a vital interest is at stake no longer retain a blocking minority in the event of a vote by qualified majority. But at the time of the 1982 vote, France had made it clear that it still regarded the Luxembourg *acquis* as en essential feature of the institutional structure, but that it could only be invoked in connection with the question actually under discussion, and not in a tactical way. For a comment on this position, see Jacqué *supra* n. 26.

46. *Bull. EC* 12/86 at p. 87.

47. *General Report of Activities 1987* at p. 31.

B. A NEW ROLE FOR PARLIAMENT

Even if it is based on a cautious approach, the White Paper programme clearly implies a more systematic use of Community powers, and hence an increased legislative burden on the institutions. The question therefore arose of the role the European Parliament was to play in this respect. On a more political plane, it was also felt that Member States had to provide some kind of response to Parliament's pressure in favour of greater involvement in decision-making. Here again, the response provided by the Single Act was hot devoid of ambiguity. In a way, the complex architecture set up in Luxembourg proved that Spinelli was correct in saying that the Community decision-making system assigned clear limits to national governments' capacity to alter the institutional structure: if invited to react to the Parliament's Draft Treaty, they could only do in this respect what they had done in the past, and adopt one of those compromises for which the Community had become famous.[48]

At face value, the new prerogatives granted to the European Parliament appear extremely modest. Co-decision was established only for the admission of new members[49] or for association agreements.[50] As regards the internal market, a *cooperation* procedure[51] was established in most fields where majority voting is now possible.[52] Broadly speaking it reproduces the two-readings system which exists in the budgetary procedure.[53] After a first round of cosultation, a 'common position' adopted by the Council is submitted to the Parliament, which must take a position within three months: it can accept the common position, propose amendments or reject it altogether. If amendments are proposed, the Commission can act as mediator, for it must decide whether to accept them or not. Once integrated in the Commission's revised proposal, Parliament's amendments can be modified by unanimous decision only. Unanimity is also required in order to adopt an act in accordance with a common position which has been rejected by the Parliament.[54]

So much has already been written on this new procedure that I need not dwell at length on its technical aspects.[55] But it is worth mentioning here that for all the changes it has introduced, it did not alter the Council's power

48. See in this respect his lecture *Verso l'Unione Europea*, Florence, European University Institute, 1983.
49. Art. 237.
50. Art. 238.
51. Art. 149 para. 2.
52. But not in all: see Art. 6 of the Single Act, which does not mention Art. 70(1) on capital movements and Art. 84(2) on air and sea transport.
53. Art. 203.
54. The same rule applies as regards amendments which have not been accepted by the Commission.
55. In addition to the works mentioned *supra* n. 23, see R. Bieber, J. Pantalis and J. Schoo, 'Implications of the Single Act for the European Parliament', 23 C.M.L.Rev. (1986), pp. 767–792; M. Domestici-Met, 'Les procédures législatives communautaires après l'Acte unique', RMC (1987), pp. 556–571. See also Louis and Waelbroeck (eds.), *Le Parlement européen dans l'évolution institutionnelle*, Bruxelles, Institut d'études européennes, 1988.

of last word, since no text can be adopted without its formal consent.[56] One could even say that the Single Act did little more than formalize what was previously possible, since nothing prevented the Commission from modifying its proposals to incorporate suggestions put forward by the Parliament – it actually did so before adoption of the Single Act. The only new power given to Parliament is the right to reject the Council's common position, but precisely because of its negative character, this prerogative is a most delicate one: if too frequently used, it might backfire and damage the European Parliament's credibility.

However, the other side of the coin has not been sufficiently stressed. The importance of the fact that the tripolar dialogue between Commission, Council and Parliament has been enshrined in a formal text should not be underestimated, for it is likely to alter the quality of the relationships between the institutions. While adding to the transparency of the dialogue, the obligation imposed on the Council to justify its position at the end of the first reading forces is to consider with greater care the opinions expressed by Parliament.[57] In the first year of working cooperation procedure, some 40% of the amendments adopted by Parliament in first reading have been accepted by the Council.[58] For the first time, Parliament has also been given the right to comment in second reading on texts which have been debated in the Council; it can therefore use this opportunity to react to the arguments put forward by national delegations.[59]

Parliament has realised that, given the limited powers which it has been granted, it must try to channel its pressures somewhat. Its rules of procedures bear the mark of this concern. Thus, rule 41 has established a follow-up of negotiations in the Council, so as to monitor how the Commission fulfills its commitments concerning the amendments adopted by Parliament on first reading. Rule 51 stipulates that on second reading, amendments are admissible only if they seek to restore amendments adopted by Parliament on first reading or if they are based on a compromise with the Council.[60] To

56. Art. 149(2)(f) provides that if the Council cannot reach a decision in the three months period that follows the European Parliament's opinion, the Commission proposal shall be deemed not to have been adopted.
57. Art. 149(2)(b).
58. Report drawn up by Mr. Graziani on the results obtained from implementation of the Single Act, *E.P. Documents*, A 2-176/88 of 26 Sept. 1988 at p. 16.
59. Its capacity for persuasion is of course lower at this stage. Less than a quarter of the amendments adopted in second reading have been ultimately accepted by the Council (Graziani Report, *supra* n. 58 at p. 17).
60. This can give rise to difficulties if new elements have been introduced by Commission or by Council into the text under discussion after first reading. Some therefore argue that the second reading should focus only on the amendments tabled by Parliament, so as to avoid any difficulty. See for instance Glaesner, 'La procédure de coopération' in Louis and Waelbroeck, *supra* n. 55 at pp. 71–77 and Jacqué, *supra* n. 23 at pp. 592–593, but the Commission has stressed that Art. 149 para. 3 EEC did not assign any explicit limit to its power of modifying its proposal during the cooperation procedure. However, the practical implications of these apparently conflicting views might be similar, since a modification which would go beyond the changes suggested by Parliament would probably amount to a 'substantial' modification, which requires a re-consultation of Parliament. See case 41/69, *Chemiefarma*, ECR (1970) 661.

that end, a dialogue between the Council and the competent committee is envisage.[61] Lastly, the need to secure the support of an absolute majority of members to adopt amendments or to reject the Council's common position has led to a considerable change in parliamentary life, for it is now essential for a large number to be present when a vote must be cast.

All these changes must seem relatively minute when compared to the status Parliament had hoped to reach by adopting its Draft Treaty. Far from establishing a genuine co-decision, the cooperation procedure vests in Parliament a review function which is normally exercised by upper houses in federal systems. Actually, with its two-readings system, the cooperation procedure is very close to the processes whereby the German *Bundesrat* is consulted;[62] the main difference being of course that, by contrast with what happens in federal states, at Community level the political will of the Member States still prevails over that of the popularly elected chamber.[63] In a way, this comparison offers a good image of the peculiar nature of the Community system, which is much more decentralised than a federation. But, more importantly, the *Bundesrat*'s example also provides evidence that, by skilful use of its competences, even an assembly deprived of full decision powers can exert real political influence.

In spite of its clear limits, the cooperation procedure might therefore contain the seeds of a more radical change. After hardly more than one year of practice, it already appears that, by the pressures exerted on the other institutions, Parliament is now able to play a specific role in the legislative process which will lead to the completion of the single market,[64] thanks in part to the greater discipline it has imposed to itself. There are of course several ways of viewing this evolution, as is often the case with institutional changes. If one thinks of the great ambitions assigned to Parliament in a not so distant past, the result certainly appears limited; but, compared to Parliament's previous weight in the legislative process, the same result might just as well be perceived as a real achievement. This evolution might also indicate an alternative scheme to strengthen Parliament's position in the institutional structure of the Community: not as a real legislator (*i.e.* in the Community context, as an equivalent to the Council), but as a partner which can play a decisive role thanks to the pressures it exerts on those who hold the legislative power.

IV. IMPLEMENTING THE INTERNAL MARKET PROGRAMME: OUTSTANDING INSTITUTIONAL ISSUES

Having reviewed both the programme and the institutional setting in which it will be made operational, we can now turn to some of the issues which

61. See rule 47(5).
62. See for instance Arts. 76 and 77 of the German *Grundgesetz*.
63. Whereas in many federations the lower house is regarded as the only true legislator; see for instance the wording of Art. 41 of the Austrian constitution.
64. For evidence of this, see R. Bieber, 'On the Legislation for the Establishment of the Single Market', 25 CML Rev. (1988).

could give rise to difficulties at the implementation stage. We will deal here only with the most important ones. As will be seen, they all involve – albeit to a different extent – basic questions on the nature and working of the Community system, such as: how can additional efficiency be reached? Does it necessarily involve a reduction in democratic cheks on the decision-making process? Is the increased institutional complexity generated by the Single Act not threatening to trigger a series of institutional controversies?

A. DELEGATION OF POWERS: EFFICIENCY V. DEMOCRACY?

We have seen that the internal market programme was framed under the assumption that no major alteration to the key principle of decision-making by consensus was likely to take place in the near future. In spite of the long-term effects they might possibly have, the modifications contained in the Single Act did not fundamentally change the nature of the problem. If a leap forward is to be realized, it is therefore necessary to think of alternative ways of avoiding the protracted bargaining to which decision-making by consensus amounts most of the time.

One such way is of course to reduce the legislative agenda, which is as we saw one of the main advantages of the principle of mutual recognition. Another way is to limit the Council's work-load by delegating more decision-making powers to other bodies. This latter way has been more actively explored at Community level in recent years, be it in the field of standardisation or through an increase in the Commission's powers as regards the implementation of Community legislation. Although these two techniques involve different kinds of problems, they raise similar political issues.

The new strategy defined by the Commission in the wake of *Cassis de Dijon* not only limits the extent to which harmonisation is necessary, but also involves a new approach to ways of harmonisation. The basic feature of this new line is the distinction drawn between essential safety requirements, which must be adopted at Community level, and technical specifications, the defining of which can be entrusted to private standardisation bodies. This new approach was defined by the Council even before the White Paper on the internal market was finalised.[65] Later on, the 'Model directive' on technical harmonisation made it clear that although standards defined by European bodies like CEN or CENELEC – or, in their absence, by national bodies – were to retain their non-mandatory character, products manufactured according to these technical specifications were to be regarded as conforming to the essential requirements laid down by the directives.[66]

One of the reasons used to justify this mechanism is that since harmonisation is of direct interest to the industry and industrialists have a more direct knowledge of the technical problems involved, it would be unwise to give

65. See the Conclusions on standardisation adopted on 16 July 1984, *supra* n. 9.
66. See point B, V of the Model Directive: see n. 68.

this task to an already overburdened Community legislator.[67] It is clear that the reference to standards can also ease the updating of technical regulations, which is often a delicate matter. But this search for greater efficiency cannot ignore the basic requirements of the Commission legal system. It has been stressed that since compliance with standards entitles a product to free movement, the reference to standards in directives amounts to a delegation of competence from the Council to private bodies.[68] It can therefore only be made in accordance with the general principles laid down by the Court of Justice: delegated powers must be of a clearly defined executive nature and subject to the same conditions as those imposed on the delegating institution, such as the duty to state reasons and the necessary of judicial control.[69] These requirements are in a way the transportation in legal terms of more general concerns. If reference to standards is to become a permanent feature of Community regulatory policy, the transparency of this process must be ensured so as to guarantee that the interests of all parties concerned (the industry, of course, but consumers as well, for instance) are duly taken into account.[70] In other words, a balance must be struck between public and private concerns.

How could the requirements laid down by the Court be satisfied? It has been suggested that standards could be published as an annex to which harmonisation directives will refer, in order to make judicial control possible.[71] To some extent, the difficulty was also anticipated by the Model Directive. The need to assign clear limits to the delegated powers surfaces in the description which is given of the essential requirements to be covered by harmonisation directives:

> 'The essential safety requirements . . . shall be worded precisely enough in order to create, on transposition into national law, legally binding obligations which can be enforced. They should be so formulated as to enable the certifications straight away to certify products as being in conformity, having regard to those requirements in the absence of standards.'[72]

67. Schmitt Von Sydow, 'The Basic Strategies of the Commission's White Paper', in: Bieber, Dehousse, Pinder and Weiler, *supra* n. 1 at p. 95.
68. R.H. Lauwaars, 'The "Model Directive" on Technical Harmonisation', in: Bieber, Dehousse, Pinder and Weiler, *supra* n. 1 at pp. 165–167.
69. See case 9/56, *Meroni* v. *High Authority*, ECR (1957–58), p. 133.
70. For this reason, the constitutional admissibility of a similar system which exists in the Federal Republic of Germany has been the object of controversies. See in general Ch. Joerges, 'The New Approach to Technical Harmonization and the Interests of Consumers: Reflections on the Requirements and Difficulties of a Europeanization of Product Safety Policy', in: Bieber, Dehousse, Pinder and Weiler, *supra* n. 1 at pp. 206–215.
71. See Lauwaars, *supra* n. 68 at p. 167, who refers to Art. 4(4) of Dir. 82/130/EEC of 17 Sept. 1984 (OJ L 300).
72. *Supra* n. 9 at point B III 1. Apparently, these requirements were not met by the 'Low Voltage' Directive of 19 Feb. 1983 (OJ L 77 of 26 March 1973), which first used the reference-to-standards technique at Community level. See Joerges, *supra* n. 70 at p. 210.

While this line of conduct is probably able to reconcile the somewhat contradictory requirements of legitimacy and efficiency, the practical difficulties should not be underestimated: whereas too much discretion given to private bodies could be regarded as incompatible with the guidelines given by the Court, a too detailed directive would amount to no less than a return to the 'old approach'. The implementation of the new approach will therefore be no easy task.

A similar problem arose regarding the implementating powers to be conferred on the Commission. In its proposals at the time of the intergovernmental conference, the Commission had made it clear that it hoped to be invested with general competence for implementation of measures adopted by the Council with a view to completing the internal market.[73] The advantage of this proposal was twofold. First, on a procedural level, it solved once and for all the awkward problem of determining which institution should be given the power to implement each and every Community provision. Second, on the merits this time, it allowed the Council to download onto the Commission part of its legislative burden. At these two levels, the Commission's proposal was therefore able to bring about a considerable progress. At the same time, it could be thought that this solution would not threaten the interests of Member States, since those interests would certainly be taken into consideration during the legislative phase.

However, the intergovernmental conference did not reach an agreement on this proposal. The Single Act has supplemented Article 145 with a new paragraph in which a more systematic delegation of powers is envisaged, but it was left for the Council to decide what requirements this power was to be subject to. It was also specified that the Council could reserve the right, in specific cases, to exercise certain implementing powers directly itself. This notwithstanding, it appears from the wording of this new provision that the delegation of implementing power is to be regarded as the rule, and their retention by the Council as the exception. Furthermore, by determining the 'principles and rules' governing the Commission's implementing powers in a framework decision, the Council could pave the way for more rational and disciplined use of the delegation of powers technique, since adoption of a pre-determined set of rules could put an end to the endless debates on the procedure to be followed in each case.

The Commission presented a draft decision even before the Single Act came into force.[74] The scope of this proposal was limited: it simply outlined three types of procedures (advisory committee, management committee, regulation committee) without specifying in which case each could be used. This approach was largely dictated by tactical considerations, for the Commission feared a theological debate in the Council if it tried to provide more

73. The Commissions proposals have been published as an annex to Ehlermann, *supra* n. 23 at pp. 405–409. See in particular Art. 3 of the paper dated 16 Sept. 1985.

74. OJ C 70 of 25 March 1986. On the legislative history of this proposal, see C. Ehlermann, 'Compétences d'exécution conférées à la Commission – La nouvelle décision-cadre du Conseil', RMC (1988), pp. 232–239.

precise indications in this respect.[75] Seen retrospectively, this caution appears as a risk. The Council decision of 13 July 1987[76] does confirm that, as a matter of principle, the Commission should be vested with implementing powers.[77] But two variants have been added to the procedures suggested by the Commission, including *inter alia*, as far as regulation committees are concerned, the possibility of preventing the Commission from acting even if the Council, to which the measures envisaged must be submitted if they are not approved by the committee, cannot reach agreement.[78] Furthermore, a safeguard clause, with a similar variant, has also been introduced.[79]

It cannot be overlooked that the Commission's autonomy will be subject to strict limitations at implementation level: in four of the seven procedures envisaged by the decision, the final word will belong in whole or in part to the Council. More importantly, the absence of any criteria to determine when each procedure can or must be used could threaten the efficiency of the entire system. True, the Council now has to choose among a limited number of procedures, but this can still prove insufficient given the wide number of possibilities available:[80] it is therefore far from sure that the decision on the powers to grant to the Commission will be significantly simplified. Indeed, the third report on the implementation of the internal market programme states that difficulties do subsist for matters like health and marketing requirements for foodstuffs and drinks.[81]

The problem here is not limited to the efficiency of these mechanisms, for the European Parliament had made it clear that it felt it ought to be consulted each time a problem of implementation was submitted to the Council. This possibility was not envisaged in the Council's decision, which may explain why Parliament chose to challenge it before the Court of Justice.[82] The action was rejected by the Court, which denied that Parliament had a *locus standi* ex Article 173 of the EEC Treaty,[83] but the problem remains: greater efficiency can and must be sought, but not at the price of a reduction in democratic control. The debate is by no means limited to the Community system; all Parliaments face difficulties in controlling delegated legislation. It must not be thought, however, that the two objectives cannot possibly be

75. See the intervention by Ehlermann before the House of Lords Select Committee on the European Communities, in: *Delegation of Powers to the Commission*, Session 1986–87, 3rd Report, London: HMSO, at pp. 17–19.
76. OJ L 197 of 18 July 1987.
77. Art. 1.
78. Variant (b) of Procedure III. This procedure was used in the past in veterinary, sanitary and phytosanitary directives.
79. Art. 3.
80. The only indication available is the declaration adopted by the intergovernmental conference, which invites the Council 'to give the Advisory Committee procedure ... a predominant place ... for the exercise of the powers of implementation conferred on the Commission within the field of Article 100A of the EEC Treaty.'
81. COM (88) 134 of 23 March 1988.
82. Although the grounds invoked to justify the proceedings were limited to the fact that by restricting to a considerable extent the Commission's autonomy, the Council had violated Art. 145. See OJ C 321 of 1 Jan. 1987.
83. Case 302/87, *European Parliament* v. *Council*, judgment of 25 Sept. 1988, not yet reported.

reconciled: it is likely that the European Parliament, like its national counterparts, would be content if the proposed implementation measures were to be tabled in Parliament so that they could be discussed if deemed necessary.

B. THE PROBLEM OF LEGAL BASIS

The institutional changes introduced by the Single Act have given additional importance to the question of the legal basis pursuant to which Community legislation should be adopted. The question is not merely academic for, in the Community system, the procedure governing the legislative process can vary to a considerable extent: the choice of a legal basis will have implications on the way the Council can take a decision or on the rights of Parliament, and can therefore have a strong incidence on the very content of the measures to be adopted. The difficulty is not new: as regards veterinary and phytosanitary controls, for instance, the Council has relied for many years not only on Article 43, which provides for qualified majority voting, but also on Article 100, which requires unanimity. But the Single Act, because of the changes it has introduced and because of its frequent invitations to take different concerns into account contemporarily,[84] gives a new dimension to this kind of problem.

It is therefore not surprising that the Court of Justice has been called to intervene in the discussion in the last two years. In a first ruling, it stated very clearly that the choice of legal basis should be determined according to objective elements like the content and purpose of the proposed measure, and was subject to judicial review.[85] Later on, in the 'hormones' case,[86] the Court indicated that if a directive falls entirely in a field covered by one provision, the mere fact that it pursues other objectives, which could be covered by other provisions, does not imply that it must be based on the two provisions, for this interpretation would restrict the scope of the first one. Thus, a directive on the use of hormones in meat need not be based on Article 100 if it is entirely covered by Article 43.[87] Classical legal constructs, like the *lex specialis* or the *lex posterior* principles, can also be of help in this respect. It is clear for instance that harmonisation measures aiming at the completion on the internal market should be based not on Article 100, but on Article 100A.

84. See for instance Art. 8C, inviting the Commission to take into account the difficulties of backwards economies when drawing up its proposals on the internal market, or Art. 100A para. 3, which envisages the adoption of a 'high level of protection' in approximation proposals concerning health, safety, environmental or consumer protection.

85. Case 45/86, *Commission* v. *Council*, judgment of 26 March 1987, not yet reported.

86. Case 68/86, *United Kingdom* v. *Council*, judgment of 23 Feb. 1988, not yet reported. See also case 131/86, *United Kingdom* v. *Council*, not yet reported.

87. The Court indicated that the practice followed in the past by the Council was not able to modify Treaty rules and could not therefore be regarded as a binding precedent (see point 29). It has, however, confirmed in a later case that if the Community competence rests on two different provisions, this competence must be exerted pursuant to both of them (case 165/87, *Commission* v. *Council*, judgment of 27 Sept. 1987, not yet reported.)

However, this kind of concern could have a negative impact on the decision-making process, for each institution will be tempted to use legal arguments in order to maximise its own power. In the wake of case 45/86, the Commission, whose role is primary here because of its right of initiative, has decided that it would as far as possible give preference to one single legal basis, so as to avoid resort to different procedures and to allow majority voting whenever possible.[88] The Rules of Procedure of the European Parliament now provide for specific verification of the validity and appropriateness of the legal basis for each provision.[89]

Very often, the concerns of the two institutions – efficiency on the one hand, democratic control on the other – will coincide, since the cooperation procedure is always synonymous with majority voting. But the reverse is not always true, which can occasionally lead to conflicts. To give but one example, the Commission and the Parliament had divergent views on the legal basis to be used for a proposed regulation on maximum permitted levels of radioactive contamination of foodstuffs:[90] whereas the Commission's proposal was based on Article 31 of the Euratom Treaty (which envisages the adoption of basic standards for the protection of health), Parliament instead favoured the use of Article 100A, according to which the cooperation procedure must be used. No agreement was reached and Parliament eventually rejected the proposal, which was, however, adopted on the basis of the Euratom Treaty. Parliament then decided to bring an action against the Council for breach of essential procedural requirements.[91]

Several conflicts of the same kind have set the institutions against each other.[92] Given the sometimes conflicting values which are attached to the new procedures established by the Single Act, there is therefore a very real risk of seeing Member States and the institutions resort more frequently than in the past to judicial litigation in order to solve their political conflicts, which would of course render decision-making rather chaotic and reduce legal security.

C. THE ROLE OF MEMBER STATES IN THE IMPLEMENTATION OF THE INTERNAL MARKET PROGRAMME

It is well known that Member States play a crucial role as regards the application of Community law. Increasing attention has been paid in recent years to the problems which arise at the implementation stage,[93] but the implications the internal market programme will have at this level remain largely

88. *Vade mecum* on institutional questions, quoted in Domestici-Net, *supra* n. 55 at p. 568. The problem would of course be less acute if voting had remained an exceptional practice.
89. Rule 36(3).
90. OJ L 371 of 30 Dec. 1987.
91. Case 70/88, OJ C 90 of 7 April 1988. This was, however, decided before the Court had ruled that Parliament had no *locus standi* to act on the basis of Art. 173.
92. See the examples given in Bieber, *supra* n. 64.
93. See for instance G. Ciavarini-Azzi (ed.), *The Implementation of Community Law by the Member States*, Maastricht, EIPA, 1985.

unexplored. Although it noted that some 60% of the complaints received each year by the Commission relate to Articles 30–36 of the EEC Treaty, the White Paper on the internal market did not really address this issue: it only indicated that it would be necessary to improve the Commission's internal procedures in order to correct violations more rapidly and effectively since, at present, the Commission can hardly settle one third of these cases.[94] Thus, the only remedy envisaged to improve compliance with Community law appears to be a reinforcement of the Commission's prosecuting capacity under Article 169.[95]

All I wish to say here is that this approach – which can certainly be termed classical – should now be revised in the light of the new internal market strategy. In fact, the new division of labour between the Community and its Member States on which this strategy rests will have a clear bearing on the profile of Community legislation. Not only should it normally result in a more Community acts being adopted, but it will be legislation of another type since it should be restricted to those elements which are deemed essential to remove obstacles to free movement. The scope of the new Community norms being more limited than in the past, they should leave large avenues open to national regulations.[96]

Two considerations are worth being made at this level. First, it is generally felt that implementation problems are in the main due to administrative inertia and to a lack of information on the part of national administrations; deliberate, conscious violations of Community law remain the exception. Second, a majority of the cases dealt with by the Commission involve non-transportation or an improper incorporation of directives in the national legal sphere. As far as the internal market is concerned, for instance, this kind of violation of Community law accounts for about 80% of the infringement proceedings initiated each year.[97] Even when directives are eventually implemented, it is often with considerable delay. Some Member States, like Italy and Belgium, have a notoriously poor record in this respect. A number of difficulties can be attributed to a lack of coordination between specialised departments and the national spokesmen in the Community institutions: very often, the latter do not have a complete view of their country's regulations in given fields, and the former are not fully informed of their obligations.[98]

Seen against this background, the new approach might clearly pose problems on the implementation side. With more Community acts to be transposed into national law and less precise guidelines as to what the content of national rules should be, the risk of non-compliance appears higher. What is

94. *Completing the Internal Market*, *supra* n. 10 at points 153–154.

95. For a critical analysis of this strategy, see Weiler, 'The White Paper and the Application of Community Law', in: Bieber, Dehousse, Pinder and Weiler, *supra* n. 1 at pp. 337–358.

96. *Supra*, para. B.

97. See the figures given in the Commission's fourth report on the application of Community law, *supra* n. 4 at pp. 20–21.

98. See Ciavarini-Azzi, *supra* n. 93, where the problem is mentioned in several national reports.

at stake is no less than the success of the new strategy – hence of the whole internal market programme, for it is clear that the behaviour of European industries will be largely determined according to the steps taken by Member States to comply with decisions adopted at the Community level. It may of course be that the momentum generated by the Commission's proposal to realise a single market by 1992 will help to make national administrations more sensitive to their duties in this respect, but it is doubtful that this will suffice. It is therefore necessary to think of additional means in order to reconcile the subsidiarity principle with a concern for faithful implementation of Community law.

The first way that might be suggested relates to the type of measure used at Community level. As is known, Article 100A provides for the adoption of *measures* – which seems to imply that regulations may be used instead of directives. This possibility meets with some reluctance from several quarters; the intergovernmental conference has explicitly invited the Commission to give precedence to the use of directives 'if harmonisation provisions involve the amendment of legislative provisions in one or more Member States'. The rationale of this suggestion is that directives were envisaged by the EEC Treaty as a means to define common ends which can be reached by Member States through different methods, whereas regulations do not offer the same kind of flexibility. This is no less than a transportation of the subsidiary principle at a legal level, and the principle was worth recalling, since there has in the past been an increasing tendency towards extremely detailed directives.

But, it might be argued, this logic should not apply where the *content* of harmonisation provisions is already governed by the principle of subsidiarity. If those provisions are to be restricted to essential health and safety requirements, for instance, those objectives are *ex hypothesi* so central that they can be regarded as forming the very end of Community action, which should be given full effect. In other words, the thrust of the new strategy is itself so much inspired by the idea of subsidiarity that guarantees as to the type of measure to be used can be regarded as redundant. So circumscribed, the use of regulations for the approximation of national law would certainly be politically more acceptable. This solution would of course be politically more acceptable. This solution would of course present great advantages, since regulations do not have to be transposed into national law: the rules adopted at Community level would therefore be given their full effect without delay.[99] Naturally, regulations based on the new approach would have to provide for supplementary legislation by the Member States more frequently than 'traditional' regulations normally do.[100]

Greater attention should also be paid to the possibility of reinforcing the prevention of violations of Community law. Much has been said above on

99. Incidentally, no doubt would arise as to their 'horizontal' direct effect. See in general A. Easson, 'Approximation and Unification of Laws in the EEC', 2 *Journal of European Integration* (1979), pp. 375–390.

100. See R.H. Lauwaars, 'Implementation of Regulations by National Measures', LIEI (1983/1), pp. 41–52.

the control mechanisms introduced by Directive 83/189, which have allowed the Commission to prevent the adoption of national provisions incompatible with Community law. Systems of this kind are bound to play a crucial role in a Community where the sphere of action of the Member States will remain important. The Commission is now trying to adapt to this new role in which the emphasis is much more on supervision and on guidance than on repressive action. It has already announced its intention to issue interpretive communications indicating the obligations imposed in a particular sphere, the measures to take, and the procedures to be followed in order to comply with Community rules.[101] Specific procedural requirements could be envisaged to draw Member States's attention on the measures which have to be modified in order to adjust to Community law: prior to the adoption of Community measures, national administrations could be asked to submit a list of the provisions which would have to be modified in order to comply with the line put forward in a Commission proposal. This exercise would force them to dedicate some thought to implementation issues even during the decisional phase; it would also make the monitoring of implementation by the Commission easier.[102]

This latter remark stresses how narrow the borderline between prevention and enforcement concerns can sometimes be. Very often, one single mechanism will be helpful at both levels. If they are given enough publicity, the communications envisaged by the Commission will also make individuals more aware of their rights and provide legal circles with ammunition to use to challenge the compatibility of national rules with Community law. Indeed, the Commission makes no mystery of its wish to encourage decentralisation through more systematic use of the judicial possibilities offered by Article 177.[103] This strategy is certainly worth pursuing, but its limits must be stressed. For a series of reasons, one of which is the discretion enjoyed by national courts in deciding whether to refer a case to the ECJ, proceedings based on Article 177 are not equally popular, nor is the propensity to question the validity of national provisions identical, in all Member States.[104] Prevention must therefore remain a central priority.

V. CONCLUSION: THE POLITICS OF INSTITUTIONAL REFORM

The evolution of the Community in the last few years teaches us a series of lessons on what might be called the politics of institutional reform. The first

101. Fourth Report on the Application of Community Law, *supra* n. 4 at p. 7.
102. A similar concern has led to a modification of Dir. 83/189, which now imposes on Member States the duty to inform the Commission of the follow-up done on the detailed opinions issued by the Commission (Art. 8 of Council Dir. of 22 March 1988, OJ L 81 of 26 March 1988).
103. *Ibid.* at point 20.
104. The survey conducted by the European University Institute on all preliminary rulings rendered by the Court of Justice ex Art. 177 until the end of 1985 has evidentiated wide differences at these two levels. The percentage of cases involving a review of national measures varies between 33% in France and 78% in Germany. The results of the project will be available in 1989.

conclusion to be drawn from this experience is that institutional reform is easier to arrive at when it is not pursued for its own sake, but emerges as a logical implication of other political choices. Once the general idea of completing the internal market by 1992 had been accepted, it proved possible to convince even the most reluctant Member States that a shift towards more majority voting was necessary. Had the objective itself not met with consensus, the change would not have been possible. The same logic is apparent in the Single Act's provisions on economic and social cohesion, on research and technological development or on the environment. In all these sectors, unanimous agreement is needed in order to define the objectives to be pursued at Community level; it is only at a second stage that resort to majority voting can be envisaged.[105] The rationale of all these provisions is the same: when a decision of principle is to be taken, Member States must be able to preserve what they regard as their essential interests but, precisely because they have been given this guarantee, no vital interest to be harmed at the implementation stage; the 'Community interest' – and in particular the necessity of an efficient decision-making system – can therefore be given precedence.

Thus, most of the developments which have taken place in these years find their origin in the Commission's capacity to capitalise on the political pressures exerted by the Parliament and to define a 'new frontier' which would be acceptable to all Member States. But the way in which the institutional reform was accomplished also deserves attention. The main feature of the process was certainly its piecemeal character, which is often the case with compromises achieved in decentralised systems.[106] As is known, the Single European Act was not the result of an inspired exercise in constitution-making, but the product of strenuous international negotiation. This cumbersome process had a direct incidence on the final result, which reflects the various aspirations and fears of more or less all Member States. In a typical *quid pro quo* exercise, France and Germany secured the adoption of provisions on political cooperation, and the backward countries a general commitment in favour of the reinforcement of economic and social cohesion within the Community, while several countries managed to limit the Community's capacity to act autonomously as far as the environment is concerned. Several of the institutional problems mentioned above are linked to the complexity of the structure which eventually emerged. The lengthy discussions on the subject of legal basis offer good examples of difficulties connected with the ambiguity of the compromises made at the time of drafting the Single Act.

With the White Paper on the internal market, questions which were previously considered as essentially technical gained the status of major political objectives. This change was paralleled by an evolution in the decision-making process: the creation of an internal market Council, with its

105. Arts. 130E, 130Q and 130S.

106. For a similar judgment on the Canadian constitutional reform of 1982, see A.C. Cairns, 'The Politics of Conservatism', in: Simeon and Banting (eds.), *And No One Cheered – Federalism, Democracy and the Constitution Act*, Toronto, Methuen, 1982, at pp. 29–58.

induced effects at national level,[107] has made it easier to coordinate national and Community action in this sphere. The introduction of majority voting has had a similar effect. Even if is not systematically used, the possibility of a vote reinforces the weight of political decision-makers over that of specialised departments, which are to a large extent deprived of the veto right they had in the past.

These changes account for the relatively positive results reached so far. The Commission has now presented most of the proposals envisaged in the White Paper; approximately one third of them have been adopted so far, which certainly represents no meagre achievement. However, these figures should not generate an excessive optimism, for the most delicate matters – tax harmonisation, the free movement of persons, and the social dimension of the internal market – remain to be dealt with. It is therefore not unreasonable to think that the pace of implementation of the White Paper programme will slow down in coming months. Much will certainly depend on the Commission's capacity to forge the coalitions which are needed for the adoption of its proposals, and to transpose into operational terms the choices made in the White Paper. It is one thing to make a conceptual distinction between what is essential and what is not, and quite another to draw a clear line between the two in different sectors.

In spite of all the difficulties which can be foreseen, it is clear that the Community has now embarked on an era of dynamism which few expected a couple of years ago. Part of this dynamism finds its origin in external factors like the economic growth experienced in recent years; but it is equally clear that the momentum generated by the White Paper would not have been possible without its healthy institutional pragmatism. Not only did this approach make possible advances generally regarded as beyond reach not so long ago; but it might lead to even further-reaching results. For whether it is achieved by 1992 or only later, completion of the internal market could well generate its own dynamic. It has, for instance, often been argued that the liberalisation of capital movements in a Community with stable exchange rates will make it more difficult for Member States to pursue autonomous macroeconomic policies.[108] If at some stage two thirds of the economic and social legislation will have to be adopted at the Community level, as President Delors recently hinted, Community citizens and interest groups might press for a stronger voice in the decision-making process. At the same time, Member States might also realises that more systematic resort to voting, or a stronger involvement of Parliament in the legislative process, do not necessarily mean unbearable threats to their national interests.

It might thus very well be the case that the coalescence of all these ele-

107. Several Member States have have entrusted to a specialised department the task of coordinating the preparation of the 1992 deadline: Portugal and Belgium now have a State secretary for internal market problems, and the portfolio of European affairs has been given the status of a fully-fledged ministry in the French government.

108. See for instance the report submitted by the Padoa-Schioppa group, *Efficiency, Stability and Equity – A Strategy for the Evolution of the Economic System of the European Community*, Brussels, 1987.

ments will lead to a profound change in the Community system. If this is so, then the low profile line followed by the Commission in the institutional debates of the early 1980s will have had more far-reaching implications than many of the radical proposals put forward in the past. It has already generated a shift which has not been sufficiently noticed: surprising as it might appear at first sight, it is now those who fear such a radical change and the implications it might have who feel it necessary to engage in theological debates on the virtues and limits of European integration and to issue clear warnings. The speech delivered by the British Prime minister in September 1988 in Bruges, and the absence of official reaction on the Commission's part, are emblematic of this evolution. Such a shift of the burden of proof is not only of great tactical importance; it is also indicative of the fact that a reinforcement of the Community is regarded as some likely even by those who do not especially favour it.

Name Index

www.ingramcontent.com/pod-product-compliance
Lightning Source LLC
LaVergne TN
LVHW102106300926
849161LV00014B/3057
9780814779569